Thomas Moran's West

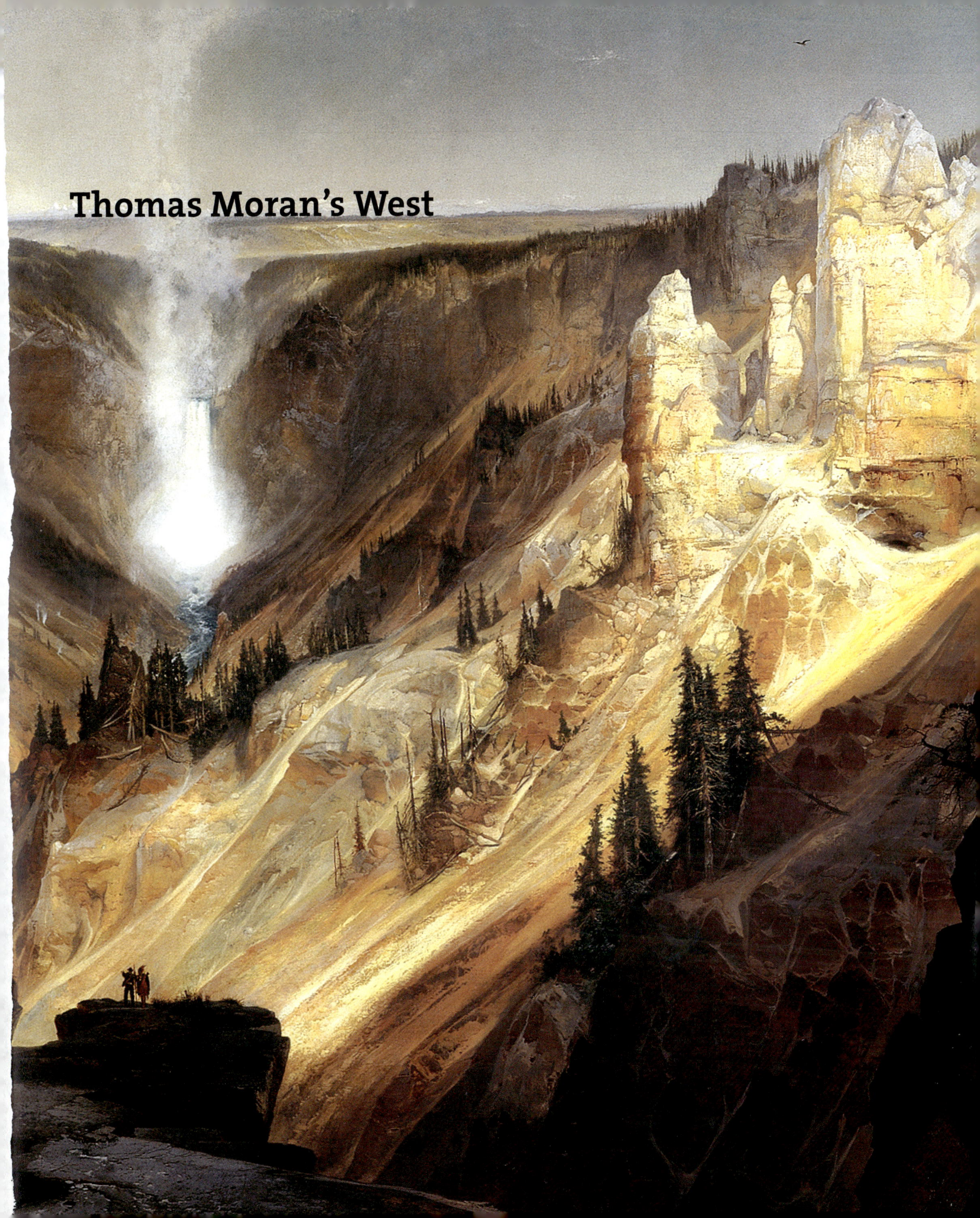

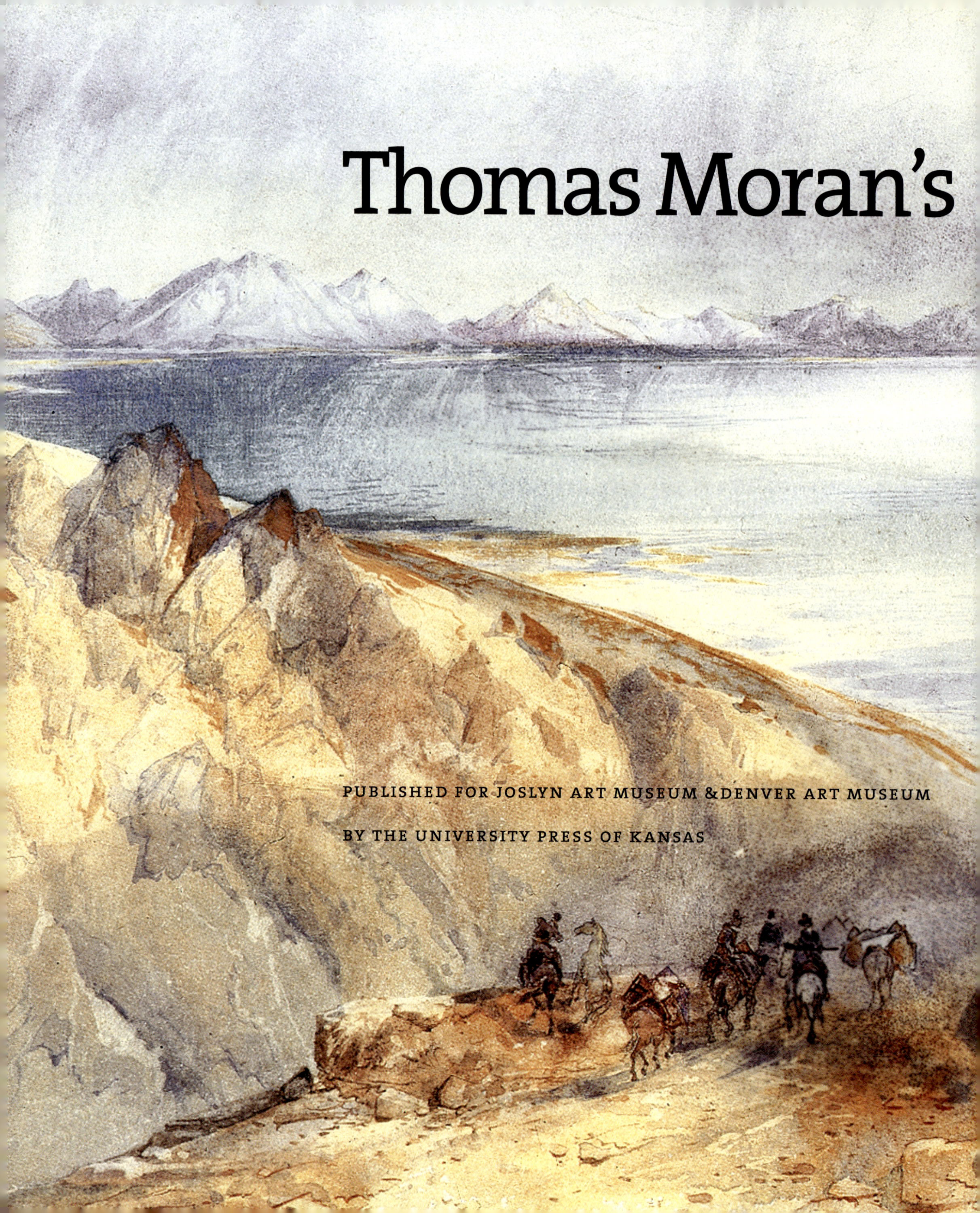

Thomas Moran's

PUBLISHED FOR JOSLYN ART MUSEUM & DENVER ART MUSEUM

BY THE UNIVERSITY PRESS OF KANSAS

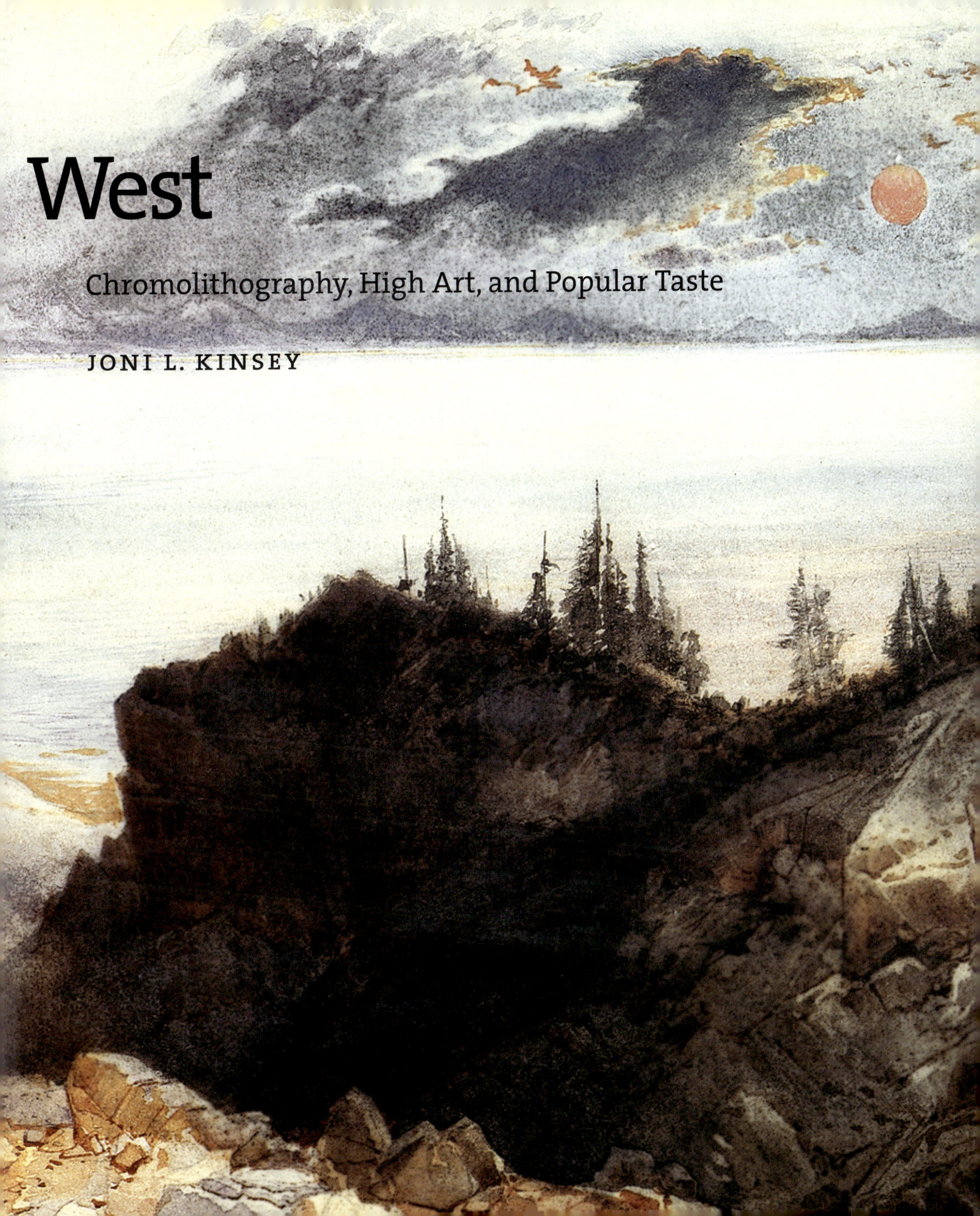

Thomas Moran and the Picturing of the American West

Chromolithography, High Art, and Popular Taste

JONI L. KINSEY

Details of illustrations :
page i: fig. 32; ii–iii: fig. 127;
vi: fig. 51; 11: fig. 15; 47: fig. 34;
83: fig. 53; 159: fig. 145; 183: fig. 64;
207: fig. 166.

Published by the University Press of Kansas (Lawrence, Kansas 66045), which was organized by the Kansas Board of Regents and is operated and funded by Emporia State University, Fort Hays State University, Kansas State University, Pittsburg State University, the University of Kansas, and Wichita State University

Library of Congress Cataloging-in-Publication Data
Kinsey, Joni.
Thomas Moran's West : chromolithography, high art, and popular taste / Joni L. Kinsey.
p. cm.
"Published for Joslyn Art Museum by the University Press of Kansas."
Includes bibliographical references and index.
ISBN 978-0-7006-1413-4 (cloth : alk. paper)
1. Yellowstone National Park—Pictorial works. 2. Yellowstone National Park—In art. 3. West (U.S.)—Pictorial works. 4. West (U.S.)—In art. 5. Moran, Thomas, 1837–1926—Influence. 6. Chromolithography — Yellowstone National Park. 7. Chromolithography—West (U.S.) 8. Art and society—United States—Case studies. 9. Moran, Thomas, 1837–1926. 10. Lithographers—United States—Biography. I. Moran, Thomas, 1837–1926. II. Joslyn Art Museum. III. Title.
F722.K47 2005
978.7′52′00222—dc22 2005015801

British Library Cataloguing-in-Publication Data is available.
Printed in China

10 9 8 7 6 5 4 3 2

The paper used in this publication meets the minimum requirements of the American National Standard for Permanence of Paper for Printed Library Materials Z39.48-1984.

Contents

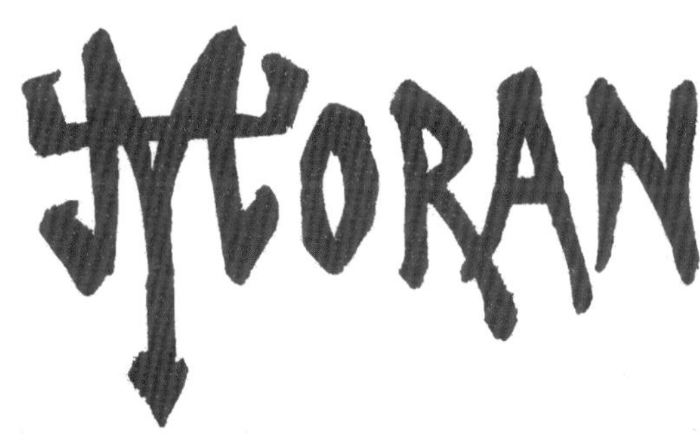

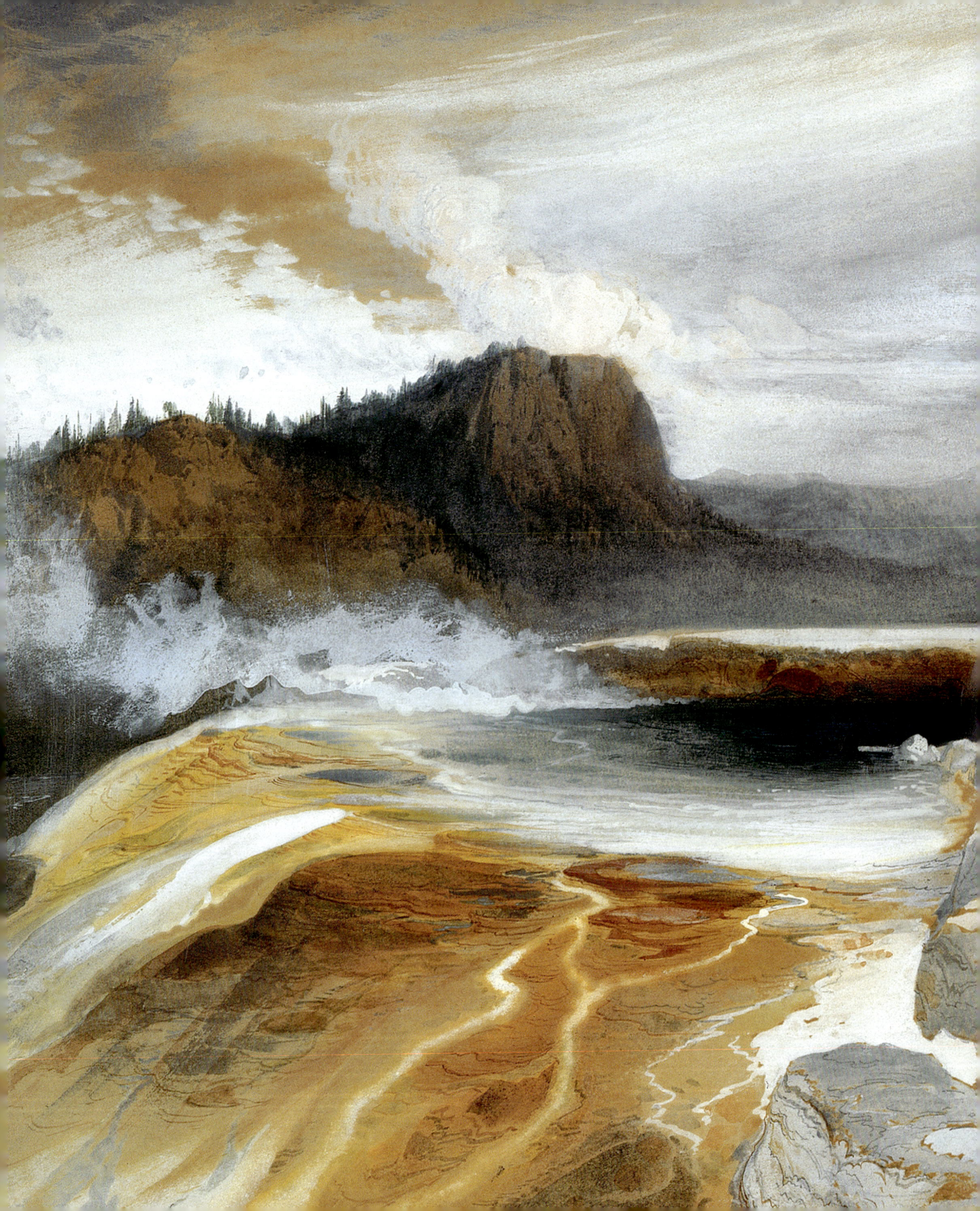

Foreword to the Second Printing

When *Thomas Moran's West* was originally published by Joslyn Art Museum in 2006, it was expected that this would be a popular volume with both scholars of nineteenth-century art history and lovers of the western landscape. There was no way to anticipate, however, the enthusiasm of its reception, and the edition quickly sold out. Recognizing the continuing demand for this book, Toby Jurovics, Chief Curator and Holland Curator of American Western Art at Joslyn Art Museum and Thomas Brent Smith, director of the Petrie Institute of Western American Art at the Denver Art Museum, proposed a second printing in conjunction with an exhibition of Moran's chromolithographs in Omaha, Denver, and the Gilcrease Museum in Tulsa. We are certain the second printing of *Thomas Moran's West* will continue to find an eager audience, a testament to Joni L. Kinsey's peerless scholarship and the never-ending popularity of Moran's inspirational vision of the American West.

The original publication of *Thomas Moran's West* was prompted by a gift to Joslyn Art Museum of Moran's 1876 portfolio *The Yellowstone National Park, and the Mountain Regions of Portions of Idaho, Nevada, Colorado and Utah* from Gail and Michael Yanney and their daughter and son-in-law, Lisa and Bill Roskens, and made possible through the support of Joslyn's Bodmer Society. We remain grateful for their generosity, which set this project in motion more than a decade ago.

Jack Becker, Ph. D.
Executive Director and C.E.O.
Joslyn Art Museum

Christoph Heinrich
Frederick & Jan Mayer Director
Denver Art Museum

FOR ELLEN

Acknowledgments

This project began in the fall of 2002 when Marsha Gallagher, curator at Omaha's Joslyn Art Museum, informed me that the museum had recently acquired a remarkable set of chromolithographs designed by Thomas Moran for Louis Prang's 1876 publication, *The Yellowstone National Park, and the Mountain Regions of Portions of Idaho, Nevada, Colorado and Utah*. The group is unique since it includes a number of publisher's proofs, complete with registration marks and penciled notations. Recognizing that the series represented a little-studied but important aspect of Moran's career, Gallagher asked if I would curate an exhibition presenting the development of the prints and their historical context. Over the ensuing two years, we located nine of the fifteen original watercolors from which the prints were made, identified an array of preparatory studies, field photographs, and later paintings that visually demonstrate the subjects' evolution in Moran's oeuvre, and delved into the fascinating history of the commission and that of his other chromolithographs. Although the exhibition was unfortunately canceled in 2005 for budgetary reasons, I am extremely grateful for Joslyn Art Museum's continuing support of the book then and for its renewed interest now with this second printing and the exhibition's revival.

A project of this scale could not be achieved without the assistance of a great many people. It draws on a wealth of previous scholarship, acknowledged individually in the accompanying notes, and I am indebted to those who have paved my way. Too, I have drawn on research I first conducted in the late 1980s as I wrote my dissertation and first book on Moran's western art, so I want to thank again the many librarians, curators, and scholars that I acknowledged in those studies. Since that time we have been blessed with the wonders of the Internet, and I would like to express my appreciation for the countless unknown librarians and their assistants who have so painstakingly digitized the electronic sources that now make historical research so much easier than in the past. These databases represent a revolution in scholarship, and they have been an invaluable asset to the writing of this book.

More immediately, a number of individuals generously opened their collections to me, answered my persistent questions, fulfilled requests for information, and offered leads to additional sources. Anne Morand, former curator of the Gilcrease Museum in Tulsa and long-time friend, offered me virtually unlimited access to the museum's unparalleled Moran collection, as did Kathryn Turner, curator, and Thomas Dewey, librarian, at the Jefferson National Expansion Memorial in St. Louis. At the Boston

Public Library, Sinclair Hitchings, keeper of prints, and Jane Winton, print librarian, were remarkably hospitable and generous with their substantial collection of Prang materials and extremely encouraging about the project. Eric Frazier, rare books librarian, and Janice Chadbourne, curator of the Fine Arts Department at the Boston Public Library, also kindly offered important access to sources. At the Boston Athenaeum, curator Sally Pierce spent an entire morning showing me prints in the collection, and Marlene Merrill, independent scholar in Oberlin, Ohio, was exceptionally generous in sharing information. I am especially indebted to her for lending me her National Archives microfilm of Hayden's letters to Prang and for sorting through the various movements of the 1871 Hayden survey with me.

I also thank those who helped locate works in private collections: Steve Good, head of the Thomas Moran catalogue raisonné project in Denver, Colorado, offered many important contacts and leads. Nancy K. Anderson, curator of American art at the National Gallery of Art; Eleanor Jones Harvey, senior curator, and William Truettner, curator, at the Smithsonian American Art Museum; and Alexis Thoman of Sotheby's Department of American Paintings all facilitated my correspondence with owners of important images in this book. To the owners of the works themselves, many of whom chose to remain anonymous, I offer special thanks for allowing their precious objects to be included here.

Conversations and correspondence with many individuals yielded essential information. Helena Wright, curator of graphic arts at the National Museum of American History, was very generous with her collection and her expertise. Others I am indebted to include Kay Wisnia, Denver Public Library; Georgia Barnhill, American Antiquarian Society; George Miles, curator of special collections at Yale University's Beinecke Library; Joe McGregor, curator of photography, United States Geological Survey, Denver; Sue Walsh Reed, curator of prints and drawings, Boston Museum of Fine Arts; Barbara Jones, curator, Westmoreland Museum of American Art, Greensburg, Pennsylvania; and Katie Schrimff, reference librarian, Hayner Public Library, Alton, Illinois. Mike Dooley, Smithsonian Fellow, investigated several Washington archives for me; David Monteith helped determine the location of Yellowstone's Excelsior Geyser and its relationship to Moran's *Great Blue Spring;* and Dr. Graeme D. Eddie of Edinburgh University's library clarified several points about the Scottish reception of the Prang portfolio.

At the University of Iowa, art history students Shanshan Chen and Marie Gernes served as very able research assistants, saving me valuable time as they tracked down countless sources; Rijn Templeton, art librarian, helped with a number of questions; and Sidney Huttner, head of the university libraries' special collections, allowed me to digitize Moran's wood engravings from several fragile volumes. David Thor, University of Iowa computer lab technician, was a godsend as he digitally corrected those images for reproduction; and Mary Bennett, curator at the State Historical Society of Iowa, offered additional assistance in locating period photographs. Holly Carver, director of the University of Iowa Press, was a true friend as she consulted with me on several occasions about the publication. The assembled audience of the University of Iowa American Studies lecture series in the fall of 2004 offered useful insights and suggestions as I presented a lecture on Prang, Moran, and the chromo controversy.

At Joslyn Art Museum, I am grateful to Marsha Gallagher for her collaboration throughout the original project. Larry Menschling spent long hours ordering the book illustrations, and Ruby Hagerbaumer cheerfully edited the book manuscript and did the final assembly of the illustrations. These relatively thankless tasks are essential to any publication, and I am grateful for the tireless efforts of these good people. More recently, I owe special thanks to Toby Jurovics, Chief Curator and Holland Curator of American Western Art at Joslyn Art Museum, Thomas Brent Smith, director of the Petrie Institute of Western American Art at the Denver Art Museum, and Fred Woodward, director of the University Press of Kansas, who have been enthusiastic about reviving the project.

The University Press of Kansas has been a pleasure to work with. Editor Nancy Jackson has been unfailingly enthusiastic about the project, adept in finding astute reviewers for the manuscript, and persistent in seeing it through publication. To those reviewers I extend my profound appreciation for their thoughtful comments and suggestions and for the record speed with which they produced them.

More personally, I would like to thank friends Susanna Strode and Rob, Laura, and Paul Cornell for their continual encouragement, friendship, and invaluable provision of child care; Wayne Fields, my best reader, who listened patiently to ongoing reports on the project's trials and triumphs and critiqued the manuscript even as he was finishing one of his own; and my parents, Barry and Carmen Kinsey, who looked after my young daughter while I made several research trips and who are, as always, my most ardent supporters. And finally I am most grateful to Ellen, who managed to grow, thrive, and delight me throughout the long months of difficult work. In gratitude for your companionship and tolerance of my distraction by other things during your first years, I lovingly dedicate this book to you. I hope you one day visit the places pictured here and are as inspired by them as I have been. Even their glories cannot rival the wonder you are to me.

Joni L. Kinsey

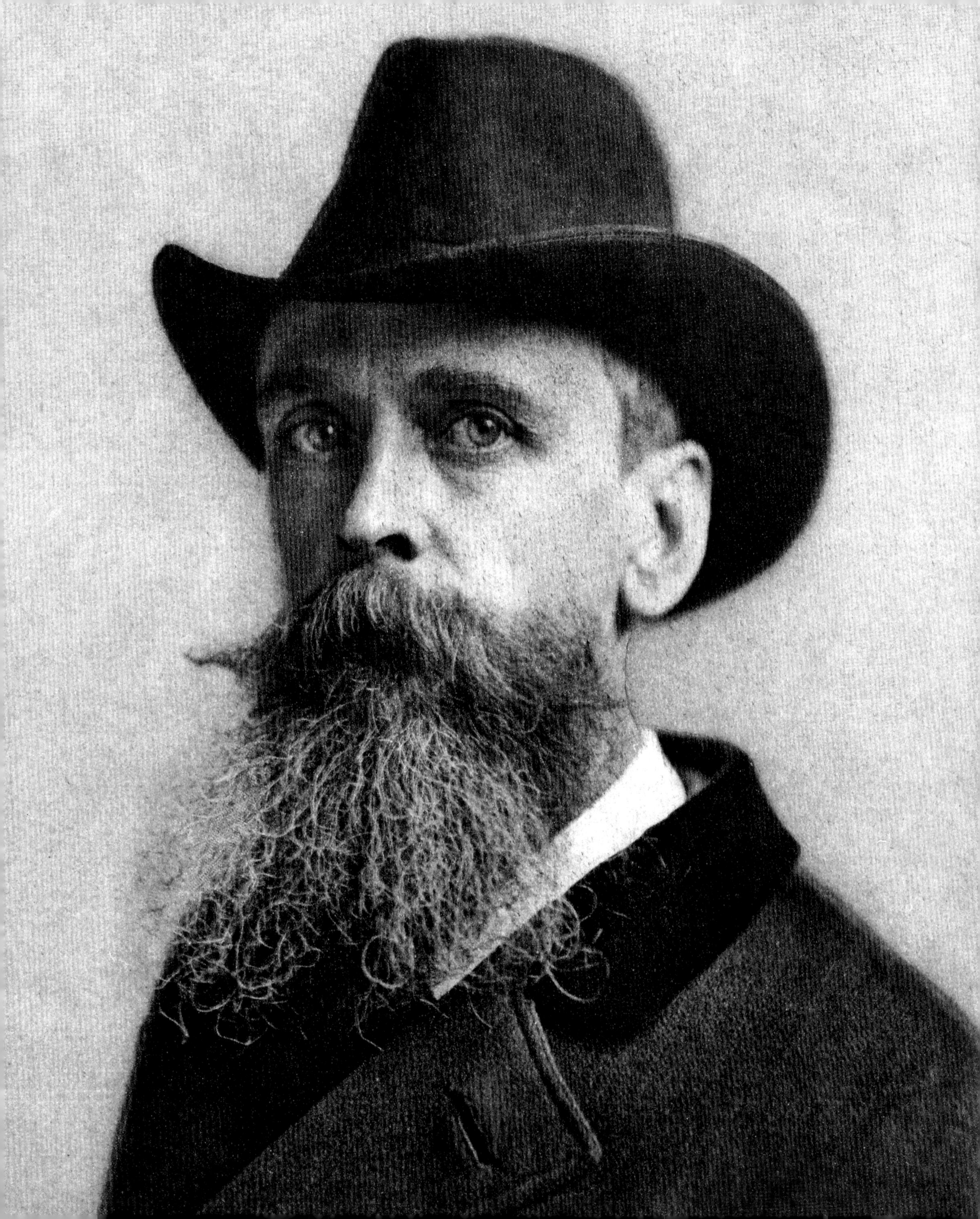

Introduction

Before many years have passed we shall see artists mounted on horseback riding in my Central Park who would have gone on foot all their days, but for the reproduction of their works by chromolithography.
—James Parton, "Popularizing Art," Atlantic Monthly, *1869*

For nineteenth-century audiences no less than for us today, the American West was a place so large and strange it could contain both wonder and woe. Its powerful character transformed the people who claimed it and influenced the United States to a degree difficult to estimate. As the West was explored, cultivated, and incorporated into the national identity, its forbidding and spectacular people and landscapes were revealed to the world, setting the stage for them to be endlessly imagined through scientific discoveries, the written word, the new medium of photography, and the artist's pen and palette. Countless industries developed to address this desire, bringing the West to the public through books, magazines, theatrical performances, scholarly lectures, exhibitions, and educational presentations, each creating the region anew as it sought to represent these places.

One of the least appreciated of these media has been the chromolithograph, a relatively modest type of printed color image that, for a brief time, galvanized the art world, polarizing opinions about taste and the place of art in American life. Chromolithographs appeared after the Civil War depicting subjects of all sorts, but their portrayal of the American West is an especially fascinating story, particularly in regard to the imagery of Thomas Moran (1837–1926, fig. 1), an artist better known for his monumental oil paintings but whose work also appeared in a wide array of commercial forms, including chromolithography. His art, ranging from enormous canvases in the U.S. Capitol to almost ubiquitous wood engravings in an array of popular magazines, contributed significantly to defining the image of the West for many Americans in the 1870s and after, especially in the era of chromolithography's heyday.

Moran had gotten his start as an apprentice wood engraver while still in his teens and, over approximately six decades, produced more than two thousand designs for publication.[1] Illustrative commissions provided him a more reliable income than painting alone, brought opportunities for travel, and introduced his name and art to an extremely large audience. He did commissioned work for some of the best firms of his time, both popular and art presses, in books, magazines, guidebooks, and advertisements, and by the 1890s reproductions of his paintings were sold as independent "works of art," the precursors of the modern poster. The majority of Moran's published imagery was reproduced through the most common reproductive medium of his time, wood engraving, but his landscapes also appeared as steel engravings, lithographs, chromolithographs, and, toward the end of his life, as photographically produced halftone gravures. He recognized that his art reached the widest audience

FIGURE 1. *Thomas Moran,* ca. 1871, photograph. Gilcrease Museum, Tulsa, Oklahoma

through publications, and he was committed to having it reproduced through the best technology available. Throughout his career he understood that such imagery was fundamental to his artistic development and success.

Moran's art was chromolithographed a number of times, but the most notable instance was in 1876 when the Boston lithographic firm, L. Prang & Co., published a suite of fifteen reproductions of his watercolors, collectively entitled *The Yellowstone National Park, and the Mountain Regions of Portions of Idaho, Nevada, Colorado and*

FIGURE 2. Title page, *The Yellowstone National Park,* 1876, L. Prang & Co. Gilcrease Museum, Tulsa, Oklahoma

THE

YELLOWSTONE NATIONAL PARK,

AND THE MOUNTAIN REGIONS OF PORTIONS OF
IDAHO, NEVADA, COLORADO AND UTAH.

DESCRIBED BY

PROFESSOR F. V. HAYDEN,

GEOLOGIST-IN-CHARGE OF THE UNITED STATES GOVERNMENT EXPLORING
EXPEDITIONS TO THE YELLOWSTONE VALLEY, AND OF THE
UNITED STATES GEOLOGICAL AND GEOGRAPHICAL
SURVEY OF THE TERRITORIES.

ILLUSTRATED
BY CHROMOLITHOGRAPHIC REPRODUCTIONS OF
WATER-COLOR SKETCHES,
BY

THOMAS MORAN,

ARTIST TO THE EXPEDITION OF 1871.

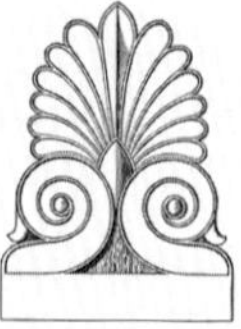

BOSTON.

L. PRANG AND COMPANY,

1876.

Utah (fig. 2). Accompanied by the authoritative text of the federal geological survey leader Ferdinand V. Hayden (1828–1887) and issued as a deluxe boxed portfolio (fig. 3), the prints are now widely regarded as a beautiful selection of views, the finest examples of chromolithography ever produced, and a landmark publication about the American West. The chromolithographs were the first printed color images of the first national park and many other notable regions of the West, and the prints remain highly valued, for both their quality and their significance within the history of American art. Several other Moran paintings were chromolithographed as well, one as late as 1913 after the process had been rendered obsolete by more modern reproductive techniques. When issued, these prints brought the colorful landscapes of the American West to large numbers of people and influenced attitudes and ideas about the region. Perhaps even more importantly, they were part of a revolution in American visual culture, one that transformed the value system of the art world and our relationship to the printed image.

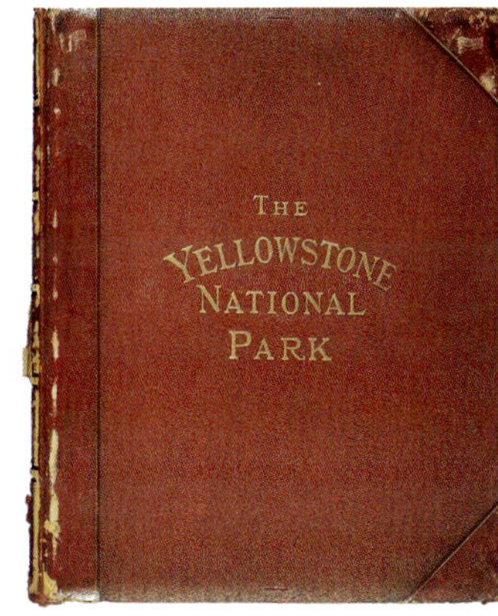

FIGURE 3. Portfolio cover, *The Yellowstone National Park*, 1876, L. Prang & Co. Gilcrease Museum, Tulsa, Oklahoma

THE TECHNIQUE OF CHROMOLITHOGRAPHY

Chromolithographs are highly detailed and intricately colored pictorial reproductions that in their best versions visually rival the oils and watercolors from which they were copied. Invented in 1796 by Alois Senefelder, lithography ("litho" meaning stone and "graphy" meaning writing) is based on the principle that oil and water do not mix. Creating the image entails drawing or painting on a very smooth-surfaced slab of absorbent limestone with a grease-based medium. The stone is then wet with water, saturating the areas not covered by the oily image. Next the stone is covered with a grease-based ink, which adheres only to the image, and paper is pressed to the stone and then lifted, transferring the ink onto it. Lithography, a "planographic" (or flat) process, has several advantages over "intaglio" printmaking (engraving and etching processes carry the ink in grooves that are incised in a metal plate or wood block), since it can reproduce continuous tone images—smooth gradations from light to dark—rather than only simulating those effects through line, as intaglio does. The images on lithographic stones are also more durable than those on intaglio plates, which wear more quickly with each print, eventually degrading the image. But lithography, like any printing process other than serigraphy and monoprinting, which can be manipulated to produce several hues simultaneously, is limited to reproducing only one color per stone or plate. Achieving a full-spectrum image requires either manually tinting a black-and-white print or creating a separate stone for each desired color within the final picture. Printings from these color-separated stones, all carefully "registered" to be in perfect alignment, result in a final synthesis that optically conjoins the individual hues into the final image (figs. 4–7).

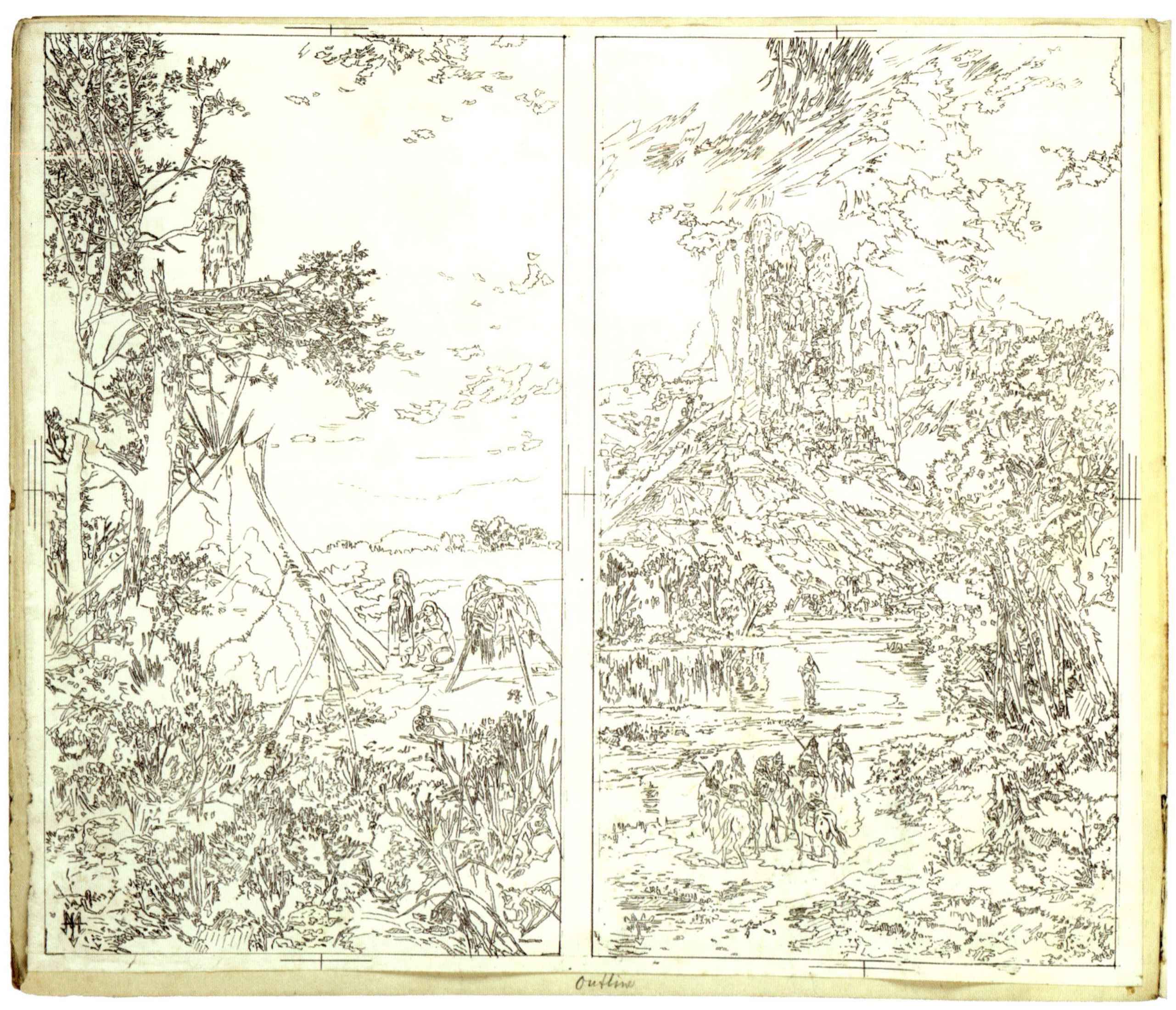

FIGURE 4. After Thomas Moran, progressive proof book of *On the Lookout* and *Cliffs of the Upper Colorado*, ca. 1879, page from bound book of chromolithographs, L. Prang & Co. Yale Collection of Western Americana, Beinecke Rare Book and Manuscript Library, gift of Paul Mellon

Unlike modern processes that photomechanically isolate the components and achieve a faithful reproduction with only four transparent inks (yellow, cyan or blue, magenta or red, and black), nineteenth-century chromo stones were manually drawn and based only on human observation. Working from a full-color original image (usually a painting or a watercolor), a skilled color lithographer, called a *chromiste,* would determine how many tints and shades were involved. Using transfer paper to copy the image to each stone, he would draw in only the parts of the picture that used a single chromatic element before going on to the next stone and its specific color. Precision was essential for accurate results, and the finest chromolithographs, including the

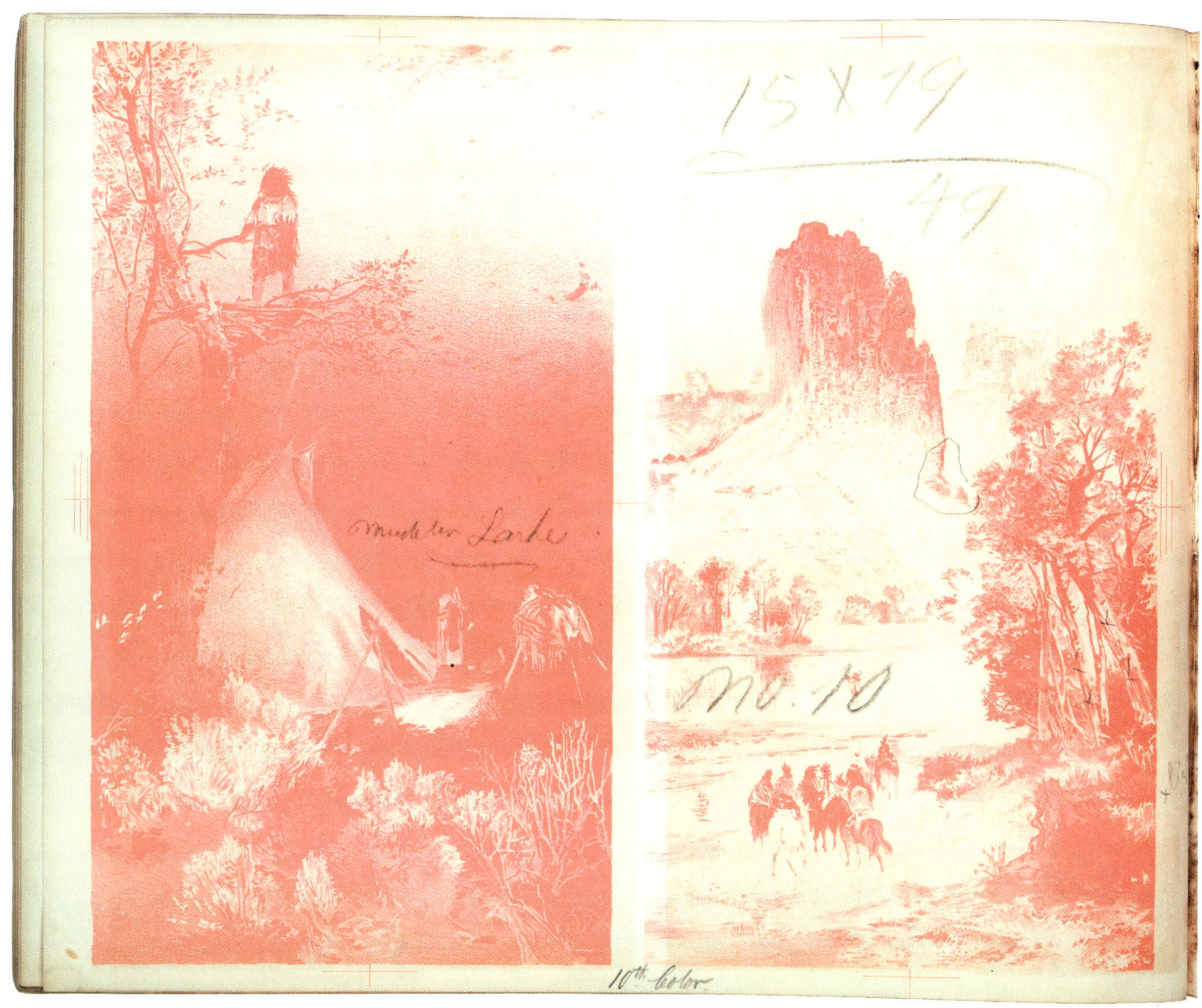

series Prang produced from Moran's watercolors in 1876, were created from as many as fifty-six carefully registered stones.[2] The process was expensive, time-consuming, and required great skill to do well, and Prang's chromos are regarded as among the finest examples of the medium.

FIGURE 5. After Thomas Moran, progressive proof book of *On the Lookout* and *Cliffs of the Upper Colorado*, ca. 1879, page from bound book of chromolithographs, L. Prang & Co. Yale Collection of Western Americana, Beinecke Rare Book and Manuscript Library, gift of Paul Mellon

MORAN'S CHROMOS BY L. PRANG & CO.

Louis Prang began publishing a wide array of chromolithographic products in the early 1860s, and his colorful cards, collectible keepsakes, and fine art reproductions revolutionized popular American visual culture by bringing color imagery to the

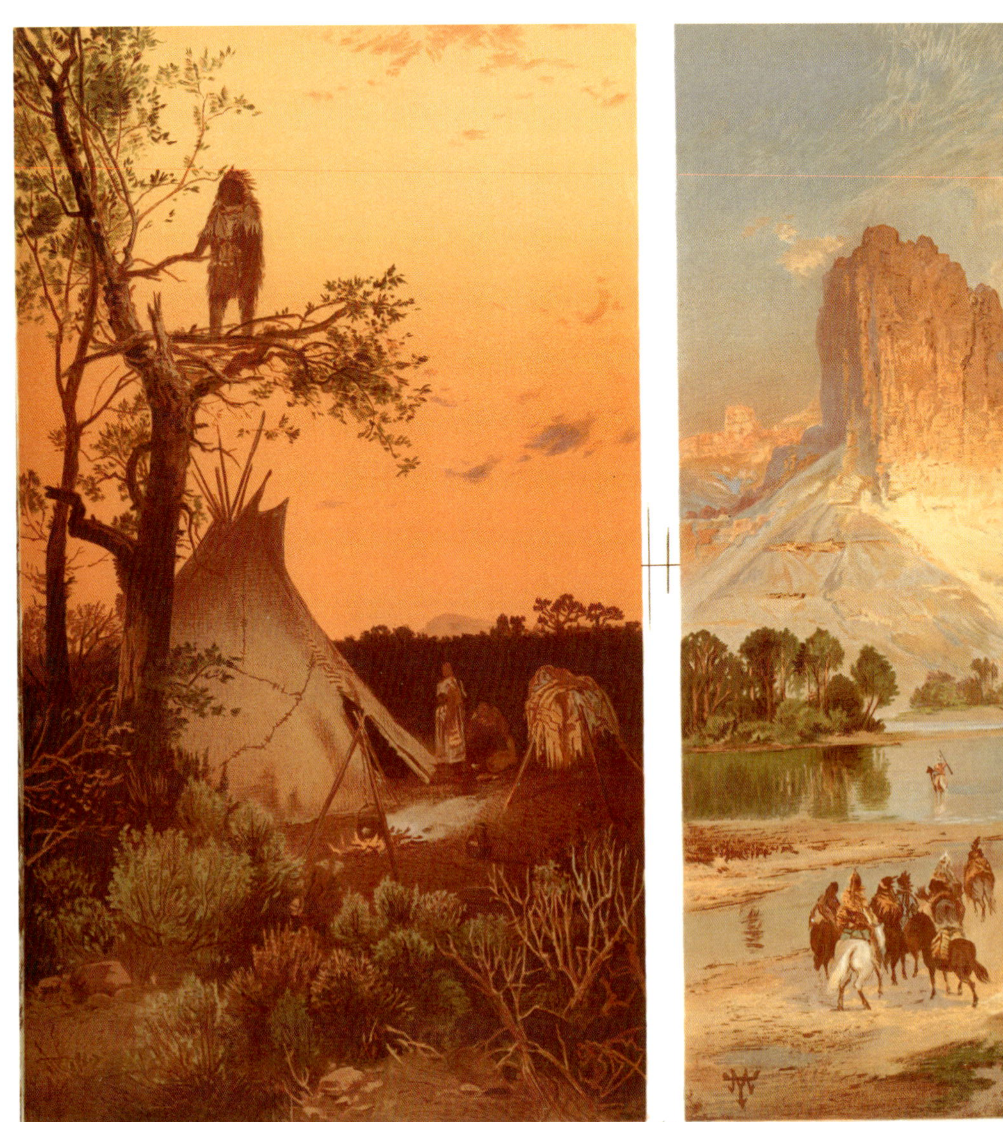

FIGURE 6. After Thomas Moran, progressive proof book of *On the Lookout* and *Cliffs of the Upper Colorado*, ca. 1879, page from bound book of chromolithographs, L. Prang & Co. Yale Collection of Western Americana, Beinecke Rare Book and Manuscript Library, gift of Paul Mellon

masses in what he called the "democracy of art." His work became highly controversial with art critics, however, for its ambitious replication of original paintings and the eagerness with which the public embraced the copies. Prang embarked on *The Yellowstone National Park* portfolio of chromolithographs from Thomas Moran's watercolors at the height of that debate, hoping to counteract the criticism with a distinguished and serious publication that would present the very best examples of his cherished medium.

The portfolio includes some of the artist's favorite subjects, themes Moran returned to repeatedly throughout his long and prolific career. Such repetitiousness was

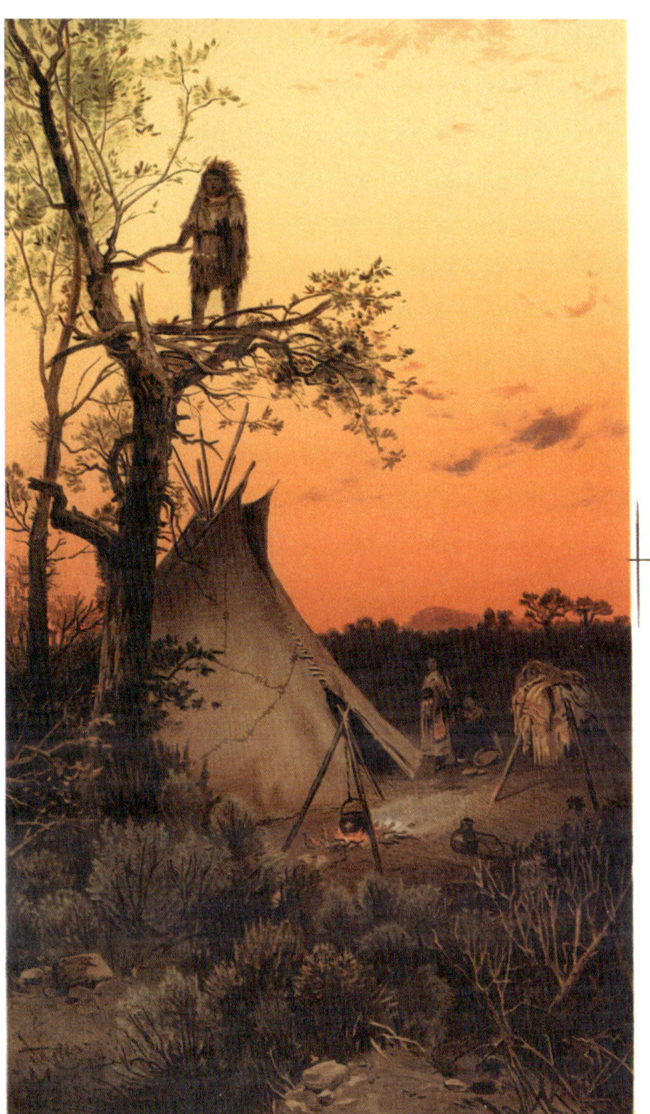

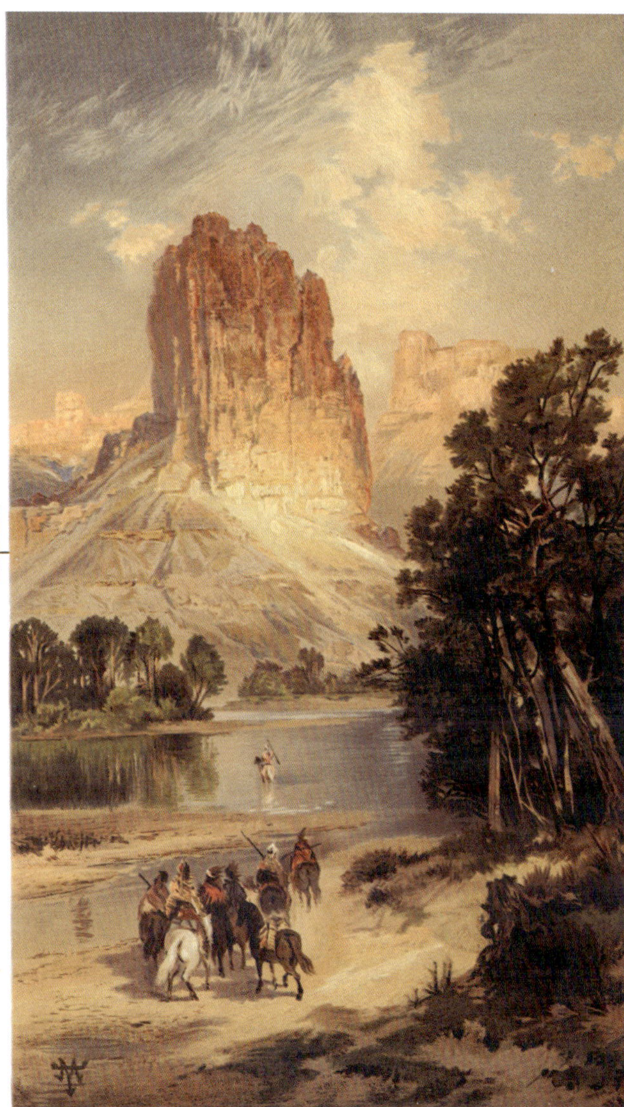

surely a practical issue as it allowed him to produce a large quantity of work relatively quickly, drawing upon the sketches and photographs in his studio collection, but it also testifies to the power of the places he depicted and their appeal to a broad audience. The recurrence of similar images in different media, sizes, and levels of finish in his work allows us to examine his artistic process through a variety of versions, from field studies and sketches to highly polished studio watercolors and oils, and then in popular reproductive imagery, from wood engravings to colorful chromolithographs. His published art, although ultimately executed by technicians for inclusion in books, magazines, and advertisements, was central to Moran's career in a variety of ways, and

FIGURE 7. After Thomas Moran, progressive proof book of *On the Lookout* and *Cliffs of the Upper Colorado*, ca. 1879, page from bound book of chromolithographs, L. Prang & Co. Yale Collection of Western Americana, Beinecke Rare Book and Manuscript Library, gift of Paul Mellon

he regarded these projects not as "mere" commercial assignments but as a mode of creative expression that should be valued no less than "original" work. Furthermore, he was very mindful that printed images disseminated his vision to a wide public and raised awareness of and interest in the vast reaches of American landscape.

Although the *Yellowstone National Park* chromolithographs are considered the outstanding specimens of their genre, they are still relatively little known and have never been the focus of a scholarly study. Two large Grand Canyon chromolithographs from Moran's paintings that were issued late in his life have received passing attention in other contexts, most notably in my own study of his work that resulted from the United States Geological Surveys and my chapter in the National Gallery of Art's book *Thomas Moran* (1997), but several other lesser-known chromos—two that were issued by *The Aldine* in 1874, two later images he did for Prang, and a series of four that appeared in Ferdinand Hayden's government report in 1883—have barely been acknowledged in the scholarly literature.

As reproductive rather than original prints, the chromolithographs are usually relegated to discussions of commercial art and admired primarily as finely crafted curiosities of an obsolete technology. Although the Prang chromos have been included in several exhibitions of Moran's art, including the National Gallery of Art's 1997 retrospective, which toured nationally, they have always been overshadowed by the artist's more dramatic oil paintings and other original works.[3] Some of the individual subjects of the series have been explored, but others have never been examined either for their significance in the artist's oeuvre or for their role in the visual culture of the nineteenth-century American West. Many are here linked for the first time to their sources in photographs and sketches and to versions of their themes that Moran created for other patrons.

Louis Prang's remarkable career and the prominence of his publishing house have received attention in several studies. Mary Margaret Sittig's 1970 master's thesis, "L. Prang & Company, Fine Art Publishers," is excellent and well documented and contains appendixes of primary materials not available elsewhere. Larry Freeman's *Louis Prang: Color Lithographer, Giant of a Man* (1971) and Katherine McClinton's *The Chromolithographs of Louis Prang* (1973) present an overview of Prang's products, and Peter Marzio's *The Democratic Art: Chromolithography, 1840–1900, Pictures for a Nineteenth-Century America* (1979) is the authoritative text on the phenomenon of chromos generally and includes sections on Prang's work. Recent studies by Michael Clapper, including an article in *American Art* and his 1997 dissertation, "Popularizing Art in Boston, 1856–1910: L. Prang & Co. and the Museum of Fine Arts," delve more deeply into the context of Prang's work and its cultural relevance.[4] While all these authors (and others) discuss the portfolio Prang produced with Moran and acknowledge it as a major achievement, their treatment is necessarily superficial within their larger discussions of his publishing house and its prolific production. The fascinating documents relating to *The Yellowstone National Park*'s production and marketing have never been discussed, nor has the publication been considered in the context of the "chromo-controversy" that raged around it. The embodiment of the uneasy balance between the imagined and the authentic that these chromos represented—in the context of aesthetics, of the American West, of scientific inquiry, and in regard to class and gender—has never been investigated, and the struggles surrounding their creation and reception are revealing about these issues. Their confluence deepens our appreciation of Moran's achievement throughout his career and sheds new light on the developing American publishing industry in the second half of the nineteenth century, especially the challenges that new technologies brought to long-standing traditions in art and visual culture.

Despite *The Yellowstone National Park*'s reputation as a landmark in the history of art and publishing, the story of the 1876 Prang portfolio and that of the other Moran chromos is a tale of trial as well as triumph. Undertaken by a publisher more accustomed to creating novelty items and single art reproductions than selling books, written by a man consumed with his own professional concerns, crafted as a hybrid of several formats with an unusual subject matter, and issued at a time of economic downturn and at the height of controversy over chromolithography, the publication was ultimately a significant disappointment for its creators. Nevertheless, the spectacular chromolithographs from Thomas Moran's art are rendered more intriguing for the challenges of their origins. They offer a range of insights about the artist's development, the shaping, packaging, and presentation of the American West as a visual commodity, the complex evolution of the publishing industry, the relationship of fine artists to commercial work, and the emerging tensions between notions of reproductions versus original art that were increasingly debated at the end of the nineteenth century. These fascinating objects stand apart from hundreds of contemporary illustrated and informational publications in their quality, their position within the prominent careers of their creators, and their lavish use of art to promote the American West. Most relevant to our own time, perhaps, Thomas Moran's chromolithographs offer early lessons in the important role of visual technology in an increasingly modern society, an issue that remains pertinent and compelling nearly a century and a half later.

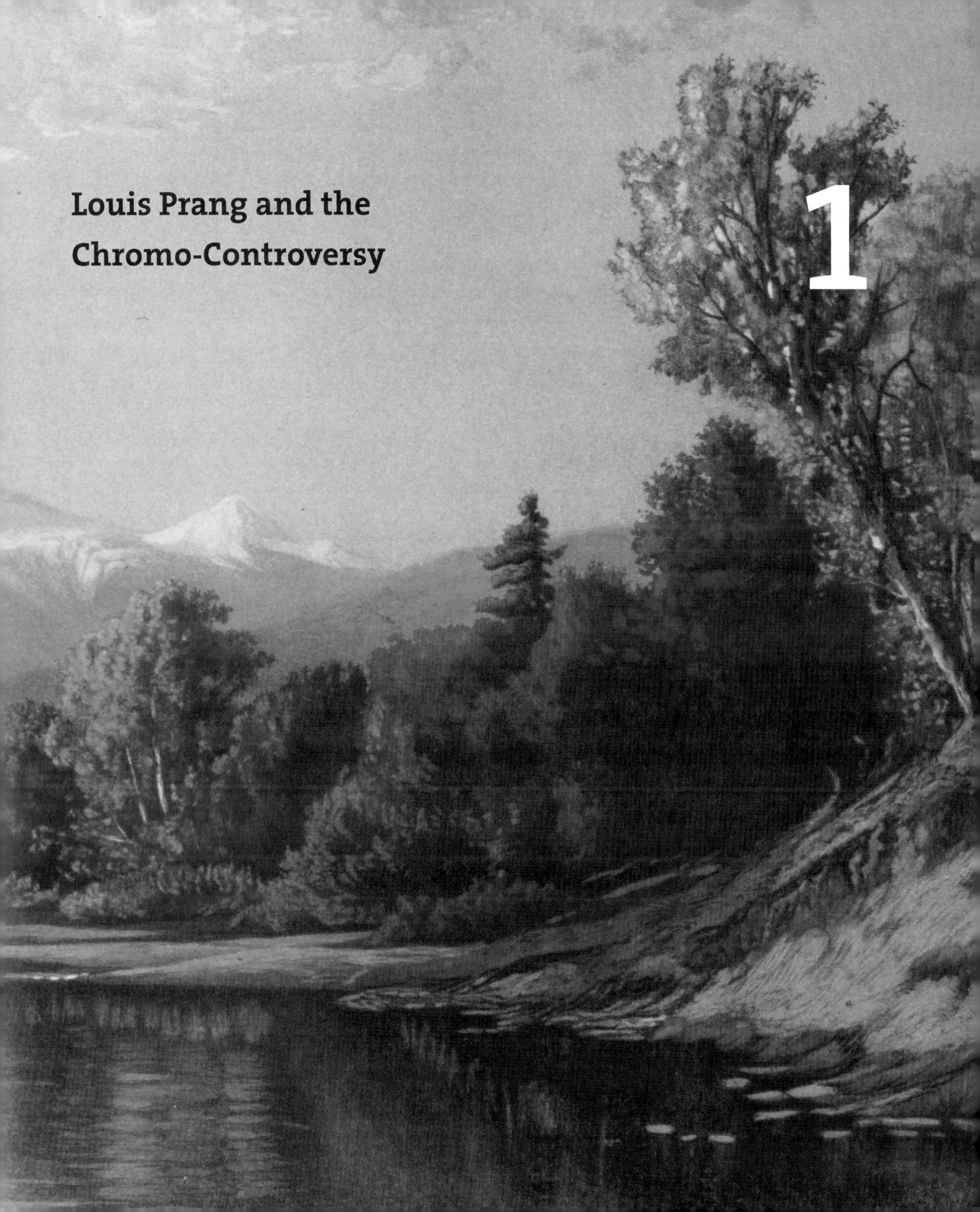

1 Louis Prang and the Chromo-Controversy

The exquisite little "Chromo" pictures, published by Prang & Co., are becoming very popular. They have much of the character of oil paintings, but they are so cheap that every household where taste presides may have at least one specimen.
—Philadelphia Daily Evening Bulletin, *1867*

The employment of chromolithography to imitate the synthetic colour of painters is one of those pernicious mistakes by which well-meaning people do more harm than they imagine.
— Philip Gilbert Hamerton, 1882

The impact of Louis Prang's vivid chromolithographs on American society is difficult to appreciate today in our image-saturated culture. When he began producing color prints in the early 1860s, only the wealthy who could afford originals had full-color art. Beautiful "gift books" and a host of more common newspapers and magazines such as *Harper's Weekly* and *Scribner's Monthly* offered images to the average person, but although these publications were profusely illustrated, the pictures were engravings — line art in black-and-white. Firms such as Currier and Ives had begun producing hand-colored lithographs at modest prices in the 1850s, but most of their images were printed only in black with watercolor added later, which resulted in a limited chromatic and tonal range. Chromolithographed cards, novelty items, and large, well-executed art reproductions, however, especially those created by L. Prang & Co., revolutionized American visual culture by making naturalistic color pictures as available as the printed word.

The period's rapid industrial growth and technological innovations brought major changes to many aspects of American life. Nowhere were they more visible than in the enormous quantities of inexpensive illustrated materials that were newly available to the average person. Between 1865 and 1870, for example, the number of magazines in the United States grew at a rate of about 100 per year, and many of these, along with an equally impressive number of new newspapers and books, contained illustrations in greater quantity and quality than ever before.[1] As the *Cosmopolitan Art Journal* wrote in 1857, "Illustration mania is upon our people. . . . nothing but illustrated works are profitable."[2]

In addition to an increasingly literate public and a rising middle class hungry for reading material, the boom was fueled by several major developments in printing technology. Foremost among these were new steam-driven presses that were faster and more efficient in their use of the vast quantities of cheaper papers that were now available. The first machines to produce "web" paper (rolls rather than sheets) were invented in 1798, and wood-pulp paper technology followed in 1843.[3] Although the wood composition also introduced the problem of impermanency since it is highly acidic, pulp paper was vastly cheaper than rag-based, enabling the production of inexpensive printed materials on a massive scale. Just as important was the new ability to print images and text on the same page. Illustrated books had formerly been both rare and expensive, as images had to be printed separately and then "tipped in" or pasted onto text sheets by hand. New platemaking processes solved this problem and led to a boom in pictorial weeklies, magazines, and books after 1850.[4] Improved engraving and platemaking techniques also raised the quality of printed pictorial imagery while keeping costs low. These included at first wood engraving and stereotyping, then electrotyping, and, later, photographic reproduction through halftone screens.[5] Various methods for reproducing photographs were attempted, and some illustrated books of the period did contain mechanically printed photographs, but generally these techniques were not very satisfying. Photographs appeared in special books with tipped-in prints, but photographic reproduction for the masses had to wait until halftone screen processes were perfected in the 1890s.

Even as the tremendous growth in illustrated materials brought a wealth of images to millions of Americans, most of them lacked a fundamental artistic element—color. Until the development of chromolithography in the middle of the century, color could be added to printed images only by hand, one page at a time.[6] This laborious process limited quantity, and it suffered qualitatively since it could not adequately reproduce or emulate the tonal subtleties of fine art. Chromolithography, on the other hand, offered the desired gradations of tone and color, and, although drawing each component color of a full-color image on its respective printing stone and the printing itself were all still manual processes, if done well, the resulting prints could replicate the qualities of a painting to a remarkable degree. The appeal of these inexpensive, well-executed color images for people accustomed only to black-and-white engravings was enormous.

As Peter Marzio has written, some 500 firms produced, published, or sold chromolithographs in America's eight largest cities in 1879. More than 100 were in operation in New York alone, and other large contingents were in Boston and Philadelphia. Chromolithography had first emanated from Boston's lithographers, and by the late 1860s L. Prang & Co. of that city was the most famous.[7] Over a century later, the firm stands out for the quality of its work and its impact on popular taste. Louis Prang did not invent chromolithography, but he brought the technique to its fullest realization as both a commodity and an art form. He distributed an extensive array of products but was especially known for his reproductions of European and American paintings. Advertising that they were indistinguishable from original art, he credited his flagship products with "refining the taste of the American people in art."[8] Passionate enthusiasts agreed, recommending the chromos to parents, schoolteachers, ministers, and others for their decorative contributions to interior spaces and their educational value in a democratic culture.

The popularity of Prang's fine art prints and their ability to blur the distinctions between originals and reproductions so unnerved connoisseurs, however, that they launched a campaign to discredit the prints for what they saw as chromos' contribution to a dangerous erosion of aesthetic values. Prang himself took an active role in the argument, ardently defending his products and his ideals for democratizing art. Although he never convinced his critics, his colorful prints won the hearts of the public and led the way for other reproductive methods that have permeated modern life. The detractors also succeeded, however, to the degree that "chromo" became synonymous with "fake," and the fundamental terms of the art world shifted away from considering published imagery as an art form to an exclusive privileging of originals.

Prang's 1876 portfolio of Thomas Moran's western chromolithographs was the publisher's most ambitious effort to present his cherished process to a sophisticated audience, and it may have been a direct effort to quell his critics' concerns about the medium. Although the publication has important ties to other issues—including the popularization of the American West, Thomas Moran's own career, and the history of the particular sites the series portrayed—the "chromo-controversy" is perhaps its most immediate context. *The Yellowstone National Park* ultimately failed to turn the tide of criticism in favor of chromolithography, and its own reception suffered for its association with that critique. But the interrelationships among the project, the debate over art reproductions, and Prang's career generally offer fascinating insights into Moran's chromolithographs and the tensions between art and industry at the end of the nineteenth century, a saga that has important implications for the visual culture of our own time.[9]

L. PRANG & COMPANY

Louis Prang (fig. 8) was born in Breslau, Silesia (present-day Poland), in 1824, the son of an engraver and calico-printing-factory manager who joined his father in the business at age thirteen. Prang later wrote, "My favorite theme is color. I was brought up a colorist and color mixer in connection with my special training for superintending a cotton printing and dyeing establishment in my native city," and indeed color would be a lifelong preoccupation.[10] He worked in the textile-printing industry until 1847, when he became active in revolutionary German politics. On the losing side of the upheavals there in 1848, he was forced to emigrate, joining the legions of "forty-eighters" who fled to the United States.[11] Prang eventually established himself in the printing industry in Boston, laboring for a time as a wood engraver for *Gleason's Pictorial* under its art department head, Frank Leslie, who would go on to create his own notable weekly newspaper. This experience with the new industry of illustrated publications inspired him to capitalize on the demand in new ways.[12]

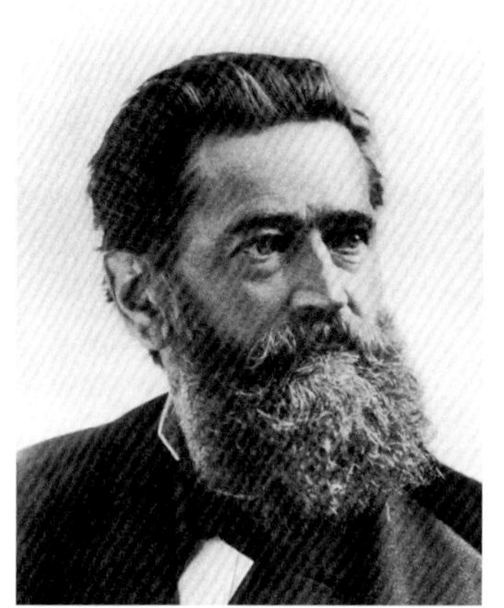

FIGURE 8. Anonymous, *Louis Prang*, ca. 1880, photograph. Courtesy of Hallmark Archives, Hallmark Cards, Inc., Kansas City, Missouri

In 1857 Prang formed a partnership with lithographer Julius Mayer. Although this relationship was short-lived, it contributed to Prang's development by introducing him to lithography and its potential. In 1859 Prang bought out Mayer and established L. Prang & Co. Desperate for customers at the beginning of the Civil War, he developed a steady trade in lithographed "War Telegram Marking Maps" that he issued quickly after major battles, complete with red and blue pencils to mark the army's movements. He produced other war-related imagery as well, such as portraits of leading generals and several series of Union camp scenes drawn by Winslow Homer (fig. 9). Most of these were printed only in black, but some reveal Prang's movement toward color lithography; Homer's small and often humorous *carte de visite* series develops from early plates that include only a hint of color to later images that display three hues in addition to the basic black.[13]

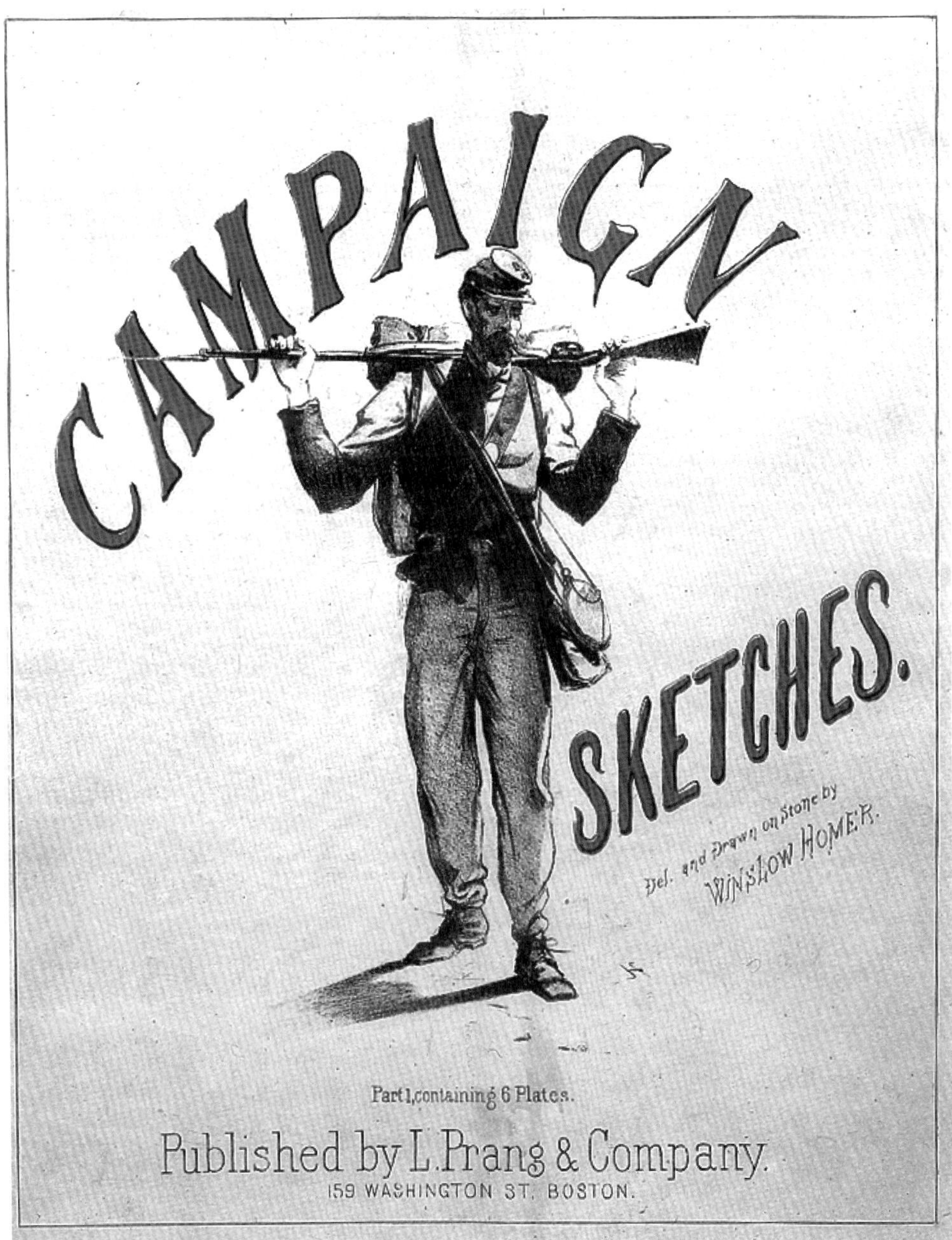

FIGURE 9. After Winslow Homer, *Campaign Sketches* (title page), 1863, lithograph, L. Prang & Co., 14 × 11 in. (35.6 × 27.9 cm). Boston Athenaeum

After the war Prang expanded his line, moving quickly to an almost exclusive emphasis on chromolithography. He produced all manner of printed materials (fig. 10), including trade, greeting, and religious cards, calendars, advertisements, scientific and natural history images, and a few books, appealing to a broad audience with a great range of imagery, from floral motifs to genre scenes. Always looking for what was or would become fashionable, he introduced new products regularly, sometimes creating a vogue, such as the Christmas cards he introduced to America in 1874. His company certainly influenced the Victorian-era passion for scrapbooks and pictorial albums, selling thousands of "Album Cards in Oil Colors," thematic sets of small colorful cards that cost as little as 50 cents for twelve.[14] These could be collected and pasted into books that Prang also sold; the most modest, selling for 15 cents, held twelve cards, and the largest, accommodating a thousand cards, cost $18.

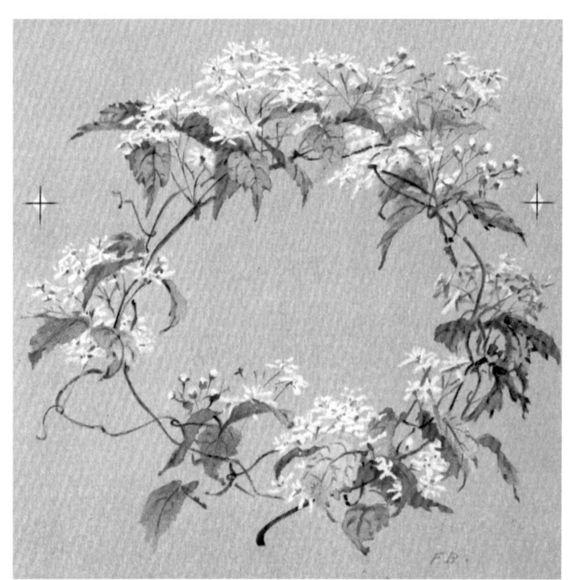

FIGURE 10. Anonymous, *May Friends Surround You Like a Wreath of Flowers!* motto card, L. Prang & Co. Hallmark Historical Collection, Kansas City, Missouri

Prang's business was hugely successful. By 1869 he had a new factory in the Boston suburb of Roxbury (fig. 11) that he called his "printory," running forty-five steam presses and employing ninety workers.[15] The plant was a model of modern industry. One important advance, for example, was the move to using zinc plates rather than lithographic stones for the drawing of each component color within any given image. At some point, possibly in the 1870s, Prang determined that not only were litho stones heavy, unwieldy, fragile, and difficult to store, they were also much more expensive than zinc plates. The zinc plates could be kept indefinitely and, when needed, the images they held could be moved via transfer paper to litho stones for printing. The expensive stones could be held in much smaller quantities and used repeatedly.[16] Another important advantage of the zinc plate/transfer method was that it worked as today's "offset lithography" does, in that the original art could be copied exactly as it appeared—the image would be "flopped" (rendered backwards) in its transfer to the stone, and then "flopped" again in the printing to achieve the proper orientation in the final version. And, finally, zinc plates enabled the "ganging up" of multiples of small images on a single stone.[17] Once printed, the sheets were easily cut into individual prints, an efficient saving of labor and materials. It is not known whether *The Yellowstone National Park* chromolithographs were produced with zinc plates, but whether that method or the more traditional one was used, their color separations would have been printed from lithographic stones (fig. 12).

PRANG'S AMERICAN CHROMOS

Prang became especially known for Prang's American Chromos, the fine art reproductions that were his firm's most aesthetically significant products (fig. 13). Even though the term "chromo" had been in use for some twenty years, Prang took credit for coining it. "I offered these pictures," he wrote, "to the public under the title of 'chromo,' a word that I thought I could use as a sort of trade mark for my best oil color prints."[18] Prang's Chromos made the word popular, but it soon began to be abused by other manufacturers of color prints with degeneration of its original meaning. Usually measuring about 10 × 12 inches, but sometimes as large as 32½ × 21¾ inches,

FIGURE 11. Anonymous, *Exterior View of Louis Prang's Chromolithographing Printing Factory at 2182 Washington St., Roxbury, Built in 1868,* photograph. American Antiquarian Society, Worcester, Massachusetts

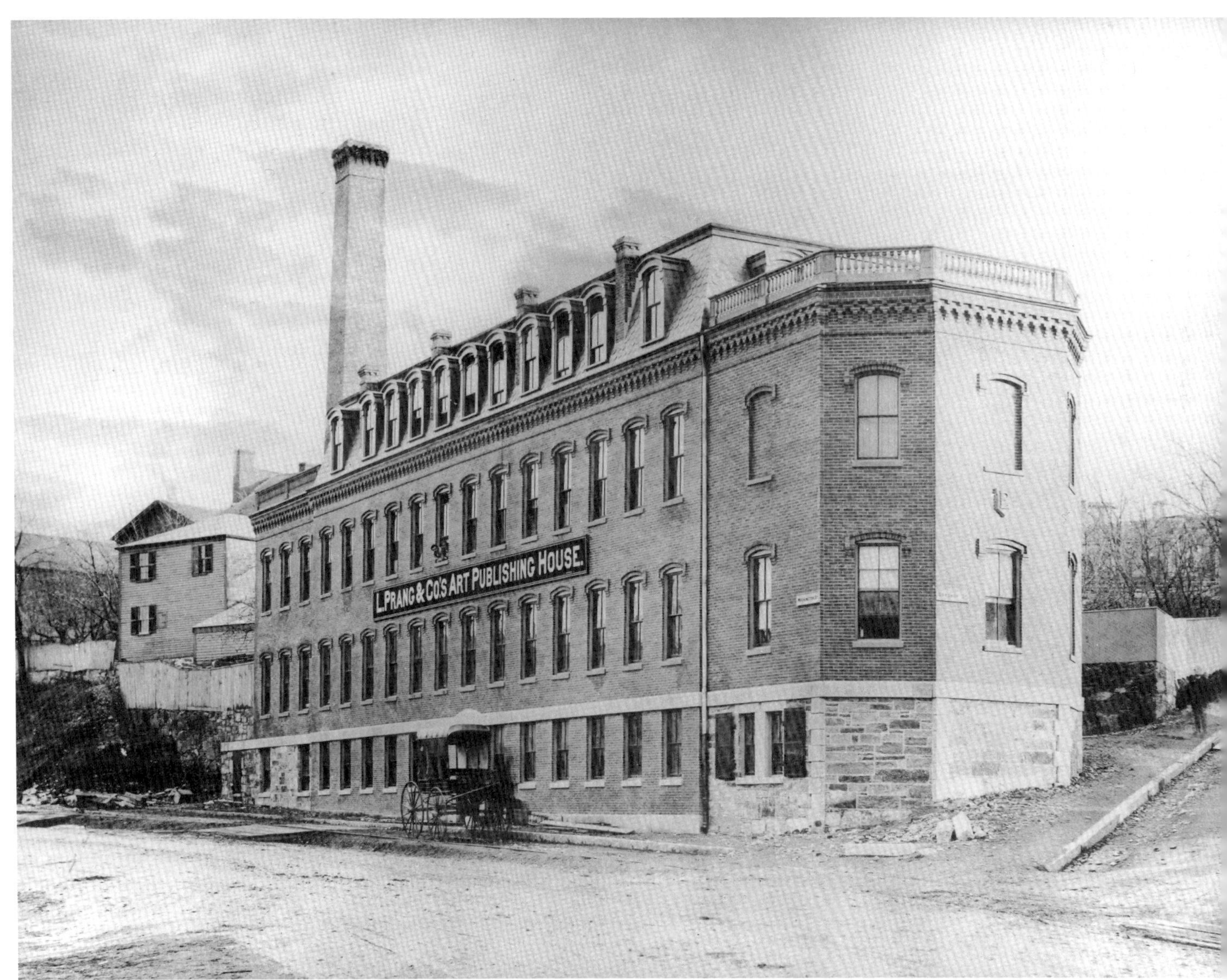

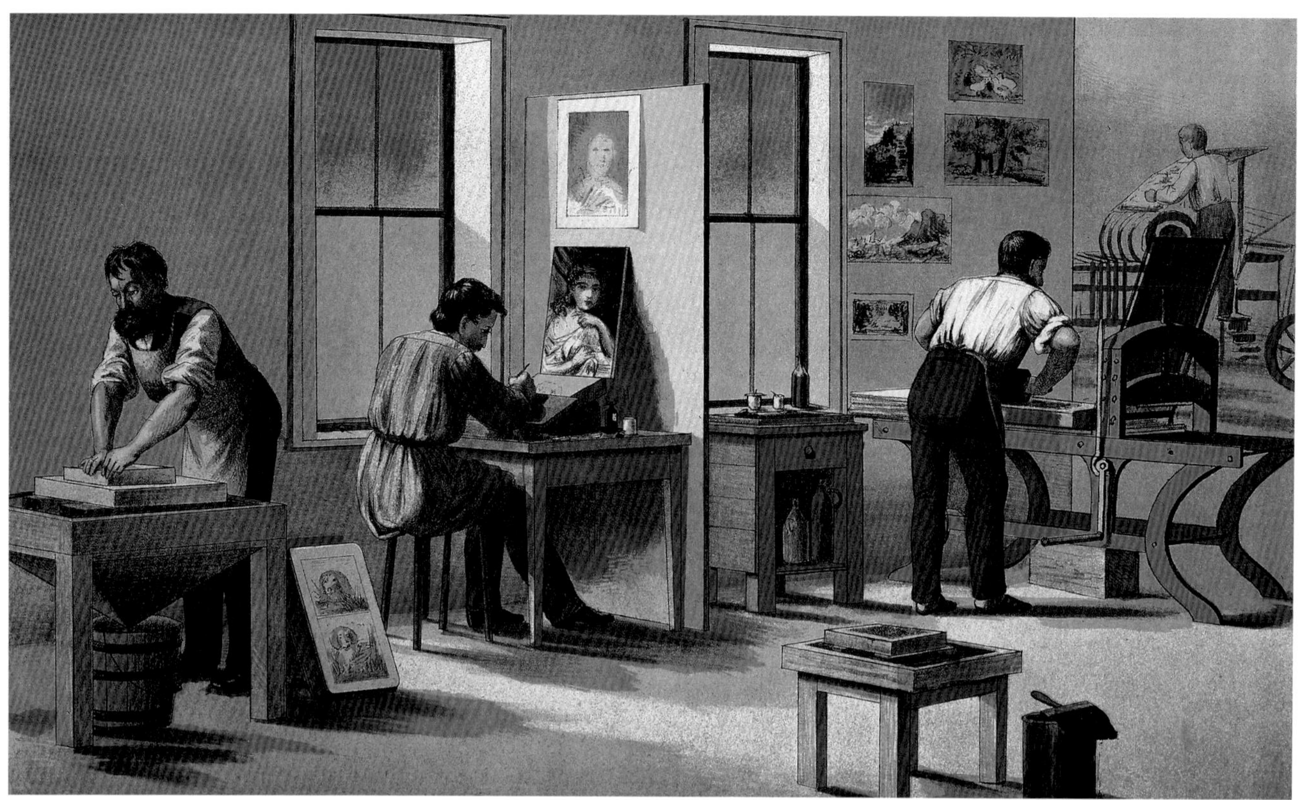

FIGURE 12. Anonymous, *Aids for Object Teaching, Trades and Occupations*, pl. 5, *"Lithographer,"* 1874, chromolithograph. Courtesy of Boston Public Library, Print Room

Prang's chromos ranged from portraits, still lifes, and animal scenes to genre subjects and landscapes, and they sought to replicate the appearance of the paintings from which they were copied in virtually every way, a point emphasized in the company's advertisements:

> Prang's American Chromos are reproductions of Paintings by the marvellous process of Chromo-lithography. The Paintings chosen for that purpose are mostly the works of distinguished American Artists, and every one is a gem of its class. Our chromo prints are absolutely fac-similes of the originals in color, drawing and spirit, and their price is so low that every home may enjoy the luxury of possessing a copy of works of art which hitherto adorned only the parlors of the rich.[19]

What distinguished Prang's American Chromos from other color imagery in Prang's own line and from art reproductions by other firms was their exceptional color range and level of finish, the result of laborious and precise color separation and printing with from eighteen to forty or more lithographic stones. Prang used oil colors since they had a greater luminosity than other inks, and, when dry, the prints were varnished using a special process that replicated both the sheen and texture of oil paintings. The actual method of obtaining this effect remains uncertain, but it

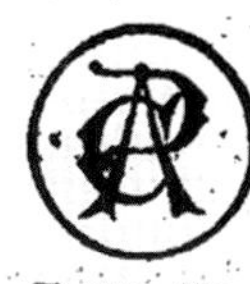

PRANG'S AMERICAN CHROMOS.

"THE DEMOCRACY OF ART."

PRANG'S AMERICAN CHROMOS are reproductions of Paintings by the marvellous process of Chromo-Lithography. The Paintings chosen for that purpose are mostly the works of distinguished American Artists, and every one is a gem of its class. Our Chromo prints are absolutely *fac similes* of the originals in color, drawing and spirit, and their price is so low that every home may enjoy the luxury of possessing a copy of works of art which hitherto adorned only the parlors of the rich.

LIST OF SUBJECTS, DECEMBER, 1869.

Subject	Price
WOOD MOSSES AND FERNS, after Miss E. Robbins	$1 50
BIRD'S NEST AND LICHENS, after Miss E. Robbins	1 50
GROUP OF CHICKENS, after Tait	5 00
GROUP OF DUCKLINGS, after Tait	5 00
GROUP OF QUAILS, after Tait	5 00
SIX AMERICAN LANDSCAPES, after Bricher, per set	9 00
EARLY AUTUMN ON ESOPUS CREEK, after Bricher	6 00
LATE AUTUMN IN WHITE MOUNTAINS, after Bricher	6 00
THE BULFINCH, after Cruikshank	3 00
THE LINNET, after Cruikshank	3 00
THE BABY, OR GOING TO THE BATH	3 00
THE SISTERS (companion to the Baby)	3 00
THE POULTRY-YARD, after Lemmens	5 00
POULTRY LIFE—A / POULTRY LIFE—B } after Lemmens, per pair	4 20
AUTUMN LEAVES (Maple)	1 00
AUTUMN LEAVES (Oak)	1 00
FLOWER BOUQUET	6 00
BLACKBERRIES IN VASE, after Lilly M. Spencer	6 00
CORREGGIO'S MAGDALENA	10 00
UNDER THE APPLE-TREE / REST ON THE ROADSIDE } after Niles, per pair	5 00
CHERRIES AND BASKET, after Miss V. Granbery	7 50
STRAWBERRIES AND BASKET, after Miss V. Granbery	7 50
THE KID'S PLAYGROUND, after Bruith	6 00
A FRIEND IN NEED	6 00
EASTER MORNING, after Mrs. James M. Hart	10 00
WHITTIER'S BAREFOOT BOY, after E. Johnson	5 00
WILD FRUIT (companion to Barefoot Boy), after George C. Lambdin	5 00
SUNLIGHT IN WINTER, after J. Morviller	$12 00
SUNSET (California scenery), after A. Bierstadt	10 00
HORSES IN A STORM, after R. Adams	7 50
OUR KITCHEN BOUQUET, after Wm. Harring	5 00
UNCONSCIOUS SLEEPER, after L. Perrault	6 00
THE TWO FRIENDS, after Giraud	6 00
THE DOCTOR, after Henry Bacon	3 00
DEAD GAME, after G. Bossett	3 00
FRINGED GENTIAN, after H. R. Newman	6 00
THE HARVEST (NORTH CONWAY), after B. B. G. Stone	5 00
THE CROWN OF NEW ENGLAND, after George L. Brown	15 00
SIX CENTRAL PARK VIEWS, after H. A. Ferguson	7 50
RASPBERRIES, after Miss V. Granbery	7 50
CURRANTS, after Miss V. Granberry	7 50
THE BOYHOOD OF LINCOLN, after Eastman Johnson	12 00
FRUIT PIECE No. 1, after C. Biele	5 00
SPRING, after A. T. Bricher	6 00
AUTUMN, after A. T. Bricher	6 00
WINTER, after J. Morviller	6 00
BABY IN TROUBLE, after Charles Verlat	6 00
POINTER AND QUAIL, after Tait	5 00
SPANIEL AND WOODCOCK, after Tait	5 00
SPRING TIME, after A. J. Van Wyngaerdt	5 00
SUNSET ON THE COAST, after M. F. H. De Haas	15 00
LAUNCHING THE LIFE-BOAT, after E. Moran	15 00
AFTER THE RAINS / BEFORE THE FROSTS } Companions, after Miss Florence Peel } ea.	3 00
NEAR BETHEL, on the Androscoggin, after S. Colman	4 00
THE BIRTHPLACE OF WHITTIER, the Poet, after Thomas Hill	15 00
A FAMILY SCENE IN POMPEII, after Joseph Coomans	20 00

ADDITIONS CONTINUALLY MADE.

"PRANG'S AMERICAN CHROMOS," which we guarantee as true *fac similes* of the originals, bear our trade mark and name on the back. They are for sale at all respectable Art and Picture stores.

PRANG'S "CHROMO JOURNAL," issued quarterly, contains a complete descriptive catalogue of our Chromos, with special information about the art. Specimen copies of the JOURNAL sent to any address on receipt of stamp.

L. PRANG & CO., FINE ART PUBLISHERS, BOSTON.

FIGURE 13. L. Prang & Co. advertisement for Prang's American Chromos, from *The Galaxy* 9 (June 1870): n.p. Special Collections, University of Iowa Libraries, Iowa City, Iowa

seems to have been a combination of a subtle embossing of the paper to simulate raised brushstrokes and a screened application of varnish that produced a canvaslike surface and the gloss of a fine painting. As one Prang advertisement read, quoting an "eminent critic": "The chromo-lithograph is a perfect facsimile of the original painting, reproducing not only the brush-marks, but the very lines of the canvas, in a way that surprises by its ingenuity. Mr. Prang tries with all his might to make his imitations absolutely deceptive, not for the purpose of deceiving, but in order to put faithful copies, 'as good as the originals,' within the reach of small purses."[20]

The glossy embellishments to printed chromos were not entirely unique to Prang; in Europe chromos treated in this way were known as *oleographs,* and although the term never caught on in the United States, it was not unknown either.[21] Prang made a specialty of the effect, and his chromos were particularly associated with this final touch that made them almost undistinguishable from the paintings they copied. Although Moran's chromolithographs in *The Yellowstone National Park* series were not given this final flourish, presumably because they originated in watercolor paintings with a matte surface, they were nevertheless part of Prang's series of high-end chromolithographs that were the hallmark of his company.

It took months for Prang's artists to draw the color separations from an original onto individual zinc plates or stones, and the transfer, printing, and finishing were no less arduous, but due to his production volume, Prang's chromos sold for modest amounts, usually no more than $5 to $10 each and many for as little as $3.[22] But even that price was significantly more than other reproductive prints of the time; Prang rightly assumed that people would pay a premium for premium products. For customers of more modest means he offered "Half Chromos," smaller prints (approximately 4 × 6 inches) with less subtle visual effects that were produced from fewer stones and lacked the final texture and varnish. Prang did not sell his chromos with frames but offered those separately, along with advice for customers who wished to do the framing themselves.[23]

To demonstrate the remarkable mimetic effects of chromos, Prang created a showroom gallery in his factory (fig. 14) "in which the proprietor sometimes hangs, side by side, an oil painting and the chromo-lithograph taken from it, both framed alike. . . . not even the artist who painted the picture could always tell them apart."[24] Taking this showroom on the road, he frequently mounted substantial displays of his wares at trade shows and fairs, including the Centennial Exposition in 1876 and the World's Columbian Exposition in 1893. At the more modest Massachusetts Charitable Mechanic's Association Exhibition in 1884, the *Bay State Monthly* reported that the L. Prang & Co. display of chromos with the original paintings from which they were drawn made viewers "puzzled to distinguish which was which." "Altogether," the review continued, "their exhibit with its large collection of elegant satin prints, its

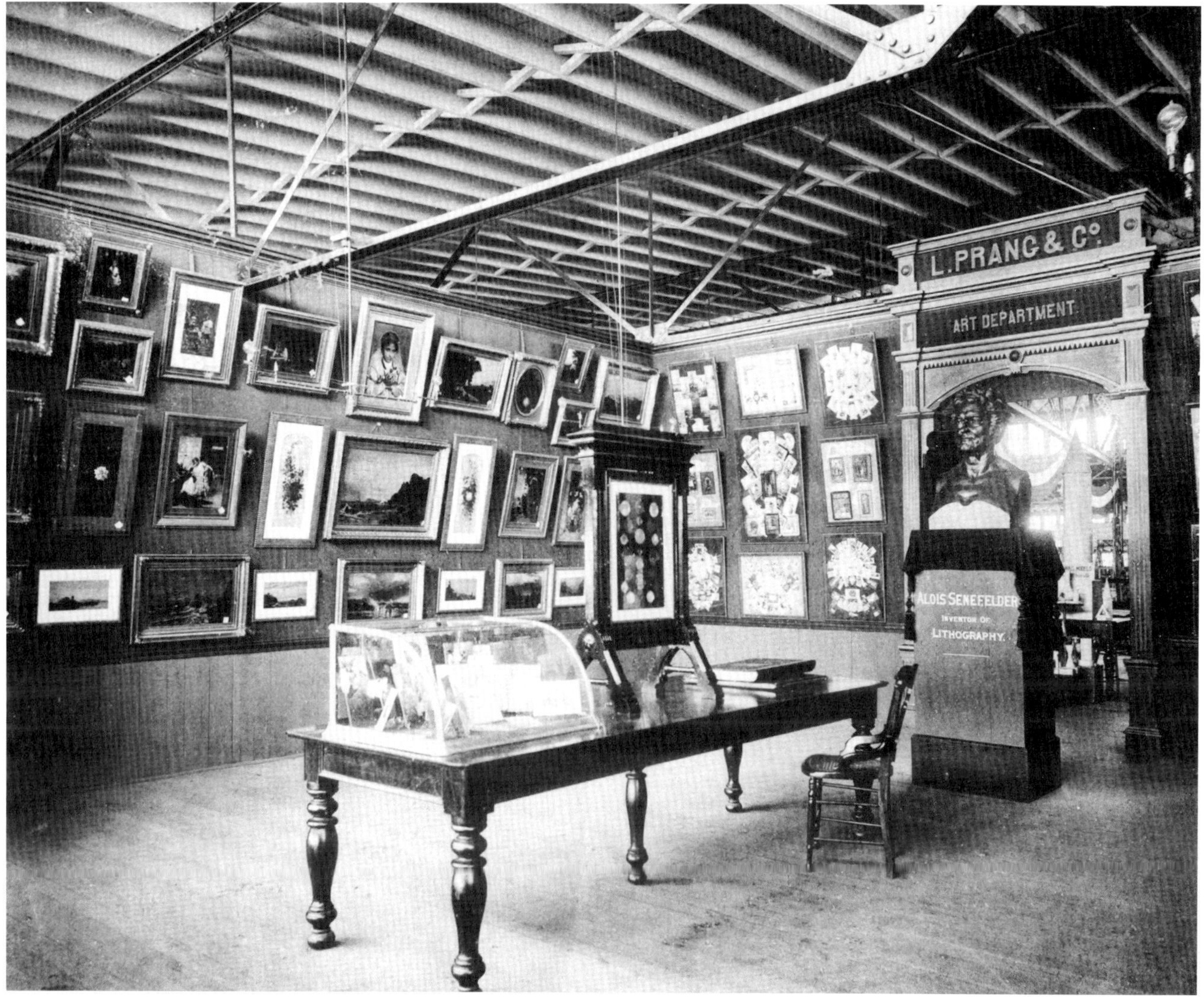

FIGURE 14. Anonymous, *Prang's Factory Showroom*, photograph. Courtesy of Hallmark Archives, Hallmark Cards, Inc., Kansas City, Missouri

studies for artists, its historical feature, . . . its interesting illustration by successive printings of how their pictures are made, and its instructive and artistic arrangement of their collection made it one of the most attractive features at the fair."[25]

Prang sold his most prestigious products through agents and directly from his factory "by subscription." Other items were available via mail order, general merchandise retailers, and stationery shops. To help explain the complex process of chromolithography to customers and justify to them the relatively high cost of his chromos compared to other publishers, Prang provided "progressive proof books" to retailers and salesmen. These remarkable binders include prints from each of the many stones required for a full-color chromolithograph, arranged to sequentially demonstrate the development of the image as it was printed (figs. 4–7). On the left side of each opened

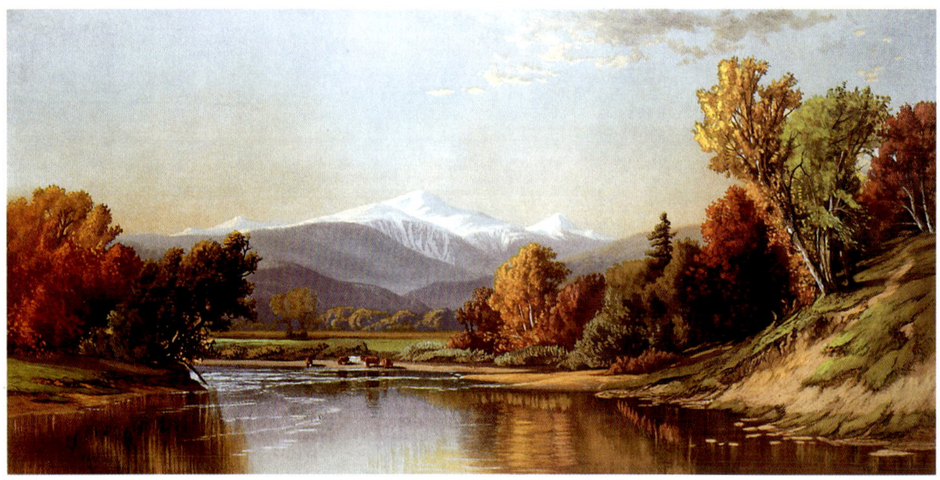

FIGURE 15. After A. T. Bricher, *Late Autumn in the White Mountains*, ca. 1865, chromolithograph, L. Prang & Co. Courtesy of Boston Public Library, Print Room

book is a page printed in the single color from one stone. Facing it on the right is the same image printed with that color *and* all those that have preceded it. As viewers turn the page, they thus see the cumulative effects of each color's addition to the developing picture. Through these virtual demonstrations, clients were able to envision the labor involved in chromo production and appreciate the final result significantly more than by simply viewing a finished image.[26] The progressive proof books were so useful that Prang published a commercially printed, bound version, *Prang's Prize Babies: How This Picture Is Made,* demonstrating the sequence of plates used to print Ida Waugh's popular chromolithograph of cherubic infants.[27]

By 1869 Prang's list of "full" chromos was up to almost fifty subjects, and it has been estimated that from 1866 to 1894 he published well over eight hundred fine art chromolithographs. The most important years were the decade of 1866 to 1876; after that, competition from Europe altered the publisher's emphasis to more "sentimental Victoriana" in his American Chromos and to other ventures such as Christmas cards and educational materials.[28] Most of the artists he reproduced were members of the National Academy of Design, and, although many are not well known today, some remain significant, including Asher B. Durand, Martin Johnson Heade, Lily Martin Spencer, Theodor Kaufmann, Alfred Thompson Bricher, and Jerome Thompson.

LANDSCAPE CHROMOS

Although the subject matter of Prang's American Chromos ranged widely, Prang's first and many of his most important later chromos were landscapes (fig. 15). His autobiography recounts that after hiring William Harring, his principal color separation artist, or *chromiste,* in 1864, "I began with his help to issue in 1865 two landscapes after oils by A. T. Bricher."[29] It is not always possible to determine the dates of creation for Prang's chromos since many were published repeatedly over a number of years, but other prints from about the same time included album cards of Hudson River and White Mountain views and a set of six larger Cuban scenes by Granville Perkins (1830–1895).[30] Prang's choice of landscape as an early emphasis is not surprising; it had been at the forefront of American art since the 1830s and it steadily grew in popularity through the 1860s.

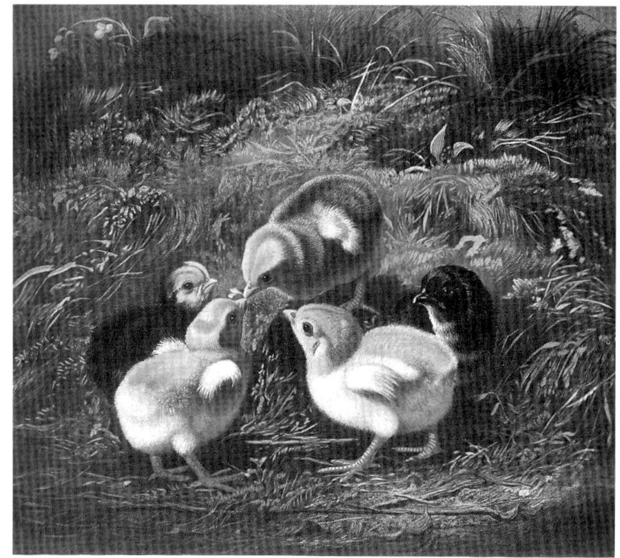

FIGURE 16. After Arthur Fitzwilliam Tait, *Group of Chickens*, 1866, chromolithograph, L. Prang & Co., 10 × 12 in. (25.4 × 30.5 cm). Courtesy of Boston Public Library, Print Room

At first the landscape chromos failed to sell well, in part because the price of $6 (for the full chromos) was significantly more than other chromolithographers' products. Prang's phenomenal success with Arthur Fitzwilliam Tait's *Group of Chickens* (fig. 16) and Eastman Johnson's *Barefoot* Boy in 1866–1867, however, turned the tide for all of his wares and proved that his pricing had been astute.[31] As Prang recalled, "Once the attention of the people [was] aroused, the landscapes which had previously fallen flat on the public were sought for, [and] it was a revelation to the trade. I could not produce fast enough—these prints and other choice subjects—everything sold."[32] Landscapes subsequently became a staple at L. Prang & Co., both as single chromos and as sets, and they were well received by most critics. Of George Loring Brown's view of Mt. Washington entitled *The Crown of New England,* for example, which Prang issued in 1869, the *Philadelphia Photographer* wrote, "This picture meets our ideas of what Messrs. Prang & Co., should make a *specialty,* i.e., large chromos of our own unequalled American scenery."[33]

Prang was already making strong efforts in that direction. In the late 1860s he approached a number of leading American artists, including Frederic Edwin Church (1826–1900) of *Niagara* fame, for what he later called an "Album of American Artists." According to his newsletter, *Prang's Chromo,* the original lithographs were to be commissioned from leading artists (rather than being drawn by others at L. Prang & Co.) and they would be issued as a "book." The publication would "be one of the most magnificent ever issued here and it will mark an epoch in the history of American art publications."[34] Although only six lithographs by J. Foxcroft Cole seem to have been produced for the project, Church apparently was intrigued with the idea:

> I believe I expressed to you, when I had the pleasure of receiving you in my studio, how much I sympathized with you in your patriotic purpose of publishing a portfolio of the works of American artists. And I should have been glad to have added my name to the copious list of artists who have promised to furnish works for publication. But this European trip has been one of too much play and too little work to permit of my making any fresh engagements; . . . I am happy to say that I

have seen nothing in Europe to cause me to change my opinion of the high excellence of the chromos you have done.[35]

Church's work was reproduced in chromolithography by other publishers, but not by L. Prang & Co.[36] Thomas Moran's request in 1875 that Prang print his lithographs *Solitude* and *Desolation* (see Chapter Two) may have been part of an effort to revive the Album of American Artists project, but neither those nor the album ever materialized. Although *The Yellowstone National Park* chromos in 1876 were reproductive rather than original prints, their presentation in portfolio was in keeping with the aspirations of the earlier project and indeed did mark "an epoch in the history of American art publications."

Two other views of American scenery that Prang reproduced at about the same time as he was corresponding with Frederic E. Church were Thomas Hill's *Yosemite Valley* and Albert Bierstadt's *Sunset in California* (also called *Sunset—California Scenery*), which Prang published in 1868 (fig. 17). These chromos were from oil paintings rather than from watercolors and were larger than the Moran prints would be. The Bierstadt chromo was the first print produced in Prang's new Roxbury factory, and, perhaps because of its significant size, it was priced at the unusual sum of $10.[37] Of the work, *Prang's Chromo* said, "We predict for this brilliant picture a large sale, as it is not only beautiful in itself, but illustrates a variety of scenery hitherto never produced in chromo."[38] As with many of Prang's other American Chromos done from oil paintings, these were also issued with a textured varnish, a surface not found on the Prang/Moran chromos because the watercolors from which they were produced had a matte finish.

Western scenery would continue to be an important subject for L. Prang & Co. About the same time as he was working with Moran, Prang also produced a group of fifteen California views after works by John R. Key (these were not accompanied by text or as lavishly packaged as the Moran chromos), and in 1878 he issued "Prang's Gems of American Scenery," small half chromos that sold in sets of six for a dollar. The first set was a series of Yosemite Valley views; another was a variety of scenes from the eastern United States. Even after his difficulties with the Moran portfolio, Prang continued to issue landscapes in his American Chromo series, although never as ambitiously presented as the 1876 Yellowstone prints. The subtle variations within landscapes may have been more difficult to produce than other types of paintings; one contemporary report indicated that Eastman Johnson's *Barefoot Boy* took twenty-six stones to print. Some landscapes required fifty-two.[39]

These extra color separations and printing, of course, cost significantly more than for chromos with fewer colors. But landscapes, like most of Prang's American Chromos, were also profitable. Prang's innovative products captured the fancy of thou-

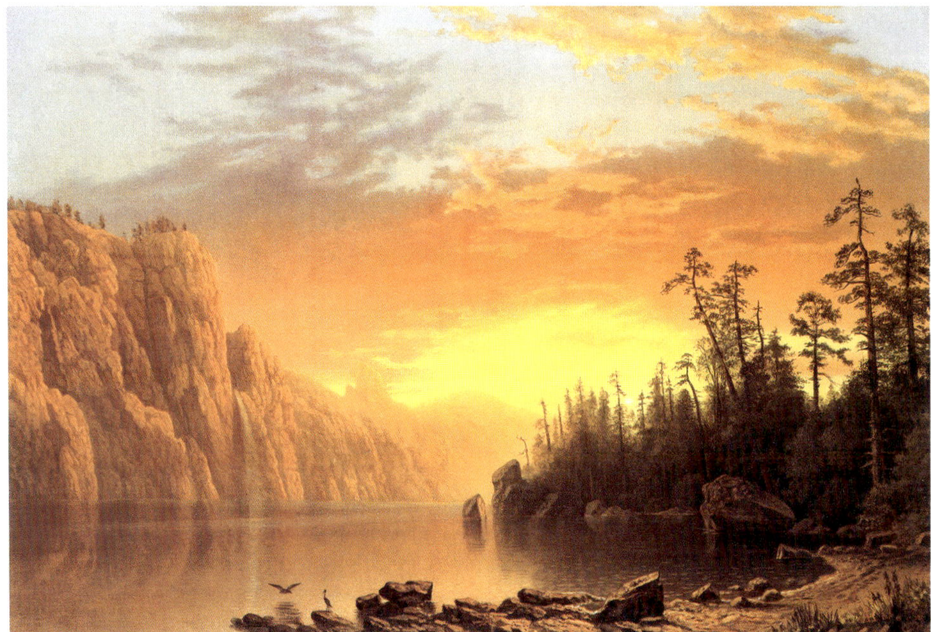

FIGURE 17. After Albert Bierstadt, *Sunset — California Scenery*, 1868, chromolithograph, L. Prang & Co. Courtesy of Boston Public Library, Print Room

sands of middle-class people in the United States and abroad, catapulting him and his company to international fame. As one reviewer noted, "It would be hard to find a house or school-room in which there is not somewhere a bit of brilliancy executed at [Prang's] establishment."[40] Substantial articles about his work appeared in magazines, newspapers, and trade journals, most of which extolled the virtues of his fine art reproductions, expressed delight in his extensive line of products, and marveled at his factory's efficiency. The immense popularity of his products, however, combined with the American Chromos' unnerving resemblance to original paintings, prompted a flurry of discussion about the effects of these prints on American culture. It was a debate that would have far-reaching implications, not only for *The Yellowstone National Park* and the art world, but also for many other areas of modern life.

THE CHROMO-CONTROVERSY

At least a century before Walter Benjamin's watershed article, "The Work of Art in the Age of Mechanical Reproduction," that discussed the aura of works of art and the implications of reproductions, people recognized that mass-produced imagery was having a significant impact on modern material life and aesthetic values.[41] Although many simply enjoyed the new abundance of pictorial imagery, a vigorous argument began in the mid-1860s about the virtues and corruptions of reproductions, with some participants extolling them as an enlightening force that offered art's elevating and educational benefits to a wide audience, and others claiming that they eroded the public's taste so severely that they threatened the positive development of culture. Chromolithographs generally and Prang's products in particular became the focus of the controversy, and although his *Yellowstone National Park* portfolio of Thomas Moran's images was never directly implicated, Prang probably intended the seriousness and quality of the 1876 publication as a rebuke to critics who sought to denigrate his work.

Chromolithographs were targeted because they most vividly represented the perceived problem. Unlike other forms of reproductions, such as wood engravings, which did not seek to be something they weren't, chromos were not only illusions but *successful* illusions. Their visual effects presented the first serious threat to the sanctity of the original and the power it symbolized, and they seemed to be *everywhere*. Prang's American Chromos were considered especially egregious since they replicated works of art with unprecedented verisimilitude, and Prang's effective marketing had taken them into nearly every corner of American life.[42] With their coats of varnish and gilt frames like those of fine oils, the modest prints were transformed into trompe l'oeil facsimiles of the art they reproduced, fooling all but connoisseurs.[43] The gravity of the delusion is difficult to appreciate today, but the veracity of chromos was so startling and the eagerness with which the masses embraced them so dramatic in the 1860s that the prints seemed to challenge the very premise of genius and privilege that had undergirded western culture since the Renaissance.

The lowly chromolithograph was only the most vulnerable example of what some considered to be a problematic trend extending far beyond art. Popular imagery generally, a variety of consumer goods, architectural revivalism, and many aspects of public entertainment were also accused of altering the very nature of American society—for the worse.[44] As Miles Orvell explained in his book, *The Real Thing: Imitation and Authenticity in American Culture:*

> The question first posed by industrial technology in the nineteenth century would become the question we are still trying to answer: how has the machine, with its power to produce replicas and reproductions, altered our culture? Has it, for example, degraded the quality of civilization by flooding our world with sham things? Or has it enlarged and democratized the base of culture? That question was debated during the years following the Civil War in terms, especially, of the ubiquitous chromolithograph, which became a symbol of the new culture. The whole problem of the cheap art reproduction sums up a good deal of the class conflict surrounding the advent of a culture of imitation.[45]

Significantly, even though chromolithographs were merely one of the most visible manifestations of a much larger issue, the word "chromo" came to represent the crisis as a whole, sometimes appearing as a hyphenated noun (e.g., "chromo-civilization").

Much to Prang's dismay, since he used the term to represent the highest of aspirations, even as "chromo" became a household word it also came to connote all that was mass produced, false, tasteless, and lacking in high moral value. And although thousands of chromolithographs by many different publishers permeated American society, as the *Boston Illustrated* reported in 1872, "when American chromos are mentioned it is usually his [Prang's] that are meant."[46] Depending on the perspective of the writer, Prang received most of the credit or the blame for chromos and their impact on American life.

As Michael Clapper has pointed out, chromos were targeted for two basic reasons: their mechanized nature dehumanized art, and their inherent deceptions degraded the public's taste. But the complaints were complex, addressing issues of quality, the relative merits of other reproductive media, the corruption of the marketplace, the ubiquity of reproductions, and so on. Supporters of chromos offered rebuttals to each of the detractors' concerns and added several important counterpoints, including the nationalistic distinction of mechanization and mass production and its positive effects on the quality of life, the educational benefits of chromos, and the democratic value of bringing art and design to millions who would otherwise go without. All of these contributions, they argued, enhanced national and cultural progress and should be cause for celebration.

Most significantly, however, the issue was a moral one, since the chromo problem required grappling with the slippery notion of truth and the issue of self-determination and the locus of power in a democratic society. Who would dictate the terms and directions of culture—the critics who cherished the sacrosanct aura of the unique and were determined to protect their ability to set the standards, or the public who, with their new access to things that had long been beyond their reach and by their sheer numbers were changing American social assumptions and practices? Since the issue struck at the very identity and authority of the critics, the vitriol of their attack should not be surprising.[47]

ATTITUDES TOWARD REPRODUCTIVE IMAGERY IN 1860

When Prang first began creating his American Chromos, reproductive prints were widely regarded as an important art form and a respectable means of disseminating art and its ideals. In 1865, for example, just before he issued his first art reproduction, *The Nation,* a journal that would later become an ardent critic of chromos' effects on modern life, published a two-part article entitled "Multiplied Art" that strongly advocated the value of reproductions even as it noted "the need for great improvement in this department." Citing educational merits, the article argued, "If one has a child to educate in beauty and thought as seen in graphic art, he can find no way so simple, and no simple way so good, as to familiarize his pupil with the best multiplied art he can procure." Crediting reproductions with even more popular relevance than fine art, it asserted, "It is certain that Americans can get more good from the contents of their portfolios [of reproductions] than from anything they see of a statelier kind of art. More comfort can often be got even out of *Harper's Weekly,* and a few illustrated books such as the English send us, than in the picture galleries." And recognizing the impact reproductions were having on visual culture, *The Nation* noted prophetically that

> it has seemed to the best and wisest of those who in our times have given thought to the fine arts, that multiplied and popular art is of as much importance to the world as art of any description whatever. . . . It is difficult for us even to estimate the greatness of its influence over past ages. Of its immense value at present we can judge more truly every day, and every day shows some new influence it already exerts, and some new field open to it but not yet occupied. Of its value to the future intellectual life of men, and of the influence it may exert over that life, we can only speculate. But, "judging the future by the past," we cannot doubt of this, that the greatest minds will give their thoughts to the keeping of the steel, the stone, and the wooden block and the manifold impression on white paper.[48]

Whether or not Louis Prang read these lines as he sought new directions for his lithography business in 1865, he certainly recognized the significance and potential of multiplied art, and he hoped, of course, that he would be among those "greatest minds."

This philosophy was echoed by most of the art societies, academies, and journals throughout the period from the 1850s to the 1880s, and many notable artists embraced illustrative and reproductive commissions, realizing that publication provided a reliable source of income and enabled their art to reach many more eyes than their singular oils and watercolors.[49] Publishers such as Currier and Ives, the American Art Union, and, of course, Louis Prang built their reputations on this premise and in turn actively encouraged it. Other efforts to democratize culture characterized the period as well, of course, as countless public museums, libraries, and other cultural institutions were established, and many of these reinforced the appreciation for reproductions and their ability to disseminate cultural ideas to a wide audience.

Principally dedicated to the ideal of art education rather than fine art connoisseurship in those early years, many nineteenth-century art museums in both America and abroad routinely filled their galleries with casts, copies, and reproductions on paper to present a comprehensive history of art. Moreover, reproductions were not necessarily segregated as a different medium but were often hung within displays of originals.[50] The most notable example of such institutions was the enormously popular South Kensington Museum in London (now the Victoria and Albert Museum), founded after the Crystal Palace Exposition in 1851, and in both its educational ideals and its celebration of a wide variety of objects, it served as an important model for many American museums. The Boston Museum of Fine Arts (BMFA) was one of these, founded after the Civil War as "a comprehensive gallery of reproductions, through plaster casts of the many treasures of Antique and Medieval Art, or photographs of original drawings by the most renowned artists of all periods."[51] As Clapper has discussed, as late as 1883, the BMFA's *Annual Report* reported that acquisition funds would continue to be directed toward copies. "It seems then, too plain for argument," the Committee on the Museum reasoned, "that we must rely principally on the liberality of others for original works of art, and that we should spend the greater part of the money available for purchases in buying reproductions. Upon what plan these should be bought is the important point to determine."[52] The BMFA was far from unique in this practice, but, although copies and reproductions continued to be prominently displayed in many museums after the turn of the century, by 1900 new theoretical hierarchies were emerging that gradually purged these objects from the galleries. In 1909, the influential BMFA secretary and president of the American Association of Museums, Benjamin Ives Gilman (1852–1933), wrote guidelines specifically advising against exhibiting reproductions due to the "radical inferiority of most copies," among other things, and his advice became a fundamental principle for art museums in the twentieth century.[53]

Within such an initial climate of appreciation for both the aesthetic and educational value of reproductions, however, it is hardly surprising that chromolithographs would have been so enthusiastically embraced when they were introduced shortly after the mid-nineteenth century. Not only were they virtually the first color images since hand-stitched samplers that were available to the multitudes, they were also the first color reproductions of paintings to be mass produced, and their ability to replicate paintings' tonal effects was far superior to engravings or etchings. The *Philadelphia Daily Evening Bulletin* wrote as early as 1856:

> Among the many advances which have been made of late years in Art, that of printing in colors is beyond question the most remarkable. It was thought almost from the beginning that it was difficult to foresee what would ultimately result from the discovery, and it is now evident that by it the most exquisite paintings of the first masters can be reproduced in all their beauty, with every shade true to the original, and at a cost far less than any other copy of equal excellence could be afforded.[54]

The potential for chromos to bring pleasure and enlightenment seemed unlimited.

The most ardent advocate of chromos, of course, was Louis Prang himself. He promoted his products and ideas in newspaper and journal articles and in his own publications and advertisements (fig. 18), the most notable of which was a quarterly

6 *CHROMOS.*

FLOWER PIECES, ETC.

Easter Morning. After Mrs. James M. Hart. Size, 14 by 21 . . . . **$10.00**
***The Same.** Size, 6¾ by 10¼ **3.00**
***Easter Morning, No. 2.** / ***Easter Morning, No. 3.** } Comps., after Mrs. O. E. Whitney. Size of each, 6¾ by 10⅜. Each **2.00**
***Easter Morning, No. 4.** / ***Easter Morning, No. 5.** } Comps., after Mrs. O. E. Whitney. Size of each, 6¾ by 10⅜. Each **2.00**
***After the Rains.** / ***Before the Frosts.** } Companions, after Florence Peel. Size of each, 9⅜ by 6⅝ . . . Each **3.00**
***Flowers of Hope.** After M. J. Heade. / ***Flowers of Memory.** After Miss E. Remington. } Comps. Size of each, 14⅜ by 8½. Each **5.00**
***Wild Flowers, No. 1.** / ***Wild Flowers, No. 2.** } Comps., after Miss Ellen Robbins. Size of each, 10 by 7 . . . Each **2.00**
Flower Bouquet. Size, 13¼ by 16⅜ **6.00**
***Fringed Gentian.** After H. R. Newman. Size in mat, 14 by 17 . . . . **2.00**
***Wild Roses.** After Mrs. Nina Moore. Size, 12⅛ by 9 . . . . **3.00**
***Gatherings by the Wayside. Mementoes of Old England.**

1. The Primroses at Home.
2. The Hedge-Sparrow's Mansion.
3. Spring's Delights.
4. Bramble and Wild Plums.

Comps. After C. Ryan. Size of each, mounted on gray board, 14 by 11 . . . . . **2.00**

White Lily. / **Calla Lily.** / **Roses.** } Comp., after Geo. C. Lambdin. Size of each, in mat, 21 by 28 . . . . . Each **5.00**
The Lily Pond. After Mrs. O. E. Whitney. Size, in mat, 11 by 14 . . . . **1.50**

DINING-ROOM PICTURES.

Strawberries and Basket. / **Cherries and Basket.** / **Currants.** / **Raspberries.** } Companions, after Miss Virg. Granberry. Size of each, 18 by 13 . . . . Each **$7.50**
Trout. / **Pickerel.** } Companions, after Geo. N. Cass. Size of each, 24 by 14 . . . . Each **7.50**
Fruit Piece, No. 1. After C. Biele. Size, 16 by 12 . . . . **6.00**
Our Kitchen Bouquet. After William Harring. Size, 18¼ by 13⅜ **5.00**
Blackberries in Vase. After Lilly M. Spencer. Size, 13¼ by 16⅜ **6.00**
Dead Game. After G. Bossett. Size, 11⅛ by 8⅜ **3.00**
***Dessert No. 1.** / ***Dessert No. 2.** } Companions, after R. D. Wilkie. Size of each, 10¼ by 15 . . . . . . Each **5.00**
***Dessert No. 3.** / ***Dessert No. 4.** } Companions, after C. P. Ream. Size of each, 10 by 12 . . . . Each **5.00**
Dessert No. 5. / **Dessert No. 6.** } Companions, after C. P. Ream. Size of each, 25⅝ by 20½ . . . . . . Each **12.00**
***Dessert No. 7.** After I. Wilms. Size, 10 by 12 . . . . **5.00**
Game Piece No. 1. / **Game Piece No. 2.** } Companions, after Geo. N. Cass. Size of each, 18⅜ by 24. Each **7.50**

MELANOPOLYCHROMES.

These pictures are entirely new in style as well as in subjects. They are from the originals of a gentleman known in the art-world under the assumed name of "Pilule," with whom the style originated, and who makes a specialty of it.

Size of each, in double mat, 14 by 17 . . . . Each **$2.50**

1. April Showers bring forth May Flowers.
2. R. S. V. P. ("Reply, if you please.")
3. Our Mutual Friend.
4. There's never Smoke without Fire.
5. One Touch of Nature makes the whole World kin.
6. The Missing Link.
7. The Chain Complete.

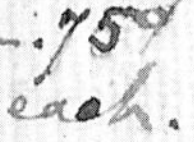

FIGURE 18. L. Prang & Co. advertisement, *Atlantic Almanac* (1870), back cover. Courtesy of Boston Public Library, Print Room

newsletter, *Prang's Chromo: A Journal of Popular Art,* that he published from December 1867 until 1871 (fig. 19).[55] Part advertisement and part propaganda, the tabloid-sized newspaper described his prints in detail, offered original or reprinted articles about the value of chromolithography for American society, and published testimonials from notable individuals on the technical and educational merits of his prints. To Prang's credit, he provided both sides of the chromo-controversy, although he hardly let his critics go unchallenged. His motivation was not simply to reinforce or enhance his products' appeal but was also a genuine desire to deliver the benefits of art to the people.[56]

THE CRITICS

The most dramatic of the early salvos launched at chromos appeared in the *New York Daily Tribune.* At first the paper's opinion was charitable. In April 1866 it wrote that the chromo of Tait's *Group of Chickens* "surprises by its ingenuity. Mr. Prang tries with all his might to make his imitations absolutely deceptive, not for the purpose of deceiving, but in order to put faithful copies . . . in the reach of small purses." But the critic put Prang on notice: "We shall not quarrel with him as to the methods of interesting people in art. He has . . . our trust that he will do his best to educate the class he works for, in the love of what is true as well as beautiful."[57] A long article the next month entitled "Concerning Chromo-Lithography" explained the process at some length and said that Tait's *Chickens* was "the most credible piece of work of this class yet produced." It was even more supportive of Prang's motives: "We trust they [L. Prang & Co.] will receive the encouragement necessary to enable them to continue their labors, which have a tendency to raise the standard of art among us, and educate the taste of the masses, by placing within their reach *fac-similes* of the finest works of the great masters in painting."[58] This gentle beginning was followed just six months later, however, with a much more pointed critique. Of several new chromos, it wrote, "None . . . are quite equal to Mr. Prang's previous publications," noting that the "cheap imitations" were "evidently intended for an uncritical market" and that they "hinder progress" in art.[59] The paper would be among the most vocal and acerbic of many that believed that the chromolithographs' quality and popularity were cause for concern.

In an era when increasing numbers of Americans aspired to refined tastes, the influence of critics who offered such advice was significant.[60] The *New York Daily Tribune*'s art critic, the presumed author of its reviews of Prang's chromos, and "the most influential commentator of his generation" was Clarence Cook (1828–1900), whose judgments could make or break artistic careers.[61] He had joined the *Tribune* in 1865, and in addition to the many columns he wrote for it until 1883, he also wrote several leading books on taste and art, including *The House Beautiful* (1876), *What Shall We Do with Our Walls?* (1881), and *Art and Artists of Our Time* (1888). These joined a host

Prang's Chromo.

A Journal of Popular Art.

Vol. II. BOSTON, CHRISTMAS, 1869. No. 7.

PRANG'S AMERICAN CHROMOS.

A full list of our American chromos and half-chromos, with size and retail price, will be found on the last page of this paper.

In presenting to our patrons wood-cut illustrations of some of our latest, as well as earlier publications, we feel compelled to remind them of the fact that these illustrations are merely indications, as it were, of the character of the pictures they represent. It is impossible to compress into so small a compass all the beauties of drawing and detail to be found in the originals, while the charms of color must of necessity be wanting entirely.

We are confident that we cannot offer anything more acceptable as a holiday gift to the art-loving public, than the splendid chromo, after the painting entitled "Family Scene

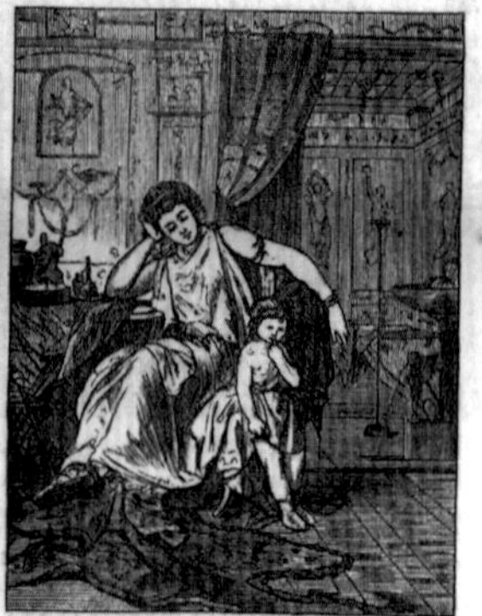

in Pompeii," which we place at the head of our list in this issue. The original, which is in our possession, is the production of Mr. Joseph Coomans, a Belgian artist of high renown, who has devoted himself almost entirely to the delineation of the family life of Greek and Roman antiquity, and whose works stand unrivalled in regard to delicacy of finish and softness, yet brilliancy, of coloring. The specimen which we have chosen combines these qualities in an eminent degree; and to do justice to the artist, as well as to ourselves, we have spared no pains and no outlay of money in producing the fac-simile. No less than forty-three stones, the greatest number ever employed, were necessary for the drawings, and the amount of time spent upon this triumph of the chromo-lithographic art will be more fully realized when we say that the *printing alone* of each edition requires fully six months for its completion. The "New York Evening Mail," speaking of our firm and the chromo under consideration, remarks:

"We knew that this enterprising house had spared neither money nor pains in its effort to hold high rank as chromo-lithographers, yet, remembering the many disadvantages by which the pursuit of a specialty of this kind is accompanied here, we did not dare to hope that an American house would take the highest rank so soon. And yet, if we are to judge from the admirable specimen of the art now before us in this chromo of Cooman's 'Family Scene at Pompeii,' on exhibition at Goupil's, there is no second place for Prang & Co. This is truly a wonder of Lithography, rich, yet delicate in color as the original — wanting in no important feature by which the painting is distinguished."

We now pass to another of our late issues: "The birth-place of Whittier, the Poet."

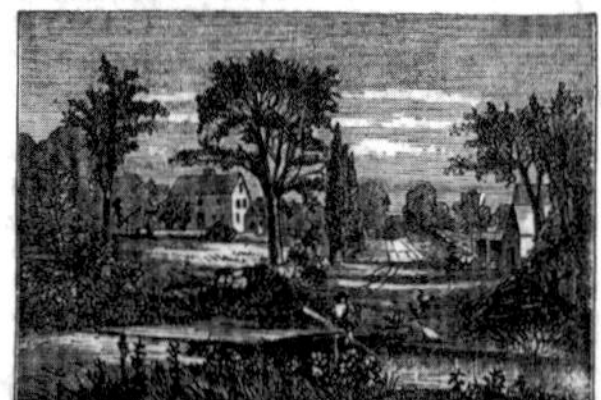

After an original, painted expressly for us by Mr. Thomas Hill, the celebrated painter of California scenery. Mr. Hill's great picture of the "Yosemite Valley" (recently sold in San Francisco, by the way), is still fresh in the memories of the people, and the chromo which we published after it, by subscription, has secured it a place in many an American home. But aside from the name of the artist, which in itself is sufficient to challenge attention, there is also something in the subject of the present picture calculated to awaken pleasant thoughts and recollections in thousands of hearts all over our country. True, the scene is not grand. The homely looking old farmhouse, the tall poplars at the gateway, the old pump in the garden, the dilapidated stable across the road, the little brook running through the foreground — all these are things to be met with daily, and to be passed by unnoticed. But it is typical of the comfortable country homes of New England; those homes, which, in the midst of their congenial associations, have reared up some of the brightest lights of our civilization, which have been the birthplaces of some of the highest aspirations of our day, and to which all those who have gone forth from them look back as to the abodes of bliss. And when to this is added, that here was born the good man and sweet poet, who is more firmly than any other enshrined in the hearts of his countrymen, then, indeed, is the humble homestead surrounded with a halo of imperishable glory!

We have Mr. Whittier's testimony, that he considers the picture a perfect portrait of the locality, as he has himself described it in his "Yankee Gipsies."

Playing Mother.

Although the grandeur of antiquity, as well as the charm of poetry, is wanting to the little picture now claiming our attention, yet we are confident that we are prophesying aright when we bespeak for it a universal popularity. Its title,

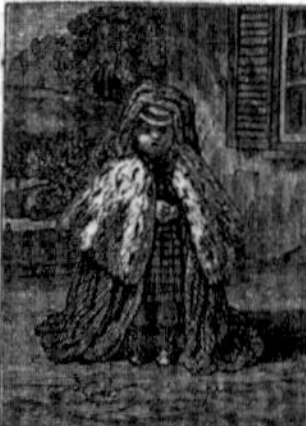

"Playing Mother," fully explains the story told by it, and it will be sufficiently recommended to all art-lovers, when we say that it was painted by Mr. John G. Brown, of New York. Mr. Brown has become quite famous by his successful delineations of American children, so much so, that he has already been styled "Children-Brown," similar to some of the old artists, who were also sometimes styled after the subjects to which they devoted special attention, such as Honthorst, who was called Gherardo delle notte (after his night pictures), or Carlo Maratti, who had to put up with the nickname of Carluccio delle Madonne, since his brush was mainly devoted to the glorification of the Virgin, and others. We may as well mention here that this chromo is of the same size with that most popular of all our publications, "The Barefoot Boy," which will be found described on another page. We shall soon have the pleasure of presenting to the public some of the larger creations of Mr. Brown's brush.

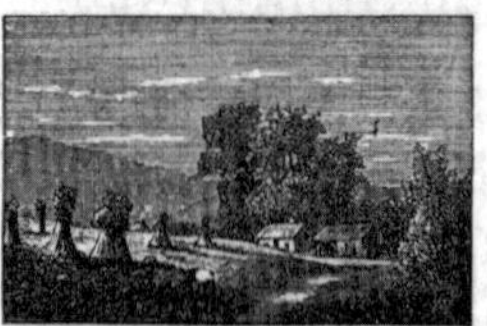

"Harvest" and "Springtime," near North Conway, are the titles of our next two illustrations. The first of the pair, painted by an American artist, Mr. B. B. G. Stone, of Catskill, has been before the public for some time, and has proved to be one of its favorites. Like "Whittier's Birth-place," it recalls the memories of the pleasant old country home, snugly nestled in a lovely valley.

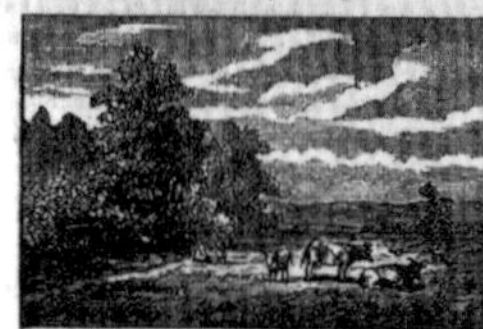

"Springtime," its companion-piece, will be new to most of our readers, having but recently been added to our list. The original is from the hands of Mr. A. J. Van Wyngaerdt, a Belgian landscape artist, of great merit. The cool, green meadow, upon which cows and sheep are quietly grazing, the outskirts of the grove, closing the picture upon the left, the blue hills, which arrest the eye in the far distance, and the translucent sky, studded with fleeting white clouds, which overarches the whole, — all these elements combine to produce one of the sweetest idyls ever fixed upon canvas.

As we are speaking of landscapes, we will stop to notice a few chromos of which we cannot present the cuts to our readers at present. All those who have followed our progress and have noted the many good pictures which we have made accessible to the people at large, will remember with delight the two beautiful landscapes by Mr. A. T. Bricher; entitled "Early Autumn" and "Late Autumn." We have now added some further specimens of the work of this favorite artist to our list, in the shape of three pictures, illustrative of the three seasons, "Spring," "Summer," and "Autumn," these being also the titles of the pictures. Of these three, "Spring" and "Autumn" are now ready, while "Summer" is in the hands of the printers and will soon be issued. To complete the series of the seasons, we have added a fourth picture, "Winter," after the late J. Morviller. This chromo is not altogether new to our patrons, as it embodies part of the scene represented in our chromo, entitled "Sunlight in Winter."

of publications on aesthetics by many different authors, ranging from theoretical treatises for scholars and artists to practical how-to books about home decoration. Most critics concerned themselves with high art issues, focusing on trends in painting and sculpture and comparing American art to the achievements of European art. But as the number of printed reproductions grew, these critics began to take more notice of them. As *The Nation* recognized in 1865:

> Criticism in America has been occupied rather too exclusively with oil pictures in gilt frames arranged in huge annual exhibitions. The periodical press, from which criticism mainly issues, seems not to acknowledge the existence of any other kind of art. And yet it would seem that if multiplied and popular art is anywhere useful, it must be peculiarly so in America. It would be well, therefore, to discuss its capacity and its limitations and to speak briefly of some of the most excellent works of multiplied art which are within reach of our people.[62]

The response to this call was both a blessing and a curse to Louis Prang and the reputation of chromolithographs.

Prang was keenly aware of the power of these texts to influence public opinion. Instead of waiting for financial ruin or, alternatively, "crying all the way to the bank," he took an active and articulate role in his own defense and continued to issue fine art chromos that he hoped would turn the tide toward populist art. He quickly responded to critics in print, and he often reprinted the exchanges in *Prang's Chromo*.[63] In the case of the negative *Tribune* review, he responded, "All the good which you and we expected from the introduction of this new helpmaid to Art education will be injuriously affected if the fallacy of your critic's assertion is not at once made evident," and in a lengthy commentary he countered the criticism point by point. Not one to allow Prang the last word, the *Tribune* printed a long rejoinder a few days later. Acknowledging that the publisher was "welcome to his opinion," it added dryly, "We do not greatly care to discuss the subject with him," but then went on for an entire column. Prang had similarly unpleasant encounters and "discussions" with other publications, including *The Galaxy*, *Putnam's Monthly*, and *The Nation*.[64]

CHROMOS' EDUCATIONAL AND DEMOCRATIC MERITS

The most persistent claim for chromolithographs was the intertwined theme that chromos were inherently democratic and educational—that they brought to the people important objects and ideas that had previously been attainable only by the wealthy. In an era of profound pedagogical change and rising disparities of class in America, these were compelling arguments. Prang wrote, "The *chief* use of chromolithographs is to cultivate the aesthetic taste of *the people*, to popularize art by scattering broadcast over the land highly finished copies of popular works of art."[65] As the

FIGURE 19. *Prang's Chromo: A Journal of Popular Art* 2 (Christmas 1869), printed newsletter, 12 × 10 in. (30.5 × 25.4 cm). Courtesy of Boston Public Library, Print Room

"people's art," illustrations and reproductive prints were to be admired and supported for their contribution to building an educated and cultured society. A wide range of individuals and prominent journals agreed, and their arguments were remarkably persistent, lasting into the 1890s and even beyond.

Some took the educational issue to an extreme, valorizing almost any color imagery and virtually beatifying Prang. In 1884, for example, one enthusiast credited even tawdry billboards with pedagogical merit: "Every . . . lithographer who sends out well drawn, well colored, well composed theatrical posters to adorn the streets of a large American city, is materially assisting in the art education of a nation."[66] Such indiscriminate advocates probably assisted Prang's critics more than they helped chromos' reputation, but the remark demonstrates how widely the visual benefits extended, at least in some people's minds. *The Aldine* gave a poetic tribute to Prang: "As an educator Mr. Prang deserves a high place in our annals. He has made 'things of beauty' and put them within the attainment of the humblest; and the love of the beautiful, but before dormant in many a soul, has been aroused by his works to an activity which clothes the whole world in brighter hues, and makes life itself a poem."[67]

At the opposite end of the spectrum, the most humble educational rationale for chromos was that the prints were merely another form of publication, little different, at least theoretically, from books, the undisputed bedrock of learning. Prang himself said, "Chromo-lithography is for the painter what the type is for the writer. . . . the education of millions demanded the power-press for literature and now it claims Chromo-lithography for the art of painting."[68] As late as 1894 *Century Magazine* echoed the same sentiment:

> Censuring a chromo because we do not enjoy it is as narrow and illiberal as it would be to condemn the publication of a poem because we would prefer to read it in the author's handwriting; for it is only another form of publishing the works of great masters, so that those who cannot afford the originals may relish and be educated by the copies. If farmers are too poor to buy pictures, give them cheap and inferior art rather than no art at all, and so let them have their chromos as broadcast as their barley.[69]

An equally modest aspiration was chromolithographs' usefulness for introducing children to art (fig. 20). The idea would be echoed by many: "These works should adorn the walls of school-rooms, and should accustom the eyes of the children from the earliest age to what is excellent in art, thus watching over and cultivating taste as well as sharpness of reasoning and clearness of intellect."[70] Countless teachers took this reasoning to heart, and although art instruction remained minimal in American public schools, chromolithographs decorated classrooms well into the twentieth century.

Similarly, it was said that adults who were "just developing a taste for art" could, through chromos, "obtain gems of art, every way superior to the average copies of celebrated pictures, and thus awaken a love for the really beautiful which will grow until it makes the humble purchaser in time a munificent patron of art."[71] Prang himself argued that chromos had this effect, retorting to the *New York Daily Tribune*'s Clarence Cook that "a poor picture is better than none, and in the course of time will create a demand for better and for the best. Our Chromos, which your critic will, we hope at least, place a step higher in the scale of Art than the cheap colored prints of former and recent times, could never have been sold to the present extent had not millions of poorer pictures paved the way for their reception. . . . the demand for good original paintings will become immeasurably greater as art education advances." Some critics, however, turned the same progressive argument to the negative, as in the *Putnam's Monthly* comment:

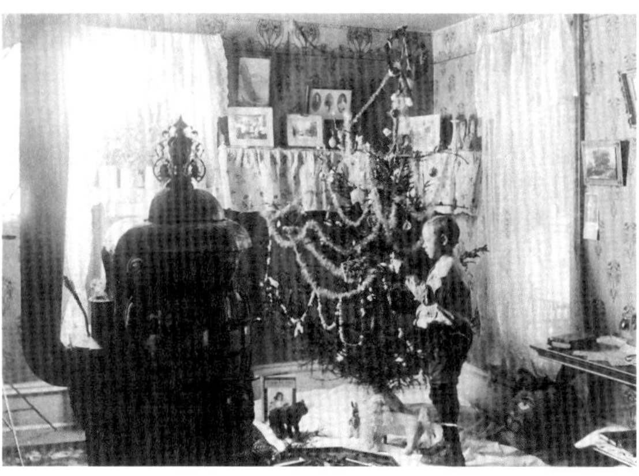

FIGURE 20. Attributed to McFarland Photographic Studio, Fulton, Illinois, *Roy McFarland and Christmas Tree*, ca. 1915. Special Collections, State Historical Society of Iowa, Iowa City

> We believe that taste for them will pass away. . . . They have no lasting attraction. As people advance in taste and appreciation of art, they begin to doubt the beauty of chromolithographs. They feel the mysterious and undefinable loveliness of color in the works of true artists, they will scorn the mechanical sameness and dullness of the lithographic tints. The lack of variety of gradation, of harmony will grow upon them, until they will no more think of admiring a counterfeit painting, than they would of passing a counterfeit bank note.[72]

Those who saw chromos as inferior generally agreed with this description and believed that the only thing the prints could teach was poor taste. One of the most straightforward in making this charge was the *Tribune*'s Cook, who summed up the widely held objection:

> We are trying our best to teach people what is good Art and what is bad, and we believe he [Prang] thinks he is working as hard in the same cause as we. It happens that we differ as to the means it is best to employ to secure the desired end. We are trying to elevate people by teaching them to seek for and admire what is true. . . . Mr. Prang's method is to teach people to admire what is false.[73]

Even the most ardent critics of chromos acknowledged that Prang was working to educate people about art, but they disagreed with both his method and his message.

COPIES AND CHROMOS: THE FALSENESS ISSUE

One of the most frequent criticisms of chromos was that they were deceptive. As Clarence Cook charged, "A clever imitation is nothing but an imitation after all. It can teach nothing, nor benefit anybody; and as every art has its own particular application and field of work, we hinder progress by every effort to wrest it to the cheap imitation of the results of some other art."[74] *The Nation* added acidly, "At the bottom of this disgust we shall find the sensation of sham, of a swindle which disappoints even as it deceives."[75] Prang, however, never shied away from presenting his process as a reproductive one, even as he claimed that his works were indistinguishable from originals. He wrote in reply to Cook, "Chromo-lithography is in itself an art *to reproduce, to imitate, not to create.* It never can obtain an 'individual and independent character,' as your critic claims for its proper sphere."[76] But Cook responded that chromos "are in the same category as false diamonds, false hair, false teeth, and with the innumerable false appliance by which homely people try to make themselves look pretty and succeed in making themselves hideous."[77] He was referring, in part at least, to what many critics took issue with—the finish of the American Chromos, what *The Nation* described as "the dreadful printing of them all over with lines as of the threads of canvas, and with a gloss as of painter's varnish." *The Nation* preferred that chromos be "flat and rather pale," such as those published by the Arundel Society, which were "wholly without pretense of being fac-similes or imitations."[78]

The deception charge was problematic for critics, however, not only because of the slippery philosophical concept of Truth upon which they depended, but also because high art critics supported the traditional practice of artists manually copying works of art. Painted copies were considered not only important study tools but also respectable substitutes for originals, and, as demonstrated by the Boston Museum of Fine Arts, they were even displayed in museums. But "what is it that is 'false' in chromos that is not 'false' in canvas copies," the *Philadelphia Photographer* asked bluntly.[79] The critics would probably have pointed out the difference between *good* painted copies by serious students of the great masters and *daubs,* since they placed chromos between the two in the hierarchy of copies.[80] "Of course, no one would prefer a fine chromo to a fine painting," wrote the *Boston Daily Evening Transcript,* "but I think every one—even the 'high art' critics—would choose a fine chromo before a poor painting or a *daub.*"[81] "Daubs" were not only bad paintings by untalented artists but were, more specifically, works produced assembly-line-style by picture mills for the undiscriminating mass market.[82] James Parton of the *Atlantic Monthly* noted with satisfaction in 1869 that chromos would probably put such sweatshop studios out of business, but in 1889 *Harper's Weekly* asked, "Does anybody suppose that the battle between the Daub and the Chromo has resulted in the routing of the Daub?" The answer was no, of course. Indeed, today such mass-produced original oil paintings remain widely available at furniture stores, "blowout sales" at hotels and convention centers, and, increasingly, on the Internet.[83]

Some people argued that traditional hand-painted copies of paintings (not daubs) provided important income and training for artists and believed that mass-produced reproductions would deprive them of a market, thus damaging the progress of art. Prang addressed this directly in "Word to Artists" in *Prang's Chromo:* "Has literature suffered from the multiplication of books?" he wrote. "Have not the discoveries of modern science, as applied to the printing-press, tended constantly to dignify, increase, and render more lucrative the profession of the author? No one can doubt it. The same result to artists will follow the perfection which we seek to attain in the production of chromos."[84] In another issue he claimed, "One good chromo after a popular picture will do more to give fame to an artist than a dozen pictures hidden away in private galleries. And yet, where an unknown artist will sell one picture to a collector, an artist whose name has become famous will sell six. So the way to the private gallery lies through the chromo."[85]

Some of Prang's own artists disagreed with this rosy assertion. Arthur Fitzwilliam Tait, the artist of the enormously popular *Group of Chickens* chromolithograph and several other subjects that Prang reproduced, complained to the publisher that sales for his originals had dropped when chromos of them were issued.[86] Nevertheless, the supportive press continued to believe that the demand could support both. "We may rely upon it," wrote Parton in the *Atlantic Monthly,* "that the persons who now buy expensive works will continue so to do, and that these chromos will enhance, rather than diminish, the value of originals; because the possession of an original will confer more distinction when everyone has copies; and it is *distinction* which the foolish part of our race desires."[87] In a letter to Prang, Parton also offered a novel reason why chromos would help artists improve their original art. "What a future there is for art where a great picture can adorn a hundred thousand homes, instead of nourishing the pride of one and when an artist can draw a steady revenue from the copyright of his works, instead of eating up one picture while he anxiously and hurriedly completes another![88] Ultimately, Thomas Moran would indeed benefit from this system, selling copyrights to his paintings independently of the paintings themselves, thereby getting double returns from each picture.

Ironically, the same critics who castigated chromos for their imitative aspirations had no problem with engraved reproductions of paintings. As *The Nation* had said bluntly in 1870, "A certainly more democratic art to which no aristocratic art objects, is the wood-cut."[89] In another article it explained more fully: "A black and white engraving or wood-cut or lithograph is a true reproduction of the forms and of the light and shade of a picture, if it is only truthfully made. But a color reproduction must be perfect or it is nothing."[90] This preference was being expressed even as late as 1892 in *Scribner's Magazine:* "Woodcuts and photo-gravures from the designs of competent artists, in the illustrated papers and magazines, are far better food for the people in homes distant from the art-centres, than the cheap chromos and cheaper steel engravings that used to be about all there was in such houses in the way of pictures of any description."[91]

The ostensible reason for privileging engraved copies over chromolithographed copies was that engravings did not seek to be more than they were, that they were more "honest" than chromos, which sought to deceive. Since the logical conclusion to this preference was that the public would be limited to owning black-and-white line art and seeing color images only in galleries and museums, the aristocratic and hegemonic agendas of the high art critics are intriguing to contemplate.

QUALITY

To separate hand-painted copies (which they respected) from chromos (which they did not), critics discredited chromos' quality. They pointed to several shortcomings, including the brilliance of color or the lack of it, faulty draftsmanship, or just a vague characterization of the prints as "poor" or "cheap." The most reliable fault, however, was their "mechanical" feel that lacked the artist's touch. *Putnam's Monthly* said, "No person of refined taste in art can look at these pictures, without feeling the utter impossibility of supplanting the master's hand by any mechanical contrivance." And with a more sweeping hand it asserted: "Mr. Prang claims that his chromo-lithographs are the best in the market. This claim can hardly be allowed. . . . sometime he may justly make this claim, and have it allowed, but not yet."[92] Prang's most ardent supporter, James Parton, countered, "It is an error to regard these works as mechanical. . . . it is unjust to reduce to the rank of artisans the skilful [*sic*] and patient artists who know how to catch the spirit and preserve the details of a fine work, and reproduce in countless copies all of both which the public can discern."[93] A more subtle comment emphasized the chromolithographic industry's moral purpose. In an 1884 article in *Wide Awake* magazine, a teacher and several female students tour Prang's factory and marvel at its wonders. As they emerge from the stone polishing room, the teacher muses, "But so do the patience and far-reaching forethought and labor, of both God and man, underlie all beauty and blessing, both of nature and art."[94]

When chromos did "catch the spirit and preserve the details of a fine work," they ironically only fueled the critics' ire. As the English aesthete Philip Gilbert Hamerton wrote in 1882: "The employment of chromolithography to imitate the synthetic colour of painters is one of those pernicious mistakes by which well-meaning people do more harm than they imagine. . . . the better they are the worse they are, for when visibly hideous they would deter even an ignorant purchaser who had a little natural taste, whereas when they are almost pretty they allure him."[95] The critics, in essence, had it both ways. When a chromo was badly done, it was castigated for its poor quality. But the more faithful the reproduction, the more "harmful" the image, because, like the fabled sirens of classical legend, its beguiling appeal led viewers away from all that was morally uplifting and true. According to such reasoning, the superb *Yellowstone National Park* chromolithographs that Louis Prang created from Thomas Moran's watercolors in 1875–1876 would have been among the most "harmful" images of all.

Despite Prang's efforts to present chromos to distinguished audiences and regardless of his and others' claims about the excellence of his products, by the 1880s the chromos that were permeating American life were indeed increasingly poor-quality prints by other publishers. It was a short step for people to associate "chromo" with "cheap" and "tawdry," and, by the end of the century, the term was synonymous with "sham" or "fake." Most interestingly, "chromo" was used beyond the art world with little or no reference to visual imagery. Thus, we can read of badly written novels described as being in the "chromo stage of development," since they were suited to "the greatest number of readers . . . [and] move in a plane of absolute mediocrity," or even of Emperor Maximilian, the puppet dictator of Mexico, being characterized as a "chromo emperor."[96] The term fell out of general use as chromos themselves became outmoded, but like any slang it needed no explanation in its heyday. As late as 1939, in *Take It Easy,* Damon Runyon wrote, "His sister . . . is the chromo sitting behind him. . . . She is older than he is, and has a big nose and a mustache."[97]

PRANG AND WOMEN'S ART

One of the unspoken reasons that critics attacked chromos so vociferously may have been related to gender bias. Many of Prang's most successful images were created by women artists, and the subject matter and affordability of his products appealed to a female clientele. The prints were enthusiastically advocated *by* women *for* women as affordable art for the home that could benefit their families' moral and intellectual development, and thousands of chromos of all sizes and shapes were also collected for albums, given to schoolchildren mostly by female teachers, and sent as "favors" to friends. The feminine appeal and domestic utility of chromos alone diminished chromos' standing in the male-dominated art world, but the new authority they opened for women—the responsibility for choosing images that could ultimately influence the moral foundation of society—represented a significant threat to the established order. As Michael Clapper has argued, if chromos were simply decorative they would not have been so controversial. "Freighted with the tasks of moral, intellectual, and cultural edification, as well as adornment, art of the middle-class home became an important ideological battleground."[98] In an age of pronounced sexism, chromos represented an unprecedented degree of autonomy for women that seriously threatened the hegemony of masculine art critics.

Other than Lily Martin Spencer (1822–1902) and Dora Wheeler (1856–1940), most of the female artists whose work L. Prang & Co. reproduced are virtually unknown

FIGURE 21. *The Finishers and Embellishers,* 1884, wood engraving, *Wide Awake* 10 (December 1884): 63

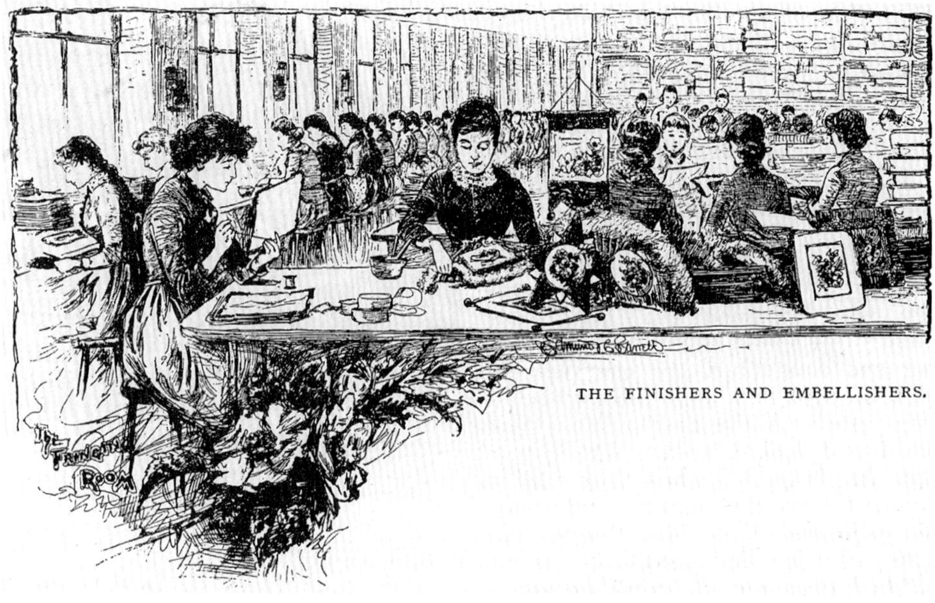

today, even to specialists in American art, but Prang gave them equal billing with male artists who produced imagery for him. He also employed "a hundred happy-looking girls . . . at their dainty labors" in his factory's finishing room, where his greeting cards were adorned with laces, ribbons, and other manually applied embellishments (figs. 21, 22).[99] This was not unusual, of course, in an age when women were an increasing percentage of the labor force, especially in industries that involved traditional women's handiwork such as garment or ceramics manufacturing, but since their employment at or by L. Prang & Co. was especially well advertised, this reliance on feminine labor may have been an additional stain on chromos' reputation.[100]

Prang never mentioned what percentage of his customers were women, and in an era before market research, he probably did not know, but he recognized them as a significant market since he emphasized feminine subject matter in his products and often addressed his advertising to "the ladies." "Your home is not complete without good pictures," a typical ad read, "pictures that cultivate the taste and elevate the soul; pictures the pleasant recollection of which will accompany the child through all his life's wanderings. Next to a masterly painting a good reproduction of such in chromo-print will answer your purpose."[101] He had a section in *Prang's Chromo* entitled "Prang's Gifts for Ladies" that included illustrated biblical bookmarks and cards, "psaligraphy" kits for "the art of cutting pictures in black paper," and "elegant" boxed sets of cards of all sorts of which he said, "No prettier or more chaste present can be given to a lady."[102] Flowers, children, baby animals, and "dining room" imagery such as food-related still lifes were prominent subjects throughout his line, as were sentimental mottoes and poems, albums and album cards, all of which he directed to Victorian-era American women and their ambitions as the primary guardians of their families' spiritual and moral well-being.

Prang's assertion of chromos' domestic value found reinforcement in everything from leading newspapers to books and magazines that spread the word directly to a female audience. The *New York Times* said, "They not only enliven a room, but they cheer the home and elevate the tastes and educate the minds of its occupants."[103] The *Ladies Repository* wrote, "The art of chromolithography in its perfected state is one of the first educators in our land. . . . every picture becomes a teacher," and it offered anecdotal examples of this effect."[104] *The American Woman's Home* (1869), by Catherine Ward Beecher and her famous sister, Harriet Beecher Stowe, gave practical advice for crafting frames and artful embellishments for reproductions and advised, "The educating influence of these works of art can hardly be over-estimated. Surrounded by such suggestions of the beautiful, and such reminders of history and art, children are constantly trained to correctness of taste and refinement of thought, and stimulated—sometimes to efforts at artistic imitation, always to the eager and intelligent inquiry about the scenes, the places, the incidents represented."[105] While other texts, including Clarence Cook's own *The House Beautiful* (1878), sneered at chromos, the affordability of the prints, their appealing subject matter, and the reassuring sanction of supportive authors rendered them enormously popular, a new means for women to quietly assert their role as guardians of family values.

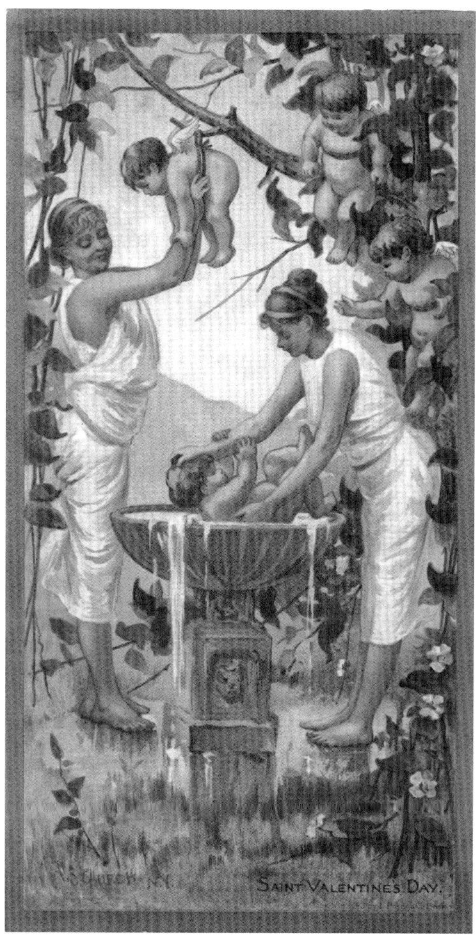

FIGURE 22. After F. S. Church, *Valentine Card*, 1885, fringed card, L. Prang & Co. Hallmark Historical Collection, Kansas City, Missouri

Even more unsettling to high art critics than relinquishing aesthetic responsibility to a female domain, however, was women's rejection of their authority in matters of taste. This was no more evident than in Harriet Beecher Stowe's 1869 *Atlantic Almanac* editorial, "What Pictures Shall I Hang on My Walls?" that exposed the tactics of the high art critics for what they were. She tells of "honest John Stubbs," who wants to buy a picture simply because it pleases him, but he is stopped by his neighbor "Don Positivo . . . who writes art-critiques for the 'Ne Plus Ultra' and solemnly informs him that it is a duty he owes to society to protest against everything that isn't high art. . . . Don Positivo tells him with a lordly air that he can buy such things if he pleases, but he feels it his duty to inform him how very trashy they are." Stowe confidently asserted, "We have little sympathy with the scornful style in which some self-important art critics have condemned or ridiculed efforts that are bringing beauty and pleasure to so many thousand homes that otherwise poverty would keep bare." Most especially, she reassured her readers that they could trust their own judgment. "The great value of pictures for home should be, after all, in their *sentiment*. They should express sincere ideas and tastes of the household, and not the tyrannical dicta of some art-critic or neighbor."[106] The critics responded, of course, instilling anxiety in place of the independent self-assurance that Stowe sought to reinforce and offering their authority as a moralizing salvation from the horrors of domestic uncertainty. *Harper's Monthly* wrote in 1876, for example, of "the doctrine of the new gospel of household art" as "always beautiful, elevated, and refined" and characterized the "apostle Clarence Cook" and others of his sort as "missionaries whom every intelligent heart will wish godspeed. For they lift up their voices to tell us what great multitudes doubt." Household art was a "mystery" for which they alone had the solution, offering "magic" that would "transform deformity into grace and ugliness into beauty." "If a person whom you know to be an expert assures you that this paper and that carpet are harmonious . . . and you really do not know," the article concluded, "why should you not trust him?"[107] With such condescending and patriarchal authority imposing paralyzing guilt on insecure homemakers, it is remarkable that Prang sold any chromos at all!

CHROMO-CIVILIZATION

Fearlessly following their own instincts rather than those of the dictatorial critics, however, Americans did buy chromos by the thousands (fig. 23). The description of Camelot's dreary, barren interior in Mark Twain's *A Connecticut Yankee in King Arthur's Court* offers an amusing example:

> And not a chromo. I had been used to chromos for years, and I saw now, that without my suspecting it a passion for art had got worked into the fabric of my being, and was become a part of me. It made me homesick to look around over this proud and gaudy but heartless barrenness and remember that in our house at East Hartford, all unpretending as it was, you couldn't go into a room but you would find an insurance chromo or at least a three-color "God Bless Our Home" over the door; and in the parlor we had nine.[108]

Twain's description, fictional as it is, points to one of the few things upon which nearly everyone could agree: by about 1870 chromos seemed to be everywhere, finding their way into everything from parlor walls to Henry James's *The Bostonians*.[109] Even some enthusiasts feared they would become too common, saying that with "wholesale gratuitous distribution their office will be degraded and they will rank as Sunday School picture cards."[110] But others celebrated their abundance as a sign of national progress. Charles Coffin wrote in the *Atlantic Monthly* in 1879, "A half century ago, a large part of the people of the United States lived in houses unpainted, unplastered, and utterly devoid of adornment. . . . how many dwellings were adorned with pictures? How many are there now that do not display a print, engraving, chromo, or

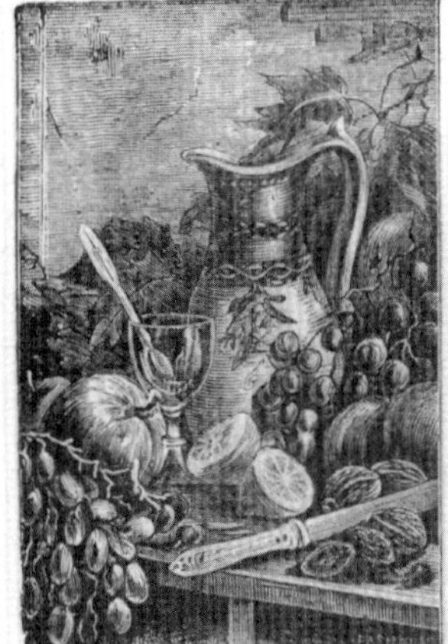

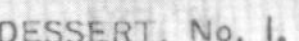

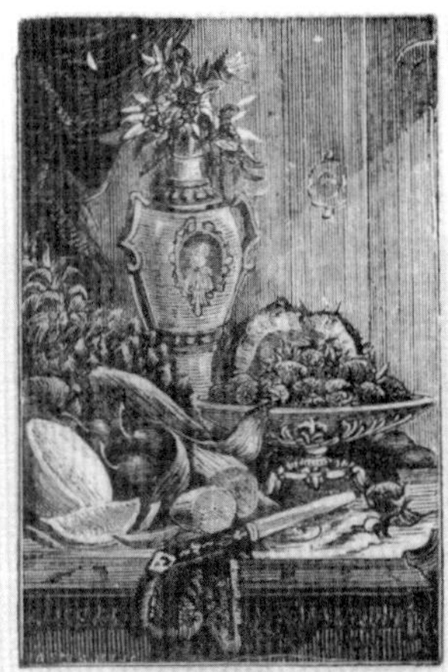

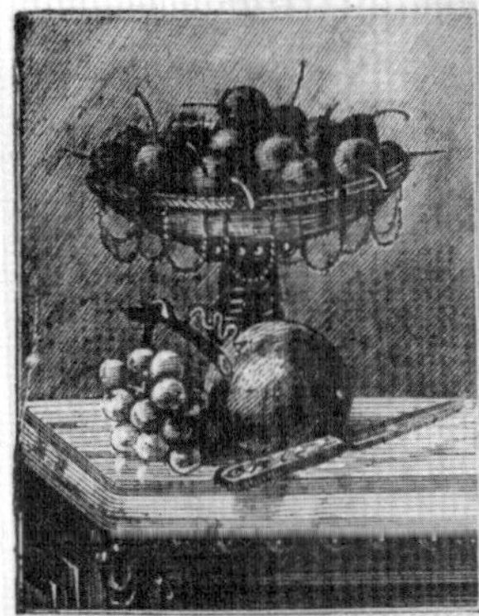

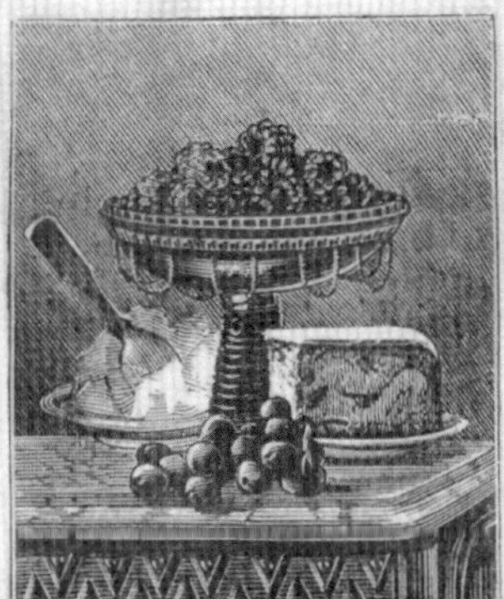

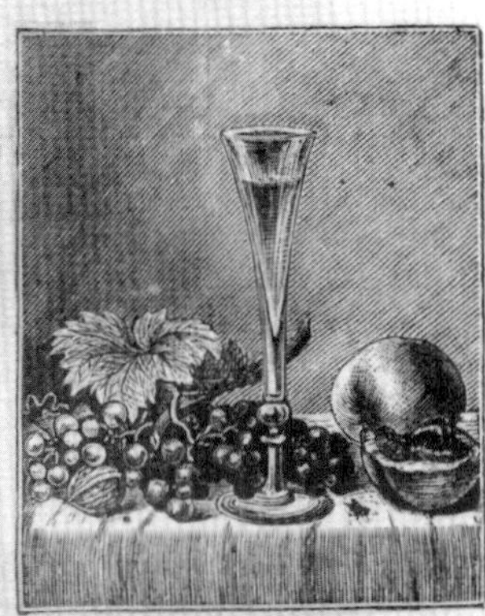

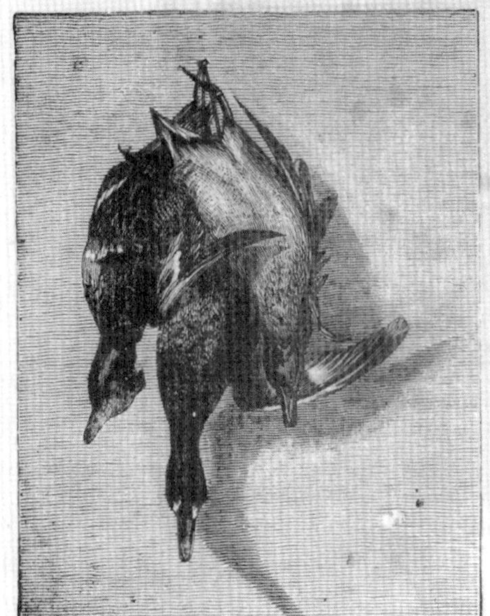

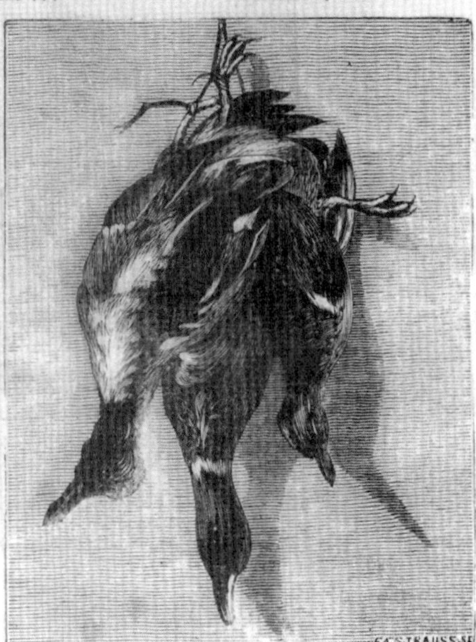

FIGURE 23. *Dining Room Pictures,* ca. 1876, catalog, L. Prang & Co. Courtesy of Boston Public Library, Print Department

lithograph?"[111] The *Boston Daily Advertiser* proclaimed that chromolithography itself "is art republicanized and naturalized in America," and James Parton called the availability of chromos "a kind of national blessing."[112]

Others saw the new availability of good reproductions as a critical tool in the process of reconciliation as the country emerged from its most harrowing crisis, the Civil War, and an aid to integration as it absorbed legions of foreign immigrants. James Parton believed, "These people, as well as the emancipated slaves of the South, it devolves upon us of this generation and the next to convert into thinking, knowing, skilful, tasteful American citizens. Mr. Prang has finished his new manufactory just in time. By his assistance we may hope to diffuse among all classes of the people that feeling for art which must precede the production of excellent national works."[113]

For critics, however, chromos were a corruption of culture. Their poor qualities debased taste and their good qualities seduced, their mechanization undermined the role of the artist, their domestic appeal removed them from the public sphere and challenged patriarchal authority, and their middle-class ownership threatened the privileged status of elites. Bringing all these ills together into what it deemed a cultural crisis was *The Nation,* which published a sweeping critique in 1874 that characterized modern society as on the road to ruin. Framed around the recent scandal in which the prominent minister Henry Ward Beecher (brother of Catherine and Harriet) stood accused of adultery, the article never actually mentioned chromolithographs but nevertheless subsumed all the cultural degradation of the current moment under the title "Chromo-Civilization." One paragraph about the "mischievous effects of the pseudo-culture" is especially revealing:

> A society of ignoramuses who know they are ignoramuses, might lead a tolerably happy and useful existence, but a society of ignoramuses each of whom thinks he is a Solon, would be an approach to Bedlam let loose, and something analogous to this may really be seen in parts of this country. A large body of persons has arisen under the influence of the common-schools, magazines, newspapers, and the rapid acquisition of wealth, who are not only engaged in enjoying themselves after their fashion, but who firmly believe that they have reached, in the matter of social, mental, and moral culture, all that is attainable or desirable by anybody, and who therefore tackle all the problems of the day—men's, women's, and children's rights and duties, marriages, education, suffrage, life, death, and immortality—with supreme indifference to what anybody else thinks or has ever thought and have their own trumpery prophets . . . whom they worship with a kind of barbaric fervor. The result is a kind of mental and moral chaos, in which many of the fundamental rules of living, which have been worked out painfully by thousands of years of human experience, seem in imminent risk of disappearing totally.[114]

In this summation, E. L. Godkin, the editor of *The Nation,* revealed the fundamental threat that chromos symbolized. With a "supreme indifference" that only made it more abhorrent to him, they embodied an erosion of privilege and authority—his own and that of others like him. When James Parton had written, referring specifically to art, that "the possession of an original will confer more distinction when everyone has copies; and it is *distinction* which the foolish part of our race desires," he was astute. The antagonism against chromos was, at its core, based on class pretensions and antidemocratic inclinations.[115]

Louis Prang understood this from the outset. In his initial response to Clarence Cook in 1866 he had written: "The American people want pictures, they delight in color pieces . . . [and it] is just as legitimate with them as with the aristocracy who can afford to hang their galleries with paintings of the old and new masters. Why then should the only invention of our day which comes to their aid be condemned and driven out of this land of promise? You, sir, who labor so faithfully for the people, cannot allow ideas so aristocratic in their tendencies."[116] He would be more pointed in later publications, pointing to "the cloven hoof of aristocracy covered up by the mantle of aesthetic culture."[117] But even as Prang sought to mollify the critics with works especially crafted to appeal to their prestige, such as his assemblage of Thomas Moran's images in *The Yellowstone National Park,* he bemoaned the ambivalent or negative response they received and finally became increasingly aware that he would never be able to break through the boundaries the authorities had established.

Ultimately, however, critics were also stymied, unable to counteract Prang's chromos and their troubling effects on art, society, and elite culture—so they did the only thing they could—they changed the rules of the game.[118] Replacing the value system that had previously embraced reproductions with one that privileged the original exclusively, they established the aesthetic hierarchy of the modern era. Reproductions became even more ubiquitous but were utterly excluded from consideration in the art world except as mere tools. The barriers between "high" and "low" were thus reinvented and the divisions solidified by similar developments, both theoretical and practical, to keep lesser art (such as that produced by most women, certain types of subject matter and media, and even, increasingly, representational art itself) at bay. Many of the basic issues that characterized the chromo-controversy and that affected the careers of both Louis Prang and Thomas Moran persist today as fundamental tensions in contemporary society, a fact that makes their work together on *The Yellowstone National Park* especially intriguing.

Thomas Moran and the Published Image

2

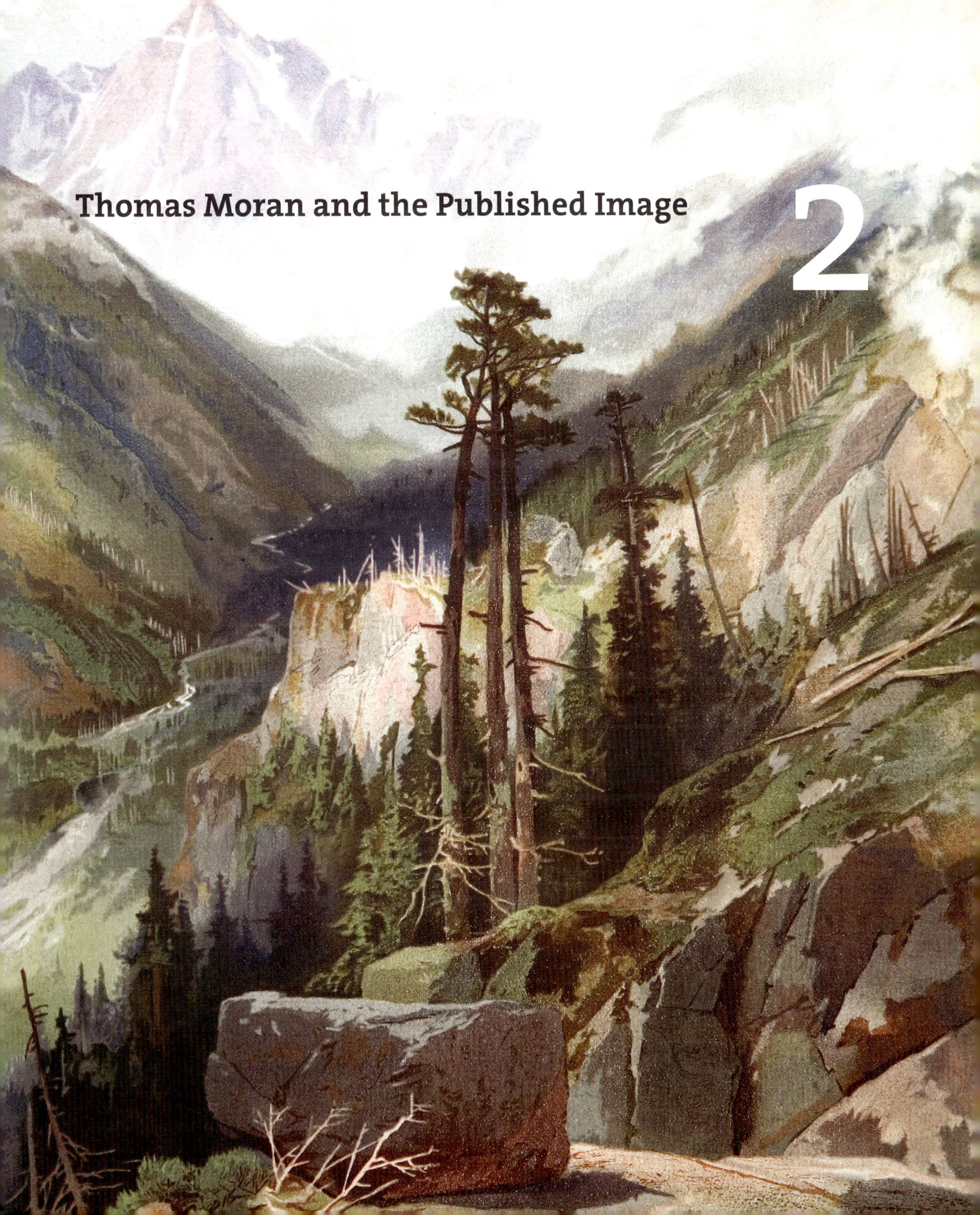

Illustration mania is upon our people. . . . nothing but illustrated works are profitable.
—Cosmopolitan Art Journal, *1857*

When Louis Prang conceived the idea to produce *The Yellowstone National Park* portfolio sometime in 1873, he was the leading chromolithographic publisher in America and Thomas Moran was an established artist who was becoming well known for monumental canvases of the western landscape and a wide array of published imagery. The two men, with the assistance of U.S. geological survey leader Ferdinand Hayden, timed the debut of *The Yellowstone National Park* to coincide with the nation's centennial celebration in 1876 and carefully crafted the portfolio to appeal to distinguished book collectors, natural historians, and art connoisseurs. With its exquisitely printed images by an artist at the height of his fame and its text by a famous supervisor of a massive, multiyear federal expedition, the work was positioned to capitalize on the public's growing fascination with the exotic landscapes of the West and stand as a significant contribution to scholarship, science, and fine art.

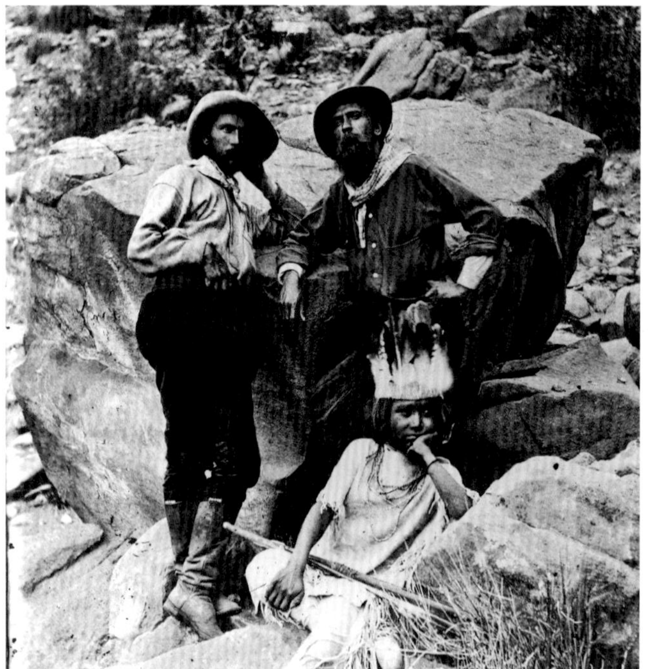

FIGURE 24. John (Jack) Hillers, *Thomas Moran* [at right] *and Justin Colburn with Paiute Boy*, 1873, photograph. National Anthropological Archives, Smithsonian Institution (1592-B)

Thomas Moran (fig. 24) was a well-chosen partner. A relative newcomer to western scenery in 1873, he had recently been catapulted to fame by the prominent sale of a major Yellowstone painting, and, during the course of the production and marketing of *The Yellowstone National Park* chromos, he produced two more monumental oils of national significance. He had twenty years of experience as an artist for the publishing industry, a thorough knowledge of printmaking, and a familiarity with the most prestigious formats and traditions within the book arts. Moreover, he was a colorist renowned for his unusual western American landscapes with a demonstrated interest in seeing his work appear through reproductions.

Moran's career had originated in published imagery, and it preoccupied him throughout his long life in addition to his original art. He remembered that as a child, "I said I was going to be a painter, and make pictures like those on the banknotes then."[1] The pictorial images on those banknotes, like those on the currency of today, were engravings, and a number of well-known American artists (such as Asher B. Durand) had done such commissions.[2] Following that inclination, Moran's serious study of art began with his apprenticeship to the engraving firm of Scattergood and Telfer in Philadelphia in 1853, when he was still in his teens. Although he considered this training "fortunate," he also readily admitted that he "never worked very hard for them, in fact did not take to engraving easily."[3] He later recalled that the work was tedious and that he had spent more of his time drawing than carving. His employers fortunately recognized his talent, and before long he was creating images for others to carve. He stayed at the shop for four of his seven years of indenture, becoming familiar with a great range of wood engraving, a knowledge that served him well in his later work in the medium. Understanding the process gave him a greater appreciation for the strong chiaroscuro drawing style that best translated into line, and by incorporating that into his designs, he was assured a better result in the finished prints.[4]

Moran published in nearly every available medium, but most of his commercial work was reproduced through wood engraving until about 1890, when mechanically produced halftones printed through photogravure gained favor. Not to be confused with woodcuts which had been printed for centuries from the surface of carved planks, or with intaglio (printed from incised grooves), wood engravings were carved into the end grain of boxwood and could then be transformed into metal printing plates with exceptionally fine detail.[5] "To such a degree and beauty has it been brought," *The Knickerbocker* wrote in 1853, the first year of Moran's apprenticeship at Scattergood and Telfer, "that in a great measure it supersedes the copper and steel engravings which used formerly to be employed for that purpose. And although it is doubtful whether wood-engraving can ever be brought to equal the delicacy of the plates . . . [of] mezzotint, yet for figures, for views of places and things, for landscapes, and especially for vignettes of the most exquisite finish and beauty, wood-engravings are now almost universally used."[6]

Wood engraving, however, like all printed media of the day other than chromolithography, was limited to a single color, and it was restricted to line that could only suggest tonal effects. Wood engraving also required technicians to engrave the blocks, a secondary translation by other hands that altered the original image, sometimes to an unfortunate degree. Moran sought to ensure a good outcome by drawing directly on the blocks so his images would not have to be redrawn, and he preferred to work with publishers who employed only the best engravers.[7] This meant, however, that his drawings were destroyed as they were engraved, a fact that accounts for the lack of original sketches that correspond precisely to his published work.[8] Nevertheless, the wide array of wood engravings that emanated from his hand stand among the best of the era and, with his other printed work, recall a long tradition of fine art in published form.

MODELS IN ILLUSTRATED PORTFOLIOS AND BOOKS

As with many artists of his time and before, Moran studied from illustrated books, and these were useful models for his work with Prang on *The Yellowstone National Park* portfolio.[9] In 1854, for example, he began trading watercolors for books and portfolios of prints at C. J. Price and Co.'s Philadelphia bookshop. His most notable acquisitions were the famous British artist J. M. W. Turner's (1775–1851) *Liber Studiorum* (1807–1819, fig. 25); Turner's *Rivers of France* (1833–1835); and Claude Lorraine's *Liber Veritatis* (engraved in the 1770s), upon which Turner had modeled his *Liber Studiorum*.[10] Moran also studied some of the original drawings for Turner's prints at London's National Gallery in 1862. According to one account, the director of the museum there was so impressed with his copies of Turner's work that "he offered him a small private room where he might work undisturbed by spectators. Pictures were taken from the wall and brought to him and many pictures from the *Liber Studiorum*, then stored in the basement, were placed at his service."[11] Turner's wash drawings were widely copied by students during the time, and, as the originals for a printed portfolio, they were an important example for Moran's watercolors for Prang's chromolithographic series.[12] Turner had envisioned the *Liber Studiorum* as a manual for young artists, and Moran was one of its most able pupils.

As he was learning the craft of engraving and etching and becoming more interested in painting in the mid-to-late 1850s, Moran and his brother Edward began informally studying with James Hamilton (1819–1878), a prominent Philadelphia

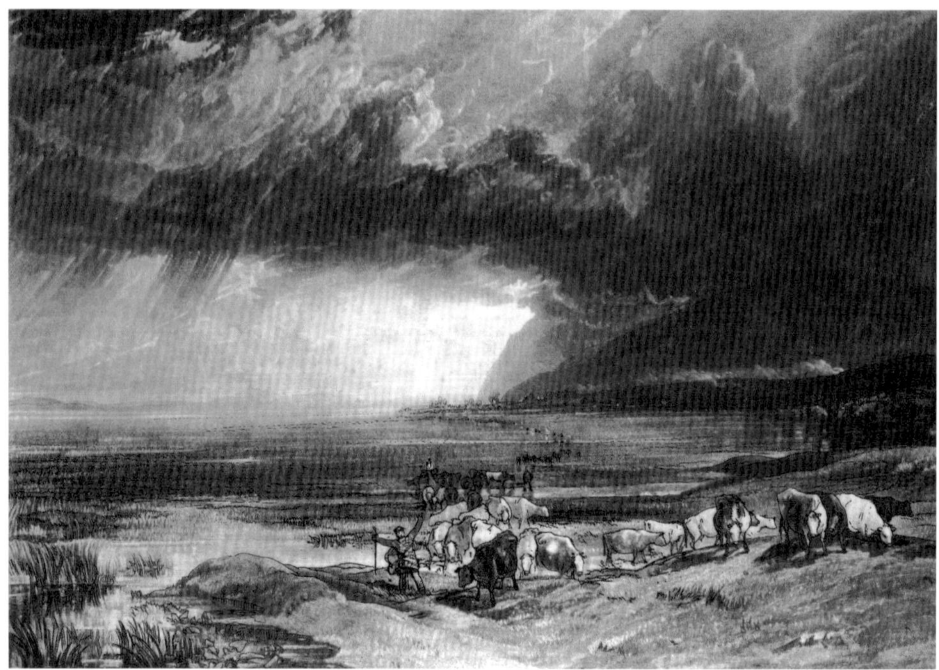

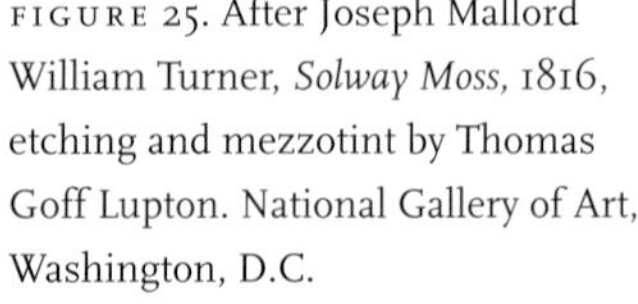

FIGURE 25. After Joseph Mallord William Turner, *Solway Moss*, 1816, etching and mezzotint by Thomas Goff Lupton. National Gallery of Art, Washington, D.C.

painter who was in his own day called "the American Turner," an appellation Moran would himself assume in his later years.[13] At that time Hamilton was working on two publication projects, transforming photographs from John C. Frémont's 1853 western expedition into publishable illustrations and similarly working up sketches made by artists who had been on Elisha Kent Kane's 1853 trip to the Arctic.[14] Although Frémont's report was never published, Kane's *Arctic Explorations* (1856), with Hamilton's images, was a beautiful gift book that was said to have joined the Bible on "every parlor table in America."[15] A noted artist who combined fine art and commercial work into a successful career, Hamilton was an important role model for the young Moran.

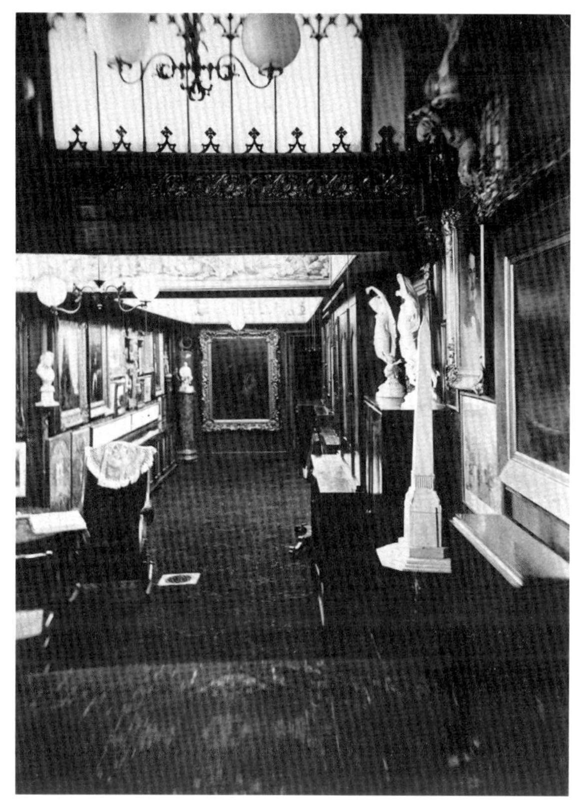

FIGURE 26. Anonymous, *John Sartain Home at 728 Sansom Street: Library, view looking from the parlor,* 1880s, albumen print. Courtesy of Pennsylvania Academy of the Fine Arts, Philadelphia, Archives

Another important individual for introducing Moran to the potential for the illustrated gift book and similarly well-illustrated periodicals such as *The Aldine* was the engraver/publisher John Sartain (1808–1897), with whom Moran lived and studied in 1860 and 1861 (fig. 26). Sartain was a prominent member of Philadelphia's art community, an engraver of many leading painters' work, and a contributor to some sixty gift books.[16] Sartain also published a journal of art criticism and commentary, *Sartain's Union Magazine of Literature and Art,* which ran from 1847 until 1852. An avid collector of prints and illustrated publications, he made his library available to young artists and took an active role in introducing them to publishers and other potential patrons.[17] As early as 1840 he had written that "a good engraving of a good picture, in its effect on the mind, is incomparably superior to a painting of ordinary merit. . . . The painter therefore should regard the engraver as his best friend."[18] In 1849 he spoke specifically of wood engravings: "We use them because for the sake of real illustration, as in the discussion of works of Art, and in the Fashion and Floral articles, they are by all odds better adapted to the purpose than anything yet invented."[19] Sartain believed that reproductive art was vital to the progress of art, and his distinguished example was a major influence on Moran. The two men maintained close ties for many years, and in 1876, when Sartain supervised the art galleries of the Centennial Exposition in Philadelphia, he facilitated the prominent display of both Moran's oil paintings and Prang's *Yellowstone National Park* chromos.[20]

In addition to creating designs that others would engrave or otherwise reproduce for publication, Moran was an accomplished original printmaker.[21] The majority of his prints are etchings, especially after 1880 when he was active in the great "etching revival" that swept both Europe and America, but he also created several original lithographs and *cliché-verre* images as early as the 1860s. Perhaps drawing on Sartain's example or recommendation, he also planned to publish portfolios of prints at least twice in his career, first in the late 1860s with a lithographic series he called "Studies and Pictures" and then again in 1875 with a series of wash drawings he made for his brother Peter to etch of scenes from Henry Wadsworth Longfellow's famed epic poem, *Hiawatha* (fig. 27).[22] Neither project was ultimately published, but they reveal Moran's interest in the commercial possibilities for printed work and were important precedents for *The Yellowstone National Park* portfolio.

Moran embarked on the *Hiawatha* project either as he completed *The Yellowstone National Park* watercolors or shortly afterward, because sixteen of the *Hiawatha* drawings were in progress by the end of 1875 when his work for Prang was finished. In December, the *Boston Daily Evening Transcript* looked forward to the Longfellow publication:

> Mr. Moran is a popular illustrator of books of travels and poems, some of the most sumptuous volumes ever published in this country having been enriched by the productions of his pencil. . . . Mr. Moran is at present engaged upon the most elaborate work which he has yet undertaken—a series of twenty-five illustrations of Longfellow's poem of "Hiawatha" which his brother, Peter Moran a most skillful etcher, is reproducing on steel. These etchings will, we think furnish evidence of a versatility and originality of talent which entitles Mr. Moran to a foremost rank.[23]

Thomas and Peter Moran planned to publish the *Hiawatha* portfolio themselves, and, in contrast to the difficulties L. Prang & Co. would encounter in marketing *The Yellowstone National Park,* the brothers enticed an impressive cadre of subscribers even before the drawings were complete, including President Ulysses S. Grant, General William Tecumseh Sherman, the railroad magnate Collis P. Huntington, Mark Twain, and Longfellow himself.[24] As early as May 1876, however, Moran reported that "work on the etchings of *Hiawatha* has come to a stand still," and the project was never finished.[25] Although the reasons for its abandonment remain unclear, the ill-fated *Hiawatha* publication remains an important parallel to the work he did with Louis Prang.[26]

Another example of Moran's interest in fine art publication is revealed in his 1875 request that Prang make prints from two lithographic stones he had drawn several years earlier, a pair entitled *Solitude* (1869, fig. 28) and *Desolation* (ca. 1869, fig. 29). Moran, or others on his behalf, had already attempted their printing, but he was dissatisfied with the results.[27] The artist explained in his letter to the publisher:

> The stone of "Solitude" gave very good results on French india paper when it was printed from some 3 years ago; but may have deteriorated by want of care in the

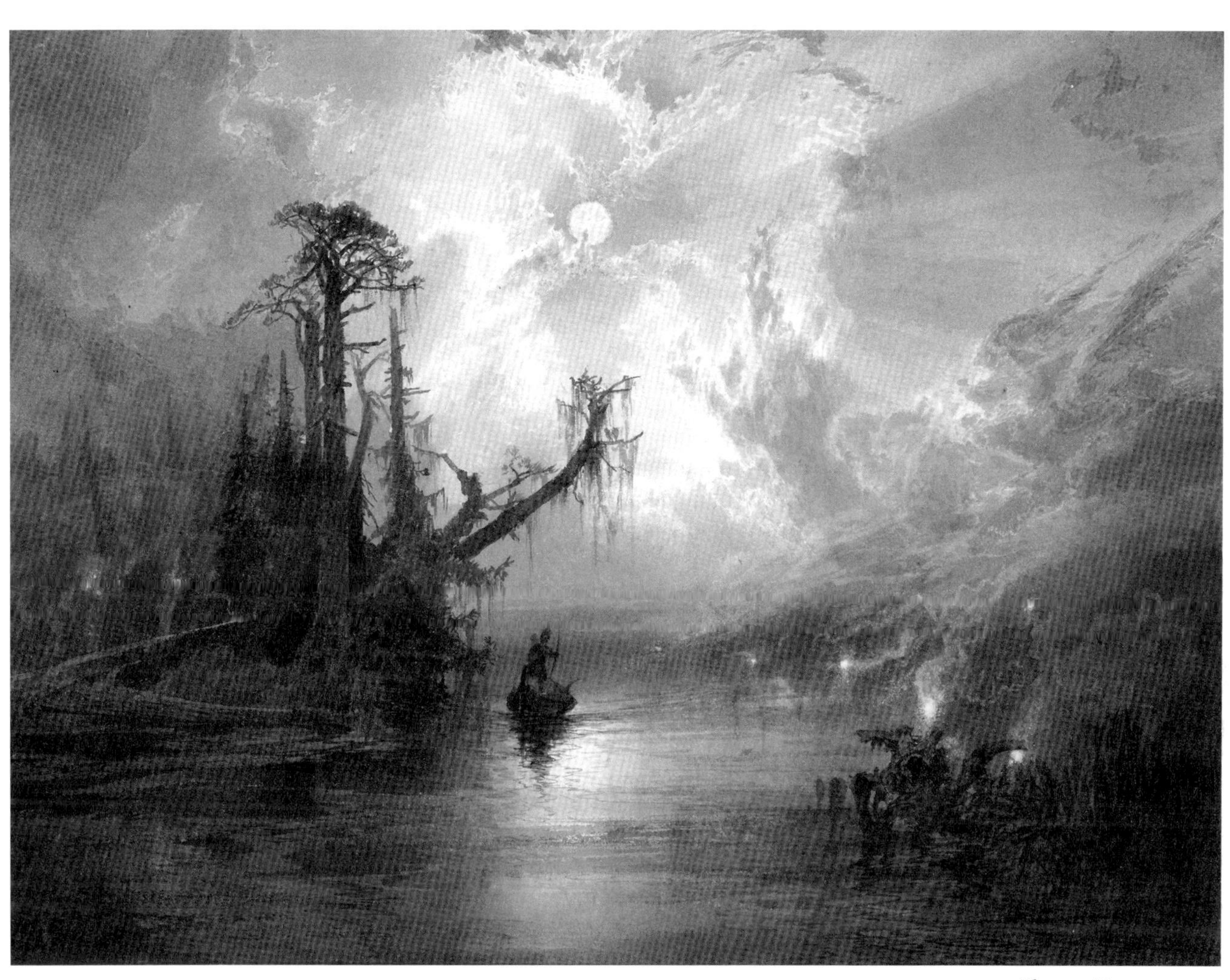

FIGURE 27. Thomas Moran, *Nokomis Falling from the Moon,* from the *Hiawatha* series, ca. 1875, wash on paper. Gilcrease Museum, Tulsa, Oklahoma

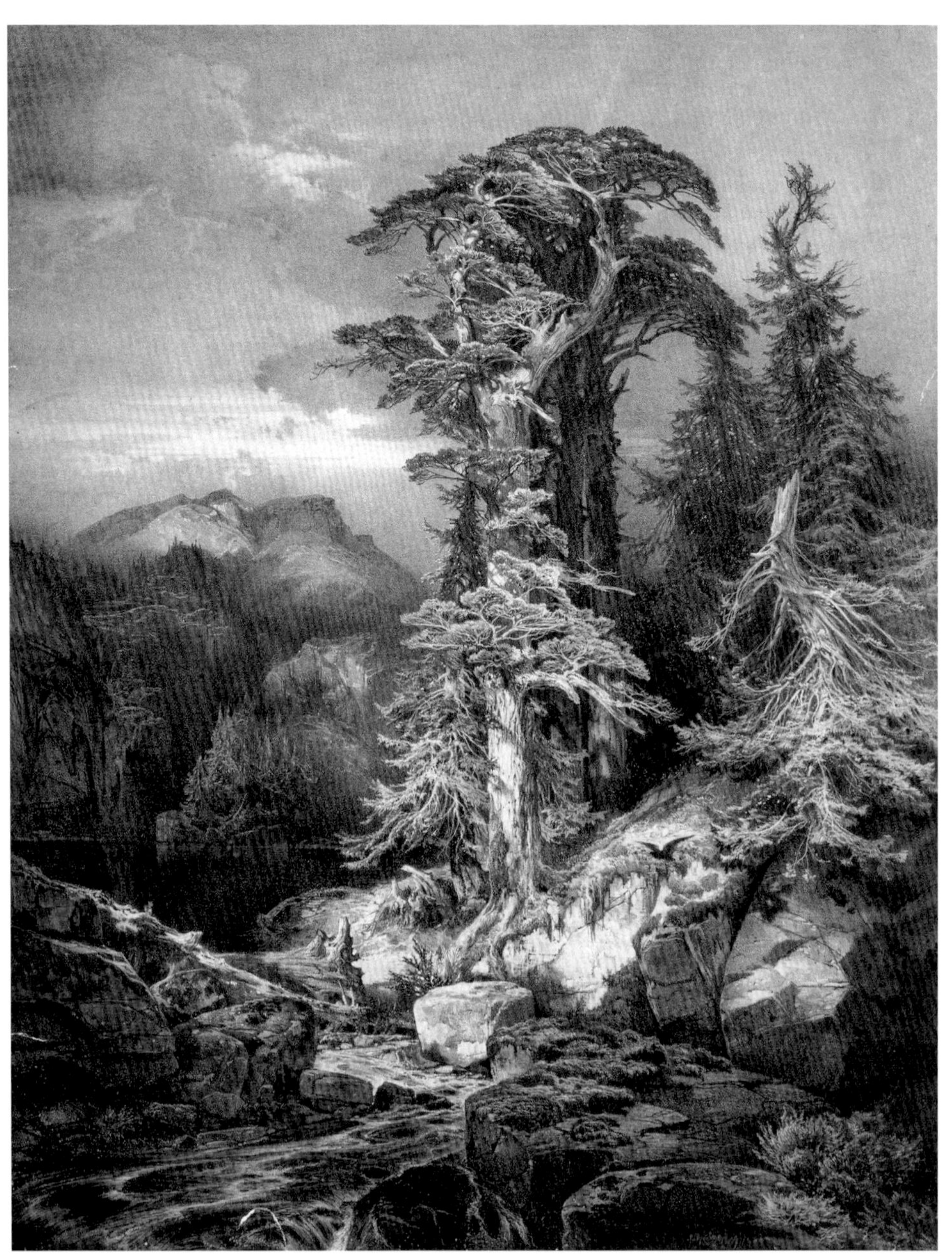

FIGURE 28. Thomas Moran, *Solitude*, 1869, lithograph, 20¾ × 16¼ in. (52.7 × 41.3 cm). Gilcrease Museum, Tulsa, Oklahoma

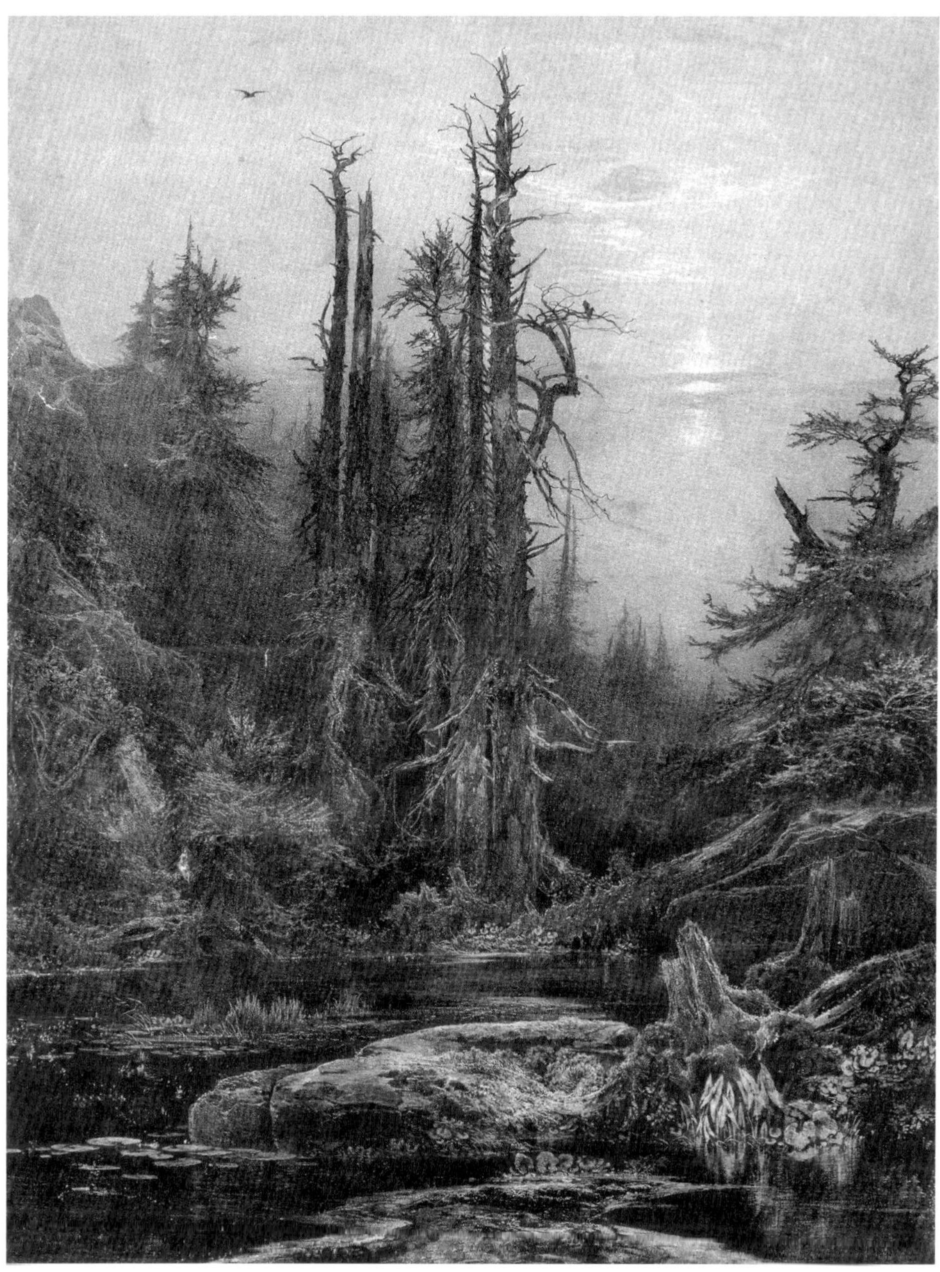

FIGURE 29. Thomas Moran, *Desolation*, ca. 1869, lithograph, 22½ × 16¼ in. (57.2 × 41.3 cm). Gilcrease Museum, Tulsa, Oklahoma

> meanwhile. The other one "Desolation" was never printed from save an experimental proof and I judge it might work up as good as it ever was. Both were somewhat spoiled in the original preparation of the stone by too much acid. I am desirous that you should try further and work them into the best possible condition and then send me proofs on French india paper (Buff Color) or if you have not got that, or cannot get it, on ordinary india paper. I should be sorry if the two drawings were now worthless through neglect.[28]

It remains unclear whether Prang fulfilled Moran's request, and we do not know what plans might have been envisioned for the prints, but the correspondence demonstrates that the two men's relationship was one of mutual respect and that the artist recognized the value of working with the publisher in a variety of ways.

THE STATUS OF REPRODUCTIVE WORK FOR MORAN AND HIS CONTEMPORARIES

Moran regarded his printed designs as no less important than his work in other media. Not prone to extensive commentary on any subject, when questioned late in life if he thought modern commercialism was dangerous to art, he replied simply, "No; the real artist will express himself anyway, and without thinking what will sell best. When he must work for his bread, it is no hindrance to his art, so long as he does his best."[29] Although the "anyway" might suggest a certain ambivalence about artistic expression within a commercial context, it should be noted that Moran said this in 1916, well after the paradigm shift rendered commercial work inappropriate for serious artists, and the qualification was surely to point out his awareness of that distinction. Other than this comment, he was never explicit about the significance of his illustrative work. Except for brief mentions of profits or assignments and passing references to being pleased or dissatisfied with projects, he rarely mentioned individual commissions. Moran's extensive work with the publishing industry, especially between 1860 and 1885, however, demonstrates that he regarded the work as an important aspect of his artistic career.

Moran was not alone in that belief. Indeed, a large number of his contemporaries had similarly multifaceted oeuvres. Winslow Homer's is perhaps the most well known, but the list is long and includes Asher B. Durand, George Catlin, Christian Schussele, Howard Pyle, John La Farge, and Albert Bierstadt, to name a few. That most of these artists were working to distinguish their art within a highly competitive system where a scarcity of galleries, patrons, and dealers made illustrative work a financial necessity is less important than the fact that the art world of the day regarded their diversity of media as an asset that could reveal their talents in a range of ways. La Farge asserted, for example, that the illustrator's "task calls upon all the powers of the artist."[30] As Michele Bogart has argued, published imagery was a respected form of artistic expression within the culture of the time.[31]

This respect, as we have seen in the example of the Boston Museum of Fine Arts, was supported by institutional practice. In 1875, for example, the National Academy of Design exhibited three of Moran's wood engravings within a larger show dominated by his paintings, and these were critically acclaimed. "The mountain scenery of Utah," one review read, "is represented with much force and grandeur in three large engravings on wood by Thomas Moran, that rank high as genuine works of art."[32] Nearly twenty years later, in 1892, for his retrospective exhibition at the Denver Art League, Moran included 160 published works among 260 total objects, including *The Yellowstone National Park* chromos. One review called special attention to the published images:

> Of equal importance [to the oils] are fifty etchings and photogravures, all proofs, varied in method and treatment as well as subject. The list includes many wood engravings, lithographs and a large number of photographs from drawings and paintings. Of especial value to the student, as the reproduction of drawings in black and white is so important as a factor in the art education of the country today, is a collection of drawings for illustration, which includes ten illustrations to "Hiawatha" in indian [*sic*] ink. The comprehensive exhibition closes with a list of water-color reproductions of Yellowstone Park color drawings.[33]

Such praise of the artistic value of reproductions was not uncommon, and many newspapers reserved special sections for notices of illustrated publications, sometimes crediting artists by name. That *The Yellowstone National Park* chromos were highlighted indicates that even at that late date, as chromolithography was being superseded by more modern processes, the prints were still considered artistically significant. The 1892 exhibition was the only comprehensive showing of Moran's art during his lifetime, and his inclusion of reproductions in such a major event in his career demonstrates both his own regard for such work and its acceptance by the art world.

MORAN AND THE WEST

Moran worked steadily as both an illustrator and a fine artist throughout the 1860s, publishing his images in a great range of periodicals and books and creating increasingly significant paintings, mostly of eastern American landscapes and European sites he visited on two trips during that decade. He exhibited his canvases at the Pennsylvania Academy of the Fine Arts, the National Academy of Design, and other important venues, but by 1870 he still had not produced the truly distinctive work that would elevate him to the forefront of his profession.[34] Albert Bierstadt's phenomenal success with western paintings throughout the 1860s had not escaped his attention,

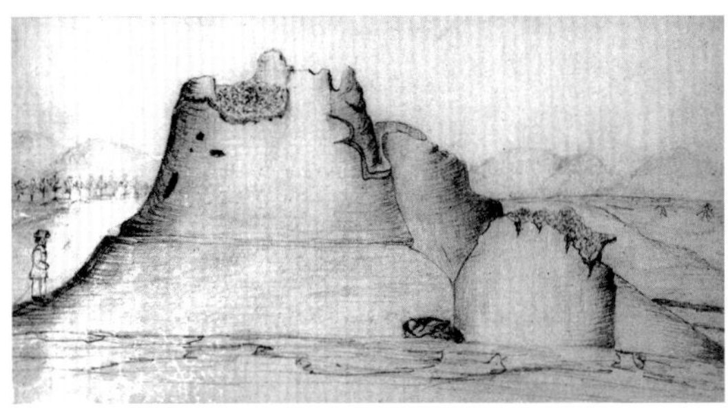

FIGURE 30. Walter Trumbull, *Castle Geyser Cone,* 1870, graphite on paper. Courtesy of National Park Service (Yellowstone National Park)

but other than a brief trip to the Pictured Rocks of Lake Superior in 1862, Moran had not yet encountered the exotic scenery that would distinguish his art from that of his contemporaries.[35]

With the inauguration of a new magazine, *Scribner's Monthly,* in 1870, however, Moran obtained both a new client and the opportunity to search out novel artistic material. The impetus was a commission to rework several amateurish drawings (figs. 30 and 31) from the 1870 Washburn/Doane Yellowstone expedition for a two-part article entitled "The Wonders of the Yellowstone."[36] That expedition had, for the first time, brought back definitive, if incomplete, information about the region known as Colter's Hell, and the magazine editors recognized that the remarkable geyser-filled area contained a wealth of sites of interest to its readers. The government took notice, too, and authorized Ferdinand V. Hayden's Geographical and Geological Survey of the Territories, which had explored eastern Wyoming in 1870, to systematically investigate the Yellowstone region. During the spring of 1871, as Hayden planned his expedition and Moran worked on the *Scribner's* illustrations, it was suggested (the specific events and instigator of the idea remain unclear) that the artist join the survey as a guest. With a loan of $500 each from *Scribner's Monthly* and the Northern Pacific Railroad, which also had a vested interest in obtaining information about the area as it planned its route through the region, Moran ventured west for the first time.[37] It would be the first of many western trips for the artist and the foundation for *The Yellowstone National Park* commission he would soon do for Prang.

Although the West had been explored and traversed by Euro-Americans for decades by 1871, vast sections of the region remained little known and visually undocumented for eastern audiences, including most of those areas that Moran would become famous for portraying. Dozens of artists and several photographers had already created countless paintings, daguerreotypes, and photographic prints, a wide array of popular engravings and lithographs, and a great range of illustrated books, magazines, guidebooks, and government reports about the West.[38] These images were the most visible aspects of a national preoccupation with the frontier after the Civil War, fueled by increasing excitement about the region's commercial potential, awareness of persistent problems with Native Americans, greater accessibility via the new transcontinental railroad, and a national understanding that in the West lay the key to America's future and its emerging identity. At the same time, despite the growing interest, the region's exotic terrain, people, and animals, its vast extremes of climate and topography, and its sheer expanse remained almost incomprehensible to most Americans. Visual images, as virtually no other medium could, helped make the place imaginable, and they contributed enormously to attitudes and perceptions about the West and its possibilities. So many of these in the antebellum period were either poorly executed,

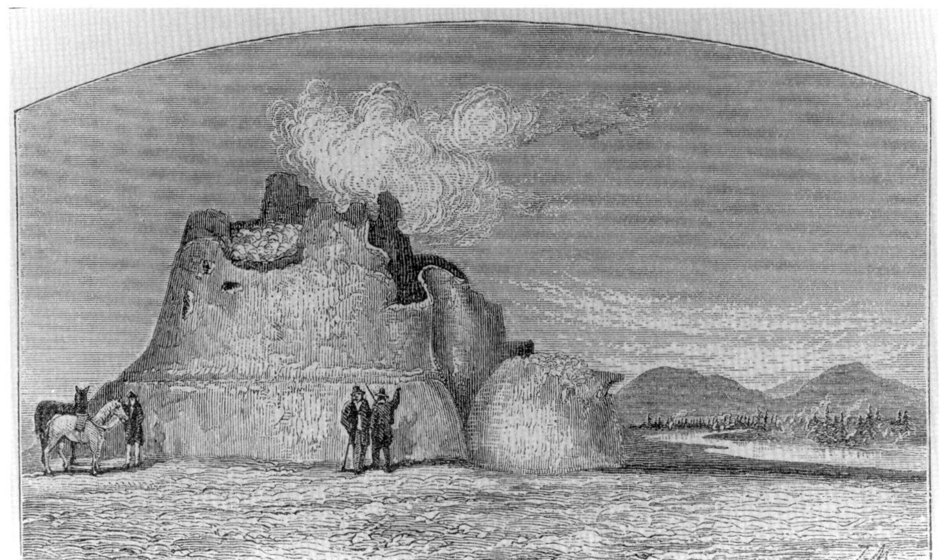

FIGURE 31. After Walter Trumbull and Thomas Moran, *Crater of the Castle Geyser*, 1871, wood engraving, 2⅞ × 5 in. (6.7 × 12.7 cm). *Scribner's Monthly* 2 (June 1871): 125

romantically inclined, or outright inventions, however, that they often contributed to misconceptions or fantasies about the West as much as they clarified them. In 1871, as Moran journeyed to rendezvous with Hayden's federal survey, he was joining a massive undertaking to factually document the region, an enterprise that would, it was hoped, bring back irrefutable and scientifically valid information that could definitively determine the character of the West and its potential for America. His images would be a part of that achievement in a number of ways.

The U.S. government had already sponsored dozens of explorations of the West, but prior to the Civil War most of these had been focused on the practical matters of reconnaissance, mapmaking, route planning, and the establishing of military authority. The information these expeditions brought back was valuable but sketchy, and the majority of it lacked scientific validity. To address this deficiency, in the late 1860s Congress sponsored four large surveys, called Great Surveys, each of which was vast in scope, comprehensive in mission, and multiyear in duration. With one exception, these surveys were led by scientists rather than military officers (Ferdinand Hayden, John Wesley Powell, Clarence King, and Lt. George Wheeler), and the teams that accompanied them were composed of experts with many different specialties, from topography and paleontology to geology and botany. Assigned to different areas of the West, these surveys were ordered to bring back as much information as possible about their territories that could be used for future determinations about their use.[39]

Photographers and artists were among the teams. They often worked together in the field, sometimes portraying the same sites in different media. Upon their return east, their work augmented the written reports and artifacts the expedition leaders submitted to Congress, but it was also circulated in publications, displayed in national expositions and in the U.S. Capitol, and sold widely, especially in the form of stereographs that were a popular parlor entertainment for many average Americans. The different media—photography and the more traditional arts of drawing, painting, and illustration—functioned differently, however, with photography offering undeniably accurate representations of the region's unusual topographical features and art providing both color and a romantic aura that enhanced the appeal of the remarkable terrain. The two types of imagery complemented each other in important ways, essentially through a symbiotic relationship that combined to present the West with an unprecedented authority. This authenticity and veracity, as well as the work's fascinating subject matter and exotic appeal, was of critical importance as the United States worked to establish the region as a resource and an integral component of the national identity.

In the case of the Yellowstone region, this synergistic visual dynamic was especially important. Yellowstone is among the most unusual areas of the West. Its surreal terrain, formed by an exceptionally active geothermal field, was so bizarre as to be unbelievable to most Americans of the 1870s without the indisputable proof of pictures. Photography could definitively confirm the conformations of the remarkable sites, but the formations required the color of traditional art to fully convey their exceptional qualities. Working together, and with scientific validation in the form of written and oral testimonials from Ferdinand Hayden and others who had witnessed the scenes, photography and painting not only convinced doubtful eastern viewers of the reality of Yellowstone but also intrigued them with its charms.

The transformative consequences of this process are fascinating. Before the Hayden expedition, for example, Yellowstone was described primarily as a hellish place of smoking geysers, boiling springs, and satanic sites such as the Devil's Hoof, Satan's Slide, and the Witches' Cauldron. After the expedition, however, with stunning images that displayed both the beauty and the color of the unusual formations, scientific data about the area's geology, and a new prospect for the region as the first national park, publicity shifted to a celebration of its marvels. Yellowstone's reincarnation into "wonderland" was due to many factors, not the least of which was intense lobbying for the National Park bill throughout the winter of 1871–1872 by those (such as the Northern Pacific Railroad) with vested interests in seeing the area as a tourist attraction, but at their foundation lay the combined power of photography and art to persuade audiences that the region was indeed a national treasure.[40]

Upon his return from the expedition in the fall of 1871, Thomas Moran created dozens of depictions of the Yellowstone area, and his illustrations, watercolors, and oil paintings, along with the photographs of his colleague, William Henry Jackson, helped catapult the region, Hayden's name, and his own reputation to national fame.

Moran's work was directly influential in convincing Congress to pass the Yellowstone National Park bill in the spring of 1872, and within a month he unveiled his first major painting, *The Grand Cañon of the Yellowstone* (1872, fig. 32), an enormous 7-x-12-foot oil painting that he immediately shipped to Washington, D.C., for exhibition. It caught the attention of congressmen, who appropriated $10,000 for its purchase, and it thus became the first landscape painting by an American artist in the United States Capitol.[41] Moran's name would be forever associated with Yellowstone for these achievements, and he was immediately invited on other trips, both by Hayden, who was delighted at the attention the dramatic picture had brought to his survey, and John Wesley Powell, another federal survey leader who hoped Moran might portray his expedition through the Colorado River region and Grand Canyon with equal success.

Moran declined, however, and traveled in the summer of 1872 with his wife via the transcontinental railroad through the Sierra Nevada Mountains to California where he visited Yosemite, encountering the scenery he would portray in *Lake Donner* and *Summit of the Sierras* for Prang.[42] In the summer of 1873 he did join Powell's expedition, taking the train to Salt Lake City and traveling south to what is now Zion National Park and the Grand Canyon in Arizona, a trip that would inspire his Utah subjects in *The Yellowstone National Park*. And in 1874, having committed by then to do the chromolithographic project, Moran returned west for a fourth visit, this one with Hayden's survey again, traveling to see the Mountain of the Holy Cross and witnessing along the way the Colorado subjects that he would paint for Prang. In all three instances of Moran's participation with the federal surveys, however, the artist was included as a guest rather than an employee. His compensation derived from the work he produced either during or out of the experience, and the most reliably lucrative of these was commercial illustration.

Similarly, most of Moran's trips, at least until he began doing less illustrative work in the mid-1880s, were made possible by publishing commissions, and he traveled frequently throughout the eastern United States, to Mexico, and to Europe. Of course, a large portion of his time and attention concerned the oil paintings for which he is best known, but the circumstances for those canvases were also facilitated by the commercial work that often provided the impetus and funding for his travel. The imagery he produced in both original and reproductive media was also usually closely related. Travel, painting, and commercial work were interdependent for him and would remain so throughout most of his life.[43]

Moran created a major painting from each of his first trips west with the federal surveys and also from two later western expeditions in 1892 and 1900. His second large work, produced from his experiences on the Powell expedition and which he was working on when Louis Prang contacted him for the chromolithographic project, was *The Chasm of the Colorado* (1873–1874, fig. 33), a 7-by-12-foot extravaganza of Arizona's

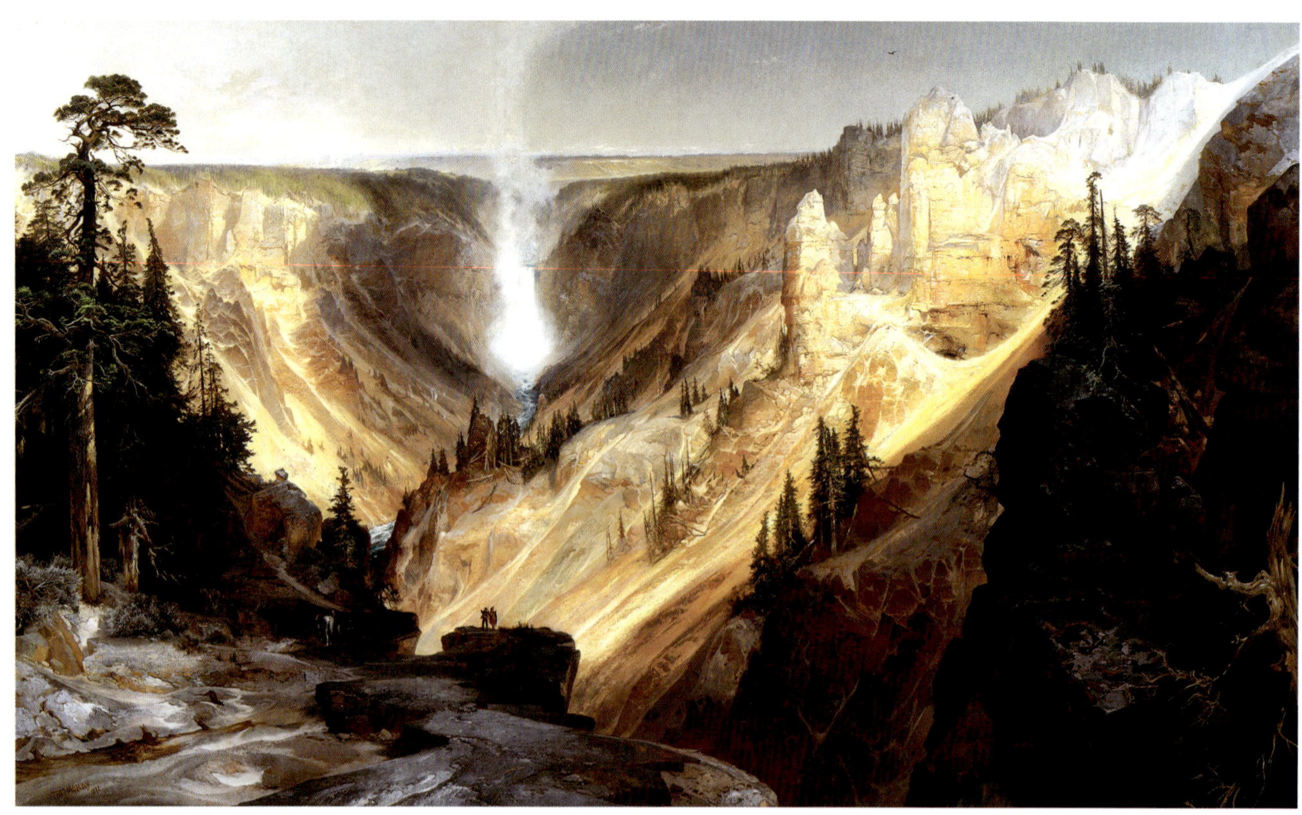

FIGURE 32. Thomas Moran, *The Grand Cañon of the Yellowstone,* 1872, oil on canvas mounted on aluminum, 84 × 144¼ in. (213 × 266.3 cm). Smithsonian American Art Museum, the Department of the Interior Museum (L.1968.84.1)

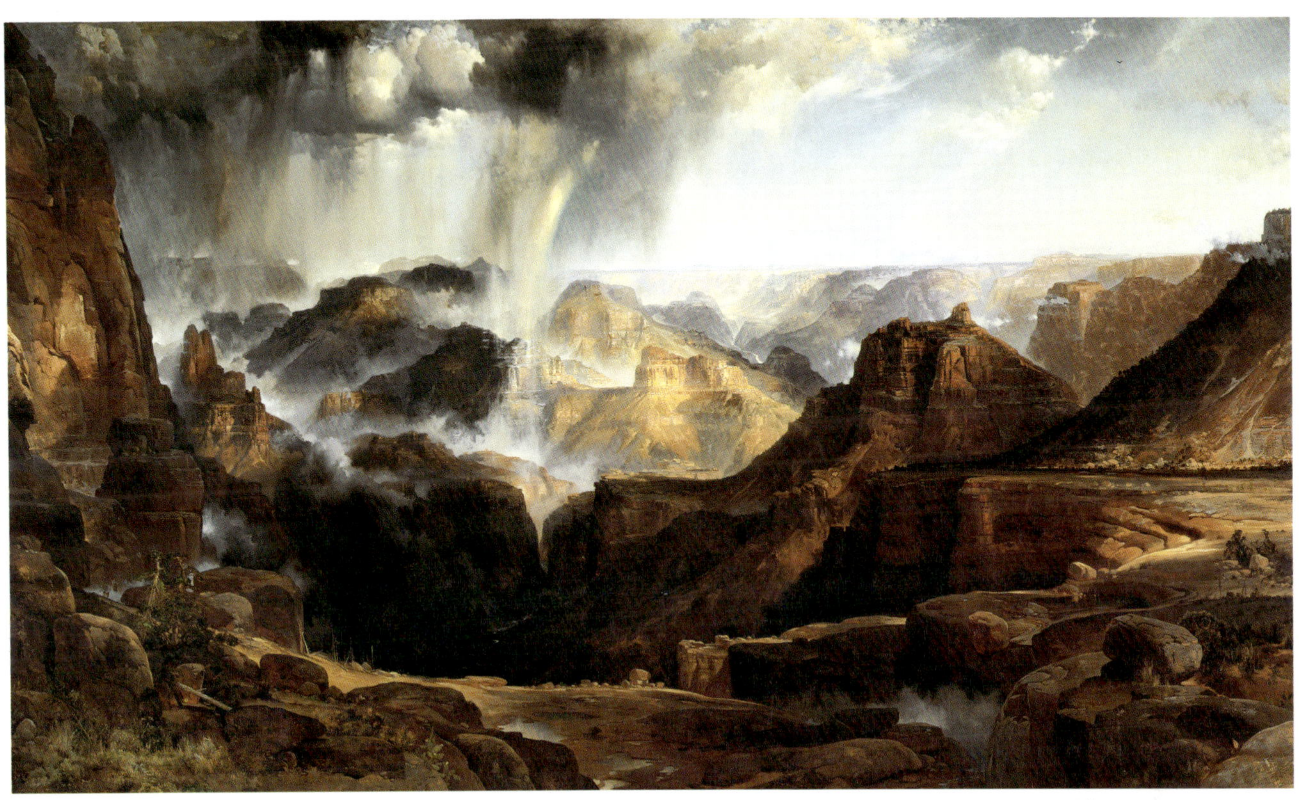

FIGURE 33. Thomas Moran, *The Chasm of the Colorado,* 1873–1874, oil on canvas mounted on aluminum, 84¾ × 144¾ in.(214.3 × 367.6 cm). Smithsonian American Art Museum, the Department of the Interior Museum (L.1968.84.2)

Grand Canyon, designed as a companion to his identically sized Yellowstone painting in Washington. Congress purchased it for another $10,000, and it joined the first work in the Capitol. After Moran's second venture with Hayden, this time to Colorado in 1874, he painted a third big picture, *The Mountain of the Holy Cross* (1875, fig. 34), the concluding scene of a remarkable triptych that, unfortunately, was not exhibited together until the late 1990s (fig. 35).[44] In each instance he worked from his own sketches, from photographs taken on the surveys, and in careful consultation with geologists Hayden and Powell, who would play an important role in verifying the truthfulness of his imagery when it was exhibited. He was scrupulous in his attention to detail, writing, for example, to Hayden with the request that he critique the geology as pictured in *The Grand Cañon*.[45] When the picture was publicly unveiled, Moran made sure that the survey leader was on hand to answer questions and testify that his rendering was indeed correct.[46] He was acutely aware that without such reinforcement even the best portrayal of Yellowstone's strange formations and coloration would be subject to skepticism, if not outright ridicule, from a dubious audience. Although the painting was received with acclaim, the question of accuracy would be an issue for some viewers of *The Yellowstone National Park* chromolithographs, perhaps because in that case the garishly colored oddities were being presented in a medium whose chromatic fidelity and authenticity were already in question.

Moran produced other large western works throughout his career, most notably a second, even larger, *Grand Cañon of the Yellowstone* (1892, Smithsonian American Art Museum) and a monumental *Shoshone Falls* in 1900 (fig. 36). He also painted countless smaller versions of western subjects throughout his life, and, indeed, although he depicted other regions, most notably Long Island, Mexico, Venice, and parts of Europe, he was best known both in his own day and in ours for his portrayals of the American West. Through these works Moran became one of the preeminent portrayers of the region that was, in the closing decades of the nineteenth century, intensely fascinating to large numbers of Americans and, whether they realized it or not, at the center of an emerging national identity. Moran's authority as an artist for federally sponsored surveys, as the creator of a congressionally sanctioned painting (with another in the works), and, perhaps most importantly, with the reputation as an accurate and effective portrayer of the western landscape would be key to his appeal for Prang, as the publisher sought to distinguish his firm and refute the critics who challenged the legitimacy of his chromolithographs.

FIGURE 34. Thomas Moran, *Mountain of the Holy Cross*, 1875, oil on canvas, 82¾ × 64¾ in. (210.2 × 164.5 cm), Museum of the American West collection, Autry National Center, Los Angeles

MORAN'S FIRST CHROMOS

When Prang approached Moran to do the *Yellowstone National Park* project late in 1873, it was not the first time the artist's work had been commissioned for a chromo project. In 1872 Ferdinand Hayden had ordered four watercolors from Moran, plan-

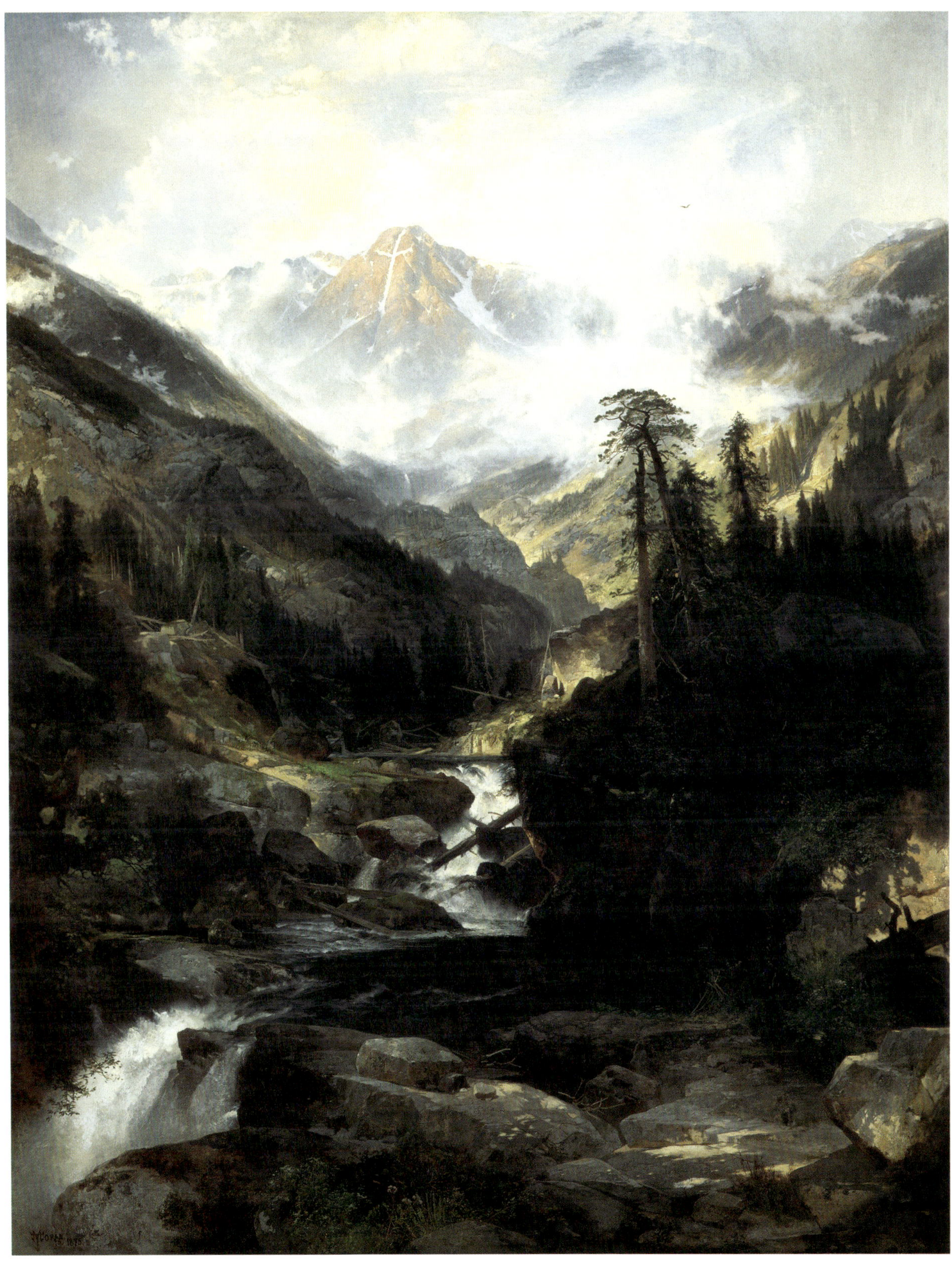

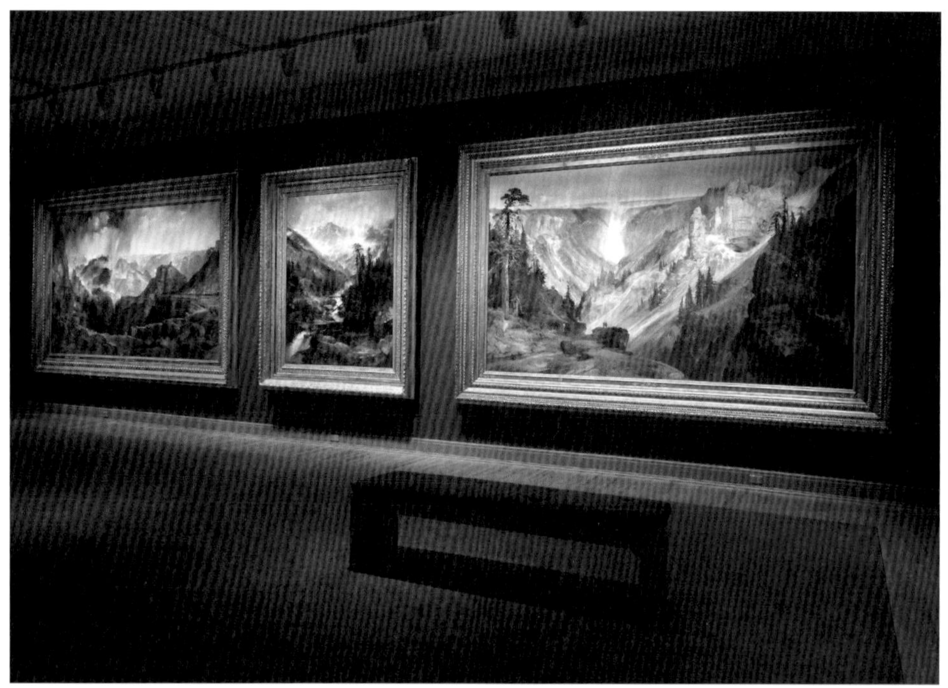

FIGURE 35. *Moran Triptych at Gilcrease Museum*, 1997, photograph. Gilcrease Museum, Tulsa, Oklahoma

ning to have them reproduced in chromolithography for his report. This was unusual; the pictorial imagery in Hayden's reports was sparse, and the survey leader usually tried to save his limited allocations by obtaining reproductions from other sources. Moran wrote to Hayden once about the project:

> The four drawings that I was to make for you are not all finished as yet, but I can complete them by the end of this week. The main reason why they are not all finished is because the exact subjects have not been fixed upon; and as the original plan embraced more than four, I desire to again consult with you before completing the four. As they are for the purpose of reproducing by chromo, I should think that subjects in which color is the remarkable feature should be chosen. I have finished two drawings of the Hot Springs, the "Upper Pools," & Diana's Baths, & I suggest The Cliffs of the Cañon & The Great Blue Spring of Fire Hole River as the other two, but if you prefer any other subjects write immediately and I will do them at once. I am overrun with work on the Yellowstone and the interest in them seems to increase.[47]

Although Hayden did not publish the chromos until 1883 (in what was a delayed report for his 1878 season), when it was issued, *The Castle Geyser* that Moran mentioned indeed appeared but with only one view of *Mammoth Hot Springs* (fig. 37). The other two images were, as Moran described, *The Grand Cañon of the Yellowstone*

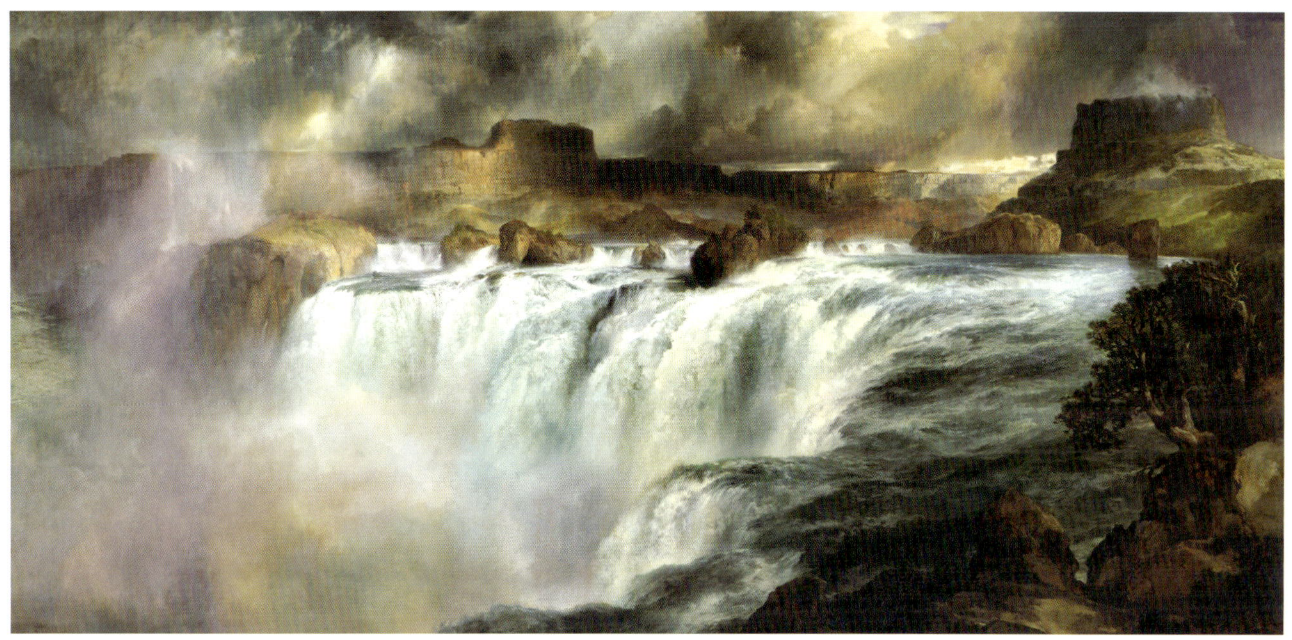

FIGURE 36. Thomas Moran, *Shoshone Falls on the Snake River,* 1900, oil on canvas, 72 × 144 in. (182.9 × 365.8 cm). Gilcrease Museum, Tulsa, Oklahoma

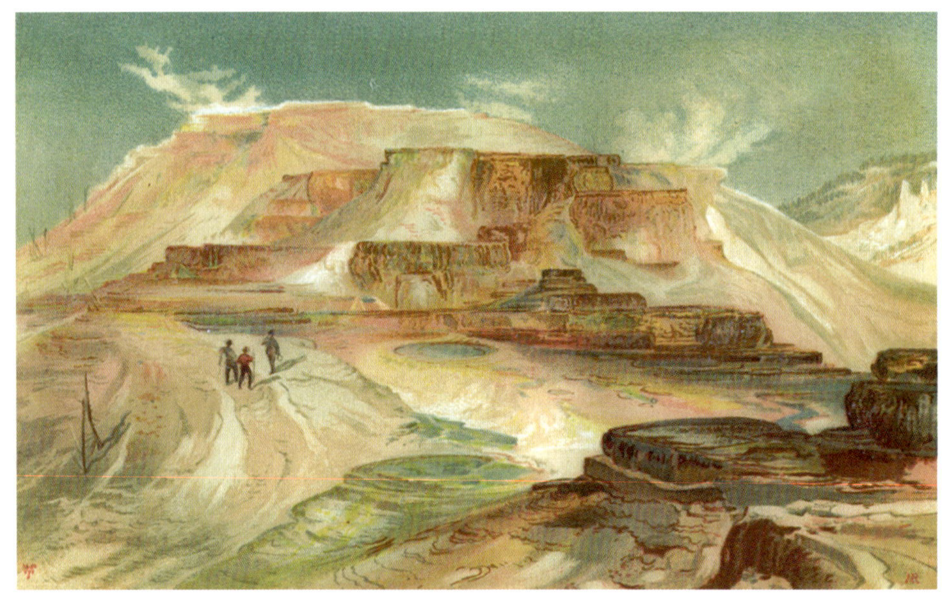

FIGURE 37. After Thomas Moran, *Pink Terraces, Mammoth Hot Springs, Gardiner's River,* n.d., chromolithograph, 4½ × 7½ in. (11.4 × 19 cm), from F. V. Hayden, *Twelfth Annual Report of the United States Geological and Geographical Survey of the Territories: A Report of Progress of the Exploration in Wyoming and Idaho for the Year 1878* (Washington, D.C.: U.S. Government Printing Office, 1878): 2, facing title page. University of Iowa Libraries, Iowa City, Iowa

and *The Great Blue Spring.*[48] Printed for Hayden by one of the leading chromolithographic firms in Philadelphia, Thomas Sinclair & Son, these chromos are less colorful than the corresponding plates in the Prang portfolio and significantly smaller (4½ × 7½ inches), but in other respects they differ only subtly from the 1876 images. Consequently they represent a mystery: if the Hayden report chromos were simply redrawn by Sinclair in 1882 from the 1876 Prang chromos, what happened to the four identical subjects Moran had created for Hayden in 1872? Or, if the Sinclair chromos were done from those 1872 watercolors, why do they so closely resemble the Prang versions? Moran often created very similar scenes for different patrons, but usually varied them slightly; the relationship between the Sinclair/Hayden chromos and the Prang images, by contrast, is almost exact. The answers may never be known, but whatever the circumstances, Hayden's original 1872 commission was the first time Moran's work was planned for chromolithographic reproduction.

The other precursor to the Prang project was two chromos published for *The Aldine,* an art periodical that specialized in high-quality reproductions. Late in 1873, shortly before Prang contacted Moran with *The Yellowstone National Park* commission, the journal advertised that it was offering two Moran chromolithographs as a gift to its subscribers. One view depicted the White Mountains (fig. 38), the other the Green River, views chosen for their symbolism of East and West.[49] The publicity touted their nationalistic significance:

> Every subscriber to The Aldine for the year 1874 will receive a pair of chromos. The original pictures were painted in oil for the publishers of TA [*The Aldine*]

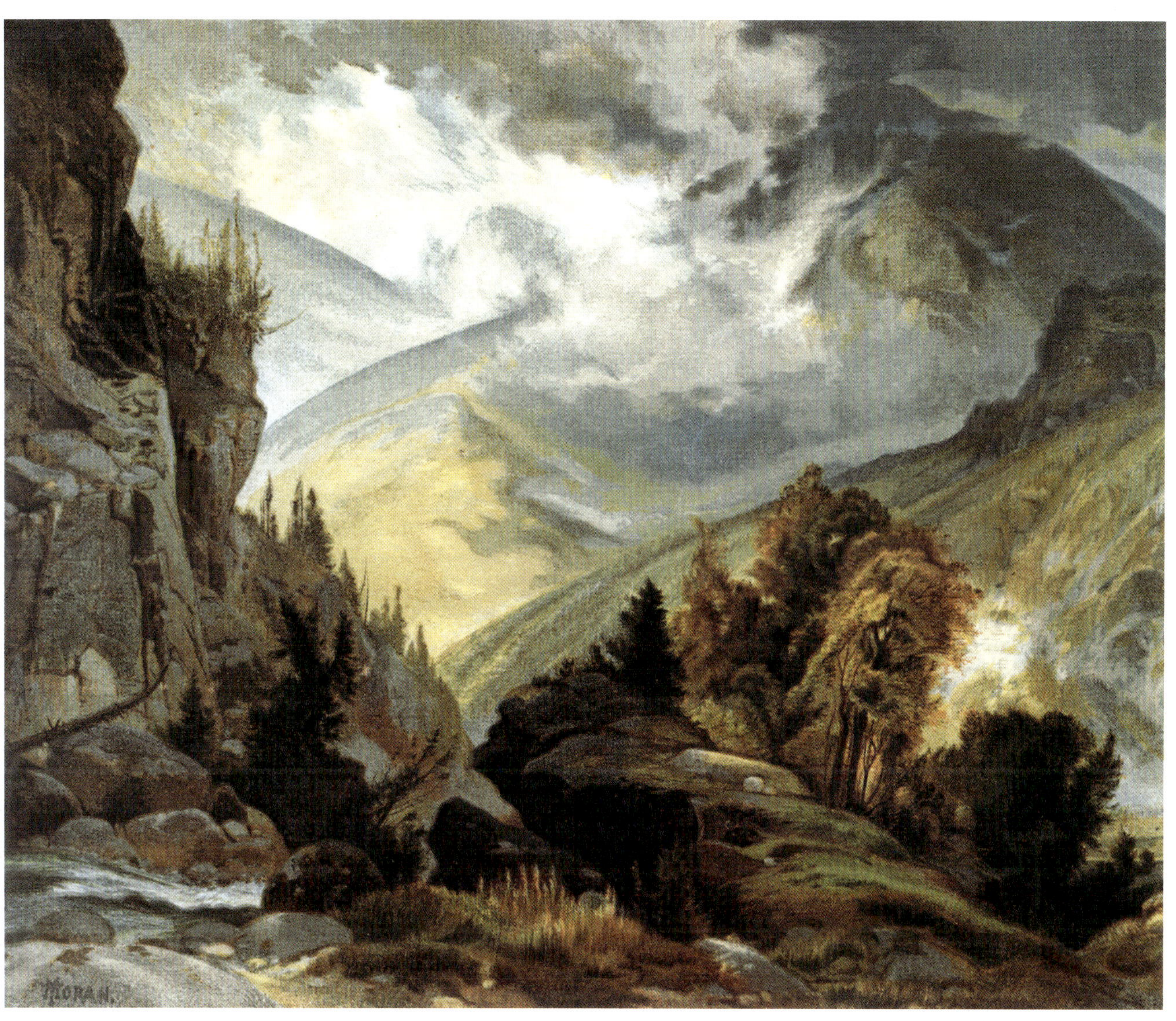

FIGURE 38. After Thomas Moran, *The White Mountains — New Hampshire,* ca. 1873, chromolithograph, 11 × 15½ in. (27.9 × 39.4 cm). Courtesy of Zaplin-Lampert Gallery, Santa Fe, New Mexico

> by Thomas Moran, whose great Colorado picture was purchased by Congress for $10,000. The subjects were chosen to represent "The East" and "The West." One is a view in the White Mountains, New Hampshire; the other gives the Cliffs of Green River, Wyoming Territory. The difference in the nature of the scenes themselves is a pleasing contrast, and affords a good display of the artist's scope and coloring. The chromos are each worked from thirty distinct plates, and are in size (12 × 16) and appearance exact facsimiles of the originals. The presentation of a worthy example of America's greatest landscape painter to the subscribers of TA was a bold but peculiarly happy idea, and its successful realization is attested by the following testimonial over the signature of Mr. Moran himself: Newark N.J., September 20, 1873. Messrs. James Sutton & Co. Gentlemen: I am delighted with the proofs in color of your chromos. They are wonderfully successful representations by mechanical process of the original paintings. Very respectfully, Thos. Moran.

Although *The Aldine* had worked with Prang for similar chromolithographic promotions since 1869, the Boston publisher was not mentioned in the advertisement. Moran's letter to the journal acknowledges only James Sutton & Co., the publisher of *The Aldine.*[50]

As the notice continued, *The Aldine* echoed Louis Prang's own rhetoric about the value of chromolithographic reproductions. Emphasizing the subject's nationalistic significance, it also reminded readers that the works were products of native talent and industry:

> These chromos are in every sense American. They are by an original American process, with material of American manufacture, from the designs of American scenery by an American painter, and presented to subscribers by the first successful American Art Journal. If no better because of all this they will certainly possess an interest no foreign production can inspire, and neither are they any the worse if by reason of peculiar facilities of production they cost the publishers only a trifle, while equal in every respect to other chromos that are sold singly for double the subscription price of The Aldine. Persons of taste will prize these pictures for themselves—not for the price they did or did not cost, and will appreciate the enterprise that renders their distribution possible.[51]

In offering chromolithographs of such symbolic significance to subscribers as a bonus to the lavishly illustrated journal, *The Aldine* was clearly attempting to demonstrate its versatility as an art publisher and position itself, like Prang, prominently at the forefront of developing issues in American art and culture. That the editors turned to Moran for such a purpose demonstrates that his works were widely recognized for their ability to convey nationalistic values to a wide audience. That ability, of course, would be one of the primary reasons that Prang would seek out Moran to create the imagery for his most ambitious project to date.

INSPIRATION AND COMPETITION: ILLUSTRATED BOOKS AND PORTFOLIOS

Prang almost certainly would have heard about Moran from the publicity *The Grand Cañon of the Yellowstone* had received since the summer of 1872 when Congress had purchased it for the Capitol building in Washington, D.C. The specific idea to focus on Moran's work in a portfolio project, however, might have been sparked by a *Scribner's Monthly* review of one of the artist's several series of Yellowstone watercolors, a group now known as the "Blackmore" set that appeared at Goupil's Gallery in New York City in January 1873. The review claimed that "these drawings are the most brilliant and poetic pictures that have been done in America thus far" and admiringly remarked: "Mr. Moran's water colors show a strong man rejoicing to run a race; and with all his sense alive for rich and strange and tender shimmering color, rainbow and mist, with fleeting cloud, and more hues than Iris with her purpled scarf can show. His love of form is strong as his love of color, and his lines betray the same innate grace of spirit, the same delicately moving mind."[52] The writer noted that another series was in the works (probably the one Moran was making for Jay Cooke) and expressed the "hope that when these are finished the general public may one day have the means of seeing them." With his acute sense of what appealed to American audiences, Louis Prang would undoubtedly have read these words with interest.

As the publisher envisioned a chromolithographic series from Moran's watercolors that would be distinguished enough to stand up to his critics, he looked to several existing types of publications. Gift books were beautifully bound, lavishly illustrated, extremely fashionable, and potentially lucrative. Portfolios of reproductive prints (mostly engravings) designed for elite collectors such as Turner's *Liber Studiorum* had a long and distinguished tradition in the art world. Illustrated natural history publications such as John James Audubon's massive *The Birds of America* (1828–1838) combined some of the merits of gift books and portfolios and were often both beautiful collections of art and highly respected works of science. And finally, the recent phenomena of photographic books, especially those about the American West, were heightening interest in the region even as they challenged long-held assumptions about the efficacy of traditional pictorial imagery. Combining aspects of all these publications with an emphasis on western scenery—one of the most intriguing subjects of the time—would, the publisher hoped, distinguish *The Yellowstone National Park* as a serious publication as well as render it a lucrative endeavor.

Many of these books had a nationalistic premise at their core—to represent America through the work of native artists—and Prang and Moran's *The Yellowstone*

National Park touted this ideal as well. Such patriotism was not a gratuitous appeal to readers but rather an effort to create a "school" that would counteract the reliance on European imagery that had long been a staple in American publications. As the influential *American Literary Gazette and Publisher's Circular* had bemoaned in 1869, "Although our pages contain a tolerably extensive list of Illustrated Books, it is unfortunately true that few are original American productions. The growing practice of American publishers, of manufacturing books out of all sorts of odds and ends that may be available, gluts the market with books whose value may only be measured by pounds and tons: while original literary productions are scarce." It continued with a direct reference to Prang: "Books with colored illustrations are extremely rare, being confined chiefly to juvenile works. The few that have made their appearance this season are poor, and show but little proficiency in the art. It is strange that we should be so much behindhand in this respect while Prang publishes the finest chromolithographs in the world."[53]

Such a compliment, coupled with the call for American illustrations, may have been all the encouragement Louis Prang needed to consider how he might position his chromos in the lucrative and burgeoning market of high-quality gift books.[54] Not only did they promise considerable financial reward, they also carried a high degree of prestige. Prang had already attempted an "Album of American Artists" in the late 1860s, but this never materialized as an assembled set. He hoped that *The Yellowstone National Park*, packaged as a deluxe portfolio that was part gift book, part art collection, part natural history treatise, all within the context of the novel scenery of the West, would finally confirm chromolithography's value as a reproductive process and definitively refute the characterization of his products as lacking in sophistication and artistic merit.

Between 1825 and 1860, approximately 1,000 gift books were published in the United States.[55] Not to be confused with print portfolios, these were bound volumes that ranged from relatively small to more substantial tomes. Most were adorned with gilded or embossed covers, sometimes of leather, and most were replete with engraved illustrations. Unlike large-scale print portfolios, these were relatively affordable, with many fine titles available for under $5. A relatively new emphasis in these books in the 1860s and 1870s was American scenery, and Moran and his mentors, Hamilton and Sartain, were each involved with contributing to their pages. Some did exceptionally well, most notably the richly illustrated, two-volume *Picturesque America; or The Land We Live In* (1872–1874, fig. 39), whose sales have been estimated at nearly a million copies. Originally priced at about $24 a set, depending on binding, the volumes are filled with imagery, including a steel engraving after Moran, but all of it is black-and-white.[56] Prang and Moran's publication, of course, had the added appeal of color, but as a large, usually unbound publication (several sets *were* bound), it was distinct from most gift books, even the lavish *Picturesque America*. *The Yellowstone*

National Park was nevertheless linked to these publications in its similar appeal to the growing market for published imagery of American scenery.

The portfolio's physical composition, of course, more closely resembled the presentation of traditional art reproductions, usually engravings or etchings that were issued both as single images and as portfolio sets. A staple in the art world since the Renaissance, these had been the focus of significant attention in mid-nineteenth-century America, especially with the rise of art unions that commissioned reproductive prints of American artists' work and disseminated them widely. Many artists, such as George Caleb Bingham and William Ranney, had become known as much for prints from their work as for their original canvases.[57] More immediate print precedents for Prang and Moran's project, however, were probably the large-scale reproductions after Frederic Church's and Albert Bierstadt's work, including chromolithographs produced in London. Some of these sold for substantial amounts—in 1869, 20-x-30-inch chromos of Bierstadt's *Rocky Mountains, Lander's Peak,* and *Storm in the Rocky Mountains, Mt. Rosalie* sold for as much as $25 apiece.[58] Portfolios of American western prints that the pragmatic Prang might have recognized as models for *The Yellowstone National Park* would have included James Otto Lewis's *The Aboriginal Port-Folio* (1835–1836), a collection of seventy-two hand-colored lithographs (ca. 18½ x 11½ inches each) of Native American imagery.[59] Not long after, George Catlin had issued a series of twenty-five to thirty-one (depending on the edition) hand-colored lithographs entitled *Catlin's North American Indian Portfolio: Hunting Scenes and Amusements of the Rocky Mountains and Prairies of America* (1844–1845). Published in at least six editions in London and New York, the prints measured approximately 18½ x 25½ inches, significantly larger and more elaborate than the illustrations in his earlier book, *Letters and Notes on the Manners and Customs of the North American Indians* (1841), with the collections priced between $25 and $40.[60] From 1839 to 1843, Prince Maximilian of Wied published his monumental *Travels in the Interior of North America, 1832–34,* a two-volume narrative plus a lavish atlas of eighty-one aquatints after the work of Swiss artist Karl Bodmer, who had accompanied the prince through the American West. The atlas was available in a number of versions, with different paper stock and degree of coloration, and these were variously priced; one was advertised in the United States at $120.[61] Prang's *The Yellowstone National Park* portfolio, priced at $60 for fifteen chromos, was in the middle range of such publications, but its presentation as a boxed selection of mounted prints

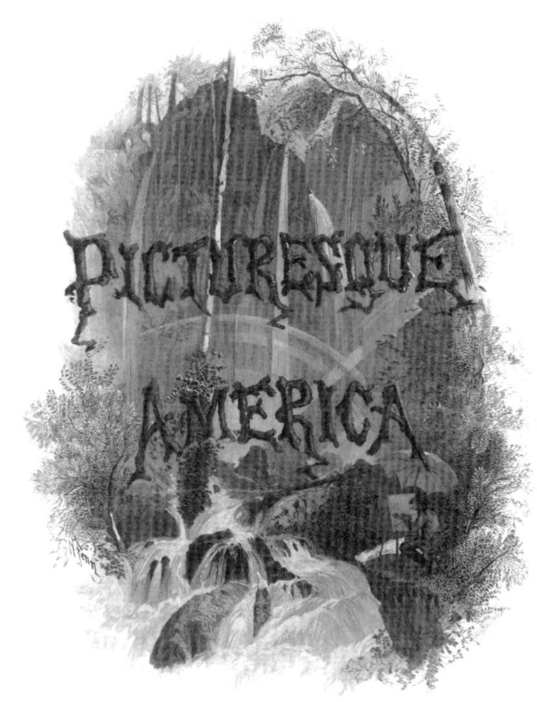

FIGURE 39. Title page, *Picturesque America,* 1872, wood engraving. Special Collections, University of Iowa Libraries, Iowa City, Iowa

was nevertheless a bow to the elite tradition of art reproductions and a response to a growing market for high-end illustrated editions of western subject matter.

In their day, many of these tomes were probably regarded more as works of natural history than as art portfolios or gift books. Indeed, as Georgia Barnhill has noted, "the illustrated book was the format chosen for much of the transmission of scientific and technical information during the nineteenth century."[62] Publications in this genre were often scientifically and artistically ambitious. Alexander Wilson's *American Ornithology* (1808–1814), for example, was a nine-volume opus with nearly one hundred plates that retailed for $120, and John James Audubon's seven-volume *The Birds of North America* (1828–1838) was priced at an astounding $1,000.[63] Portfolios of landscape prints such as Joshua Shaw's *Picturesque Views of American Scenery* (1819–1820) and Shaw and William Guy Wall's *Hudson River Portfolio* (1821) were probably regarded more as compendia of picturesque and nationalistic subject matter than as scientific contributions, but western landscapes had definitively entered the scientific realm in numerous government survey reports, especially the notable twelve-volume Pacific Railroad survey reports of 1855–1861. The Great Surveys reports that Moran himself contributed to about the time he was working with Louis Prang also added to this trend. Western scenery may have been regarded within more of a scientific context than eastern landscape, because so many of its interpreters were working within an exploratory context, and it was an association that Prang would capitalize on as he presented Moran's chromolithographed images to a scientific audience.

In shaping *The Yellowstone National Park* portfolio, the publisher may also have been responding to new books of photography that were, by the late 1860s, joining the more traditional forms of illustrated publications as significant vehicles for pictorial imagery.[64] Photographic books had been produced only since the early 1850s, made possible by high-quality paper photographs that were replacing daguerreotypes. These collections were composed of actual albumen prints tipped into the books' pages (mechanized printing of photographs was not perfected until the 1880s), and because each print had to be manually produced (with each taking up to half an hour), books containing them were of necessity limited editions.[65] The photographs were usually accompanied by text, and the volumes were often luxuriously bound. They ranged in size from relatively small, with prints of approximately 5 × 7 inches, to much larger. A. J. Russell's *The Great West Illustrated* (1869), for example, contained prints that measured 13 × 16 inches. A leather-bound album of fifty albumen prints with accompanying text, Russell's book visually chronicled the scenery along the rail line between Laramie, Wyoming, and Salt Lake City. A similar publication, although smaller, was Ferdinand Hayden's own *Sun Pictures of Rocky Mountain Scenery* (1870), composed of thirty of Russell's railroad photographs. Prang and Moran both would have known this book through their familiarity with the survey leader.

Even as Prang's *The Yellowstone National Park* portfolio echoed and emulated aspects of these other forms of published imagery, it was also in competition with them, both literally in the marketplace and figuratively in an era in which the merits of different modes of pictorial representation were contested.[66] As we have seen, Prang was acutely aware of the tensions between chromolithography, painting, and engravings, but he was also surely familiar with those between photography and manually drawn art. The issue focused on the relative accuracy, authenticity, and evocative power of the different media, with some, including Hayden in *Sun Pictures of Rocky Mountain Scenery,* extolling photography as "the nearest approach to truthful delineation of nature," and others, such as William Cullen Bryant in *Picturesque America,* explaining that "photographs, however accurate, lack the spirit and personal quality which the accomplished painter or draughtsman infuses into his work." These qualities, Bryant argued, "give to the work a value higher than could be derived from mere topographical accuracy."[67] When *The Yellowstone National Park* finally appeared, the preface emphasized its principal claim as the first full-color publication on the subject, but also underscored its authenticity:

> [Previous publications] were all wanting in one particular which no woodcut, engraving, or photograph can supply, and which nevertheless, is of the greatest importance, especially in the case under consideration. All representations of landscape scenery must necessarily lose the greater part of their charm when deprived of color; but of any representation in black and white of the scenery of Yellowstone it may truly be said that it is like Hamlet with the part of Hamlet omitted, for the wealth of color . . . constitutes one of the most wonderful elements of their beauty.

Hayden acknowledged that the portfolio's vivid hues would test viewers' credulity, but testified to their accuracy:

> So strange indeed, are the freaks of color which nature indulges in habitually in this wonderful country that it will no doubt require strong faith on the part of the reader in the truthfulness of both artist and writer to enable him unhesitatingly to accept the statements made in the present volume by the pen as well as by the brush. . . . the sketches by Mr. Thomas Moran, who accompanied me on one of my expeditions, are not only of a high order of artistic merit, [however,] but . . . they can also be relied upon as exceedingly correct renderings of their subjects, interesting alike to the man of science, the lover of art, and the admirer of nature.

Within the context of a range of types of published imagery, each competing for a position of authority within the complex and tenuously balanced ideals of truth and art, Prang positioned *The Yellowstone National Park* to offer the best of both worlds, and he saw Moran as the best artist to achieve that synthesis.

THE YELLOWSTONE NATIONAL PARK CHROMOLITHOGRAPHS

Prang approached Moran with the commission to create a series of watercolors for a special portfolio of chromolithographs in December 1873. He would later invite Hayden to write the accompanying text, but he conducted each relationship separately. Although Prang's business records have not survived, nor have any letters from the publisher to the artist, several from Moran to Prang exist, and they, along with the voluminous correspondence from L. Prang & Co. to Hayden preserved at the National Archives, reveal the progress of the project as well as the many hopes for *The Yellowstone National Park.*

It is not known when Prang and Moran first met. They may have been introduced by the artist's brother Edward who painted several works for Prang in the late 1860s.[68] Regardless, it is clear from their correspondence that the artist and publisher had collaborated before the *Yellowstone* project. When Prang approached the artist just before Christmas 1873, Thomas replied warily:

> In reply I would intimate that my previous transaction with you in a similar business was anything but satisfactory to me, inasmuch as I made to your order three illustrations from the American poets for which you were to pay me $75.00. When I sent them to you, you returned them, merely saying that you had concluded that the publication of the work would prove too expensive. That, of course, was not my business and your declining to pay for the pictures you had ordered, was, to put it in the mildest form, taking a most unfair advantage of me.[69]

Moran continued, stating that he would take on the commission, but that the order must be for at least eight watercolors for which he would receive $100 apiece, and he specified a payment schedule and the number of copies of the final prints that he would receive. He agreed to furnish at least two watercolors per month until the project was completed, and, although he did not ultimately meet those deadlines, he sent watercolors to Prang on a regular basis throughout 1874 and early 1875.

Prang must have quickly clarified the incident in question because Moran wrote an apology almost immediately, citing a misunderstanding with his brother Edward, who had apparently handled the earlier transaction for him, and he expressed relief at the resolution: "I have felt all along since that time I had been imposed upon. I now withdraw all that I said in my letter. . . . my brother Ed has the unfortunate faculty of muddling everything that he transacts for other people, and yours is not the only case where misunderstandings have arisen through very similar circumstances."[70]

Once they reconciled the misunderstanding, Moran finished several scenes for Prang within months and produced the others over the following year and a half, completing the work probably by fall 1875. This was hardly the only task that preoccupied him during that time. Indeed, in the spring of 1874 he was hard at work completing the monumental

Chasm of the Colorado (fig. 33), as well as producing a number of wood engraving designs for *Scribner's Monthly, The Aldine,* and other publications.[71] The following summer he journeyed west again for a month, this time to Colorado to see the Mountain of the Holy Cross, and that subject consumed his attention in his third large western oil (5 × 7 feet, fig. 34) until April 1875, shortly before he completed Prang's watercolors.[72]

One way to achieve such remarkable productivity was through repetition of subject matter and motifs, and indeed that is a hallmark of Moran's oeuvre. The subjects and compositions in the Prang series, for example, have similar counterparts in the artist's oil and watercolor paintings and his engraved illustrations in popular journals, brochures, railroad timetables, guidebooks, gift books, and government survey reports. Not simply a matter of expediency, such redundancy underscores Moran's belief that the subjects were important American sites and themes worthy of continued attention. The appearance of comparable scenes in different contexts, from fine art galleries to commercial publications, furthermore demonstrates the impact of his work on American culture and provides unusually rich evidence of his working methods and stylistic development. In the case of the Prang series, for example, similarly titled images in other publications are exceptionally useful in determining the probable appearance of the nine subjects excluded from the final publication.

Moran created two other very similar watercolor series shortly before he embarked on his work for Prang. One was for the Northern Pacific Railroad financier Jay Cooke, in partial payment for $500 Cooke had loaned Moran to make his 1871 Yellowstone trip. This group of paintings, like the Prang watercolors, was subsequently dispersed to disparate collections and has never been reassembled as a suite. The only series to remain intact is the sixteen "Blackmore" watercolors that Moran painted in 1872 for William Blackmore, an English industrialist, anthropologist, and guest of Hayden's 1872 Yellowstone expedition. These works are today owned by the Gilcrease Museum in Tulsa, Oklahoma, and they are extremely useful in considering the potential appearance of several unlocated works Moran made for Prang. Between 1872 and 1874, Moran executed about fifty watercolors for other patrons as well, usually as single works or small groups.[73]

Although the documentation that would reveal the exact nature of Prang's request to Moran has not survived, it is clear that the selection of subjects for the watercolor series was largely the artist's choice and that he did not begin the project with a preconceived list. When he began the work in the spring of 1874, for example, he had not yet visited Colorado. Only after his journey there that summer did he produce the four images from that area for the portfolio, two of which, *The Mountain of the Holy Cross* (fig. 40) and *Mosquito Trail, Colorado* (fig. 107), appeared in the final publication. Furthermore Moran's question to the publisher on April 18, 1874, "Shall I give you a geyser?" indicates that he was making decisions as time went by.[74]

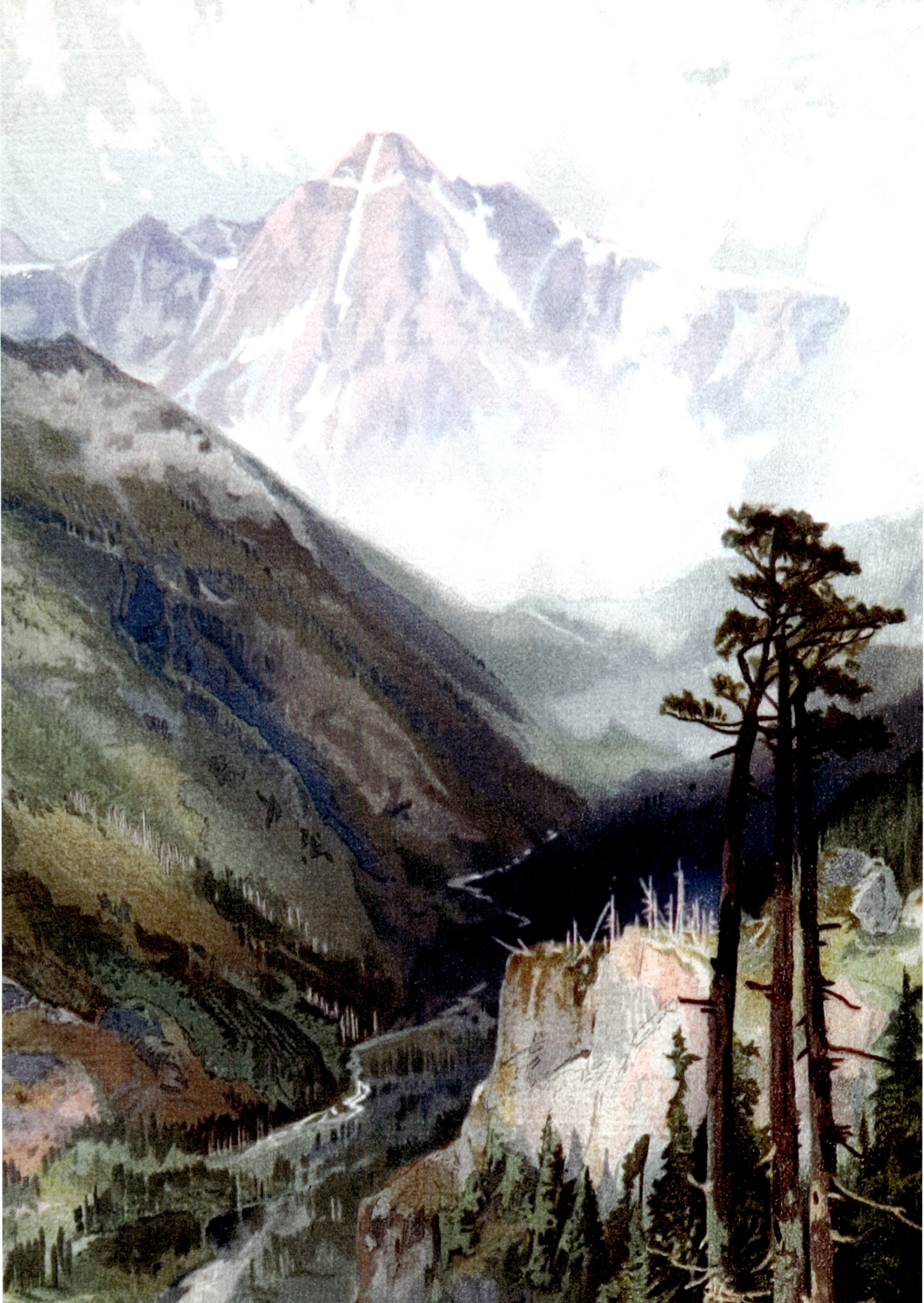

Moran worked on the Prang watercolors intermittently throughout 1874. *Gardiner's River Hot Springs, The Towers of Tower Falls* (fig. 41), and *Devil's Den* (not included in the final publication) were completed by the end of February 1874.[75] *Head of the Yellowstone River* and *Lower Yellowstone Range* were finished the next month. The artist wrote Prang in early November with an update:

> My dear Mr. Prang: Since you were here I have made but one drawing of the series, as soon after you left, I met with an accident that produced a felon on my right thumb which has prevented me from doing any work whatever up to the present time, but it is now getting better & I am once more at work. I have the designs ready to work on of Donner Lake. Twin Lake. Pikes Peak. Summit of the Sierras. Great Salt Lake & Azure Cliffs of [Green River struck out] Colorado. Will send on two the latter part of this or the beginning of next week. The "Azure Cliffs" I have finished & it is a very beautiful drawing.[76]

We will probably never know Prang's opinion about the "beautiful drawing," but it must not have been one of his favorites since of the six works Moran mentioned in the letter, only *The Great Salt Lake* and *Summit of the Sierras* appeared in the final portfolio.

One newspaper article during this period must have been enormously gratifying to Louis Prang, validating his initial investment in *The Yellowstone National Park* project. Unlike the *New York Daily Tribune* that had been so harshly critical of his chromos, the *New York Times* wrote admiringly of Prang's work in October 1874: "In this country the highest degree of perfection [in chromolithography] has, without question, been obtained in the works that are being published from time to time by Prang & Co., of Boston. Very many of these are of the highest order; and it must be conceded that the publishers have greatly served the interest of art by offering such work to the public." The author concluded with a special request that Prang & Co. might attempt to make chromos from watercolors.

> Wherever . . . colors can be used to the best advantage, chromo-lithography promises good results. In imitating oil painting, and in the portrayal of colored designs of any kind, its effects are very beautiful, and if the enterprising firm at Boston, which has done so much to further the progress of the art in America, can produce an equally good imitation of the delicate effects of water-colors, they will have advanced to a point where little more could be desired.[77]

Since Prang had already embarked on just such a watercolor project with Moran he must have read this challenge with both satisfaction and anticipation, looking forward to what he hoped would be equally admiring reviews of his finest creations.

FIGURE 40. After Thomas Moran, *The Mountain of the Holy Cross* (detail), chromolithograph, 13⅝ × 9⅝ in. (34.6 × 24.4 cm). Joslyn Art Museum, Omaha, gift of Gail and Michael Yanney and Lisa and Bill Roskens

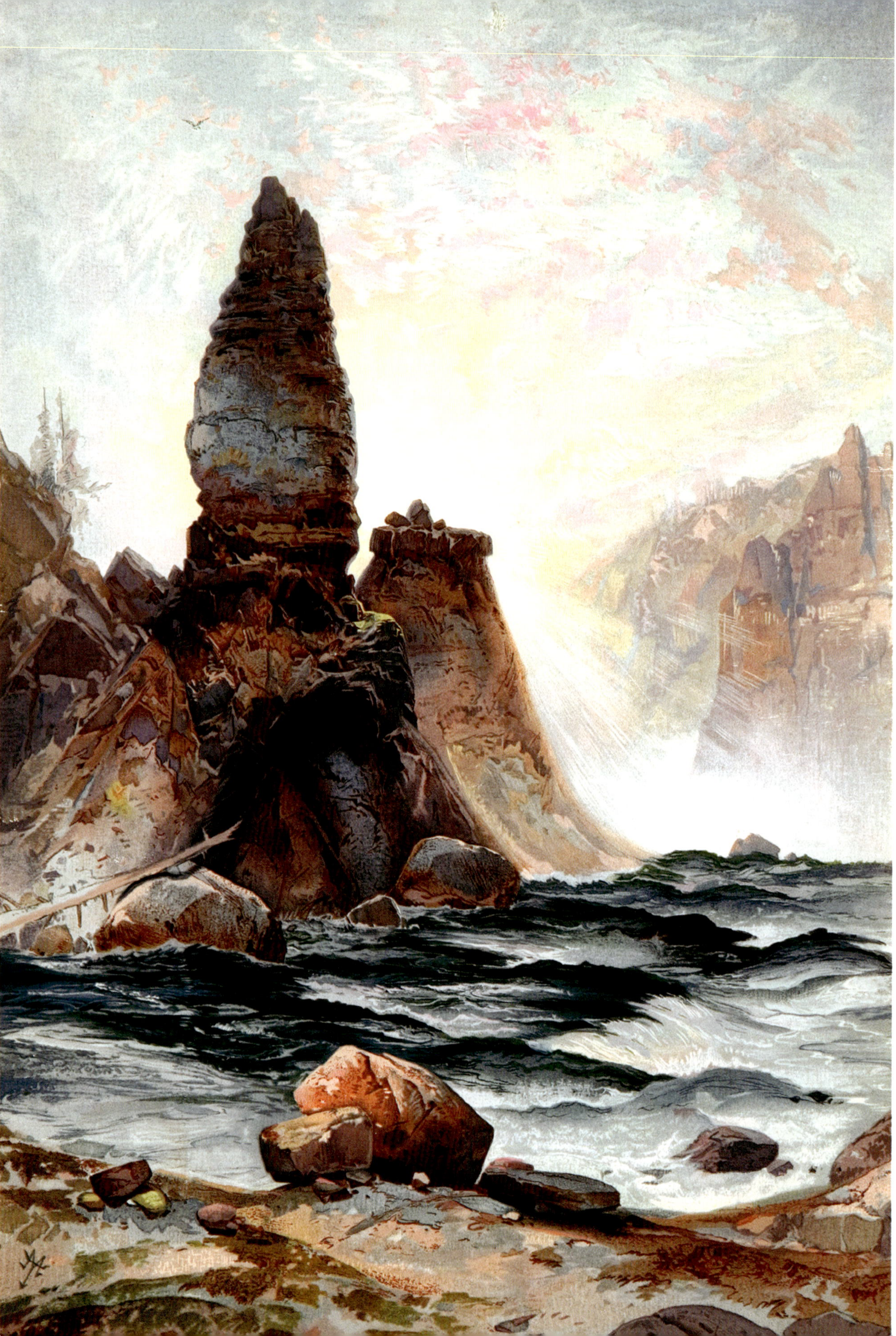

Moran apparently finished the last watercolor for Prang sometime in the middle of 1875 or shortly thereafter.[78] The number of images was substantially increased from Moran's original proposal of "at least eight" to twenty-four. The artist did receive his requested $100 for each work, twice what he had gotten for each of the sixteen Blackmore watercolors in 1872.[79] Once the paintings arrived at the Prang "printory," they were handed over to the *chromiste* (probably William Harring, who handled Prang's most important pictures). He carefully replicated them, separating out the component colors and redrawing each on a different lithographic stone. In the absence of the Prang company records, it remains uncertain whether Moran received proofs of the completed prints before the chromolithographs were pronounced finished, but considering the judicious care with which the Prang office handled Hayden's portion of the project, it is likely that he did. Several annotated impressions of the prints (complete with registration marks that indicate they were proofs), today in the collection of Joslyn Art Museum in Omaha, Nebraska, demonstrate that the chromos were carefully checked for color accuracy. Once this was done to everyone's satisfaction, Moran's role in the project was concluded, and he seems not to have been asked to help market the final publication or in any way assist with its promotion.[80]

In a letter of March 9, 1876, L. Prang & Co. wrote to Hayden with the news: "We have the pleasure of sending you, by today's express, a package containing copies of our Chromos of Western scenery, as per enclosed list. . . . These comprise all the pictures we now have in hand, and all we contemplate bringing out, before we see how the enterprise is likely to go."[81] These were proofs, as Prang indicated in early April: "The publication is not ready yet, only proofs have been printed, the regular edition . . . will not be finished in less than 6 weeks. We doubt the wisdom of beginning to deliver now (which we could to the extent of about 12 copies from the proofs) before the regular edition with text is prepared."[82] The fifteen chromos were finished by the end of the month and were sent to the Centennial Exposition for exhibition in L. Prang & Co.'s display, albeit without Hayden's text. Its production progressed in subsequent months, and by October, Prang's office reported that "the work is now being rapidly pushed forward, and will be ready for the market shortly." The final publication, with text and portfolio case, was finally ready on December 6. When Moran received his copy, he wrote Louis Prang an appreciative reply:

> It is in every respect a most sumptuous & magnificent work; and the faithfulness with which you have reproduced my water color drawings is beyond praise. It seems to me that Chromo-Lithography has, in your hands, attained perfection so skillfully have you reproduced every shade and tone of color in the originals. I naturally feel proud that a work so difficult and extensive should have been produced in America; & hope that your enterprise and skill will meet with the appreciation it deserves.[83]

FIGURE 41. After Thomas Moran, *The Towers of Tower Falls* (detail), chromolithograph, 13¾ × 9 in. (34.9 × 22.8 cm). Joslyn Art Museum, Omaha, gift of Gail and Michael Yanney and Lisa and Bill Roskens

Moran's satisfaction surely gratified the publisher enormously. It had been three years since he had first approached the artist to do the watercolors, and he too was anxious to know whether the project would "meet with the appreciation it deserves."

The 1876 Prang prints were the most important chromolithographs ever made from Moran's art. Just as they represented a long line of struggles by the publisher, they were also part of a varied artistic career within a period of transition in the world of art and publishing. *The Yellowstone National Park*'s images vividly embody many aspects of those issues, from their formal echoes of other Moran works and the artist's experiences with specific sites, to tensions between different published media and publication formats. Most importantly, as a "just subject for national pride," as Hayden described it in the preface, the portfolio was part of a larger effort to use Moran's art to popularize the American West in the second half of the nineteenth century. The Prang publication was a much larger effort to package and commodify the region, transforming it from an alien wilderness into an integral part of national identity through pictorial imagery. The portfolio participated in making the landscape's sublime expanses manageable and offered its collectors the literal ability to own its scenic wonders. This mirrored similar efforts that used Moran's art metaphorically to represent cultural domination over the region, and indeed the American landscape generally. These included everything from the physical expansion of Euro-Americans into the West to more symbolic acts of appropriation, such as that when Congress hung *The Grand Cañon of the Yellowstone* on the walls of the U.S. Capitol. By enframing the landscape, shaping it, and presenting it to viewers through the carefully constructed vehicle of either a gallery exhibition or a lavishly printed portfolio, Moran's art made the enormity and exoticism of the West approachable. That process, of composing views from the raw material of experience and transforming them into evocative symbols of American possibility, is evident in each individual scene of *The Yellowstone National Park*.

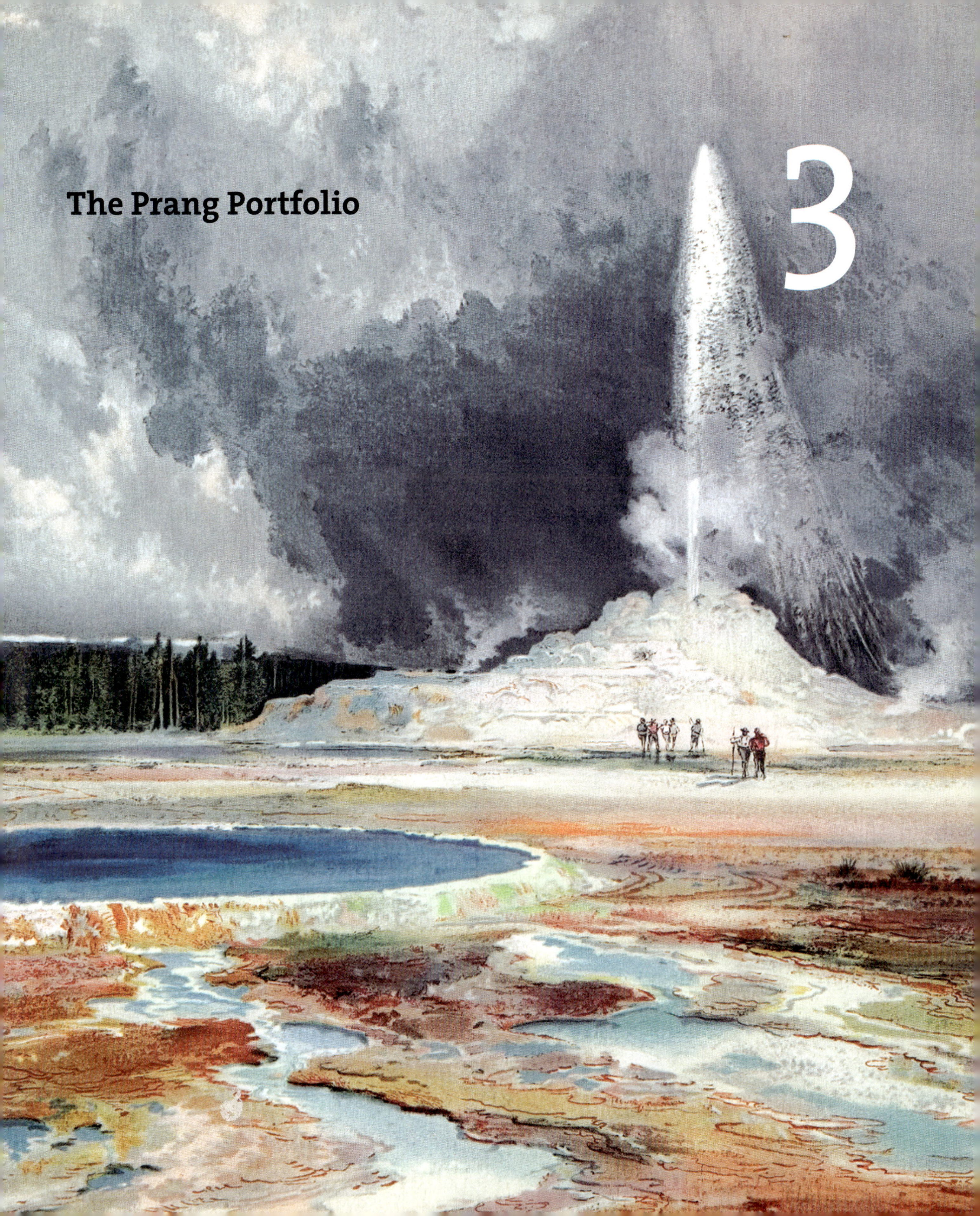

3 The Prang Portfolio

In the reproduction of Mr. Moran's water-colors Messrs. L. Prang & Co. have fully sustained the world-wide reputation to which they have attained by the conscientious and artistic practice of the difficult and beautiful process of chromo-lithography.
—*Ferdinand Hayden,* The Yellowstone National Park, *1876*

The Yellowstone National Park, and the Mountain Regions of Portions of Idaho, Nevada, Colorado and Utah is a large, boxed, folio-sized portfolio (20 × 18 inches, figs. 2 and 3) of fifteen mounted chromolithographs drawn from Moran's watercolors (image size 9½ × 14 or 14 × 9½ inches), accompanied by thirty pages of letterpress text written by Ferdinand Hayden and two annotated maps (figs. 152 and 153). The portfolio cases varied in color—some were red, some were brown, some were green, and a few copies were bound as books.[1] The press run was limited to 1,000 copies and each set sold for $60, a figure that translates to roughly $1,000 today.[2] Only about 100 copies had been sold or given away, however, before a disastrous fire at L. Prang & Co. in September 1877 reduced the remaining inventory to about fifty complete sets and odd numbers of the single plates.[3] This extraordinary reduction in the number of copies renders the extant publications and separate prints more rare and thus more valuable today than if the original edition had survived intact.

The portfolio is magnificent, but it was originally intended to be even more so. Moran produced a total of twenty-four watercolors for the project, and Prang culled them to fifteen to cut costs, although the rationale for his selections remains unclear.[4] Hayden's text was also planned to be more thorough and scientific. His twelve-and-a-half-page introduction is wholly concerned with Yellowstone's geology, ignoring all the other regions pictured in the chromolithographs, and the one-page "descriptions" that accompany the prints are relatively superficial explanations of their locations and remarkable features. Had *The Yellowstone National Park* been issued with all twenty-four images Moran created and with a text of a truly scholarly nature, the publication would undoubtedly be even more renowned than it is today.

The series is dominated by Yellowstone scenes, many of which are today's tourist attractions, but other parts of the West are depicted as well, including some of Moran's most well-known subjects, such as the Mountain of the Holy Cross and the area now known as Zion National Park. Prang deferred to Hayden about the sequence of plates: "In regard to the order of arrangement of the pictures we should prefer to take your decision, as you can doubtless arrange their sequence better than we can," but it remains uncertain whether the survey leader offered an opinion on the matter.[5] After nine Yellowstone sites at the beginning of the series, the order deviates from the title with two Colorado scenes, the single views from Nevada and Idaho, and finally the two Utah images.[6] Beyond the basic pattern, the subjects' order has no internal logic. The Yellowstone images, for example, are not arranged geographically, as they move from *Gardiner's River Hot Springs* in the northern section of the park to *The Great Blue Spring* and *The Castle Geyser* in the southwest, and then back even farther north to *The Lower Yellowstone Range,* nor do they follow the progress of any historical expedition. This is also true for the rest of the series. At the same time, the two maps in the portfolio are labeled with the chromos' titles and numbers, enabling interested readers to determine, at least roughly, their geographical locations.

The Yellowstone National Park was the first illustrated publication about the West printed in color and is an exceptional example of the book arts of its time. Nearly every study of the history of chromolithography and Prang's and Moran's careers acknowledges its remarkable achievement, but the project has never been explored in depth. Many of the prints reiterate favorite Moran themes, but these images have not been considered in relation to the actual sites or their various visual and literary sources. Other images have never been studied at all since Moran rarely depicted them. Close scrutiny of these reveals a great deal of new information about the subjects and the artist's work more generally.

The portfolio also offers a remarkable opportunity to consider the intriguing relationship between land as place and landscape as crafted presentation. For although Moran was careful to depict the component parts of his scenes accurately, he reconstructed some aspects, altering relationships in various ways. These manipulations for pictorial effect are revealed through comparisons, especially to the photographs that he used as references. These photographs, as discussed in the previous chapter, offered a different sort of authority about their subjects than did drawings and paintings, especially in representing terrain. On the other hand, Moran never claimed to mirror nature but rather saw his role as that of an interpreter who should offer what William Cullen Bryant called "a value higher than could be derived from mere topographical accuracy."[7]

The creative process that these images embody, along with Prang's strategic decisions for their presentation, offers a number of insights into how attitudes toward the West were shaped in the late nineteenth century. Even as it existed as a factual reality, the West was also being simultaneously *created* in the minds of eastern Americans. *The Yellowstone National Park* portfolio was but one contributor to that development, but it had several elements that distinguished its potential impact. Like all illustrated publications about the West, the portfolio was a selection of landscapes that could be literally owned and held, facilitating a private enactment of a much larger national impulse that regarded the West as available for the taking. Since this series was especially visually compelling, it may have made the experience more immediate. And the addition of color was critical. By comparison to wood engravings and hand-colored lithographs that all present their subjects with a contrast that hardens, the chromolithographs, like the watercolors from which they were drawn, tend to soften the scenes, rendering the terrain more beautiful than sublime. This enhanced viewers' engagement, beguiling them even as it presented scenes of an almost unimaginable power, both literal and figurative. But astute observers and readers would have recognized that proprietary presumption toward such a land of extremes carried risks. *The Yellowstone National Park* portrays some sites, for example, known for their foreboding, even sinister associations. These images were balanced in the series with more uplifting subjects, but it seems clear that the prints were carefully selected not only to celebrate the West's "wonders," but also to consider its more ambiguous aspects. By presenting this tension, *The Yellowstone National Park* chromolithographs assist in deepening the act of incorporation that brought the West into the national identity, acknowledging its challenges as well as its promise.

When all twenty-four images Moran originally created for the project are considered together as both a linear sequence and a unified work, correspondences among the plates emerge, creating a dialogue that reveals the project's full significance. Formal, geographical, circumstantial, and symbolic analogies within the array of disparate prints link seemingly different works and distantly located subjects, creating a synergism of effect that is only evident when the images are understood together within the context of their creation and their sequence within the series and through cultural associations that endowed these novel sights with meaning. *The Yellowstone National Park* was the most remarkable compendium of western views available in 1876, and although it has had many competitors since, it may be no less significant today.

GARDINER'S RIVER HOT SPRINGS

The chromolithographs in *The Yellowstone National Park* begin with *Gardiner's River Hot Springs* (fig. 42), a subject more commonly called *Mammoth Hot Springs* in other Moran portrayals and at the park itself. This distinctive formation was the first landmark within the boundaries of what would become Yellowstone National Park that the Hayden expedition encountered in 1871, and it is still a major tourist destination.[8] Graced with colorful terraces of mineral springs that form a large hill and surrounded by other geothermal features, it dominates the northern headquarters of the park today.

Moran and survey photographer William Henry Jackson spent considerable time sketching and photographing at Mammoth Hot Springs. The artist posed on the cascading ledges in some of the views, perhaps to provide a sense of scale to the exotic scene (fig. 43). Although they camped in the area for nearly three days, Moran mentioned the springs only briefly in his characteristically laconic Yellowstone journal. Another member of the survey, however, Albert Peale, was more descriptive and poetic:

> A little further on we were greeted with one of the grandest sights imaginable. Before us rose about 600 feet a mass of white sediment arranged in separate ter-

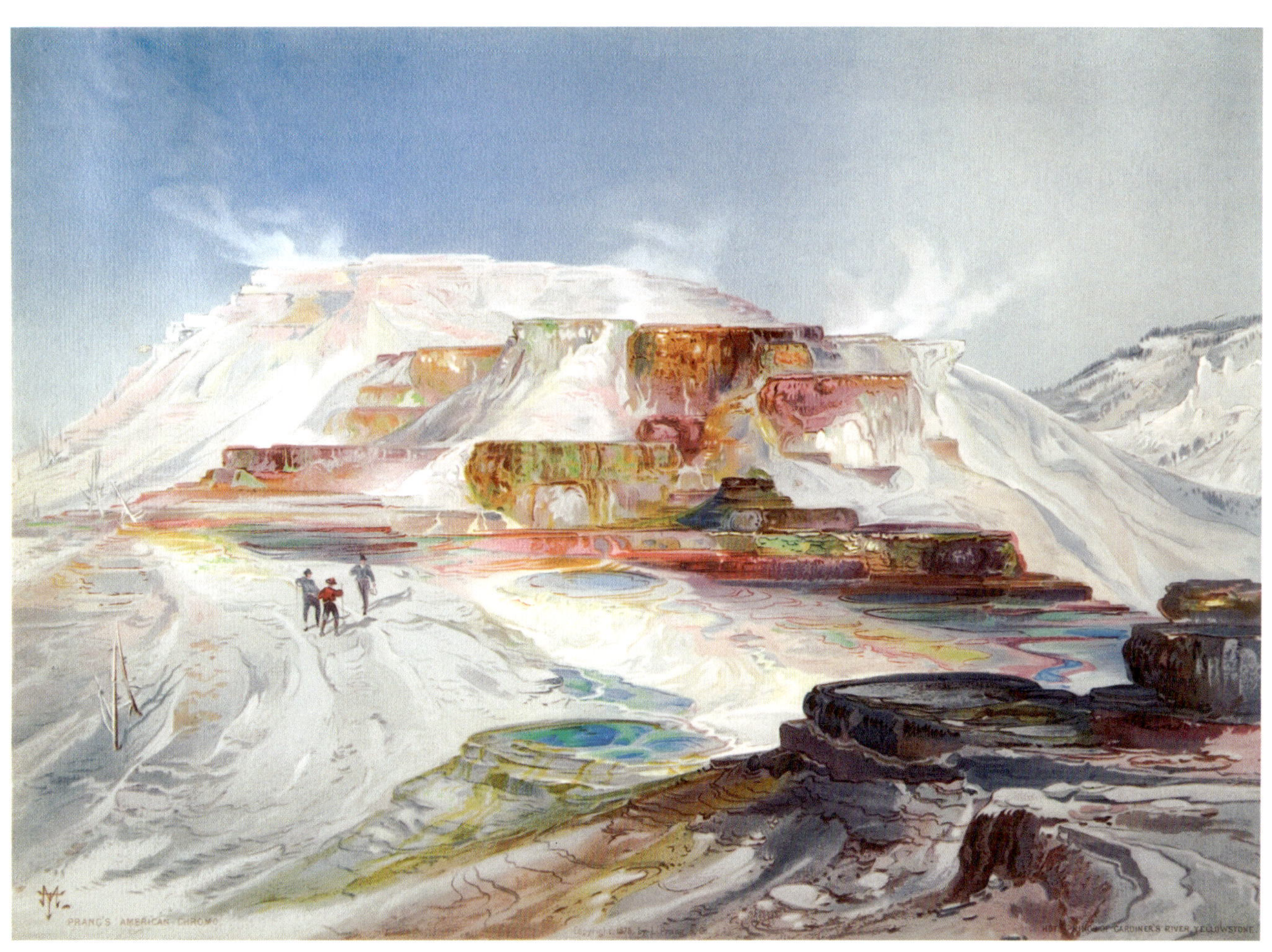

FIGURE 42. After Thomas Moran, *Gardiner's River Hot Springs,* ca. 1875, chromolithograph, 9⅝ × 14 in. (24.4 × 35.5 cm). Joslyn Art Museum, Omaha, gift of Gail and Michael Yanney and Lisa and Bill Roskens

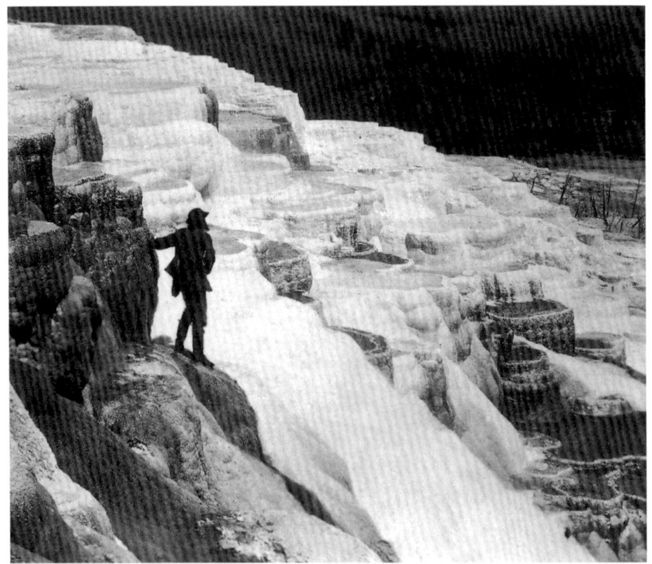

FIGURE 43. William Henry Jackson, *White Mountain Hot Springs — Group of Upper Basins [Thomas Moran on Mammoth Hot Springs]*, 1871, photograph. Courtesy of East Hampton Library, Long Island Collection

> races looking like a vast frozen cascade. Each one of the terraces has a number of hot springs, while in beautiful basins (formed of the deposit)—some of them white, others red, others of a delicate pink tint—rising one above the other were innumerable pools of water, some hot others warm and still others cold. About 300 feet above our camp there is one large circular basin about a quarter of a mile in diameter filled with pools of water which boils up in various places over the surface. It is beautifully clear, seeming to be of a greenish-blue color.[9]

This pool-filled circular basin is the area of Mammoth Hot Springs sometimes called Diana's Baths or Upper Pools, and it became a favorite subject of Moran's, luminous in its coloration and exotic in its configuration.[10]

Moran had published wood engravings of Mammoth Hot Springs before he embarked on the Prang commission, most notably in *Scribner's Monthly* early in 1872 and in *The Aldine* in the spring of 1873 (fig. 44), but those views, of course, lacked the color so critical to the distinctive formation.[11] He had also already created several watercolors of the subject before crafting the one for Louis Prang, most of them taking an oblique view of the terraces and presenting them cascading diagonally across the composition (fig. 45). The Prang composition is unusual in Moran's oeuvre since it presents the formation from a frontal perspective, the mineral mountain rising directly in the center of the scene. This perspective also appears in at least one Jackson photograph (fig. 46) that may have been a reference for Moran's composition, and it is found in a later oil, *Great Hot Springs, Yellowstone National Park* (1893, fig. 47), which Moran painted nearly twenty years after the Prang commission.

In *The Yellowstone National Park* portfolio, *Gardiner's River Hot Springs* is linked to other mountainous views, most notably *Tower Falls and Sulphur Mountain,* with its unique looming geological mass, but it also coloristically compares to *The Grand Cañon of the Yellowstone.* The impression in Joslyn Art Museum's set is a printer's proof, with a nail hole in the upper right margin and right and left registration marks on both the right and left sides.

THE GREAT BLUE SPRING OF THE LOWER GEYSER BASIN

There is no major landmark today at Yellowstone called the Great Blue Spring, but Joslyn Art Museum's proof impression of the chromolithograph (fig. 48) has a penciled notation on its verso that reveals the exact spot: "Mouth of Excelsior Geyser, Yellow-

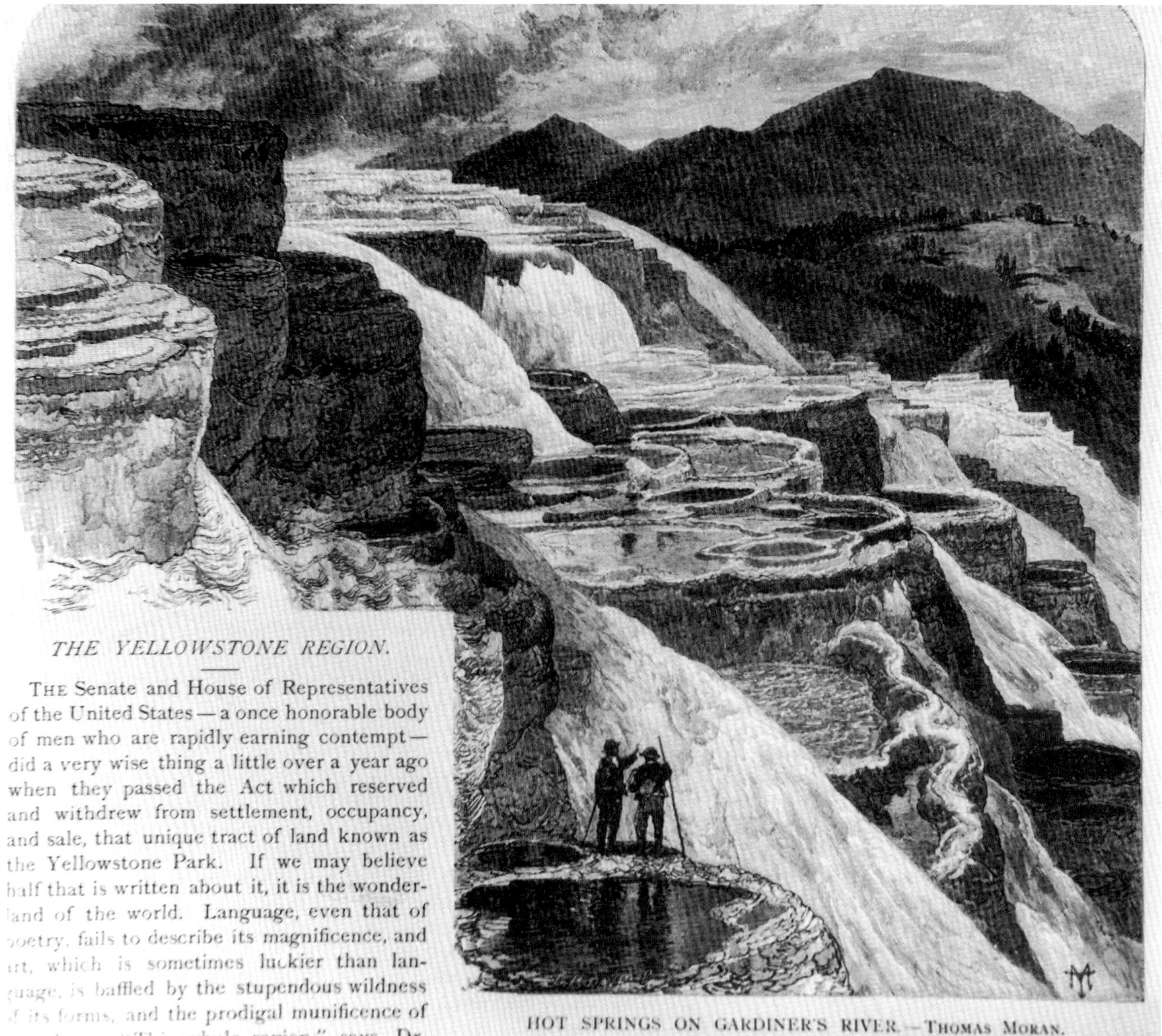

THE YELLOWSTONE REGION.

THE Senate and House of Representatives of the United States—a once honorable body of men who are rapidly earning contempt—did a very wise thing a little over a year ago when they passed the Act which reserved and withdrew from settlement, occupancy, and sale, that unique tract of land known as the Yellowstone Park. If we may believe half that is written about it, it is the wonderland of the world. Language, even that of poetry, fails to describe its magnificence, and art, which is sometimes luckier than language, is baffled by the stupendous wildness of its forms, and the prodigal munificence of ... "This whole region," says Dr.

HOT SPRINGS ON GARDINER'S RIVER.—THOMAS MORAN.

FIGURE 44. After Thomas Moran, *Hot Springs of Gardiner's River*, 1873, wood engraving, *The Aldine* 6 (March 1873): 74

stone Park."[12] Today, Grand Prismatic Spring, adjacent to Excelsior Geyser and measuring 370 feet in diameter, is more noteworthy as Yellowstone's largest spring, but Moran's view relegates that expansive pool to the far-right background and focuses instead on Excelsior Geyser, a much smaller, deep-blue pool that is distinguished by the brightly colored streams flowing from it into the adjacent Fire Hole River.[13] Located in the Midway Geyser Basin along the current road from the Old Faithful area (the Upper Geyser Basin) to Madison, Excelsior Geyser (fig. 49) erupts extremely sporadically today and its streams vary greatly in volume. But when it was especially active

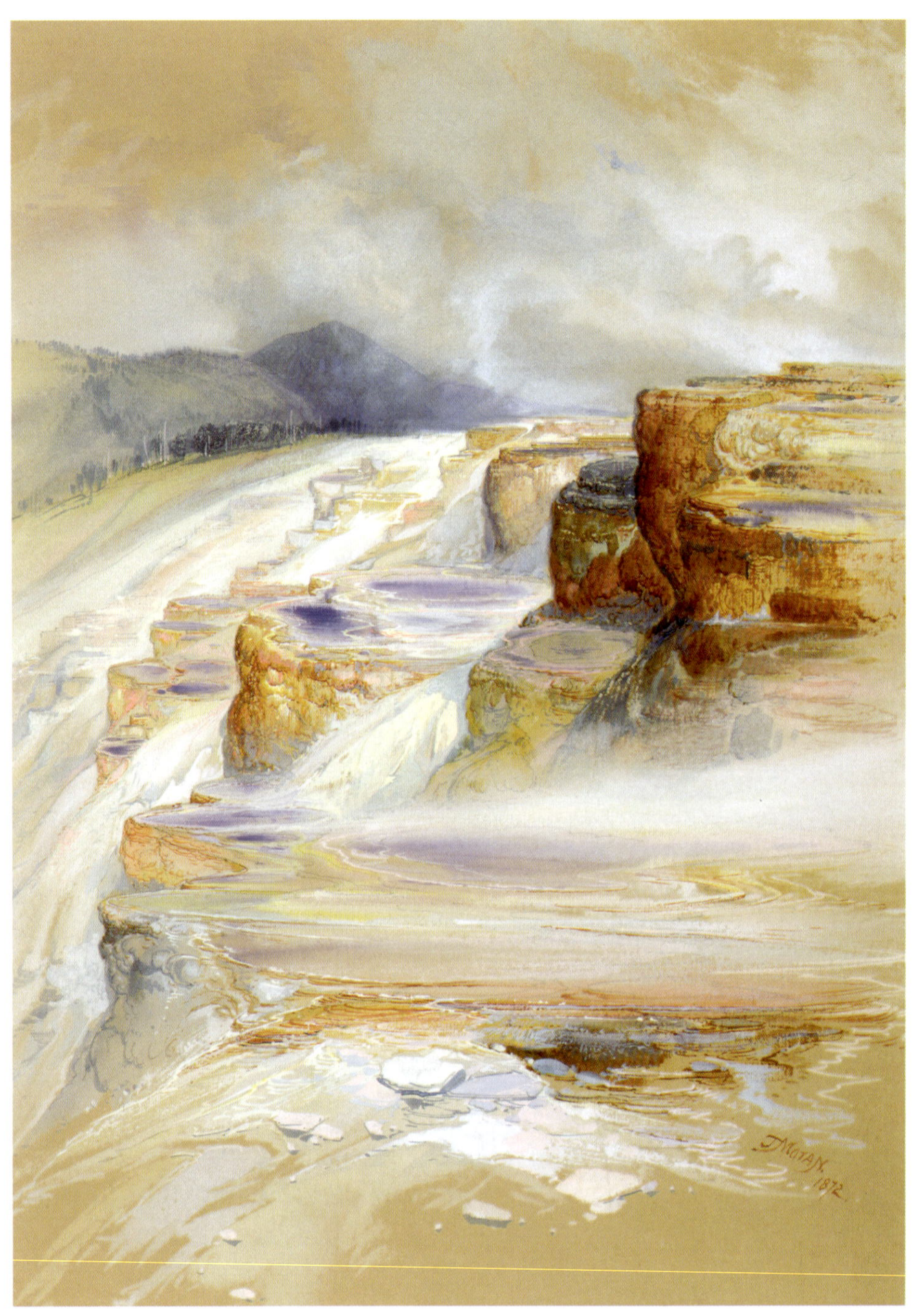

FIGURE 45. After Thomas Moran, *Hot Springs of Gardiner's River, Diana's Baths,* 1872, watercolor, 13⅜ × 9¾ in. (34 × 24.7 cm). Gilcrease Museum, Tulsa, Oklahoma

in the late nineteenth century, it was the most dramatic geyser in the world, with "fountain" eruptions that could go 300 feet high and 300 feet wide and emit enough hot water to noticeably increase the flow of the Firehole River.[14] Even when inactive, however, Excelsior still produces a huge runoff, accounting for the colorful deposits that extend to the river—surely the feature that inspired Moran to portray the site.[15] In the Prang chromo, he portrayed the geyser as steaming and bubbling rather than in full eruption, the ultramarine blue of its deepest area a dramatic contrast to the red and yellow deposits oozing into the river below.

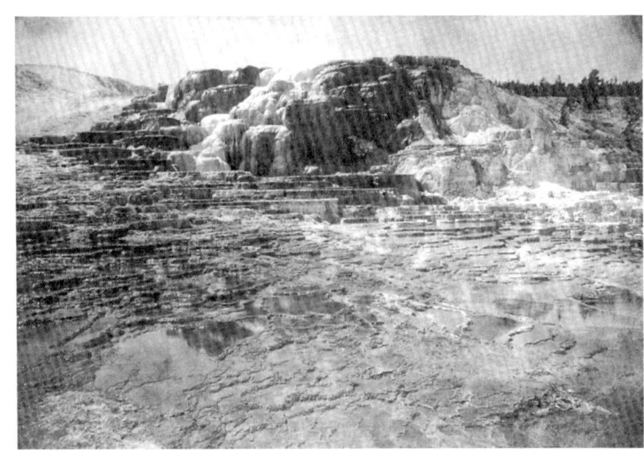

FIGURE 46. William Henry Jackson, *Yellowstone, Diana's Terrace,* 1871, photograph. Courtesy of East Hampton Library, Long Island Collection

Once encamped at Yellowstone Lake on July 28, 1871, the Hayden survey explored the surrounding region, including the geyser basins, in small foray parties. Moran probably saw the Excelsior Geyser on August 8, en route to the Old Faithful area on his last full day with the Hayden expedition. There he produced at least one watercolor field sketch (fig. 50) that he probably used as a color reference for his views of the subject in the following years. Albert Peale was a few days ahead when he encountered the Fire Hole River area on August 4, but his impression of the scene corresponds closely to *The Great Blue Spring:*

> We soon came to some huge springs—the largest we have seen yet. There was one about 200 feet in diameter. Just below this there is a huge depressed spring down in a crater 20 feet deep. There was an immense volume of steam which obscured the water, which was beautifully clear and blue showing huge boulders in the bottom. The water from these springs was considerable in amount and flowed over into the river in a beautiful cascade lined with sesquioxide of iron.[16]

In the text accompanying Moran's chromo, Ferdinand Hayden described the formation as "one of the grandest hot springs ever seen by the human eye." He noted further that

> the surface of this vast cauldron . . . is intensely agitated, and steam is constantly rising, so that only when the passing breeze sweeps it aside can we gaze into the seething pit, where the water over the deepest part of the spring appears of the most intense blue color, fading toward the edge into a green. The overflow from the spring pours over the slope in small channels, or spreads over broad surfaces where the evaporation of the water has deposited a crust of a marvelous combination of tints. The coloring is very vivid, and of many shades, from bright scarlet to delicate rose, mingled with bright and creamy yellows, and vivid green from the minute vegetation. . . . It is almost impossible to give an idea either in words or

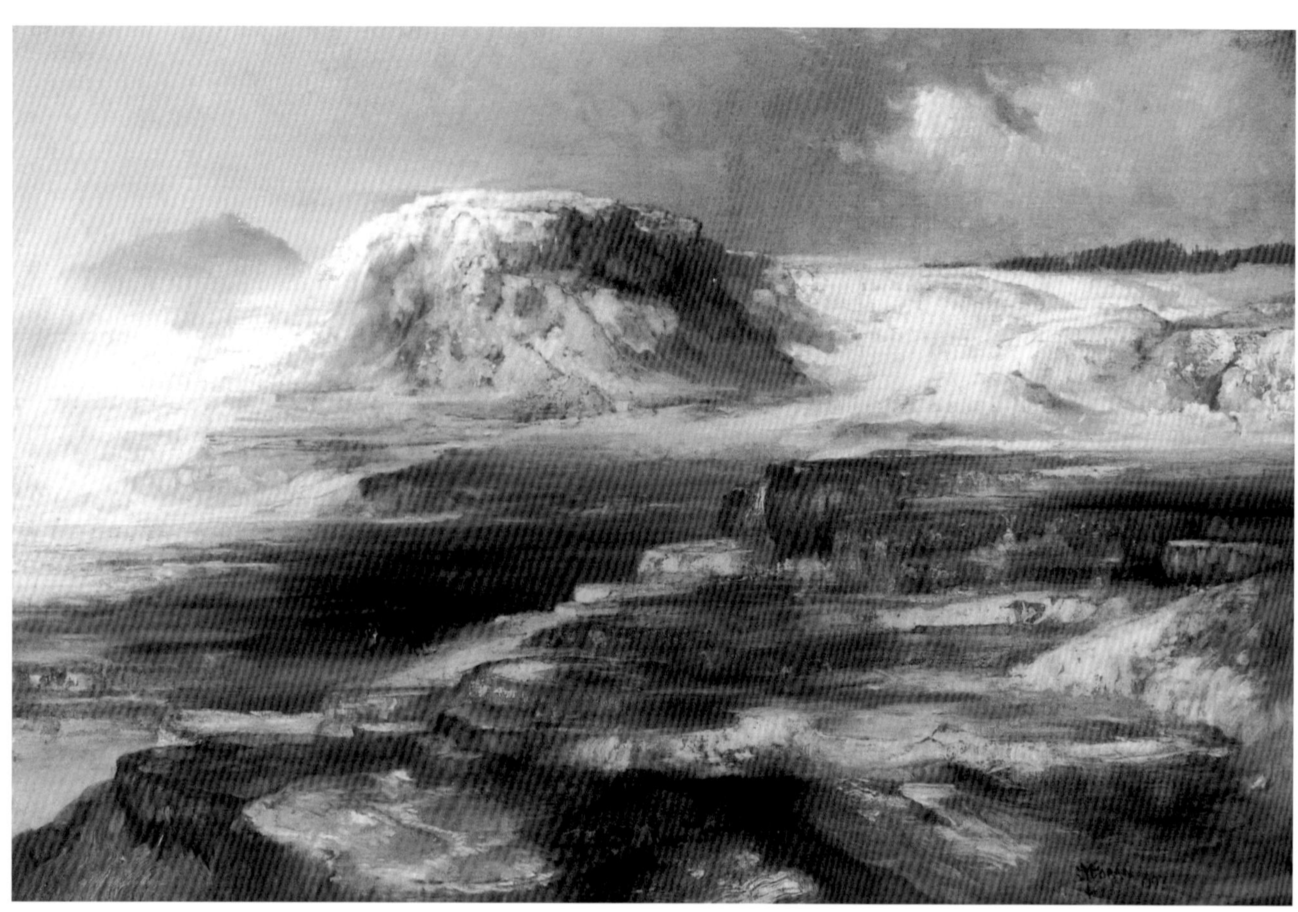

FIGURE 47. Thomas Moran, *Great Hot Springs, Yellowstone Park*, 1893, oil on canvas, 20 × 30 in. (50.8 × 76.2 cm). Gilcrease Museum, Tulsa, Oklahoma

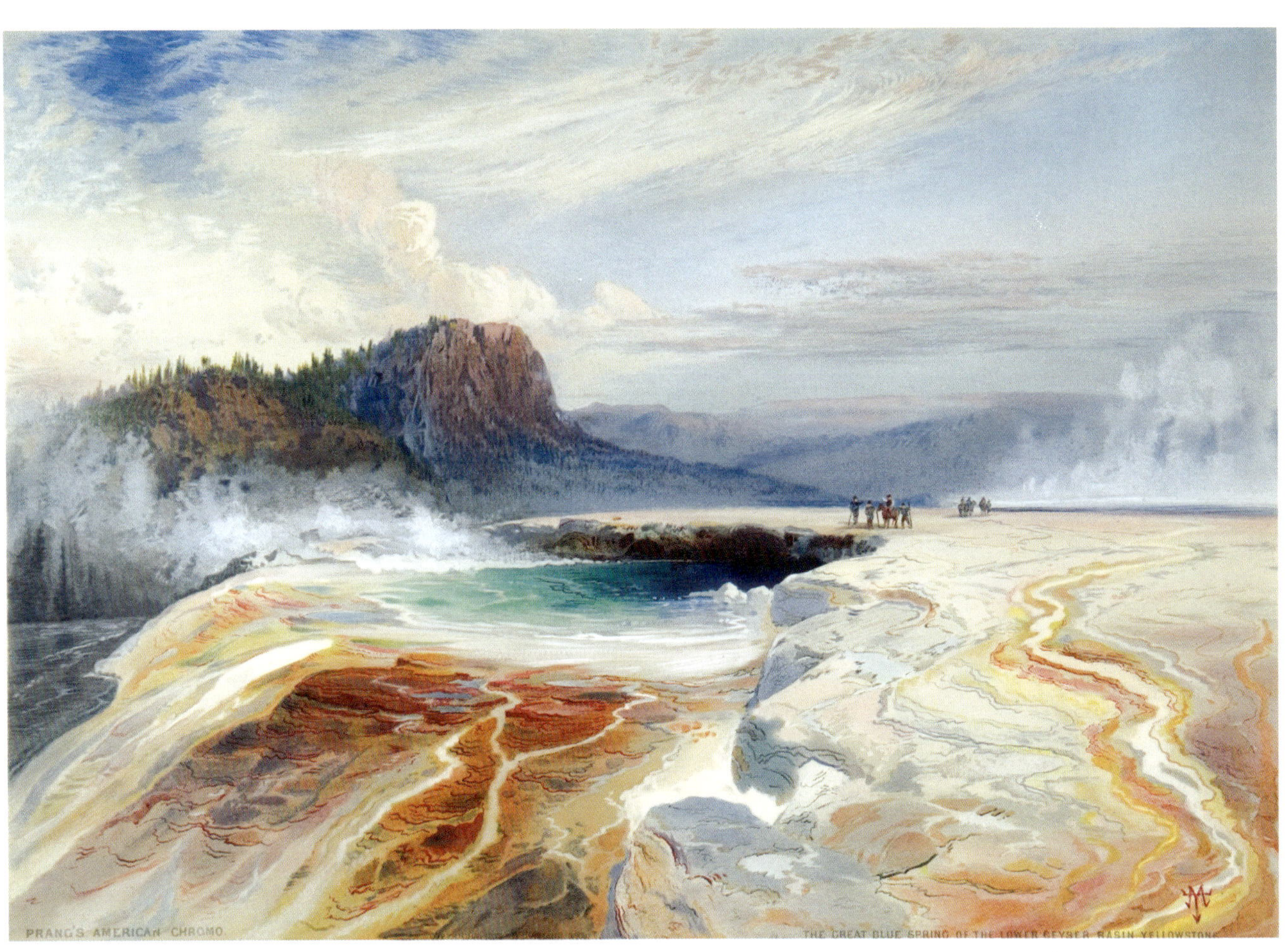

FIGURE 48. After Thomas Moran, *The Great Blue Spring of the Lower Geyser Basin*, ca. 1875, chromolithograph, 9¾ × 14 in. (24.8 × 35.6 cm). Joslyn Art Museum, Omaha, gift of Gail and Michael Yanney and Lisa and Bill Roskens

FIGURE 49. William Henry Jackson, *Excelsior Geyser,* ca. 1871, photograph. United States Geological Survey Photographic Library (jwh00549)

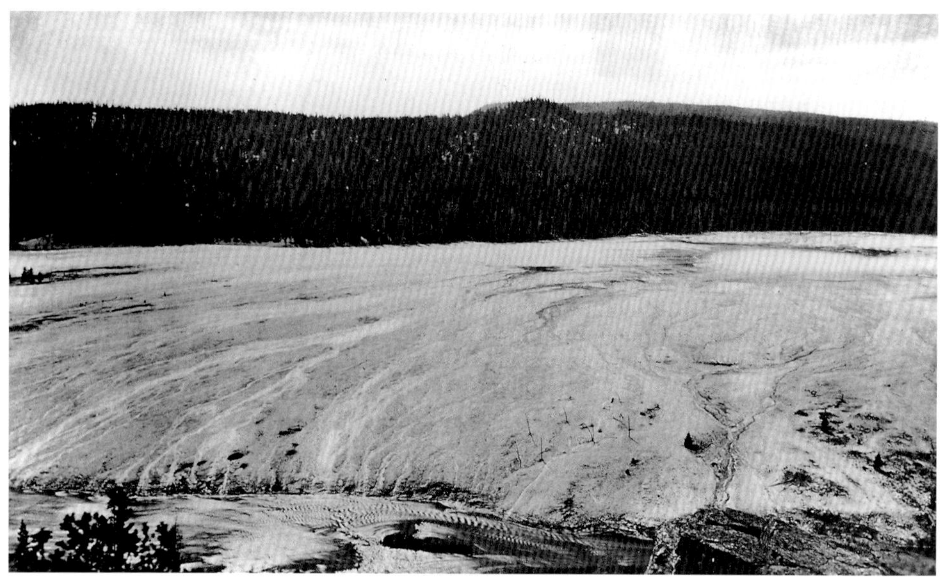

> picture of the exquisite beauty of the springs of which the Great Blue Spring is a type.[17]

Although it may have been "almost impossible," Moran did succeed in conveying this scene effectively. At the same time, this view was probably one of those that prompted critics to characterize the coloring of the Prang chromos as "bold, not to say violent."[18]

With its intense color, it is surprising that the Great Blue Spring did not become one of Moran's favorite subjects for oil paintings. Instead, he tended to depict it in watercolor, such as the one he created for Prang (fig. 51). With its sweeping expanse, chromatic array, and range of textures, from the evanescent steam to the dark looming mountain behind, the site was a natural for Moran as colorist, and his views of it are among his most striking images.

THE CASTLE GEYSER, UPPER GEYSER BASIN

The Castle Geyser, a short walk from the famous Old Faithful Geyser in the Upper Geyser Basin at Yellowstone National Park, is notable for its well-developed cone, an indicator of a very old formation. It still erupts regularly, about once every thirteen hours, in a dramatic display with a loud roar and high spray and steam, lasting about an hour in two phases, a significantly longer showing than Old Faithful.[19]

Moran created several views of Castle Geyser, his first even before he ventured west. Working from amateurish drawings by two soldiers who had accompanied the Washburn-Doane expedition through the Yellowstone region in the summer of 1870,

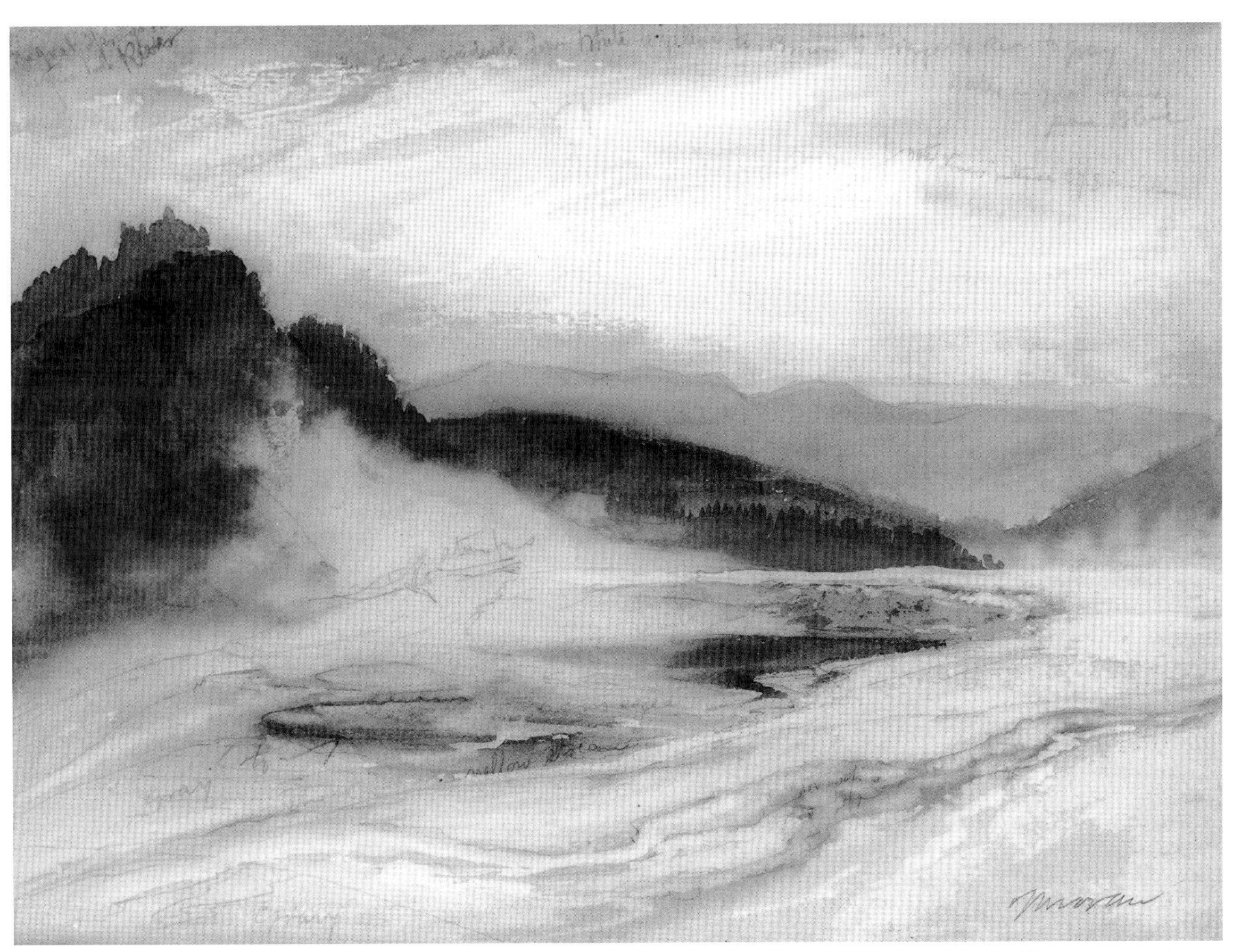

FIGURE 50. Thomas Moran, *Great Springs on the Firehole River,* 1871, pencil, watercolor, and opaque color, 8⅛ × 11⅛ in. (20.6 × 28.5 cm). Courtesy of National Park Service (Yellowstone National Park)

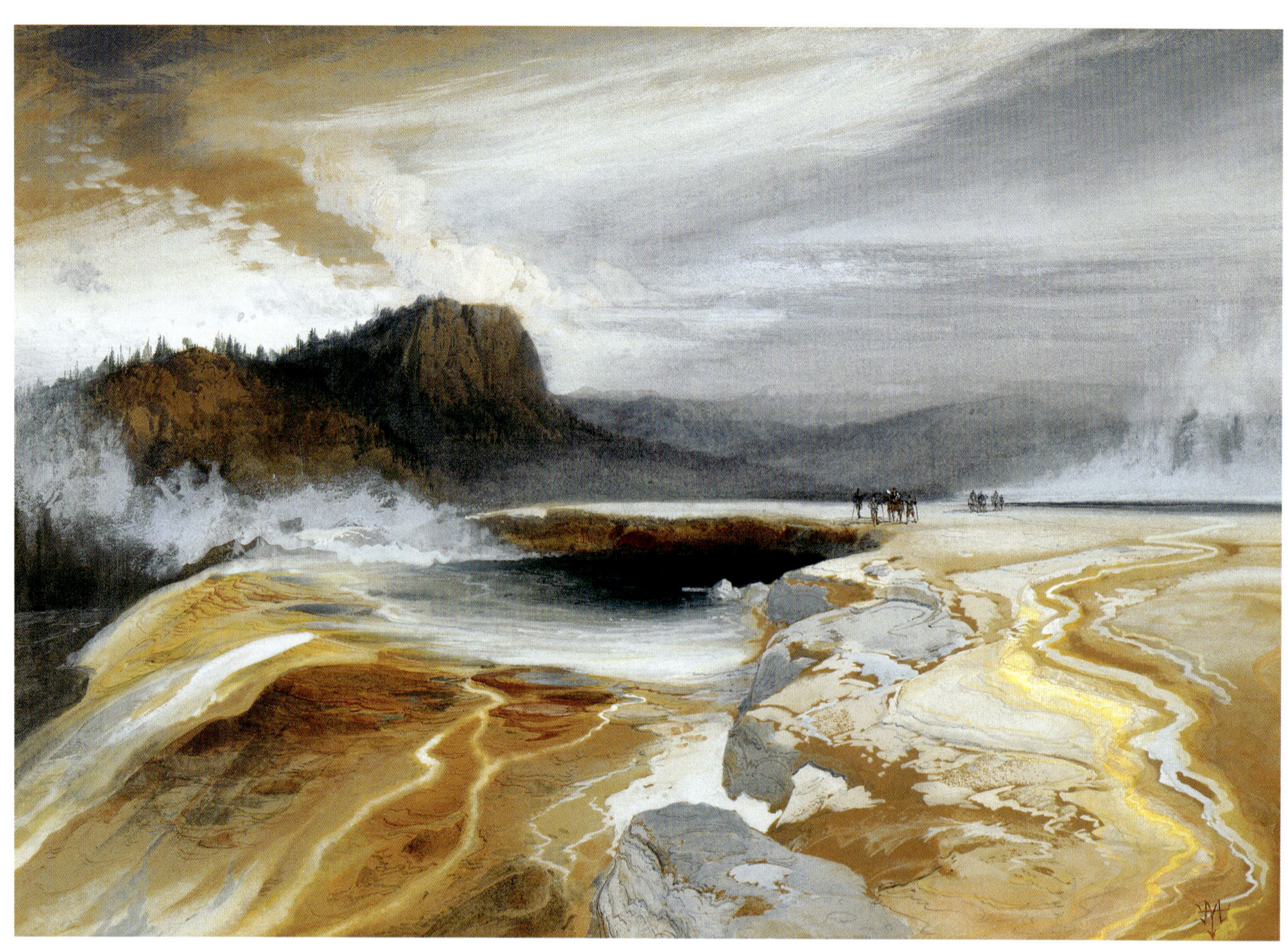

FIGURE 51. Thomas Moran, *Great Blue Spring of the Lower Geyser Basin, Yellowstone,* ca. 1873, pencil, watercolor, and opaque color, 9½ × 13¾ in. (24.1 × 34.9 cm). Private collection, Washington, D.C.

he created a series of illustrations for *Scribner's Monthly* in the spring of 1871, one of which focused on this formation (figs. 30 and 31).[20] This commission piqued his curiosity about the West and contributed to his interest in joining the Hayden expedition to Wyoming that summer so he could see the remarkable features for himself.

The geysers were among the last landmark sites Moran visited in Yellowstone before heading for home. He and Jackson paid a hasty two-day visit to the Fire Hole River at the Midway Geyser Basin, where he saw the Great Blue Spring, and to the Upper Geyser Basin, where he saw Old Faithful, the Castle Geyser, and the other notable hydrothermic features of that unique area. He recorded in his journal only: "Went to the geysers. Helped Jackson during the day [August 9] and returned by myself to camp."[21] Moran produced very few sketches of this remarkable area, probably using his limited time helping Jackson produce photographs he could use back in his eastern studio. He wrote in his journal that, "as the Wonders of the Yellowstone had been seen, I concluded to return."[22]

Jackson's photograph, *The Castle Geyser, Fire Hole Basin* (1871, fig. 52), seems to be the source for the Prang watercolor and chromolithograph (fig. 53), and also for the similar "Blackmore" version at the Gilcrease Museum (fig. 54), although he may have referred for his detail of the geyser to another version showing the formation from close range (fig. 55). In both the more panoramic photograph and the chromolithograph, the shimmering Crested Pool dominates the foreground and leads the viewer's gaze to Castle Geyser beyond. Unfortunately, this spectacular vantage point, with the continuous view from the beautiful pool to the steaming vent, is today marred by a boardwalk that cuts between the two formations.

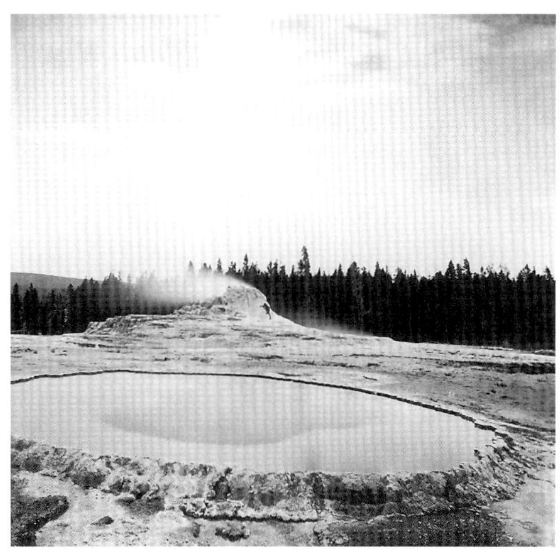

FIGURE 52. William Henry Jackson, *The Castle Geyser, Fire Hole Basin*, 1871, photograph. United States Geological Survey Photographic Library (jwh00109)

Moran suggested the subject to Prang for the chromo series, writing to the publisher on April 18, 1874: "Shall I give you a geyser? The most pictorial one is the Castle."[23] The Hayden survey's mineralogist, Albert Peale, would have agreed with this, as he had written in his diary that the Castle Geyser was the "prettiest one of all."[24] As with several images in the Prang series, the artist seems to have considered this subject most suitable for a watercolor portrayal; it did not become a favored subject for oil paintings.

THE LOWER YELLOWSTONE RANGE

The mountains depicted in this view (fig. 56) actually lie outside the northern boundary of the present-day Yellowstone National Park, as Hayden noted in the Prang publication, "about thirty miles southeast of Fort Ellis, Montana [present-day Bozeman]." Labeled the "Lower" Yellowstone Range since the peaks are downriver from the

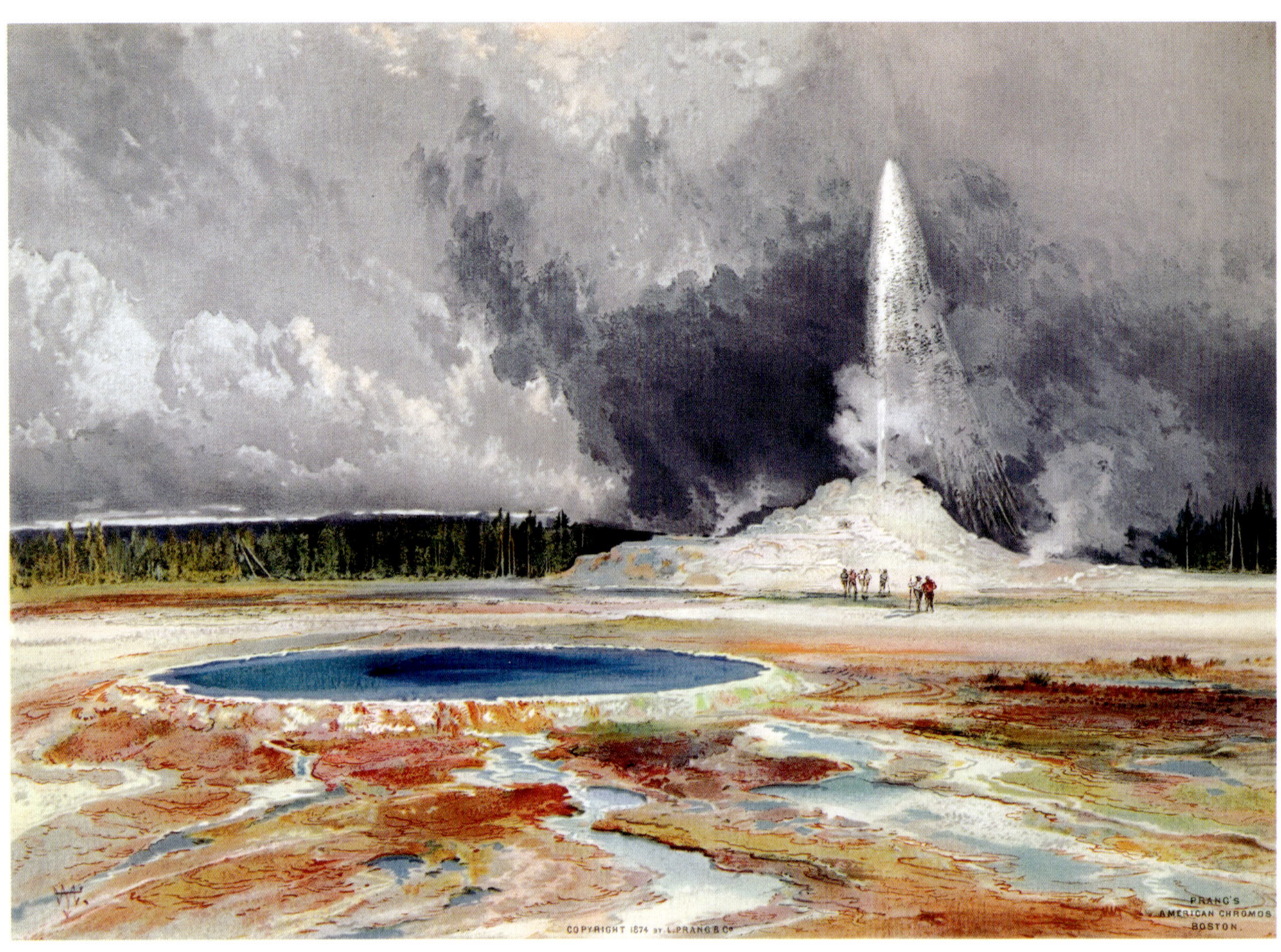

FIGURE 53. After Thomas Moran, *The Castle Geyser, Upper Geyser Basin*, ca. 1875, chromolithograph, 9¾ × 14 in. (24.8 × 35.6 cm). Joslyn Art Museum, Omaha, gift of Gail and Michael Yanney and Lisa and Bill Roskens

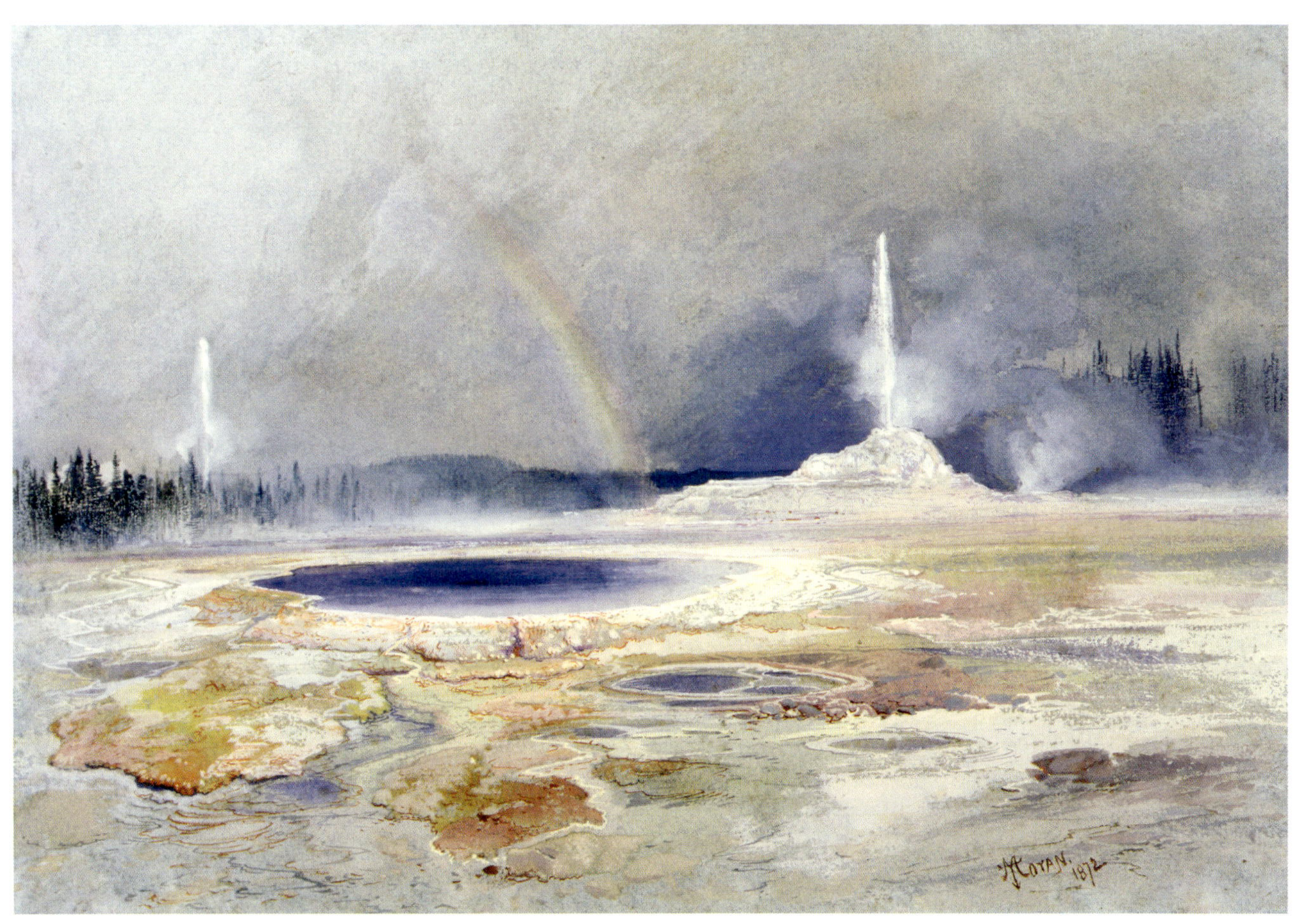

FIGURE 54. Thomas Moran, *The Castle Geyser, Fire Hole Basin,* 1872, pencil, watercolor, and opaque color on paper, 7½ × 11 in. (19 × 27.9 cm). Gilcrease Museum, Tulsa, Oklahoma

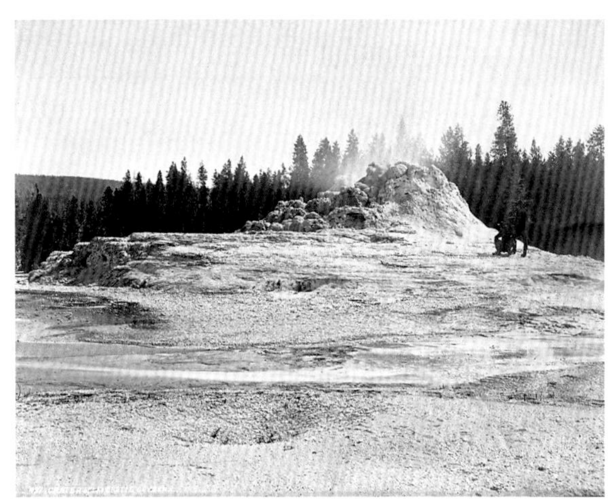

FIGURE 55. William Henry Jackson, *Crater of the Castle Geyser*, ca. 1871, photograph from Moran's studio collection. Gilcrease Museum, Tulsa, Oklahoma

headwaters in Yellowstone Lake (the Yellowstone River flows northward out of the park), they had formerly been called the Snowy Range and today are known as the Beartooth Mountains in the Absaroka/Gallatin Range. A stunningly beautiful region, the southern portion of this area can now be toured between present-day Cooke City and Red Lodge, Montana, via the Beartooth Highway, a route designated a National Scenic Byway in 1989 and recently characterized as "America's most beautiful road."[25]

Although *The Lower Yellowstone Range* is the fourth plate in the Prang portfolio, it depicts the first site in the series that Moran visited. He had taken the Union Pacific west in June 1871, making his "first sketch in the West" at the railroad station at Green River, Wyoming.[26] Continuing on, he transferred to a stagecoach at Corinne, Utah, for an arduous four-day journey northward through Idaho and joined the Hayden party at the stage stop on the Continental Divide near today's Monida, Montana, on June 30 (not in Virginia City or Fort Ellis, and not in early July as has been previously reported).[27] Together the group traveled on to Virginia City and Fort Ellis (at today's Bozeman), where they lingered before starting south toward the Yellowstone area on July 15.[28] On July 11, Moran and seven other survey members ventured to Mystic Lake, approximately twelve miles from Fort Ellis, and it was in this vicinity that he sketched *The Yellowstone Range from Near Fort Ellis* (fig. 57), the study for the watercolor he produced for Prang (fig. 58).[29]

In his journal Moran was unusually descriptive about these days, obviously excited to be out of the train and the stagecoach and finally working in the landscape. Noting that "the Mountains . . . are about 11,000 feet high . . . having snow upon them," he described them as

> bordered with great cliffs & peaks of limestone, some of them isolated & forming splendid foreground material for pictures. Sketched but little, but worked hard with the photographer selecting points to be taken. . . . The view from the Mountains south east of our Camp & on the road to the lake looking toward the Yellowstone Country glorious & I do not expect to see any finer general view of the Rocky Mountains.[30]

This statement is among Moran's most articulate in regard to a specific view. He was usually much more general and concise in his writing.

Although the source for *The Lower Yellowstone Range* seems definitive, the Prang chromolithograph's composition also closely relates to drawings Moran made on his return trip, such as *The Lower Entrance to Madison Canyon* (fig. 59), which he sketched

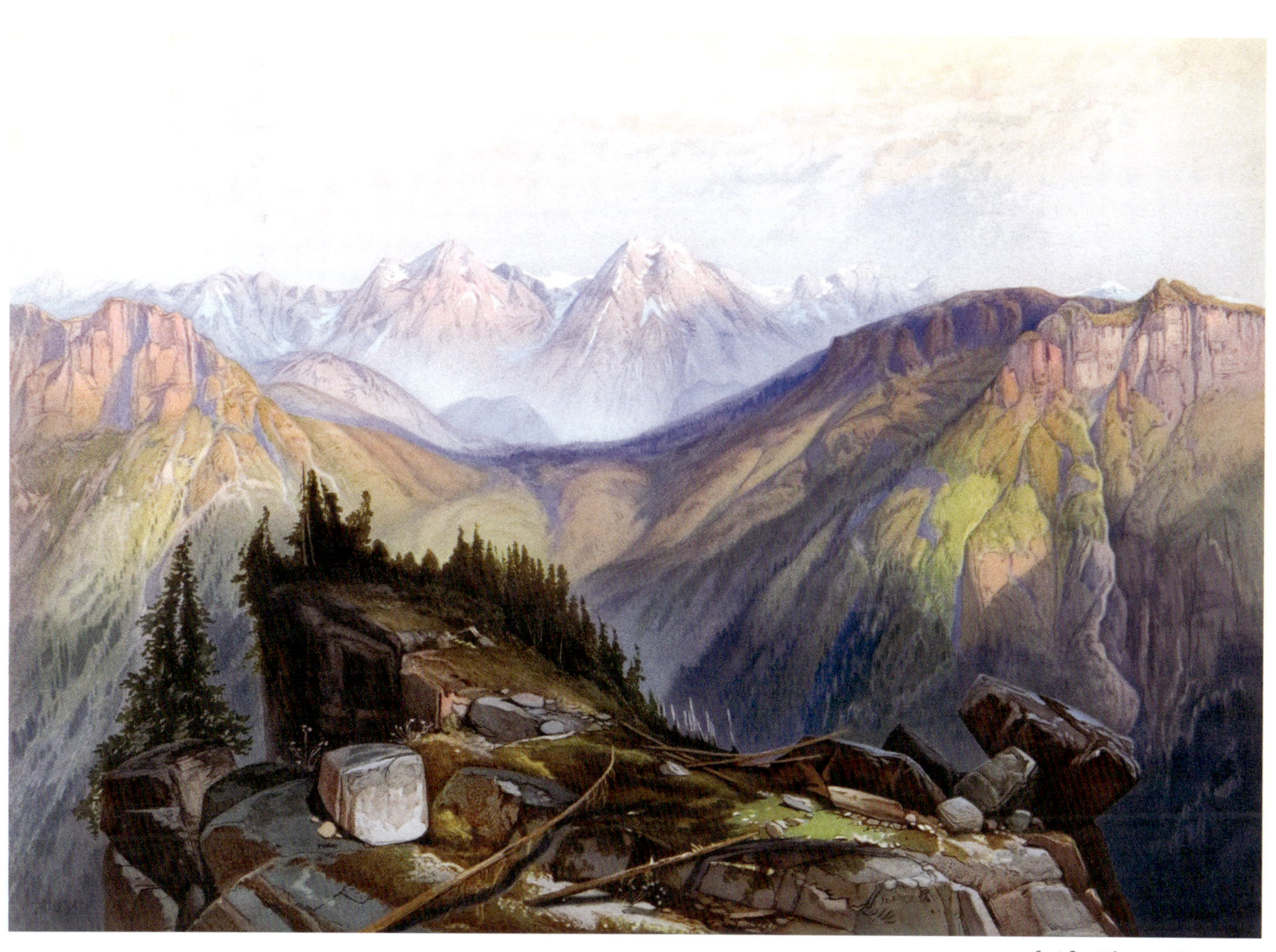

FIGURE 56. After Thomas Moran, *The Lower Yellowstone Range,* ca. 1875, chromolithograph, 9⅝ × 13⅞ in. (24.4 × 35.2 cm). Joslyn Art Museum, Omaha, gift of Gail and Michael Yanney and Lisa and Bill Roskens

FIGURE 57. Thomas Moran, *The Yellowstone Range from Near Fort Ellis*, 1871, watercolor, 10⅛ × 13¾ in. (25.7 × 34.9 cm). Courtesy of National Park Service (Yellowstone National Park)

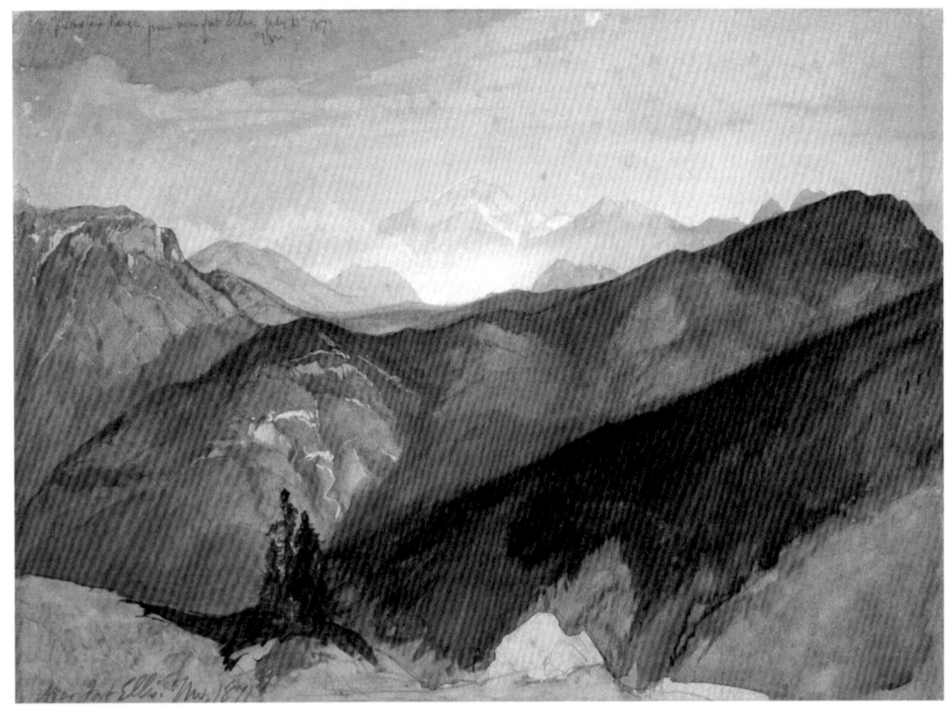

during the second week of August as he was leaving the Yellowstone region to return home.[31] Typically Moran constructed his images from a variety of studies and photographs, sometimes incorporating elements far from the actual scene depicted. He may well have compiled a number of mountainous views into his composition of *The Lower Yellowstone Range.*

The watercolor today at the National Museum of American History in Washington, D.C., is the image Moran created for Prang (fig. 58), but the artist also painted quite similar versions for William Blackmore (today at Gilcrease) and for Jay Cooke, a painting that may be the one today in a private collection in Nebraska.

YELLOWSTONE LAKE

Yellowstone Lake (fig. 60) was a central focus of the Hayden survey of 1871.[32] The party camped around it for nearly a month, the majority of its time in the region. Some of the Hayden survey members arrived at Yellowstone Lake on July 28, 1871, although Moran and Jackson remained back at the Grand Canyon sketching and taking photographs for a couple more days, joining up with the main party at the lake on August 1.[33] Moran would explore Yellowstone for only another week before heading home, but the Yellowstone Lake area was his base camp throughout that time. As expedition historian Marlene Merrill notes, "Hayden's special enthusiasm for this lake study probably derived from the fact that the 1869 [Folsom-Cook-Peterson] and

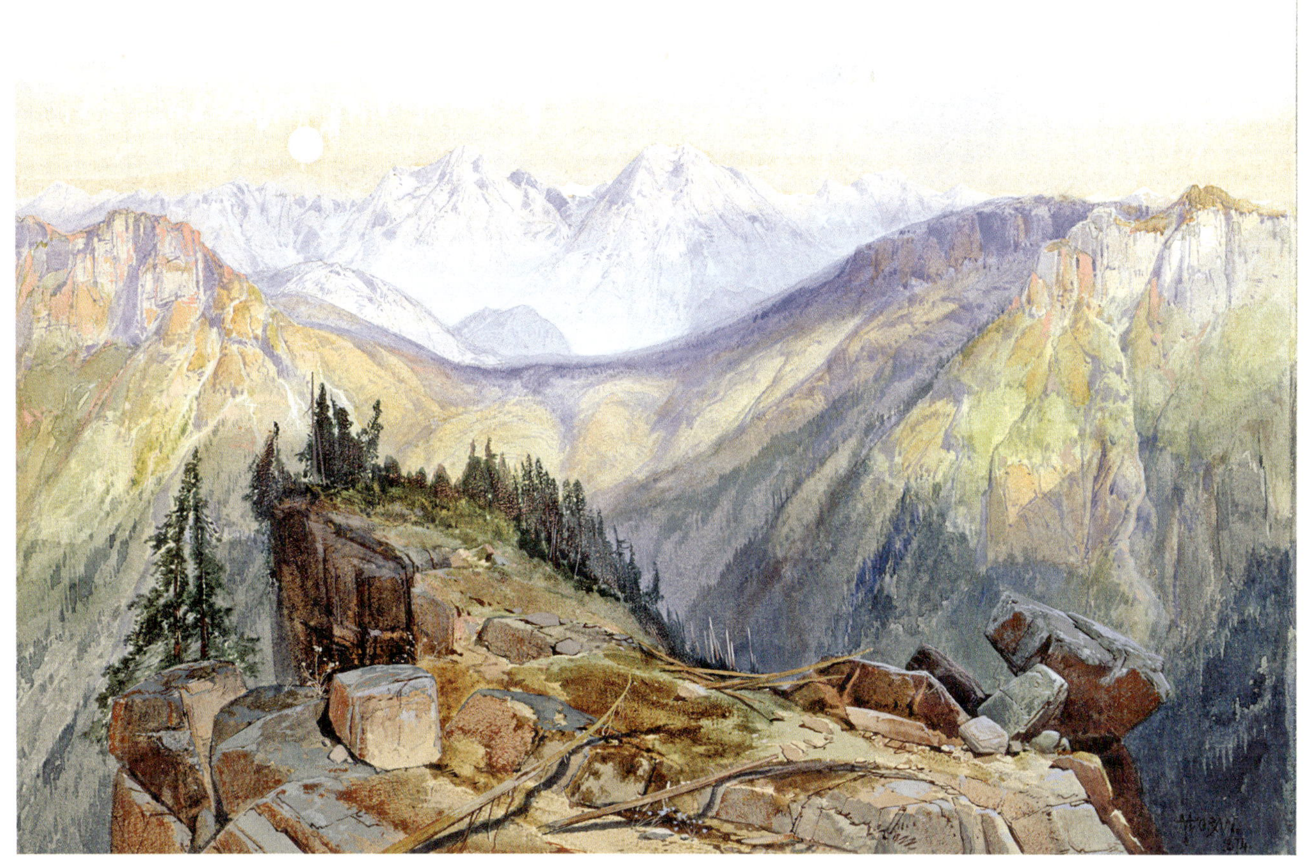

FIGURE 58. Thomas Moran, *Lower Yellowstone Range*, 1874, watercolor and opaque color, 9½ × 14 in. (24.1 × 35.6 cm). Division of Graphic Arts, National Museum of American History, Smithsonian Institution, gift of L. Prang & Co., 1883

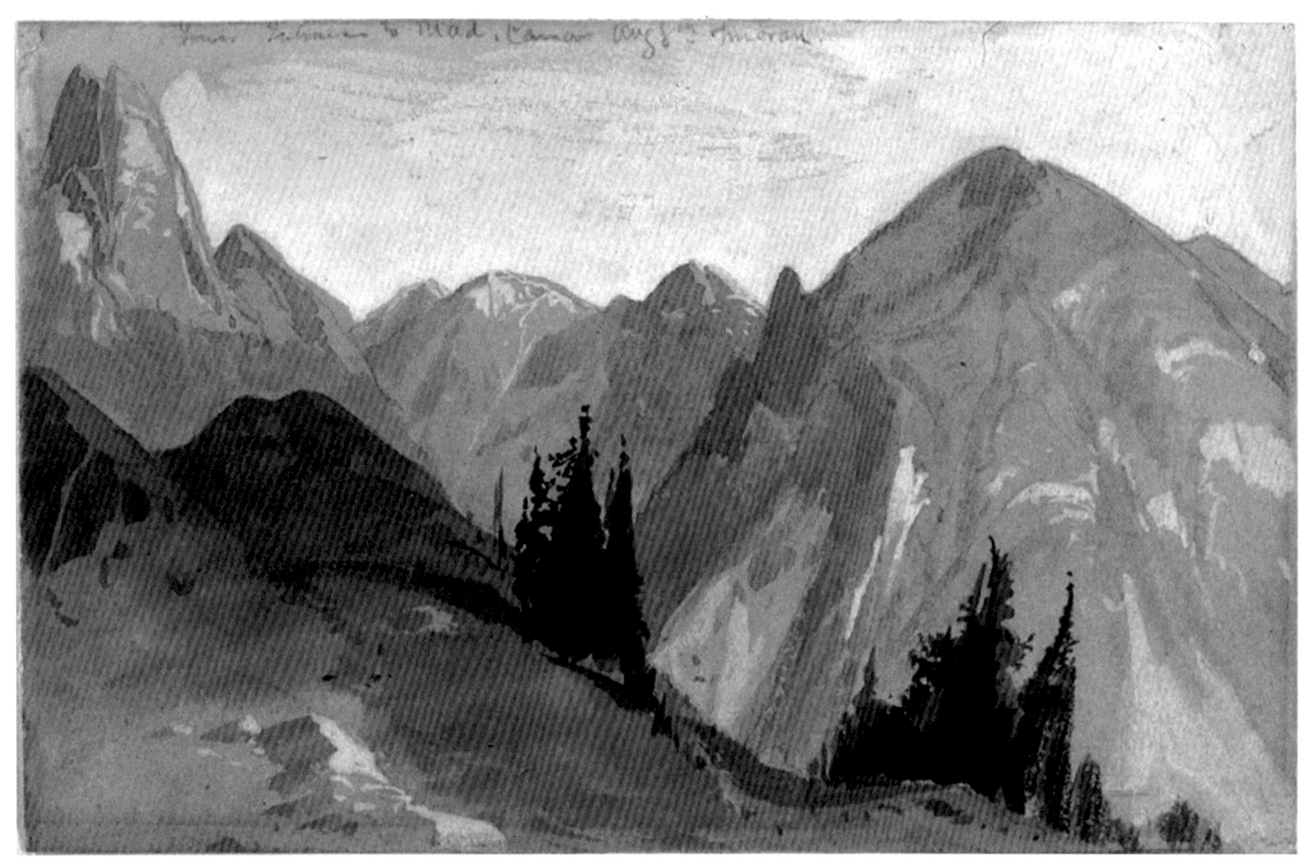

FIGURE 59. Thomas Moran, *Lower Entrance to Madison Canyon, Aug. 8, 1871*, 1871, graphite, watercolor, and white gouache on wove paper, 5¼ × 8¼ in. (13.3 × 20.9 cm). Jefferson National Expansion Memorial, St. Louis (4299)

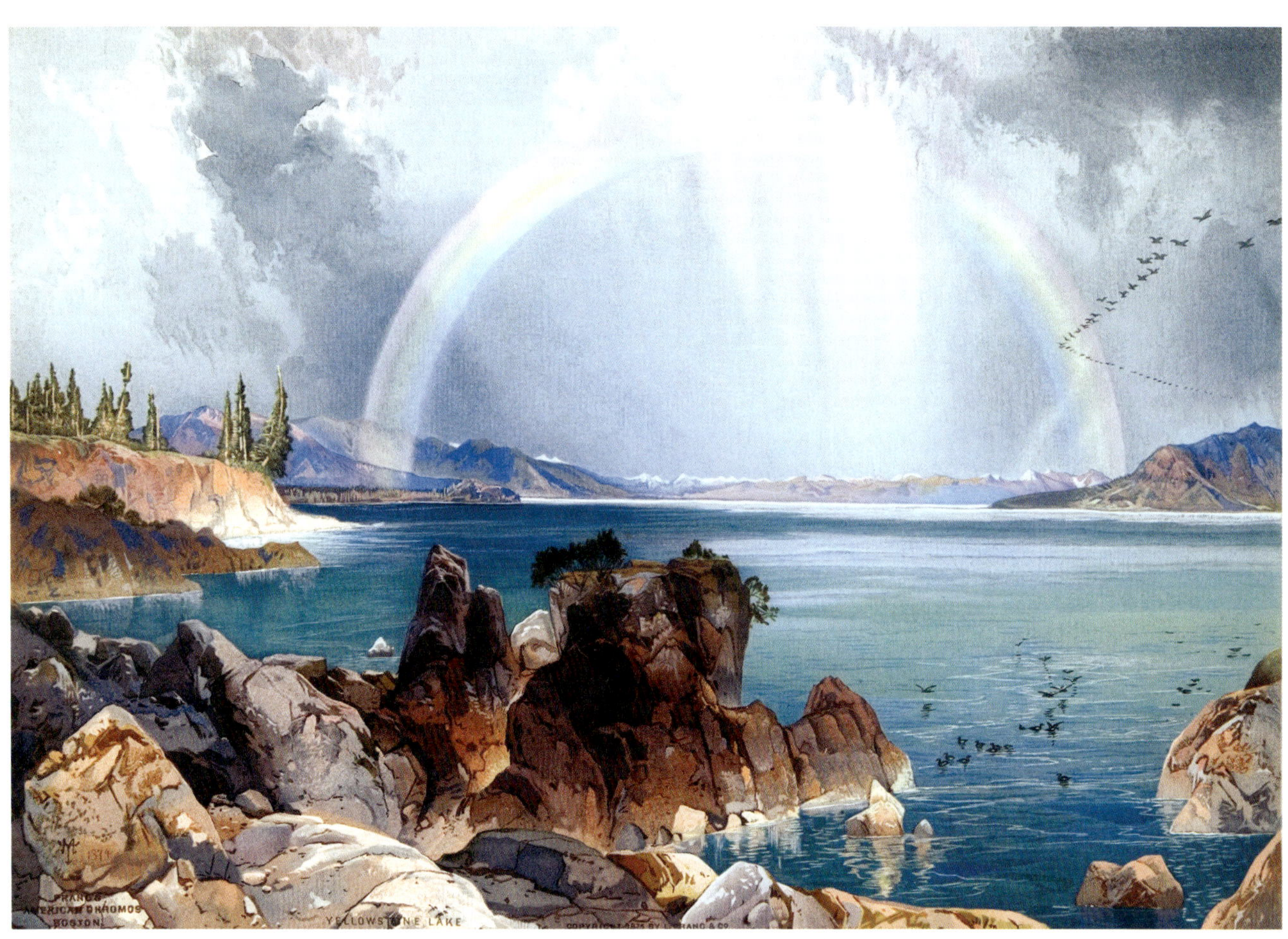

FIGURE 60. After Thomas Moran, *Yellowstone Lake*, ca. 1875, chromolithograph, 9⅞ × 14⅜ in. (25 × 36.5 cm). Joslyn Art Museum, Omaha, gift of Gail and Michael Yanney and Lisa and Bill Roskens

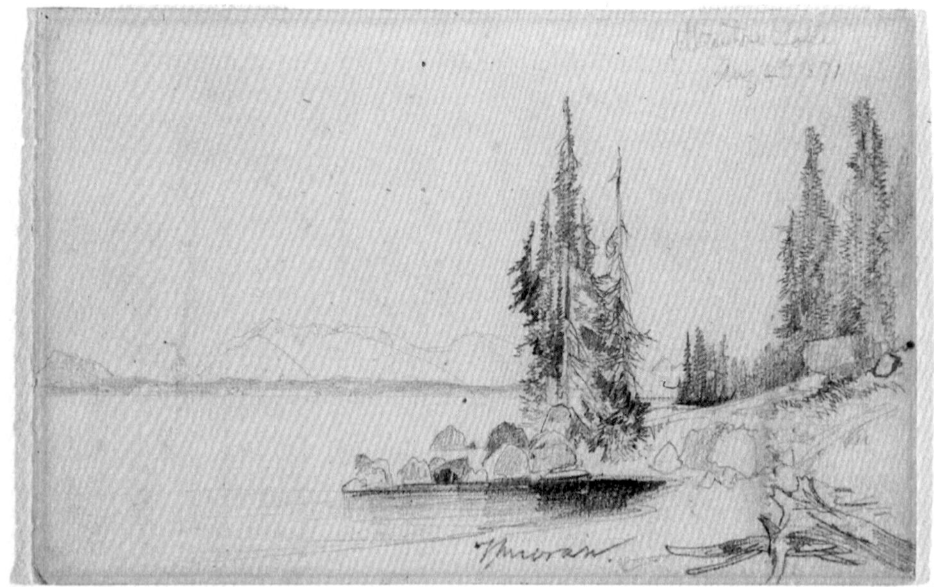

FIGURE 61. Thomas Moran, *The Yellowstone Lake,* 1871, graphite on wove paper, 4¾ × 9¾ in. (12 × 24.7 cm). Jefferson National Expansion Memorial, St. Louis (4217)

1870 [Washburn-Doane] expeditions had obtained virtually no information on either the lake or its islands."[34]

Although Moran did several sketches of Yellowstone Lake (fig. 61), the primary source for the Prang chromolithograph is probably a photograph by William Henry Jackson (fig. 62), at least in the foreground where the jutting rocks protrude out of the lake.[35] Although Moran's watercolor (fig. 63) is based on the view from a position known as Promontory Point on the south arm of Yellowstone Lake, it is a highly romantic portrayal, especially in the overarching rainbow that dominates the scene. In his emphasis on that dramatic element, Moran was almost certainly responding to the long tradition of endowing landscapes with the symbolic arc that rendered them not only more beautiful, but also evoked the biblical rainbow at the end of the flood in the Book of Genesis.[36] The motif, with the full bow over a body of water, was a favorite of his at the time; Moran did a similar view of Lake George for *The Aldine* in 1874.[37] In its biblical allusion, *Yellowstone Lake* has links in the Prang portfolio to the evocative *Mountain of the Holy Cross,* helping balance the more foreboding scenes of the erupting geysers, *Devil's Den* (which was not published), and the Devil's Hoof, more commonly known as *The Towers of Tower Falls.* It is also compositionally related to the other views of bodies of water—*Head of the Yellowstone River* and *The Great Salt Lake*—and *Upper Twin Lakes* and *Lake Donner,* had they been published in the final series.

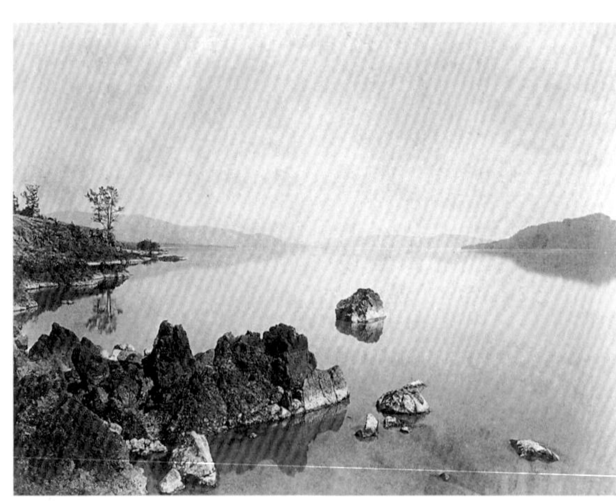

FIGURE 62. William Henry Jackson, *South Arm, Promontory Point, Yellowstone Lake,* 1871, photograph. Library of Congress, Washington, D.C. (lot 3546; repro no. LC-USZ62-84442 DLC)

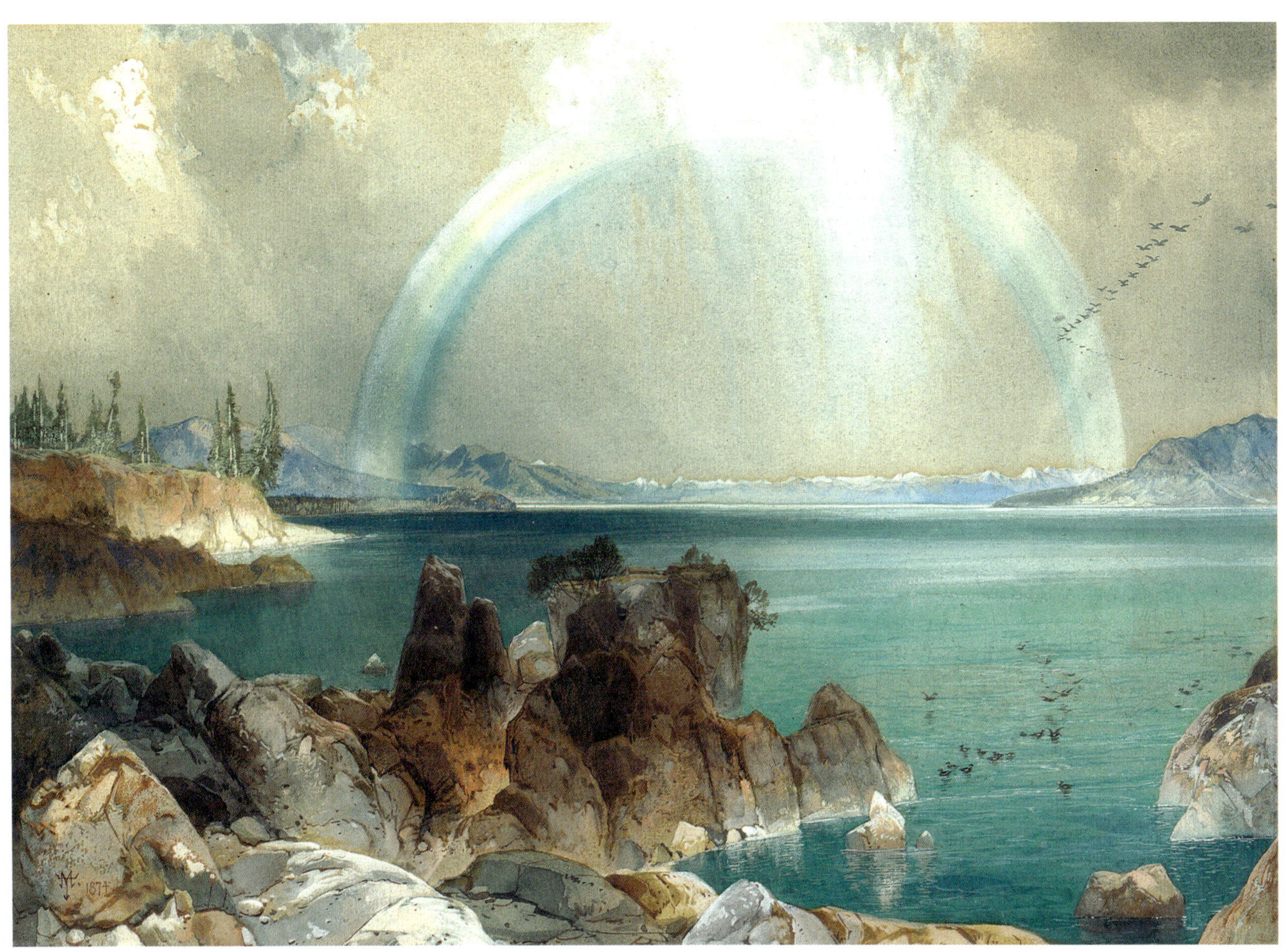

FIGURE 63. Thomas Moran, *Southern Arm of Yellowstone Lake, Yellowstone National Park, Wyoming Territory,* 1874, pencil, watercolor, and opaque color, $9\frac{7}{8} \times 14\frac{3}{8}$ in. (25.1×36.5 cm). Private collection, Wyoming

Yellowstone Lake is distinctive in the artist's oeuvre. He had created a watercolor of Yellowstone Lake for William Blackmore in 1872, but it focuses more on the shoreline hot springs than on the lake itself. Despite the subject's picturesque qualities and Hayden's intense interest in it, Yellowstone Lake would not become a significant theme for Moran in other work.

TOWER FALLS AND SULPHUR MOUNTAIN

Tower Falls was the second major landmark within present-day Yellowstone National Park that Moran visited in 1871. The party arrived there on July 25. The falls are the most notable characteristic of Tower Creek, a tributary of the Yellowstone River, and are located near the confluence of these two waterways in the north-central part of the park, about thirty miles southeast of Mammoth Hot Springs. They are especially notable for the towering rock pinnacles that surmount them as they plunge 132 feet to the creek bed below, and the site remains a significant tourist destination within the park today.

In his Yellowstone journal, Moran was characteristically brief about his visit to the falls, saying only, "Thence to Tower Falls" and "Remained at Tower Falls sketching & photographing,"[38] but he later wrote on the back of the watercolor he created for Louis Prang:

> It is certainly [one] of the most impressive scene[s] in the park. The Sulphur Mountain lies across the Yellowstone river, which flows at its base. The snowy dome of the Mountain is supported upon a base of columnar basalt of great regularity and formation. The columns of which are about 40 feet in height. Beneath these columns lies a strata of calcerous deposit intermixed with sulphur and iron given the most delicate and beautiful tints of red and yellow. This is again supported upon another mass of columnar structure.[39]

Moran portrayed Tower Falls a number of times but limited his compositions to three distinctive formats, two of which appear in the Prang publication. One that he usually called *The Tower of Tower Falls* focused on the singular pinnacle known as the Devil's Hoof as it was viewed at creek level above the falls, just before the water plummets over the precipice. Another, usually called simply *Tower Falls* (the one that was not part of the Prang commission), was a view of the falls from below, looking up at the crenellated silhouette with a "reverential gaze." And finally, in *Tower Falls and Sulphur Mountain* (figs. 64 and 65), the falls and their framing towers appear on the left side of the composition, seen from an oblique angle from the adjacent plateau, with the distinctive white dome of Sulphur Mountain looming just beyond in the center of the scene.[40] The mountain itself was a geological oddity, named for its composition of breccia and conglomerate laced with sulphur (fig. 66).

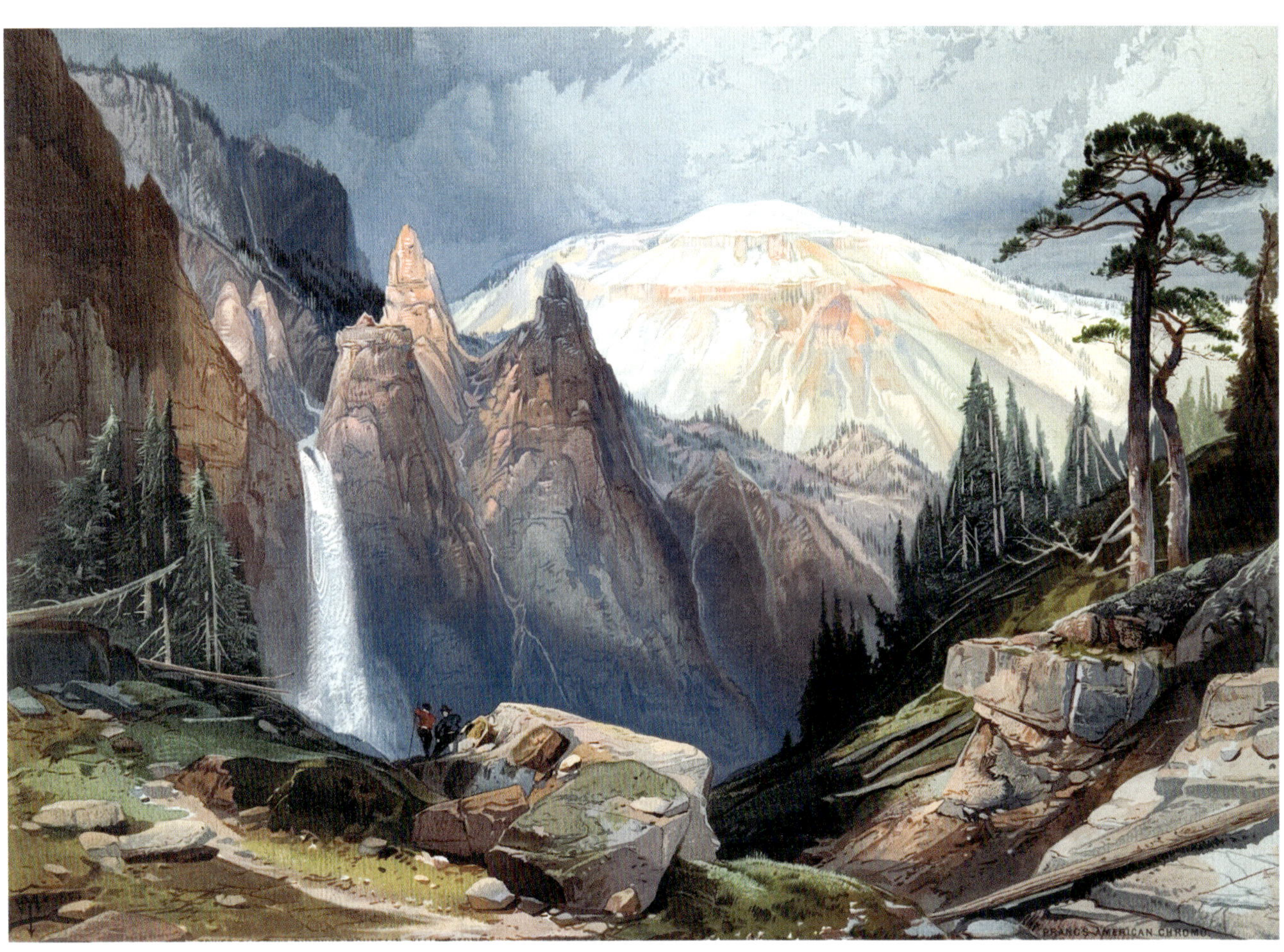

FIGURE 64. After Thomas Moran, *Tower Falls and Sulphur Mountain*, ca. 1875, chromolithograph, 9¾ × 14 in. (24.8 × 35.6 cm). Joslyn Art Museum, Omaha, gift of Gail and Michael Yanney and Lisa and Bill Roskens

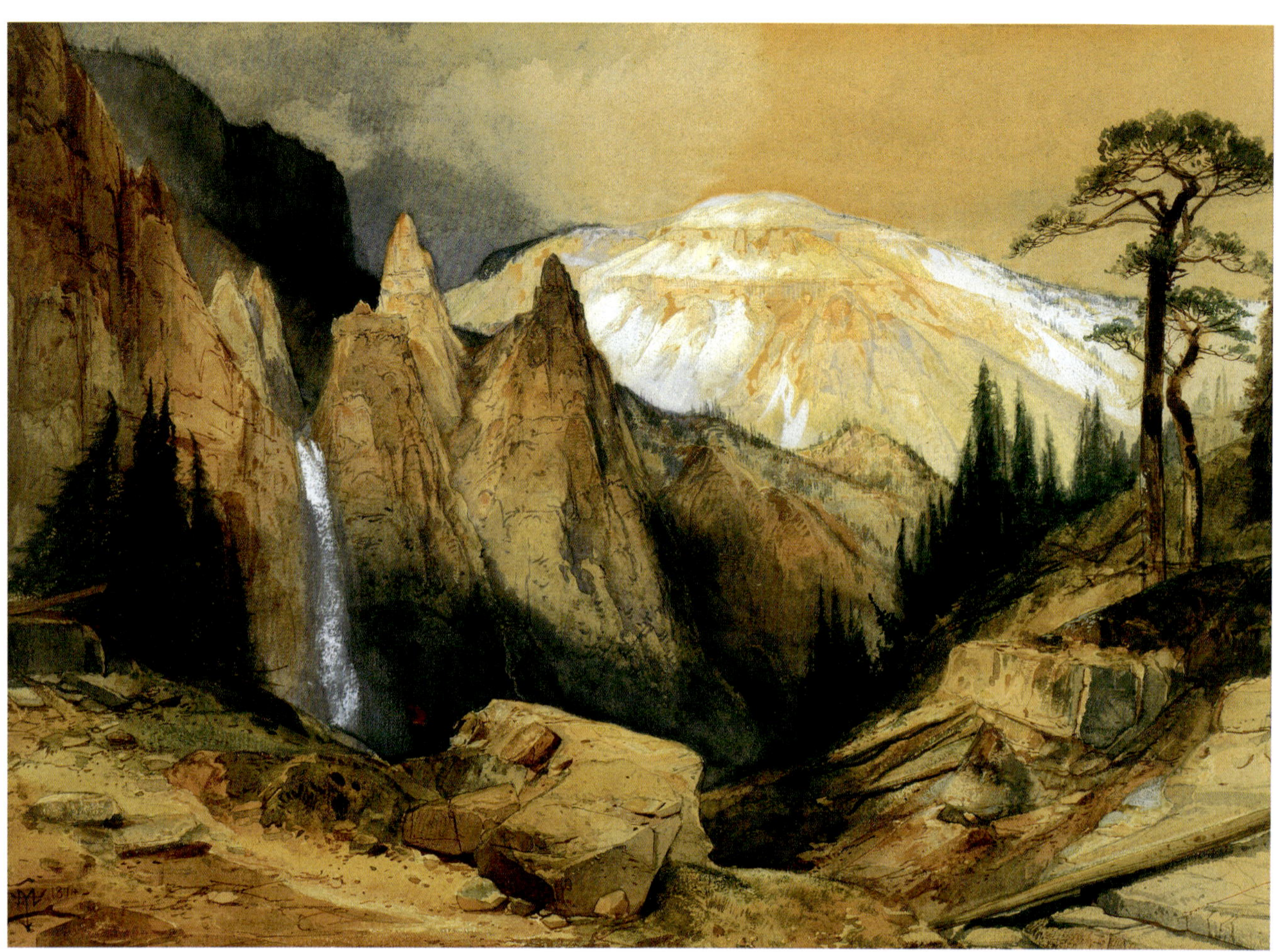

FIGURE 65. Thomas Moran, *Tower Falls and Sulphur Mountain, Yellowstone National Park*, 1874, pencil, watercolor, and opaque color, 10 × 14 in. (25.4 × 35.6 cm). Collection of the Westmoreland Museum of American Art, gift of Dr. Walter Read Hovey (1978.87)

Despite its unusual geological features, *Tower Falls and Sulphur Mountain* is a traditional "prospect" composition, with hikers placed strategically amid a V-shaped foreground, framed by trees and boulders that draw the viewer's attention to the remarkable formations beyond. Such structural conventions had been a staple of landscape painting for centuries, helping viewers visually and psychologically envision their own relationship to depicted scenes, and these visual strategies and their effects were especially important to Moran as he presented sights and formations that were almost unimaginable to his eastern audiences. Even as he relied on faithful renderings of actual topography, he did not hesitate to include elements from his imagination or other sources that would provide visual balance, scale, and proportion in his compositions and give audiences a familiar framework for viewing the extraordinary scenes. The dominant pine to the right in *Tower Falls and Sulphur Mountain,* for example, was one of Moran's favorite stock motifs, a feature that derived from an 1867 sketch of a pine in the Borghese Gardens in Rome. Moran kept his original drawing in his studio collection throughout his life and frequently included it in numerous American western views as an organic vertical element.[41]

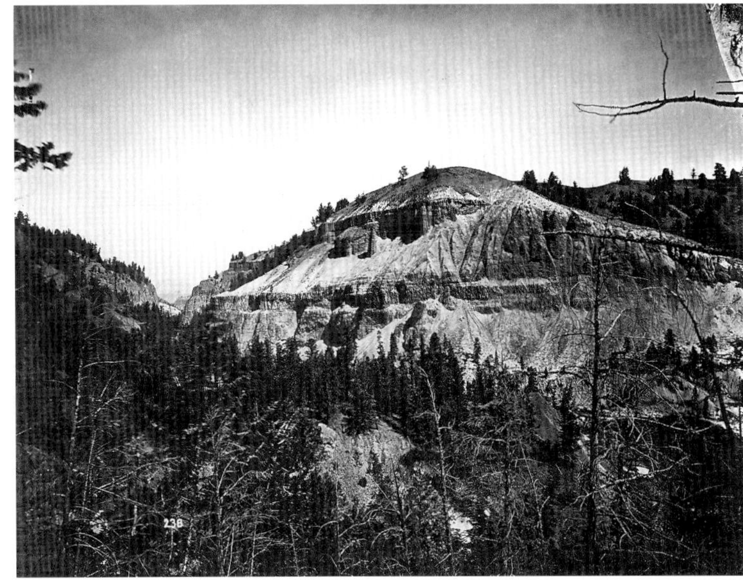

FIGURE 66. William Henry Jackson, *Sulphur Mountain,* ca. 1871, photograph. United States Geological Survey Photographic Library (jwh0081)

Tower Falls and Sulphur Mountain was not a favorite subject of Moran's for oils, but he did repeat it in several other media, including watercolor and wood engraving. The Jefferson National Expansion Memorial collection in St. Louis includes two interesting field sketches of *Tower Falls and Sulphur Mountain,* one a tiny sepia wash field sketch and a slightly larger contour drawing in pencil (figs. 67 and 68). The Gilcrease Museum also has a tiny pencil-and-wash drawing, but this one is colored and gridded for enlargement (fig. 69). Although the exact sequence of the three remains uncertain, they demonstrate that Moran spent considerable time refining the composition before he produced the several studio watercolor versions and wood engravings of it, such as that he produced for *The Aldine* in 1873 (fig. 70).

Tower Falls and Sulphur Mountain is a complex portrayal of a unique site that helps unify the Prang series in several ways. It depicts the site of *The Towers of Tower Falls* from a different point of view, and the looming Sulphur Mountain echoes other mountainous scenes in the portfolio, such as *The Mountain of the Holy Cross, The Summit of the Sierras, The Lower Yellowstone Range,* and *Gardiner's River Hot Springs.*

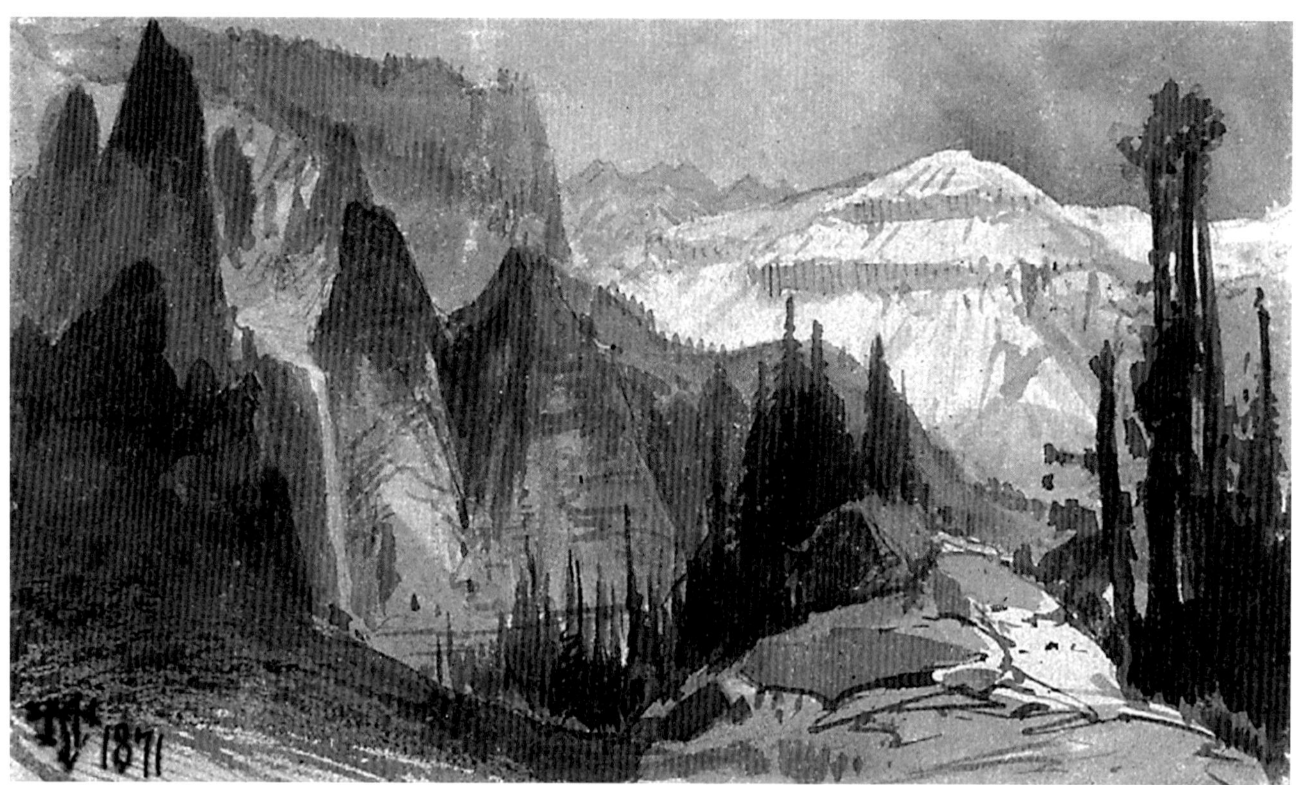

FIGURE 67. Thomas Moran, *Towers of Tower Falls [Tower Falls and Sulphur Mountain]*, 1871, pencil and wash on beige wove paper, 3 × 5⅜ in. (7.6 × 14.2 cm). Jefferson National Expansion Memorial, St. Louis (4263)

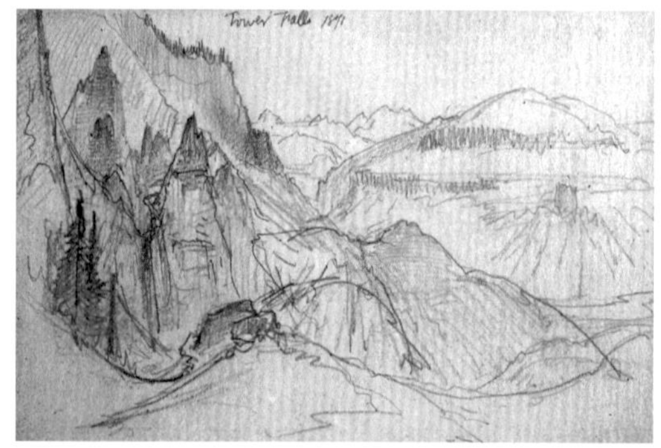

FIGURE 68. Thomas Moran, *Tower Falls*, 1871, graphite on gray wove paper, 5 × 8 in. (12.7 × 20.3 cm). Jefferson National Expansion Memorial, St. Louis (4219)

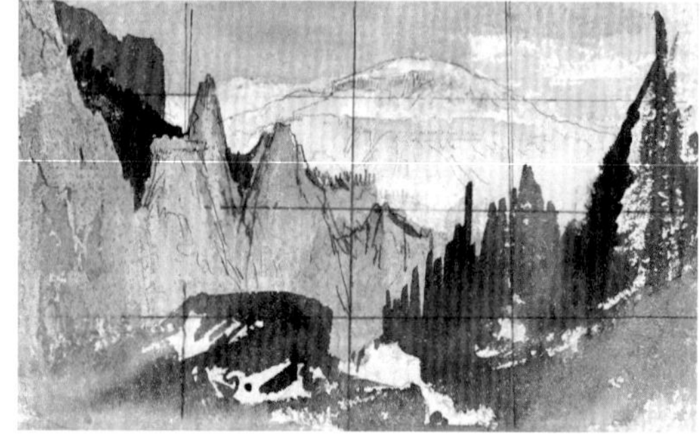

FIGURE 69. Thomas Moran, *Tower Falls and Sulphur Rock*, pencil and watercolor, 3⅜ × 5½ in. (8.5 × 14 cm). Gilcrease Museum, Tulsa, Oklahoma

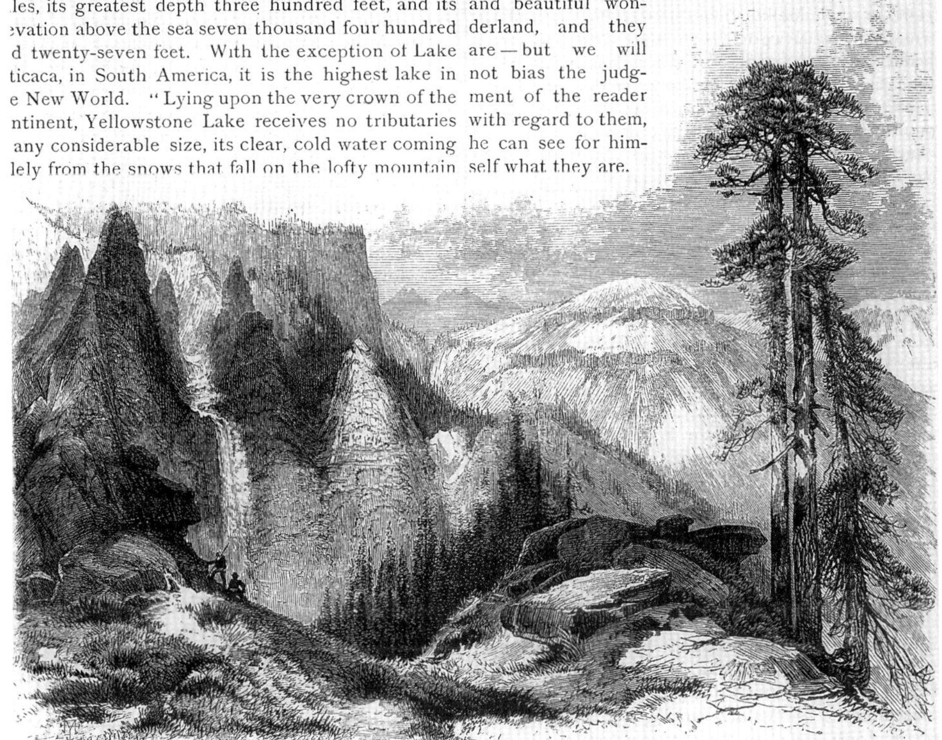

FIGURE 70. After Thomas Moran, *Tower Falls and Column Mountain,* 1872, wood engraving, *The Aldine* 6 (March 1873): 75. Courtesy of Boston Public Library, Print Room

HEAD OF THE YELLOWSTONE RIVER

This chromolithograph (fig. 71) depicts the Yellowstone River as it emerges from its headwaters in Yellowstone Lake, very near the present-day visitors' center at Fishing Bridge. In 1871, Moran and Jackson remained at the Grand Canyon of the Yellowstone for several days before joining the main survey party at Yellowstone Lake on August 1. The next day, Moran wrote in his journal, "Made photographs & sketches of the Lake & river in forenoon," among them several views (figs. 72–74) that emphasize the shoreline and distant mountains that would later appear in the published chromo.[42]

Moran probably chose *Head of the Yellowstone River* for the Prang portfolio for its beauty and significance in the region. As Hayden wrote in the text accompanying the chromolithograph, "The river passes through a great variety of scenery, but at no point can it boast of more enchanting beauty than at its very head, near the magnificent lake of which it forms the outlet."[43] Today the Yellowstone River, which flows northward through the park, is the longest undammed river in the lower forty-eight states, extending 671 miles to its confluence with the Missouri River in North Dakota. After leaving the lake it moves serenely, with a "sluggish current more like a lake than a great stream," for some ten miles, before changing into what Hayden described as a

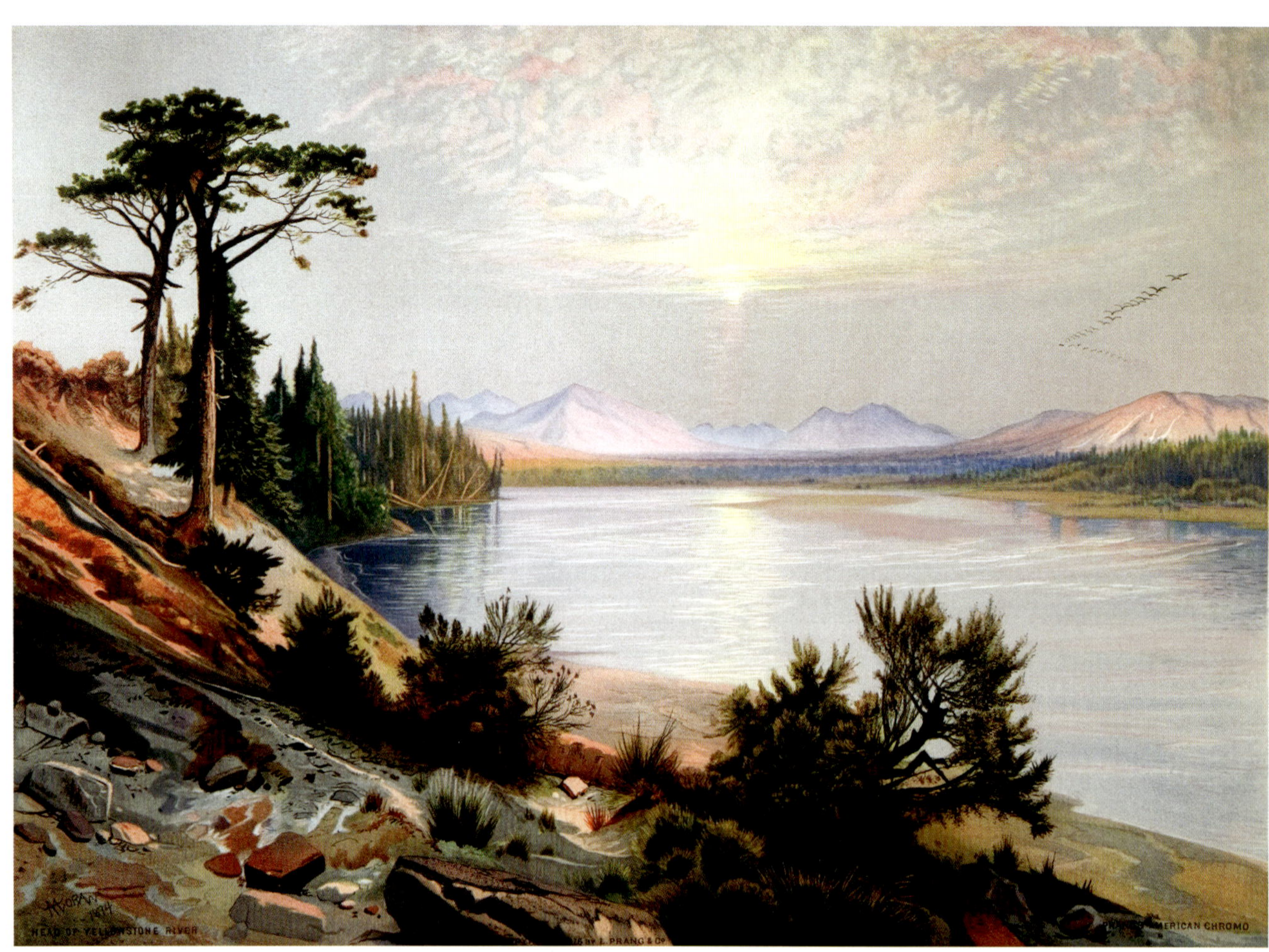

FIGURE 71. After Thomas Moran, *Head of the Yellowstone River,* ca. 1875, chromolithograph, 9⅞ × 14 in.(25 × 35.6 cm). Joslyn Art Museum, Omaha, gift of Gail and Michael Yanney and Lisa and Bill Roskens

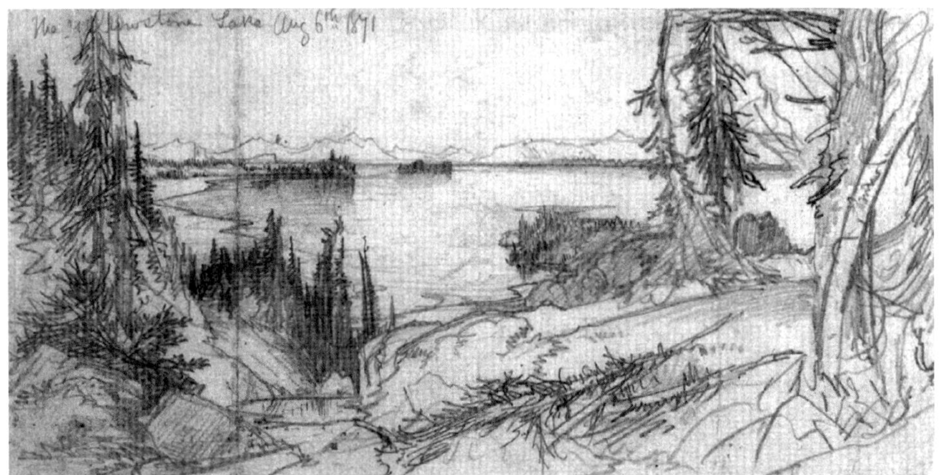

FIGURE 72. Thomas Moran, *The Yellowstone Lake, Aug. 6, 1871*, 1871, pencil, 4¾ × 9⅞ in. (12 × 25.1 cm). Jefferson National Expansion Memorial, St. Louis (5846)

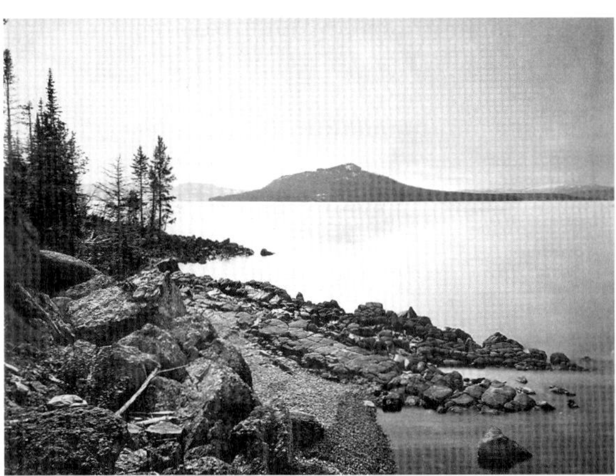

FIGURE 73. William Henry Jackson, *Yellowstone Lake,* 1871, photograph from Moran's studio collection. Gilcrease Museum, Tulsa, Oklahoma

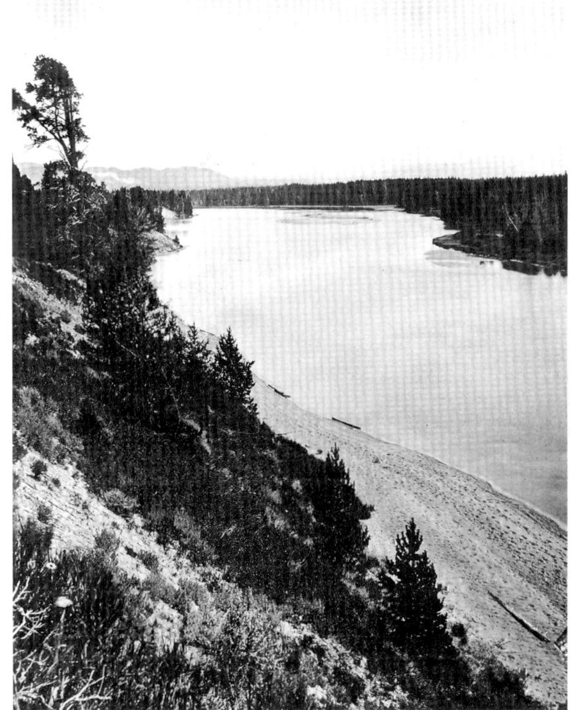

FIGURE 74. William Henry Jackson, *Head of the Yellowstone River,* 1871, photograph, United States Geological Survey Photographic Library (Jackson 97a)

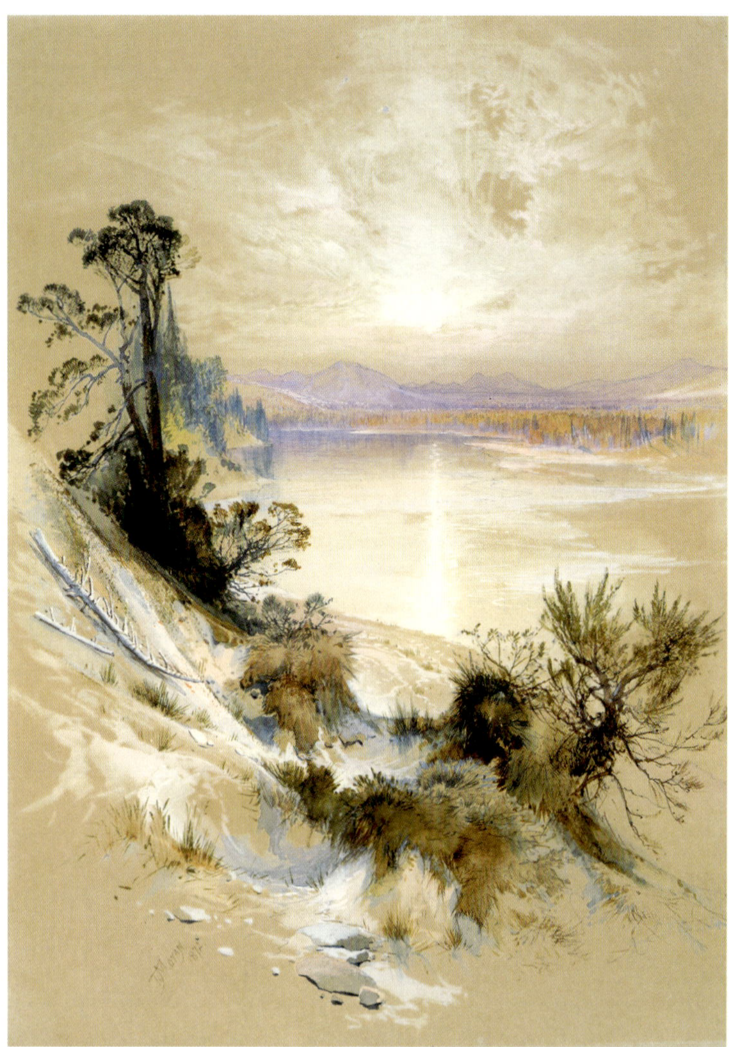

FIGURE 75. Thomas Moran, *Yellowstone River,* 1872, pencil, watercolor, and opaque color, 13 × 9½ in. (33 × 24 cm). Gilcrease Museum, Tulsa, Oklahoma

"rapid torrent, rushing along between rocky banks" as it nears the Grand Canyon of the Yellowstone.[44]

Like *Yellowstone Lake,* with which it is closely associated both geographically and formally in the Prang portfolio, *Head of the Yellowstone River* was not among the subjects that Moran would replicate frequently, perhaps because it is a relatively generic view that could be of almost any western mountain lake or river. At the same time, it is not an entirely imagined scene, as comparison to Jackson's photograph, *Head of the Yellowstone River* (fig. 74), reveals. Moran's image has the same basic composition, but the point of view is slightly lowered, his favorite Borghese Garden tree stands in for the western pine, and the chromo version is a more elongated horizontal. Moran had done a vertical version of the subject for William Blackmore in 1872 (fig. 75) that more closely resembles Jackson's photograph and then in 1879 created an original

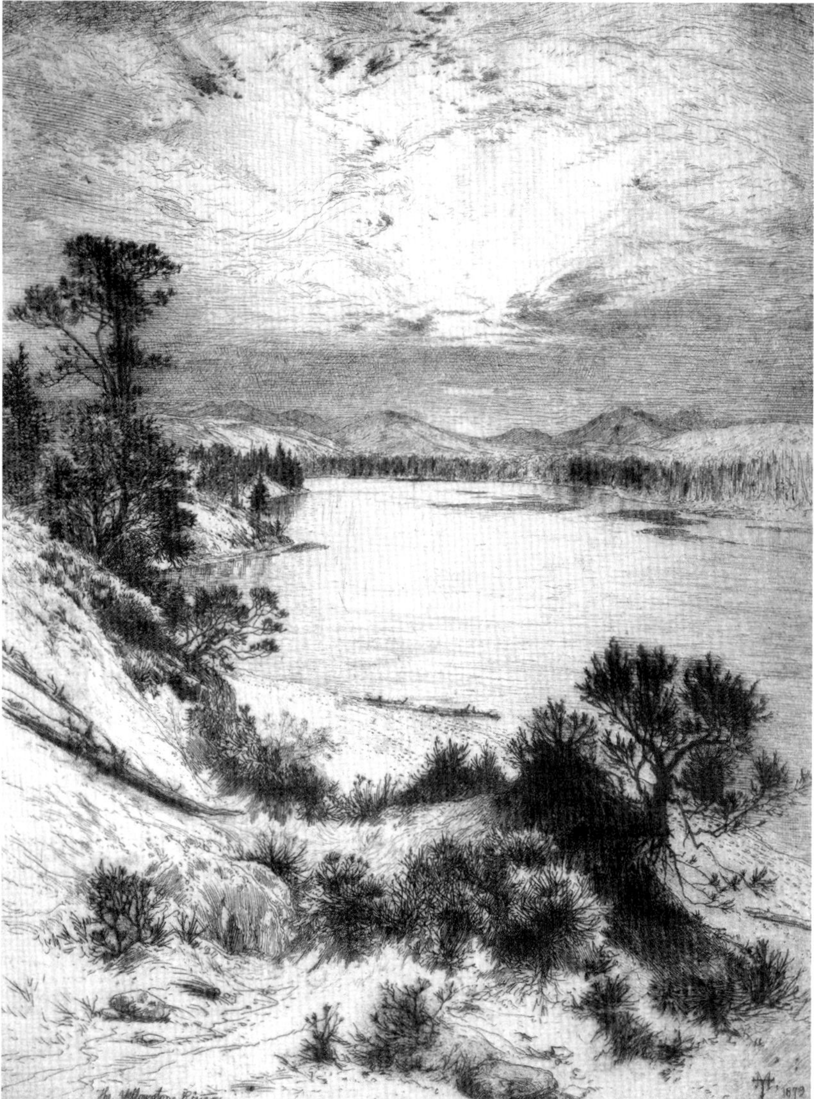

FIGURE 76. Thomas Moran, *The Head of the Yellowstone River [The Yellowstone River]*, 1879, etching, 8½ × 6¼ in. (22 × 15.9 cm). Gilcrease Museum, Tulsa, Oklahoma

etching of the scene that substitutes a lively use of line for the range of color in the earlier portrayals (fig. 76).

Despite its lack of resonance as a continual theme in the artist's work, Moran no doubt recognized that *Head of the Yellowstone River* was central to any thorough understanding of the Yellowstone region. Since it depicted the headwaters of the major river that gives the region its name, this scene was geographically important, and in the Prang series it also provided an echo for other appearances of the river, most notably in *The Grand Cañon of the Yellowstone,* but also in *Upper Falls of the Yellowstone,* one of the nine views that was ultimately excluded from the final portfolio.

THE GRAND CAÑON OF THE YELLOWSTONE

The Grand Canyon of the Yellowstone (fig. 77, which the Prang portfolio refers to with its original spelling) is arguably the most dramatic feature in Yellowstone National Park. It is a massive, curving, and extremely rugged canyon in the northeastern quadrant of the park that extends from Upper Falls (which drops 109 vertical feet) and the nearby Lower Falls (which are more spectacular at 308 feet), some twenty-four miles northward, almost to Tower Falls. As Hayden wrote in the Prang text: "It is a gorge cut into volcanic rocks. . . . The walls in many places vertical, slope to the water's edge, leaving no beach. In some places they are eroded into fantastic shapes, towers, spires, and gothic columns; in others again they present fortress-like fronts, or long slides of brilliant-colored debris; while elsewhere they consist of massive rock, separated by jointage, resembling irregular masonry going to decay."[45]

The Hayden survey reached the canyon on July 27, 1871, only a week after entering the Yellowstone Park area. Moran and William Henry Jackson spent considerable time "photographing and sketching around the Falls & Cañon," before leaving the area for Yellowstone Lake on July 31.[46] Moran sketched several views of the gorge from different vantage points (figs. 78–80) and assisted Jackson in making photographs (figs. 81 and 82) that he would later use back in his studio as he constructed large oils and finished watercolors (fig. 83), such as the one he produced for Louis Prang. Although unified and visually convincing, these studio landscapes are not usually portrayals of the scene from a single viewpoint, but rather compilations of features Moran witnessed from several positions around the canyon.[47]

The Prang chromolithographed version of Yellowstone's Grand Canyon is more formally exaggerated than many of Moran's other views of the gorge, with its protruding foreground extending toward the left and its overly dramatic cliffs rising in the right middle ground.[48] The falls, pushed deep into the distance, take a secondary role. Color and contrast are also more starkly handled than in other representations of the site, with much more white and other high-key tones and stronger contrasts of light and dark. Moran's other portrayals more typically emphasize the falls, the depth of the canyon, and the rich range of yellows and ochres of its rugged walls. Although Moran painted many sites within the Yellowstone region, he became best known for this subject, primarily due to the fame of his massive oil *The Grand Cañon of the Yellowstone* (1872, fig. 32), which Congress purchased in June 1872.[49] At the same time as he was creating his first "Big Picture," Moran had also published what may be his preliminary study of the subject in *Scribner's Monthly* (fig. 84). Another wood engraving, from *The Aldine* in 1873 (fig. 85), is very similar to the Prang chromolithograph in its pronounced emphasis on the large white cliffs that dominate the right side of the gorge. All these representations helped shape tourists' expectations of the park, eventually contributing to the construction of scenic overlooks there that provided these

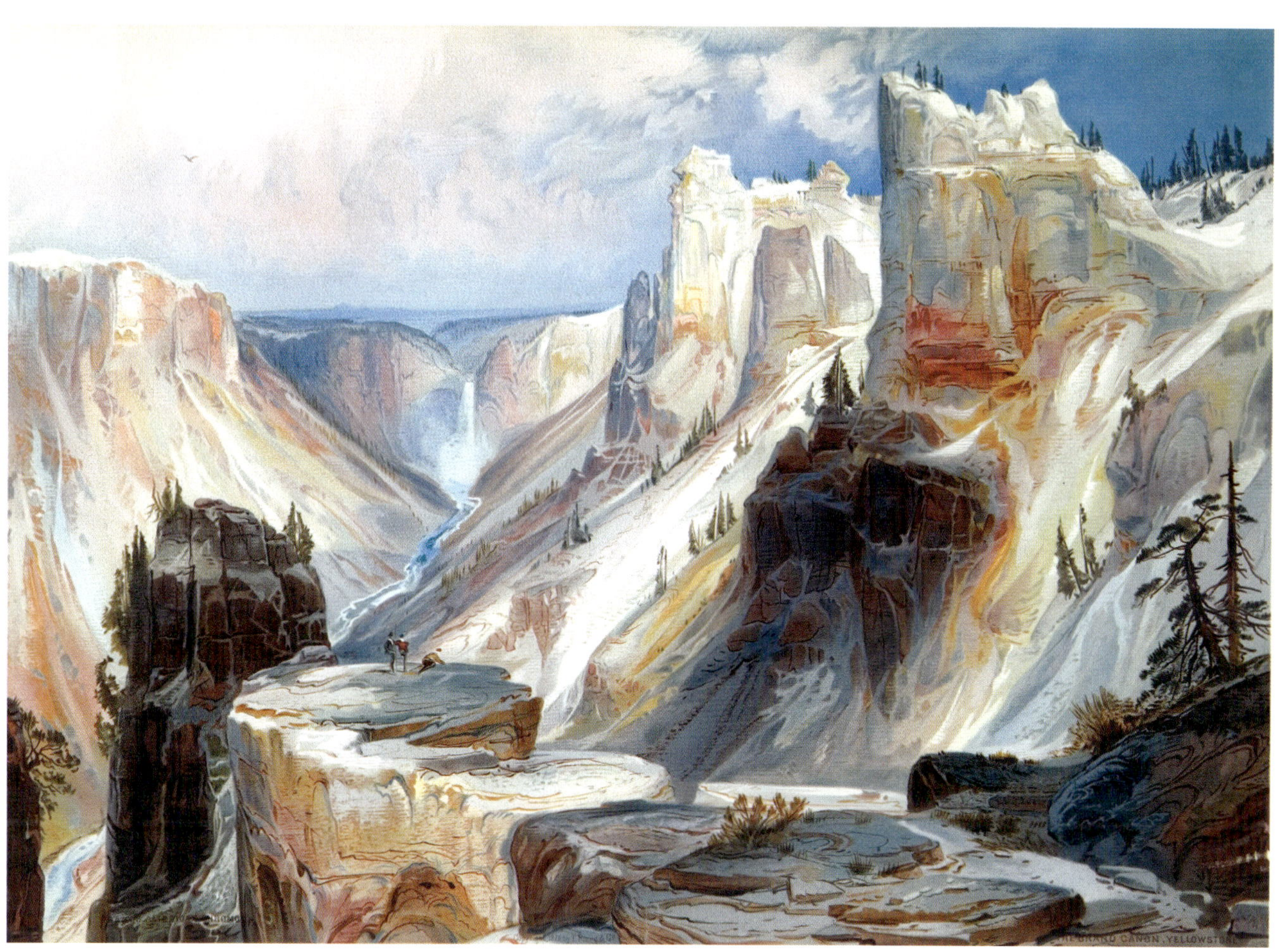

FIGURE 77. After Thomas Moran, *The Grand Cañon of the Yellowstone,* ca. 1875, chromolithograph, 9⅞ × 14 in. (25 × 35.6 cm). Joslyn Art Museum, Omaha, gift of Gail and Michael Yanney and Lisa and Bill Roskens

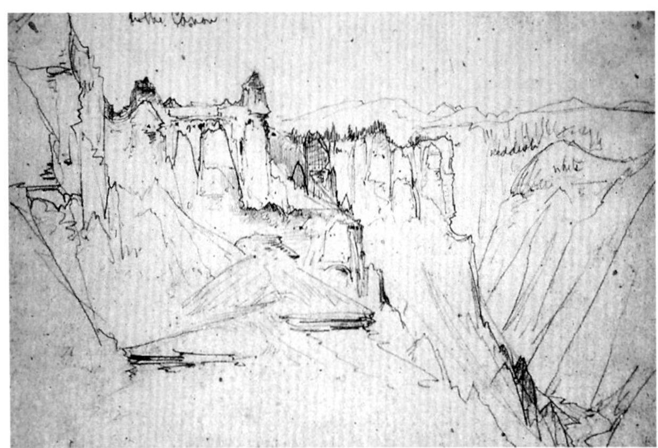

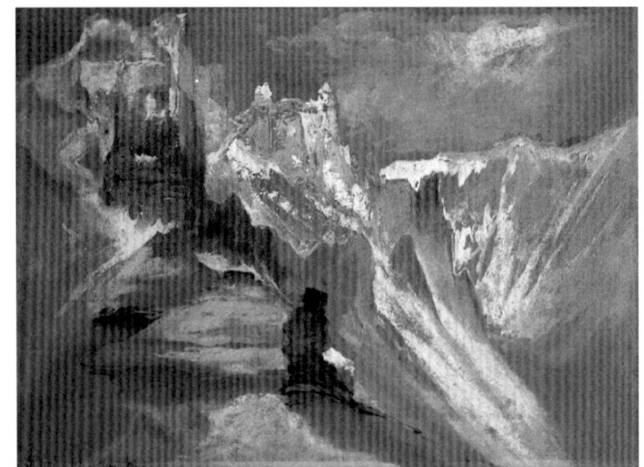

FIGURE 78. Thomas Moran, *In the Canyon*, 1871, pencil, 5⅛ × 7¾ in. (13 × 19.7 cm). Jefferson National Expansion Memorial, St. Louis (4215)

FIGURE 79. Thomas Moran, *Yellowstone Canyon*, 1871, watercolor, 10⅜ × 14⅛ in. (26.3 × 35.8 cm). Courtesy of National Park Service (Yellowstone National Park)

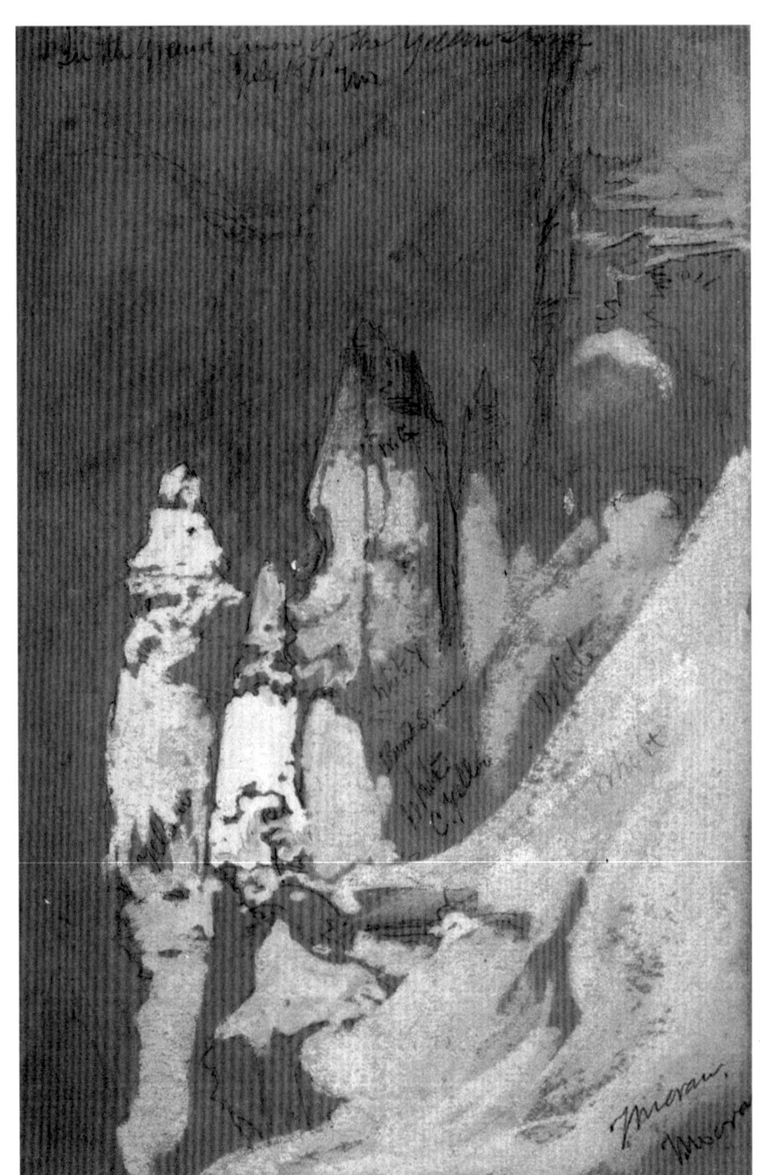

FIGURE 80. Thomas Moran, *In the Grand Canyon of the Yellowstone*, 1871, watercolor, $7\frac{11}{16}$ × 5 in. (19.6 × 12.7 cm). Courtesy of National Park Service (Yellowstone National Park)

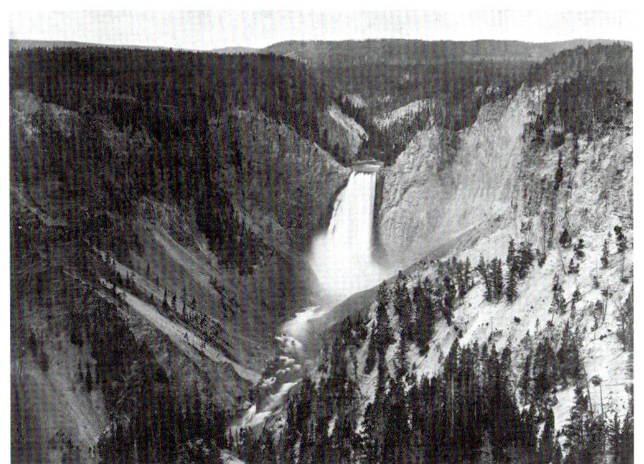

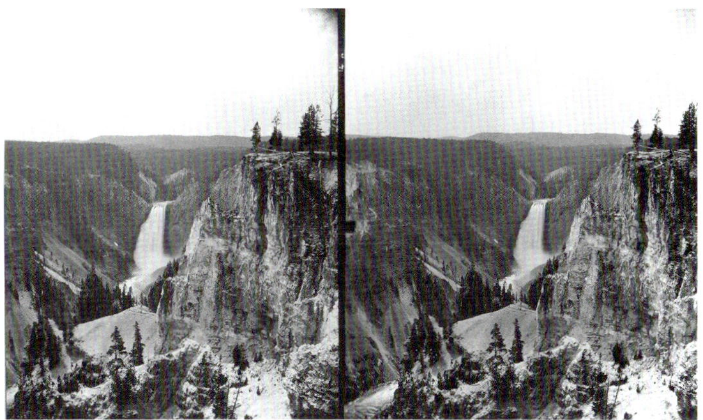

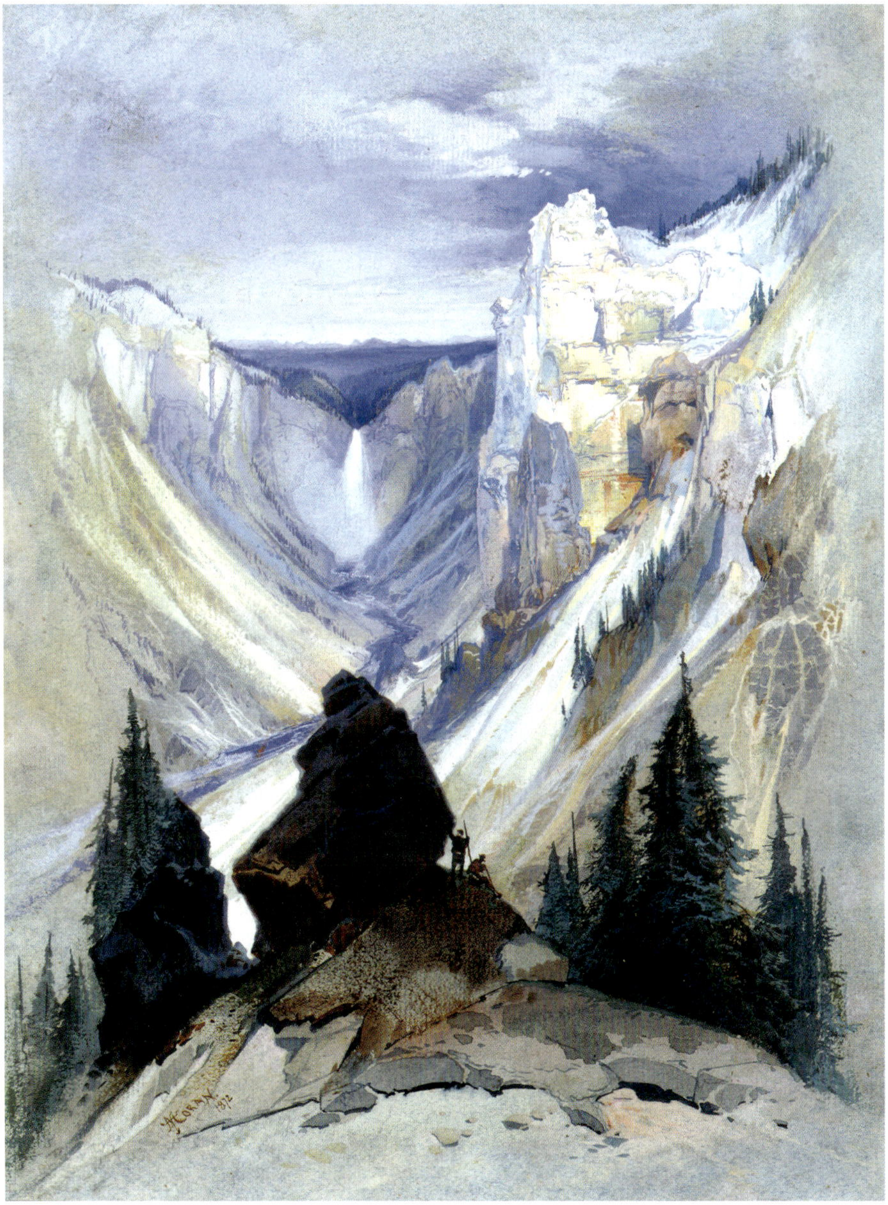

FIGURE 81. William Henry Jackson, *Lower Falls of the Yellowstone River (400 feet) [From Inspiration Point]*, 1871, photograph from Moran's studio collection. Gilcrease Museum, Tulsa, Oklahoma

FIGURE 82. William Henry Jackson, *Yellowstone Falls Viewed from Artist's Point*, photograph, U.S. Geological Survey Photographic Library (jwh00692)

FIGURE 83. Thomas Moran, *The Grand Canyon of the Yellowstone*, 1872, pencil, watercolor, and opaque color on paper, 11¼ × 8 in. (28.6 x.20.3 cm). Gilcrease Museum, Tulsa, Oklahoma

FIGURE 84. After Thomas Moran, *The Great Cañon and Lower Falls of the Yellowstone*, 1871, wood engraving, 4⅜ × 6½ in. (11.1 × 16.5 cm), *Scribner's Monthly* 3 (February 1872): 388. Perkins Library, Hastings College, Hastings, Nebraska

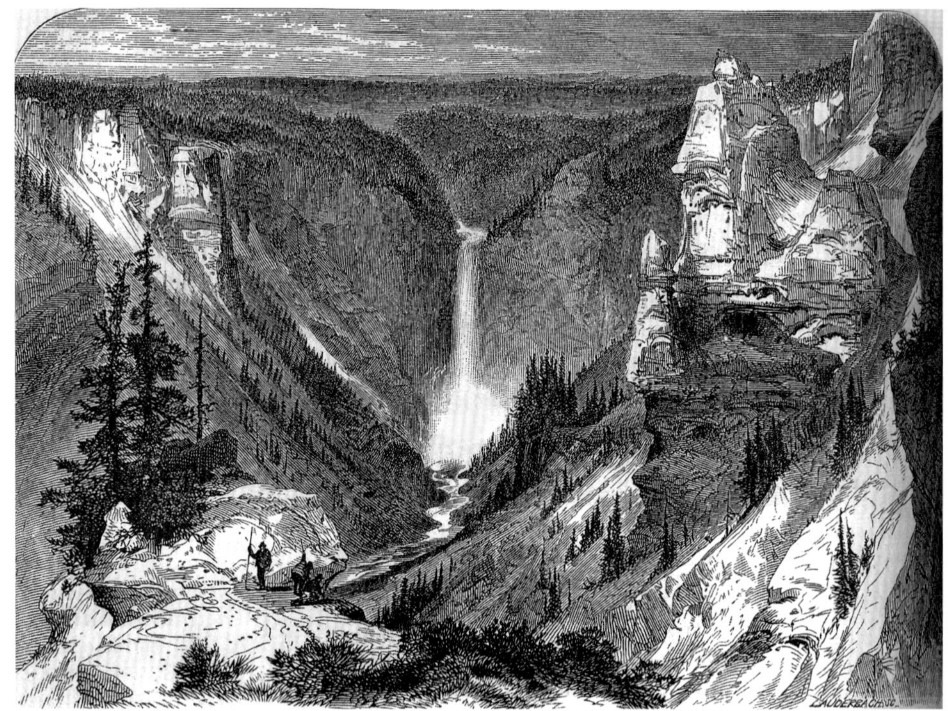

FIGURE 85. After Thomas Moran, *Cliffs in the Grand Cañon*, 1872, wood engraving, *The Aldine* 6 (March 1873): 75

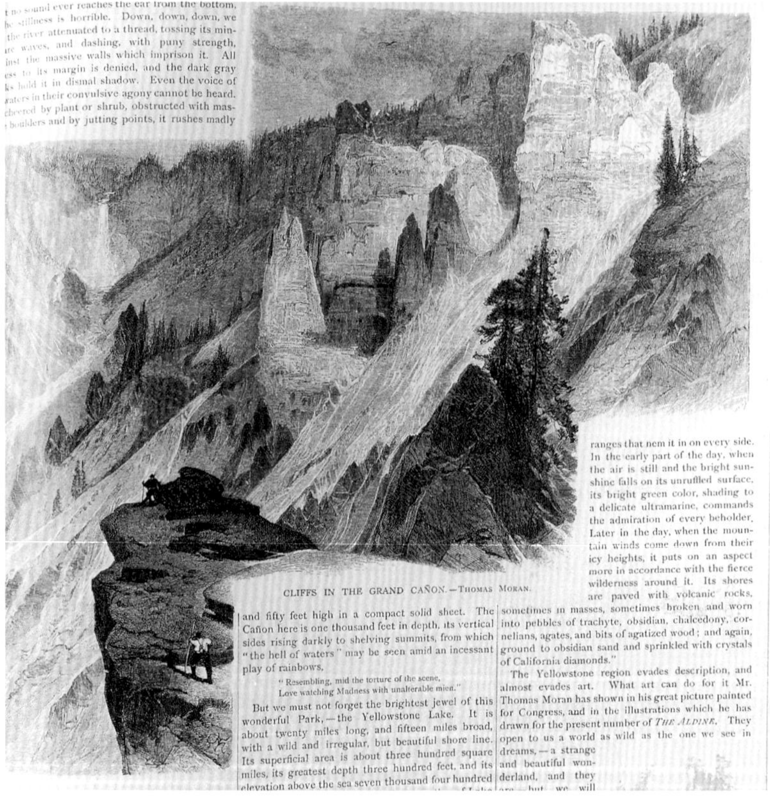

no sound ever reaches the ear from the bottom, the stillness is horrible. Down, down, down, we see the river attenuated to a thread, tossing its miniature waves, and dashing, with puny strength, against the massive walls which imprison it. All access to its margin is denied, and the dark gray rocks hold it in dismal shadow. Even the voice of waters in their convulsive agony cannot be heard. Uncheered by plant or shrub, obstructed with massive boulders and by jutting points, it rushes madly

CLIFFS IN THE GRAND CAÑON.—THOMAS MORAN.

and fifty feet high in a compact solid sheet. The Cañon here is one thousand feet in depth, its vertical sides rising darkly to shelving summits, from which "the hell of waters" may be seen amid an incessant play of rainbows.

"Resembling, mid the torture of the scene,
Love watching Madness with unalterable mien."

But we must not forget the brightest jewel of this wonderful Park,—the Yellowstone Lake. It is about twenty miles long, and fifteen miles broad, with a wild and irregular, but beautiful shore line. Its superficial area is about three hundred square miles, its greatest depth three hundred feet, and its elevation above the sea seven thousand four hundred

ranges that hem it in on every side. In the early part of the day, when the air is still and the bright sunshine falls on its unruffled surface, its bright green color, shading to a delicate ultramarine, commands the admiration of every beholder. Later in the day, when the mountain winds come down from their icy heights, it puts on an aspect more in accordance with the fierce wilderness around it. Its shores are paved with volcanic rocks, sometimes in masses, sometimes broken and worn into pebbles of trachyte, obsidian, chalcedony, cornelians, agates, and bits of agatized wood; and again, ground to obsidian sand and sprinkled with crystals of California diamonds."

The Yellowstone region evades description, and almost evades art. What art can do for it Mr. Thomas Moran has shown in his great picture painted for Congress, and in the illustrations which he has drawn for the present number of *THE ALDINE*. They open to us a world as wild as the one we see in dreams,—a strange and beautiful wonderland, and they

vistas. The artist became so associated with his perspective on the Grand Canyon of the Yellowstone, for example, that Artist's Point there was named in his honor. On the other side of the gorge is another promontory, Moran Point. Together these remind visitors, however subtly, that the Yellowstone "experience" not only has historical roots but has also been influenced by aesthetic theories and practice.

Moran visited Yellowstone only once after his initial trip to the region in 1871, returning in 1892 with William Henry Jackson. At that time he made more sketches of the canyon, from which he produced a second monumental oil of the scene. That work, measuring 10 × 14 feet, was featured in the Wyoming exhibit at the World's Columbian Exposition in Chicago in 1893 and was later given to the National Collection of Fine Arts in Washington (today's Smithsonian American Art Museum), where it usually hangs with the large 1872 version of the same subject. The two Yellowstone "periods" offer a remarkable glimpse at the transformations in Moran's artistic development, from his early linear style to his later, more fluid, almost Impressionistic handling of paint. As an example from the first, the Prang chromolithograph represented the formative era, a time in which Yellowstone's character was first being understood, and this signature image was its centerpiece.

THE TOWERS OF TOWER FALLS

The third of Moran's three favorite portrayals of Tower Falls (two of which appear in the Prang portfolio), *The Towers of Tower Falls* (fig. 86), takes its point of view at the edge of Tower Creek, looking toward the distinctive pinnacle known as the Devil's Hoof that stands just at the brink of the 132-foot cataract. The formation was named by Nathaniel Langford during the Washburn/Doane expedition of 1870 and was popularized in Langford's *Scribner's Monthly* article of May 1871. Langford's description singled out the distinctive pinnacle:

> The stream is broken into a great number of channels, each of which has worked a torturous course through a compact body of shale to the verge of the precipice where they re-unite and form the fall. The countless shapes into which the shale has been wrought by the action of the angry waters, add a feature of great interest to the scene. Spires of solid shale, capped with slate, beautifully rounded and polished, faultless in symmetry, raise their tapering forms to the height of from 80 to 150 feet, all over the plateau above the cataract. Some resemble towers, others the spires of churches, and others still shoot up as lithe and slender as the minarets of a mosque. Some of the loftiest of these formations, standing like sentinels upon the very brink of the fall, are accessible to an expert and adventurous climber. . . . Many of the capricious formations wrought from the shale excite merriment as well as wonder. Of this kind especially was a huge mass sixty feet in height, which,

FIGURE 86. After Thomas Moran, *The Towers of Tower Falls,* ca. 1875, chromolithograph, 13¾ × 9 in. (34.9 × 22.9 cm). Joslyn Art Museum, Omaha, gift of Gail and Michael Yanney and Lisa and Bill Roskens

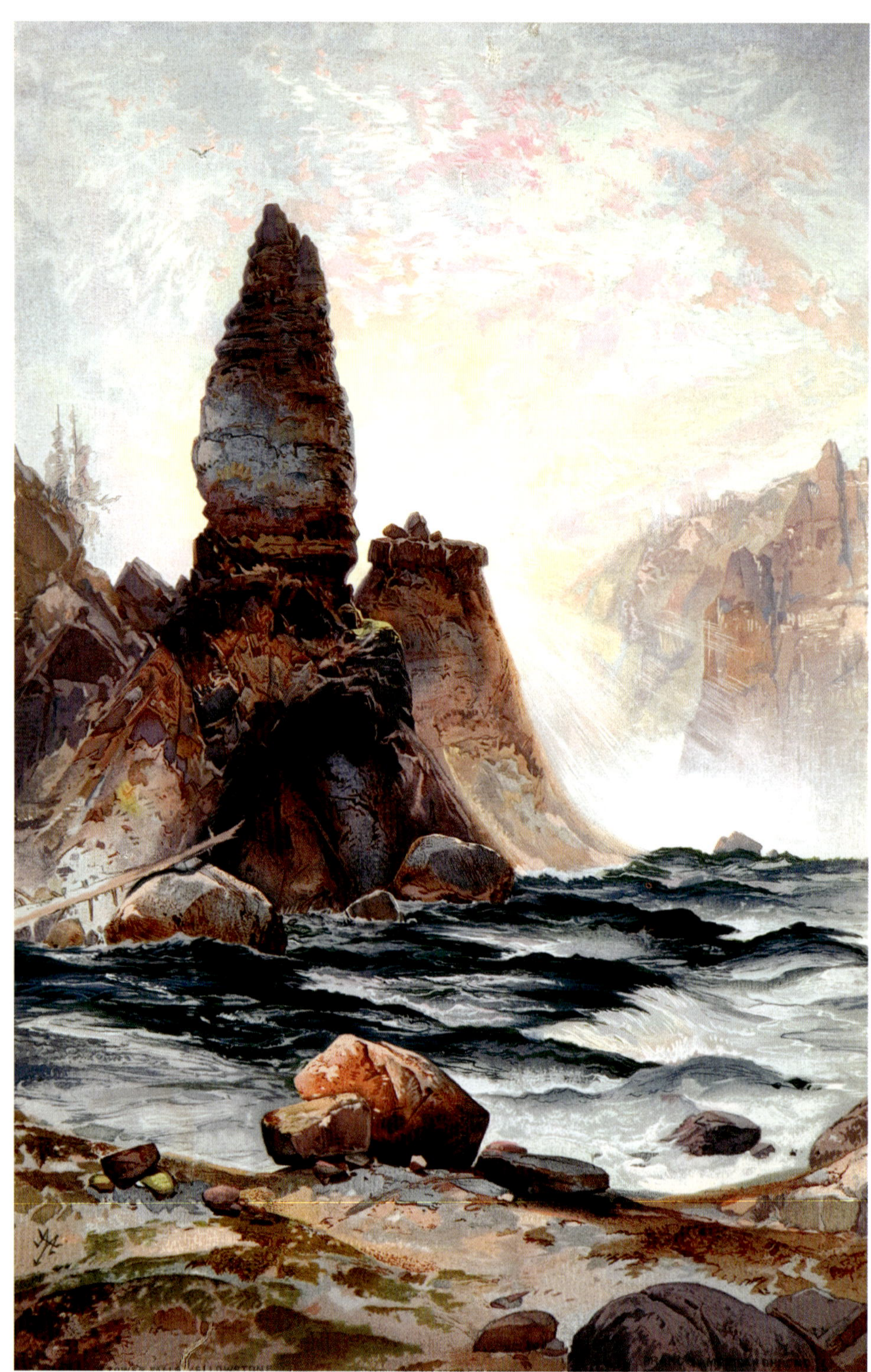

from its supposed resemblance to the proverbial foot of his Satanic Majesty, we called the "Devil's Hoof."[50]

Demonic place-names abound at Yellowstone and, although the more sinister aspects of the region were repressed during the lobbying process for the national park bill and in subsequent promotional literature, Hayden did not hesitate to quote Langford's description of this distinctive feature in his text accompanying *The Towers of Tower Falls* in the Prang portfolio. It is unlikely that the Devil's Hoof's darker associations were remembered in the late 1880s, however, when Northern Pacific Railroad selected the image for a chromolithographed brochure advertising the line as the "Wonderland Route to the Pacific Coast" (ca. 1890, fig. 87). Since the principal financier of the NPRR, Jay Cooke, had his own series of Yellowstone watercolors that Moran had produced for him in return for the $500 advance toward his 1871 trip, it might be assumed that Cooke's *Tower Creek, Yellowstone* was the source for the NPRR brochure.[51] In fact, however, Cooke had withdrawn from the NPRR with the fall of his powerful banking house in the Panic of 1873, and its designer probably referred instead to the Prang chromolithograph, which corresponds to the brochure's image in virtually every detail.[52]

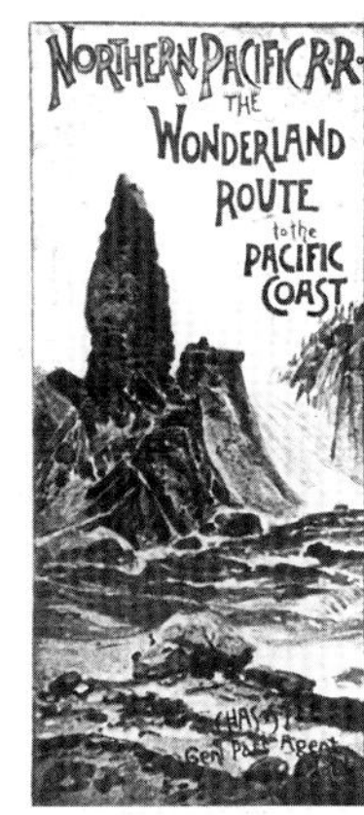

FIGURE 87. After Thomas Moran, *Northern Pacific R.R.: The Wonderland Route to the Pacific Coast*, ca. 1890, chromolithographed promotional brochure

For his classic composition of the Devil's Hoof, Moran seems to have worked from a Jackson photograph (fig. 88), noticeably removing the pine that grows awkwardly from the lower formation. He also had his own field drawings (figs. 89 and 90), which lack the clarity of the final version but also emphasize the vertical pinnacles. These are also related to an exceptional wood-engraving design that Moran created for the frontispiece for the April 1873 edition of *The Aldine* (fig. 91).

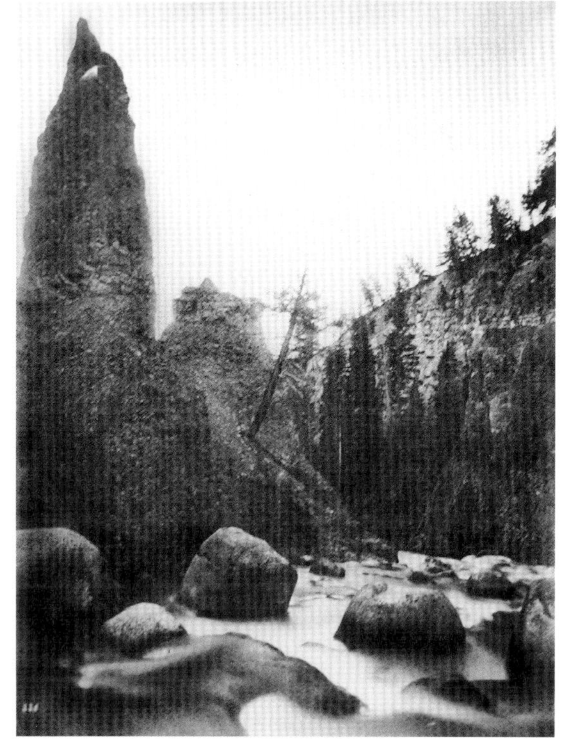

FIGURE 88. William Henry Jackson, *Tower of Tower Falls*, ca. 1871, photograph. United States Geological Survey, Special Collections, Reston, Virginia

Moran created at least four finished watercolors of this subject in the early 1870s, each varying only slightly in its details (fig. 92), and he also created several other related views looking up at the distinctive towers from below the falls.[53] He produced at least one oil version about the same time and then returned to the theme in a misty late work (fig. 93). At the height of his interest in original etching in the 1880s, he dedicated two remarkable prints to the subject (figs. 94 and 95), infusing the already lively scene with an ecstatic profusion of movement and vibrancy through a highly expressive use of line.[54] One striking feature of the chromolithographed version is echoed in these etchings: the sunset that glows behind the pinnacle, spreading its rays through the spray that rises as the water plummets over the edge. This effect has at once a heavenly aura and, for those with more fortitude,

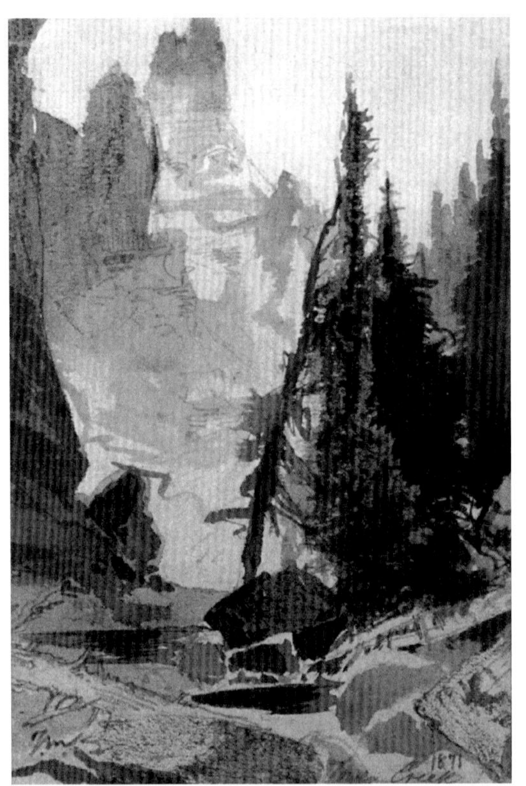

suggests something of the mouth of Hell, beckoning beyond the "foot of his Satanic Majesty." With its demonic allusions, *The Towers of Tower Falls* stands in the Prang portfolio as an interesting, if subtle, contrast to the plate that follows it. *The Mountain of the Holy Cross* depicted a more obvious symbol, but when paired, these two scenes exemplify some of the most profound extremes of the American West and the region's suggestive associations for nineteenth-century viewers.

THE MOUNTAIN OF THE HOLY CROSS

The Mountain of the Holy Cross is an actual mountain, one of Colorado's "14,000 footers," located in the Sawatch Range about 100 miles west of Denver.[55] It was "discovered" in the late 1860s and documented by the Hayden survey in 1873, but despite the fame that Jackson's photographs, Moran's art, and a poem by Henry Wadsworth Longfellow brought the site in the mid-1870s, the mountain has nevertheless remained a relatively obscure site. Although access has been greatly facilitated by modern roads, a close view of the cross is still only obtained by strenuous hiking to the summit of Notch Mountain, the peak's immediate neighbor. Notch Mountain hides

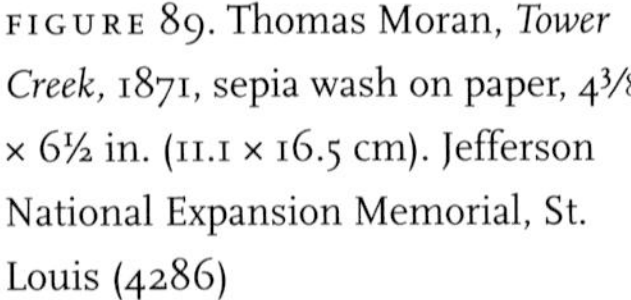

FIGURE 89. Thomas Moran, *Tower Creek,* 1871, sepia wash on paper, $4\frac{3}{8} \times 6\frac{1}{2}$ in. (11.1 × 16.5 cm). Jefferson National Expansion Memorial, St. Louis (4286)

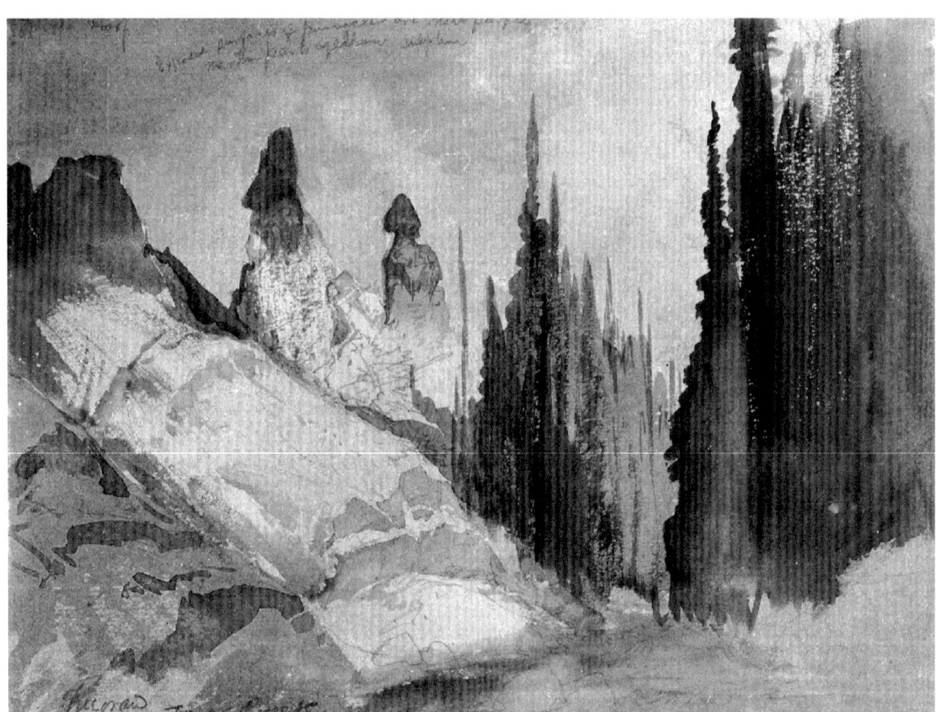

FIGURE 90. Thomas Moran, *Tower Creek,* 1871, watercolor, $7\frac{3}{4} \times 10\frac{9}{16}$ in. (19.7 × 26.8 cm). Courtesy of National Park Service (Yellowstone National Park)

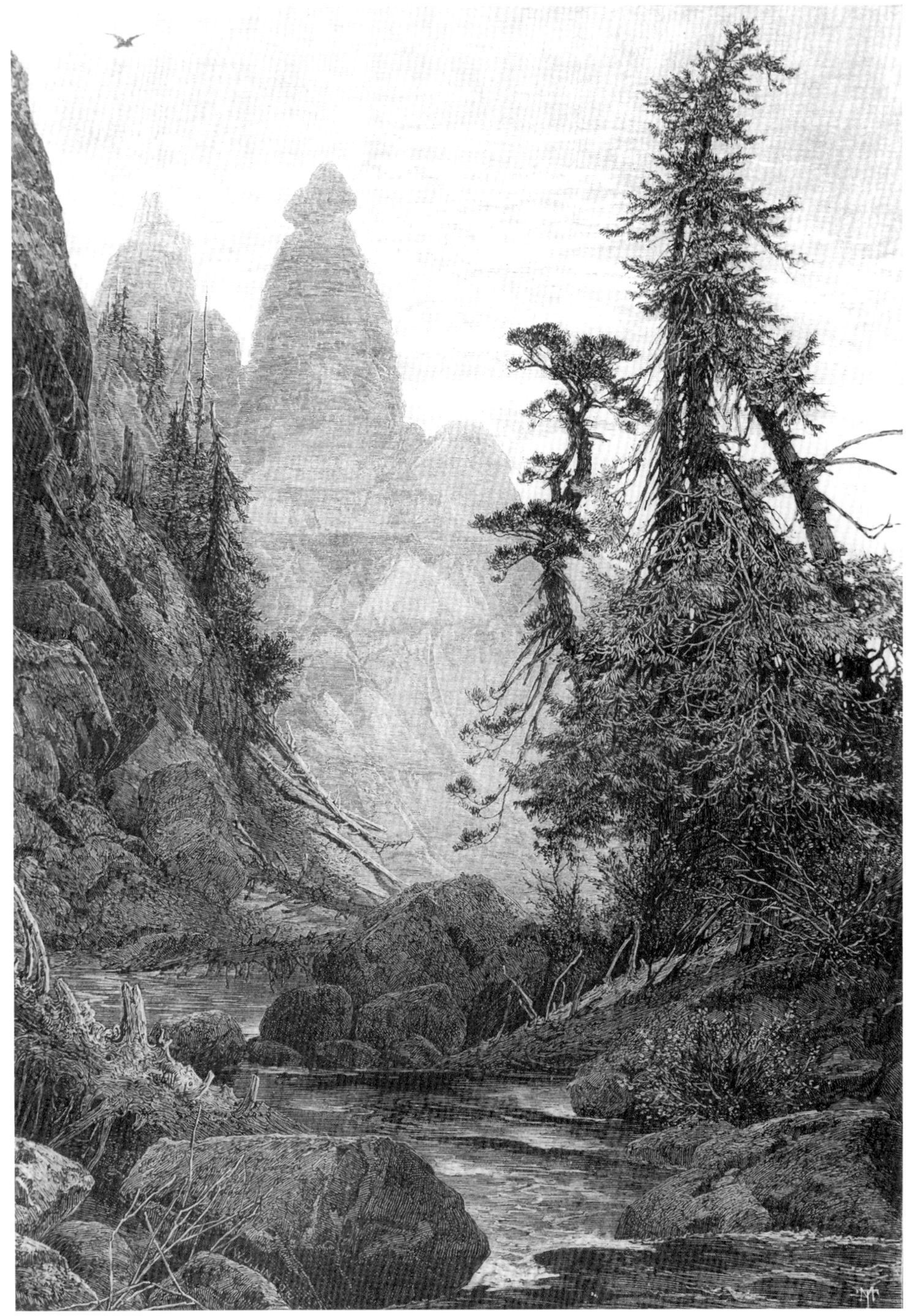

FIGURE 91. After Thomas Moran, *Tower Creek,* ca. 1873, wood engraving, 12¾ × 8¾ in. (32.4 × 22.2 cm), frontispiece, *The Aldine* 6 (April 1873). Collection of the author

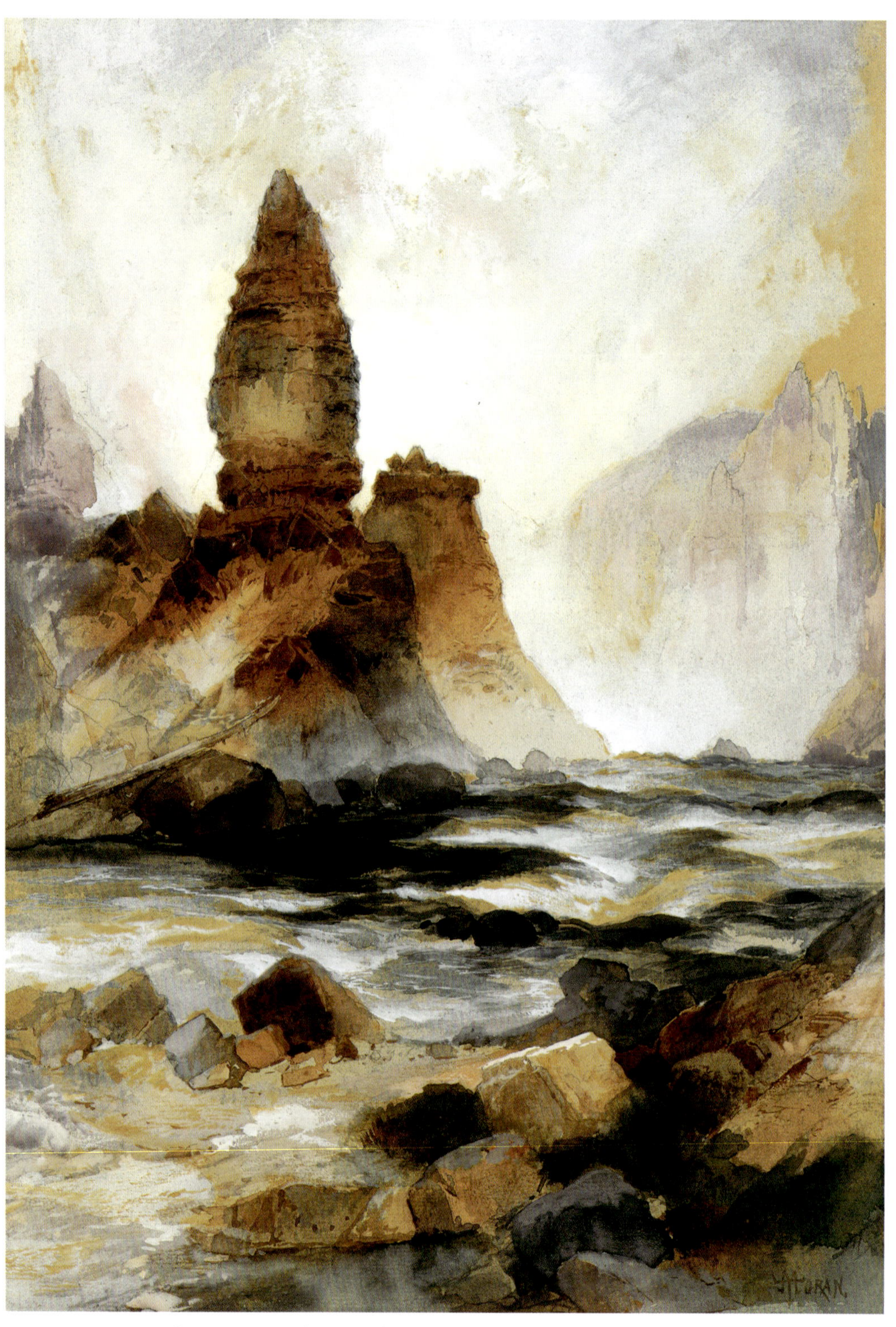

FIGURE 92. Thomas Moran, *The Tower of Tower Falls,* 1874, pencil, watercolor, and opaque color, 14½ × 10½ in. (36.8 × 26.7 cm). Collection of Michael S. and Leslie Engl

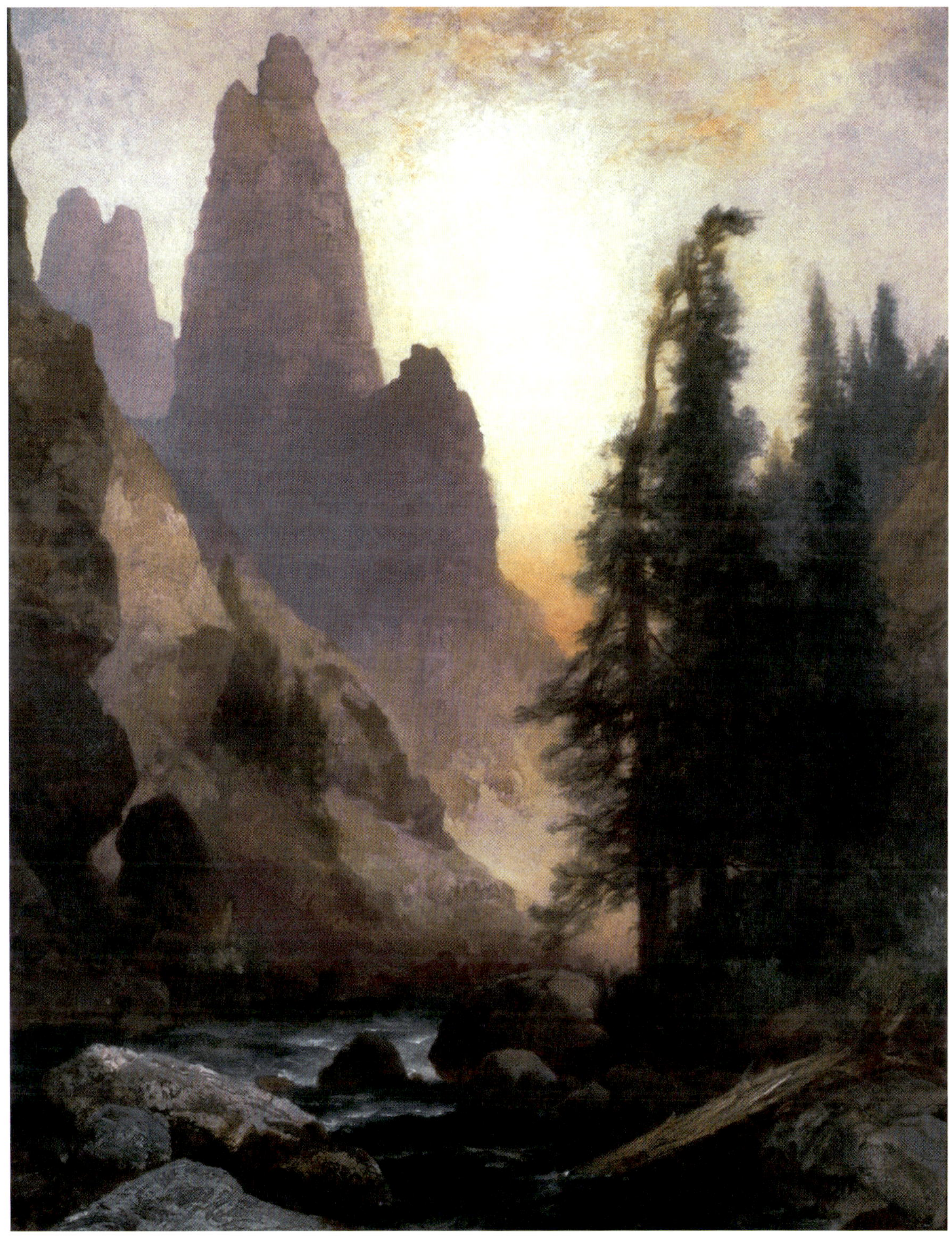

FIGURE 93. Thomas Moran, *Above Tower Falls,* 1917, oil on canvas, 14¾ × 11½ in. (37.4 × 29.2 cm). Guild Hall Museum, East Hampton, New York

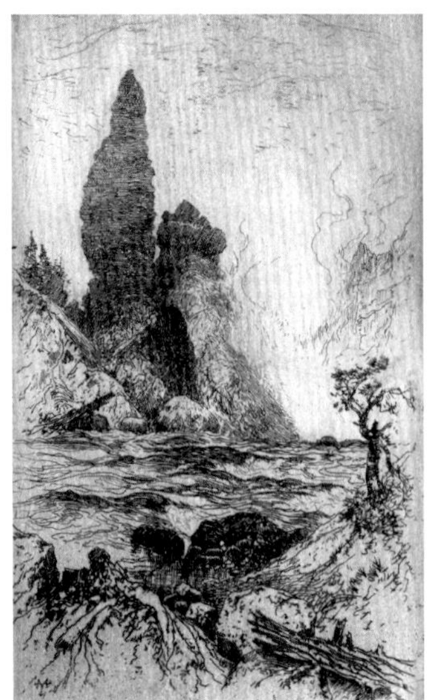

FIGURE 94. Thomas Moran, *Tower Falls*, 1880, etching, 6 × 3½ in. (15.2 × 8.9 cm). Gilcrease Museum, Tulsa, Oklahoma

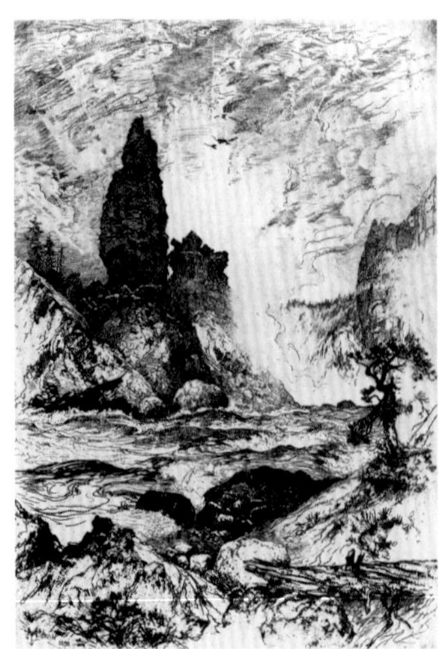

FIGURE 95. Thomas Moran, *Tower Falls, Yellowstone Park*, 1880, etching, 11⅛ × 7¾ in. (28.3 × 19.7 cm). Gilcrease Museum, Tulsa, Oklahoma

the cross except from very distant vantage points, and of course it is snow-covered except in late July and August when warm weather reveals the formation.[56] The remarkable configuration is hardly "conspicuous," as Hayden described it in the Prang publication.

The monumental version of *The Mountain of the Holy Cross* had profound implications for Americans, and the Prang chromolithograph both drew upon and advanced that significance, since it popularized the image and the place more widely than the painting itself could. As a dramatic natural embodiment of the preeminent Christian symbol, the view represented (especially in the centennial year of 1876) the culmination of decades of Manifest Destiny, the notion that had fueled expansionism throughout the century—that it was American's divine mission to claim, civilize, and Christianize the continent. The sacred mountain also seemed the ultimate validation of the quasi-religious movement known as Transcendentalism, which had characterized literary and philosophical writings since at least the 1820s. As Ralph Waldo Emerson wrote in his 1836 essay, *Nature,* "The noblest ministry of nature is to stand as the apparition of God. It is the organ through which the universal spirit speaks to the individual, and strives to lead back the individual to it."[57]

Inspired by Jackson's 1873 photographs of the cross (fig. 96), Moran may have portrayed the Mountain of the Holy Cross even before he traveled to view it himself. He created a wood engraving for *Picturesque America,* which was published in 1874 (fig. 97), the same year that he traveled to Colorado with the Hayden expedition, and the dating of the production is uncertain. The Prang chromo of the next year (fig. 98) is remarkably different from both this view and Moran's monumental oil (fig. 34), since it portrays the mountain from the adjacent mountain range rather than from the floor of Holy Cross Creek Valley. In all his portrayals, however, the artist took liberties with topography, as the side of the peak that contains the cross formation is not actually visible from either point of view. To more dramatically present the sacred symbol, Moran effectively turned the mountain to present its distinctive face. In the oil he created what Albert Boime has called "the reverential gaze," looking up at the mountain, but the Prang chromo offers a "magisterial gaze" across the intervening valley from a neighboring ridge.[58] Even though Moran manipulated the landscape in both versions, the elevated view of the valley in the Prang chromo was something he actually experienced. This is verified by Jackson's photographs, by his own sketches, and by a letter the artist wrote to his wife. Moran described the scene to her:

> Thursday [August 20] we began the ascent of the intervening mountain between us and the Roche Mountonée Valley, & of all the hard climbing that I have experienced, this beat it. Almost perpendicular, covered with burnt & fallen timber, lying 3 or 4 deep. It was only by slow & persevering effort that the horses could get

through & we had to walk a good part of the way. When we got to the top the view was perfectly magnificent. 2,000 feet below us lay the Mountonée Valley with the Holy Cross Creek rushing through it & at the head of the valley the splendid peak of the Holy Cross with the range continuing to the left of us.[59]

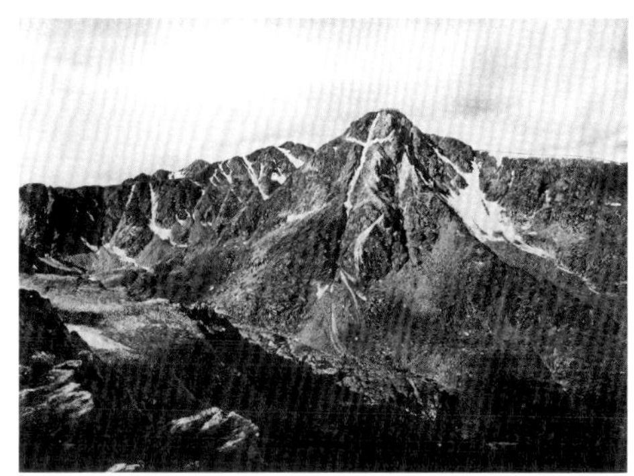

FIGURE 96. William Henry Jackson, *Mountain of the Holy Cross*, 1873, photograph, United States Geological Survey Photographic Library (jwh01276)

Moran did sketch the view from this vantage point (fig. 99) and helped Jackson photograph it (fig. 100) before moving down the valley and up Notch Mountain to see the cross itself (figs. 101 and 102). The journey took several days and was a trying "pilgrim's progress," as the party struggled through the rugged terrain. As he described the climb to his wife:

> Horror!!! the way up the Valley was infinitely worse than anything we had yet encountered. A swamp, covered with the worst of fallen logs & projecting through which were the Roche Mountonée or Sheep Rocks, rounded and smooth & slippery, varying from 10 to 40 feet high. We worked our way as best we could, without any serious accident, except one of the horses slipping off a rock about 20 feet & punching a hole in his belly & a fir bough striking me in the eye. . . . Added to all this it rained on us all the time, making the logs and rocks extremely dangerous & slippery. . . . these two miles took us three hours to make. The next day . . . [we] began the ascent of the Mountain . . . the toughest trial of strength that I have ever experienced. . . . After lunch we again started through the timber upward and at 2½ o'clock were at 12,000 feet. Here we were in clear view of the Cross & although still 800 feet from where we intended to reach, we were all so tired that we concluded we had gone far enough. We rested half an hour and then started on the back track, getting back to camp in about 3 hours. In the Valley is one of the most picturesque waterfalls that I have ever seen. I shall use it in the foreground of the picture. . . . I have not done much sketching, but I have done a good deal of looking.[60]

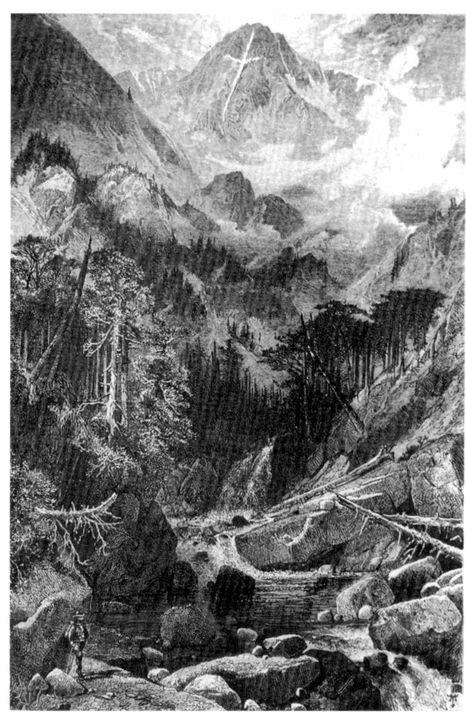

FIGURE 97. After Thomas Moran, *Mountain of the Holy Cross*, ca. 1873, wood engraving, 9½ × 6⅝ in. (24.1 × 16.7 cm), from *Picturesque America* (New York: D. Appleton & Co., 1874), 2: 501

The torturous climb toward the image of Christian salvation was both a practical reality and a symbolic journey that Moran would allude to in his representations of the site, including in the watercolor he would make for Prang.

Back east, Moran produced his third large western oil painting, *The Mountain of the Holy Cross* (1875, fig. 34), which he seems to have envisioned as the final component of a triptych with *The Grand Cañon of the Yellowstone* (1872, fig. 32) and *The Chasm of the Colorado* (1873–1874, fig. 33). Although he never exhibited the three together (the

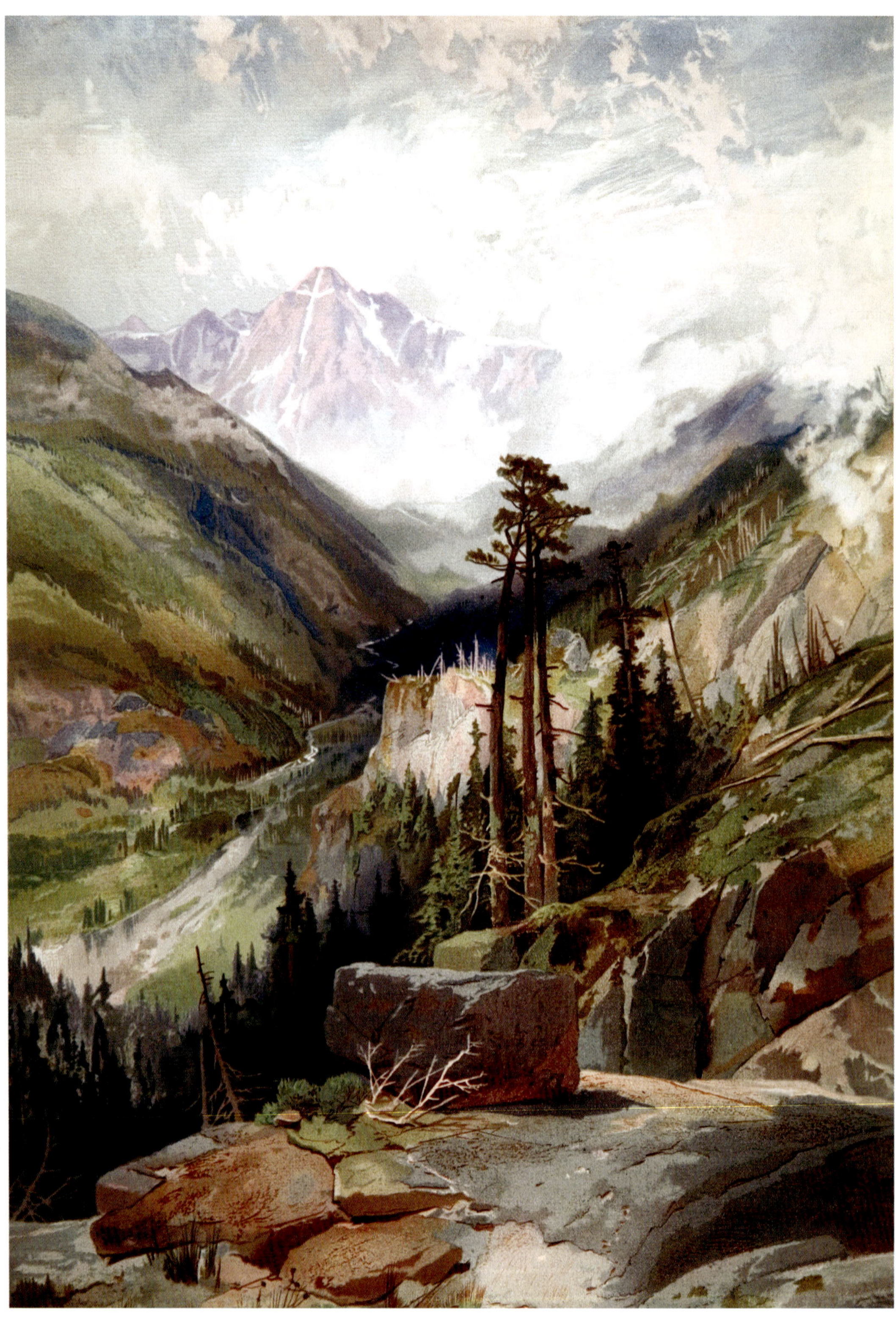

FIGURE 98. After Thomas Moran, *The Mountain of the Holy Cross*, 1875, chromolithograph, 13⅝ × 9⅝ in. (34.6 × 24.4 cm). Joslyn Art Museum, Omaha, gift of Gail and Michael Yanney and Lisa and Bill Roskens

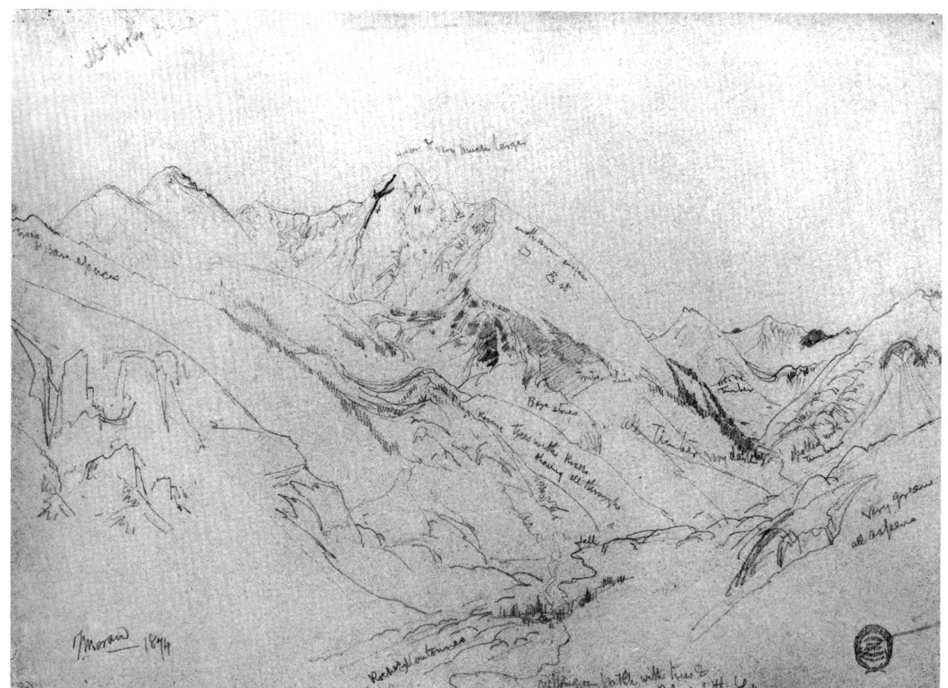

FIGURE 99. Thomas Moran, *Mt. Holy Cross*, 1874, graphite on blue-gray paper, 10¾ × 15 in. (27.3 × 38.1 cm). Cooper-Hewitt National Design Museum, Smithsonian Institution, gift of Thomas Moran, 1917-17-30 (photo: Ken Pelka)

FIGURE 100. William Henry Jackson, *[From] Roches Mountain, Near the Mountain of the Holy Cross*, 1873, photograph. United States Geological Survey Photographic Library (Jackson 1340)

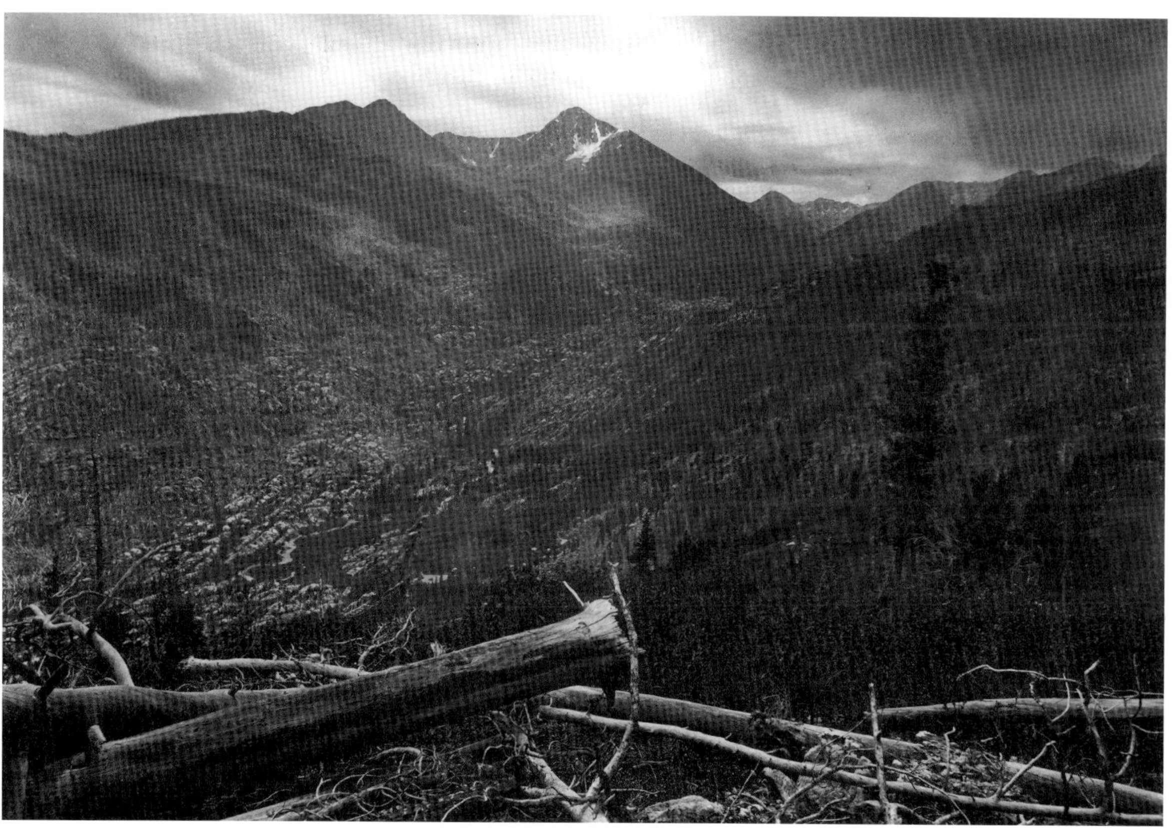

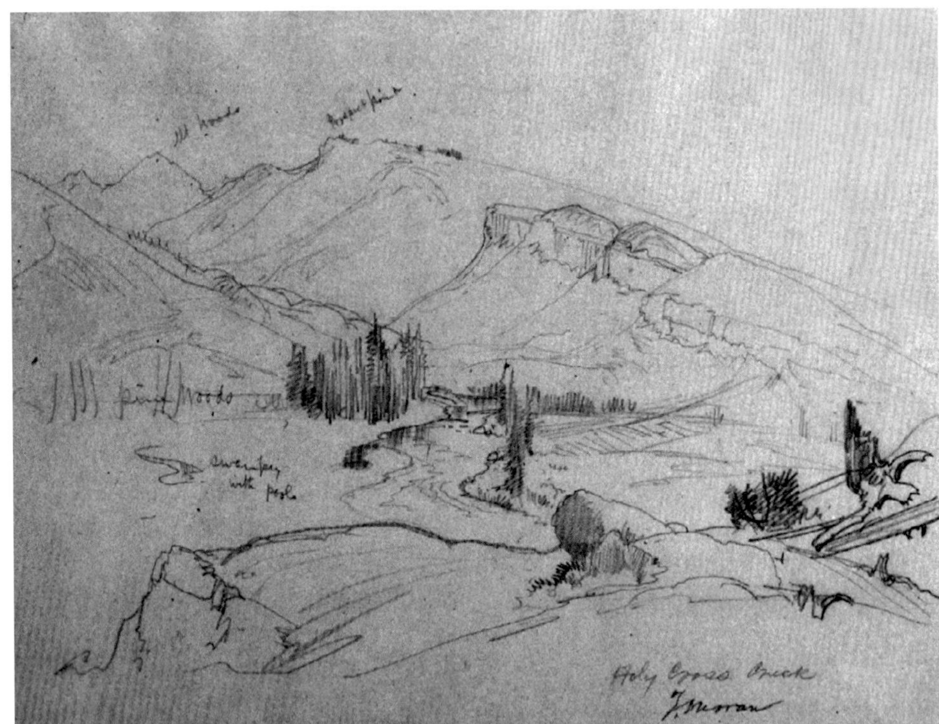

FIGURE 101. Thomas Moran, *Holy Cross Creek,* 1874, pencil on paper, 9 7/8 × 12 13/16 in. (25.1 × 32.6 cm). Jefferson National Expansion Memorial, St. Louis (5858)

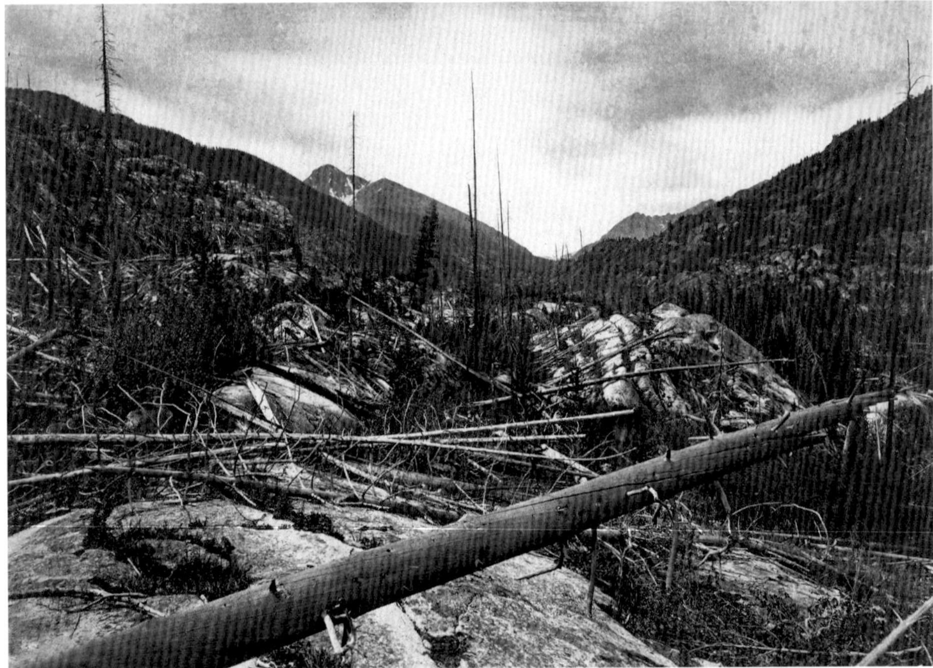

FIGURE 102. William Henry Jackson, *Roches Mountonées, Mountain of the Holy Cross,* 1874, photograph from Moran's studio collection. Gilcrease Museum, Tulsa, Oklahoma

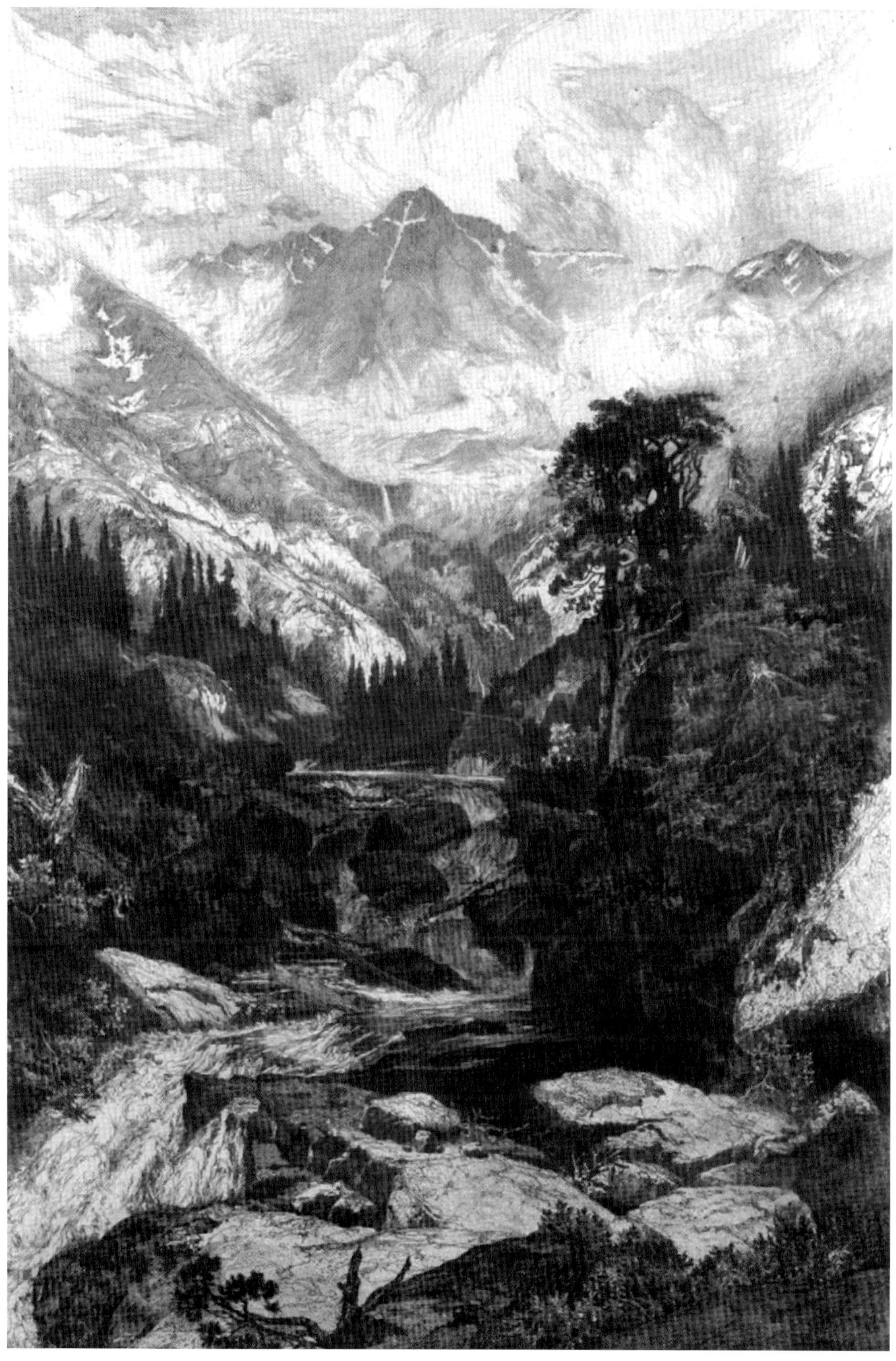

FIGURE 103. Thomas Moran, *Mountain of the Holy Cross, Colorado,* 1888, etching, 30⅝ × 21¾ in. (77.8 × 55.2 cm). Jefferson National Expansion Memorial, St. Louis (4279)

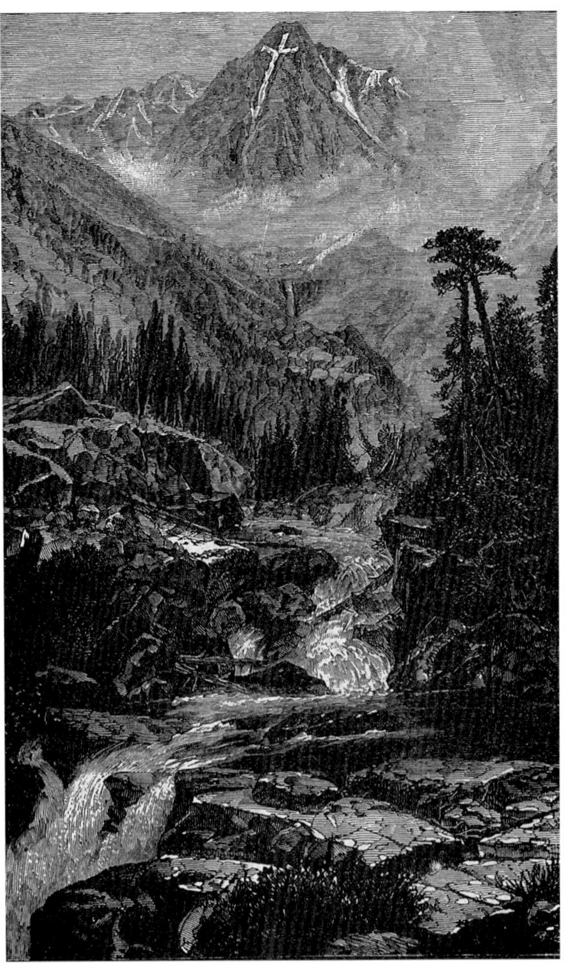

FIGURE 104. After Thomas Moran, *Mountain of the Holy Cross*, 1880s, wood engraving, ca. 6½ × 4½ in. (16.5 × 11.4 cm), in *Tourist Tickets from Chicago and St. Louis to the Rocky Mountains*, Passenger Department, Chicago and Alton Railroad, 1884. Warshaw Collection of Business Americana — Railroads, Archives Center, National Museum of American History, Smithsonian Institution

first two were purchased by Congress for the U.S. Capitol), he did submit *The Mountain of the Holy Cross* to the Centennial Exposition in Philadelphia in 1876 and asked that Congress loan the other two to the exhibition, a request that was unfortunately denied.[61] The three works were first publicly linked in my book, *Thomas Moran and the Surveying of the American West*, and then actually displayed together for the first time in the 1997 Thomas Moran retrospective exhibition at the National Gallery of Art in Washington, D.C., and the Gilcrease Museum in Tulsa (fig. 35).

Moran continued to paint the Mountain of the Holy Cross into the 1880s. An original etching (fig. 103) and a design for a Prang Christmas card (fig. 161) reveal its continuing relevance for his work and echo many of the elements of the 1875 painting (fig. 34). The subject's Christian symbolism would also become intertwined with western commerce during this era, as well, after Dr. William Bell, an English physician and vice president of the Denver and Rio Grande Railway (D&RG), purchased the large oil version of *The Mountain of the Holy Cross* and installed it in a special skylit niche in his home in Manitou Springs, Colorado. Bell and the D&RG were fashioning Manitou as a health resort, and he displayed the painting for years as an almost public shrine. When the creek flowing from the snowy cross is understood as holy water, it powerfully symbolized the efficacy of the "water cure" that was Manitou's regimen for a host of ailments, from tuberculosis to hysteria.[62] To advertise its services, the D&RG reproduced Moran's image in guidebooks, advertisements, and other promotional materials even into the early twentieth century (figs. 104–106). Eventually the Mountain of the Holy Cross became an actual pilgrimage site and representations of it appeared on all sorts of printed materials, including playing cards, the masthead for the *Rocky Mountain Herald* newspaper in Denver, and a U.S. postage stamp as late as 1951.[63] The mountain itself was named a national monument by presidential proclamation in 1929, although this status was revoked in 1950 because of declining visitation and the fact that the cross's right arm had eroded, diminishing the formation. It remains today a landmark within the Holy Cross National Forest.

THE MOSQUITO TRAIL, ROCKY MOUNTAINS OF COLORADO

Moran painted four Colorado subjects for Louis Prang, but only two were included in *The Yellowstone National Park*. Considering Pike's Peak's fame, it may be surprising that Prang chose instead the mountainous view *Mosquito Trail* (fig. 107), a work that is compositionally linked in the portfolio to the other summit scenes, *The Lower Yellowstone Range* and *The Summit of the Sierras. Mosquito Trail* has long been considered a rather generic alpine view of the Rocky Mountains, but it actually portrays a specific site, a route called Mosquito Pass that links Leadville and Fairplay, Colorado. Although the terrain there is exceptionally rugged, Mosquito Trail was the main stage road between Denver and Leadville until 1881, and, at 13,185 feet, it is today the highest open mountain pass in the United States accessible to two-way traffic.[64] A recent Web site notes that the name "Musquito" derived from a nearby mining camp, founded in 1861 between Park City and the London Mine. In a meeting to name the fledgling community (which no longer exists), "someone noticed a mosquito squashed between the pages of one of the city record books."[65] A misspelling rendered the town "Musquito," and, indeed, Moran replicated this spelling in his ledger entry about the Prang watercolor.[66]

In the Prang portfolio, Hayden identified the mountains in

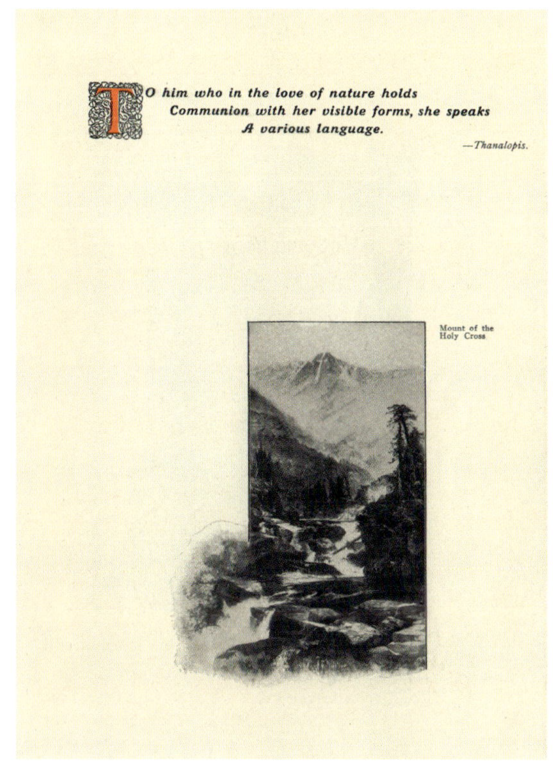

FIGURE 105. After Thomas Moran, *Mount of the Holy Cross,* ca. 1906, photomechanical book illustration in *With Nature in Colorado,* Passenger Department, Denver and Rio Grande Railway, 1906. Warshaw Collection of Business Americana — Railroads, Archives Center, National Museum of American History, Smithsonian Institution

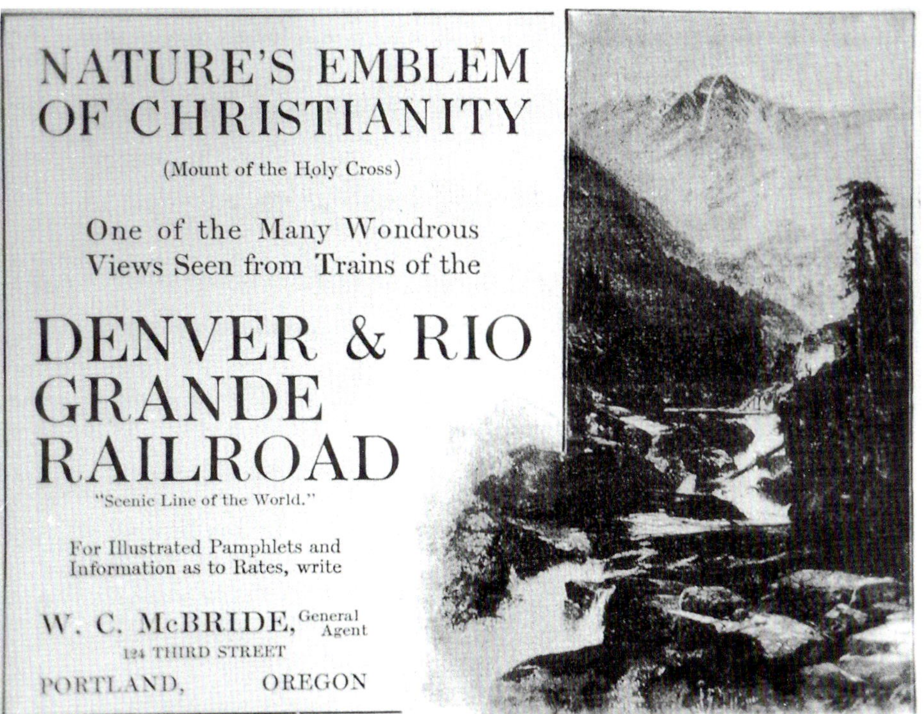

FIGURE 106. After Thomas Moran, *Nature's Emblem of Christianity,* 1906, magazine advertisement, *Pacific Monthly,* 1906. Gilcrease Museum, Tulsa, Oklahoma

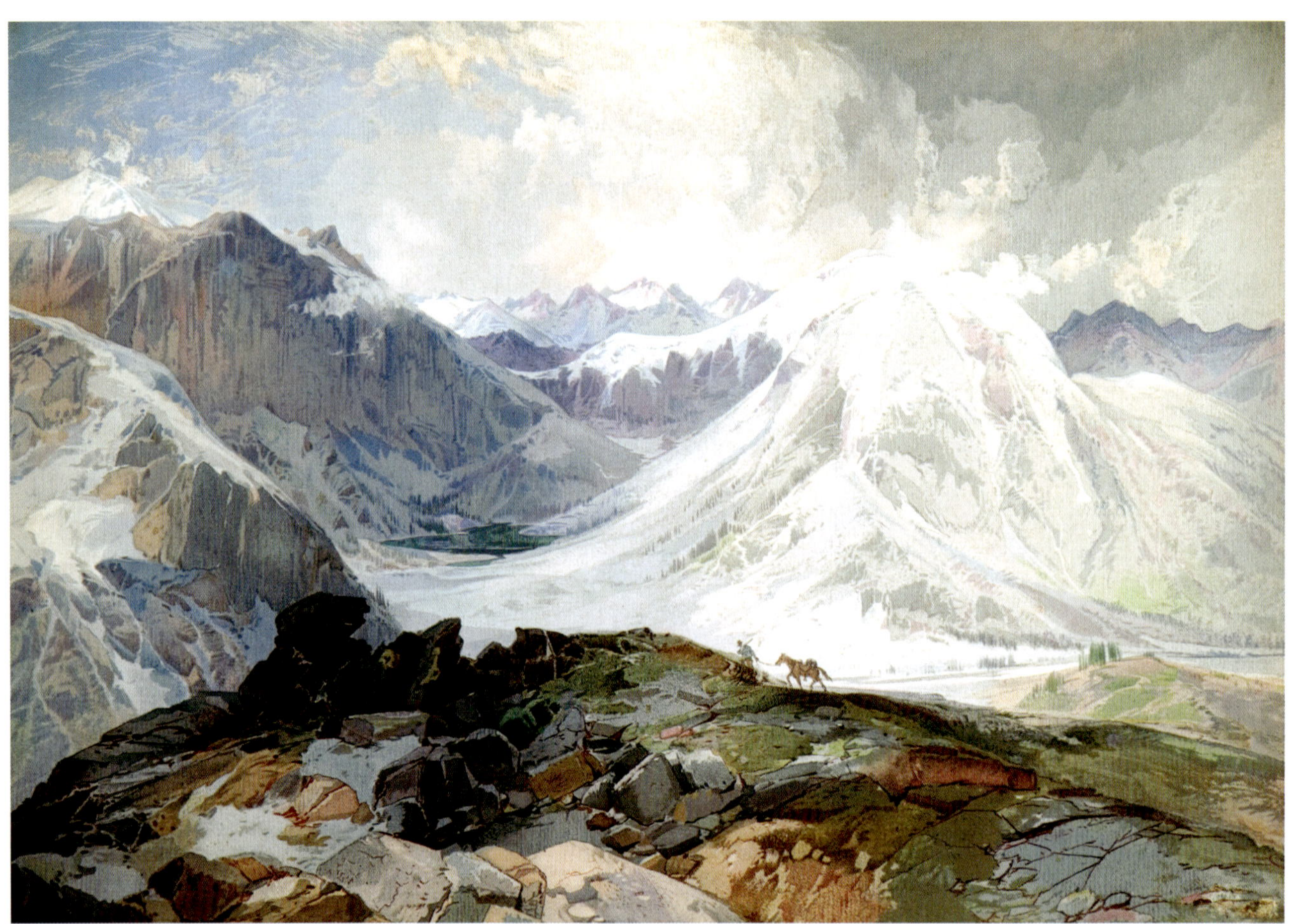

FIGURE 107. After Thomas Moran, *The Mosquito Trail, Rocky Mountains of Colorado,* 1875, chromolithograph, 9¾ × 14¼ in. (24.8 × 36.2 cm). Joslyn Art Museum, Omaha, gift of Gail and Michael Yanney and Lisa and Bill Roskens

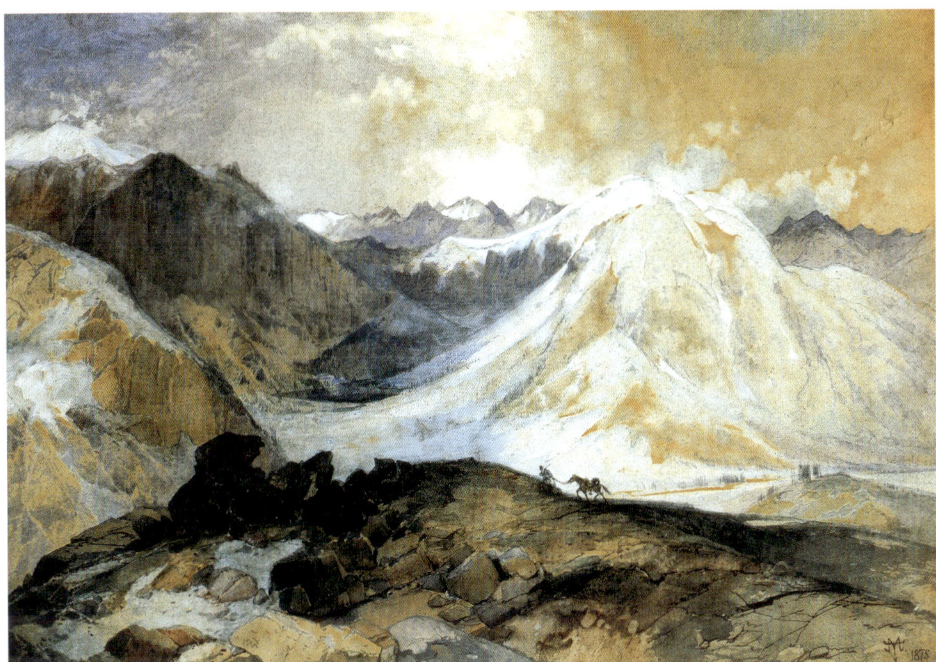

FIGURE 108. Thomas Moran, *Mosquito Trail, Rocky Mountains of Colorado*, 1875, pencil, watercolor, and opaque color, 9¾ × 14¼ in. (24.8 × 35.2 cm). Private collection, New York

Mosquito Trail as the "great Park Range, which forms the west wall of the South Park," and noted that the water in the middle ground was "the beautiful Twin Lakes" to the west. He went on to name the surrounding peaks, most of which reach above 14,000 feet, including Holy Cross. The Twin Lakes' appearance in this chromo is significant since one of the other watercolors Moran made for Prang was *Upper Twin Lake, Colorado*. Had it been included in the publication, Moran would have essentially been moving the viewer from a distant point of view in *Mosquito Trail* to a close-up perspective on the lake in *Upper Twin Lake*, a linking not unlike the chromos of Tower Falls that depict it from two different vantage points.[67]

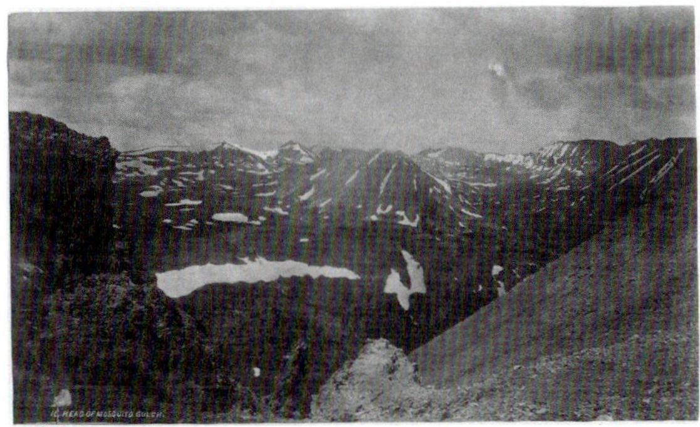

FIGURE 109. William Henry Jackson, *Head of Mosquito Gulch*, 1873, albumen print. George Eastman House, Rochester, New York (74:0041:0037)

Although there are a number of field sketches from many different sites in Moran's oeuvre that have similar compositions to *Mosquito Trail* and Jackson also produced several views of the area, including one with similarities to Moran's image (fig. 109), no single source has emerged for the Prang composition. At the same time, several annotated drawings dated from August 23 to August 26, 1874, depict the mountains around the Twin Lakes area (fig. 110). With the location of Mosquito Pass confirmed, these views can therefore be associated with the watercolor and chromolithograph of *Mosquito Trail* (figs. 107 and 108).[68] One of these (fig. 111) depicts a cabin in the foreground where the rocky

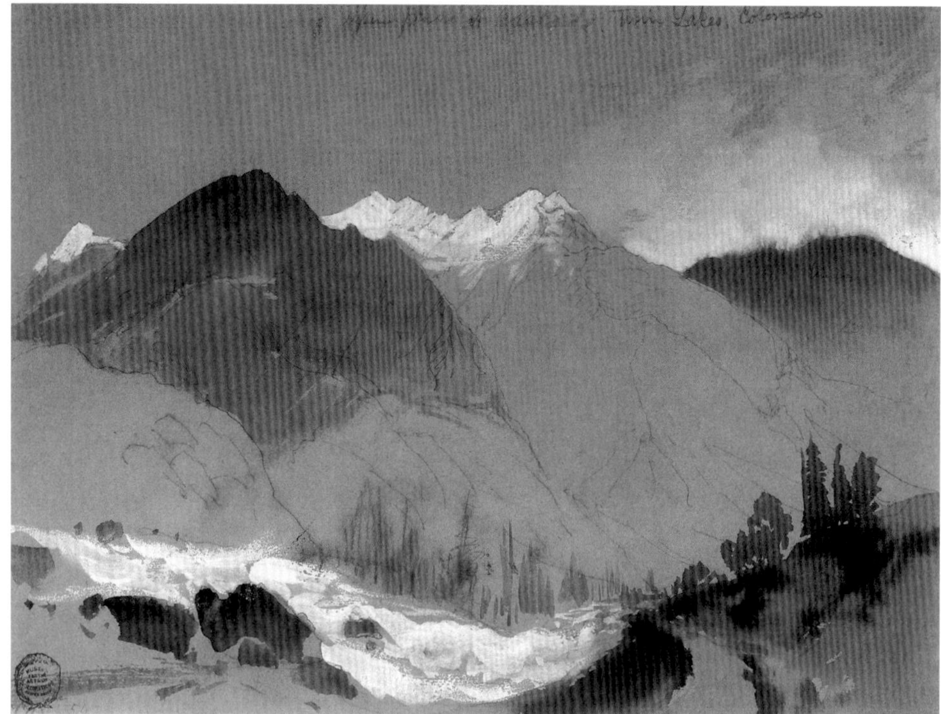

FIGURE 110. Thomas Moran, *Alpine Pass at Cascade, Twin Lakes, Colorado,* 1892, watercolor, white gouache and graphite on gray paper, 9 3/8 × 12 5/8 in. (23.8 × 32.1 cm). Cooper-Hewitt National Design Museum, Smithsonian Institution, gift of Thomas Moran, 1917-17-71 (photo: Matt Flynn)

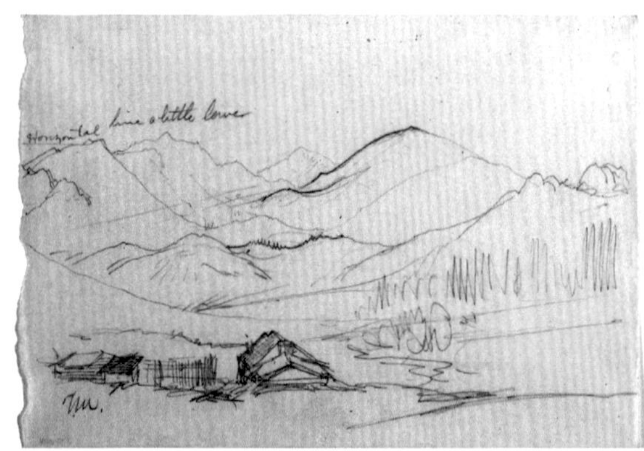

FIGURE 111. Thomas Moran, *Holy Cross Trip* [descriptive], 1874, pencil, 5½ × 8 in. (14 × 20.3 cm). Jefferson National Expansion Memorial, St. Louis (5857)

rise looms in the final composition. In the chromo, Moran substituted the lone figure leading his packhorse to suggest the travails of traversing the high country and represent the miners who worked the rich gold and silver mines that abounded about the time he visited the area with the Hayden survey in 1874.

THE SUMMIT OF THE SIERRAS

Although the Sierra Nevada Mountains are most often associated with California, Moran's title for this view he created for Prang was *Summit of the Sierras, Nevada* (figs. 112 and 113). It is difficult to pinpoint the exact location of the view, but the photograph of Mount Shasta and Shastina with the intervening Whitney Glacier, taken by Carleton Watkins on the Clarence King survey in 1870 (fig. 114), compares to contours of the two central peaks in Moran's portrayal.

Moran himself traveled on the transcontinental railroad through the Sierra Range in the summer of 1872 on his way to California. Upon his return, he produced a series of designs for *Picturesque America,* among them a wood engraving, *Summit of the Sierras,* that appeared in the article "The Plains and the Sierras" (fig. 115).[69] The illustration is extremely similar to the chromolithograph, altered only in its slightly more accessible foreground and the small group of trees that appear on the middle left edge.

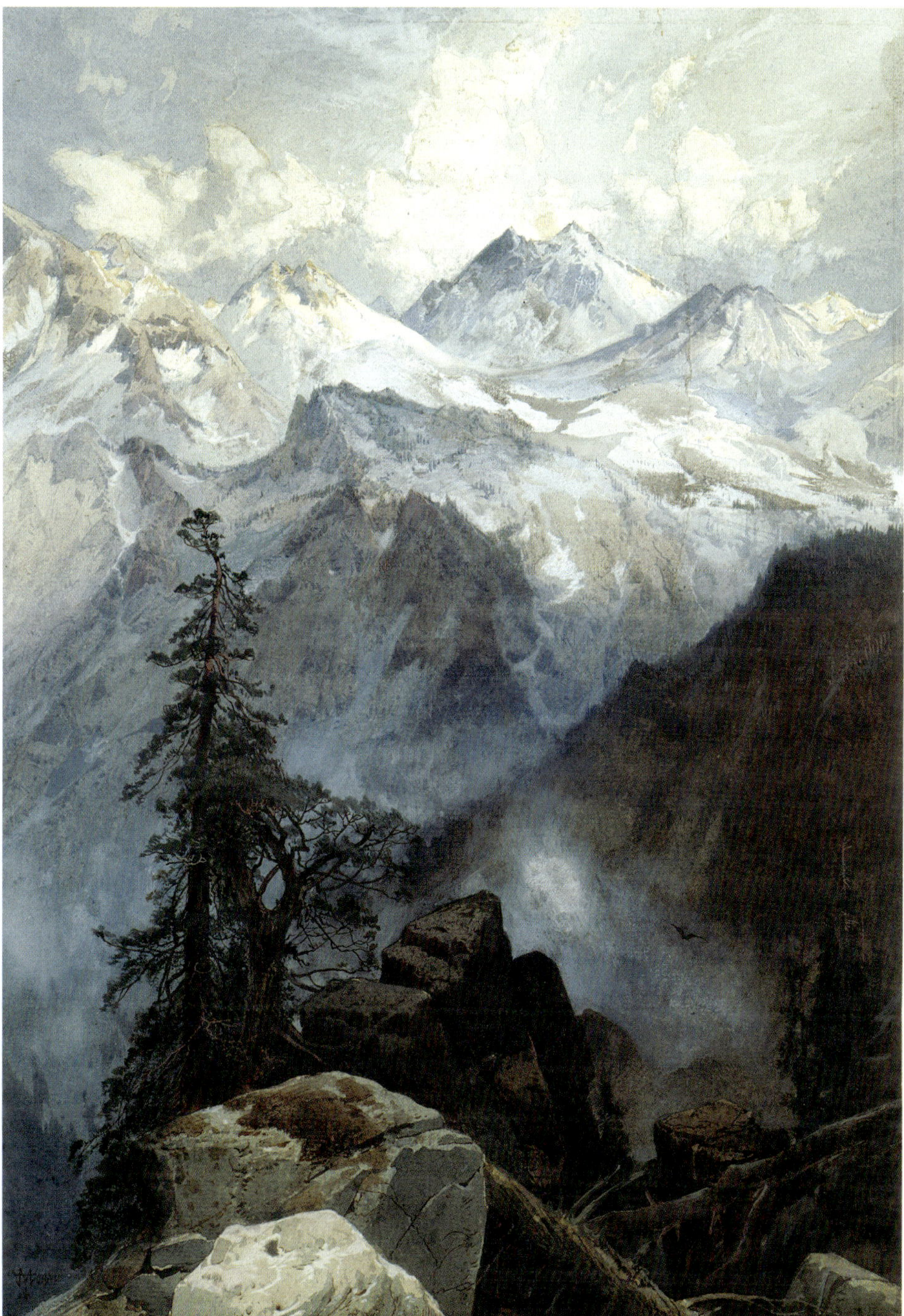

FIGURE 112. Thomas Moran, *Summit of the Sierras, Nevada*, 1874, watercolor and opaque color, 14 1/5 × 9 4/5 in. (36 × 25 cm). The Art Institute of Chicago, gift of Mrs. Byron Harvey (1965.852)

FIGURE 113. After Thomas Moran, *The Summit of the Sierras*, ca. 1875, chromolithograph, $3\frac{5}{8} \times 9\frac{5}{8}$ in. (34.6 × 24.4 cm). Joslyn Art Museum, Omaha, gift of Gail and Michael Yanney and Lisa and Bill Roskens

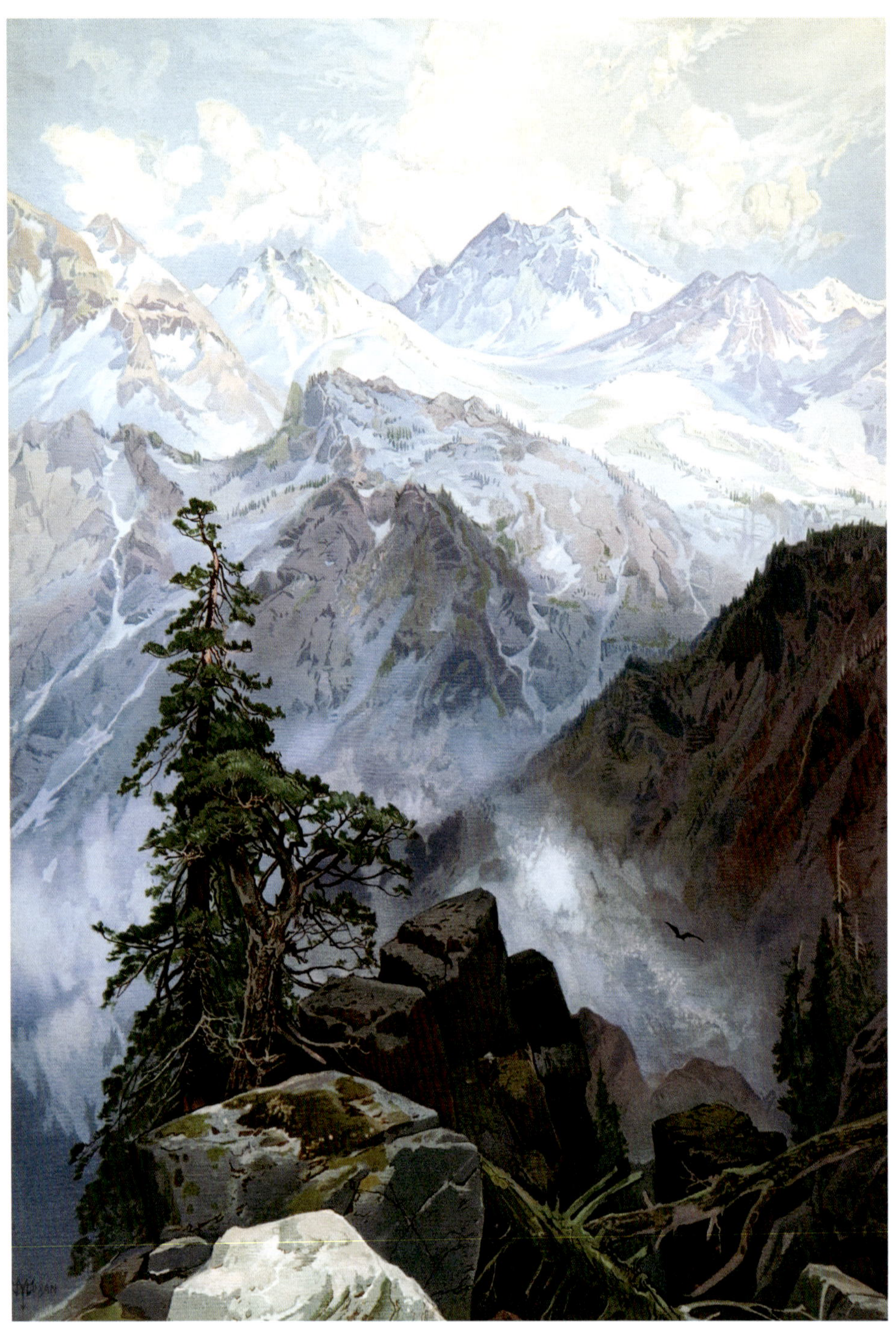

Moran did not make use of his California and Nevada experiences for paintings as much as he might have, probably because Albert Bierstadt, Thomas Hill, and others had already "claimed" much of that territory by the time he visited there. As one of his relatively few images of the region, therefore, *The Summit of the Sierras* is distinctive. Furthermore, it is among the most classically beautiful images of the Prang series. The watercolor from which the chromo was drawn today resides in the collection of the Art Institute of Chicago and is an expressive example of Moran's virtuosity in the medium, revealing, for example, a much more subtle array of color and value than the final chromolithograph.

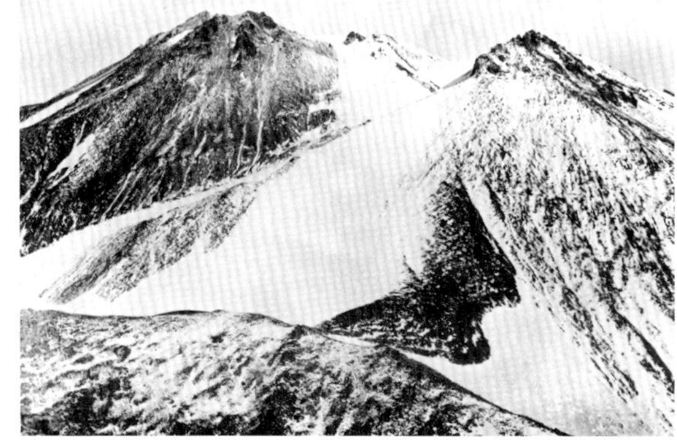

FIGURE 114. Carleton Watkins, *Mount Shasta and Shastina with Whitney Glacier*, 1870, photograph, United States Geological Survey Photographic Library (Kingp063)

As a mountainous scene from the heights, *The Summit of the Sierras* shares its lofty perspective most especially with *The Lower Yellowstone Range* and *The Mosquito Trail*, which immediately precedes it in the portfolio, but its point of view from a prospect is also found in *The Grand Cañon of the Yellowstone* and *The Mountain of the Holy Cross*. Had *Lake Donner* been included in the final series, it would also have added to this theme, the "magisterial gaze" that was such an important element in *The Yellowstone National Park*'s conceptual significance and its appeal to American audiences. *Lake Donner* also, of course, portrayed a site in the Sierra Nevada and would have been an important geographical link to *The Summit of the Sierras*.

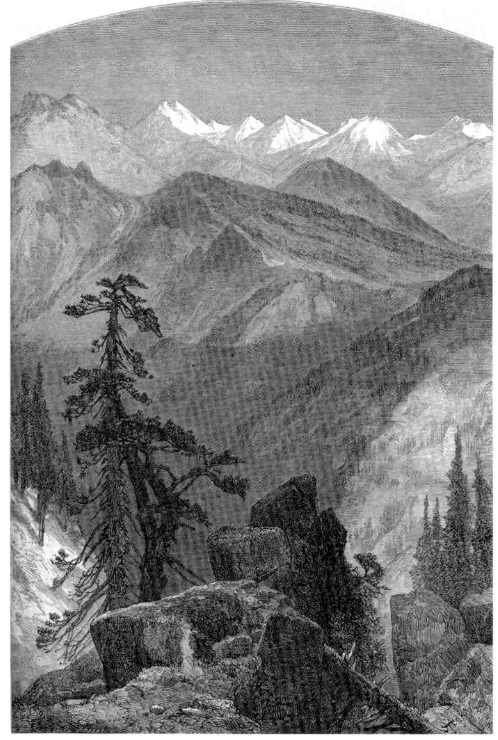

FIGURE 115. After Thomas Moran, *Summit of the Sierras*, ca. 1873, wood engraving, *Picturesque America* (New York: D. Appleton & Co., 1874), 2: 199

THE GREAT FALLS OF SNAKE RIVER, IDAHO TERRITORY

The Great Falls of Snake River, better known as Shoshone Falls, is located in south-central Idaho, southeast of Boise and just outside the town of Twin Falls. The Snake is a major tributary of the Columbia, with a volume greater even than the Colorado River, and Shoshone is its most prominent cataract. Because of its wide breadth and its vertical drop of 212 feet, the falls were called the Niagara of the West.[70] In 1907, the formation was altered, however, by a hydroelectric dam that significantly diminishes the volume of the falls, except in times of extremely high water, and consequently the view Moran presented in *The Great Falls of Snake River* (fig. 116) is today a rare sight.

When Moran created the watercolor for Prang (fig. 117), he had not yet visited Shoshone Falls, although he had traveled near the site and crossed the Snake River repeatedly as he traveled through southern Idaho on his way to his rendezvous with Hayden's expedition in 1871. He also encountered the Snake River on his 1879 trip to Idaho to see the Tetons, but that did not include a visit to the falls either.[71] He finally saw them in 1900 and went on to produce a major oil of the

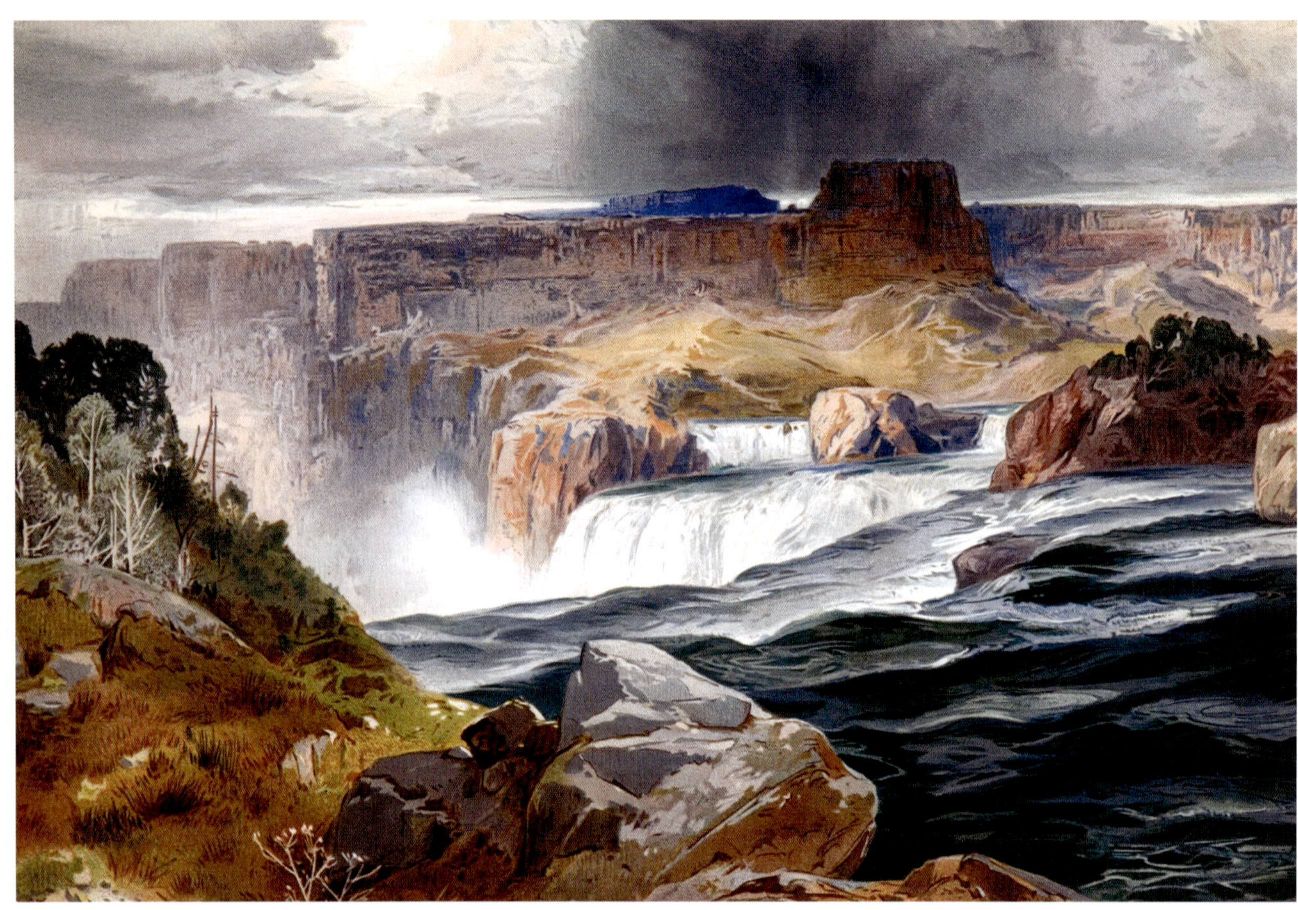

FIGURE 116. After Thomas Moran, *The Great Falls of Snake River, Idaho Territory,* ca. 1875, chromolithograph, 8 × 12 in. (20.3 × 30.5 cm). Joslyn Art Museum, Omaha, gift of Gail and Michael Yanney and Lisa and Bill Roskens

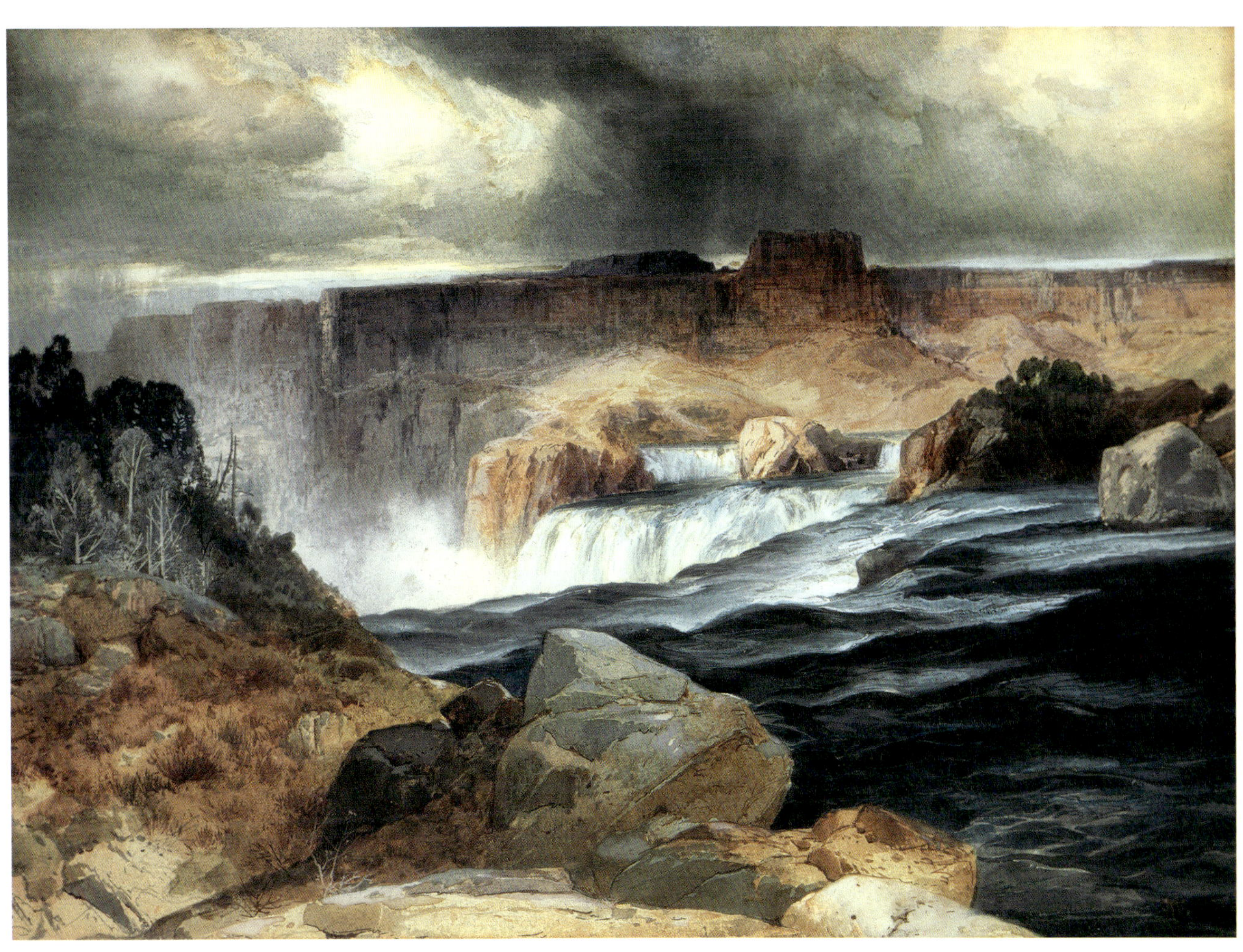

FIGURE 117. Thomas Moran, *Shoshone Falls, Snake River, Idaho,* ca. 1874–1875, watercolor on paper board, 10 × 14 in. (25.4 × 35.6 cm). Chrysler Museum of Art, Norfolk, Virginia, gift of Hugh Gordon Miller (60.52.47)

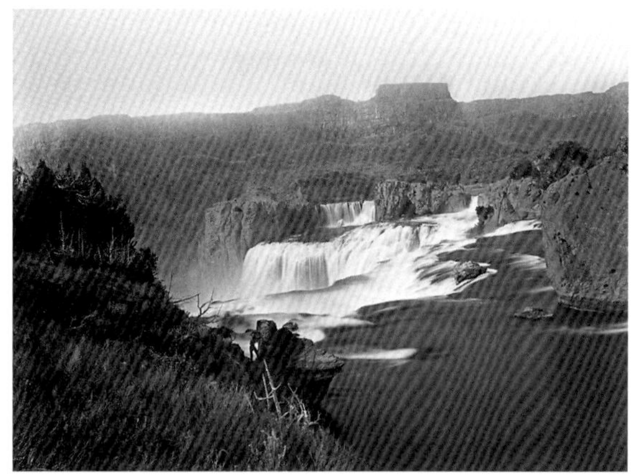

FIGURE 118. Timothy O'Sullivan, *Shoshone Falls, Snake River, Idaho, View across the Top of the Falls*, 1874, albumen print, 8 × 10¾ in. (20.3 × 27.3 cm). National Archives, Still Picture Division (77-KS-4-118)

subject (*Shoshone Falls*, 1900, fig. 36) that echoes Frederic Edwin Church's heralded painting of *Niagara* (1857, Corcoran Gallery of Art) in a much more monumental format (6 × 11 feet), echoing his own earlier "Big Pictures" of Yellowstone, the Grand Canyon, and the Mountain of the Holy Cross.[72]

For his 1874–1875 Prang watercolor, Moran worked from the photographs that Timothy O'Sullivan had taken in 1868 during his work for Clarence King's survey (fig. 118).[73] Moran probably also read the description of the cataract in King's *Mountaineering in the Sierra Nevada* (Boston, 1872), a text Hayden liberally quoted in the Prang portfolio:

> A few miles in front the smooth surface of the plain was broken by a ragged, zigzag line of black, which marked the edge of the farther wall of the Snake Cañon. A dull, throbbing sound greeted us. Its pulsations were deep, and seemed to proceed from the ground beneath our feet. . . . We looked down into a broad, circular excavation, three-quarters of a mile in diameter, and nearly seven hundred feet deep. . . . the wall of the gorge opposite us, like the cliff at our feet, sank in perpendicular bluffs nearly to the level of the river. . . . A horizon as level as the sea; a circling wall, whose sharp edges were here and there battlemented in huge, fortress-like masses; a broad river, smooth and unruffled, flowing quietly into the middle of the scene, and then plunging into a labyrinth of rocks, tumbling over a precipice two hundred feet high, and flowing westward in a still, deep current, disappears behind a black promontory.[74]

Since O'Sullivan's image was in black-and-white, King's vivid description of the topography's coloration was probably especially useful to Moran, as he had never seen the place himself:

> It is a strange and savage scene: a monotony of pale blue sky; olive and grey stretches of desert, frowning walls of jetty lava, deep beryl-green of river-stretches, reflecting here and there the intense solemnity of the cliffs, and in the centre a dazzling sheet of foam. . . . Upon the foam of the cataract one point of the rock cast a cobalt-blue shadow. Where the river flowed around the western promontory, it was wholly in shadow, and of a deep sea-green. . . . Dead barrenness is the whole sentiment of the scene. The mere suggestion of the trees clinging here and there along the walls, serves to heighten rather than relieve the forbidding gloom of the place. Nor does the flashing whiteness, where the river tears itself among the rocky islands, or rolls in spray down the cliff, brighten the aspect. In contrast with its brilliancy, the rocks seem darker and more wild.[75]

As King noted, the falls' brilliant drama was heightened by the oppressiveness of the barren, arid landscape. It was an effect noted by other visitors, including one in 1888 who wrote, "There was never a day during our Shoshone visit that, for a moment the region did not become a hideous reality from which I longed to escape."[76] Moran's treatment, however, renders the scene lively and even inviting with its colorful rocks and stormy sky that contrasts vividly to King's "monotony of pale blue." This, as Peter Boag has pointed out, is more akin to Yellowstone and southwestern landscapes than the "olive and grey stretches of desert" that actually surround Shoshone Falls.[77]

King concluded his article by comparing Shoshone Falls to the two most well-known American cataracts, Niagara and Yosemite. Characterizing Shoshone as a "Dantean gulf" in contrast to the more welcoming landscapes that surround the other two falls, he wrote, "You ride upon a waste—the pale earth stretched in desolation. Suddenly you stand upon a brink. As if the earth had yawned, black walls flank the abyss. Deep in the bed a great river fights its way through the labyrinth of blackened ruins, and plunges in foaming whiteness over a cliff of lava. You turn from the brink as from a frightful glimpse of the Inferno, and when you have gone a mile the earth seems to have closed again."[78] The sinister associations that the scene evoked were not unlike those prompted by Yellowstone's unsettling features, and this was an important, if subtle, implication that linked the subjects in the Prang portfolio. Despite these foreboding qualities, Shoshone Falls regularly appeared in print as early as 1866, and the site became something of a tourist destination by the mid-1870s. At the same time, however, since it was not served by a railroad and because its surroundings were exceptionally stark, the waterfall did not become a major attraction.[79]

As Linda Hults has discussed, Shoshone Falls was frequently compared to Niagara Falls, and Moran's interest in the western cataract was undoubtedly influenced by the countless representations of Niagara that dated back at least to 1760.[80] Moran saw the most famous of them all, Frederic Edwin Church's *Niagara,* at the 1867 Exposition Universelle in Paris, an exhibition that also included his own *Children of the Mountain* (1866, Anschutz Collection, Denver). Moran proclaimed Church's oil the most wonderful painting ever created and modeled his late monumental oil, *Shoshone Falls* (fig. 36), on its example.[81] As Moran's daughter later recalled, when he finally visited Shoshone in 1900, he was "tremendously impressed by the Falls, and told me . . . that not since his first sight of the Yellowstone and the Grand Canyon had he been so stirred and thrilled . . . the Fall was in full water[,] there were no houses nor people to spoil the grandeur of the mighty torrent of water[,] and it was beyond words magnificent."[82]

Moran's earlier views of the falls, including the Prang version and a similar, vertical wood engraving in *The Aldine* in 1876 (fig. 119), are more intimate than the monumental oil of 1900, and not simply in their smaller size.[83] They offer the viewer a

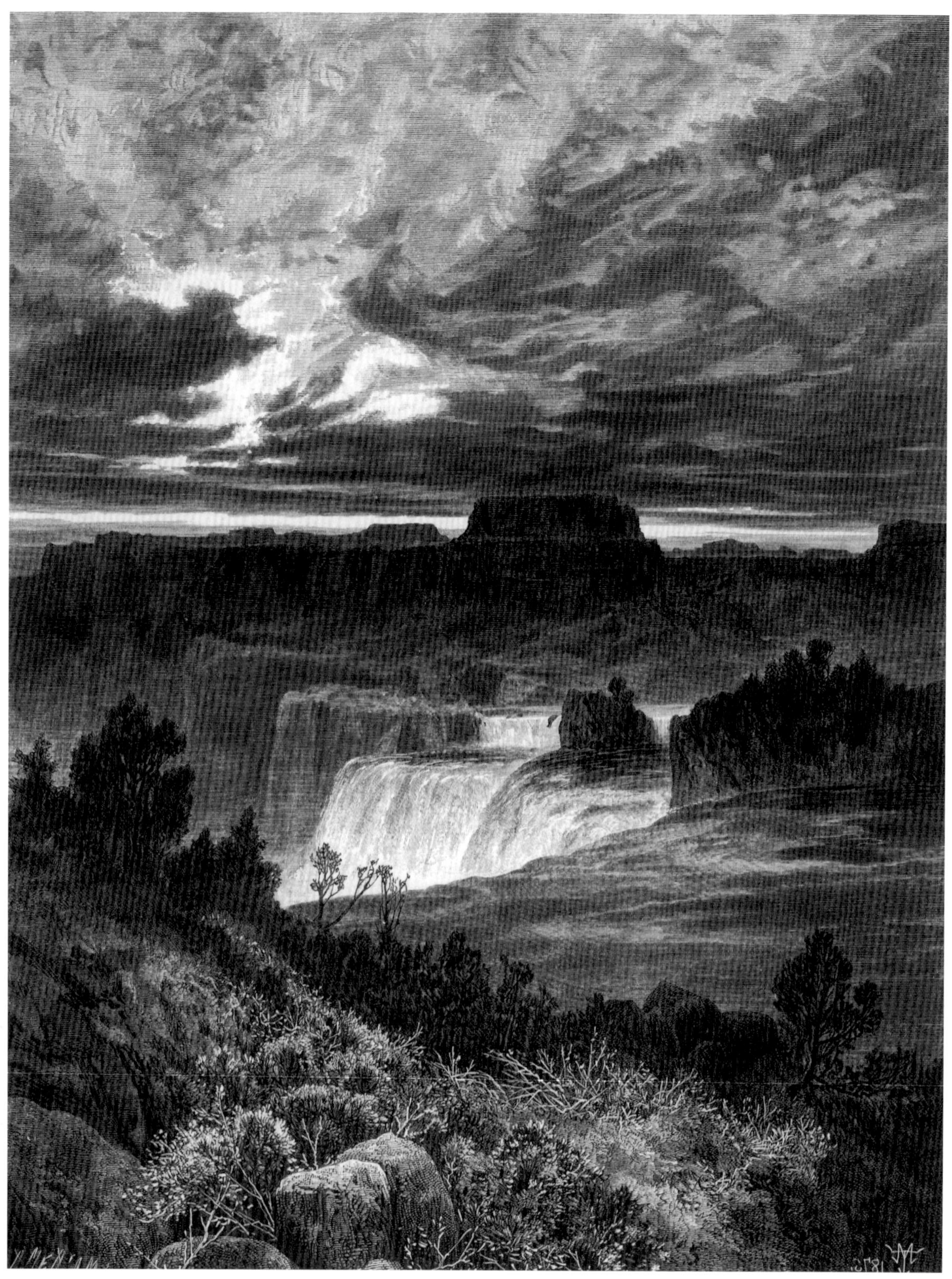

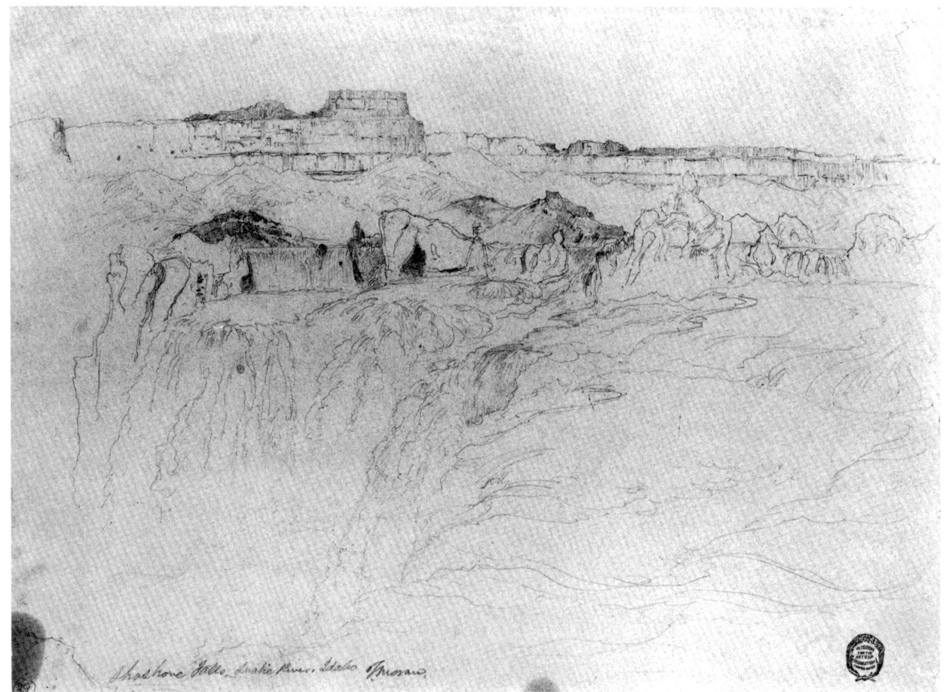

FIGURE 120. Thomas Moran, *Shoshone Falls, Snake River, Idaho,* graphite on blue-gray paper, 10 13/16 × 14 15/16 in. (27.5 × 38 cm). Cooper-Hewitt National Design Museum, Smithsonian Institution, gift of Thomas Moran (1917-17-29) (photo: John Parnell)

more secure foreground on the lower right, and their point of view is slightly upriver, lessening the drama of the falls as it plummets over the brink. These features render the sublimity of the scene, so useful in the monumental version, more picturesque and more appropriate for a handheld viewing experience.

Within the Prang commission, *The Great Falls of Snake River* echoes other waterfalls, including those in *The Grand Cañon of the Yellowstone, Tower Falls and Sulphur Mountain, The Towers of Tower Falls,* and the unpublished *Upper Falls of the Yellowstone.* Of these, it is probably closest to *The Towers of Tower Falls,* since that work also portrays a river just before it plummets and was a formation infamous for satanic associations.

An undated Moran drawing in the Cooper-Hewitt Museum (fig. 120) closely resembles the Prang version of *The Great Falls of Snake River,* and, although probably done on the artist's 1900 visit, the image reveals his continuing interest in the point of view of the Prang watercolor he had done twenty-five years earlier. Had Moran managed to make the visit earlier, in the heyday of the "Big Picture" era, his immense *Shoshone Falls* and the site it depicts would probably have become as famous as Yellowstone and the Grand Canyon.[84] The painting would have catapulted the site to landmark status in the American West and rendered the Prang chromolithograph even more noteworthy than it is today.

FIGURE 119. After Thomas Moran, *The Falls of the Snake River,* ca. 1876, wood engraving, "Idaho Scenery," *The Aldine* 8 (June 1876): 195. Courtesy of Boston Public Library, Print Room

VALLEY OF THE BABBLING WATERS, SOUTHERN UTAH

The imprecise title of *Valley of the Babbling Waters* (fig. 121) has rendered it less well understood than if Moran had named it "Canyon of the Rio Virgin" or "Little Zion Valley." The remarkable sandstone buttes the chromolithograph depicts lie along the Virgin River in the area of southwestern Utah now known as Zion National Park. Moran first visited that spectacular region in 1873 as he traveled with John Wesley Powell's federally sponsored expedition through the tributaries of the Colorado River and on to the Grand Canyon in Arizona. Although the scene is highly stylized in Moran's presentation, it depicts the central portion of the park, an area now called Zion Canyon, and the central butte has been identified as the one known today as Angel's Landing.[85] Moran's composition is more of a compilation of features than a portrayal of a specific point, but it appears to have been roughly positioned from what is now called Emerald Pools Trail.

Moran's letters to his wife in 1873 told of their side trip to the Rio Virgin area as the survey party journeyed south toward the Grand Canyon, but he offered few details about the scenery he seems to have found so artistically intriguing:

> In my last letter to you I mentioned, that as we could not get away from here [southern Utah] for a few days, we were going on a trip of a couple of days to the Cañon of the Virgin. We left on Friday morning, travelled about 20 miles and camped for a night in view of the cliffs. . . . The next morning we started for the cliffs about 8 miles distant where we arrived about 10 o'clock. The view was very fine and I made one sketch. We started back about 1 o'clock and camped for the night in Cottonwood Cañon about 8 miles from here reaching Kanab the next morning.[86]

Moran created three watercolors of the Rio Virgin area for Prang's series, but only *Valley of the Babbling Waters,* which remains unlocated, appeared as a chromolithograph in the portfolio. All three designs, *Valley of the Babbling Waters* (fig. 122), *Temple of the Virgin, Mu-Koon-Tu-Weap Valley* (fig. 140), and *The Narrows, North Fork of the Rio Virgin, Utah* (fig. 141), were replicated in wood-engraved form in "The Scenery of Southern Utah," an April 1875 article in *The Aldine.* The first (fig. 122) is a virtual replica of the chromolithograph, and the other two are probably equally similar to the two unpublished Prang watercolors (see Chapter Four).

For both the Prang and *The Aldine* versions of *Valley of the Babbling Waters,* Moran may have referred to photographs by John (Jack) Hillers taken on the Powell expedition, although no comparable views have been identified. Several of the artist's sketches, however, contain elements of the final scene, most notably *The Cathedral/Rio Virgin* (fig. 123), which shares its basic composition, including the winding river, clump of foreground trees, distinctive angled cliffs of the canyon's right wall, and the central butte of Angel's Landing (although the sketch shows it more accurately

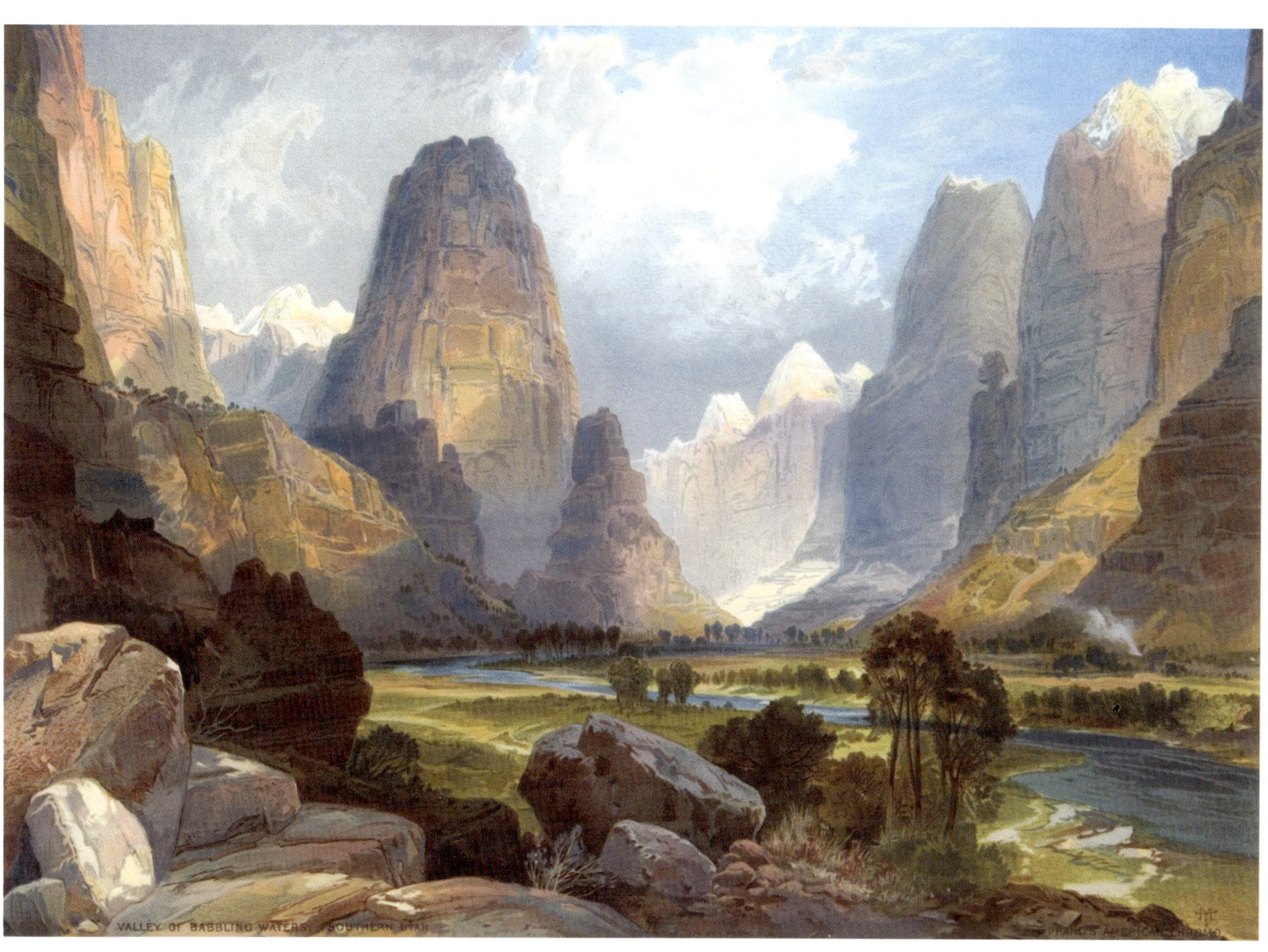

FIGURE 121. After Thomas Moran, *Valley of the Babbling Waters, Southern Utah*, ca. 1875, chromolithograph, 9¾ × 14 in. (24.8 × 35.6 cm). Joslyn Art Museum, Omaha, gift of Gail and Michael Yanney and Lisa and Bill Roskens

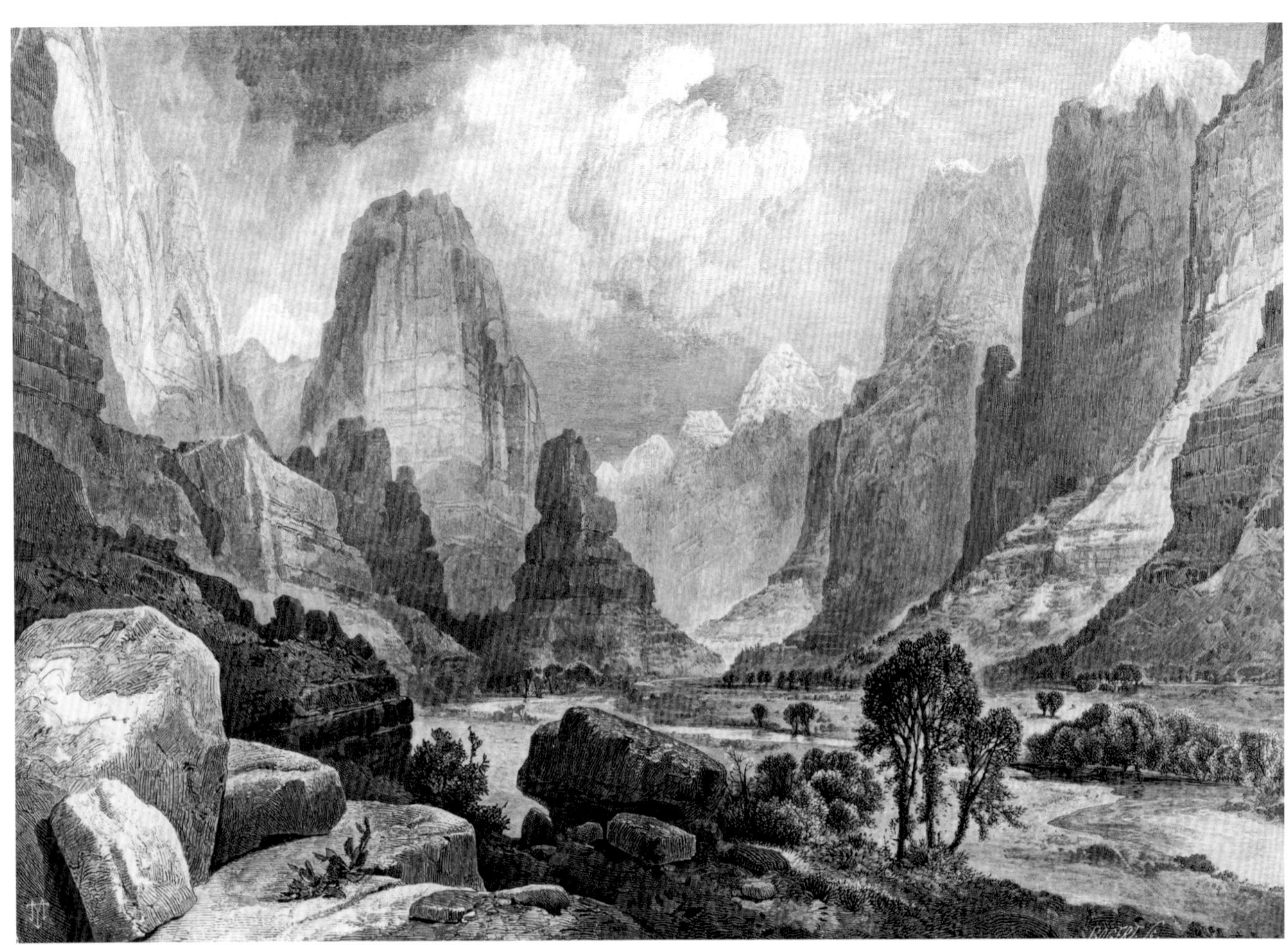

FIGURE 122. After Thomas Moran, *Valley of the Babbling Waters, Utah,* ca. 1875, wood engraving, 8⅞ × 12¾ in. (22.6 × 32.3 cm), *The Aldine* (April 1875): opposite p. 307. Gilcrease Museum, Tulsa, Oklahoma

angled). Other drawings from the valley floor (figs. 124 and 125), however, also contain elements of the finished scene, indicating that, like Moran's composite portrayal of the Grand Canyon of the Yellowstone, *Valley of the Babbling Waters* was probably a compilation from several points of view.

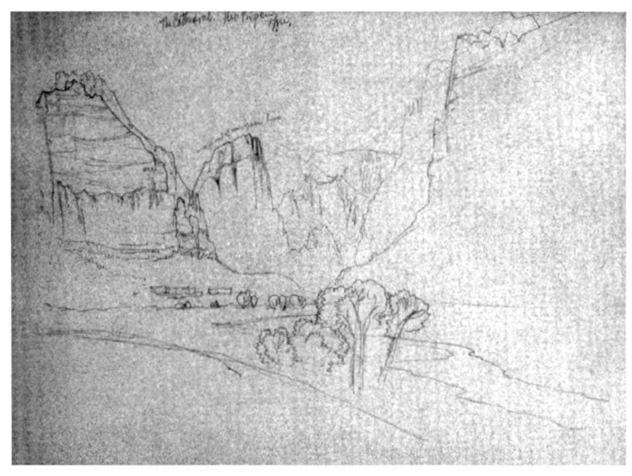

FIGURE 123. Thomas Moran, *The Cathedral/Rio Virgin*, 1873, pencil on blue wove paper, 10¾ × 15 in. (27.3 × 38.1 cm). Jefferson National Expansion Memorial, St. Louis (4244)

As Moran reported in his letter, another name for Rio Virgin canyon was *Mu-Koon-Tu-Weap*, which John Wesley Powell explained in *Scribner's Monthly* was a Paiute word for "straight canyon." Recently this has been pointed out as a linguistic misinterpretation, with the term probably closer to "red country," but the name is nevertheless still specifically associated with the North Fork of the Virgin River.[87] A related word, *Pa-ru-nu-weap*, which Powell defined as "Roaring Water Canyon," refers to the East Fork of the Virgin River, especially in the area of the Narrows. These names are relevant to the two unpublished Utah scenes from the Prang series, but also are relevant to the region's later history, since it was proclaimed Mukuntuweap National Monument in 1909. It was renamed Zion National Monument in 1918 and expanded and designated a national park the following year.[88]

With all of its unusual buttes, cliffs, and colors, *Valley of the Babbling Waters* shares some compositional similarities with *The Grand Cañon of the Yellowstone*, and its focus on towering rock formations echoes the formations in the two depictions of Tower Falls. Pinnacles and buttes were a recurrent motif for Moran, not only because such distinctive forms are landmarks throughout the West but also because they were often endowed with symbolic meaning—biblical associations such as those that fill today's Zion National Park.[89] As *The Aldine* explained, "Probably no portion of the American continent embodies more natural glories [than Utah]. . . . The mind of man cannot conceive anything in nature more truly blending the beautiful and the awful than 'Valley of the Babbling Waters,'" and "awful," of course, meant "sublime," with all of its implications of reverence and awe.[90]

THE GREAT SALT LAKE OF UTAH

The only other Utah subject that appeared in the Prang portfolio was the Great Salt Lake, the largest inland body of water west of the Mississippi that remains today a distinctive feature northeast of Salt Lake City. It extends north and westward as far as Promontory, Utah, near the historic conjunction of the Central Pacific and Union Pacific Railroads. A landlocked remnant of prehistoric Lake Bonneville, it is fed from streams originating in the surrounding mountains, but it has no outlets and maintains its level primarily through evaporation. This renders it extraordinarily saline and devoid of most life other than tiny crustaceans known as brine shrimp. At the

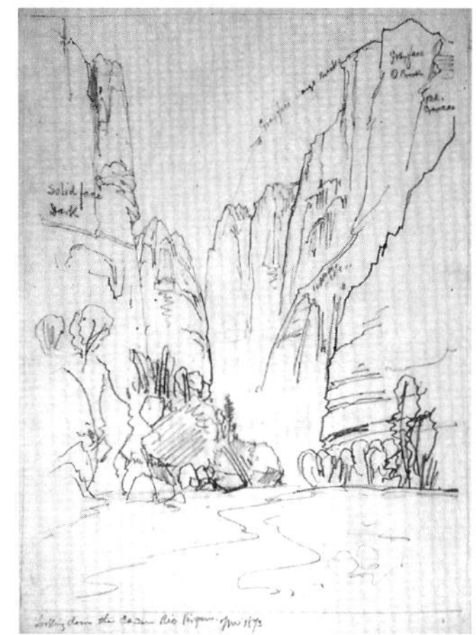

FIGURE 124. Thomas Moran, *Looking down the Cañon Rio Virgin*, 1873, pencil on paper, 15 × 10¾ in. (38.1 × 27.3 cm). Jefferson National Expansion Memorial, St. Louis (5851)

FIGURE 125. Thomas Moran, *The Canyon of the Rio Virgin, South Utah,* 1873, graphite on tan paper, 10 11/16 × 15 1/16 in. (27.2 × 38.3 cm). Cooper-Hewitt National Design Museum, Smithsonian Institution, gift of Thomas Moran (1917-17-22) (photo: Ken Pelka)

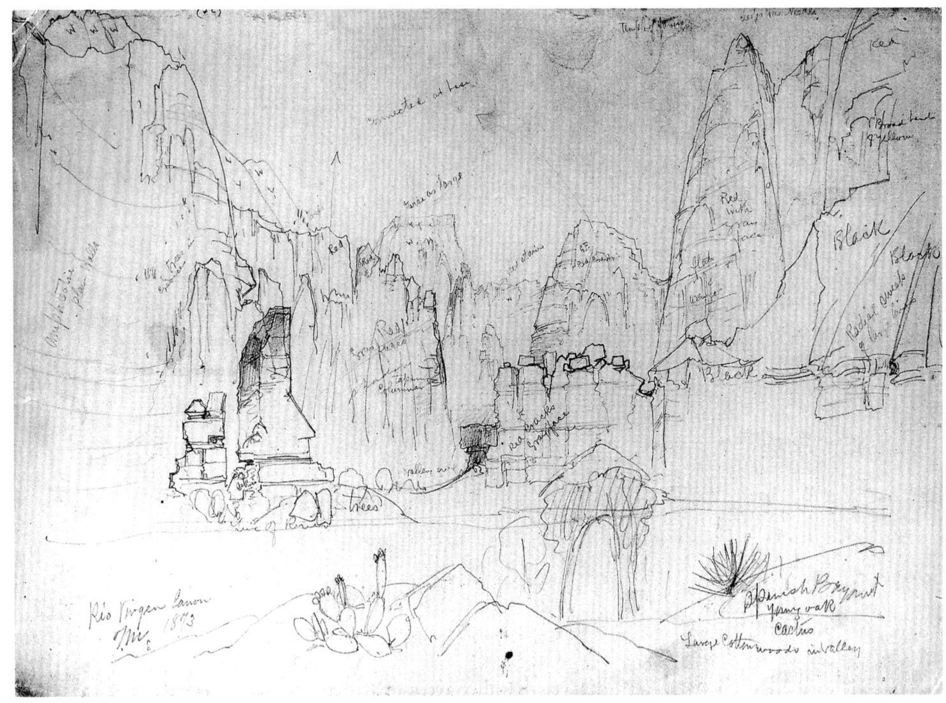

same time, it has long been a recreational site; its waters were advertised to tourists in the 1880s, and large resorts and bathhouses were built along its shores early in the twentieth century.[91]

Moran visited Salt Lake City in the summer of 1873 as he journeyed to rendezvous with John Wesley Powell's expedition to the Grand Canyon, but he did not mention the lake in his letters, nor did his fellow traveler, *New York Times* correspondent J. E. Colburn, in his newspaper columns.[92] It is not certain that Moran actually saw the lake except perhaps from a distance. But the area was already well known by the time he arrived, and he could have constructed his view from any number of visual sources or descriptions or from his own experience and imagination.

The Salt Lake Valley had been discovered by Euro-Americans in the 1820s and was settled by the Mormons in the late 1840s.[93] It had been a focus of interest for numerous topographical and geological surveys well before Moran's time and was documented in several illustrated publications.[94] The famous explorer John Charles Frémont had described the view of the lake from the mountains to the east in 1843–1844, a view that seems to correspond to Moran's watercolor for Prang (fig. 126). Frémont described the lake from there as "the object of our anxious search—the waters of the inland sea, stretching in still and solitary grandeur far beyond the limits of our vision." It was a vision realized in Moran's painting.[95]

Moran produced remarkably few sketches of the Great Salt Lake, but as with most of the other Prang images, he did several published versions of the subject that cor-

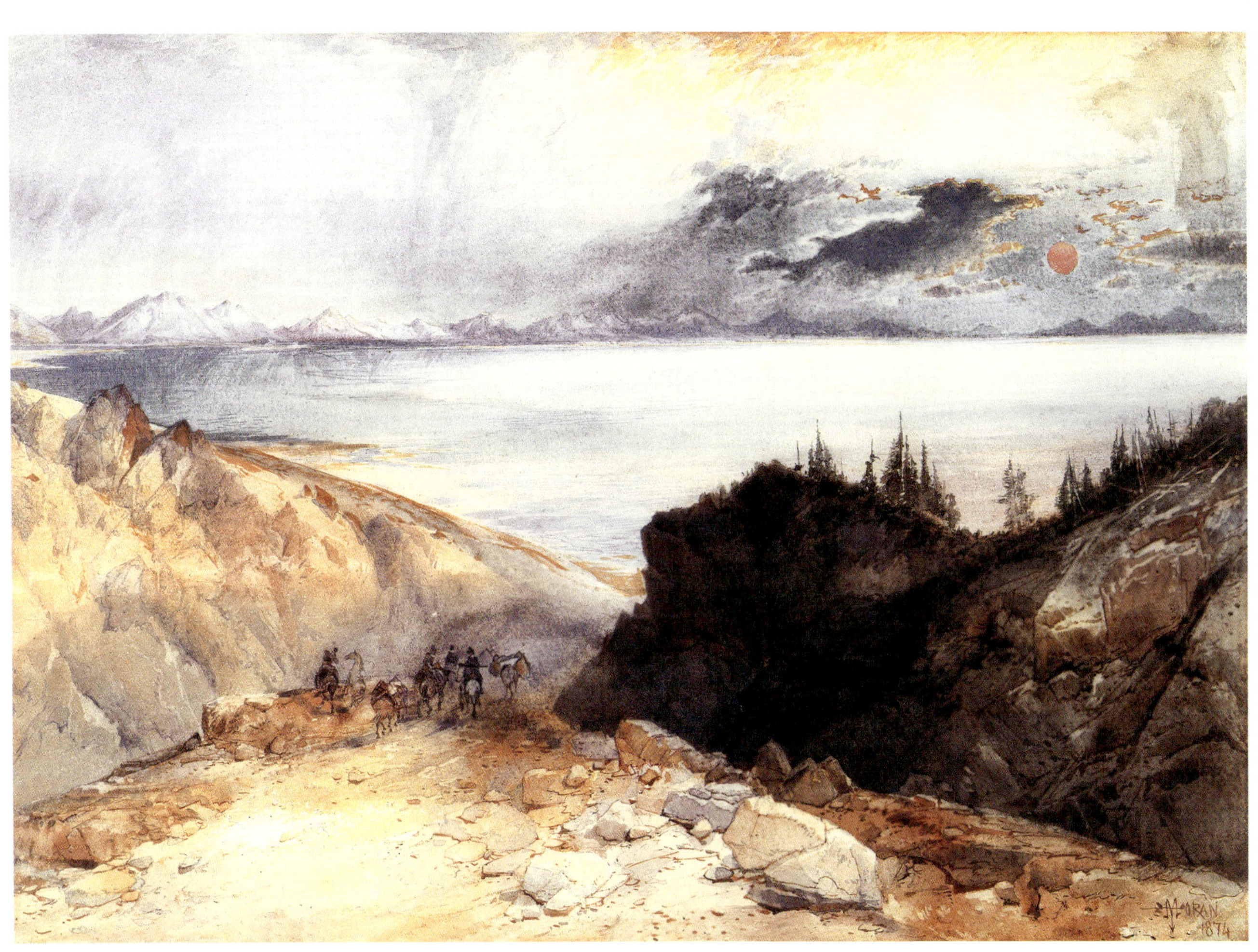

FIGURE 126. Thomas Moran, *The Great Salt Lake of Utah*, 1874, pencil, watercolor, and opaque color, 9½ × 14 in. (24.1 × 35.6 cm). Private collection, New York

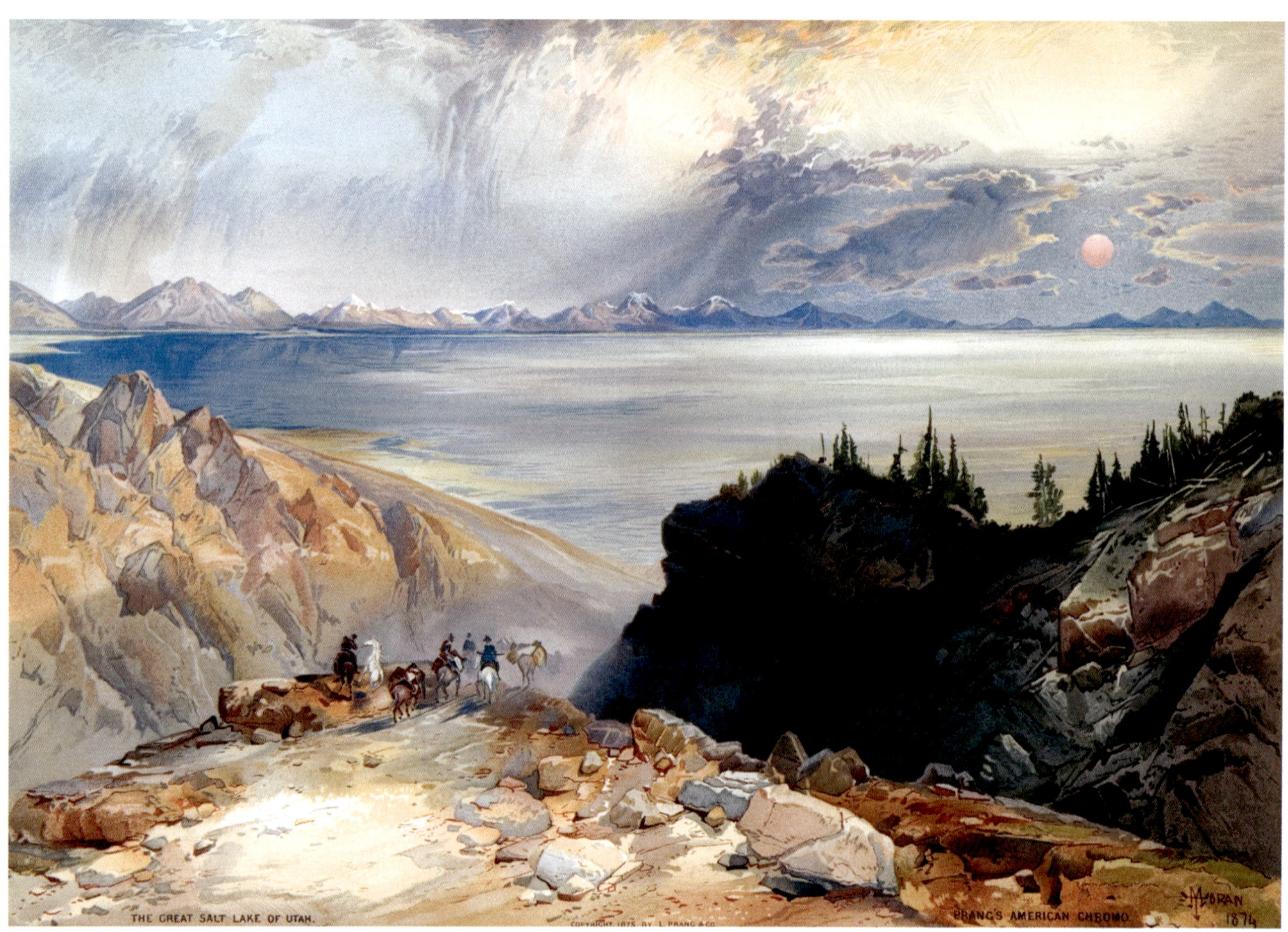

FIGURE 127. After Thomas Moran, *The Great Salt Lake of Utah,* ca. 1875, chromolithograph, 9¾ × 14⅛ in. (24.8 × 35.9 cm). Joslyn Art Museum, Omaha, gift of Gail and Michael Yanney and Lisa and Bill Roskens

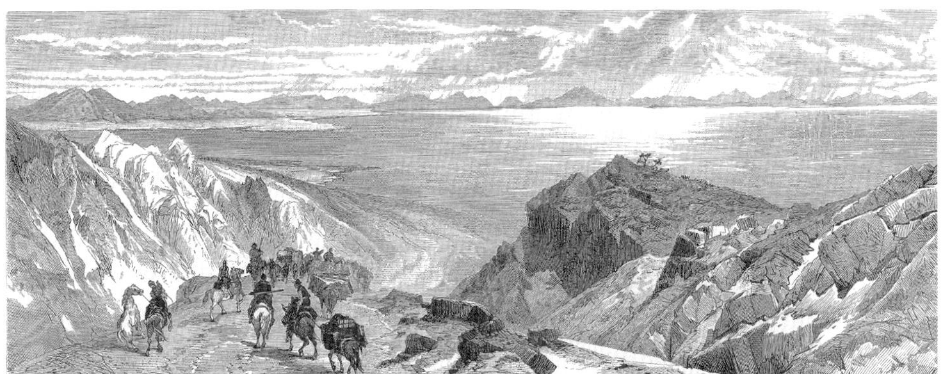

FIGURE 128. After Thomas Moran, *Salt Lake*, ca. 1874, wood engraving, *Picturesque America* (New York: D. Appleton & Co., 1874), 2:186

respond closely to the chromolithograph (fig. 127). One appeared in *Picturesque America* in 1874 (fig. 128), and another in an 1890 Denver and Rio Grande guidebook.[96] Hayden described the Prang view as looking in "a westerly direction . . . standing on the [Wasatch] mountain-range which forms the eastern side of the lake basin." He went on to say, however, that "just underneath the mountains in the foreground is located Great Salt Lake City," an observation that suggests that Moran's scene is oddly composed, simultaneously greatly foreshortened and expanded as it reduces the city to invisibility at the same time as it extends across the lake to the horizon. The geographical inconsistency may derive from an entirely different source, a Jackson photograph of Ogden, Utah (fig. 129), which, although not an exact match, shares a number of features with the painting, even though it looks south toward Salt Lake rather than west.

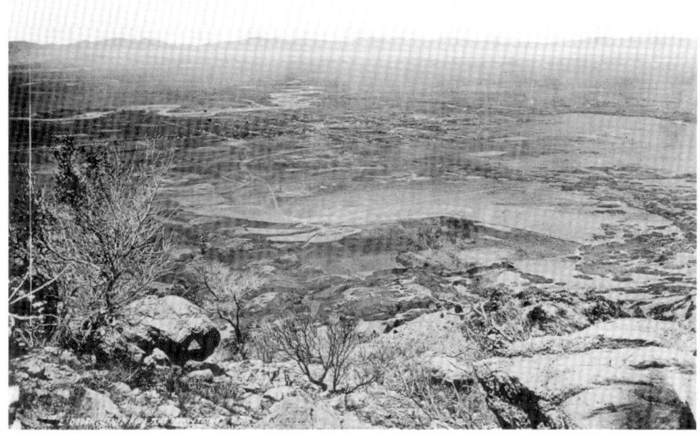

FIGURE 129. William Henry Jackson, *Ogden, Looking Down into Salt Lake Valley over Ogden, to Salt Lake*, 1871, photograph, United States Geological Survey Photographic Library (jwh00140)

Within the Prang portfolio, *The Great Salt Lake* has a significant position as the last chromolithograph of the series and as a final echo of expansive water that *Yellowstone Lake* and *Head of the Yellowstone River* presented earlier. *Upper Twin Lake, Colorado* and *Lake Donner* would also have made important additions to this theme if they had been included in the final portfolio.

Taken together, the plates in *The Yellowstone National Park* present a region of dramatic extremes through balanced groupings of scenes across a vast geographical range. When the unpublished watercolors that Moran intended for the portfolio are considered with the chromolithographs, each territory would have been represented by a lake (with the exception of Idaho); a mountain/summit scene; pinnacles, towers, or dramatic monumental rocks; and a waterfall. They offer viewers intimate encounters with their subjects and sweeping vistas that emphasize a magisterial gaze.

This simultaneous appeal to the personal experience and the larger aspirations of the nation epitomizes the power of nineteenth-century landscape art to embody and promote cultural values toward land generally and the American West in particular. Offering the first published glimpse of these scenes in color, these remarkable chromolithographs created a new perspective on their subject at the same time as they reinforced prevailing attitudes toward it.

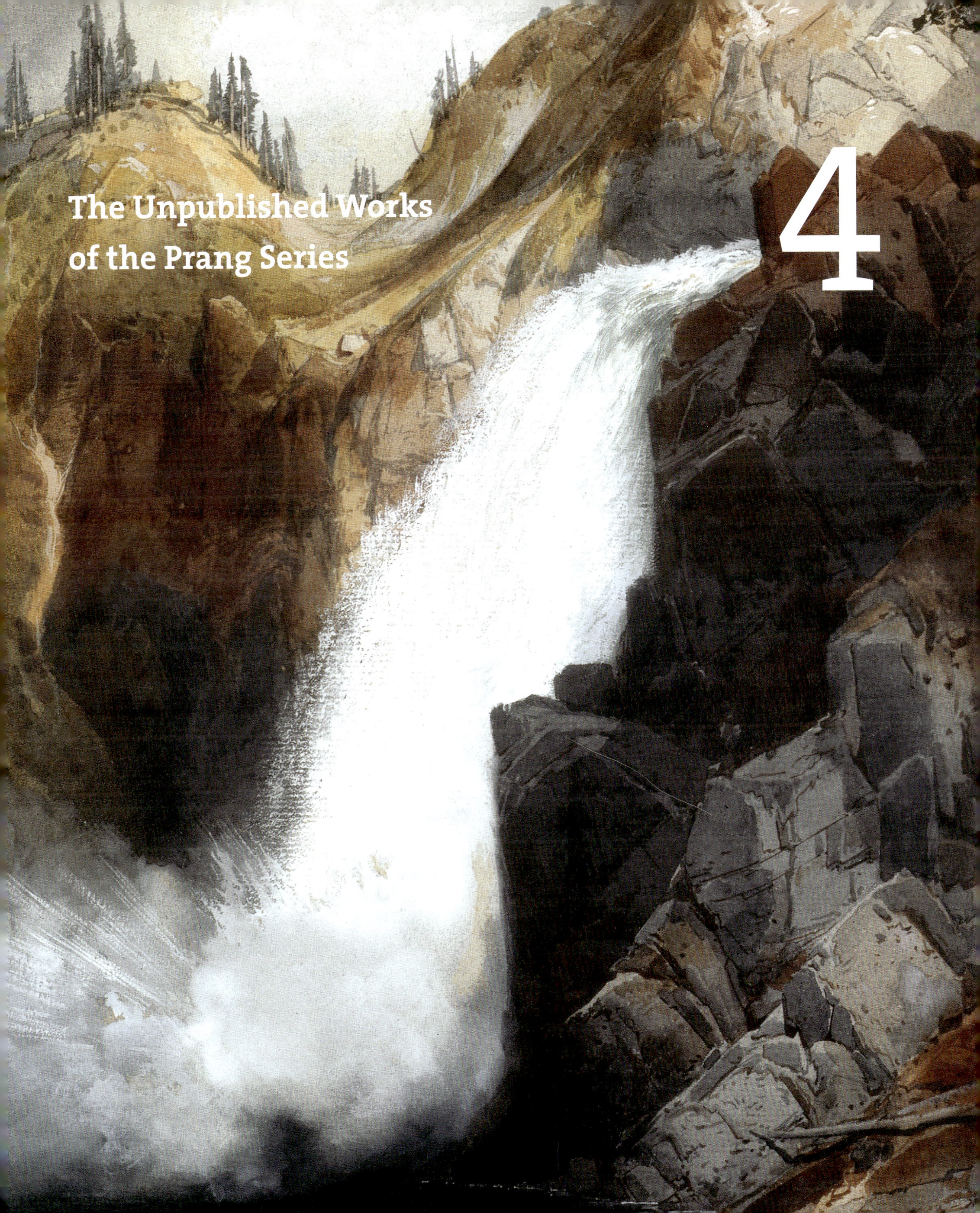

The Unpublished Works of the Prang Series

4

All representations of landscape scenery must necessarily lose the great part of their charm when deprived of color; but of any representation in black and white of the scenery of the Yellowstone it may truly be said that it is like Hamlet with the part of Hamlet omitted.
—*Ferdinand Hayden,* The Yellowstone National Park, *1876*

Nine of the twenty-four watercolors Thomas Moran created for Louis Prang in 1874–1875 were never produced as chromolithographs and were not included in *The Yellowstone National Park* portfolio. These images have never been identified or discussed in the Moran and Prang scholarship, and all but one have remained unlocated today even after diligent searching. Since they were part of the geographical and artistic effect the artist originally envisioned, however, these "unpublished nine" views constitute an important part of the project. They helped balance its geographical range, complementing the other subjects and compositions in a variety of ways. With all twenty-four images, the publication would still have focused most fully on the Yellowstone region—with eleven scenes—but also would have included five Utah views, four from Colorado, two of the Sierra Nevada Range, and two of Idaho/Wyoming (not in Yellowstone). The project's remarkable synergism of effect is only apparent when the lost works are considered with those in the portfolio.

Since the Prang & Co. records that would have provided titles for the complete series have been lost and Moran himself did not leave a full account, the identity of all nine unpublished watercolors is not easy to determine. Three of the paintings' subjects are indisputable, since they were listed in the sale catalog of Prang's art collection in 1892: *Upper Twin Lake, Colorado; Lake Donner, Nevada;* and *Gunnison's Butte, Azure Cliffs of Green River, Utah.*[1] Moran's ledger books offer additional clues, but these can be confusing since he often used alternate or shortened titles that are sometimes interchangeable with other works.[2] Adding to the difficulty, several scholars have speculated on various aspects of the commission, but, although most of their research is sound, some of their assumptions are contradictory. The probable list may be found in the appendix of this book.

Even with only one of the unpublished watercolors located, it is still possible to discuss the nine images, and even to estimate their appearance, since Moran published comparable wood engravings in several publications. As we have already seen, he often maximized his artistic material by replicating the same subjects in different media, sometimes with only slight variations. This fortuitous coincidence facilitates the identification and description of the unpublished Prang works, providing a fuller picture of the entire project than has previously been achieved. For the first time, the entire endeavor can be understood as a unified effort that combined site, representation, presentation, and perception into a remarkable portrayal of the American West.

UPPER TWIN LAKE, COLORADO

Perhaps because Moran traveled to Colorado with Hayden's survey in 1874, during the period of his most intense work for Prang, he devoted four scenes of the region to the chromolithographic project (*The Mosquito Trail; The Mountain of the Holy Cross; Upper Twin Lake, Colorado;* and *Pike's Peak*). Only the first two appeared in the final portfolio. The year of *The Yellowstone National Park*'s publication, 1876, was also when Colorado achieved statehood, and the planned emphasis may have been a calculated effort to capitalize on growing public interest in the new state. Included in the 1892 Prang sale, *Upper Twin Lake* depicted a Rocky Mountain region already known for intense mining activity as well as stunning beauty.

As Hayden wrote, the "beautiful Twin Lakes" were "nestled in the glacier-worn gorge of Lake Fork" and were visible in the distance of *Mosquito Trail* (fig. 107). Today this area is located on Route 82 between Leadville and Aspen, with the town of Twin Lakes as its commercial hub. Hayden predicted that "at some period in the future [the lake area] will become one of the most attractive watering places in the West," and, indeed, this assessment proved prophetic. As early as the 1880s the Twin Lakes area was attracting tourists via the Denver and Rio Grande Railway, and it remains a thriving recreational destination today.[3] D&RG publications of the period included Twin Lakes among the sights along its line, noting in its 1887 guidebook, *Rhymes of the Rockies,* that they were "easily reached by an hour's ride from Granite, a station on the Leadville Branch" and that "numerous sail and row-boats and fishing tackle can always be obtained. . . . Twin Lakes is one of the highest of the popular Rocky mountain resorts and furnishes an unfailing 'antidote' for hot weather."[4]

In the absence of the watercolor, it is revealing to turn to Moran's illustrations of Upper Twin Lake in *The Rhymes of the Rockies* and in William D. Rideing's article, "The Rocky Mountains," in *Picturesque America* (fig. 130) and also to William Henry Jackson's photograph of 1873 or 1874 (fig. 131).[5] The *Picturesque America* view offers a wider panorama than the *Rhymes* version and its point of view is slightly elevated. The *Rhymes* engraving's proportions, however, are closer to those of the Prang chromos,

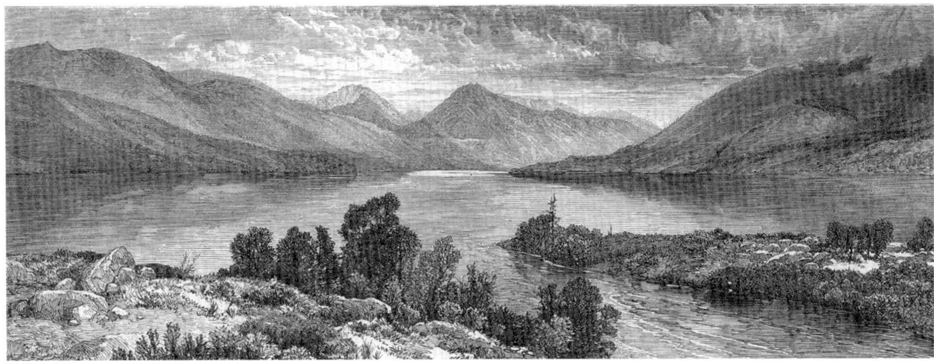

FIGURE 130. After Thomas Moran, *Upper Twin Lake,* ca. 1874, wood engraving, *Picturesque America* (New York: D. Appleton & Co., 1874), 2: 496

FIGURE 131. William Henry Jackson, *Upper Twin Lake, Colorado*, ca. 1873, photograph, United States Geological Survey Photographic Library (Jackson 1327)

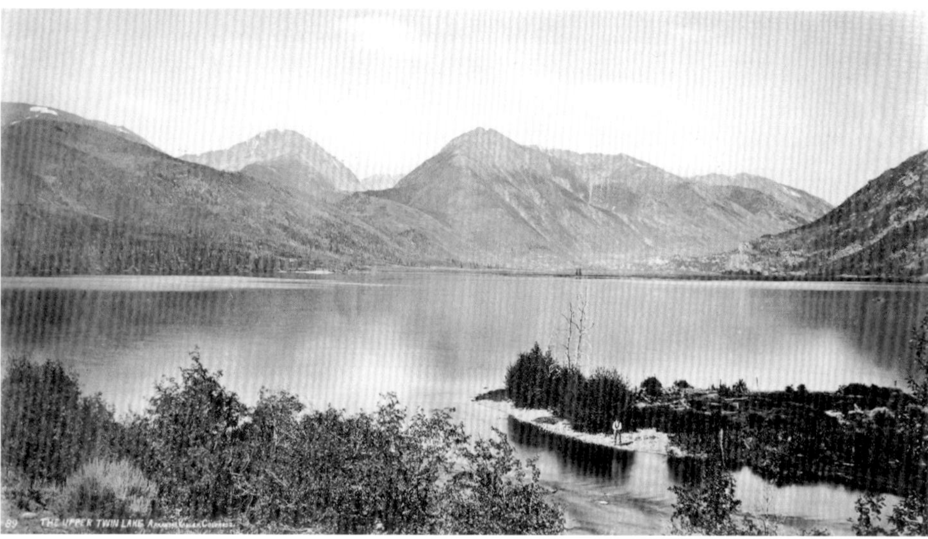

and it may be closest to the original watercolor. In both versions, Moran provided his characteristic foreground that offers entry into the tranquil scene, and the serene lake occupies the middle ground, surrounded by gently sloping mountains. The snowpack that dominates *The Mosquito Trail* has been replaced by full summer growth, including small trees. The wood engraving's close correspondence with Jackson's photograph indicates that it was a principal reference for Moran.

Referring readers to Moran's illustration, *Picturesque America* wrote of Twin Lakes:

> The larger is about two and a half miles long and mile and a half wide; the smaller about half that size. At the upper end they are girt by steep and rugged heights; below they are bounded by undulating hills of gravel and bowlders. A broad stream connects the two, and then hurries down the plain to join and swell the Arkansas [River]. Our illustration does not exaggerate the chaste beauty of the upper lake, the smaller of the two. The contour of the surrounding hills is marvellously varied: here softly curving, and yonder soaring to an abrupt peak. In some things it transports us to the western Highlands of Scotland, and, as with their waters, its depths are swarming with the most delicately flavored, the most spirited and largest trout. Sportsmen come here in considerable numbers; and not the least charming object to be met on the banks is an absorbed, contemplative man, seated on some glacier-thrown bowlder, with his slender rod poised and bending gracefully, and a pretty wicker basket, half hidden in the moist grass at his side, ready for the gleaming fish that flaunts his gorgeous colors in the steadily lapping waters.[6]

Upper Twin Lake's picturesque and pastoral qualities would have been a useful addition to *The Yellowstone National Park*, balancing the more sublime and unusual views of several of the other subjects.

The Prang auction catalog of 1892 noted that "*Upper Twin Lake* has a wonderful effect of rainbow and mist."[7] Missing, of course, from the black-and-white version, the rainbow in the watercolor would have made an interesting counterpart to that in *Yellowstone Lake,* had *Upper Twin Lake* been published in the chromolithographic series. At the same time, the subject's geographical relationship with *The Mosquito Trail* was clear since the lakes distantly appeared in that view. Coupled with *The Mountain of the Holy Cross* and *Pike's Peak,* these images would have made an impressive selection of Colorado scenes had they all appeared in the portfolio.

PIKE'S PEAK

Pike's Peak is the large, distinctive, and still-famous mountain just west of Colorado Springs, Colorado, on the front range of the Rocky Mountains. Named for Zebulon Pike (1779–1813), who ascended the peak on the first American expedition to the region in 1806–1807, the mountain has long been an important landmark, especially since it can be seen for miles across the plains that extend to the east.[8]

Moran noted payment from Prang for a Pike's Peak watercolor in May 1875, along with "*Musquito Trail, Mi [Mu]Koon Tu Weap Valley, Pike's Peak,* and *[Upper] Twin Lake.*"[9] He had just visited Colorado the previous summer with Hayden's expedition but had portrayed Pike's Peak even earlier for *Picturesque America,* using Jackson's photographs as a reference (figs. 132 and 133).[10] The resulting wood engraving may afford a glimpse of the lost Prang watercolor.[11] In what has become the classic portrayal, the mountain is framed by the Garden of the Gods, with the snowy dome beckoning in the distance.[12] The dark protruding rocks of the "gateway" make an interesting contrast, both in their irregular contours and in their dark coloration. At the site itself and in oil versions such as Moran's later *Pike's Peak, through the Gateway Rocks* (1880s, private collection, Dallas), these rocks are distinguished by their rich range of terra-cottas that greatly enhance the brilliant peak.[13] Calling the scene "strangely impressive" and the foliage "gloomily pathetic," *Picturesque America* remarked that the monumental forms "remind us of the valley of the Yellowstone."[14]

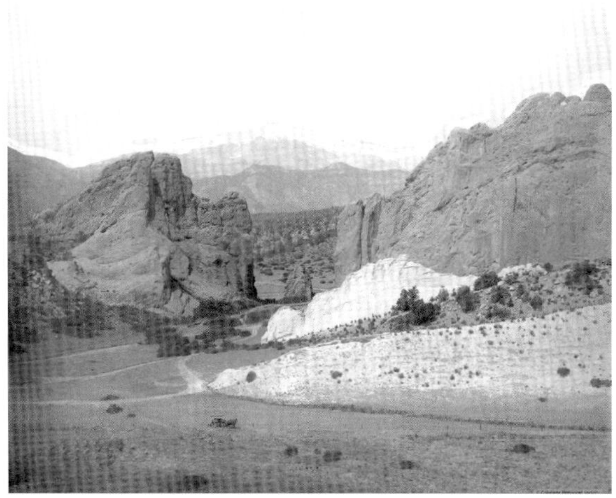

FIGURE 132. William Henry Jackson, *Pike's Peak [from] Garden of the Gods,* 1880–1900?, photograph. Colorado Historical Society, Denver (CHS. J3815)

Moran wrote his wife from Colorado after seeing the mountain for himself: "The scenery since yesterday noon was very beautiful as we are fairly into the Rocky Mountains. One view, in particular, was magnificent. It was a view of Pikes Peak, 50 miles away. I did not make a sketch as we were on the march at the time, but I can remember it near enough."[15] At the time Moran could not have known how important the site would become for him in the 1880s, when William A. Bell, an English physi-

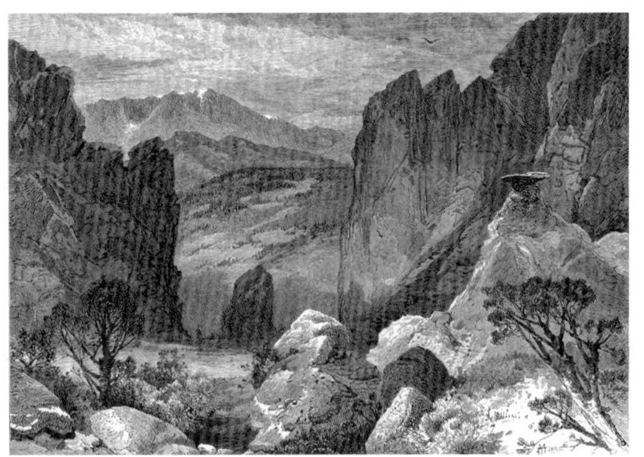

FIGURE 133. After Thomas Moran, *Pike's Peak, from Garden of the Gods,* ca. 1874, wood engraving, *Picturesque America* (New York: D. Appleton & Co., 1874), 2: 495

cian and vice president of the Denver and Rio Grande Railway, purchased his third large western oil painting, *The Mountain of the Holy Cross* (1875, fig. 34), for his home in Manitou Springs near the foot of Pike's Peak. Moran visited Bell there several times and produced a number of watercolor sketches and illustration designs of the surroundings. One of these trips was in 1881 with William Henry Jackson and writer Ernest Ingersoll, and their collaborative work resulted in a lavishly illustrated book, *Crest of the Continent: A Record of a Summer's Ramble in the Rocky Mountains and Beyond* (1885), which included another Pike's Peak wood engraving and a description of the site from the very perspective of the Moran view:

> To pass in between massive portals of rock in brilliant terra-cotta red, and enter on a plain miles in extent, covered in all directions with magnificent isolated masses of the same striking color, each lifting itself against a wonderful blue Colorado sky with a sharpness of outline that would shame the fine cutting of an etching; to find the ground under your feet, over the whole immense surface, carpeted with the same rich tint, underlying arabesques of green and gray, where grass and mosses have crept; to come upon masses of pale velvety gypsum, set now and again as if to make more effective by contrast the deep red which strikes the dominant chord of the picture; and always as you look through or above to catch the stormy billows of the giant mountain range tossed against the sky, with the regal, snow crowned massiveness of Pike's Peak rising over all, is something, once seen, never to be forgotten.[16]

Had a chromolithograph of *Pike's Peak* appeared in the Prang publication, it would have been linked geographically with the other Colorado scenes, especially *The Mosquito Trail,* since Hayden mentioned that the mountain was among the distant peaks visible in that scene. The towering rocks in the foreground in the Garden of the Gods would have also provided formal analogies to the pinnacles of *The Towers of Tower Falls* at Yellowstone, *Gunnison's Butte,* and the Rio Virgen *Narrows* in Utah. The latter two, of course, like *Pike's Peak,* were excluded from the final portfolio.

LAKE DONNER, NEVADA

Moran noted payment from Prang for a Donner Lake watercolor in an undated entry in his ledger.[17] It was an unusual subject for the artist since he rarely did paintings of Nevada and California. He had traveled through Donner Pass on the transcontinental railroad in 1872, but this was territory that Albert Bierstadt had already made famous through spectacular monumental paintings, and Moran may have been reluctant to compete with his example. Nevertheless, *Lake Donner* has close ties to his rival's precedent.

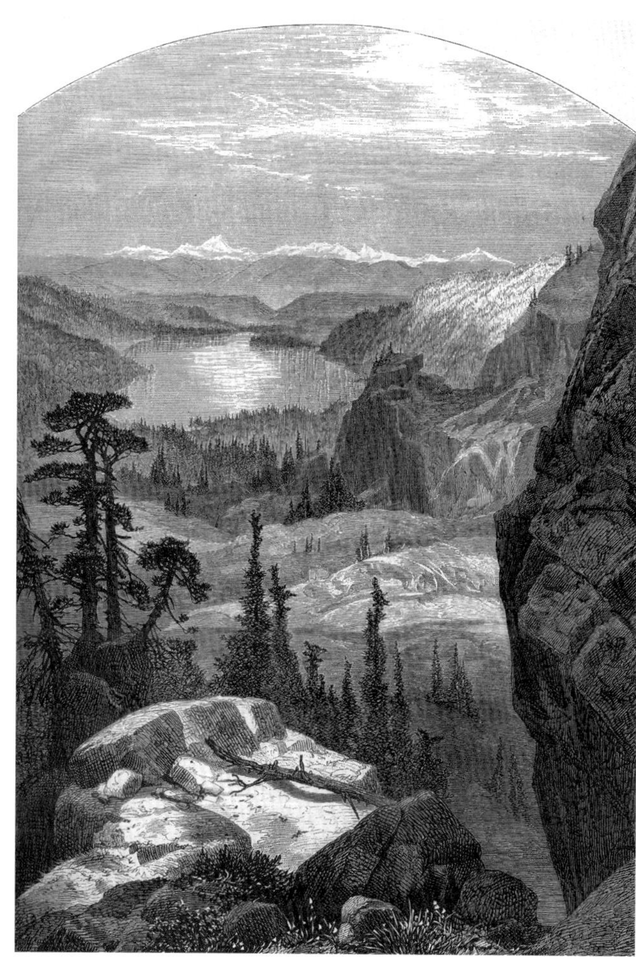

FIGURE 134. After Thomas Moran, *Lake Donner*, ca. 1874, wood engraving, *Picturesque America* (New York: D. Appleton & Co., 1874), 2: 195

Two Moran sketches of Donner Lake may have served as studies for his Prang watercolor. One of them, owned today by the Gilcrease Museum, is undated.[18] The other, a drawing in the Cooper-Hewitt Museum, is clearly inscribed "1879," but it is still possible that that work was actually done in 1872, since Moran sometimes inaccurately titled and dated his sketches years after they were drawn.[19] One point that would certainly argue for an 1872 origin for the Gilcrease sketch, *Donner Lake,* is its similarity to a wood engraving of the subject that Moran drew for *Picturesque America* shortly after his return from the 1872 California trip (fig. 134). A slightly different version, *Donner Lake,* had appeared in the serial *Appleton's Journal,* also published by D. Appleton & Co.[20] Both of these probably resemble the unlocated *Lake Donner* watercolor that Moran created for Prang, especially since his other Nevada view in the chromolithographic portfolio, *The Summit of the Sierras,* also appears in wood-engraved form in both articles.

California was, of course, already an important and well-publicized destination for transcontinental travelers, and the Sierra Nevada was a high point on the route there. Donner Lake was not only a remarkable scenic vista along the way, but was also infamous for the disaster that had claimed the lives of most of the ill-fated Donner party in the winter of 1846–1847 and had resulted in the horrifying outcome of cannibalistic activity on the part of some survivors. The valley had subsequently been portrayed by several artists, and Moran and Prang were surely aware of Americans' morbid fascination with the area.

Timothy O'Sullivan had photographed Donner Pass while working for Clarence King's U.S. Geological Exploration of the Fortieth Parallel (fig. 135), but an even closer source for Moran might have been Albert Bierstadt's portrayals of Donner Lake. Bierstadt had unveiled a massive panorama created for railroad magnate Collis P. Huntington in January 1873, a sweeping horizontal view.[21] Closer still to Moran's *Picturesque America* composition (and presumably to his watercolor for Prang) is Bierstadt's oil sketch (1871–1872, fig. 136). Both vertical scenes take their point of view at the summit of Donner Pass, looking west to the lake, which shimmers in the distance, and both are framed with a large vertical pine on the left and dark rugged outcroppings on

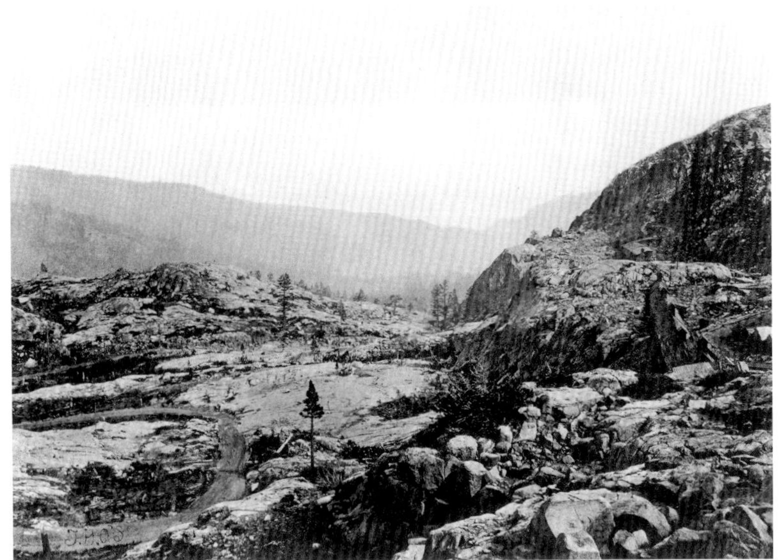

FIGURE 135. Timothy O'Sullivan, *Donner Lake Pass in the Sierra Nevada Mountains of California*, photograph. United States Geological Survey Photographic Library (Kingp052)

the right. An 1872 *Scribner's Monthly* article described Bierstadt's painting in progress in terms almost equally applicable to Moran's version:

> The scene is on the route of the road, and the point of view is near the place where, some fifteen years ago, a party of emigrants perished within a short distance of the civilization they were seeking. . . . The rocky summit from which the view is taken is high, and thus a vast extent of mountain, lake, and valley is embraced. The line of the railroad is beheld, a mere thread, where it enters the scene some thirty miles off, and the eye follows it, coming nearer still, along the perilous path cut for it in the trap and granite sides of the great hills which tower above it. In the middle distance is Donner Lake, the central point of interest, and beyond it range after range of hills until the horizon meets them.[22]

As the writer noted, in Bierstadt's painting, extending from the right into the middle ground is a small but unmistakable line of snowsheds that helped keep the Central Pacific's track clear in the heavy snows of the Sierra Mountains' winter. These were in their day an impressive feat of engineering and thus an important element in the scene for Huntington as patron of the work. The snowsheds are absent in Moran's wood engraving, but in his view a secure, if rugged, foreground stands in place of Bierstadt's precipitous gorge. *Lake Donner, Nevada* was among the watercolors sold at the 1892 Prang auction, and the accompanying text noted that it similarly had "an attractive distance and a very imposing foreground."[23]

Since the Sierra Nevada region had been so thoroughly "claimed" by Bierstadt and others, Moran's portrayal of the area for Prang is unusual. He may have chosen the subject since he had the *Picturesque America* designs readily in hand, or the publisher may have asked for something from the area that would capitalize on readers' interest in the region and make the publication more comprehensive. Had *Lake Donner* been included in the final publication, it would have represented another site that suggested both grandeur and the awesome power of nature, echoing some of the same cultural challenges as the other scenes in the portfolio. Prang's reasoning for excluding *Lake Donner* from the final portfolio remains unclear, but as he crafted the publication to appeal to an elite audience, he may have wished to avoid the grisly associations that the site evoked.

GUNNISON'S BUTTE: AZURE CLIFFS OF GREEN RIVER, UTAH

The Green River, with its distinctive and colorful buttes, was among Moran's favorite subjects. He addressed it in as many as forty versions throughout his career in a variety of media.[24] He first glimpsed the river as he traveled west to join Hayden in 1871 at a point where it crosses the Union Pacific line in southern Wyoming. It was there he made his *First Sketch in the West,* a Green River scene with a broad sweeping riverbed foreground. The unusual formations and colors of the buttes along the waterway would be the focus of some of Moran's most beautiful paintings.[25]

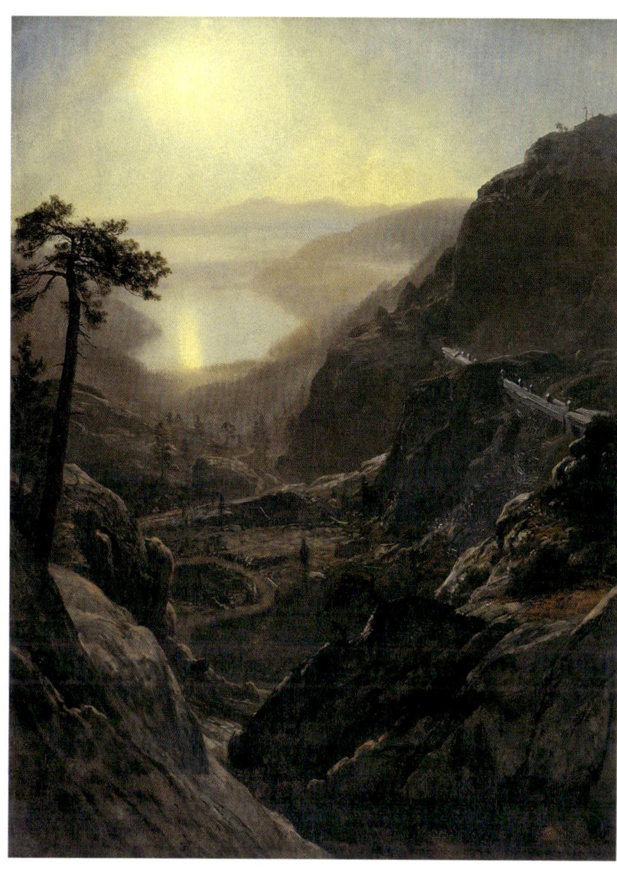

FIGURE 136. Albert Bierstadt, *View of Donner Lake, California,* 1871–1872, oil on paper mounted on canvas, 29¼ × 21⅞ in. (74.3 × 55.6 cm). Fine Arts Museums of San Francisco, gift of Anna Bennet and Jessie Jonas in memory of August F. Jonas, Jr. (1984.54)

The Green River is the largest tributary of the Colorado River, running from its headwaters in the Wind River Range south through Wyoming and eastern Utah to its confluence with the Colorado southwest of Moab. Gunnison's Butte is today a landmark just north of the town of Green River, Utah (not to be confused with Green River, Wyoming), in the east-central portion of the state, and it stands near the mouth of Gray Canyon at a point that was known in the 1870s as Gunnison['s] Crossing.[26] John Wesley Powell described the area in his 1869 journal, noting the "azure beds and cliffs on either side of the river." He described the site as an "Indian crossing. . . . we see evidences that a party of Indians have crossed within a very few days. This is the place where the lamented [John] Gunnison crossed, in the year 1853, when making an exploration for a railroad route to the Pacific coast."[27] Moran's 1873 trip with Powell through Utah (toward the Grand Canyon in Arizona) had led them south and west from Salt Lake City rather than east to the area of Gunnison's Butte, but he did have access to John (Jack) Hiller's photographs of the formation from the Powell survey (fig. 137).[28]

Moran actually produced two Green River views for Prang. The unpublished portfolio image, *Gunnison's Butte: Azure Cliffs of Green River, Utah,* was listed among the Moran watercolors in the 1892 Prang sale, but the painting remains unlocated today. The second, *Cliffs of the Upper Colorado River, Wyoming Territory,* was listed in 1879 and was published as a smaller chromo than the prints in *The Yellowstone National Park* series (fig. 156).[29] *Cliffs of the Upper Colorado,* like most of Moran's Green River scenes, portrays one of the distinctive buttes in the Palisades group near Green River, Wyoming.

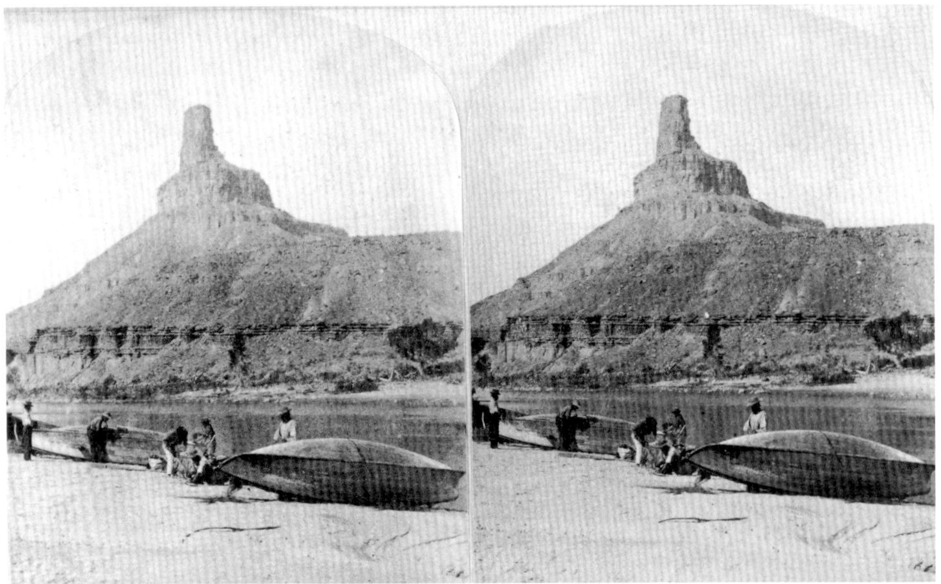

FIGURE 137. John K. (Jack) Hillers, *Canyons of the Green River, Cathedral [Gunnison's] Butte, Blue Cliffs,* ca. 1871, photograph. United States Geological Survey Photographic Library (hjk00992)

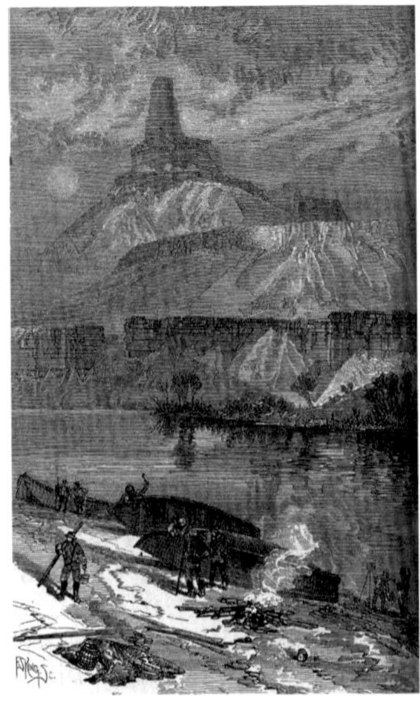

FIGURE 138. After Thomas Moran, *Repairing Boats at Gunnison's Butte,* ca. 1874, wood engraving, *Scribner's Monthly* 9 (January 1875): 310

The possibility of a glimpse of the lost *Gunnison's Butte: Azure Cliffs of Green River* watercolor may exist in Powell's *Scribner's Monthly* article of January 1875, which includes a Moran wood engraving, *Repairing Boats at Gunnison's Butte* (fig. 138). Moran also published a similar view in *The Aldine* in January 1876 under the title *Azure Cliffs of the Green River* (fig. 139).[30] Both the *Scribner's* and *The Aldine*'s scenes depict a much more slender tower than those at the Palisades. The formation rises from a mountainous base on the other side of the river, and a small group of boatmen work in the foreground. These details compare directly to Hiller's photograph (fig. 137).

The Aldine's text offered an interesting geographic and historical context for Moran's image of *Gunnison's Butte:*

> The present picture conveys the feature of "The Azure Cliffs of Green River," lying not less than one hundred miles south of the spot where the Pacific road crosses that river, and yet bearing so many similar characteristics that the resemblance is instantly to be recognized. Few such spires of rock, thus buttressed and terraced, rise even in the wonderful mid-continent; and there is a matter of historical interest in the alternate name of the bold bluff with its rocky spiral tower—that of "Gunnison's Butte." For here it was that the lamented explorer, Lieutenant [John W.] Gunnison, made his crossing of the Green River in 1853, when taking those first surveys for a contemplated Pacific road, only four years after the discovery of gold in California, and when none could have anticipated the present greatness of our Western Empire, or the magnificence of the lines of travel crossing the continent and giving access to it. Undoubtedly the "Azure Cliffs" are among the most

> notable features of a wonderful land; and they certainly supply, from the pencil and burin combining to illustrate them, a picture of exceptional beauty as well as the historical interest thus attaching to them. Gunnison dying in a noble cause, has a noble monument, worthy of its present unexceptional setting.[31]

Lt. John W. Gunnison was a member of the U.S. Army Corps of Topographical Engineers and had explored Utah in 1849 with Capt. Howard Stansbury. He had subsequently written a history of the Mormons (1852) and was killed by Native Americans near Utah Lake in 1853.[32] Moran was probably attracted to the formation he drew for Prang because of its unique configuration, but also perhaps because he knew that Gunnison's name would be familiar to American audiences, providing a reference point in what would be, for most viewers, an alien landscape.

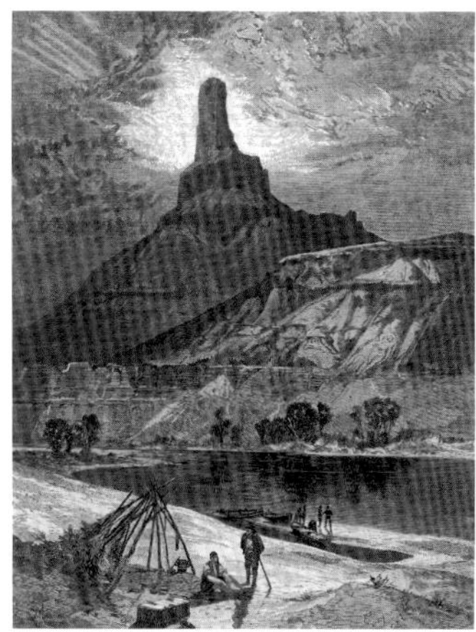

FIGURE 139. After Thomas Moran, *Azure Cliffs of the Green River,* ca. 1875, wood engraving, *The Aldine* 8 (January 1876): 34. Courtesy of Boston Public Library, Print Room

The 1892 sale catalog of Prang's paintings described the remarkable chromatic range of *Gunnison's Butte* as "beautiful in color with its azure, emerald, and topaz tints, as translucent as the colors of gems."[33] A comparable watercolor, today in a private collection and probably somewhat sketchier than the Prang version, displays this same chromatic subtlety, offering a tantalizing glimpse at a scene that would have made a striking addition to *The Yellowstone National Park.*[34] There its pinnacle formation would have augmented the vertical elements in *The Towers of Tower Falls* and the *Valley of the Babbling Waters,* and its status as a Utah landmark would have complemented that image, *The Great Salt Lake of Utah,* and the two *Mu Koon Tu Weap* scenes.

MI [MU] KOON TU WEAP VALLEY

The Utah subjects depicting the area now known as Zion National Park are the most problematic of the unpublished watercolors. Moran noted in his ledger book: "In all I made 24 drawings for Mr. Prang for his work in chromo of the National Yellowstone Park in which work he used 15 of them. Mr. Kirkpatrick of Newark afterward bought two of them [from Prang,] the Cañon of the Rio Virgen & the Upper Fall of the Yellowstone."[35] The "Cañon of the Rio Virgen" could be *Valley of the Babbling Waters* since Moran's own offprint copy of the wood-engraved version from *The Aldine* (fig. 122) contains a pencil notation, "Cañon of the Rio Virgen," next to the printed title, probably in Moran's hand. But Carol Clark's 1980 catalogue raisonné of Moran's watercolors lists Kirkpatrick's *Cañon of the Rio Virgen* as a vertical image (her no. 102). *Valley of the Babbling Waters,* of course, is horizontal and furthermore is listed separately in Clark's catalog (no. 138). Thurman Wilkins offers a clue to the confusion in his Moran biography when he notes that "Moran pictured Mu-koon-tu-weap for *The Aldine,* under the caption "Valley of the Babbling Water," a rough translation of the Indian name."[36] In fact, as described above in Chapter Three, two other Moran illustrations in *The Aldine* (April 1875) are associated with that Indian term for the Rio Virgin or "Babbling Water." They are *Temple of the Virgin, Mu-Koon-Tu-Weap Valley, Utah,* and *The Narrows, North Fork of the Rio Virgen, Utah.* Indeed, in his ledger, Moran noted payment from Prang for two works with similar titles: *Mi [Mu] Koon Tu Weap Valley* and *Mu Koon Tu Weap Narrows,* but he did not mention *Valley of the Babbling Waters* by name at all.[37] Clark lists a watercolor, *Mu Koon Tu Weap Valley,* dimensions unknown (no. 129), but she does not seem to have known of *Mu Koon Tu Weap Narrows.* Since both Prang watercolors, *Mu Koon Tu Weap Valley* and *Mu Koon Tu Weap Narrows,* were also probably vertical images (based on *The Aldine* versions—see discussions of each below), either could ostensibly be the vertical Kirkpatrick *Cañon of the Rio Virgen.*[38]

In the end, and somewhat tentatively since what Moran called *Mu Koon Tu Weap Valley* in his ledger could still be the published view called *Valley of the Babbling Waters,* it seems that Moran produced *three* views of the Zion region for Prang—*Valley of the Babbling Waters,* which is the horizontal work published in the final portfolio, and two vertical images, *Mu Koon Tu Weap Valley* and *Mu Koon Tu Weap Narrows.*

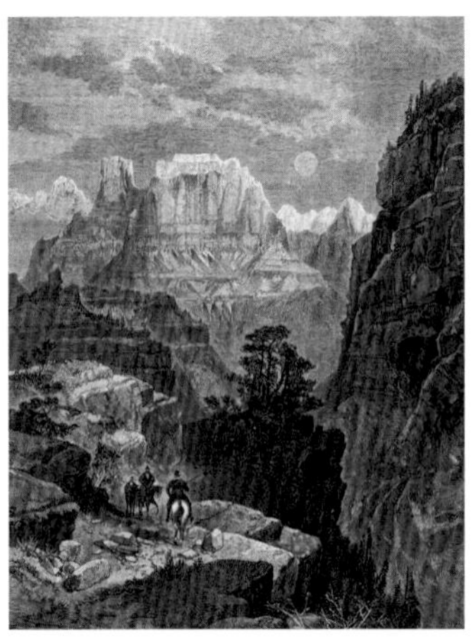

FIGURE 140. After Thomas Moran, *Temple of the Virgin, Mu-Koon-Tu-Weap Valley, Utah,* ca. 1874, wood engraving, *The Aldine* 7 (April 1875): 307. Courtesy of Boston Public Library, Print Room

The Aldine's wood engraving, *Temple of the Virgin, Mu-Koon-Tu-Weap Valley, Utah* (fig. 140), is probably a version of the unpublished Prang watercolor *Mu Koon Tu Weap Valley.* It is a vertical view with a rocky foreground occupied by three horsemen riding in from the left, a rugged dark cliff rising on the right, and a distinctive light-colored butte dominating the central background. A full moon dots the sky. Although the vantage point is elevated, the dramatic cliffs rise to meet our gaze, much as they do throughout Zion itself, where the dramatic cliffs and outcroppings both contain the view and enliven it. In her discussion of Moran's work in the area of what is now Zion National Park, Gaell Lindstrom states that this view probably portrays the formation now known as "West Temple."[39]

Moran's traveling companion on the 1873 trip that took him to Utah on the way to the Grand Canyon, Justin E. Colburn, may have been referring to that "temple" in one of his *New York Times* articles when he wrote, "Moran and myself, with a guide and a pack horse, took an excursion of four days into and through the most interesting and beautiful region we have ever seen. It is called by the Mormons 'Little Zion Valley.' . . . at the foot of the valley, on the west, stands a mass of cliffs, 4,500 feet above the valley, called the Temple of the Virgin, which alone is worth the trip from Washington to Southern Utah."[40] Powell also briefly mentioned the "tower-rocks" known as the "Temples of the Virgen" in his description of the 1873 trip in *Scribner's Monthly.*[41] Late in his life, Moran was interviewed about his Utah landscapes and specifically mentioned the Mu-Koon-Tu-Weap area of Zion:

> There is a canyon off the Rio Virgin, known in the Indian Vernacular as Mu-Koon-Tu-Weap, that for glory of scenery and stupendous scenic effects cannot be surpassed. Its cliffs rise up in rugged massiveness for 5000 feet with some of the

> most peculiar formations noticeable toward the top. It is a marvelous piece of nature's handiwork that is worth going a long distance to see. I think southern Utah is unsurpassed in the class of scenery that characterizes it, and any one who admires desert landscape need go nowhere else to see it in all its weird, fantastic attractions.[42]

With such an affinity for the remarkable formations of the area, it is not surprising that Moran would have presented Prang with three watercolors.

Had *Mu Koon Tu Weap Valley* been included in the Prang publication, its looming composition would have further amplified the mountainous theme that recurs in *The Mountain of the Holy Cross, Gardiner's River Hot Springs, The Summit of the Sierras, Pike's Peak, The Three Tetons,* and *The Mosquito Trail.* Furthermore, in its direct and indirect biblical reference it would have both complemented *The Mountain of the Holy Cross* and helped balance the satanic themes in *The Devil's Den, The Towers of Tower Falls,* and even *The Great Falls of the Snake River.* Closely linked as well with the other three Utah scenes (in addition to those discussed here, there is *The Great Salt Lake,* of course), *Mu Koon Tu Weap Valley* represents an interesting omission by Louis Prang, and ultimately an unfortunate one, since the image would have enhanced the portfolio in so many ways.

MU KOON TU WEAP NARROWS

Facing the wood engraving of *Temple of the Virgin, Mu-Koon-Tu-Weap Valley* in *The Aldine*'s April 1875 issue is *The Narrows, North Fork of the Rio Virgin, Utah* (fig. 141). This is probably a version of the unpublished watercolor, *Mu Koon Tu Weap Narrows,* that Moran created for Prang. *The Aldine*'s image also compares closely to a *Scribner's Monthly* illustration and a Moran watercolor field sketch today in the Gilcrease Museum.[43] *The Aldine*'s vertically oriented image is striking in its arched composition, framing the rising buttes through the aperture of a cave. The point of view is low, emphasizing the rocky foreground at the river's edge, but the gaze rises quickly in the middle ground to the soaring rocks that block further access and lift our attention to their irregular, silhouetted tops.

The Narrows is a unique 2-mile section of the North Fork of the Virgin River in present-day Zion National Park. In places it is only 20 to 30 feet across, with canyon walls on each side that rise to 2,000 feet. Today it is a unique hiking route, or more accurately a wading route, since it involves walking in the river, sometimes in water as high as chest deep. Considering the extreme constriction of the space, it seems that in his portrayal Moran was depicting the *entrance* to the passage rather than a view of that confined space itself. Indeed, the composition suggests an invitation into an enclosed realm, the flanking walls of the cave beckoning to the enclosure in the distance.

FIGURE 141. After Thomas Moran, *The Narrows, North Fork of the Rio Virgin, Utah*, ca. 1874, wood engraving, *The Aldine* 7 (April 1875): 306. Courtesy of Boston Public Library, Print Room

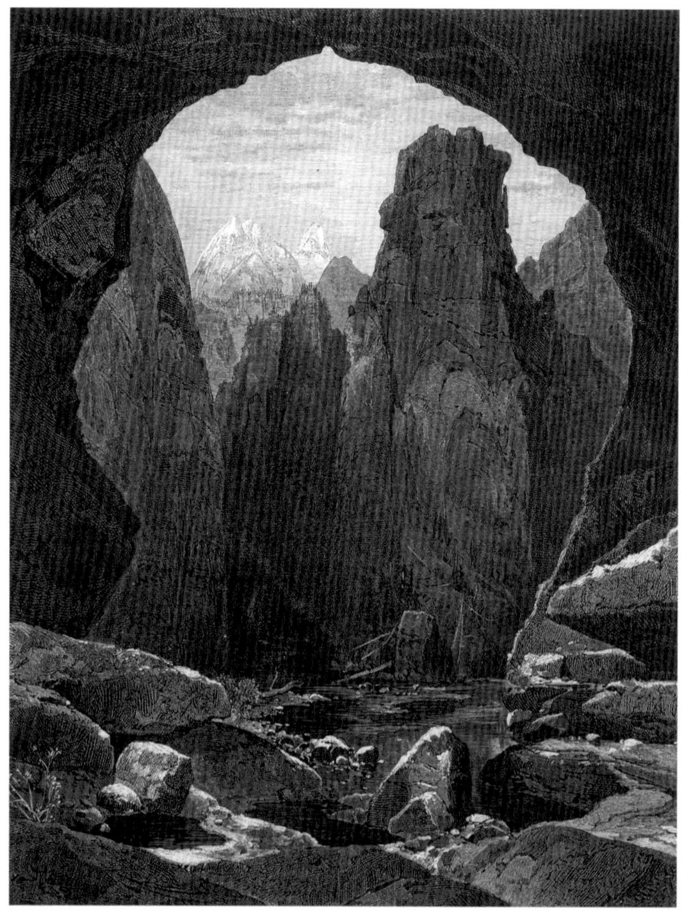

Although it is doubtful that Moran waded the Narrows himself, he could have learned about its inner recesses from the Powell survey members. Powell himself described the area in *Scribner's Monthly* in October 1875:

> The cañon was 1200 feet deep, but we found it steadily increasing in depth, and in many places exceedingly narrow—only twenty or thirty feet wide below, and in some places even narrower—for hundreds of feet overhead. There are places where the river, in sweeping past curves, has cut far under the rocks, but still preserves its narrow channel, so that there is an overhanging wall on one side, and an inclined wall on the other. In places a few hundred feet above, it becomes vertical again, and thus the view to the sky above is entirely closed. Everywhere this deep passage is dark and gloomy, and resounds with the noise of rapid waters.[44]

The "dark and gloomy" atmosphere of the Narrows, as well as its focus on a singular butte within a canyon, would have reinforced a number of other images in *The Yellowstone National Park* series, especially *The Towers of Tower Falls* and *Devil's Den*.

Echoing the other river scenes, it would have nevertheless contrasted with the open and light-filled scenes of lakes and alpine views, its constricted composition offering a unique balance to the whole.

UPPER FALL[S] OF THE YELLOWSTONE

It is not surprising that Moran created a version of *Upper Fall[s] of the Yellowstone* for the Prang series. Marking the beginning of the Grand Canyon of the Yellowstone as the river winds its way some twenty-five miles north from Yellowstone Lake, Upper Falls would be a primary tourist attraction in any area less replete with remarkable features. Although a notable landmark at Yellowstone National Park, it is considered something of a stepchild to the more famous and more dramatic Lower Falls that is the focal point of the canyon just downriver.

Moran had portrayed Upper Falls for *Scribner's Monthly* (fig. 142) even before he visited the region, redrawing a sketch by Private Charles Moore, a soldier who had

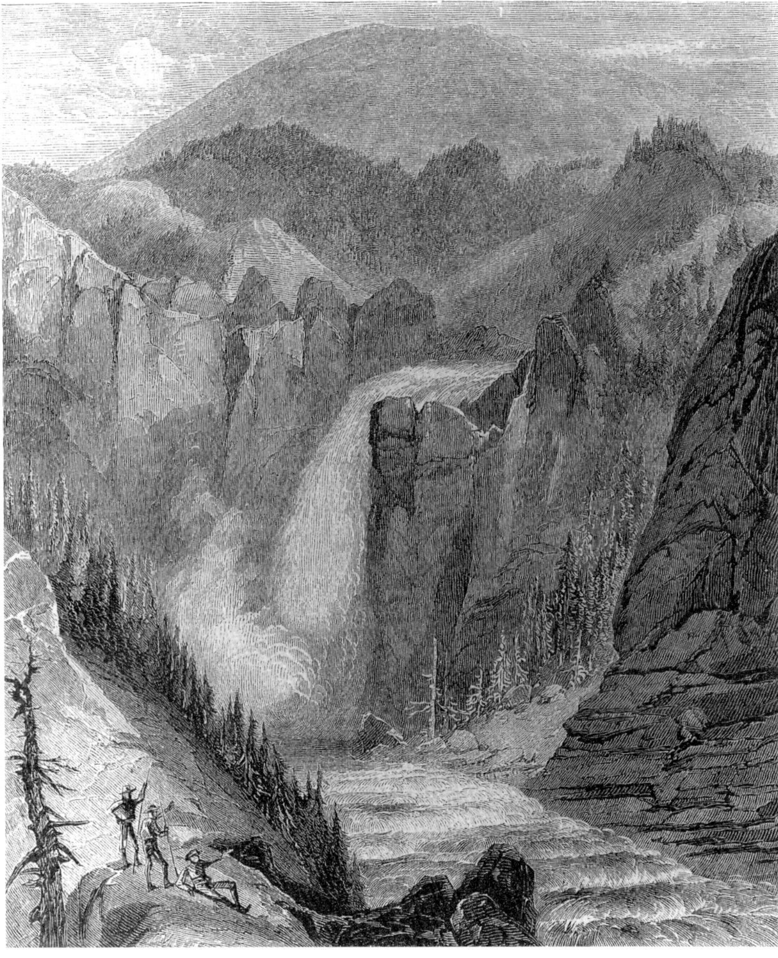

FIGURE 142. After Thomas Moran, *Upper Falls of the Yellowstone, Wyoming*, 1872, wood engraving, *Scribner's Monthly* 2 (May 1871): 14

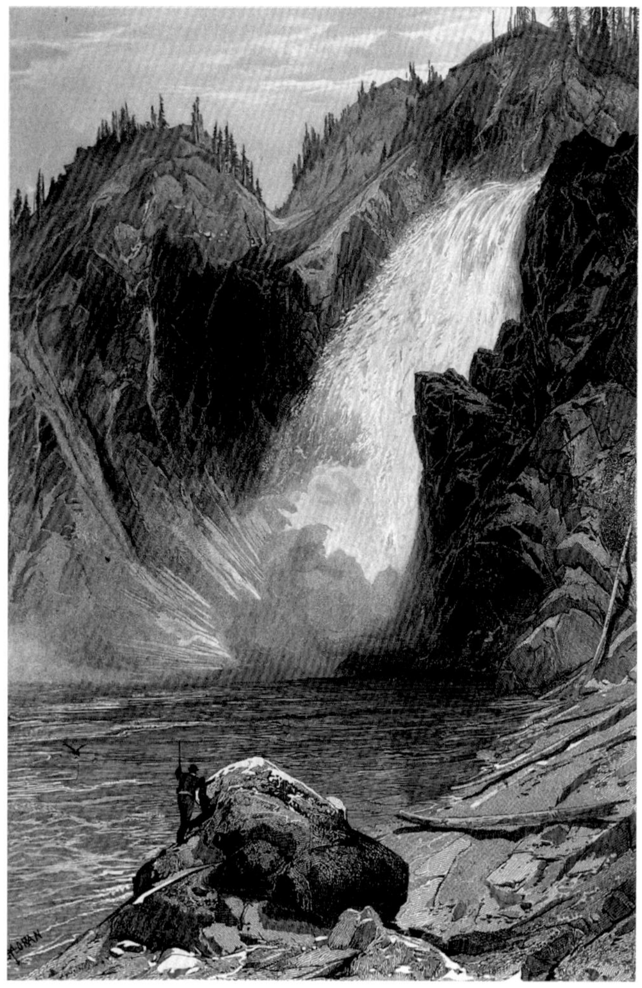

FIGURE 143. After Thomas Moran, *Upper Yellowstone Falls*, ca. 1872, steel engraving, *Picturesque America* (D. Appleton & Co., 1872), n.p. Collection of Joslyn Art Museum, Omaha

accompanied the 1870 Washburn/Doane Yellowstone expedition.[45] Of the many images in that article, the view of Upper Falls is probably the most accurate and convincing in its resemblance to the actual site, and as such serves as a useful comparison to Moran's later portrayals. After Moran had seen the cascade for himself in 1871, Upper Falls became a favorite in his Yellowstone repertoire. Before the Prang commission, he had painted it in watercolor for William Blackmore (1872, Gilcrease) and had created the design for a steel engraving in *Picturesque America* (fig. 143), possibly using one of Jackson's several photographs of the falls as a reference (fig. 144).[46]

Moran noted in his ledger that Prang sold *Upper Fall[s] of the Yellowstone* and *Cañon of the Rio Virgin* to a "Mr. Kirkpatrick." Although Carol Clark apparently did not realize the Kirkpatrick/Prang link when she listed the work in her catalogue raisonné of Moran's watercolors (no. 61), it is clear that this Upper Falls is the work today in the Philbrook Museum of Art in Tulsa, Oklahoma (fig. 145). As such it is the only one of

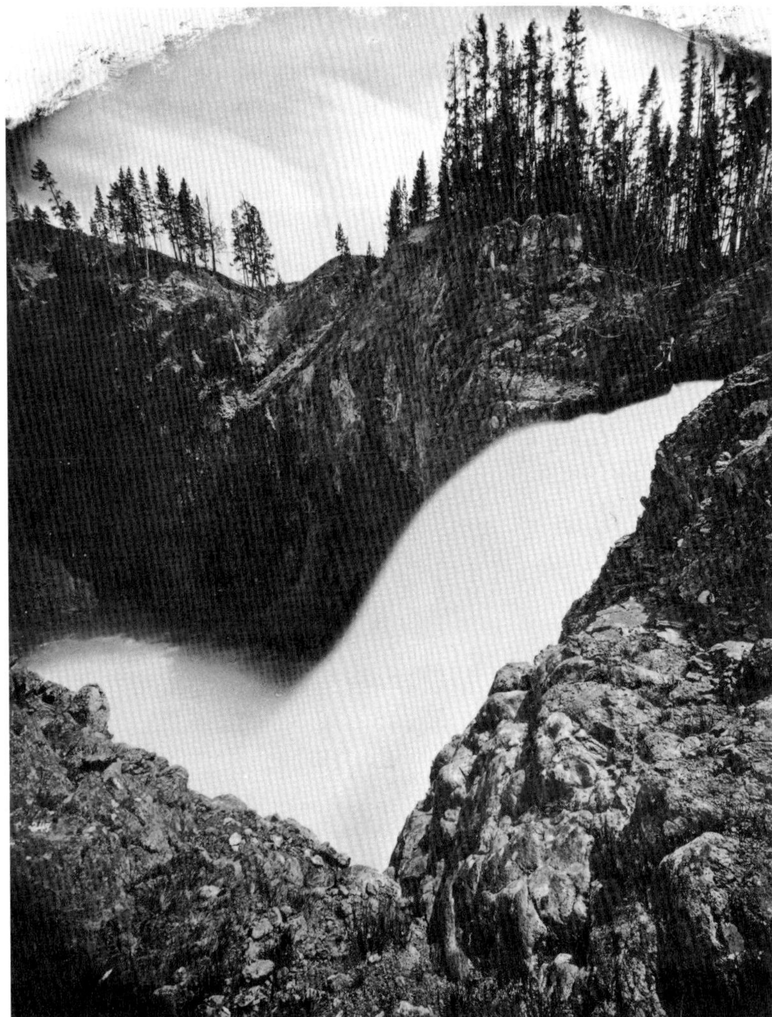

FIGURE 144. William Henry Jackson, *Yellowstone National Park, Upper Falls of the Yellowstone River, near the View from the West Side*, 1871, photograph. United States Geological Survey Photographic Library (jwh00085)

the nine "unpublished" works that Moran produced for Prang whose location is currently known. Philbrook's *Upper Falls* differs only slightly from the Blackmore version and the *Picturesque America* engraving. It is a little darker overall, and its foreground is somewhat more detailed, but generally Moran's portrayals of Upper Falls were remarkably consistent. The verso of the Philbrook watercolor, however, contains a unique feature, a handwritten note by the artist, perhaps written to assist Prang and Hayden as they composed its accompanying text for the published portfolio:

> About 25 mi below the Yellowstone Lake the river makes the first grand leap over a Basaltic ledge of rock, a distance of 125' into a vast black looking cauldron, worn by the waters in their tremendous rush. Unlike the lower Fall (half a mile below) it is broken in its descent by the projecting rocks, tearing the waters into clouds

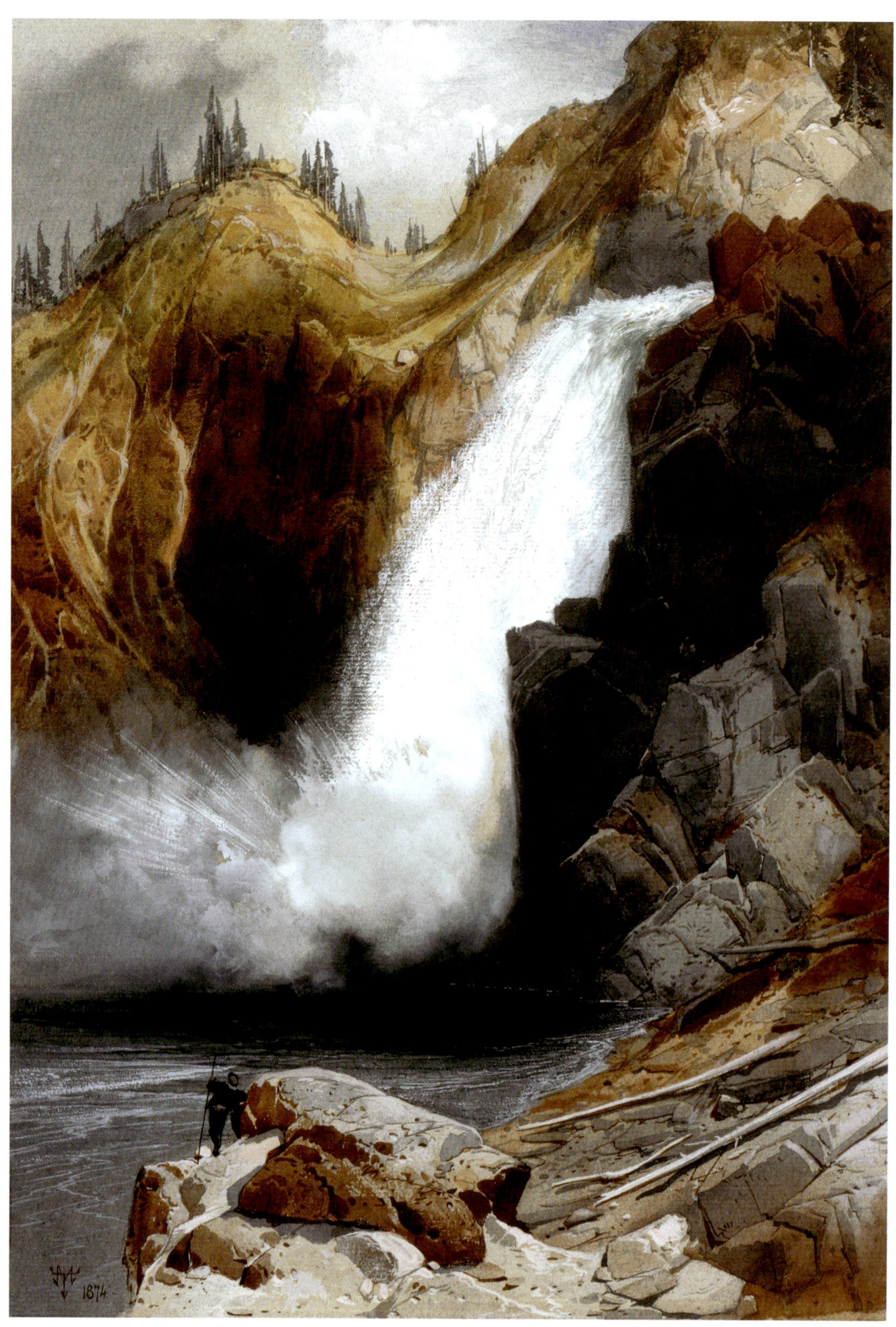
1874

> of spray ere it reaches the bottom and giving the peculiar rocket-like discharge of water points shown in the picture. This point is the proper head of the Grand Cañon and the river makes a fitting entrance into it. A curious fact is that all fish caught in the river below these falls are free from a worm which is found in the flesh of nearly all those caught above.[47]

In all of his versions of Upper Falls, Moran highlighted the spray he mentioned in this comment, and in keeping with his written description, its thunderous visual explosion as it plummets into the river is the most arresting aspect of the scene.

DEVIL'S DEN

Another close and gloomy space was Devil's Den in Yellowstone, which Moran painted for Prang, noting payment on February 27, 1874.[48] Named by the Washburn/Doane expedition in 1870, the thin canyon occupies an approximately half-mile stretch above Cascade Falls on Cascade Creek, a tributary of the Yellowstone River.[49] The two waterways join between the Upper and Lower Falls, just above the Grand Canyon of the Yellowstone. The Hayden survey party camped on Cascade Creek on July 26, 1871, en route from Tower Falls to the Grand Canyon, and they may have even carried the May 1871 *Scribner's Monthly* article in which Nathaniel Langford described where Cascade Creek "passes through a gloomy gorge, of abrupt descent, which on either side is filled with continuous masses of obsidian that have been worn by the water into many fantastic shapes and cavernous recesses."[50] In his own *Scribner's Monthly* article in February 1872, Hayden also mentioned the canyon, noting that

> the gorge is so narrow and deep that the traveler looks down from the margin above into an abyss so dark and forbidding that a very appropriate name came almost involuntarily to one's lips—the "Devil's Den." The sides of the gorge are very rugged, composed of angular masses of basalt and obsidian cemented with volcanic ashes. There is also a large amount of sulphur mingled with the ashes so that the debris looks like the remains of an old furnace.[51]

Hayden's description contrasts with Moran's Blackmore version, *Devil's Den, Cascade Creek* (fig. 146), which is hardly gloomy but rather a relatively tranquil and light-filled view of a creek flanked with rugged outcroppings. The wood-engraved illustration that accompanied Hayden's article (fig. 147) is more forbidding, although this may be due in part to limitations of the medium itself. Taken together, however, we may see something of the lost *Devil's Den* watercolor of the Prang series.[52]

As Hayden noted in *The Yellowstone National Park,* satanic place-names abound at Yellowstone, although these were deemphasized during the national park campaign in favor of the more positive associations of "wonderland."[53] It is interesting to

FIGURE 145. Thomas Moran, *Upper Falls, Yellowstone,* 1874, watercolor, 14 × 9¾ in. (35.6 × 24.8 cm). The Philbrook Museum of Art, Tulsa, Oklahoma, gift of John Zink

speculate that the *Devil's Den* might have been excluded from the Prang portfolio for that reason, in an effort to stress Yellowstone's wondrous aspects rather than its more sinister qualities. *The Towers of Tower Falls,* of course, was also known as the Devil's Hoof, but that nickname was not part of the work's title. Had *Devil's Den* appeared in the Prang publication, it nevertheless would have complemented that work, offering an interesting contrast to the sacred themes of *The Mountain of the Holy Cross,* the biblical allusions at Zion, and the rainbow in *Yellowstone Lake.* It would also have had formal and topographical links to the other canyon and river views, especially those that depicted confined scenes such as *Mu-Koon-Tu-Weap Narrows.*

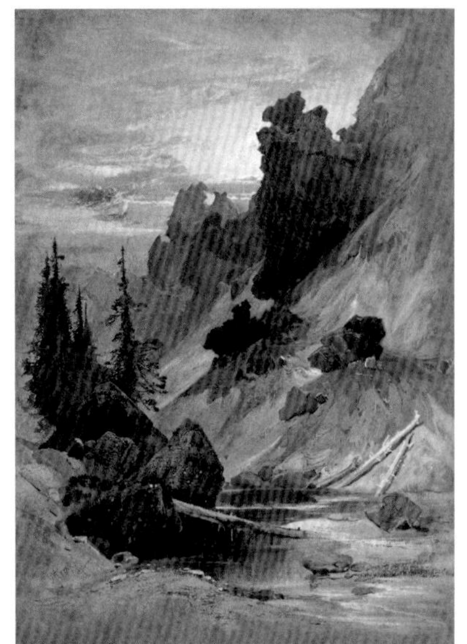

FIGURE 146. Thomas Moran, *Devil's Den, Cascade Creek,* 1872, watercolor, 13⅛ × 9⅞ in. (33.3 × 24.5 cm). Gilcrease Museum, Tulsa, Oklahoma

THE THREE TETONS

The last entry in Moran's ledger about *The Yellowstone National Park* commission lists *The Three Tetons,* but it remains unclear why the title, accompanied by the notation "[$]100.00" that indicates that Prang paid him for the work, is struck through with a line.[54] It is the only one of the entire list to appear this way. The Tetons, of course, are the remarkable mountain range extending northward between Jackson Hole, Wyoming, and Yellowstone National Park. Rising spectacularly from the western edge of the relatively planar glacial moraine that makes up the Snake River Valley, they are especially rugged peaks that are rendered even more dramatic because of the great distance from which they can be viewed. Today, they are the focal points of Grand Teton National Park.[55] Although located in Wyoming, they are also visible from Idaho, and Moran may have considered them an additional Idaho scene to *Shoshone Falls,* balancing the geographic array in the Prang project more thoroughly.

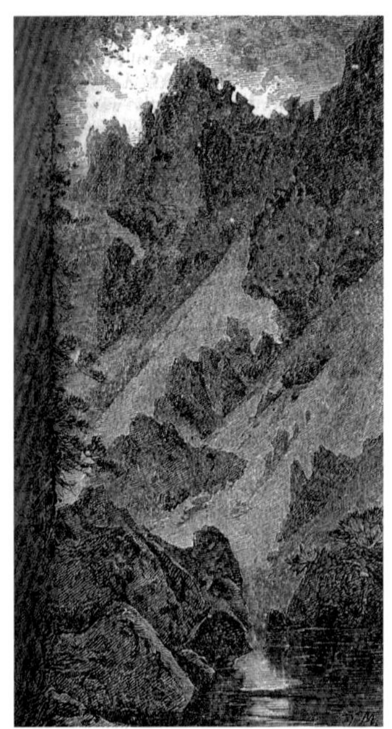

FIGURE 147. After Thomas Moran, *The Devil's Den,* 1871, wood engraving, *Scribner's Monthly* 3 (February 1872): 393. Perkins Library, Hastings College, Hastings, Nebraska

Moran had not actually seen the Tetons when he painted them for Prang, except perhaps from a distance on the Idaho side in 1871 as he traveled north from Salt Lake City to join Hayden's expedition at Monida, Montana. In 1872, however, Hayden's survey ventured south of Yellowstone into the Teton region and brought back photographs that Moran probably used to compose his Prang watercolor (fig. 148).[56] On that trip several members of Hayden's party ascended the tallest peak and named it Mount Hayden, although it was later renamed Grand Teton. Another of the Tetons they named Mount Moran, the massive 12,605-foot peak just north of the three tallest Tetons, distinctive for its large bulk and unique contours.[57] This homage to the artist remains today, along with a crossroads named Moran Junction and a nearby town, Moran, Wyoming. The artist was extremely pleased by the recognition, writing to Hayden that he was "delighted to be so honored."[58] Hayden himself was so excited by the mountains that he admonished the artist, "The next great picture you paint must be the Tetons."[59] Although Moran reserved his "great pictures" for sites that he had personally visited, his watercolor of the Tetons for Prang may have been a response to this exhortation as well as an indication of his personal affiliation with the western peak.[60]

In June 1876, *The Aldine* published a Moran wood engraving, *Mount Hayden and Mount Moran* (fig. 149), that may offer a glimpse of the lost Prang watercolor, although the correspondence between the two images remains uncertain.[61] He had already provided another version, *Mount Hayden and Mount Moran—From the West* (fig. 150), based on one of Jackson's photographs, for Nathaniel Langford's article "The Ascent of Mount Hayden" in *Scribner's Monthly*. *The Aldine* version is a more compelling view, even as it alters the distinctive silhouette of the Tetons. With its rugged foreground and angled mountainside that frames the peaks beyond, it seems a more finished, composed view appropriate for a studio watercolor treatment.

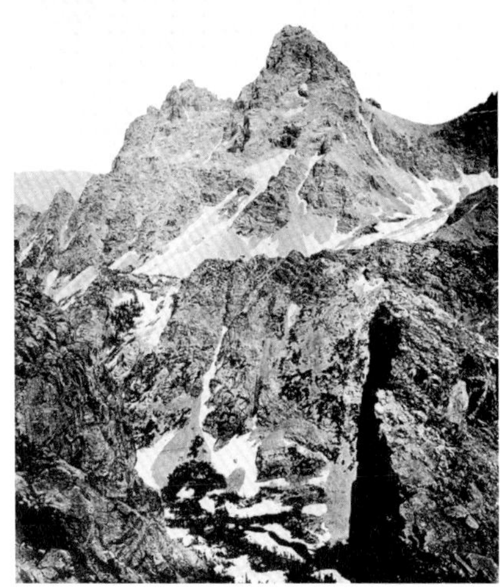

FIGURE 148. William Henry Jackson, *The Grand Teton, Originally Named Mount Hayden*, 1872, photograph. United States Geological Survey Photographic Library (jwh00162a)

After his 1879 trip to see the Tetons for himself, Moran created additional images of the mountains, including several significant oils.[62] Of those, *The Three Tetons* (1895, the White House), *The Teton Range* (1897, Metropolitan Museum of Art), and *In the Teton Range, Idaho* (1899, Kimbell Art Museum, Fort Worth) are among the most notable. Even though he never actually saw the Tetons from the most spectacular viewpoint on the eastern side, Moran nevertheless said that the peaks were "perhaps the finest pictorial range in the United States or even in North America."[63]

THE ABSENT WONDERLANDS

Although the full title of *The Yellowstone National Park* limits the geographical area of the portfolio's scope to Yellowstone, Idaho, Nevada, Colorado, and Utah, it is interesting to consider why Moran did not include several other famous sites of the West in his series for Louis Prang. Yosemite, the Giant Sequoias, and, especially, the Grand Canyon in Arizona are three of the most notable omissions. Moran had visited at least two of the three, the areas had received significant attention by 1876, and audiences were hungry for information about them. Their absence, especially when the artist portrayed other more obscure sites for the project, is curious.

When Moran visited Yosemite in 1872 he created a number of sketches, but he never made much of them in his paintings or published work. He seems not to have sketched the Big Trees at all, which is surprising since the stunning Mariposa Grove of monumental redwoods is nearby. As mentioned in the previous chapter, however, these attractions had already been quite publicly "claimed" by other artists, especially by his chief rival, Albert Bierstadt, and Moran may have been loath to invite more comparisons with him than his work already had. By 1876, Bierstadt's work was receiving criticism for its hyperbolic qualities, and any

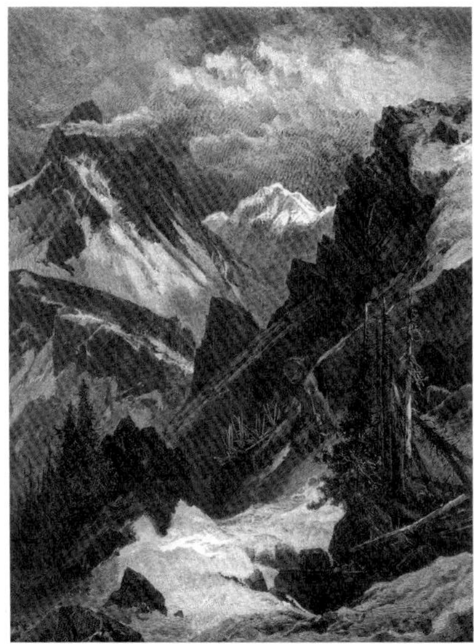

FIGURE 149. After Thomas Moran, *Mount Hayden and Mount Moran*, ca. 1875, wood engraving, *The Aldine* 8 (June 1876): 194. Courtesy of Boston Public Library, Print Room

portrayals Moran might have made of the same sites would undoubtedly have invited similar commentary.

The absence of Arizona's Grand Canyon from the portfolio, however, is harder to understand. It was the site Moran had most recently visited when Prang approached him to do the chromolithographic project, and it remained one of his most important subjects throughout his life. Two Utah images from Moran's 1873 trip west were included in the Prang portfolio, but the real destination that summer and the highlight of the experience was the Grand Canyon. After his return east in the fall, and as he began the Prang commission in early 1874, Moran was also hard at work on his second major western oil painting, *The Chasm of the Colorado* (1873–1874, fig. 33). At the same time and through much of that year, he was also busy producing some thirty Grand Canyon illustrations for *Scribner's Monthly*.[64] These appeared early in 1875, about the time Moran finished the Prang watercolors, and they were also reprinted in Powell's report the same year.[65] Had Prang or Moran been interested in including the Grand Canyon among the chromolithographs, any of these compositions would have been readily available for watercolor treatments.

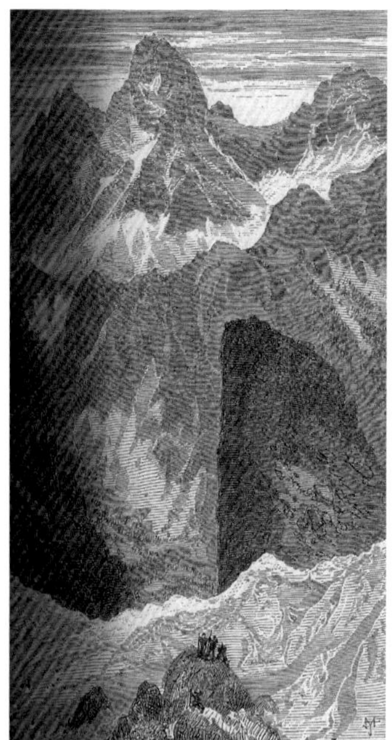

FIGURE 150. After Thomas Moran, *Mount Hayden and Mount Moran — From the West*, ca. 1873, wood engraving, *Scribner's Monthly* 6 (June 1873): 143

Until letters are found between the publisher and artist that might explain the omission, we are left to speculate about the Grand Canyon's absence from the Prang series. The obscurity of the location might have been a factor. Although this massive chasm now presides as the most famous and well-visited western wonderland, in the mid-1870s it was an extremely remote location that few Americans had seen, and despite *Scribner's* and Powell's efforts to visually publicize it, it had not received the attention that had made Yellowstone so prominent. The Grand Canyon would not become easily accessible until 1901, when the Atchison, Topeka, and Santa Fe Railway built a spur line to the south rim and constructed El Tovar Hotel there, a facility still in use today.

The site of *Valley of the Babbling Waters* in present-day Zion National Park was equally remote. Indeed, Hayden's text emphasizes that fact:

> The whole of the region here described may be said to be almost inaccessible. In attempting to traverse it, one would be obliged to cross gorge after gorge with nearly vertical walls, three thousand feet or more in depth. Hence this great country, above two hundred miles in length and one hundred and fifty in width, and rich in scenes as grand as the one before us, must ever be dedicated to nature, for it can never be inhabited by man. It is unique, grand, barren, and desolate.[66]

Although "barren and desolate," the Zion canyon was also "unique" and "grand." And while *The Aldine* also called *Valley of the Babbling Waters* "awful," it combined that term with "beautiful." The Rio Virgin valley was remote, but it was endowed with the redeeming qualities of beauty and sacred associations.

This was not the case for the Grand Canyon in the 1870s. Although Congress had validated Moran's *Chasm* painting with its purchase, most people regarded the site and the painting as an apocalyptic landscape, calling it everything from "the wildest and . . . [most] diabolical scene man ever looked upon" and "Dante's Inferno," to a "grand transformation scene gone wild." The art critic of the *Atlantic Monthly* wrote: "Here there is no loveliness for hundreds of miles, nor anything on which the healthy human eye can bear to look. . . . this scene is only the concentrated ghastliness of a ghastly region." He found nothing to recommend in the landscape and concluded with, "The only aim of art is to feed the sense of beauty; it has no right to meddle with horrors and desolation."[67] And even Moran's friend, *Scribner's Monthly* editor Richard Watson Gilder, had said: "It is awful. The spectator longs for rest, repose, and comfort . . . from all this chaos and tumult."[68] With such a negative response to the subject, it is hardly surprising that Louis Prang might have declined a Grand Canyon view if Moran had suggested one. He was anxious to please the critics with his beautiful portfolio of western landscape chromolithographs, and "chaos and tumult," he surely thought, was not the way to do that.

The nine subjects that Moran created for *The Yellowstone National Park* leave unresolved some of the Prang project's most intriguing questions. Until the watercolors are found, we can only imagine how they would really appear. But even without them, it is possible to understand that their subject matter would have augmented the final publication significantly, solidifying the compositional and formal patterns of the plates and deepening the tension between the sacred and the profane that the portfolio embodies in interesting and important ways. Whether their addition to the publication would have helped or hurt its reception when it was issued can never be known, but they certainly would have added to the artistic significance of the final product.

Even without the intriguing contributions the unpublished nine watercolors might have provided, *The Yellowstone National Park* was the apogee of chromolithographic reproduction and a remarkable assemblage of some of Moran's most effective paintings. The combined forces of misfortune, poor management, and preconceived critical attitudes toward Prang's chromolithographs, however, rendered the publication much less well received than it deserved to be. The nine scenes that were omitted would probably have had no effect on the outcome, but their original contribution is significant nevertheless. With the fifteen views that were chromolithographed, they give a unique portrayal of the American West, one that would have been even more compelling had they taken their rightful place within the pages of the completed portfolio.

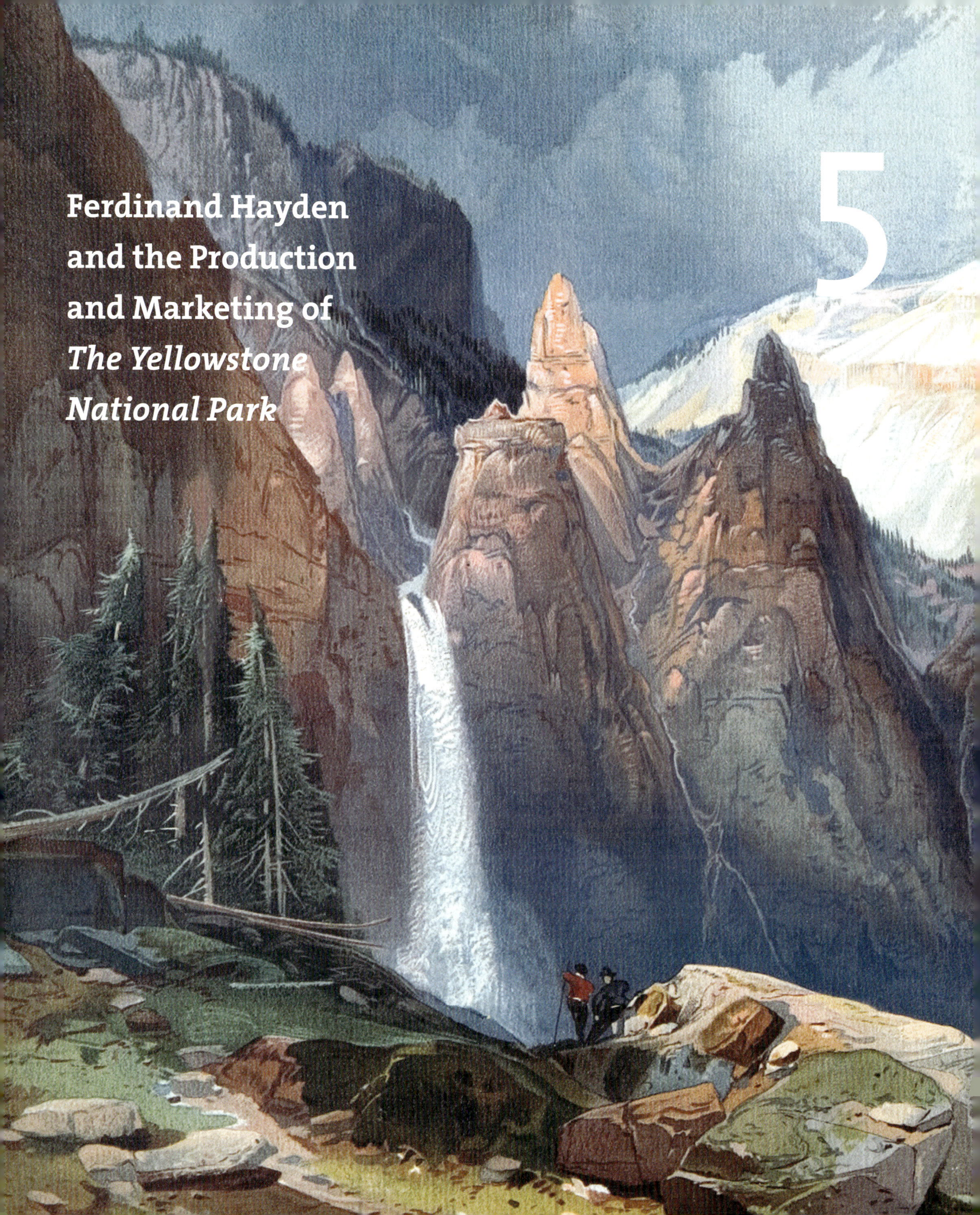

5

Ferdinand Hayden and the Production and Marketing of *The Yellowstone National Park*

The public must now decide whether there is sufficient appreciation for work of so high a standard in the country, and whether the publishers were justified in incurring the very considerable outlay involved in its production.

—*Ferdinand Hayden,* The Yellowstone National Park, *1876*

When Ferdinand Hayden (fig. 151) wrote the text for the Prang portfolio, he was already a veteran explorer, paleontologist, physician, writer, and congressional lobbyist. He had served as a doctor in the Civil War and had launched his expeditionary career in 1867 with a survey of Nebraska. An energetic promoter of his own endeavors, he had been active in publishing extensive scientific reports of his expeditions and had quickly recognized the value of pictorial imagery for drawing public attention to his survey work. In 1869, as he moved his explorations into eastern Wyoming, he hired an artist, Henry Wood Elliott, to make topographical studies of the territory; the following year he signed on William Henry Jackson as photographer. That same year he published a photographic book, *Sun Pictures of Rocky Mountain Scenery,* a selection of thirty photographs by A. J. Russell of scenes along the Union Pacific Railroad between Laramie and Salt Lake City. He also welcomed the painter Sanford Gifford, who was already traveling in the West the summer of 1870, for a brief stint with the party. Gifford's visit did not result in any substantial paintings, but the fact that Hayden invited him back the next year seems to demonstrate the value that he placed on having a well-known landscape artist portray the scenery through which the expedition traveled.[1] Gifford declined the opportunity, but when Hayden was preparing to embark on what would become his landmark exploration of the Yellowstone region in the spring of 1871, he was more than willing to accept the proposal that Thomas Moran accompany him, "an artist," the painter's letter of introduction read, "of much genius, who desires to take sketches in the upper Yellowstone region, from which to paint some fine pictures on his return. That he will surpass Bierstadt's Yosemite we who know him best fully believe."[2] Moran accompanied the expedition as a guest, with funding from *Scribner's Monthly* and the Northern Pacific Railroad, but he was a de facto member of the survey. He worked closely with Jackson on the trip, helping make photographs, and his remarkable imagery would be a major asset to Hayden, who would become famous as the leading explorer of the Yellowstone region. Moran maintained a close relationship with Jackson, Hayden, and other U.S. geological survey members in subsequent years.

Hayden was shrewd in using Jackson's images and Moran's sketches from Yellowstone to advance his professional agenda; in fact, he spent so much time promoting his survey that he has been characterized as much as a popularizer of the West as a scientist. He showed the images to congressmen as the national park bill was debated in the winter of 1871–1872, prevailed upon *Scribner's Monthly* to let him use the wood engravings Moran had produced for the magazine in his own government reports, and was extremely active in encouraging other publishers to present his expedition in print, often sharing photographs and the electrotypes of Moran's illustrations he had obtained from *Scribner's* with them.[3] His efforts were rewarded as his survey received increased appropriations and heightened fame. So when L. Prang & Co. approached him in 1875 to help with *The Yellowstone National Park* chromolithograph publication, he "cheerfully assented to take charge of the literary part of the work."[4] The portfolio promised to be a prestigious vehicle that would call his name and research to the attention of distinguished individuals and the wider public, bringing even more renown to his endeavors.

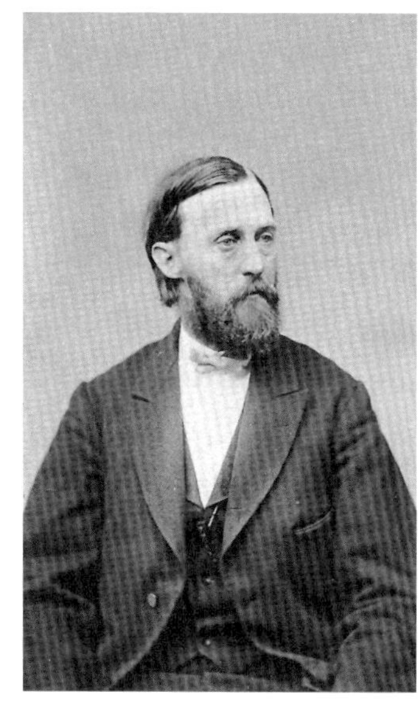

FIGURE 151. Anonymous, *Ferdinand Vandiveer Hayden (1829–1887)*, ca. 1875, albumen silver print. National Portrait Gallery, Smithsonian Institution, Washington, D.C.

In contrast to the limited documentation on Moran's interactions with Prang, the archive regarding Hayden's involvement is extensive, since he received his mail at a government office where all incoming correspondence was preserved. Between December 1874 and November 1878, Prang's office wrote Hayden almost ninety letters about the project, many quite detailed. The correspondence is usually signed "L. Prang & Co.," but most of it was probably written by Prang's "business manager and literary critic" or "technical manager," Sylvester Koehler (1837–1900), who would go on to become an important figure in the Boston art world.[5] Louis Prang occasionally wrote to Hayden as well, and the two men visited personally several times during the course of the project. Although we only have the publisher's side of the conversation, the letters, now at the National Archives in Washington, D.C., are exceptionally useful for understanding the progress of *The Yellowstone National Park* portfolio, its production and marketing, the hopes for its success, and, ultimately, its unfortunate reception and outcome. The saga reveals the challenges of creating and distributing books during a period of severe economic recession when transition and intense competition characterized the American publishing industry. Moreover, it represents the perils of presenting a controversial popular medium in a format cherished by wealthy and conservative collectors.

Probably hearing of the chromo project from Moran, with whom he was in close touch, Hayden asked L. Prang & Co. about the publication's progress in December 1874 and was told that it was still far from completion and that he would receive proofs when they were ready. The next contact was in June 1875, when Prang himself wrote the survey leader: "Learning of your visit to this city I wish to invite you to see what we are doing in the way of reproduction of Thomas Moran's sketches 'Yellow Stone Valley.'"[6] The next letter, in September, indicates that the meeting never took place, but it was accompanied by several proofs of the chromos and a promise of eight more by November. Included with the pictures were several questions:

> First. If all these sketches are connected with your explorations, and if they can be put forward in connection therewith. Second. How much text in your opinion will they receive and what ought be the character of it. Third. How much will you charge us to prepare the text and when could you have it ready for us. Fourth. In the event of your preparing suitable text and connecting this publication of the pictures with your expedition would the enterprise in your opinion merit and in any tangible way receive the support of the government or of the Smithsonian Institution?[7]

This inquiry suggests that Prang had discussed a prospective text with Hayden but was unsure which images had originated with which survey (some had derived from Moran's experiences with Hayden, others with Powell, and still others with the artist's own trip to California). Moran, of course, had chosen the subjects and had probably explained to Prang only that he had seen most of the sites during his travels with federal expeditions.[8]

As its question about government interest in the publication indicates, L. Prang & Co. requested the survey leader's assistance on many more aspects of the project than just the text. Asking about everything from the title of the work to Hayden's opinions on issuing the publication serially, the publisher especially solicited his help in marketing the final product, something modern authors are asked to do only to the extent of attending book readings and signings. Throughout the relationship, Hayden was an exceptionally busy man for whom the Prang publication was a valued but relatively minor sideline, and although he corresponded with the firm regularly, he was often slow in answering their requests. Since he was simultaneously concerned with lobbying Congress for funding, planning his next expedition and arranging its many details, traveling several months of the year, supervising staff both in Washington, D.C., and in the West, writing his research into official reports, scientific publications, and popular accounts and seeing them through publication, and answering hundreds of requests from many quarters for photographs, information, and assistance, it is remarkable that Hayden was able to respond to L. Prang & Co.'s numerous and persistent needs at all.[9] That he did so frequently and with relative thoroughness seems nothing short of extraordinary.

THE TEXT

In October 1875, with all of Moran's watercolors in hand and Hayden's willingness to write the accompanying text assured, Prang's office presented the survey leader with a deadline: "We should like the text to be ready when the pictures are; and we hope to have the latter completed by March next [1876]."[10] Two months later, with printing of the chromos under way, the editors wrote Hayden, "It is therefore time we were arranging for the text and the details of publication."[11] With no results forthcoming, another letter followed with a more specific charge regarding the chromolithographs: "We desire text for them, which shall be descriptive of each picture and which shall comprise one or two pages of introductory matter and then detailed description of each picture."[12]

L. Prang & Co. struggled for months to get Hayden to write the copy. At the end of April, the editor wrote: "Please pardon our importunity, but we beg to say that we have got our Chromos all ready for the Centennial, and are very desirous of presenting them there, as the great feature of our Exhibit. We need the text to present the work in its completeness and trust therefore, you will be able to send the copy to us very shortly. May we expect it within a few days?"[13] Hayden finally came through with some copy by the first week of May, but it was apparently just a short passage for the first "number," an initial installment with just a few chromos. The process for the full publication continued.

Still hopeful of having something substantial to show at the Centennial Exposition, the editors detailed their desires for the introduction again at the end of June: "It need not be long, but should set forth the object of your expedition, and such general points of interest in the portions of country illustrated, as may seem to warrant the publication of so extensive a work. Then too, in the introduction, you could say, once and for all, what is necessary to be said about Mr. Moran's sketches, and the faithfulness of our reproduction."[14] With no response forthcoming, the prints went on to Philadelphia with only a preliminary "circular" as textual accompaniment.

The Yellowstone National Park chromolithographs were a prominent component of Prang's exhibition in the Centennial Art Building in the summer of 1876. The galleries were supervised by none other than Moran's old friend and mentor, John Sartain, who had long been an advocate of reproductive imagery as well as of fine art generally, and he personally saw to it that both Moran and Prang were well accommodated in their exhibitions. He promised Moran good placement of his several paintings in the main halls and consulted with Louis Prang on the fabric coverings for the walls of his area to ensure they would be of "a style suitable to hang chromos on with advantage."[15] This inside ally was a significant asset; Moran's newly completed 5-by-7-foot *Mountain of the Holy Cross* painting, for example, was given a prominent spot in a major gallery in Memorial Hall and Prang's display was well positioned and appointed.[16]

At the fair, *The Yellowstone National Park* chromolithographs attracted the favorable notice of *Frank Leslie's Historical Register of the United States Centennial Exposition,* although this commemorative publication was not issued until 1877, some months after the exhibition had closed. "Visitors to Memorial Hall should not fail to pass some time in Gallery X," the reviewer explained in a passage of several paragraphs, "which lies very near the exit toward the Annex, and where can be seen a number of chromolithographic reproductions of water-color sketches by Mr. Thomas Moran, illustrating the Yellowstone region and that of the Colorado, as also oil paintings by the same artist." The review listed all the titles, attesting that "the sketches are accurately executed and brilliant in color," and went into detail about several images and their origin in the federal surveys. Although Prang's company was not named, the publisher would surely have been pleased at this attention to its creations.[17]

The Centennial Exposition, of course, was a vast fair with millions of exhibits, so this relatively elaborate review attests to the significance of the Prang display. With its presentation of colorful views of western scenery at a time of heightened nationalism when western events were at the forefront of American news, the Moran chromos were a timely attraction. Colorado was a brand-new state, and many other areas depicted in the series were newly accessible via the transcontinental railroad. And then, immediately after the opening of the fair, news of the Battle of the Little Bighorn in Montana turned all eyes westward. Tensions had been rising in the region for years, of course, but had been especially prone to conflict since the 1874 discovery of gold in South Dakota's Black Hills. The ensuing resistance by the Native Americans of the region had dominated headlines throughout June 1876, and the Centennial Exposition and the national celebrations were almost overshadowed by the loss of Custer and his entire regiment. Within such a context, western scenery, regardless of how beautiful, colorful, or intimately portrayed, must have seemed truly sublime in the Burkean sense, a region of terrible power.[18]

A SCIENTIFIC EMPHASIS

The presentation of *The Yellowstone National Park* chromos at the Centennial Exposition gave the Prang editors new ideas to consider in their aspirations for the publication, and they offered Hayden extended instructions about how he might shape his text to fit them. The most important of these was an increased emphasis on the scientific importance of the publication. Although the portfolio's reputation today is as a remarkable artistic and technological achievement, its contribution to science was the primary concern for L. Prang & Co. The editors voiced their belief that a scientific bent would aid sales, but they may have also thought it might address the problem that had plagued Prang since the late 1860s—the characterization of chromos as lacking in real cultural significance. As discussed in Chapter Two, serious scientific books had a long history of lavish illustration, and presenting Moran's scenic imagery within this context would, it was hoped, align them with that tradition of distinguished publications. An even more subconscious aspiration in crafting the portfolio as a scientific contribution may have been to appeal primarily to male readers, thus subverting the implicit association that Prang's products were largely the domain of a female clientele for decorative or social purposes.

The editors stressed their desire for a scientifically noteworthy work to Hayden several times, but no more explicitly than when the text he finally offered them in early July 1876 did not meet their expectations:

> As regards the "Introduction," we must take the liberty of saying that we have been somewhat disappointed by it. We had hoped it would be much fuller, and more scientific, although still popular in its character. For these reasons we spoke of the forthcoming work in our circular as "the most important contribution yet made to the illustrated *scientific* literature on 'our great western territories.'" With the present text that statement would hardly be warranted and might lay us open to the charge of overstating. With your permission we will outline what we thought the Introduction ought to contain.
>
> 1.) A concise account of the discovery of the Yellowstone region and of the early expeditions to it, and the adjacent regions.
>
> 2.) A short account of your own expeditions and labors, not only in the Yellowstone Valley, but also elsewhere in the West.
>
> 3.) A *general* description of the whole region comprised in the illustrations, and a statement of the reasons which caused Congress to establish the Yellowstone National Park. The Act of Congress might here be given.
>
> 4.) A short description of the geological character of the region, and a statement of the scientific results which have grown out of its exploration. If any new views have been gained for the formation of the earth or of its crust, or if any of the older hypotheses have been either strengthened or upset by the results obtained that fact ought to be stated.
>
> 5.) The geological peculiarities of the region, as far as they can be seen in the sketches, ought to be pointed out with reference to each separate plate.
>
> The Introduction here mapped out, would, we believe, give a real scientific value to the work, and together with the picturesque descriptions already in our hands, would make the work as complete as we would like to see it.[19]

Hayden promptly complied with the request to rewrite, and the editors decided that the new draft he submitted toward the end of July "will do very nicely."[20] They then turned their attention to the descriptions that accompanied each plate, deciding quickly that those also needed substantial editing:

> Reading through some of the descriptions which are about to be set up in type, it appeared to us, that by a little rearranging and a few verbal changes, they might be made somewhat clearer for the general reader. We have therefore had three of them rewritten. . . . We will now have the rest of the Descriptions carefully read, and if we have any more changes to suggest we will report to you immediately, so that you may

decide before leaving [for the West]. We beg pardon for these suggestions, but we are convinced that you will receive them in the spirit in which they are offered. It is your own as well as our interest to have this work go forth as perfect as may be, and our only object in suggesting the changes indicated is to make the text as clear and concise as possible. You know from experience that what is quite clear to an author familiar with his subject is sometimes not as clear to the uninformed reader.[21]

After several revisions, printing was begun on the text by the end of August. The editors had one final suggestion, the addition of a preface, and for that they decided to expedite matters by writing it in-house. Hayden approved their copy, which was published with his signature, and the final portfolios, with chromos and text, were at last in hand by December 1876.

Hayden's written commentary in *The Yellowstone National Park* is indeed more scientific than literary and artistic, but despite Prang's acceptance of it, the text was hardly "the most important contribution yet made to the . . . *scientific* literature on 'our great western territories.'" After a rather romantic opening paragraph, he briefly recounted the history of Yellowstone's exploration and offered lengthy instructions for reaching the area, noting that "at no distant period the Park will be as easily accessible as almost any other mountain region now visited by those who travel for pleasure." He then launched into a geological discussion of the park, paying special attention to the sites depicted in the chromos, and added a table comparing the various geyser eruptions and their chemical compositions. His introduction concluded with the text of the congressional park act and a list of the chromos and the locations of their subjects. At twelve and a half pages of printed text, the essay was relatively cursory, exclusively focused on Yellowstone, and entirely a summary of previous publications. The other regions represented in the plates were only mentioned in the "descriptions" that accompanied each plate.

POSITIONING *THE YELLOWSTONE NATIONAL PARK* IN THE MARKET

As L. Prang & Co. worked with Hayden to shape *The Yellowstone National Park,* the company carefully considered the appeal of nearly every aspect of the publication. Stung by the criticism Prang's American Chromos had received at the hands of the art critics, the publisher was determined to present a work that would appeal to intellectual tastes. The title, for example, was crafted to emphasize its association with the U.S. geological surveys, and "after much hammering on the idea, and balancing of phrases," the editors sent several for Hayden's review, saying that "our main idea is, to get as much official identification of the work with your expedition as possible."[22] As the editors made even more clear in their next letter, they hoped the scientific nature of *The Yellowstone National Park* would ensure the publication's appeal beyond the art market. It was especially important, they believed, to deemphasize the decorative quality of the imagery and position the publication as a scholarly endeavor that would capture the attention of scientists and serious book collectors:

> In our last letter we omitted to state one point which it appeared to us, ought not to be lost sight of in writing the title. It is this, that the title ought to appeal as strongly as possible to the *scientific* world and that, consequently, everything ought to be avoided in it, which might convey the idea that the work is simply a collection of pretty pictures. We therefore kept the words "Illustrations," "Views," and "Scenes" (all of which were considered) carefully out of the title, and strove to emphasize the fact that the illustrations are *primarily* of a scientific character, which we believe to be the true state of the case. We are compelled to appeal to two classes of the public with this publication, the one the picture loving class, the other the scientific class. To reach the first we must trust to the pictures themselves. If we can induce the other class to look at our work upon the strength of the impression received by reading the title, as advertised, we shall have gained a point worth making. Generally speaking pictures as such do not interest the scientific world sufficient to induce its members to go to any trouble in looking them up. We must therefore make it clear in the title that the scientific character of the work is the leading feature, that art has in this instance been in the service of science, and that scientific accuracy has not been sacrificed for the mere purpose of producing "pretty pictures." If we can make this clear we may also hope for the sympathy of the libraries, in this country as well as in Europe. Libraries do not care for mere picture-books, but they are *compelled* to take notice of all works of a scientific character.[23]

Such careful consideration of the audience and the potential reception of the work is hardly surprising since the project was a major investment of both time and money, but the emphasis on science is especially noteworthy, as this sort of book represented a major departure from anything L. Prang & Co. had done before. In this fascinating passage, the company reveals that it was feeling its way into a new arena, hoping to position itself as a publisher of serious imagery and not just popular chromos and novelty items. Distinguishing between the classes of readers, the "picture-loving class" and the "scientific class," the editors nevertheless hoped to appeal to both, with a hybrid publication that would principally impress with its substance and then beguile with its beauty.

One element that helped make *The Yellowstone National Park* more scientifically valid was the inclusion of two maps that pinpointed the scenes portrayed in the chromolithographic plates (figs. 152 and 153). Adding these did not occur to the Prang staff until June 1876 as they were working with the textual component of the publication, and they wrote Hayden with a suggestion: "It has occurred to us that it might be well

FIGURE 152. *Map of the Yellowstone National Park,* 1876, from *The Yellowstone National Park* (Boston: L. Prang & Co., 1876). Gilcrease Museum, Tulsa, Oklahoma

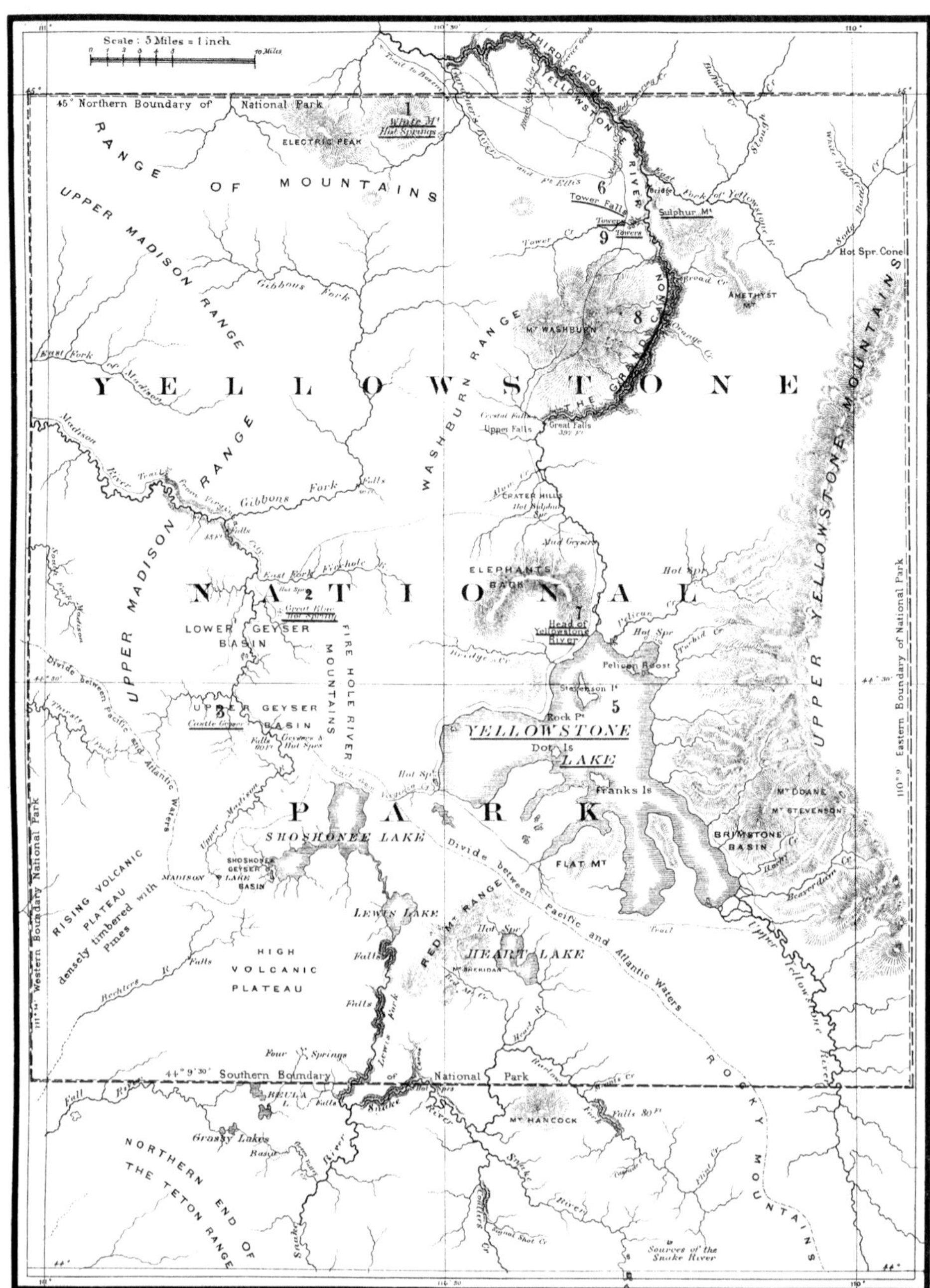

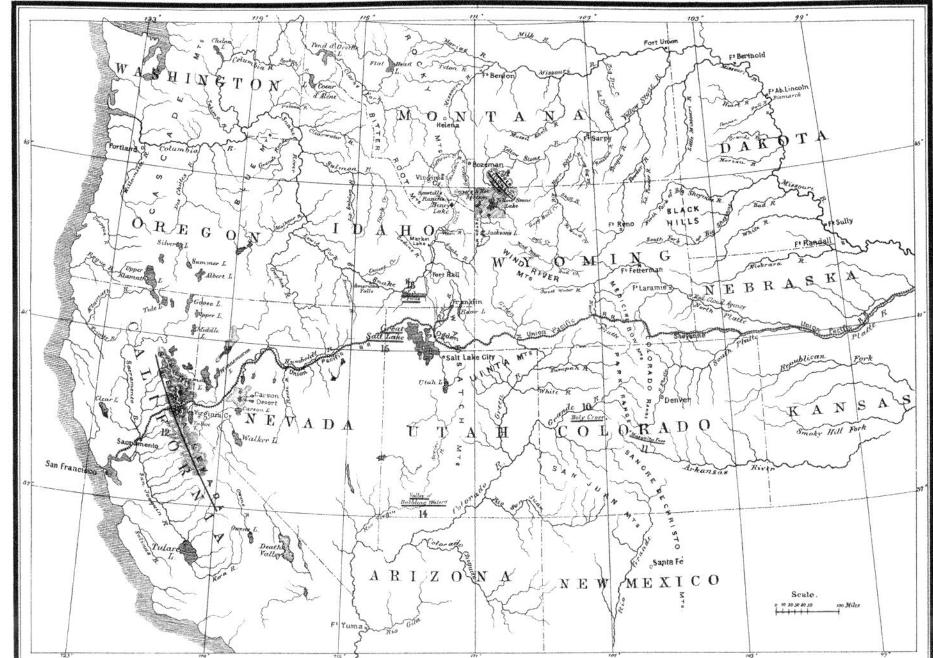

FIGURE 153. *Map of Western U.S.*, 1876, from *The Yellowstone National Park* (Boston: L. Prang & Co., 1876). Gilcrease Museum, Tulsa, Oklahoma

to add an outline map of the territory covered by the descriptions and on which the locations of the various views represented in Mr. Moran's sketches should be indicated. If you think well of this idea, can you furnish the material for such a map, and will you please allude to it in your introduction?" On July 8, only days after word of the Battle of the Little Bighorn reached the East, the publisher asked him to note specifically "those parts where General Custer met with his late terrible fate, to give a clear idea of the roads bearing in and out," reasoning that "such a publication would be of special interest at present and might be made to aid in advertising our publication."[24] Hayden supplied the maps (noting only the location of the Little Bighorn River), and they are indeed a highly useful component to the portfolio, whether they are considered from a scientific perspective or from an artistic one, as we chart Moran's images and his travels.

Although *The Yellowstone National Park* was usually sold as a complete boxed set, L. Prang & Co. seems to have issued a few serial installments of the chromos before the finished work was ready. This was not uncommon; many expensive publications at the time, including *Picturesque America*, were marketed this way. The company asked Hayden his opinion about the strategy as early as January 1876: "What do you think of issuing these in numbers—two pictures in each number or part with a few pages of text. The price we shall have to put rather high $10 for numbers, and would like your judgment as to how many copies we should be likely to sell through official and scientific channels."[25] Still undecided about both the installment question and the price, the editor wrote again in March: "We have not yet determined whether we shall publish them all at once, or whether we shall issue them in parts containing three pictures. The prices at which we shall publish them will be $5.00 for a single picture, parts of three pictures $12.00, the whole series $50.00."[26] Although the pricing of both single images and the complete publication would change, the serial offering seems to have been decided by the summer when Hayden was told: "As we want to issue the first part at once, we trust you will send it [the text] to us without delay. We have already the text for the first three numbers printed."[27] Once the portfolio was complete, however, L. Prang & Co. restricted sales of the single pictures for a time, preferring to market the work as a unified publication.

The lack of advance notices was a concern for L. Prang & Co., as it wrote to Hayden in early August:

> This work has now cost us fully $15,000—and we have not yet seen one Dollar in return, nor have we received one word of encouragement except from you. We think you know from experience that we have spared neither labor nor expense to make this publication an artistic as well as a scientifically reliable work! We are, of course, quite willing to show our gratitude to any person who may assist us in this matter, as far as it can be done without incurring any suspicion of "bribery."[28]

By the end of the year, the completed production cost totaled $25,000, nearly $500,000 in today's money.[29] L. Prang & Co. had a significant investment in the project, both financially and in regard to its reputation, and with the final portfolio finally in hand, the company turned to its intensive marketing early in 1877.[30]

THE CRITICAL RECEPTION OF *THE YELLOWSTONE NATIONAL PARK*

When it was finally circulated in the first months of 1877, *The Yellowstone National Park* portfolio did not provoke the sort of controversy that Prang's earlier chromos had elicited. Neither, however, did it receive the wholehearted acclaim that the publisher expected or that such a high-quality production probably should have warranted. Some important journals and newspapers indeed praised it highly, but many more chose either to ignore the work or to give it only a brief notice. Such a lack of recognition is highly ironic today, considering the portfolio's reputation as a rare and valuable publication and a landmark in the history of art and color printing.

Because of the criticism the *New York Daily Tribune* and *The Nation* had meted out to Prang's chromolithographs in the past, the publisher coveted their approval of *The Yellowstone National Park* above all other reviews. Immediately after the portfolio's completion, in early January 1877, his firm began courting the critics at these two publications. "The newspapers we shall also take in hand now," the office wrote Hayden, "and we shall commence by turning our attention on the 'N.Y. Tribune' and 'The Nation.' Our Mr. Clark will see the editors of these papers personally, and will endeavor to work them into a fit state for writing about the book *enthusiastically.*"[31] After meeting with the first, the editors wrote hopefully: "We believe the 'Tribune' will come out all right. Mr. Ripley personally promised our Mr. Clark that we should have a good notice."[32]

The *Tribune's* review was apparently not written by its noted critic, Clarence Cook, and although not overtly negative, was perfunctory. A short column more descriptive than analytical, it recounted the essential features of the publication and paraphrased Hayden's text about Yellowstone's characteristics. The closest it got to negative commentary was saying that the scenery there "bears a closer resemblance to the fairy scenes produced on the stage than to the woods and hills which are usually seen in Nature," and it concluded with a compliment: "The volume . . . presents a striking and singularly attractive view of the unique picturesque resources of the great mountain region to which it is devoted."[33] But upon reading the review, Prang's business manager, Sylvester Koehler, bluntly expressed the publisher's dismay: "The notice in the 'Tribune' is an outrage, and speaks badly for the people who work on the paper. It reads as if the merest penny-a-liner had written it—a fellow who was afraid to speak his own mind, as he feared to betray his ignorance, and therefore did not dare to do more than to pick out a few phrases here and there from the book itself and to string them together. If this notice is a fair specimen of Tribune '*criticism,*' then we pity the paper and the people who read it!"[34]

The Nation was initially quite complimentary of *The Yellowstone National Park* in some ways, saying that Hayden's text was "well written" and testifying that the reproductions were indeed faithful to the originals. It praised Prang, albeit with something of a backhanded jibe at chromolithography: "There can be no doubt that this work of Mr. Moran's was worth doing, and worth doing so well; and it is especially to be commended that Mr. Prang was willing to undertake so costly an enterprise, the copying of such works as these being one of the things that lithography is undeniably fitted to effect, and, indeed, its chief reason for existence." As the commentary went on, however, it grew increasingly more critical, first damning Moran with faint praise as it "cheerfully" asserted that "he is at his best with working on paper instead of on canvas." And then, even as the reviewer admitted ignorance of the sites and could not "pretend to judge" the views, he called them "crude and shocking" and their coloration "bold, not to say violent."[35]

Prang was horrified. As his office wrote to Hayden, "We can assure you that we were as much chagrined when reading the article in this paper, as you were. But how can we help it? We have no control over these gentlemen, and cannot compel them to do justice, if they will not do it of their own free will. The papers of the U.S. appear almost to be bent on snubbing the work, especially the 'high-toned' ones of the 'Nation' and 'Tribune' class. These people are so 'high-toned' that they have lost the appreciation of everything which does not emanate from their own ring."[36] The battle that Prang had been fighting with these publications and their notions of chromolithography's value since the 1860s had not abated and, unfortunately, this time he would not be able to take consolation in either his products' popularity or their financial rewards.

The scientific press that Prang had so eagerly sought to interest as they had shaped the Yellowstone portfolio virtually ignored the book. *The American Journal of Science and Arts* did review it, after Prang's office specifically solicited its editor. "We have sent a copy of the 'Yellowstone' to Prof. [James] Dana," the publisher wrote, "and we have the promise of a *long* notice in the 'Journal of Science and of Arts.' This promise was given before he had seen the work (in reply to a letter of ours, asking permission to send the copy). A recommendatory letter we have not yet received from him, but we presume we shall get it."[37] Even though Dana never apparently wrote the testimonial letter,[38] he did publish a short, complimentary review of the publication:

> This volume of colored sketches, illustrating some of the most striking points in Rocky Mountain scenery, is magnificent in scale and beautiful in execution. The colors of the landscapes will be thought too brilliant by those who have not visited the region, and perhaps in one or two cases the artist has allowed his feelings in that exhilarating atmosphere to influence in some degree his brush. But in other cases, that for example of the scenery along the Cañon of the Yellowstone, as we understand from one who has visited the region, the colors even fall short of the reality.[39]

The review continued, quoting from Colonel William Ludlow, who had toured Yellowstone in 1875 and who verified the vivid coloring of the sites. After listing the chromolithographs, it noted that, "as specimens of chromo-lithography and of artistic effect, the plates are of unusual excellence," before concluding with a brief mention of Hayden's qualifications for writing the text. Despite the glowing remarks, however, Prang's office was disappointed that the review had not been long, as they had hoped, and upon reading it remarked dryly to Hayden, "The notice in Prof. Dana's Journal does not amount to much!"[40]

A few publications did hail *The Yellowstone National Park* as a significant artistic achievement. As the *Newark Daily Advertiser* described it:

> The book is not a book. It is a portfolio, each of those exquisite chromos being mounted upon pure white card board of imperial size. The chromos are 14 × 10 inches; the board is 23 × 18 inches, and the letter press, a gem of typography, is on

> card board of the same size and purity of color and texture. It is a genuine triumph of American graphic art, and some of the lake views almost ripple on the beach as we look at them. The coloring is perfect and the perspective admirably maintained. The two great pictures which adorn the Capitol at Washington are almost as beautiful, in this comparatively miniature form, as they are in the originals.[41]

Thomas Moran had moved to Newark in 1872 and was well known to the local newspaper, so its reporter was predisposed to favorably review the portfolio. Nevertheless, the *Daily Advertiser*'s admiring comments surely pleased both artist and publisher even though the paper was not especially prominent.

One magazine very familiar with Moran, *Scribner's Monthly*, seems to have ignored *The Yellowstone National Park*. This is especially surprising, since the editor, Richard Watson Gilder, was a good friend of the artist and the magazine had published hundreds of his illustrations. *Scribner's* had also worked closely with Hayden throughout the period of his Yellowstone exploration, publishing his articles and helping encourage the passage of the park bill. *The Atlantic Monthly*, which had been the vehicle for James Parton's important article on chromolithography, was also silent, and a similar publication, *Harper's Monthly*, published only a short notice in its literary column. *Harper's Weekly*, however, offered a substantial commentary and a genuine recommendation, no doubt either written or encouraged by editor George William Curtis (1824–1892), to whom Prang had sent a copy. It asserted prophetically that "the *National Park* will be hoarded by special collectors and public libraries," and for the average collector it suggested that "the whole work is one of such permanent value and interest that all who are intending Christmas presents next winter should be wise in time."[42]

The Yellowstone National Park also received some favorable attention in Britain. Perhaps the most important review anywhere was an enthusiastic one in the *Times* of London, but unfortunately it was not published until November 1877—so late that it had little effect on sales. A full column offered an elaborate history and description of the Yellowstone region, important, of course, for a British audience unfamiliar with the territory, and then praised the publication unequivocally: "The magnificent portfolio . . . is in every respect worthy of the subject, creditable in the highest degree to the artist, the publishers, and American skill. [It] is strong and handsome and tasteful, no finer specimens of chromo-lithographic work have been produced anywhere; and the beautifully printed descriptive text . . . is all that could be desired of a work of this kind."[43]

Like most of the other reviews, the *Times*'s opinion had been influenced by association. Prang wrote to Hayden in early February 1877: "Our English agent wrote a few days ago. He has very strong hopes of getting a *good* notice in the 'Times' through a gentleman named Blackmore, who claims to be a friend of yours, and who is reported to be very enthusiastic about the book."[44] Sir William Blackmore was a wealthy British investor who had accompanied Hayden's second expedition to Yellowstone in 1872 and who had also, it will be remembered, commissioned a series of watercolors similar to Prang's from Moran.[45] Relying on Blackmore's familiarity with both the region and Moran's art, the *Times* took care to refute the concern expressed by so many others that Moran's images were exaggerated and fantastical, and it added that the artist had also provided "all the touches necessary to raise them to the level of works of art." Most gratifying for Prang was the praise for the quality of the reproductions: "Equal success has attended the efforts of the copyist in his, perhaps, more difficult task. . . . no more masterly specimens of this kind of work have ever been produced." A delighted L. Prang & Co. wrote Hayden: "Have you seen the splendid notice of your book in the London Times of Nov. 23. It is 1¼ columns long, and all together excellent. We have written for a number of copies." The next day the publisher remarked that the article was "certainly effective," since John Kasson, the American ambassador in Vienna, had requested a copy on its recommendation to "present to a high personage here." The firm wistfully asked the survey leader, "Could not other of our ambassadors be influenced to follow [his] example?"[46]

The other British review that Prang received with pleasure appeared in Scotland's most important newspaper, the *Scotsman,* and was reprinted in several American sources, including the *Denver News* and *A Journal of Outdoor Life.*[47] Dr. Thomas Croxen Archer (1817–1885) of Edinburgh had received an early copy of the portfolio and wrote Prang: "I think so highly of the book that I shall hope to get a notice of it in the 'Scotsman,' the leading paper of Scotland. It is in every respect most beautifully got up and I am better able to judge, from having seen Mr. Moran's original drawings at Washington."[48] The review was indeed glowing:

> Mr. Moran's beautiful drawings bear testimony to the fact that no pains had been spared to make them faithful representations of the remarkable scenes they represent. To give equally trustworthy reproductions of these drawings was most desirable so that the marvels of Wonderland, as it is often now called, might be seen by all the world. This has been done in a very magnificent volume published by Messrs. Prang & Co., of Boston, U.S. It contains fifteen chromoliths of such excellence, that we are surprised to find that firm, eminent as it is, bringing out so large a work in a style which would do credit to the Imperial State Printing Establishment of Austria, long so famous for its perfection in the glyptic arts. There is a softness and aerial depth not often seen in chromoliths, and as the work has been brought out under the careful supervision of the eminent geologist who surveyed the country, we have ample guarantee that the drawings are faithful representations. The work

is necessarily a costly one, but no public library can well do without it; and to those who can afford to put it in their libraries, it will be a great source of pleasure.[49]

The comparison to the Imperial State Printing Establishment of Austria was no doubt especially gratifying to Prang, and the recommendation that libraries acquire it was exactly what the publisher wished more reviews would emphasize.

Since *The Yellowstone National Park* is considered today such an exemplary publication, it may be surprising that it was not universally and eagerly hailed in its own day, but it is also important to recognize that Prang's name was widely associated with mass appeal rather than prestige. Moran's and Hayden's reputations bolstered the work's credibility, helping it meet with the approval of some distinguished art collectors, bibliophiles, and scientists, but this cachet was obviously not enough to change the opinions of the critics, especially those at the *New York Daily Tribune* or *The Nation*. And conversely, the publication was not popular enough (and inexpensive enough) to attract the regular Prang constituency—the large numbers from the middle class—who might have ensured its success through sheer numbers. In today's terminology, the portfolio was targeted at a very rarified niche market, and because it was unusual, expensive, and had baggage it was a difficult sell.

Throughout the spring and summer of 1877, as the critical reception of *The Yellowstone National Park* was unfolding, L. Prang & Co., with the help of Ferdinand Hayden and others, was also working energetically to sell the portfolio. Perhaps influenced by the paucity of good reviews and hampered by the same factors that restricted those, that process proved even more frustrating and ultimately disappointing to the publisher than publicizing it had. The process would conclude, however, with a surprising twist of fate that rendered the publication and its legacy infinitely more valuable to subsequent history than its early troubles might suggest.

SELLING THE PORTFOLIO

When L. Prang & Co. launched *The Yellowstone National Park* late in 1876, the country was still in the throes of a crippling depression brought on by the Panic of 1873, and hard times would linger until 1879. The company acknowledged the economic conditions directly in only one instance: "Times are as bad in Europe as they are here, and therefore against us," but the poor economy was surely a factor in the continual difficulties the firm faced in selling the publication. Other contributing factors that are less easily documented probably included the refusal of many critics and potential collectors to adjust their negative perceptions of chromos and the portfolio's unorthodox and ambiguous position between the worlds of science and art, but it is also abundantly clear that the company lacked experience in selling prestigious publications and that it failed to develop an effective marketing strategy.

From the outset of its relationship with Hayden, the publisher hoped that the survey's position in the federal government would provide special opportunities for bulk sales. Just as the company was beginning to work with him on plans for the text in the fall of 1875, the editors asked: "We would like to know if there is any prospect of any copies being taken by the Government. Should any be taken we should have to make special provision for them in the printing of our edition."[50] The theme recurred throughout their correspondence. Appealing to Hayden to use his influence in Washington on their behalf, the editors wrote:

> In Europe a work of such magnitude, value and national interest would be sure to receive the support of the governments, if not in the shape of a direct subvention, at least by the purchase of a good number of copies for distribution among libraries, etc., and as gifts to foreign scientific institutions. Here these things are almost out of the question. . . . We should think that some of the Western states and territories, whose interest it is to have their resources and their attractions brought prominently to the notice of the world might perhaps be willing to aid in circulating the work. If you can direct attention to the work in the proper quarters, or if you can name to us the person with whom we might correspond on the subject, we should be indebted to you. . . . if a *state* should take a number of copies, we are quite willing to allow a discount.[51]

Prang's staff worked a number of angles to elicit official interest in *The Yellowstone National Park,* sending copies to several governors, senators, congressmen, and others affiliated with government agencies, but the sizable orders they hoped for never materialized.

Since Prang was primarily a publisher of cards, novelty items, and single fine art reproductions, the firm was unfamiliar with the complex world of bookselling and especially the marketing of high-end publications. The company routinely placed advertisements in journals and newspapers but relied on stationery retailers and direct mail for most of its regular sales. In the 1870s, lists of "Books Received" were a staple in most journals and newspapers and, of course, retail bookstores operated in most cities, but even established publishing houses sold their most significant publications, including large portfolios such as *The Yellowstone National Park,* through "canvassers"—independent salesmen or agents who paid personal visits to prospective clients, selling their wares one at a time. This individualized attention, especially when conducted by "gentlemen" with the proper letters of introduction, was essential to attract the distinguished clientele who bought high-end books. In turn those collectors were sometimes asked to write testimonial letters that could be used in circulars to encourage others of the same class or pretensions to purchase the work.

When Hayden asked about advertising early in the process, the publisher reasoned:

> There is no use in stirring up the public through the press, as long as we cannot follow this up by bringing the book forward. No agent being ready to show the work and no copies of it being for sale in the bookstores, those interested in it would forget about it, for there are but few people who will take the trouble to write and there are probably none, who would buy on the strength of a newspaper circular. The book is too expensive for that and people want to *see* it, before ordering.[52]

L. Prang & Co. recognized that it had a choice "whether the book must go to the trade, or whether it can be worked through agents," but as the editors explained to Hayden,

> we adhere to the opinion that the work ought to be *canvassed,* but the difficulty is to get the right man. We have tried hard to interest the best canvassing agent in Boston in the book, but in vain. He likes the work exceedingly well, but is afraid to touch it. We are now going to see another canvassing firm in regard to it and our Mr. Clark has taken a copy to Philadelphia, with the intention of conferring with Gebbie and Barry.[53]

Unfortunately, like the Boston canvassing firm, the Philadelphia company of Gebbie and Barry also decided "not to touch the work," and L. Prang & Co. continued to search for "a thorough gentleman, for we think that no other kind of person will be fit."[54] The editors told Hayden, "Your book is quite an exceptional character, and must be managed in an exceptional way. Wherever we can get the right sort of a man, we mean to make people feel that they are not dealing with an ordinary book canvasser, but with a gentleman, who has a right to be respected. But of course the difficulty of finding such men, makes the whole management of the book a difficult task!"[55]

L. Prang & Co. ultimately did find sales representatives in England, New York, Chicago, and Philadelphia, and Hayden himself agreed to handle Washington, D.C., receiving "the 40% commission which we would have to pay any other agent." Even though Hayden was sometimes slow in providing letters of introduction for the sales agents, lists of potential buyers, and suggestions for appropriate agents to represent *The Yellowstone National Park,* considering his many other obligations and interests, he was remarkably engaged with the project. He did, for example, distribute dozens of circulars. L. Prang & Co. expressed relief, saying gratefully, "We shall consider Washington as well attended to and shall trouble our minds no further in regard to it," but the nearly constant stream of letters about the lack of sales indicates that their worry hardly abated.[56]

To acquire testimonials for a significant promotional circular that could accompany presentations of *The Yellowstone National Park,* the firm gave or sold the portfolio to a host of noteworthy individuals. Queen Victoria of Britain and President Ulysses S. Grant and, later, President Rutherford B. Hayes, General William Tecumseh

Sherman, the emperor of Brazil, poet Henry Wadsworth Longfellow, Smithsonian secretary Joseph Henry, California governor Leland Stanford, and Professor James Dana all received copies.[57] Hayden offered to give one to the prominent statesman Carl Schurz (1829–1906), who would soon serve as secretary of the interior in the Hayes administration, but the publisher, perhaps unwisely, discouraged the gift of yet another copy. "In the case of a book like yours," the editors reasoned, "the testimony of political celebrities is not as valuable as that of scientific and literary men and of men of acknowledged taste in matters of art."[58] For all Prang's generosity to those with "acknowledged taste," however, only a few of the distinguished recipients wrote the cherished endorsements. In early February the office reported that, "so far, of all the letters promised us we have only the one by Genl. Sherman. This of course delays us greatly, because we cannot issue a circular until we get more letters."[59] The lack of response, either by neglect or intent, was a source of extreme frustration to Prang.[60]

The balance between science and art that L. Prang & Co. had thought would be *The Yellowstone National Park*'s real distinction seems to have been, in the eyes of many potential buyers, either too much of one thing or too little of the other. The scientific community was unenthusiastic. The School of Mines in England considered the book "too artistic."[61] James Dana, the editor of the *American Journal of Science and Arts,* declined to write a letter of support, and his journal notice, although positive, was cursory. The American Geographical Society refused to buy a copy, pleading "a lack of funds," and L. Prang & Co. wrote: "It is really tremendous—the leading Geogr[aphical] Society of the country has no money to buy one of the most important works ever published on the geography of the U.S.! . . . We shall *give* a copy to the poor 'Society,' so as to make sure of a letter from its President."[62] But art patrons were not interested either. "A great patron of the arts," the crown prince of Germany, "returned the copy sent him with the remark that he was 'too poor' to buy it!" August Belmont (1816–1890), a major patron and member of the elite "Four Hundred" at the top of New York's social register, returned his copy "accompanied at least by a polite note, stating that Mr. B. was obliged for the privilege of looking at the book, but that he did not wish to increase his library!" Prang wrote, "We are simply disgusted."[63]

Not *all* the news was bad. The publisher was greatly cheered that even though Queen Victoria considered writing a testimonial beneath her, she had taken "much interest in the subject as well as in the artistic style of the illustrations that adorn the book and has given her Commands to deposit the book in her Royal Library."[64] *Harper's Weekly* political editor, George William Curtis, "wrote a very nice letter" for the circular, as did the Smithsonian secretary, Joseph Henry (1797–1878), and prominent journalist and lyceum lecturer James Redpath (1833–1891) offered assistance in soliciting congressional interest in the publication. Such bright spots, however, were few and far between in the spring and summer of 1877.[65]

By March the news was becoming familiar. "In New York and Boston the story is the same old one," Hayden was told. "Not a single copy sold, with exception of two copies to friends to whom we allowed the agents discounts."[66] At the end of April, Prang's office informed the survey leader, "You certainly have sold more than any agent we have in America," but since that was only about fifty copies, it was a hollow compliment.[67] Boston, of course, as home to L. Prang & Co., should have been one of the most receptive markets for the firm's achievements, but the situation there was the worst. At the end of 1877, after a full year of promotion, the company reported, "The City of Boston is good for nothing as far as the 'Yellowstone' is concerned," and "We have sold just *one* copy of the book this fall! All the upper ten in New York have been tried, but they turn up their noses at it. If it were *English,* it would take!"[68]

DISASTER: A BLESSING IN DISGUISE?

Despite all the best efforts, *The Yellowstone National Park* failed to attract buyers. Whether the poor sales were due to the uneasy balance of science and art that the publication represented, the stigma of the chromo-controversy, its characterization as a decorative art form that appealed to women, the reputation of L. Prang & Co. as a lowbrow publisher, the lack of an effective marketing strategy in a time of significant economic recession, or some combination of these remains unclear. Most of the limited edition of 1,000 copies languished unsold in Prang's warehouse. Then, on September 27, 1877, only nine months after *The Yellowstone National Park* had been completed, disaster struck. A fire broke out at the plant and destroyed all but about fifty copies of the portfolio and a few hundred individual chromos.[69] As the *Boston Post* reported, "The building was filled with valuable plates, chromos, etc., and the loss will amount to nearly $50,000, of which about $15,000 is on the building. A valuable collection of oil paintings was almost entirely destroyed, and most of the stock of chromos was rendered worthless."[70] The article continued with a long list of the company's insurance coverage, which makes it clear that even if the losses were higher (as some have reported), Prang was well prepared for such a setback.[71]

Nevertheless, the fire was a major blow to the company, and it severely altered the long-term legacy of *The Yellowstone National Park.* At the same time, however, since the portfolio had sold so poorly, the disaster may have been something of a relief to Prang. He would be reimbursed for most of the $25,000 he had invested in the project, which he had been unlikely to recoup anyway, and the loss of most of the stock saved him from the task of continuing to market an unprofitable and disappointing product. Most important in retrospect is that the calamity drastically reduced the number of prints, rendering the few remaining sets infinitely more valuable for their rarity. This is more relevant to modern collectors, of course, than it would have been to Louis Prang, but it is highly significant to understanding the importance of the surviving chromolithographs.[72]

In the early stages of promoting the complete portfolio, L. Prang & Co. had declared: "We shall not *sell* single pictures, as that would undoubtedly interfere with the sale of the work itself. People must take *all* or *none!*" But the company revised this stance after a few months as hopes for profits dissolved.[73] Seeing some interest in single copies of the prints, Hayden offered to market them individually in early May 1877, and the publisher regretfully complied:

> We beg to say that we would gladly send you the 70 views gratis, if there were any chance at all of our getting back even some of our money on the 'Yellowstone.' As it is, the chances are more likely that we shall be the sad losers. Under these circumstances you will, perhaps, not think it unfair if we send you only one half the number you asked for (i.e., 35), gratis, and charge you at the rate of $1.50 for the others.[74]

In May 1878 the firm consigned more of the remnants with Hayden, pricing each mounted chromo at $4.[75] Although Prang's American Chromos usually sold for about $6 apiece and even for as much as $10, the company's catalogs listed the remaining Moran prints for as little as $1.50 as late as the 1890s (fig. 154).[76]

With few copies of the complete portfolio left to sell after the September 1877 fire, L. Prang & Co. essentially stopped promoting *The Yellowstone National Park*. It continued to "dispose of" its remaining copies for years and did have a few noteworthy sales. In 1882, for example, the preeminent aesthetician and English art critic, John Ruskin (1819–1900), whom Moran met in England that year, bought a copy for the Sheffield Museum, along with several of the artist's etchings and paintings and prints by his wife, Mary Nimmo Moran (1842–1899).[77] This purchase was comparable to Clarence Cook purchasing a Prang print, since Ruskin had formerly expressed an abhorrence of chromos.[78] Ruskin wrote to the artist in mid-February 1883 with some artistic advice, asking Moran to "give up for a while all that flaring and glaring and splashing and roaring business," but he also mentioned the portfolio: "I had so much to say to you about your book that I could not say it when it came. But it will be spoken of, I hope not in a way displeasing to you, at my first Oxford lecture in my account of the new energies of western art—and meantime, in practice to myself."[79] Ruskin was true to his word and mentioned *The Yellowstone National Park* in a lecture entitled "Fairy Land" a few months later.[80] The comment was brief: "Nor are any descriptions of the Valley of Diamonds, or the lake of the Black Islands, in the *Arabian Nights,* anything like so wonderful as the scenes of California and the Rocky Mountains which you may . . . see represented with most sincere and passionate enthusiasm by the American landscape painter, Mr. Moran, in a survey lately published by the Government of the United States."[81] Although Ruskin was mistaken about the publisher, which must have annoyed Prang, for an aesthete who "believed all chromos should be burned," the purchase and acknowledgment of the portfolio was a significant compliment to Moran.[82]

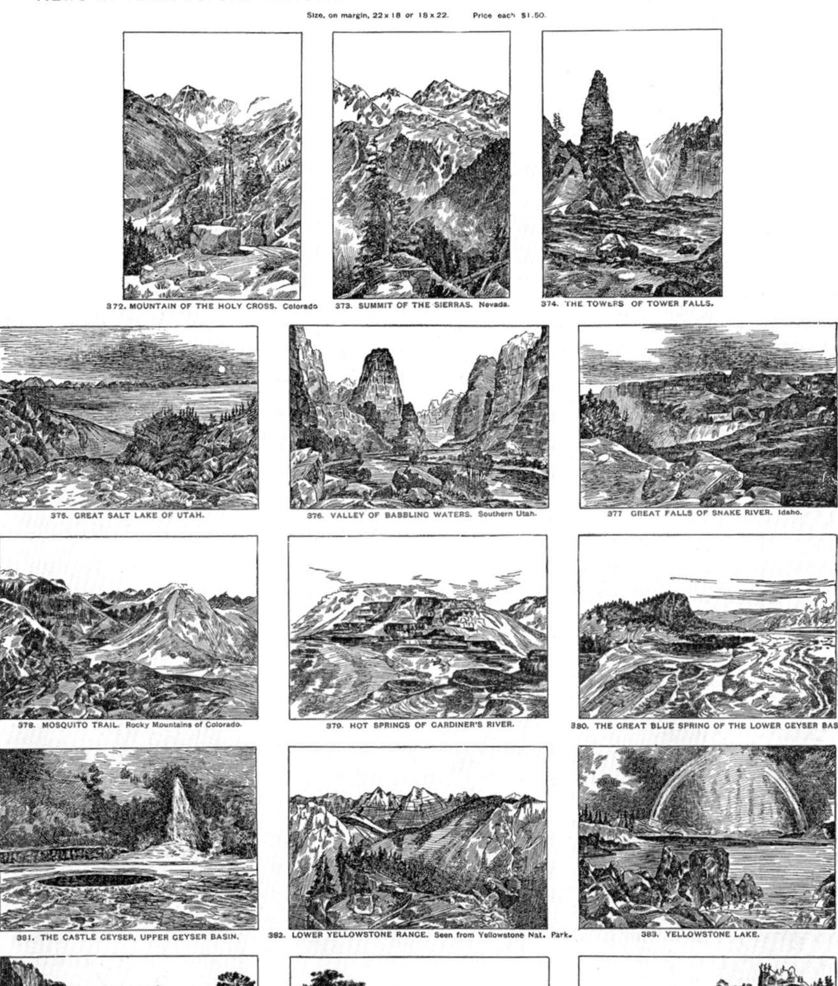
PRANG'S ART STUDIES. 19

VIEWS IN YELLOWSTONE NATIONAL PARK AND NEIGHBORHOOD. By THOMAS MORAN.

Size, on margin, 22 x 18 or 18 x 22. Price each $1.50.

372. MOUNTAIN OF THE HOLY CROSS. Colorado

373. SUMMIT OF THE SIERRAS. Nevada.

374. THE TOWERS OF TOWER FALLS.

375. GREAT SALT LAKE OF UTAH.

376. VALLEY OF BABBLING WATERS. Southern Utah.

377. GREAT FALLS OF SNAKE RIVER. Idaho.

378. MOSQUITO TRAIL. Rocky Mountains of Colorado.

379. HOT SPRINGS OF GARDINER'S RIVER.

380. THE GREAT BLUE SPRING OF THE LOWER GEYSER BASIN.

381. THE CASTLE GEYSER, UPPER GEYSER BASIN.

382. LOWER YELLOWSTONE RANGE. Seen from Yellowstone Nat. Park.

383. YELLOWSTONE LAKE.

384. TOWER FALLS AND SULPHUR MOUNTAIN.

385. HEAD OF YELLOWSTONE RIVER.

386. THE GRAND CAÑON OF THE YELLOWSTONE.

FIGURE 154. *Views in Yellowstone National Park and Neighborhood by Thomas Moran,* from *Illustrated Catalogue of Fine Art Studies, Water Color Studies, Pictures, etc.* (Boston: L. Prang & Co., 1890), p. 19. Graphic Arts Division, National Museum of American History (GA G947)

Although Prang's business continued to flourish with new ventures, the last correspondence from his office to Ferdinand Hayden was a dejected personal note from the publisher in November 1878. Citing financial pressures "on all sides and to such an extent that I am obliged to look after every Dollar due us, like a starving man will look after a dry crumb stored away in the corner of his cupboard," he asked the survey leader for remittance of any outstanding proceeds from *The Yellowstone National Park*. "We have still 25 complete portfolios in stock, can you not possibly work them off for us before the holidays? I see no way of doing this here and I need money so bad I am obliged to push my friends to some trouble on my behalf."[83] After such a promising beginning, it was a sad conclusion to one of the most ambitious and remarkable chromolithographic projects ever undertaken.

Late in his life Prang admitted in his autobiography that "art books and booklets occupied my attention for some time, but for this work a special [concession] and special [skills] are required to command success."[84] Considering all of the heartache *The Yellowstone National Park* must have represented for Prang, however, he seems to have been proud of the portfolio. He included it, for example, as part of his company's display at the World's Columbian Exposition in Chicago as late as 1893. There it received a surprising amount of attention for a nearly twenty-year-old publication. Shortly before that, on February 18, 1892, Prang sold his remaining original watercolors that Moran had created for *The Yellowstone National Park* at the American Art Galleries in New York. They were unfortunately dispersed at that time, selling for between $50 and $109 each.[85]

In the years since, however, the complete publication and the single chromos from the series have grown in renown and, with their rarity heightened by the disastrous 1877 fire, they have become avidly sought-after and increasingly expensive collector's items. As chromolithographs have once again become intriguing to collectors and scholars, it is ever more evident that the Prang chromos of Thomas Moran's art are a paradigm of the medium. Representing its extraordinary extremes, from the sublime quality the technique could achieve to the most abject disappointment it could provoke, *The Yellowstone National Park* stands as a monument to the aspirations, anxieties, and achievements chromolithography represented in the art world in the late nineteenth century.

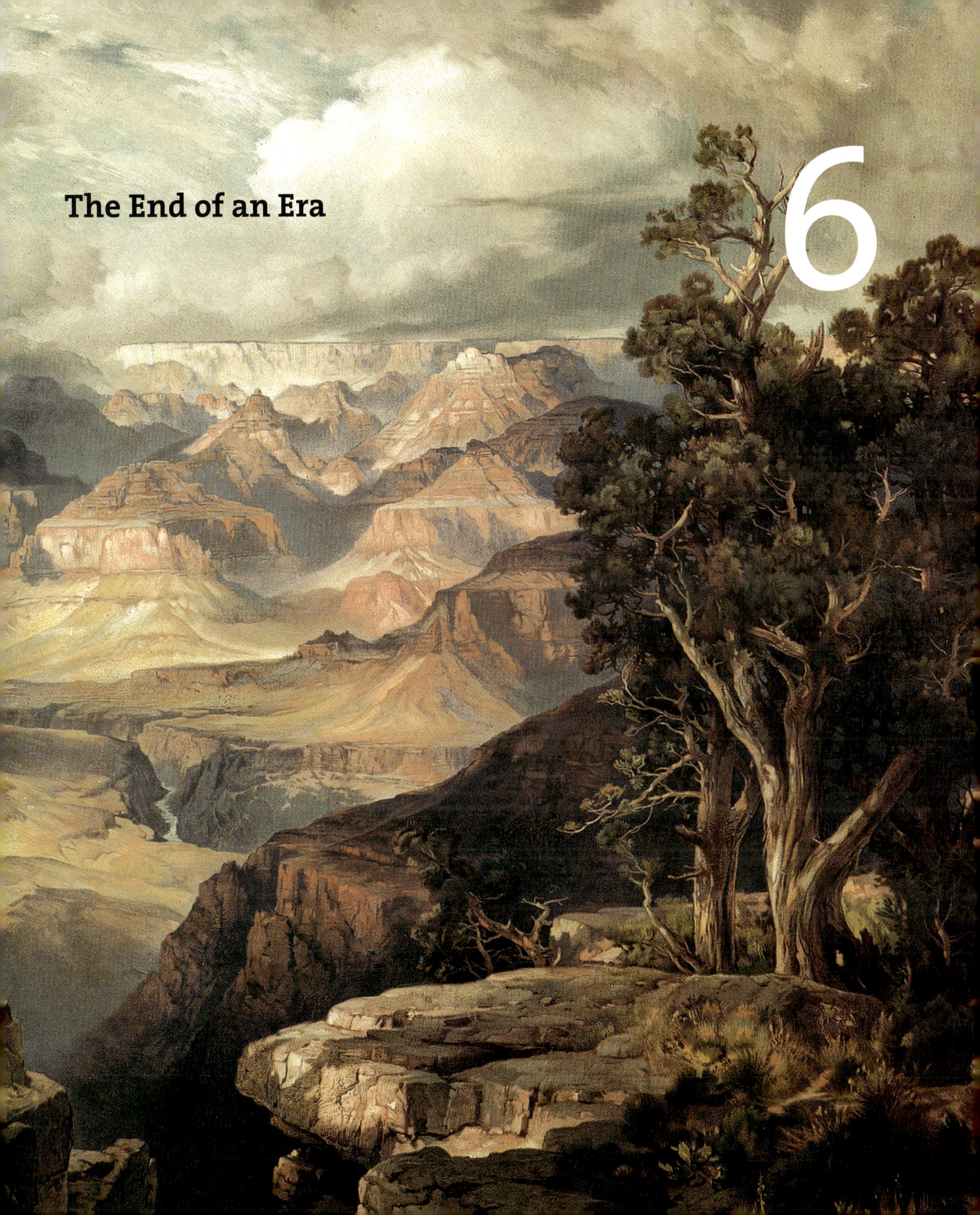

6

The End of an Era

The sketches by Mr. Thomas Moran, who accompanied me on one of my expeditions, are not only of a high order of artistic merit, but . . . they can also be relied upon as exceedingly correct renderings of their subjects, interesting alike to the man of science, the lover of art, and the admirer of nature.
—Ferdinand Hayden,
The Yellowstone National Park, *1876*

Moran did other work for L. Prang & Co. after *The Yellowstone National Park,* although never again on the scale of the lavish 1876 publication. He also did two paintings that were chromolithographed by other publishers as large frameable prints. Within the transitional period of the 1880s and 1890s when a variety of reproductive media were competing for favor, chromolithography continued to be employed for a number of purposes until it was finally rendered obsolete by photomechanical methods shortly after the turn of the century. Moran's and Prang's reproductive work during the period paralleled those changes. Although neither again confronted the continuing reproductive controversies to the degree they had with the Yellowstone portfolio, each contributed to the ongoing discourse with subsequent work. Ultimately both careers were affected by the new aesthetic hierarchy that emerged from the debates.

Prang apparently did not ascribe any of *The Yellowstone National Park*'s difficulties to Moran, since he commissioned him to paint six 7-x-12-inch paintings in about 1878, paying him $500 in December 1879. Moran did not list titles for those images in his ledger, and only two of them were issued as chromolithographs, *On the Lookout—A Ute Camp, Utah* (fig. 155) and *Cliffs of the Upper Colorado River, Wyoming Territory,* which Prang advertised in his *Illustrated Catalogue* (fig. 156).[1] Since the original for *Cliffs of the Upper Colorado* is an oil, these works were apparently not watercolors like those Moran had created for the earlier portfolio.[2] The 1879 chromos were mounted on boards measuring 14 × 9 inches, significantly smaller than the 1876 series, and they originally sold singly for 75 cents rather than being collected in a portfolio as their predecessors had been. Although the collected series had failed to sell, individual chromos were obviously still a viable product for the publisher.

Prang continued to issue single chromos from paintings that he commissioned or purchased from artists, including two late watercolors by Winslow Homer. But in the wake of *The Yellowstone National Park*'s failure, and with growing competition from other chromolithographers, he turned increasingly to other endeavors by the late 1870s. The portfolio project had been one of a number of experiments during that period. Of these, Christmas cards were the most lucrative. Prang had noticed the novelty items in England early in the decade and introduced them to the American market at about the same time that he launched *The Yellowstone National Park.* His firm had included a few holiday-related offerings in its catalogs as early as the 1860s, but by the late 1870s its Christmas cards were selling by the millions and constituted an entirely new industry (fig. 157).[3] Prang's cards dominated the market until about

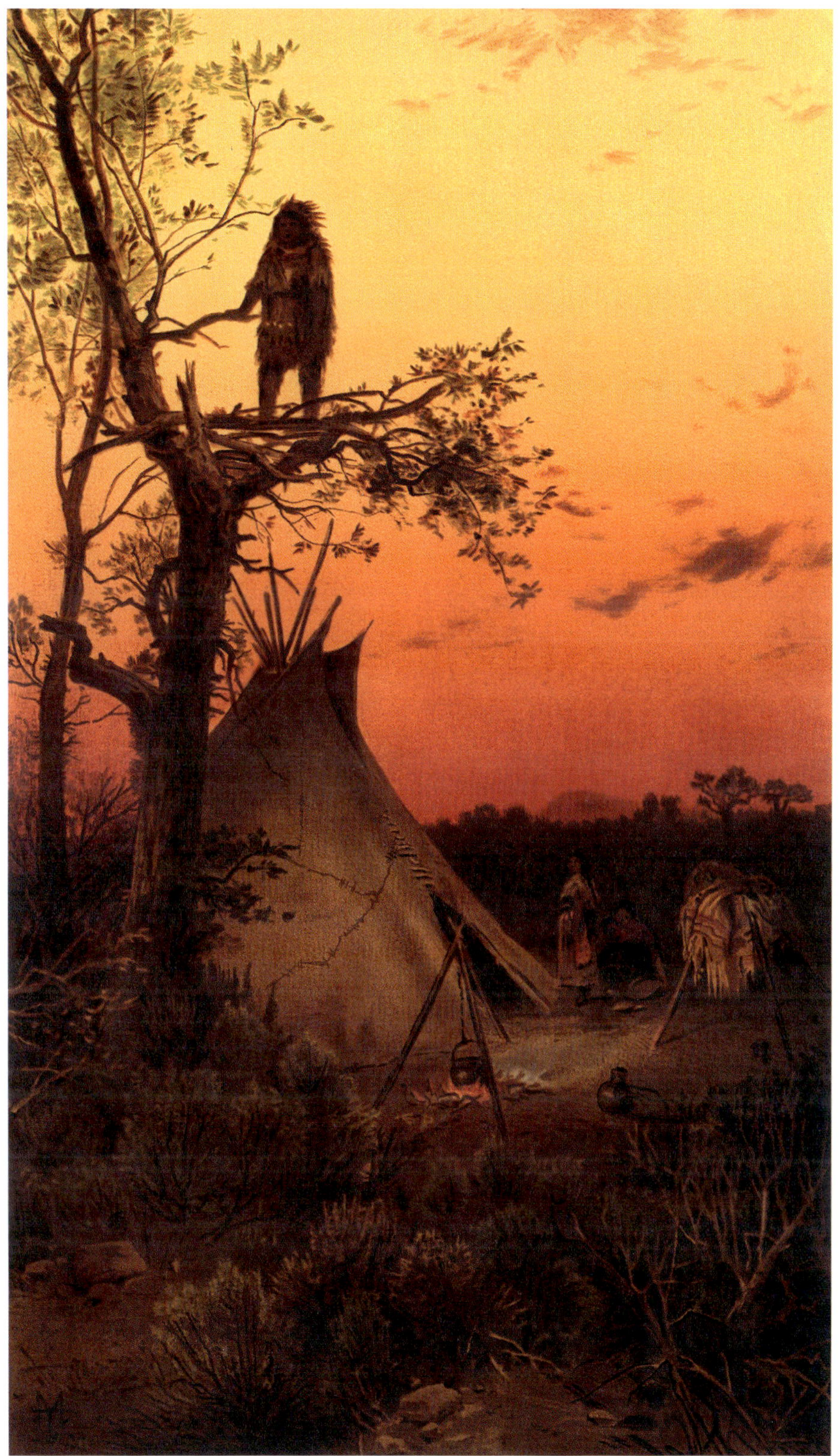

FIGURE 155. After Thomas Moran, *On the Lookout — A Ute Camp, Utah,* ca. 1879, chromolithograph, 12¼ × 7⅛ in. (31.1 × 18.1 cm). Courtesy of Boston Public Library, Print Room

FIGURE 156. After Thomas Moran, *Cliffs of the Upper Colorado River, Wyoming Territory*, ca. 1879, chromolithograph, 12⅛ × 7 in. (30.8 × 17.8 cm). Courtesy of Boston Public Library, Print Room

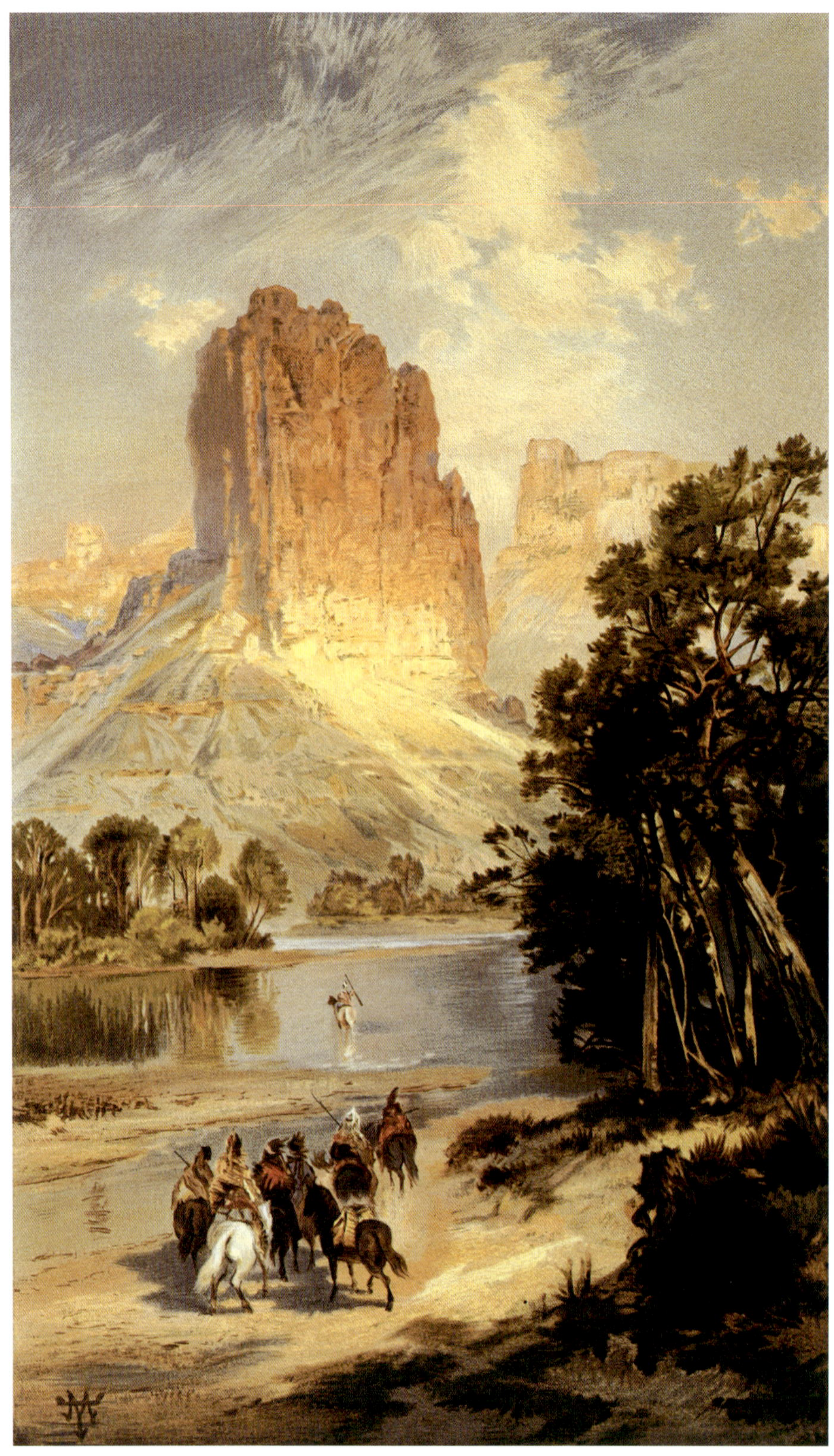

1890, and today Louis Prang is better known as the "Father of the Christmas Card" than for all his other types of chromolithographs.[4]

Prang's Christmas cards ranged from 25-cent, small boxed sets, to lavish productions as large as 7 × 10 inches with double-sided fringed designs that sold for several dollars.[5] Many people considered the latter an art form. As one woman emphasized, "My Longfellow Card stands on my cabinet, and will for many a day. I should as soon think of taking a painting down from the wall and stowing it away because it had hung a year."[6] To reinforce such attitudes, heighten interest in the cards, and elevate their prestige, Prang ingeniously engaged the services of major artists and staged well-publicized annual competitions for holiday designs from 1880 to 1884. The contests were elaborate affairs, with the original paintings displayed at the American Art Gallery in New York's Madison Square and at the Doll & Richards Gallery in Boston and with distinguished juries who evaluated the work. In 1880 the panel included the leading architect of the day, Richard Morris Hunt; Tiffany & Co.'s head silver designer, Edward C. Moore; and landscape painter Samuel Colman. Judges in subsequent years included the noted artist John La Farge and the prominent architect Stanford White. Public admission to the exhibitions was 25 cents, but artists and art critics received free tickets. Prang reserved the rights to all the prizewinning designs, as well as first option on any of the nonwinners, at prices set by their creators.[7]

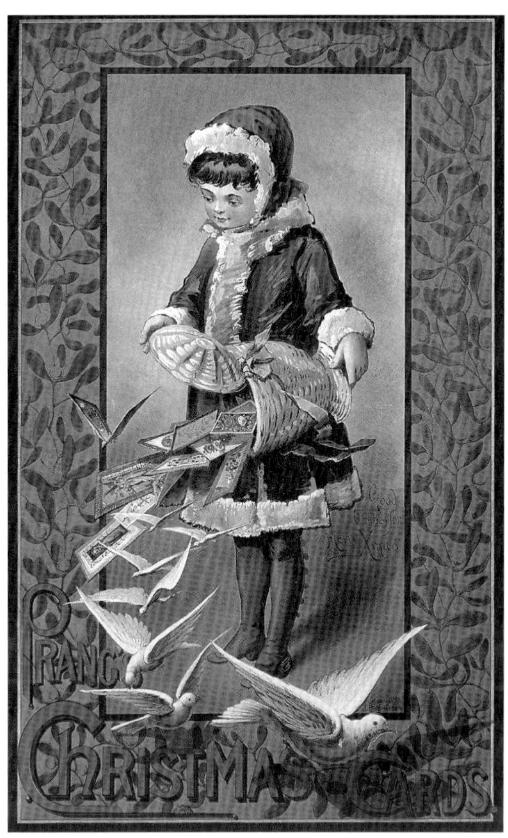

FIGURE 157. *Prang's Christmas Cards*, 1881, chromolithograph advertisement, L. Prang & Co., 22½ × 14 in. (57 × 35.5 cm) Boston Athenaeum

The response to the competitions was enormous. The first, in 1880, received nearly 800 entries, mostly from women.[8] The second year, to encourage national artistic development, the contest was limited to American artists, and it offered $2,000 in prize money, distributed at several levels of achievement. The third year, the system became more elaborate, with an elite group of preselected professional artists competing in one category for $1,000 as the top prize. An equal amount was offered in the "public prize" category, with these winners voted by exhibition visitors. Prang did leave open the possibility that a winner in the first category could also win in the second, a sort of "grand prize" that he allowed the public to decide. Although he apparently grouped the leading contenders prominently at the doorway, all the entries were displayed without attribution, to make the judging fair.[9] In the fourth and final year, Prang made the competition even more exclusive, limiting it to an invited group of twenty-two artists and presenting the exhibition in Manhattan's Reichard Gallery.[10] After that competition, for which Thomas Moran won third prize, the show traveled to Boston's Museum of Fine Arts and the Art Institute of Chicago.[11] These activities to present the Christmas card in a high art context were not only ingenious showmanship. They

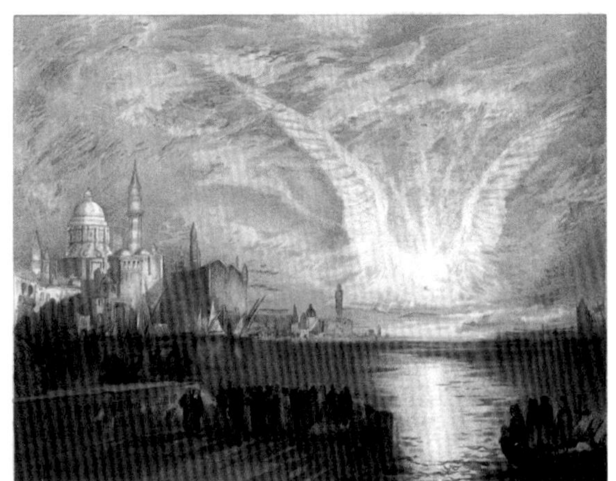

FIGURE 158. After Thomas Moran, *Unto You That Fear,* 1880s, chromolithographed Christmas card. Courtesy of Hallmark Archives, Hallmark Cards, Inc., Kansas City, Missouri (B2.6:7)

also enhanced interest in the cards and promoted sales. It was also consistent with Prang's earlier efforts to present his reproductions as art for the people, a recognition of the aesthetic and social contributions of commercial design.

Thomas Moran sold at least four Christmas card designs to Louis Prang in the 1880s. These paintings were an unusual sideline for an artist better known for his landscape views, and they add an interesting dimension to his oeuvre. Since the cards did not receive titles when they were produced and were not dated, it is difficult to determine their chronology. One, a Venetian scene, contains an inscription on a stone wall in its lower left: "Unto you that fear my name shall the sun of righteousness arise with healing in his wings" (fig. 158). The view is dominated by a remarkable sunrise (or sunset) that displays enormous, cloudlike wings in the sky. A group of figures huddles in the foreground on the stone plaza adjacent to the inscription, and another group stands in a nearby boat at the lower right.[12]

A similarly visionary design is that identified by its inscription: "And I Saw the New Jerusalem Coming Down from God out of Heaven" (fig. 159). The scene is dominated by a ghostly city floating in the clouds, flanked by an angel on the left and cherubs who hold the inscribed banner along the lower edge of the composition. Moran probably created this design in 1884, since it fits the description in the *Boston Daily Evening Transcript:* "Mr. Moran is represented by two views of medieval cities, rich and glowing in color, one of them, while the other is dark and very blue, both being injured by somewhat theatrical perspective and angels poorly drawn."[13] The latter "dark and very blue" image is the one known as *Christmas Wings* (fig. 160), which depicts a white-robed angel carrying a torch flying over what looks like an English-style town on a snowy night. The view, however, as Moran later recounted, was the scene outside his Greenwich Village studio window, and the gothic-towered structure was the Jefferson Market Police Court.[14] Despite the incongruous setting and the criticism it received for the angel's poor drawing, this design won Moran $300 for third prize in L. Prang & Co.'s final Christmas card competition in 1884.[15]

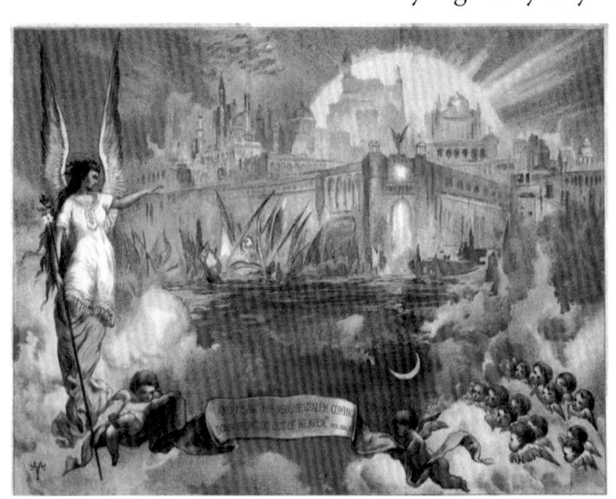

FIGURE 159. After Thomas Moran, *And I Saw the New Jerusalem Coming,* 1880s, chromolithographed Christmas card. Courtesy of Hallmark Archives, Hallmark Cards, Inc., Kansas City, Missouri (B2.6:7)

The most interesting of Moran's holiday art may be the *Holy Cross Christmas Card* (ca. 1883, fig. 161), a subject much more in keeping with his other work and certainly an appropriate theme for a Christian holiday.[16] Since he gave the original watercolor for the card as a wedding present to the daughter of William A. Bell, the Colorado owner of the monumental oil entitled *Mountain of the Holy Cross* (fig. 34), Moran sold

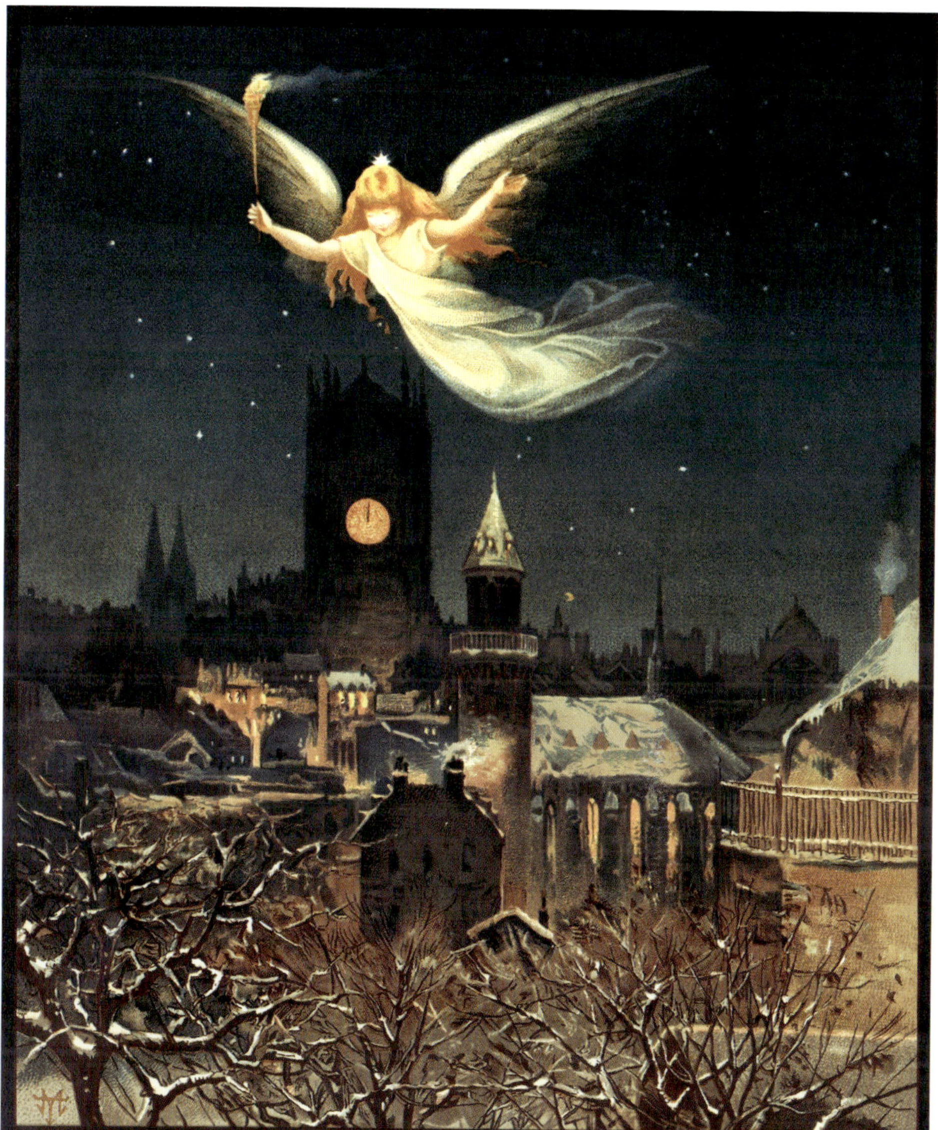

FIGURE 160. After Thomas Moran, *Christmas Wings*, ca. 1883, chromolithographed Christmas card, 7 3/16 × 6 in. (18.3 × 15.2 cm). Courtesy of Boston Public Library, Print Room

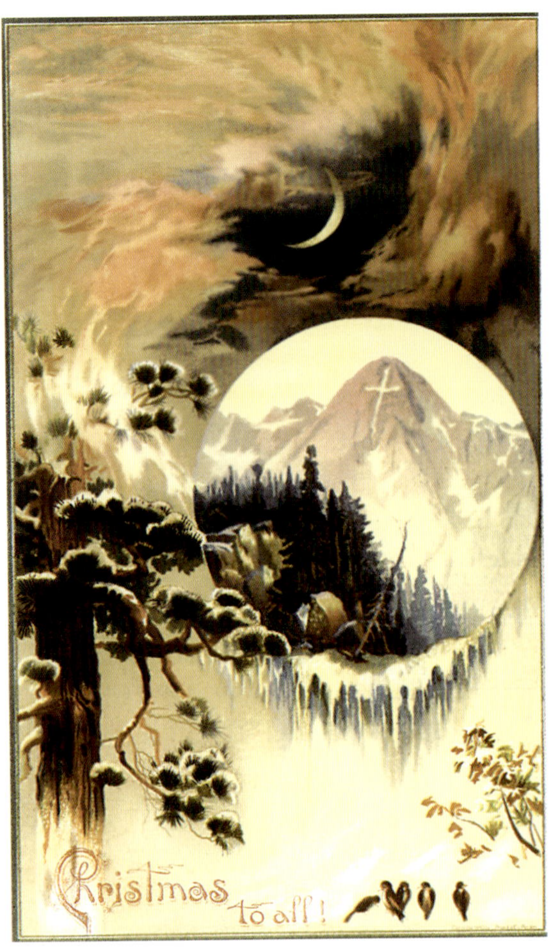

FIGURE 161. After Thomas Moran, *Holy Cross Christmas Card*, ca. 1883–1884, chromolithographed Christmas card. Courtesy of Boston Public Library, Print Room (Prang Album no. 47)

only the copyright to Prang. Considering the subject's association with the Bell family and its business interests as well as the implicit blessings of the scene itself, the small painting of the sacred mountain would have been a highly meaningful gift for the newlyweds.[17] For Prang, reproducing the view as a Christmas card was a return to the subject matter he and Moran had worked on together in *The Yellowstone National Park* eight years before.

Even though Prang exhibited the Christmas card designs in prestigious galleries, neither the paintings nor the cards made from them advanced his democratizing mission for chromolithography as directly as Prang's American Chromos. Neither were they as controversial, perhaps because they did not claim to rival art in the same ways as the chromos. Another reason for them being considered essentially inconsequential, however, may have been influenced by gender issues. Many of the designs, for example, originated with female artists, and the cards would have been purchased almost exclusively by women, rendering them less worthy of serious attention than art reproductions with elevated aspirations.[18] After *The Yellowstone National Park* had failed to appeal to masculine sensibilities with its serious scientific-related imagery, Prang may have resigned himself to a largely feminine clientele, recognizing that the divide between popular and high art was increasingly along gender lines.[19] These issues are intriguing, both in regard to Prang's situation and for the changing status of reproductions in the transition period of the 1880s to 1900. It is especially interesting to consider them in the context of twentieth-century modernism, a movement increasingly recognized as a patriarchal system that systematically minimized the interests and contributions of women.[20] Since art reproductions and holiday cards were "decorative arts" rather than significant financial investments, they were part of the realm of female consumers. Their characterization as either a "decorative" category or as women's art could be used to relegate them to a lowly position in the stratified aesthetic hierarchy.

OTHER CHROMOS BY MORAN

Regardless of the increasing gulf between high and low art, Thomas Moran continued to arrange for his work to appear in chromolithographic prints. The first of these was in 1892 when the Atchison, Topeka, and Santa Fe Railway published a large chromolithograph of a new work, *The Grand Cañon of the Colorado* (fig. 162).[21] This time the chromo, drawn by Gustave Buek of the American Lithographic Company

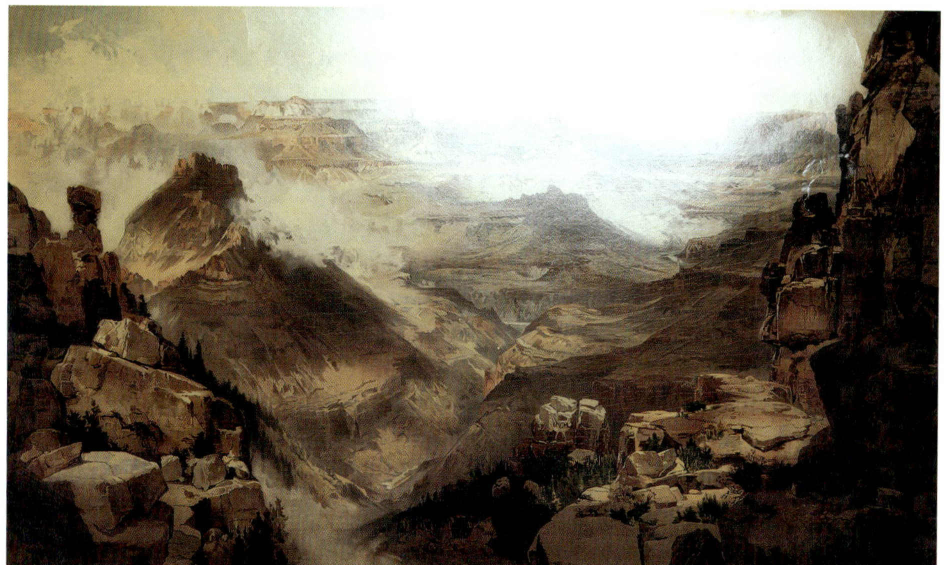

FIGURE 162. Gustave Buek after Thomas Moran, *The Grand Cañon of the Colorado*, 1892, chromolithograph. Gilcrease Museum, Tulsa, Oklahoma

in New York, was based not on a relatively small watercolor, as the Prang chromos had been, but rather on a monumental 5-x-8-foot oil painting created out of Moran's experiences on his second trip to Arizona with William Henry Jackson during the summer of 1892. The Santa Fe's painting, now in the Philadelphia Museum of Art (fig. 163), was the artist's first major treatment of the subject since *The Chasm of the Colorado* (1873–1874, fig. 33), which he had sold to Congress in 1874. The 1892 painting, which Moran reworked in 1908, is much more chromatically brilliant than the congressional picture but has a number of compositional similarities to the earlier painting, including framing elements on both sides, a vast gulf that dominates the center of the scene, and a rainstorm that suffuses the distance on the left. At the same time, the later work is significantly less foreboding than *The Chasm*, perhaps an attempt to appeal to the tourist market the Santa Fe Railway was preparing to serve as it built its route ever nearer the canyon. In contrast to the more ambiguous *Chasm of the Colorado*, which is a constructed view from various positions around the canyon, Moran identified this scene as "near the junction of the Colorado Chiquito" and from a prospect called Bissell's Point.[22]

As it completed its line to the canyon toward the end of the century, the Santa Fe was embarking on an ambitious and creative publicity campaign for its premier tourist attraction, much in the way the Northern Pacific Railroad had done with Yellowstone in the 1870s and the Denver and Rio Grande had done with various points in Colorado in the 1880s. The Santa Fe line reached as far as Flagstaff by 1892, and for his trip that summer, Moran traveled in relative comfort, a sharp contrast to the rigors of his expeditions in the 1870s. The specific circumstances of the company's commission and production of the chromolithograph remain unclear, but as Moran

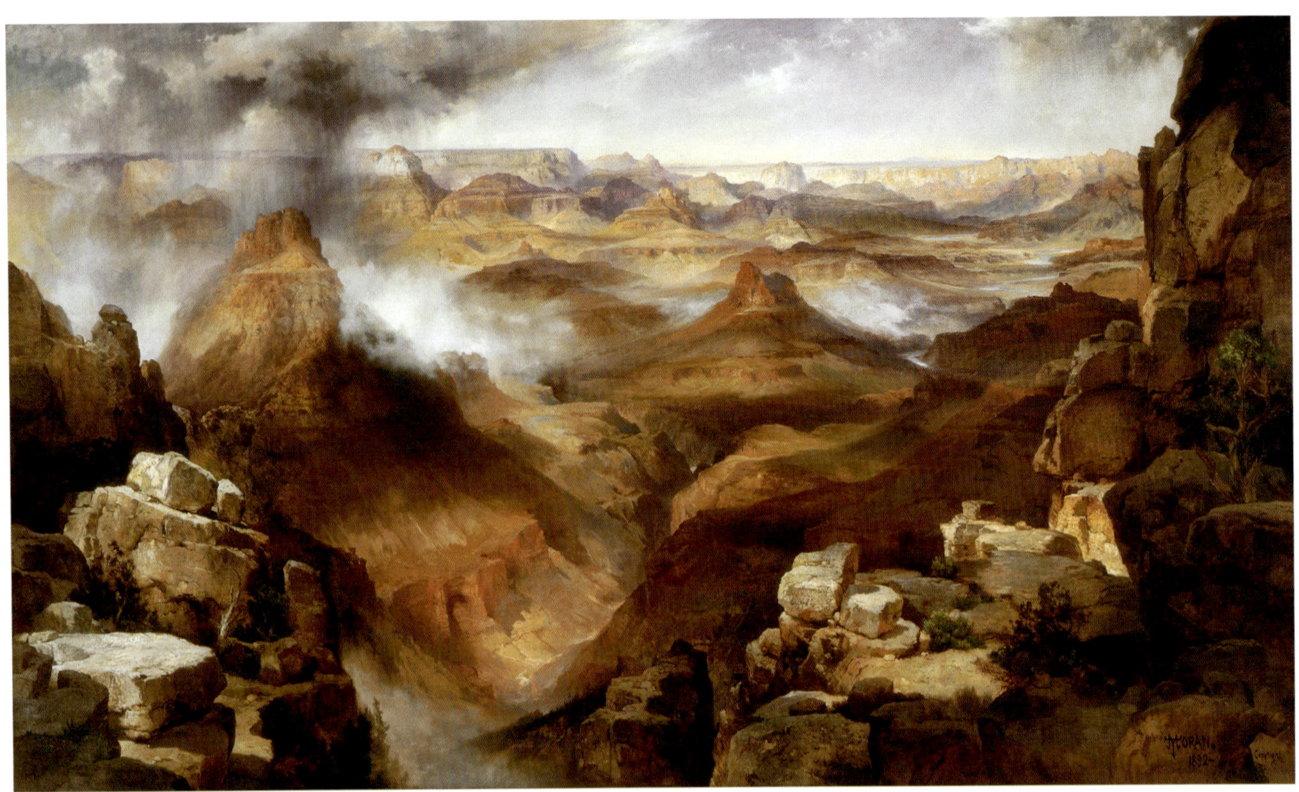

FIGURE 163. Thomas Moran, *The Grand Canyon of the Colorado River,* 1892 (reworked 1908), oil on canvas, 53 × 94 in. (134.6 × 238.7 cm). Philadelphia Museum of Art, gift of Graeme Lorimer, 1975

biographer Thurman Wilkins reports, "In return for the trip Moran agreed to assign to the Santa Fe the copyright on a single canvas, to be reproduced for publication."[23] We do know that Moran actually met the *chromiste,* Gustave Buek, since the lithographer later mentioned the visit in an article about the artist: "Knowing Moran had done excellent lithographing himself," he wrote, "I naturally approached him with considerable hesitation. No man could have received a young man, as I was, with greater cordiality than he received me."[24] The chromolithograph he created from the vivid Grand Canyon painting was reproduced in only six colors and consequently has a much more limited tonal range than either the oil version or the prints Prang had made from Moran's work in the 1870s.

The Santa Fe line reached the rim of the Grand Canyon in 1901, enabling Moran to travel to the region almost annually, especially since the railroad offered an ingenious arrangement for artists to trade pictures for transportation and lodging at the company's new rimside El Tovar Hotel. The program was facilitated by the railroad's farsighted passenger agent, William Simpson, who acquired dozens of paintings from many different artists in this way, at least until the innovative barter arrangement was outlawed by U.S. transportation regulations in 1911. (Even then the company continued the program with a nominal fee system.) Simpson thus created what may have been the first corporate collection of western art and helped found the Taos and Santa Fe art colonies by bringing artists to the region.[25]

As the first and most famous painter of the Grand Canyon, Moran remained a distinguished and valued asset to the Santa Fe Railway even into his eighties (fig. 164). He even became part of the company's promotions in a 1909 advertisement that read "Thomas Moran Sketching at the Grand Canyon" and that included his portrait and the railroad's distinctive logo (fig. 165). As late as 1915, Simpson wrote in an internal memorandum: "No doubt you know that Mr. Moran and his daughter visit the Canyon regularly each year. We have purchased several of his paintings and even if we should not purchase any more, the fact that he goes there steadily is of great advertising value. He constantly talks Grand Canyon when away from there."[26]

Moran's last work reproduced in chromolithography was also done for the Santa Fe Railway. *Grand Canyon from Hermit Rim Road* (fig. 166) was drawn from a 1912 painting (fig. 167), again by Gustave Buek. It may have been inspired by a special artists' excursion the railroad sponsored for a select group of artists in 1910 that included Moran.[27] Surprisingly, however, the Santa Fe did not purchase the painting directly from the artist but rather from Buek's American Lithographic Company, which had acquired it from Moran's Chicago dealer, Moulton and Ricketts Gallery. For $4,000, the railroad received the oil painting, 2,500 chromolithographs from it, and the reproduction rights. This print, like the 1892 Grand Canyon chromo, was also a large-format production, with even more vivid colors. The company sold or gave

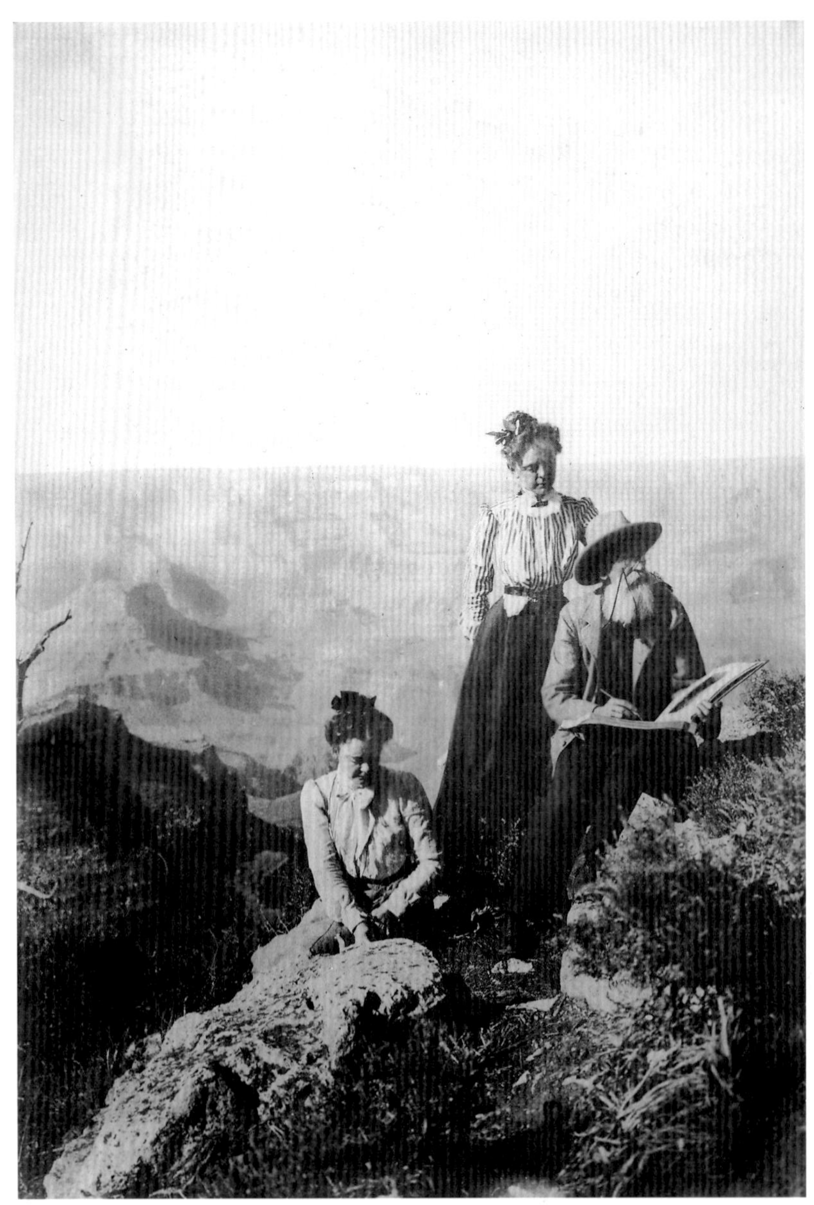

FIGURE 164. William H. Simpson, *Thomas Moran with His Daughters at Grand Canyon,* ca. 1909, photograph. Courtesy of Museum of New Mexico (103023)

Thomas Moran Sketching at

Grand Canyon

of Arizona

A large painting of the Grand Canyon of Arizona, by Thomas Moran, N. A., hangs in the National Capitol at Washington, D. C.

Mr. Moran was the first American artist of note to visit this world's wonder. He still frequently goes there to get new impressions. In his summer home at Easthampton or in his New York City studio, usually may be seen several canyon canvases under way.

Quoting from Chas. F. Lummis, in a recent issue of *Out West* magazine: "He (Moran) has come nearer to doing the Impossible than any other meddler with paint and canvas in the Southwest."

Other eminent artists also have visited the titan of chasms. They all admit it to be "the despair of the painter."

You, too, may view this scenic marvel as a side trip on the luxurious and newly-equipped

California Limited

en route to or from sunshiny California this winter.

Santa Fe

All the way

Only two days from Chicago, three days from New York, and one day from Los Angeles. A $250,000 hotel, El Tovar, managed by Fred Harvey, will care for you in country-club style. Round-trip side ride from Williams, Ariz., $6.50.

Yosemite also can be reached in winter from Merced, Cal., nearly all the way by rail.

Write for our illustrated booklets: "Titan of Chasms" and "El Tovar."

W. J. Black, Passenger Traffic Manager
A. T. & S. F. Ry. System
111 Railway Exchange, Chicago

FIGURE 165. *Thomas Moran at the Grand Canyon*, ca. 1909, advertisement, *Fine Arts Journal*, 1909

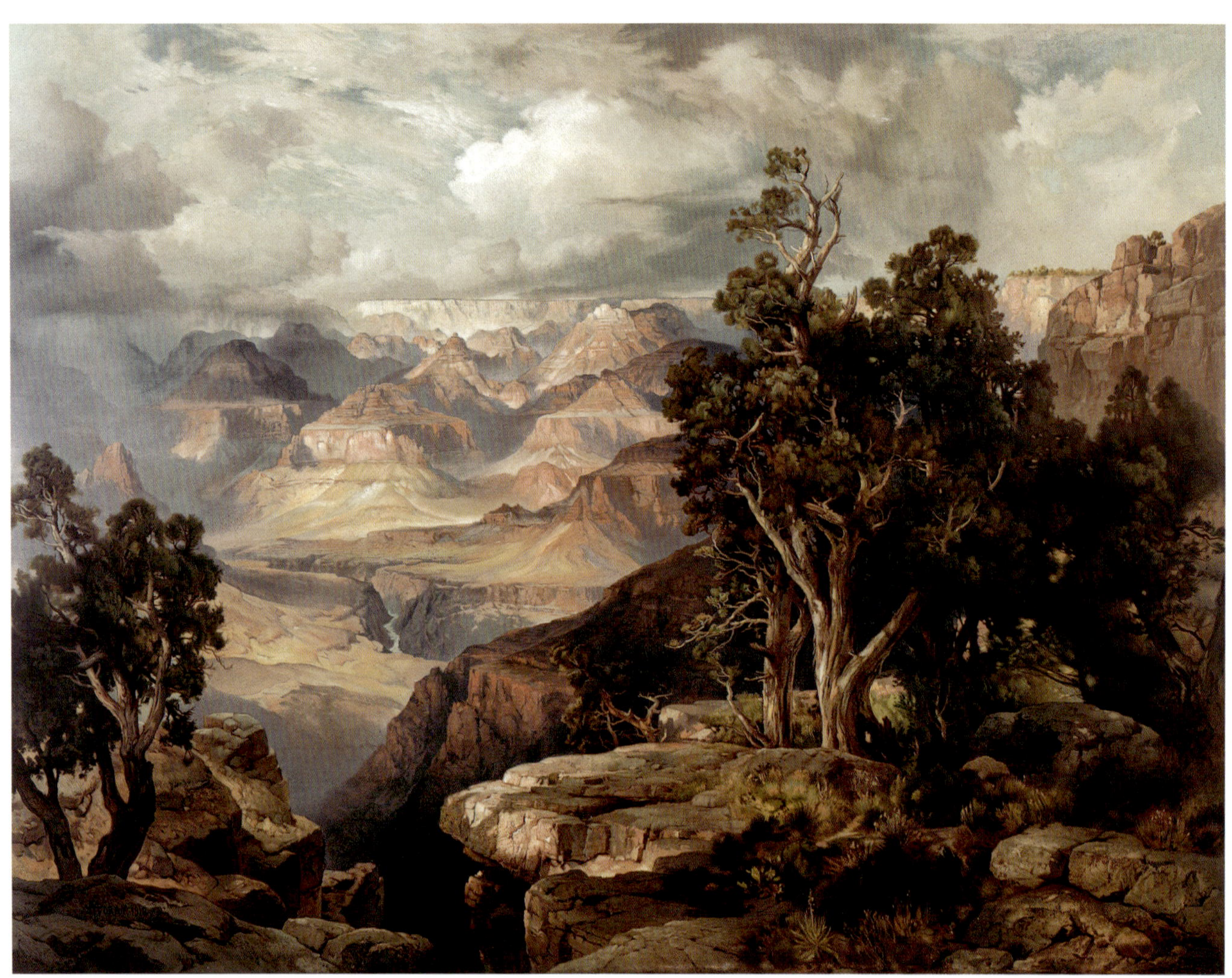

FIGURE 166. After Thomas Moran, *Grand Canyon from Hermit Rim Road,* 1913, chromolithograph, 26½ × 35 in. (67.3 × 88.9 cm). Courtesy of Zaplin-Lampert Gallery, Santa Fe, New Mexico

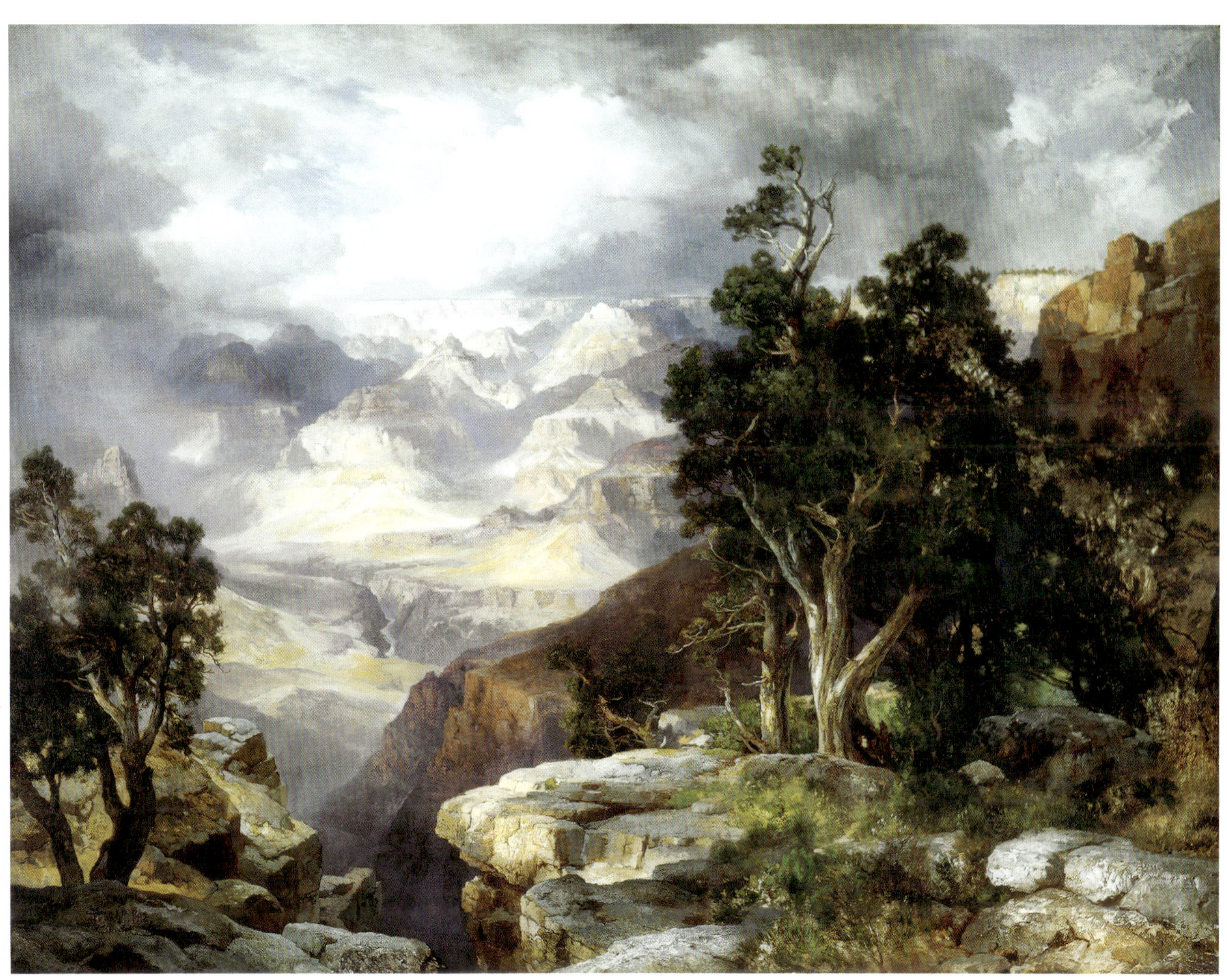

FIGURE 167. Thomas Moran, *Grand Canyon from Hermit Rim Road,* 1912, oil on canvas, 30½ × 40½ in. (77.5 × 102.9 cm). Burlington Northern/Santa Fe Railway Company Art Collection

away unknown numbers of the prints and reproduced it in smaller form on countless calendars throughout the years.[28] The corporation retained a sizable number of the chromolithographs until 1996, when it placed the remaining stock with the Zaplin-Lampert Gallery in Santa Fe, New Mexico, offering the pictures for $4,800 each.[29]

Both of the large Grand Canyon chromos were like Prang's earlier fine art reproductions in their suitability for framing. As Thurman Wilkins reported, "Over the years the publicity department of the Santa Fe would distribute thousands of chromos of the painting . . . to clubs, hotels, railway stations, schools, colleges, and universities throughout the land, indeed all over the world."[30] These prints suggest that for a brief time around the turn of the twentieth century chromolithography seems to have retained, or perhaps regained, something of the value it had held in the 1860s and 1870s as the method of choice for fine art reproduction. As newer reproduction technologies became the norm for commercial printing of all sorts, however, Moran increasingly turned to publishers who used photogravure and other modern methods to reproduce his paintings.

CHANGES IN THE INDUSTRY

Although chromos continued to be produced at least through 1915, by 1900 "halftone" images that were mechanically produced photographically and then printed through letterpress or photogravure (and later through offset lithography) were changing the industry.[31] Shifting the locus of the creative process of printed imagery to some degree, publishers began relying on artists to provide "camera-ready" art that could then be handed directly to the printer to create negatives and printing plates. Even as it facilitated illustration in some ways by making pictorial reproduction vastly less expensive, these changes also signaled a major disruption in the labor force as they displaced the artisan wood engravers who had populated the industry by the hundreds only a few decades before.

The photomechanical prints of the early twentieth century were little different from commercially produced posters of today. And like the so-called "limited edition" offset prints that sell today for relatively high prices in shopping malls, they were often sold and advertised as chromos had been for decades, as respectable substitutes for original works of art for a mass audience. The strong market for these, then as now, enhanced artists' fame, perhaps even more than earlier published imagery had, since they replicated the actual paintings without their being redrawn by others.[32] They had another advantage as well—artists could get double mileage out of a work by selling the original oils and the reproduction rights separately. Beginning in the 1890s, for example, Moran sold copyrights to many of his paintings to publishers for an average of $500 each, even as he sold the paintings elsewhere for much more. These works were photographed, printed, framed, and sold by the hundreds, enabling him to continue his substantial income from commercial reproductions long after his heyday as an illustrator and even after advanced age slowed his productivity as a painter.[33]

As if to confirm the significance of her father's artistic reputation, Moran's daughter Ruth wrote a decade after her father's death in 1926 to Osborne & Co., a publishing house that had just published a special calendar adorned with photogravure reproductions of his paintings: "It would have pleased my father, Thomas Moran, to observe with what fidelity modern machinery and skill can now reproduce these miniature facsimiles of the artist's work. And it is also a pleasure to know that the public appreciates these reproductions."[34] The sentiment echoed the artist's lifelong interest in blending the worlds of fine and commercial art, a devotion that is most vividly revealed in the remarkable western chromolithographs of the 1870s.

Louis Prang also adapted to the changes in reproductive technologies, moving into photomechanical reproductions by the 1890s, but these technical products were never a hallmark of his shop as chromos had been. The *Atlantic Monthly* noted in 1892, for example, that "L. Prang & Co. sent us two examples of photo-color prints; that is . . . pictures produced by printing in color form plates prepared for lithography from a photographic negative. The interest is in the process. The result does not strike us as differing greatly from that obtained by chromo-lithography."[35] Controversy and increased competition within the industry had already prompted Prang to diversify his business. As early as 1874, in addition to moving toward Christmas cards and trying his hand at prestigious publications such as *The Yellowstone National Park,* he had established an education department within L. Prang & Co. In 1882 he extended its emphasis on art education by creating a new subsidiary, the Prang Educational Company. Both the division and the new company worked with leading art educators of the time, including the state director of art education in Massachusetts, to produce school texts for art instruction, manuals on industrial arts for both teachers and students, and even practical art supplies, and Prang increasingly turned his attention to this arena. Most notable of his publications in this line were the "Prang Courses in Art Education," practical books that taught progressive artistic skills, beginning with very young children. He promoted the textbooks as making it "possible to begin systematic instruction on approved lines with the youngest school children" and credited the teaching with "being in harmony with the Kindergarten spirit of free observation and activity. They develop the work gradually toward a high standard of Art appreciation and technical skill."[36] Louis Prang thus continued his mission to democratize art and educate the people even after the heyday of the chromo. The Prang name continues today in the world of art education. In 1897, L. Prang & Co. merged with the Taber Art Company of New Bedford, Massachusetts, forming the Taber-Prang Co., and the descendant of this firm continues to produce crayons and other materials under the Prang trademark.

Another aspect of art education also preoccupied Louis Prang after his work with Thomas Moran. Fulfilling his lifelong interest in the theory of color, he published several books that established a standard system of reference for artists, scientists, printers, and others. His first effort in this direction was in 1877, shortly after the ill-fated Yellowstone portfolio was largely destroyed, with his company's publication of *The Theory of Color in Its Relation to Art and Industry,* written by W. Von Bezold and translated by Prang's able assistant, Sylvester Koehler. "Designed to show, by a series of simple experiments, the modern theory of color and the relation of the tones of the spectra to one another," the publication was quite important in its time and lay the foundation for many other chromatic treatises, both scientific and practical.[37] One of Prang's last efforts was his signature *Prang's Standard of Color* that he coauthored in 1898 with the head of his educational company, Mary Dana Hicks, who would become his second wife in 1900.[38]

THE LEGACY

Instead of eliminating the tensions between reproductive images and original art, the replacement of nineteenth-century reproductive technologies with more modern methods only elevated the ideal of the original further into a rarified realm. It was a phenomenon that fundamentally shaped subsequent artists' careers and the larger history of twentieth-century art. And within society more generally, it only widened the gulf between the elite and the masses. Since the high art gatekeepers were unable to stem the tide of mechanized imagery and were persistently unnerved by the chromo problem and the increasing aesthetic legitimacy accorded to women that these both represented, they basically changed the rules of the game. Whereas they had applauded reproductions and their artists when they first became so prominent in the 1850s, by the 1890s the dismayed "tastemakers" realized the full implications of published images, and they effectively established a new hierarchy of genres, one that placed illustrations and printed reproductions at one end of the scale and high art at the other. Solidifying the cult of the original, they institutionalized that aesthetic paradigm for the twentieth-century art world and beyond, relegating chromos, wood engravings, their modern descendants, and all who would associate with them, to the lowest rung on the aesthetic ladder.

This shift happened at the same time that changes in taste were moving away from the spectacular romantic landscapes that had been Moran's hallmark. Toward the end of his life, his paintings were overshadowed by more modernist trends, and his achievements as a published artist were virtually forgotten. His paintings never entirely disappeared from view, receiving attention as early as the 1930s from avid collectors such as Thomas Gilcrease and scholars such as Fritiof Fryxell, but since the resurgence of interest in American art, beginning in the 1960s, Moran's work has steadily grown in favor and prestige. In keeping with the theoretical changes that diminished published imagery's importance, however, the commercial dimension of his career was largely ignored. Since the late 1980s, however, it has increasingly been acknowledged both as a critical component of his artistic life and as a major contributor to attitudes toward the West and its cultural development. And within Moran's prodigious record of publications, *The Yellowstone National Park* chromolithographs of 1876 are by far the most respected. They have been widely hailed as the best nineteenth-century examples of American western scenery printed in color, Moran's most accomplished work for reproduction, and Louis Prang's finest effort. As Prang scholar Katherine McClinton asserted, "The prints have never been surpassed as examples of the best chromolithography. . . . Today this portfolio of chromolithographs is considered unexcelled among illustrations of the Far West." In his book *Prints of the West,* Ron Tyler calls them "among the most beautiful [chromolithographs] printed in the nineteenth century," and Peter Marzio declared that "the Yellowstone folio established the highest standards for the chromo artistry in America."[39]

As we have seen, however, *The Yellowstone National Park* chromolithographs and, indeed, all of the early color reproductions of Moran's western paintings encountered enormous challenges for recognition in their own day. Much more than a simple triumph, the complex history of their creation, publication, and presentation reveals a far more interesting achievement, one that struggled against the competing ambitions that ultimately shaped the American visual culture of our own time. As they materially brought the sublime scenery of the West to a wide audience, they simultaneously were part of a contentious debate that questioned their very legitimacy. This context alone should validate their relevance for art history. But especially when positioned within Moran's development and that of the history of the publishing industry, which wrestled with the dual interests of popular audiences and lofty aspirations for American art, the chromolithographs assume a critical value that far exceeds their identity as mere reproductive images. They were central to the debate that defined the aesthetic terms of the following century, principles that became so normalized that they have gone unquestioned until very recently.

In the intervening years, the ideals of Thomas Moran and Louis Prang for the democracy of art have been only partially realized. The gulf between high and low they sought to bridge has only widened, and commercial design, decorative arts, and reproductions remain marginalized. Nearly a century and a half after they were created, the remarkable chromolithographs that presented the colorful western wonderlands to Americans and that still stand as the finest examples of the Moran and Prang democratic aspirations for art also serve as poignant reminders of the many issues we continue to face.

Appendix Moran's Paintings for Louis Prang

The Yellowstone National Park: Published Works

1. *Gardiner's River Hot Springs,* 1874
pencil, watercolor, and opaque color, 9½ × 14 in. (24.1 × 35.6 cm)
l.l.: TMORAN/1875
Private Collection
Provenance: The artist; L. Prang & Co., Boston; Dr. John A. Mitchell's aunt (1918–1919); Dr. John A. Mitchell, Interlaken, Mass. (1919–ca. 1970); Kennedy Galleries, Inc., N.Y.; Robert Levis, II, Alton, Ill.
Bibliography: AAA-Prang (1892), no. 352; Los Angeles County Museum of Art, *The American West,* no. 100, p. 107; Kennedy Galleries, Inc., N.Y., *Kennedy Quarterly* 11, no. 4 (March 1972): illus. p. 202; Clark, no. 49

2. *The Great Blue Spring of the Lower Geyser Basin,* ca. 1873 (fig. 51)
pencil, watercolor, and opaque color, 9½ × 13¾ in. (24.1 × 34.9 cm)
l.l.: TM
Private Collection, Washington, D.C.
Provenance: The artist; L. Prang & Co., Boston; Mrs. J. D. Ratcliffe, Palisades, N.Y. (1962); Mr. and Mrs. J. William Middendorf, N.Y. (1968); Hirschl & Adler Galleries, Inc., N.Y. (1971); James Biddle, Washington, D.C.
Bibliography: AAA-Prang (1892), no. 346; Metropolitan Museum of Art, N.Y., *Watercolor Painting in America* (1966), no. 85; Metropolitan Museum of Art, N.Y., *Middendorf* (1967), no. 38, illus. pp. 56–57; Indiana University, Bloomington Art Museum, *The American Scene, 1820–1900,* no. 65, illus.; Hirschl & Adler Galleries, Inc., N.Y., *Forty Masterworks of American Art,* no. 26, illus. p. 39; High Museum of Art, Atlanta, Ga., *The Beckoning Land, Nature and the American Artist,* no. 69, illus. p. 29; The National Endowment for the Arts and the Corcoran Gallery of Art, Washington, D.C., *Wilderness,* no. 138, illus.; NCFA, *National Parks* (1972), no. 54, illus. p. 93; Hirschl & Adler Galleries, Inc., N.Y., *Retrospective of a Gallery,* illus. no. 69; MOMA, *Natural Paradise* (1976), illus. p. 81; Alan Gussow, *A Sense of Place,* illus. 1:76; Clark, no. 40

3. *The Castle Geyser, Upper Geyser Basin,* 1874
pencil, watercolor, and opaque color, 9½ × 14 in. (24.1 × 35.6 cm)
unlocated
Provenance: The artist; L. Prang & Co., Boston
Bibliography: Clark, no. 33

4. *Lower Yellowstone Range,* 1874 (fig. 58)
watercolor and opaque color, 9½ × 14 in. (24.1 × 35.6 cm)
Division of Graphic Arts, National Museum of American History, Smithsonian Institution, Gift of L. Prang & Co. (1883)
l.r.: TMORAN/1874
Provenance: The artist; L. Prang & Co., Boston
Bibliography: Wilson, "Moran," no. 35; Amon Carter Museum, Fort Worth, Tex., *The Democratic Art,* no. 54a, illus. p. 58; Marzio, *Chromolithography,* p. 310, illus. pl. 67; Clark, no. 48

5. *Southern Arm of Yellowstone Lake, Yellowstone National Park, Wyoming Territory (Yellowstone Lake, Yellowstone National Park),* 1874 (fig. 63)
pencil, watercolor, and opaque color, 9⅞ × 14⅜ in. (25.1 × 36.5 cm)
Private Collection, Wyoming
Provenance: The artist; L. Prang & Co., Boston; Sotheby's, N.Y.
Bibliography: AAA-Prang (1892), no. 354; Clark, no. 67

6. *Tower Falls and Sulphur Mountain, Yellowstone National Park,* 1874 (fig. 65)
pencil, watercolor, and opaque color, 10 × 14 in. (25.4 × 35.6 cm)
l.l.: TM/1874
Inscription on verso by Moran: "It is certainly [one] of the most impressive scene[s] in the park. The Sulphur Mountain lies across the Yellowstone river which flows at its base. The snowy dome of the Mountain is supported upon a base of columnar basalt of great regularity and

formation. The columns of which are about 40 feet in height. Beneath these columns lies a strata of calcerous deposit intermixed with sulphur and iron given the most delicate and beautiful tints of red and yellow. This is again supported upon another mass of columnar structure."

Westmoreland Museum of American Art, Greensburg, Pa., no. 1978.87

Provenance: The artist; L. Prang & Co., Boston

Bibliography: AAA-Prang (1892), no. 354; Clark, no. 57 [?]

7. *Head of the Yellowstone River,* 1874
pencil, watercolor, and opaque color, 9½ × 14 in.
(24.1 × 35.6 cm)
l.l.: T. Moran 1874
unlocated
Provenance: The artist; L. Prang & Co., Boston
Bibliography: AAA-Prang (1892), no. 356; Wilson, no. 36; Clark, no. 43

8. *The Grand Cañon of the Yellowstone,* 1874
pencil, watercolor, and opaque color, 9½ × 14 in.
(24.1 × 35.6 cm)
unlocated
Provenance: The artist; L. Prang & Co., Boston
Bibliography: AAA-Prang (1892), no. 353; Clark, no. 38

9. *The Towers of Tower Falls,* 1874 (fig. 92)
pencil, watercolor, and opaque color, 14½ × 10½ in.
(36.8 × 26.7 cm)
Private Collection, Idaho
Provenance: The artist; L. Prang & Co., Boston
Bibliography: AAA-Prang (1892), no. 351

10. *The Mountain of the Holy Cross,* 1875
pencil, watercolor, and opaque color, 9½ × 14 in.
(24.1 × 35.6 cm)
l.r.: signed
unlocated
Provenance: The artist; L. Prang & Co., Boston
Bibliography: AAA-Prang (1892), no. 349; Gustave Buek, "Thomas Moran, N.A. — The Grand Old Man of American Art," illus. p. 37; Wilson, "Moran," no. 93; Clark, no. 151

11. *Mosquito Trail, Rocky Mountains of Colorado,* 1875 (fig. 108)
pencil, watercolor, and opaque color, 9¾ × 14¼ in.
(24.8 × 35.2 cm)
l.r.: [TM monogram]/1875
Private Collection, New York
Provenance: The artist; L. Prang & Co., Boston; Mrs. J. D. Ratcliffe, Palisades, N.Y. (1962); Mr. and Mrs. J. William Middendorf II, N.Y.; Hirschl and Adler Galleries, Inc., N.Y. (1969–1973)
Bibliography: AAA-Prang (1892), no. 345; Laura Bride Powers, "Early Art of Thomas Moran, Shown in Art Club Exhibit"; Wilson, "Moran," no. 40; Metropolitan Museum of Art, N.Y., *Watercolor Painting in America* (1966), no. 87; Wilkins, *Moran,* p. 97; Metropolitan Museum of Art, N.Y., *Middendorf* (1967), no. 40, illus. p. 59; Indiana University, Bloomington Art Museum, *The American Scene, 1820–1900,* no. 67, illus.; Katherine Morrison McClinton, "L. Prang and Company," illus. no. 9a, p. 104; Clark, no. 149; Anderson, *Thomas Moran,* no. 51

12. *Summit of the Sierras, Nevada* ca. 1874–1875 (fig. 112)
watercolor and opaque color, 14⅕ × 9⅘ in. (36.0 × 25.0 cm)
l.l.: [TM monogram]ORAN
The Art Institute of Chicago, Gift of Mrs. Byron Harvey, no. 1965.852
Provenance: The artist; L. Prang & Co., Boston; Mrs. Byron Harvey
Bibliography: AAA-Prang (1892), no. 350; Ruth B. Moran, "Thomas Moran," illus. p. 45; Wilson, "Moran," no. 94; The Arts Club of Chicago, *The American Landscape,* no. 21, illus. 17; Clark, no. 98

13. *Shoshone Falls, Snake River, Idaho (The Great Falls of the Snake River, Idaho Territory),* ca. 1874–1875 (fig. 117)
watercolor, 10 × 14 in. (25.4 × 35.6 cm)
The Chrysler Museum of Art, Norfolk, Va.
Provenance: The artist; L. Prang & Co., Boston; Hugh Gordon Miller
Bibliography: AAA-Prang (1892), no. 355; Wilson, "Moran," no. 92 (as the Great Falls of Snake River, Idaho Territory); Clark, no. 176

14. *Valley of the Babbling Waters,* ca. 1874–1875
pencil, watercolor, and opaque color, 9½ × 14 in.
(24.1 × 35.6 cm)
l.r.: TM
unlocated
Provenance: The artist; L. Prang & Co., Boston
Bibliography: AAA-Prang (1892), no. 344; Wilson, "Moran," no. 95; Clark, no. 138

15. *The Great Salt Lake of Utah,* 1874 (fig. 126)
pencil, watercolor, and opaque color, 9½ × 14 in.
(24.1 × 35.6 cm)
l.r.: TMORAN/1874
Private Collection, New York
Provenance: The artist; L. Prang & Co., Boston; Sotheby's, N.Y.
Bibliography: AAA-Prang (1892), no. 347; Wilson, "Moran," no. 37; Clark, no. 186
The Yellowstone National Park: Unpublished Works

16. *Upper Twin Lake, Colorado,* 1875
pencil, watercolor, and opaque color, 9½ × 14 in.
(24.1 × 35.6 cm)
unlocated, formerly L. Prang & Co., Boston
Bibliography: AAA-Prang (1892), no. 358; Clark, nos. 62 and 159

17. *Pike's Peak,* 1875
pencil, watercolor, and opaque color, 9½ × 14 in.
(24.1 × 35.6 cm)
unlocated, formerly L. Prang & Co., Boston
Bibliography: Clark, no. 154

18. *Lake Donner, Nevada,* 1875
pencil, watercolor, and opaque color, 9½ × 14 in.
(24.1 × 35.6 cm)
unlocated, formerly L. Prang & Co., Boston
Bibliography: AAA-Prang (1892), no. 359; Clark, no. 188

19. *Gunnison's Butte, Azure Cliffs of Green River, Utah,* 1874
pencil, watercolor, and opaque color, 9½ × 14 in.
(24.1 × 35.6 cm)
unlocated
Provenance: The artist; L. Prang & Co., Boston
Bibliography: AAA-Prang (1892), no. 357; Clark, no. 291

20. *Mu-Koon-Tu-Weap Valley,* 1875
pencil, watercolor, and opaque color, 14 × 9½ in.
(35.6 × 24.1 cm)
unlocated, formerly L. Prang & Co., Boston
Bibliography: Clark, no. 129

21. *Mu Koon Tu Weap Narrows,* 1874–1875
pencil, watercolor, and opaque color, 9½ × 14 in.
(24.1 × 35.6 cm)
unlocated, formerly L. Prang & Co., Boston

22. *Devil's Den,* 1874
pencil, watercolor, and opaque color, 14 × 9½ in.
(35.6 × 24.1 cm)
unlocated, formerly L. Prang & Co., Boston

23. *Upper Falls, Yellowstone,* 1874 (fig. 145)
pencil, watercolor, and opaque color, 14 × 9¾ in.
(35.6 × 24.8 cm)
The Philbrook Museum of Art, Tulsa, Okla.
Provenance: The artist; L. Prang & Co., Boston; Mr. Kirkpatrick, Newark, N.J.; John Nicholson Gallery, N.Y.; M. Knoedler & Co.; Private collection
Bibliography: Clark, no. 61

24. *The Three Tetons,* 1875
pencil, watercolor, and opaque color, 14 × 9½ in.
(35.6 × 24.1 cm)
unlocated, formerly L. Prang & Co., Boston

Small Prang Series

1. *Cliffs of the Upper Colorado River, Wyoming Territory,* ca. 1879
oil on canvas, 11½ × 6½ in. (29.2 × 16.5 cm)
Private Collection, Dallas, Tex.
Provenance: The artist; L. Prang & Co., Boston
Bibliography: AAA-Prang (1892), no. 419; Clark, no. 104 (listed as a watercolor); Harvey, *Thomas Moran and the Spirit of Place,* p. 12

2. *On the Lookout — A Ute Camp, Utah,* ca. 1879
oil or pencil, watercolor, and opaque color, 11½ × 6½ in.
(29.2 × 16.5 cm)
unlocated, formerly L. Prang & Co., Boston
Bibliography: AAA-Prang (1892), no. 419; Clark, no. 418

Notes

ARCHIVAL SOURCES

AAA Archives of American Art, Smithsonian Institution, Moran papers

BPL Boston Public Library, Print Room, Prang papers

EHL East Hampton Free Library, Moran papers

GIL Thomas Gilcrease Museum of American History and Art, Tulsa, Oklahoma, Moran papers and art collection

HCC Hallmark Cards Collection, Kansas City, Missouri, Prang collection

JNEM Jefferson National Expansion Memorial, St. Louis, Missouri

NA National Archives, Washington, D.C., United States Geological Survey Records

SFRR Santa Fe Railway Archives, Burlington Northern/Santa Fe Corporation, Fort Worth, Moran curatorial file

WAR Warshaw Collection of Business Americana, National Museum of American History, Smithsonian Institution

YNP Yellowstone National Park Museum Collection, Yellowstone National Park, Moran papers

INTRODUCTION

1. Moran's prodigious production of art for publication was first mentioned in S. G. W. Benjamin, "A Pioneer of the Palette: Thomas Moran," *Magazine of Art* 5 (February 1882): 93. My own research has added to his estimates.

2. This process is described and illustrated in Peter C. Marzio, *The Democratic Art: Chromolithography, 1840–1900, Pictures for a Nineteenth-Century America* (Boston: David R. Godine in association with the Amon Carter Museum, 1979); and Peter C. Marzio, "The Democratic Art of Chromolithography in America: An Overview," in *Art and Commerce: American Prints of the Nineteenth-Century* (Boston and Charlottesville: Museum of Fine Arts, distributed by the University Press of Virginia, 1978), 77–102. An artist's manual on the subject explains, "If it is decided to make an imitation water-colour, then more colours will have to be used . . . because the light pink or blue tints or any other light color of the sketch will each require a separate light printing of that colour as well as a dark colour." Thomas Edgar Griffits, *The Technique of Colour Printing by Lithography: A Concise Manual of Drawn Lithography* (London: Faber and Faber, 1940), 53–54. The number of stones is reported in James Parton, "Popularizing Art," *Atlantic Monthly* 23 (March 1869): 353.

3. Nancy Anderson, ed., *Thomas Moran* (Washington, D.C., and New Haven, Conn.: National Gallery of Art and Yale University Press, 1997). Some of the Prang chromos from Moran's watercolors were also included in Anne R. Morand, Joni L. Kinsey, and Mary Panzer, *Splendors of the American West: Thomas Moran's Art of the Grand Canyon and Yellowstone* (Birmingham, Ala.: Birmingham Museum of Art in association with the University of Washington Press, 1990). Individual chromos from the series have been shown in other exhibitions from time to time.

4. Larry Freeman, *Louis Prang: Color Lithographer, Giant of a Man* (Watkins Glen, N.Y.: Century House, 1971); Katharine Morrison McClinton, *The Chromolithographs of Louis Prang* (New York: Clarkson N. Potter, 1973); Marzio, *The Democratic Art;* Michael Clapper, "'I Was Once a Barefoot Boy!': Cultural Tensions in a Popular Chromo," *American Art* 16 (Summer 2002): 17–39; Michael Clapper, "Popularizing Art in Boston, 1865–1910: L. Prang & Co. and the Museum of Fine Arts," Ph.D. diss., Northwestern University, 1997.

CHAPTER 1. LOUIS PRANG AND THE CHROMO-CONTROVERSY

1. Frank Luther Mott, *A History of American Magazines*, 5 vols. (Cambridge, Mass: Harvard University Press, 1930–1968), 3:5.

2. "Illustrated Works," *Cosmopolitan Art Journal* 1 (June 1857): 111.

3. Jo Ann Early Levin, "The Golden Age of Illustration: Popular Art in American Magazines, 1850–1925," Ph.D. diss., University of Pennsylvania, 1980, p. 28.

4. Early attempts at machine printing were greeted with derision; one of the earliest such publications, the British *Penny Magazine*, begun in 1832, received initial criticism for its imagery, but after it rose to a circulation of 200,000, it was acclaimed for having "made a revolution in popular art. . . . It had given the ordinary British reader a knowledge of art treasures of painting and sculpture which could not have been imparted by any other agency." Theodore DeVinne, "The Growth of Wood-Cut Printing," *Scribner's Monthly* 20 (May 1880): 35.

5. Because even the more durable end grain of wood blocks was subject to wear, plaster molds were made of the engraved blocks and cast, a technique first perfected around 1829 and called stereotyping. Electrotyping was an improvement on this in which molds were made from wax that provided a much better impression, and copper was deposited electrolytically rather than done as metal casting. This also improved detail. The thin copper impression was then backed with a regular printing plate and could be printed along with the typed page. This technique was only developed in the 1840s and was not generally viable until the 1870s, when the electronics of the process were perfected. Levin, "The Golden Age of Illustration," pp. 29–30.

6. Sally Pierce and Catharina Slautterback, *Boston Lithography, 1825–1880: The Boston Athenaeum Collection* (Boston: Boston Athenaeum, 1991), 10.

7. Marzio, *The Democratic Art*, p. 17. See also ibid.

8. *Prang's Chromo: A Journal of Popular Art* 1 (January 1868): 5.

9. It could be argued that the ten-volume publication *Oriental Ceramic Art: Collection of W. T. Walters* (New York: D. Appleton & Co., 1897), which included 116 chromolithographs from L. Prang & Co., was even more lavish, but Prang neither published this series nor was it the same type of project as *The Yellowstone National Park*. The critics of the 1860s would have approved of using chromolithography to reproduce decorative objects rather than paintings.

10. Quoted by Edward A. Rushford, "Lewis [*sic*] Prang, Engraver on Wood," *Antiques* 37 (April 1940): 187, without source. Prang was born on March 12, 1824; he died in Los Angeles in 1909.

11. Prang did not leave Europe until February 26, 1850, sailing to New York on the ship *Splendid*. Ibid.

12. Louis Prang, "Autobiography of Louis Prang," unpublished manuscript in private collection; reprinted in Mary Margaret Sittig, "L. Prang & Company, Fine Art Publishers," master's thesis, George Washington University, 1970, pp. 123–163.

13. The Boston Athenaeum has a fine copy of this series.

14. M. E. Hollingsworth, "How Christmas Cards Are Made," *Wide Awake* 20 (December 1884): 63.

15. The new factory is described in *Prang's Chromo: A Journal of Popular Art* 1 (Christmas 1869): 5; and also in "An Art Workshop," *Aldine: A Typographic Art Journal* 2 (July 1869): 2. It still exists at 286 Roxbury Avenue (formerly Washington Avenue). It is now an apartment building. Prang's house also still stands on nearby Centre Street behind the factory, and Louis Prang Street is located just south of the Museum of Fine Arts in Boston.

16. This process is described in Hollingsworth, "How Christmas Cards Are Made," p. 63. It is uncertain, however, just when Prang & Co. shifted to using zinc plates. See Marzio, *The Democratic Art,* pp. 67–71.

17. "Flopped" should not be confused with "reversed," which refers to a photographic negative in the printing trade. Regarding "ganging up," the Hollingsworth article recounts, "they saw nine prints taken in greasy ink from the zinc drawing. These were pasted upon a sheet of paper. This sheet was laid, print side down, upon a slab of well polished stone. . . . A strong even pressure from a heavy roller was now applied to the sheet upon the stone. Then the paper was dampened, rubbed and washed off. Behold the lines of the nine prints of the zinc drawing remained upon the stone slab [ready for printing to paper]. . . . A printing stone might contain from one, to three hundred and fifty 'transfers' — these latter tiny Scripture-text cards, and baby valentines." Hollingsworth, "How Christmas Cards Are Made," pp. 63–64.

18. Quoted in Rushford, "Lewis [*sic*] Prang," p. 189, without source.

19. Advertisement for Prang's American Chromos, *Galaxy* 9 (June 1870): n.p.

20. Although similar Prang advertisements are in a number of sources, this one appeared in *Harper's Weekly,* January 25, 1868, p. 63. Prang frequently cited reviews of "eminent critics" in his publicity.

21. See for example "Autotypes and Oleographs," *Nation* 11 (November 10, 1870): 317–318. See also Marzio, *The Democratic Art,* p. 94.

22. "The time occupied in preparing these stones for the press is about three months; and when once the stones are ready, an edition of a thousand copies is printed in five months more." Parton, "Popularizing Art," p. 351. Prang's price lists are found in many of his advertisements and in any edition of *Prang's Chromo: A Journal of Popular Art.*

23. "Hints on Framing," *Prang's Chromo: A Journal of Popular Art* 1 (January 1868): 4.

24. Parton, "Popularizing Art," p. 351.

25. "Publishers' Department," *Bay State Monthly* 2 (December 1884): 175.

26. The proof books for *The Yellowstone National Park* chromos have not been located. BPL and the Boston Athenaeum have some for other chromos, and the Beinecke Library at Yale has one for the two late Prang/Moran chromos.

27. This was published sometime in the 1890s. BPL has a copy of this publication, and several plates from it are reproduced in McClinton, *The Chromolithographs of Louis Prang,* plates a–d.

28. Sittig, "L. Prang & Company," pp. 56–57, 60–67.

29. Prang, "Autobiography," in ibid., pp. 149–150.

30. McClinton, *The Chromolithographs of Louis Prang,* pp. 151–157.

31. Prang sold 19,000 copies of *Group of Chickens* in its first year and had sold 30,000 copies by 1869. *Prang's Chromo: A Journal of Popular Art* 1 (January 1868): 1; "An Art Workshop," p. 2. For more on *The Barefoot Boy,* see Clapper, "'I Was Once a Barefoot Boy!"

32. Prang, "Autobiography," in Sittig, "L. Prang & Company," p. 150.

33. *Philadelphia Photographer* (1869): 168.

34. "Album of American Artists," *Prang's Chromo: A Journal of Popular Art* 2 (Christmas 1870): 3. This was announced in *Putnam's Monthly* as a "Gallery of American Painters," *Putnam's Monthly Magazine of American Literature, Science, and Art* 11 (April 1868): 516.

35. Frederic E. Church to L. Prang & Co., quoted in *Prang's Chromo: A Journal of Popular Art* 1 (Christmas 1868): 6.

36. Gerald Carr, *Frederic Edwin Church, The Icebergs* (Dallas, Tex.: Dallas Museum of Art, 1980), pp. 28–29.

37. Both of these are reproduced in color in Ron Tyler, *Prints of the West* (Golden, Colo.: Fulcrum Publishing, 1994), 136–137.

38. *Prang's Chromo: A Journal of Popular Art* 2 (Christmas 1869): 5.

39. Parton, "Popularizing Art," p. 353.

40. Ibid., p. 354.

41. Walter Benjamin, "The Work of Art in the Age of Mechanical Reproduction," 1936, reprinted in *Illuminations,* ed. Hannah Arendt (New York: Schocken Books, 1978).

42. The presence of color itself in a printed reproduction was a controversial issue. For more on this, see Neil Harris, "Color and Media: Some Comparisons and Speculations," in Neil Harris, *Cultural Excursions: Marketing Appetites and Cultural Tastes in Modern America* (Chicago: University of Chicago Press, 1990), 318–336.

43. This remarkable facsimile effect is not present in unvarnished chromos, and these offer no hint at what prompted such controversy. The varnished and textured chromos, however, are indeed remarkable. BPL has a number of these, as does AAA in the Margaret Sittig papers.

44. For a thoughtful essay on the importance of this issue for American intellectual history, see Harris, "Iconography and Intellectual History: The Halftone Effect," in *Cultural Excursions,* pp. 304–317.

45. Miles Orvell, *The Real Thing: Imitation and Authenticity in American Culture, 1880–1940* (Chapel Hill: University of North Carolina Press, 1989), 36.

46. Edward Stanwood, *Boston Illustrated* (Boston: James R. Osgood & Co., 1872), 97.

47. Clapper, "Popularizing Art in Boston," pp. 102–103, 113–114.

48. "Fine Arts: Multiplied Art," *Nation* 1 (July 20, 1865): 90–92; (July 27, 1865): 123–125.

49. For more on the training of wood engravers, see Ann Prentice Wagner, "The Graver, the Brush, and the Ruling Machine: The Training of Late Nineteenth-Century Wood Engravers," *Proceedings of the American Antiquarian Society* 105, no. 1 (1995): especially 182–186.

50. For more on this topic, see Michael Clapper, "The Chromo and the Art Museum: Popular and Elite Art Institutions in Late Nineteenth-Century America," in Christopher Reed, ed., *Not at Home: The Suppression of Domesticity in Modern Art and Architecture* (London: Thames and Hudson, 1996); and Clapper, "Popularizing Art in Boston," pp. 255–261.

51. Quoted without specific source in Laurence W. Levine, *Highbrow/Lowbrow: The Emergence of Cultural Hierarchy in America* (Cambridge, Mass.: Harvard University Press, 1988), 151.

52. Boston Museum of Fine Arts, *Annual Report* (1883), quoted in Clapper, "Popularizing Art in Boston," p. 183.

53. Benjamin Ives Gilman, "Aims and Principles of the Construction and Management of Museums of Fine Art," *Museum Journal* (July 1909): 28–44; reprinted in Bettina Messias Carbonell, *Museum Studies: An Anthology of Contexts* (Malden, Mass.: Blackwell Publishing, 2004), 423.

54. "Fine Arts," *Philadelphia Daily Evening Bulletin,* October 25, 1856, p. 2, col. 2.

55. Curiously, the very first *Prang's Chromo* issue was reprinted with two dates, one for December 1867 and one for January 1868, still as volume one, number one, BPL. Prang wrote numerous letters to papers defending his products and his own integrity, and he reprinted many of them. See, for example, "Art Critics Criticized," *Prang's Chromo: A Journal of Popular Art* 1 (September 1868): 6.

56. Prang used the phrase "the democracy of art" as a subtitle of his company's logo on some advertisements. See, for example, *Galaxy* 9 (June 1870): n.p.

57. "Fine Arts Items," *New York Daily Tribune,* April 27, 1866, p. 7, cols. 1–2.

58. "Concerning Chromo-Lithography," *New York Daily Tribune,* May 1866; reprinted in *Prang's Chromo: A Journal of Popular Art* 1 (January 1868): 2.

59. "Fine Arts," *New York Daily Tribune,* November 20, 1866, p. 6, col. 1.

60. For an overview, see the classic book by Russell Lynes, *The Tastemakers: The Shaping of American Popular Taste* (1949; reprint ed., New York: Dover Publications, 1980), and more recently in Levine, *Highbrow/Lowbrow.*

61. Kenneth John Myers, "The Public Display of Art in New York City, 1664–1914," in *Rave Reviews: American Art and Its Critics, 1826–1925,* ed. David B. Dearinger (New York: National Academy of Design, 2000), 45.

62. "Fine Arts: Multiplied Art," *Nation* 1 (July 20, 1865): 91.

63. "Controversy with an Art Critic," *Prang's Chromo: A Journal of Popular Art* 1 (April 1868): 2–3; and "Chromos and Critics," *Prang's Chromo: A Journal of Popular Art* 2 (Christmas 1870): 4–5.

64. See *Galaxy* 6 (November 1868): 714–715, (December 1868): 860; and "Chromo-Lithography," *Putnam's Monthly Magazine of American Literature, Science, and Art* 12 (October 1868): 507–508, (December 1868): 763–764.

65. Louis Prang, "On Theories of Chromo-Lithography," *Nation* (November 28, 1867): 437–438. The emphasis is Prang's.

66. "Street Lithography," *Art Age* (December 1884): 57.

67. "An Art Workshop," p. 2.

68. Louis Prang, "Chromo-Lithography, the Handmaiden of Painting," *New York Daily Tribune,* December 1, 1866, p. 6, col. 2. *Harper's Monthly* echoed this in 1868: "We most gladly welcome the effort of Mr. Prang to do for Art what has already been measurably done for Literature. There are few cultivated households in which the best books are not to be found. We trust that the time is not far distant when adequate representations of the best works of art will not be equally indispensable. . . . These 'Chromos' are the largest, and an altogether successful step in that direction." "The Editor's Easy Chair," *Harper's Monthly* 36 (February 1868): 398.

69. Joseph Jefferson, "The Autobiography of Joseph Jefferson," *Century Magazine* 40 (August 1890): 538–556.

70. Charles Waldstein, "The Lesson of Greek Art," *Century Magazine* 31, new ser. 9 (November 1885–April 1886): 266.

71. "The Arts of Design in the United States," in *First Century of National Existence; The United States as They Were and Are* (Hartford, Conn.: L. Stebbins, 1875), p. 343.

72. "Chromo-Lithography," *Putnam's Monthly Magazine of American Literature, Science, and Art* 12 (October 1868): 507–508.

73. "Mr. Prang's Defense," *New York Daily Tribune,* December 7, 1866, p. 5, col. 1.

74. "Fine Arts," *New York Daily Tribune,* November 20, 1866, p. 6, col. 1.

75. "Autotypes and Oleographs," 318.

76. Prang, "Chromo-Lithography, the Handmaiden of Painting."

77. "Mr. Prang's Defense."

78. "Chromo-Lithographs, American, English, and French," *Nation* (October 31, 1867): 359.

79. *Philadelphia Photographer* (1868): 115–117.

80. The *Nation* said, "There was a worse thing which this [chromolithography] is replacing — the manufacture of cheap oil-painting by the wholesale, painted in a way not dissimilar to the chromos, but very much more dingy and disagreeable in color." "Autotypes and Oleographs," p. 318.

81. "Chromos in Perfection," *Boston Daily Evening Transcript,* November 25, 1870, p. 1, cols. 3–4.

82. For more, see Saul E. Zalesch, "What the Four Million Bought: Cheap Oil Paintings of the 1880s," *American Quarterly* 48 (March 1996): 77–109.

83. Parton, "Popularizing Art," pp. 356–357; "The Picture of Commerce," *Harper's Weekly* 33 (May 18, 1889): 403. For an amusing account of daubs, see William Dean Howells, "A Counterfeit Presentiment," part III, *Atlantic Monthly* 40 (October 1877): 449. For one on picture mills, see Frank R. Stockton, "The Reversible Landscape," *Century Magazine* 28, new ser. 6 (May–October 1884): 434–439.

84. "A Word to Artists," *Prang's Chromo: A Journal of Popular Art* 1 (January 1868): 4.

85. *Prang's Chromo: A Journal of Popular Art* 8 (September 1870): 4.

86. Tait's correspondence with Prang is recounted in Warder Cadbury, *Arthur Fitzwilliam Tait: Artist in the Adirondacks* (Cranbury, N.J.: Associated University Presses, 1986), 84.

87. Ibid., p. 355.

88. James Parton to L. Prang & Co., quoted in *Prang's Chromo: A Journal of Popular Art* 1 (January 1, 1868): 1.

89. "Autotypes and Oleographs," p. 317.

90. "Color Printing from Wood and from Stone," *Nation* (January 10, 1867): 36.

91. William Coffin, "American Illustration of Today," *Scribner's Magazine* 11 (January 1892): 108. *Scribner's Monthly* ran from 1870 to 1881 and is not to be confused with *Scribner's Magazine,* which adopted the name five years after *Scribner's Monthly* became *Century Magazine.* The five-year delay was required by contract to prevent confusion with the earlier journal.

92. "Chromo-Lithography," *Putnam's Monthly Magazine of American Literature, Science, and Art* 12 (October 1868): 508.

93. Parton, "Popularizing Art," 353–554.

94. Hollingsworth, "How Christmas Cards Are Made," p. 65.

95. Philip Gilbert Hamerton, *The Graphic Arts* (London: Seeley, Jackson, and Halliday, 1882), 375.

96. "A Piece of History Worth Writing," *Century Magazine* 26, new ser. 4 (May–October

1883): 477; Charles Dudley Warner, "The Novel and the Common School," *Atlantic Monthly* 65 (June 1890): 724.

97. Damon Runyon, *Take It Easy* (New York: Frederick A. Stokes, 1938), 292, quoted in Marzio, *The Democratic Art*, pp. 209–210.

98. Clapper, "The Chromo and the Art Museum," in Reed, ed., *Not at Home*, p. 37.

99. Hollingsworth, "How Christmas Cards Are Made," p. 64. For more on the women whose art Prang reproduced, see Amelia Peck and Carol Irish, *Candace Wheeler: The Art and Enterprise of American Design, 1875–1900* (New York and New Haven, Conn.: Metropolitan Museum of Art in association with Yale University Press, 2001); and Jane Bayard Curley, "The Advent of the American Christmas Card: Prang's Christmas Card Competitions and the Rise of Women Artists," *Nineteenth Century* 22 (Fall 2002): 3–9.

100. For more on the complicated and fascinating issue of gender politics in the late-nineteenth-century art world, see Kirsten Swinth's excellent book, *Painting Professionals: Women Artists and the Development of Modern American Art, 1870–1930* (Chapel Hill: University of North Carolina Press, 2001).

101. Prang placed such ads in a variety of publications. This one, ironically, appeared in the male-oriented *Scientific American*, new ser. 15 (December 8, 1866): 397.

102. *Prang's Chromo: A Journal of Popular Art* 1 (January 1868): 7.

103. "Chromo-Lithography," *New York Times*, October 31, 1874, p. 13.

104. Mary E. Neely, "Popular Art," *The Ladies Repository: A Monthly Periodical Devoted to Literature, Arts, and Religion* 4 (December 1876): 551.

105. Catherine E. Beecher and Harriet Beecher Stowe, *The American Woman's Home: Or, Principles of Domestic Science, Being a Guide to the Formation and Maintenance of Economic, Healthful, Beautiful, and Christian Homes* (New York: J. B. Ford, 1869, and Boston: H. A. Brown, 1869), 94.

106. Harriet Beecher Stowe, "What Pictures Shall I Hang on My Walls?" *Atlantic Almanac* (1869): 43.

107. "The Editor's Easy Chair," *Harper's Monthly* 52 (April 1876): 772–773.

108. Mark Twain, "A Connecticut Yankee in King Arthur's Court," *Century Magazine* 39 (November 1889): 74.

109. See, for example, Harriett Beecher Stowe, *House and Home Papers* (Boston: Ticknor and Fields, 1865), 10; William Dean Howells, "A Counterfeit Presentiment"; Twain, "A Connecticut Yankee in King Arthur's Court," p. 74; Henry James, "The Bostonians," *Century Magazine* 30, new ser. 8 (May–October 1885): 862.

110. *Literary World* 3 (December 1872): 104.

111. Charles Carleton Coffin, "Labor and the Natural Forces," *Atlantic Monthly* 43 (May 1879): 553–556.

112. *Boston Daily Advertiser*, quoted in *Prang's Chromo: A Journal of Popular Art* 1 (January 1868): 1; Parton, "Popularizing Art," p. 357.

113. Parton, "Popularizing Art," p. 354.

114. "Chromo-Civilization," *Nation* (September 24, 1874): 201–202.

115. Parton, "Popularizing Art," p. 355.

116. Prang, "Chromo-Lithography, the Handmaiden of Painting," p. 6.

117. Louis Prang, "Chromos and Critics," *Prang's Chromo: A Journal of Popular Art* 2 (Christmas 1870): 5, col. 3. The article was a response to "Autotypes and Oleographs," in the *Nation*.

118. This is essentially the thesis of Kirsten Swinth's *Painting Professionals*, although she deals with a much broader swath of fine art history, specifically in regard to women's activities in the art world. A related argument about the displacement of women as founders of philanthropic organizations is Kathleen D. McCarthy, *Women's Culture: American Philanthropy and Art, 1830–1930* (Chicago: University of Chicago Press, 1991).

CHAPTER 2. THOMAS MORAN AND THE PUBLISHED IMAGE

1. Thurman Wilkins, *Thomas Moran: Artist of the Mountains* (Norman: University of Oklahoma Press, 1966; revised ed., 1997), 17, quoting from Moran's interview with Gussie Packard DuBois, "Thomas Moran Knows Nature and Paints It," *Pasadena Star-News*, March 11, 1916, p. 6, col. 3, in AAA, Moran papers 4, frame 556.

2. Ron Tyler, "The Prints of Life in the West, 1840–60," in Ron Tyler et al., *American Frontier Life: Early Western Painting and Prints* (New York: Abbeville Press, 1987), 184–186.

3. Wilkins, *Thomas Moran*, p. 20, from Moran Papers, GIL, Miscellaneous Notes, A25.

4. Several have noted this point. See, for example, Wilkins, *Thomas Moran*, p. 44; and T. Victoria Hansen, "Thomas Moran and Nineteenth-Century Printmaking," in Anne Morand and Nancy Friese, *The Prints of Thomas Moran in the Thomas Gilcrease Institute of American History and Art, Tulsa, Oklahoma* (Tulsa, Okla.: Thomas Gilcrease Museum Association, 1986), p. 14. For more on the training of wood engravers, see Wagner, "The Graver, the Brush, and the Ruling Machine," pp. 167–191. Wagner lists a number of nineteenth-century training manuals for wood engravers.

5. For more on the rise of wood engraving, see Jacob Kainen, "Why Bewick Succeeded: A Note in the History of Wood-Engraving," *Contributions from the Museum of History and Technology*, Bulletin 218 (Washington: Smithsonian Institution, 1959): 186–201. I am grateful to Sue Rainey for her gentle corrections to my previous misconceptions about wood engraving.

6. "Desultory Thoughts on Wood Engraving and Wood-Cut Printing," *Knickerbocker* 41 (January 1853): 52. Lithography was also a relatively new printing medium and was widely used for single images, but the thickness of the stones did not correspond to that of the printing plates used for text, and the extra steps it took to combine them in the final publication made the combination too expensive for regular use. Moran did, however, illustrate at least one publication with lithographs, *Guide-Book to the West Chester and Philadelphia Railroad* (Philadelphia: Sherman & Co., 1869).

7. *Scribner's Monthly*, Moran's most important commercial patron, usually refused illustrations drawn on paper rather than on wood. "If an artist cannot draw upon the wood, his contribution, however beautiful, must be declined, or else given to a middleman to be redrawn upon the block . . . as there were few (and there are now fewer) draftsmen of ability who *can* and *will* devote themselves to the transfer of other's work, the monotony of the publications which employ the middlemen is great, since the individuality of the artist's style is usually lost in transit." "Linton's Hints on Wood-Engraving," *Scribner's Monthly* 19 (April 1880): 793.

8. Until the advent of photographic halftone printing, which preserved original drawings, Moran provided images for publication on paper only rarely; his 1870 drawings for his first Yellowstone assignment for *Scribner's*

Monthly were one such instance. These drawings are preserved in the Moran collection at the Gilcrease Museum.

9. For a useful discussion of the history of landscape printmaking and Moran's knowledge of it, see Linda Hults, "Thomas Moran and the Landscape Print," in Morand and Friese, *The Prints of Thomas Moran*, pp. 21–38.

10. GIL 95.5317.326. For more on these publications, see Anne Lyles and Diane Perkins, *Colour into Line: Turner and the Art of Engraving* (London: Tate Gallery, 1989).

11. Moran papers, EHL 1–290.

12. Lyles and Perkins, *Colour into Line*, pp. 44, 46.

13. By one account, Hamilton became the Moran family's next-door neighbor in Philadelphia and bought some of Thomas Moran's drawings. GIL 148:5126.243. Published studies on Hamilton include Arlene Jacobowitz, *James Hamilton, 1819–1878: American Marine Painter* (Brooklyn, N.Y.: Brooklyn Museum of Art, 1966); and John I. H. Baur, "A Romantic Impressionist: James Hamilton," *Bulletin of the Brooklyn Museum* 12 (Spring 1951): 1–9.

14. The photographer on Frémont's 1853 expedition was Solomon Carvalho, but unfortunately all but one of his photographs were lost to fire at Frémont's home. For more, see Martha A. Sandweiss, *Print the Legend: Photography and the American West* (New Haven, Conn.: Yale University Press, 2002), 100–108.

15. *Dictionary of American Biography* 10 (1933): 256; cited in William Truettner, "The Genius of Frederic Edwin Church's *Aurora Borealis*," *Art Quarterly* 31 (Autumn 1968): 271.

16. Katharine Martinez, "John Sartain (1808–1897): His Contribution to American Publishing," *Imprint: Journal of the American Historical Print Collectors Society* 8 (Spring 1983): 12n24. For more on Sartain's career, see Katharine Martinez and Page Talbott, eds., *Philadelphia's Cultural Landscape: The Sartain Family Legacy* (Philadelphia: Temple University Press, 2000).

17. The members of the Sartain family, including their four children, who were close in age to Moran and his siblings, were friends of the Morans for many years. All the Sartain children were employed in their father's business in the family home, and when Moran lived with them he shared quarters with one of the sons, Samuel, and with his own future brother-in-law, Stephen J. Ferris (1835–1915), who was also there studying printmaking. Ferris married Moran's sister Elizabeth in 1862, and at least one of their children, Jean Leon Gerome Ferris, grew up to be a painter. Martinez and Talbott, eds., *Philadelphia's Cultural Landscape*, pp. 32–35. Primary sources on the relationships include GIL 93:4026.620, 119:5117.235, 231:4016.4022, and 158:4017.4013; and EHL 1–98 and 1–289.

18. John Sartain, in a lecture to the Artists' Fund Society of Philadelphia, later published in George W. Bethune, *The Prospect of Art in the United States* (Philadelphia: Artists' Fund Society, 1840): 11, cited in Martinez, "John Sartain," p. 10.

19. "To the Public: Wood Cuts," *Sartain's Union Magazine* 5 (September 1849): 12.

20. Ethan Robey, "John Sartain and the Contest of Taste at the Centennial," in Martinez and Talbott, eds., *Philadelphia's Cultural Landscape*, p. 94.

21. For an overview of Moran's original printmaking, see Thomas Bruhn, "Printmaker 'of the First Rank,'" in Anderson, ed., *Thomas Moran*, pp. 283–299; and Morand and Friese, *The Prints of Thomas Moran*.

22. For more on "Studies and Pictures," see Bruhn, "Printmaker 'of the First Rank,'" in Anderson, ed., *Thomas Moran*, pp. 290–292.

23. *Boston Daily Evening Transcript*, December 1, 1875.

24. Wilkins, *Thomas Moran*, p. 55.

25. Moran to Powell, May 29, 1876, NA, Record Group 57, mfm. 156, roll 4. The Hiawatha project was mentioned again, however, in the *Boston Daily Evening Transcript*, December 6, 1876, and also in the *Independent*, December 21, 1876, with a notice: "Mr. Thomas Moran has nearly completed his series of illustrations in India ink of Longfellow's 'Hiawatha,' which are being etched by his brother Peter, who, by the way, was the only etcher awarded a medal at the Centennial." Moran reported in his ledgers that "in 1875 I commenced the series of illustrations to Hiawatha. Up to the present time I have finished about 16 out of an intended 25" ("Old Book of Lists," GIL 4026.4048). For more on the project, see Wilkins, *Thomas Moran*, p. 55. The original grisaille wash drawings are owned by the Gilcrease Museum.

26. For more on Moran and *Hiawatha*, see J. Gray Sweeney, *Artists of Michigan from the Nineteenth Century* (Muskegon, Mich.: Muskegon Museum of Art, 1987), 33–37; and J. Gray Sweeney, *Great Lakes Marine Painting of the Nineteenth Century* (Muskegon, Mich.: Muskegon Museum of Art, 1983), 44–46.

27. *Solitude* was apparently printed by James McGuigan. See Garo Z. Antreasian, "Some Thoughts about Printmaking and Print Collaborations," *Art Journal* 39 (Spring 1980): 180–188.

28. Moran to Prang, January 15, 1875, HCC.

29. DuBois, "Thomas Moran Knows Nature and Paints It."

30. Quoted in Michele H. Bogart, *Artists, Advertising, and the Borders of Art* (Chicago: University of Chicago Press, 1995), 310n9.

31. Ibid., chapter one, "The Problem of Status."

32. *Boston Daily Evening Transcript*, April 9, 1875.

33. "The Moran Pictures," *Denver Republican* 28 (November 1892), EHL scrapbook, 56.

34. Moran was elected a National Academician in 1884. Anderson, ed., *Thomas Moran*, p. 241. Some of the most notable exhibitions to which Moran submitted works in the 1860s include the Washington, D.C., Art Association, the Pennsylvania Academy of the Fine Arts (to which he was elected as an Academician in 1861), the Sanitary Commission of Philadelphia Fair, the Artists' Fund Society of Philadelphia, and the 1867 Exposition Universelle in Paris.

35. Bierstadt took his first trip west in 1859, and his large western landscape oils of the early 1860s brought unprecedented prices in the range of $10,000 to $25,000, although he also sold pictures for far less. For a summary of his most successful sales, see Linda Ferber, "The History of a Reputation," in Nancy K. Anderson and Linda S. Ferber, *Albert Bierstadt: Art and Enterprise* (Brooklyn, N.Y.: Brooklyn Museum in association with Hudson Hills Press, 1990), 26–27.

36. Nathaniel P. Langford, "The Wonders of the Yellowstone," *Scribner's Monthly* 2 (May 1871): 1–17; (June 1871): 113–128.

37. For more on Moran's relationship with *Scribner's Monthly* and the Northern Pacific Railroad, see Joni L. Kinsey, *Thomas Moran and the Surveying of the American West* (Washington, D.C.: Smithsonian Institution Press, 1992), pp. 68–92.

38. These artists are recounted in countless studies. See, for example, William Truettner,

ed., *The West as America: Reinterpreting Images of the Frontier* (Washington, D.C.: Smithsonian Institution Press, 1991); and Sandweiss, *Print the Legend.*

39. Although several studies of individual surveys and their leaders have been recently published, the best single overview of the Great Surveys remains Richard Bartlett, *Great Surveys of the American West* (Norman: University of Oklahoma Press, 1962).

40. I discuss this transformation in greater detail in Kinsey, *Thomas Moran,* pp. 45–92. See also Aubrey Haines, *The Yellowstone Story: A History of Our First National Park,* 2 vols. (Yellowstone National Park, Wyo.: Yellowstone Library and Museum Association, 1977).

41. For more details about this, see Kinsey, *Thomas Moran,* pp. 43–92.

42. For an overview of this trip, see Anne Morand, *Thomas Moran: The Field Sketches, 1856–1923* (Norman: University of Oklahoma Press for the Thomas Gilcrease Institute of American History and Art, 1996), 38–41 and 95n50.

43. A version of the design for *The Grand Cañon of the Yellowstone* appeared as *The Great Cañon and Lower Falls of the Yellowstone,* in F. V. Hayden, "Wonders of the West II: More about the Yellowstone," *Scribner's Monthly* 3 (February 1872): 388. *The Chasm of the Colorado* appeared in wood engraving in John Wesley Powell, "The Cañons of the Colorado," *Scribner's Monthly* 9 (February 1875): 408. For more, see Kinsey, *Thomas Moran,* pp. 60, 113.

44. For more on the triptych theory that links *The Grand Cañon of the Yellowstone, The Chasm of the Colorado,* and *The Mountain of the Holy Cross,* see Kinsey, *Thomas Moran,* pp. 149–150, 175. Unfortunately, my theory about the triptych was not credited to me in the 1997 book, *Thomas Moran,* edited by Nancy Anderson, that accompanied the National Gallery exhibition. In the book and the exhibition itself the triptych was presented as a fact, something that had always been understood as Moran's intent. While I do believe that Moran envisioned the three together, the recognition of them as a triptych derived from my research, first appearing in my 1989 dissertation and then in my 1992 book.

45. Moran to Hayden, March 11, 1872, NA, roll 2, frames 468–470.

46. Richard Watson Gilder to Hayden, April 27, 1872, NA, roll 2, frame 540. Gilder was Moran's friend and the editor of *Scribner's Monthly.* Although Moran wrote directly to Hayden about other matters, in this instance he may have asked Gilder to make the request, perhaps feeling that he was already in Hayden's debt. Or, Gilder may have written to Hayden on his own, since they had been in close touch about Yellowstone matters since the previous spring.

47. Moran to Hayden, November 24, 1872, NA, roll 2, frames 655–656. Moran wrote with updates in subsequent months, mentioning the work in his letter of March 10, 1873, for example. Ibid., roll 3, frames 185–186, and March 31, frames 246–247.

48. F. V. Hayden, *Twelfth Annual Report of the United States Geological and Geographical Survey of the Territories: A Report of the Progress of the Exploration in Wyoming and Idaho for the Year 1878, by F. V. Hayden, U.S. Geologist. Conducted under the Authority of the Secretary of the Interior,* part II (Washington, D.C.: U.S. Government Printing Office, 1883). The images are facing the title page and facing pages 1, 63, and 180. The first volume of this report, "part I," has four chromos as well, but these were obviously drawn by other artists. The first one, *Pike's Peak and the Garden of the Gods,* seems curiously close to the unpublished view Moran created for Prang, but in my opinion the chromo was taken from Jackson's photograph or another artist's drawing rather than from one by Moran.

49. Moran noted the commission in his ledger and apparently planned at least a "North" view as well — a Lake Superior scene. "3 Oil pictures for Sutton & Co., viz Green River Cliffs — West 250.00/White Mountains — East 250.00/Lake Superior — North 250.00." Moran ledger, GIL 4026.4048, p. 54.

50. "Increased Attractions," *Aldine Press* 2 (May 1869): 34; cited in Janice Simon, "*The Aldine,* The Art Journal of America," p. 4 of unpublished manuscript. I am grateful to Professor Simon for sharing her research with me. On other occasions, *The Aldine* commissioned Prang to provide wood engravings of his company's "most celebrated pictures" for reproduction in the magazine.

51. *New York Evening Mail,* December 3, 1873. *The Aldine* also handled original art as an "art union." *The Aldine Art Union Prospectus — 1874–75* (November 1874) listed Moran's *The Cliffs of the Green River* in a gold frame as the most expensive "Aldine Art Union Prize, Series A" at $500.

52. "Thomas Moran's Water-Colors," *Scribner's Monthly* 5 (January 1873): 394.

53. "Illustrated Presentation and Gift Books," *American Literary Gazette and Publisher's Circular,* December 1, 1869, p. 489.

54. L. Prang & Co. did publish a few other books about the time of *The Yellowstone National Park,* but these were not focused on fine art. In 1878, *Literary World* reported that "L. Prang & Co., the noted lithographers of Boston, seem about to be embarking in a regular publishing business" (February 1, 1878, p. 169). For a sizable list of Prang's other publishing ventures, see McClinton, *The Chromolithographs of Louis Prang,* chapter 8.

55. Ralph Thompson, *American Literary Annuals and Gift Books, 1825–1865* (1935; reprint ed., New York: Archon books, 1967), cited in Gerald W. R. Ward, *The American Illustrated Book in the Nineteenth Century* (Winterthur, Del.: Winterthur Museum, 1987), 93.

56. William Cullen Bryant, ed., *Picturesque America; or The Land We Live In,* 2 vols. (New York: D. Appleton and Co., 1872–1874); for more on the history of *Picturesque America,* see Sue Rainey, *Creating Picturesque America: Monument to the Natural and Cultural Landscape* (Nashville, Tenn.: Vanderbilt University Press, 1994). Prang had already embarked on his Yellowstone National Park project with Moran when volume two of *Picturesque America* was issued.

57. This phenomenon is discussed in many histories of printmaking. For the western context, see Tyler, "The Prints of Life in the West, 1840–60," in Tyler, *American Frontier Life.*

58. Helena Wright, "Bierstadt and the Business of Printmaking," in Anderson and Ferber, *Albert Bierstadt,* pp. 267–288, especially note 26. See also Brucia Witthoff, "The History of James Smillie's Engraving after Albert Bierstadt's 'The Rocky Mountains,'" *American Art Journal* 19 (1987): 40–51.

59. The Lewis portfolio was originally issued in installments of seven prints for $2. Tyler, *Prints of the West,* pp. 41–55.

60. Ibid., p. 55, gives the prices in guineas, since Catlin published the portfolio in London. I have converted his figures according to the Economic Resources History Web site, "How Much Is That Worth Today?" at http://eh.net/hmit/compare.

61. Brandon Ruud, ed., *Karl Bodmer's North American Prints* (Omaha: Joslyn Art Museum,

in association with the University of Nebraska Press, 2004), 75n91.

62. Georgia Barnhill, "The Publication of Illustrated Natural Histories in Philadelphia, 1800–1850," in Ward, ed., *The American Illustrated Book in the Nineteenth Century*, p. 53.

63. Laura Rigal, "Empire of Birds: Alexander Wilson's *American Ornithology*," in *Art and Science in America: Issues of Representation*, ed. Amy R. W. Meyers (San Marino, Calif.: Huntington Library, 1998), 66. The figure for Audubon's *Birds* is from Tyler, *Prints of the West*, p. 63.

64. My discussion of this subject is greatly informed by Sandweiss's excellent book, *Print the Legend*, especially her chapter, "Western Photography and the Illustrated Book," pp. 273–324.

65. Ibid., p. 278.

66. Ibid., pp. 279, 285–289.

67. F. V. Hayden, *Sun Pictures of Rocky Mountain Scenery* (New York: Julius Bien, 1870), vii, quoted in Sandweiss, *Print the Legend*, pp. 171–172, and Bryant, ed., *Picturesque America*, 1:iv.

68. Edward Moran's association with Prang in 1869 produced at least one chromolithograph, *Launching the Lifeboat*. BPL Print Room has a copy of this print, as well as a photocopied letter from Edward to Prang dated October 27, 1869, from an unidentified source. The letter mentions his progress on the work, saying, "The Chromo of the Life Boat comes next in order — as regards that — I have changed it so much from the original that it would have been no use to you whatever and as the others were out I did not think it worthwhile to return it. . . . I will send you a 'few lines' to enhance the sale and increase the popularity of your chromo in which I have no pecuniary interest. If you will send me one dozen of the *Life-boat* for my own distribution to personal friends and the press. I will in reply send you a letter for the public eye that will be all that you could desire." *Launching the Lifeboat* was noted in the *Evening Post* (New York), October 22, 1869, p. 2, cols. 2–3. The 1899 Prang sale catalog also lists *Modesty, Girl with Roses, The Rice of Plenty*, and *A Winter Girl* by Leon Moran; and *Shepherdess, When the Wedding Gifts Arrive*, and *Going from the Church* by Percy Moran. One previously unnoticed work Thomas produced for Prang, *The Birth of Christ*, is included as well. Christmas designs by all three artists are listed. *Catalogue of Louis Prang's Collection, Sold by Private Auction* (Boston: Copley Hall, 1899).

69. Moran to Louis Prang, December 22, 1873, HCC.

70. Ibid., January 8, 1874.

71. For the full list of these patrons, see Moran's ledger books, GIL.

72. Wilkins offers an outline of Moran's activities during this time. *Thomas Moran*, pp. 132–143.

73. Katherine Morrison McClinton, "Thomas Moran's Yellowstone Watercolours," *Apollo* 124 (July 1986): 40. Individuals for whom Moran painted these watercolors included Alexander Drake, *Scribner's* art editor; Richard Watson Gilder, *Scribner's* editor; Mrs. George Franklin Edmunds, wife of the Vermont senator who had assisted in passage of the Yellowstone Park bill; Russell Sturgis, architect; William Henry Holmes, then draftsman for the Hayden survey; William H. Jackson, photographer; and Charles Lummis, western writer.

74. The other Colorado image was *Upper Twin Lake, Colorado*. The geyser question is found in a letter from Moran to Prang, April 18, 1874, HCC.

75. Moran's Receipt Book, in GIL, notes payment for the first three watercolors on March 3, 1874.

76. Moran to Prang, November 8, 1874, photocopy in BPL.

77. "Chromo-Lithography," *New York Times*, October 31, 1874, p. 13.

78. Moran ledger, GIL 3626.145, pp. 31–32. The dating is uncertain since Moran did not always date his entries and also since Prang's office wrote Hayden on September 24, 1875, saying that they had "some 20 sketches in all to chromo." Since the final number was twenty-four it is unclear if they were not all complete at that time or if the author of the letter was imprecise. Prang sent Hayden a partial list on October 5, 1875, that specified The Great Salt Lake Utah; The Mosquito Trail, Colorado; Summit of the Sierras, Nevada; Great Falls of Snake River, Idaho; Valley of Babbling Waters, So. Utah; The Great Blue Spring; Lake Donner, Nevada; Gunnison Butte, Utah; Pike's Peak, Colorado; and Upper Twin Lake and said that others were in hand as well. NA, roll 9.

79. Moran noted in his "Old Book of Lists," GIL 4026.4048, that "in Summer of 1872 I made sixteen water color drawings of the Scenery of Yellowstone region for Mr William Blackmore of London for $800.00." Quoted in Anderson, ed., *Thomas Moran*, p. 203.

80. Although the letters that might definitively establish this have not been located, the thoroughness of the Prang correspondence to Hayden about the marketing process suggests that if Moran had been involved with that aspect of the project, he would have been mentioned.

81. Prang to Hayden, March 9, 1876, NA, roll 9.

82. Ibid., April 5, 1876. The letter of April 28 indicates that the prints were finished and ready for the Centennial Exposition.

83. Moran to L. Prang & Co., December 27, 1876. Copy of letter without source, National Gallery of Art curatorial files.

CHAPTER 3. THE PRANG PORTFOLIO

1. The information about the color of the cases is found in L. Prang & Co. to Hayden, January 23, 1877, NA, roll 9. The cost was $5 more for a bound book, and the company considered selling it that way: "We have had one copy bound, but we don't like it as well. However, we can get any copies bound that are so desired, at an extra expense of $5.00, i.e., at $65. — for the complete work, *bound*." February 8, 1877. The next day the firm wrote the survey leader again, however, saying that this price was too low: "We find that we must make a change in the price for *bound* volumes of the 'Yellowstone.' We told you that the price for those would be $65 which at 40% off would make it $39 Net to us. We must, however, get $41 Net, or else we shall lose $2 on the binding which we cannot afford. We leave it to you to make the retail price more than $65 if you think it best to do so." February 9, 1877.

2. This figure is based on the calculator found at http://eh.net/hmit/compare, using the Consumer Price Index for comparison.

3. The remaining inventory of the single sheet chromos was detailed in a letter from L. Prang & Co. to Hayden, May 16, 1878, NA, roll 9. The most that survived of any one image was 185 copies *(The Castle Geyser)*, and many had substantially fewer. The inventory memo includes both good and damaged copies listed separately.

4. Each print is identified with the name of its subject, the identifying phrase "Prang's American Chromos," and Moran's distinctive

monogram and signature. "In all I made 24 drawings for Mr. Prang for his work in chromo of the National Yellowstone Park in which work he used 15 of them. Mr. Kirkpatrick of Newark afterward bought two of them the Canon of the Rio Virgen & the Upper Fall of the Yellowstone." Moran, "Old Book of Lists," GIL 4026.4048.

5. L. Prang & Co. to Hayden, March 23, 1876, NA, roll 9.

6. "The order of arrangement we have not determined upon, indeed that is a matter we should want your opinion on." Ibid., October 18, 1875.

7. Bryant, ed., *Picturesque America,* 1:iv. For more on Moran's aesthetic theory and methodology, see Kinsey, *Thomas Moran,* pp. 11–16, 54–57.

8. Moran and the Hayden party arrived at Mammoth Hot Springs on July 21 and stayed there three days. Anderson, ed., *Thomas Moran,* p. 198. See also Marlene Deahl Merrill, ed., *Yellowstone and the Great West: Journals, Letters, and Images from the 1871 Hayden Expedition* (Lincoln: University of Nebraska Press, 1999), 128–129.

9. Albert Peale diary, July 21, 1871, YNP, quoted in Merrill, ed., *Yellowstone and the Great West,* p. 128.

10. In his accounting ledger, Moran listed a work entitled *Upper Pools* for Prang, along with *Devil's Den* and *Tower [of] Tower Falls.* Moran ledger, GIL 4026.4048, p. 54. In another entry he listed the three again, this time calling *Upper Pools "Hot Springs."* GIL 3626.145, p. 11. It would be easy to misconstrue the two as separate works, but since *Hot Springs* is also mentioned in the context of *Devil's Den* and *Tower [of] Tower Falls,* the second list is clearly a replication of the first. Furthermore, in other instances (as in the Blackmore watercolor set at Gilcrease), Mammoth Hot Springs is sometimes called *The Hot Springs of Gardiner's River, Upper Pools,* so it seems safe to assume that *Upper Pools* in Moran's ledger is the same as *Hot Springs,* and that this was the work eventually reproduced in the Prang portfolio as *Gardiner's River Hot Springs.*

11. Hayden, "Wonders of the West II," p. 389; "The Yellowstone Region," *Aldine* 6 (March 1873): 74.

12. This impression has a nail hole toward the bottom left side and right and left register marks and pinholes.

13. Even though the map in *The Yellowstone National Park* places the site slightly north and east of the Grand Prismatic Spring in the "Lower Geyser Basin," both Moran's views of the Great Blue Spring and descriptions of it in contemporary accounts suggest that they were describing today's Grand Prismatic Spring. The 370-foot diameter measurement is a modern one; Albert Peale estimated it at "about 200 feet," and, in the Prang publication, Hayden said it was 260 feet in diameter. Merrill, ed., *Yellowstone and the Great West,* p. 147; Hayden, *The Yellowstone National Park,* p. 19.

14. After nearly a century of dormancy, Excelsior erupted again briefly in 1985, although not with its earlier force. I am grateful to David Monteith for discussing the geyser with me and confirming its relationship to Moran's *Great Blue Spring.*

15. Even in its dormant state, Excelsior emits approximately 4,500 gallons per minute or six million gallons per day. http://www.geyserstudy.org/midway.htm#excelsior.

16. Albert Peale diary, July 21, 1871, YNP, quoted in Merrill, ed., *Yellowstone and the Great West,* p. 147. Merrill notes that the color in the pool actually comes from cyanobacteria, not sesquioxicide of iron (p. 266n14).

17. Hayden, *The Yellowstone National Park,* p. 19.

18. "Fine Arts," *Nation* (February 15, 1877): 107.

19. http://www.nps.gov/yell/tours/oldfaithful/castleg.htm.

20. Langford, "The Wonders of the Yellowstone." For more on this commission, see Kinsey, *Thomas Moran,* pp. 47–48.

21. Moran Yellowstone Journal, August 9, 1871, YNP. Also quoted in Anderson, ed., *Thomas Moran,* p. 199.

22. Moran Yellowstone Journal, August 7, 1871, YNP. Also quoted in Anderson, ed., *Thomas Moran,* p. 199. The dates that Moran recorded in his journal for his activities during these closing days of his Yellowstone experience conflict slightly with those in Albert Peale's diary. For example, Peale wrote on August 7, "Getting into camp we found that Jackson, Smith, and Lieut. Doane had gone over to the geysers." Moran wrote on August 8 that he "set out with Jackson, Smith & the Escort across the Country for the Geysers in Fire Hole River led by Doane." Peale reports that Jackson returned to the main camp on August 8, but Moran records that on August 9 he "went to the Geysers [and] Helped Jackson during the day." Moran indicated that he left the main survey to return east on August 10, although Peale says on August 8 that "Mr. Moran went down the Madison, on his way back to Philadelphia, with the soldiers who went back to Fort Ellis." Anderson's quotations from Moran's Yellowstone Journal are not precisely dated, but his handwritten entries in the original at YNP are. For Peale's diary, see Merrill, ed., *Yellowstone and the Great West,* pp. 151–156. I cannot account for the discrepancies in the two diaries.

23. Moran to Prang, April 18, 1874, HCC.

24. Albert Peale diary, August 5, 1871, YNP, quoted in Merrill, ed., *Yellowstone and the Great West,* p. 148.

25. For detailed maps and descriptions, see http://gorp.away.com/gorp/activity/byway/mt_beart.htm.

26. Moran's *First Sketch in the West* is GIL 0236.882.

27. Monida is located on Interstate 15 at the border of Idaho and Montana. The diary of Hayden party member George Allen and the newspaper account written by Albert Peale (*Philadelphia Press,* July 29, 1871) definitively establish the date and location of Moran's arrival, both of which have been erroneously reported in previous Moran scholarship. Allen's and Peale's texts are quoted in Merrill, ed., *Yellowstone and the Great West,* pp. 92, 252n36. See also p. 252n33 regarding the location of the stage stop from Corinne. Basing his account on Moran's handwritten recollections (GIL 4016.3921), Wilkins notes that the stagecoach trip was about 350 miles and did not stop, "save for meals." Wilkins, *Thomas Moran,* p. 83.

28. Fort Ellis was created in 1867 to establish a U.S. military presence in the area. It was named for Colonel Augustus Van Horne Ellis, who was killed at Gettysburg. It was abandoned in 1886 and absorbed into the city of Bozeman (http://www.bozemanonline.com/history.php).

29. The group that traveled to Mystic Lake included Hayden, Jackson, George Dixon, Albert Peale, Moran, Dr. Campbell, and soldiers Norton and Jerome. Although Moran does not mention him, Peale remained with him, Jackson, and Dixon when the others returned to Fort Ellis toward the end of the day. See Peale's account in Merrill, ed., *Yellowstone and the Great West,* pp. 112–113.

30. Moran Yellowstone Journal, July 13, 1871,

YNP. Also quoted in Anderson, ed., *Thomas Moran*, p. 198.

31. Ibid., August 11, 1871. Also quoted in Anderson, ed., *Thomas Moran*, p. 200.

32. The Joslyn impression is a printer's proof, with a nail hole at the top left margin and right and left registration marks and pinholes. It is inscribed in pencil on verso, "Yellowstone Lake," and on the front has a penciled "I" and color marks in both the lower right and lower left that suggest that the printer or *chromiste* was testing the ink.

33. Moran Yellowstone Journal, August 1, 1871, YNP, and Merrill, ed., *Yellowstone and the Great West*, p. 140.

34. Merrill, ed., *Yellowstone and the Great West*, p. 22.

35. For a complete listing of these, see Morand, *Thomas Moran: The Field Sketches*, p. 148.

36. For more on this motif in Moran's work, see Kinsey, *Thomas Moran*, pp. 26–28, 98, 115–116.

37. *Aldine* 7 (April 1874): inside front cover.

38. Moran Yellowstone Journal, July 25–26, 1871, YNP. Also quoted in Anderson, ed., *Thomas Moran*, pp. 198–199.

39. Cited in Carol Clark, *Thomas Moran: Watercolors of the American West* (Austin: University of Texas Press for the Amon Carter Museum, 1980), p. 131, under her no. 56.

40. Joslyn Art Museum's impression of *Tower Falls and Sulphur Mountain* is a printer's proof, with nail holes in both the top and bottom left and right and left register marks and pinholes. On the lower right margin in reversed script is written "No. 18," and then similarly at the lower left is written "No. 18 No. 19" and maybe even "No. 22," although this is cut off. These may refer to the number of color separations as they were printed.

41. For more on this tree and some of its implications, see Kinsey, *Thomas Moran*, pp. 36–37.

42. Moran Journal, August 1, 1871, YNP. Also quoted in Anderson, ed., *Thomas Moran*, p. 199.

43. Hayden, *The Yellowstone National Park*, p. 29.

44. Ibid., p. 29.

45. Ibid., p. 31.

46. Moran Yellowstone Journal, July 31, 1871, YNP.

47. For more on this method and its effects in Moran's canyon views, see Kinsey, *Thomas Moran*, pp. 54–58.

48. Joslyn Art Museum's impression is a printer's proof, with a nail hole on the bottom right margin and right and left registration marks and pinholes.

49. For an extensive discussion of this work, see Kinsey, *Thomas Moran*, pp. 43–67.

50. Langford, "The Wonders of the Yellowstone" (May 1871): 9. Hayden's mineralogist on the 1871 survey, Albert Peale, wrote that the towers at Tower Falls were "very fine. The water makes a semicircular turn then forms a series of small falls and then rushes over the precipice falling 156 feet [actually 132 feet]. Above these there are a number of towers which rise to the height of 1000 feet above the water. My first view was from the top of one of these towers and the depth to where the water fell seemed immense. Afterwards I went down the side of the canyon to where the water fell and stood in the spray. Looking up, the sight was grand." Peale diary, 1871, cited in Merrill, ed., *Yellowstone and the Great West*, p. 134.

51. This version is Clark no. 53, now owned by Pennsylvania State University, Ogontz Campus. For more on the history of the picture, see John P. Driscoll, "Moran Watercolor Found in University Attic," *American Art Journal* 10 (May 1978): 111–112.

52. I discuss this brochure and the NPRR campaign to position itself as the "Yellowstone Park Line" in Kinsey, *Thomas Moran*, pp. 68–78.

53. Clark lists two versions of *Tower Falls and Sulphur Mountain* (nos. 56 and 57) as belonging at one time to Louis Prang. One of these, Clark no. 57, is actually a view of *The Tower of Tower Falls* but confusingly does not correspond exactly with the chromolithograph version. The other versions are Clark nos. 53, 54, 57, and possibly no. 58, although it is unclear from the title, *Towering Heights*.

54. The early oil I saw in a private collection in Washington, D.C., in 1987 is relatively small (ca. 10 × 14 inches) and closely resembles the various watercolor versions of *Tower of Tower Falls*.

55. Today the Mountain of the Holy Cross is visible, distantly, from Shrine Pass, a gravel road off Interstate 70 between Copper Mountain and Vail where a small outdoor chapel was constructed in the 1990s. The mountain itself is reached from the turnoff to Camp Tigiwon between Red Cliff and Minturn on Highway 24, plus a strenuous hike of about five miles from the trailhead to the top of Notch Mountain. For details see Kinsey, *Thomas Moran*, p. 205n1.

56. Although Hayden reported in the Prang text that the mountain is "so steep that no snow can lie on it [and so] the cross is visible throughout the whole year," he had only visited the mountain in the summer and was apparently unaware of the deep snowpack that covers the Rocky Mountains in other seasons.

57. Ralph Waldo Emerson, *Nature*, 1836. See also Barbara Novak's important essay, "The Nationalist Garden and the Holy Book," in her *Nature and Culture: American Landscape and Painting, 1825–1875* (New York: Oxford University Press, 1980), 3–17.

58. Albert Boime, *The Magisterial Gaze: Manifest Destiny and American Landscape Painting, ca. 1830–1865* (Washington, D.C.: Smithsonian Institution Press, 1991).

59. Thomas Moran to Mary Nimmo Moran, Kanab, Utah, August 24, 1874, quoted in Amy O. Bassford and Fritiof M. Fryxell, eds., *Home-Thoughts, from Afar: Letters of Thomas Moran to Mary Nimmo Moran* (East Hampton, N.Y.: East Hampton Free Library, 1967), 53.

60. Ibid., pp. 53–56.

61. On the triptych issue, see Kinsey, *Thomas Moran*, pp. 149–150, 175.

62. For a thorough discussion of this history, see ibid., pp. 141–173; and Joni L. Kinsey, "Sacred and Profane: Thomas Moran's *Mountain of the Holy Cross*," *Gateway Heritage* 11 (Summer 1990): 4–23.

63. This stamp is reproduced in Kinsey, *Thomas Moran*, p. 173, and in color in Kinsey, "Sacred and Profane," p. 17.

64. From Denver, take I–70 to Route 9 south through Breckenridge, or Highway 285 to Route 9 north. At about one mile south of Alma is County Road 12 going west through Park City. Follow this dirt road up to the North London Mill, where the trail officially starts. Follow the signs to Mosquito Pass (http://1traildamage.com.glowball.com/trails/index.php?id=41).

65. http://www.colormar.com/ColoradoPlaces/mosquito_pass.html.

66. Moran ledger, GIL 3626.145, p. 31.

67. There should be no reason to confuse *Upper Twin Lake* with *Mosquito Trail*, since Moran clearly noted both in the same ledger entry as he recorded payment for each. Ibid., undated entry.

68. *Delano Valley, Eagle River* (JNEM no. 5859, Morand no. 296), *Upper Twin Lake* (JNEM no. 4230, Morand no. 297), and another untitled sketch from the Holy Cross trip (JNEM no. 4252, Morand no. 299) also seem related to this vicinity.

69. E. L. Burlingame, "The Plains and the Sierras," in Bryant, ed, *Picturesque America*, 2:168–199. *Summit of the Sierras* is on page 199.

70. Shoshone Falls is just upriver from another cascade called Pillar Falls.

71. Fritiof Fryxell, "Thomas Moran's Journey to the Tetons in 1879," *Augustana Historical Society Publications* 2 (1932): 36–46; see also Wilkins, *Thomas Moran*, p. 179.

72. Linda Hults, "Thomas Moran's *Shoshone Falls:* A Western Niagara," *Smithsonian Studies in American Art* 3 (Winter 1989): 89–102.

73. Anne Morand, "The Camera and the Artist's Eye," *Gilcrease Journal* 10 (Summer 2002): 20. O'Sullivan visited the falls again with Lt. George Wheeler's Army Corps of Engineers survey in 1874, and his views from that expedition are similar.

74. The article also appeared as Clarence King, "The Falls of the Shoshone," *Overland Monthly* 5 (October 1870): 379–385; Clarence King, *Mountaineering in the Sierra Nevada* (Boston, 1872; reprint ed., Lincoln: University of Nebraska Press, 1970), 188–191.

75. King, "The Falls of the Shoshone," p. 318.

76. Edwards Roberts, *Shoshone and Other Western Wonders* (New York, 1888), quoted in Anderson, ed., *Thomas Moran*, p. 169.

77. For more on the Snake River region and Moran's relationship to it, see Peter C. Boag, "Thomas Moran and Western Landscapes: An Inquiry into an Artist's Environmental Values," *Pacific Historical Review* 67 (February 1998): 40–66; and Peter C. Boag, "Overlanders and the Snake River Region: A Case Study of Popular Landscape Perception in the Early West," *Pacific Northwest Quarterly* (October 1993): 122–129.

78. King, "The Falls of the Shoshone," p. 385.

79. Anderson, ed., *Thomas Moran*, pp. 162–163.

80. The visual history of Niagara is well documented in Jeremy Elwell Adamson, *Niagara: Two Centuries of Changing Attitudes* (Washington, D.C.: Corcoran Gallery of Art, 1985); and Elizabeth McKinsey, *Niagara Falls: Icon of the American Sublime* (Cambridge: Cambridge University Press, 1985).

81. Hults also argues that Moran's monumental *Shoshone Falls* was a statement about environmental preservation, especially in the context of Niagara's degradation in the nineteenth century, but Boag challenges this assumption and characterizes the painting as a more personal work that Moran produced in response to his wife's death, which occurred shortly before his 1900 trip to Shoshone Falls. Hults, "Thomas Moran's *Shoshone Falls*"; and Boag, "Thomas Moran and Western Landscapes."

82. Ruth Moran to Horace Albright, 1929, Moran papers, EHL B228, L158, quoted in Boag, "Thomas Moran and Western Landscapes," p. 59.

83. "Idaho Scenery," *Aldine* 8 (June 1876): 195.

84. Although never as famous as some of Moran's other favorite sites, Shoshone Falls was not unknown in the nineteenth century. For some of the contemporary accounts of it, see Anderson, ed., *Thomas Moran*, 167–169; and also John Codman, "The Shoshone Falls," *Century Magazine* 39 (April 1890): 924–927.

85. Gaell Lindstrom, *Thomas Moran in Utah (68th Faculty Honor Lecture)* (Logan: Utah State University, 1983), 18n8.

86. Thomas Moran to Mary Nimmo Moran, Kanab, Utah, August 2, 1873, in Bassford and Fryxell, eds., *Home-Thoughts, from Afar*, p. 35.

87. John Wesley Powell, "An Overland Trip to the Grand Cañon," *Scribner's Monthly* 10 (October 1875): 663. Clarification of the term is found in Thomas G. Alexander, "Red Rock and Gray Stone: Senator Reed Smoot, the Establishment of Zion and Bryce Canyon National Parks, and the Rebuilding of Downtown Washington, D.C.," *Pacific Historical Review* 72 (February 2003): 7n13.

88. Lindstrom, *Thomas Moran in Utah*, p. 18n8. The information on the history of Zion National Park is from http://www.nps.gov/zion/ParkProfile.htm.

89. Among the more noteworthy such features at Zion are Angel's Landing, the Three Patriarchs, and the Great White Throne. For more on the tower motif in Moran's work, see Kinsey, *Thomas Moran*, pp. 28–35.

90. "The Scenery of Southern Utah," *Aldine* 7 (March 1875): frontispiece and pp. 306–307.

91. See, for example, the Denver and Rio Grande Railway's publication, *Valleys of the Great Salt Lake, Describing the Garden of Utah and the Two Great Cities of Salt Lake and Ogden* (Chicago: R. R. Donnelley & Sons, 1890).

92. Moran wrote his wife from Salt Lake on July 9, 1873. See Bassford and Fryxell, eds., *Home-Thoughts, from Afar*, pp. 29–30. Colburn's articles appeared in the *New York Times* on July 15, August 7, and September 4, 1873, and are reprinted in Anderson, ed., *Thomas Moran*, pp. 360–366.

93. William H. Goetzmann, *Army Exploration in the American West, 1803–1863* (New Haven, Conn.: Yale University Press, 1959): 220–222.

94. Frémont, for example, visited the Great Salt Lake on his 1843–1844 expedition. The U.S. Army Topographical Engineers' exploration of the Great Salt Lake, led by Howard Stansbury in 1850, resulted in a well-illustrated government report. See Goetzmann, *Army Exploration*, pp. 219–225.

95. John Charles Frémont, *Report of an Exploring Expedition to the Rocky Mountains in the Year 1842 and to Oregon and North California in the Years, 1843–44*, p. 198, quoted in Goetzmann, *Army Exploration*, p. 91.

96. E. L. Burlingame, "The Plains and the Sierras," in Bryant, ed., *Picturesque America*, 2:186; *Valleys of the Great Salt Lake*.

CHAPTER 4. THE UNPUBLISHED WORKS OF THE PRANG SERIES

1. *Prang Auction Catalogue, 16–18 February, 1892* (New York: American Art Galleries, 1892). A number of copies of this document exist. I examined ones at BPL and AAA.

2. For example, Moran lists payment for three works twice. In his ledger, GIL 4026.4048, p. 54, he lists *Devil's Den, Hot Springs*, and *Towers [of] Tower Falls*, and then in ledger no. 3626.145, p. 11, he lists *Upper Pools, Devil's Den*, and *Tower [of] Tower Falls*. I am assuming that *Upper Pools* in Moran's ledger is the same as *Hot Springs*, the work eventually published in the Prang portfolio as *Gardiner's River Hot Springs*. Another complication in the record is Moran's strikethrough of *The Three Tetons*, an editorial change whose implications remain unclear.

3. Hayden, *The Yellowstone National Park*, p. 37.

4. "Twin Lakes," in *Rhymes of the Rockies; or What the Poets Have Found to Say of the Beautiful*

Scenery on the Denver and Rio Grande Railroad, the Scenic Line of the World, 3rd ed. (Chicago: Poole Bros., 1887), 40–41. A wood engraving after Moran appears on page 39, probably a version of the Prang chromolithograph.

5. W. H. Rideing, "The Rocky Mountains," in Bryant, ed., *Picturesque America,* 2:496.

6. Ibid., p. 498.

7. *Prang Auction Catalogue, 1892,* p. 130.

8. Goetzmann, *Army Exploration in the American West,* p. 37.

9. Moran ledger, GIL 3626.145, p. 31.

10. Jackson photographed the site from only slightly different angles countless times over at least a thirty-year period, and these are not always dated, making it difficult to determine exactly which view Moran might have used. For a large selection of these, see http://photoswest.org, an online catalog of the Colorado Historical Society, which owns a major collection of Jackson's work. There are also significant Jackson collections at the United States Geological Survey, the National Archives, and the George Eastman House in Rochester, New York.

11. Rideing, "The Rocky Mountains," in Bryant, ed., *Picturesque America,* 2:495. The same wood engraving appeared in F. V. Hayden, *Annual Report of the United States Geological and Geographical Survey of the Territories, Embracing Colorado and Parts of Adjacent Territories, Being a Report of Progress of the Exploration for the Year 1874* (Washington, D.C.: U.S. Government Printing Office, 1876), plate 6. Hayden routinely shared photographs with the managing editor of *Picturesque America,* Oliver Bunce, and in turn Bunce provided electrotypes of their engravings to him for use in his annual reports. For more on this relationship, see Kinsey, *Thomas Moran,* especially pp. 87–88.

12. In 1879, at the urging of D&RG president William Jackson Palmer, Charles Perkins, president of the Chicago Burlington & Quincy Railroad, purchased much of the land now known as the Garden of the Gods. Upon his death, his family gave the land to the city of Colorado Springs as a park, requiring that it be called Garden of the Gods and remain free to visitors (http://www.gardenofgods.com/history.htm).

13. This painting is reproduced in Eleanor Jones Harvey, *Thomas Moran and the Spirit of Place* (Dallas, Tex.: Dallas Museum of Art, 2001), 19.

14. Rideing, "The Rocky Mountains," in Bryant, ed., *Picturesque America,* 2:496.

15. Thomas Moran to Mary Nimmo Moran, Kanab, Utah, August 11, 1874, quoted in Bassford and Fryxell, eds., *Home-Thoughts, from Afar,* p. 47.

16. Ernest Ingersoll, *Crest of the Continent: A Record of a Summer's Ramble in the Rocky Mountains and Beyond* (Chicago: R. R. Donnelley & Sons, 1885), 46–47. For more on Moran's 1881 trip, see Kinsey, *Thomas Moran,* pp. 163–169.

17. Moran ledger, GIL 3626.145, p. 32.

18. *Donner Lake,* GIL 1336.664. This work is reproduced in Morand, *Thomas Moran: The Field Sketches,* p. 174.

19. Cooper-Hewitt Museum, no. 1917.17.44.

20. "With Wheeler in the Sierras," *Appleton's Journal: A Monthly Miscellany of Popular Literature* 3 (October 1877): 289–297; *Donner Lake* is on page 293.

21. For more on this, see Anderson and Ferber, *Albert Bierstadt,* pp. 94–98, 233.

22. D. O. C. Townley, "Living American Artists," *Scribner's Monthly* 3 (March 1872): 608.

23. *Prang Auction Catalogue, 1892,* p. 130.

24. See Kinsey, *Thomas Moran,* p. 29.

25. *First Sketch in the West* is GIL 0236.882.

26. Hal G. Stephens and Eugene M. Shoemaker, *In the Footsteps of John Wesley Powell: An Album of Comparative Photographs of the Green and Colorado Rivers, 1871–72 and 1968* (Boulder and Denver, Colo.: Johnson Books and the Powell Society, 1987), 151. I am also grateful to the ranger at Green River State Park in Green River, Utah, who spoke with me about the location of Gunnison's Butte but wished to remain anonymous.

27. Entry for July 13. John Wesley Powell, *Canyons of the Colorado* (Meadville, Pa.: Floyd & Vincent, 1895; reprinted as *The Exploration of the Colorado River and Its Canyons* [New York: Dover Publications, 1961]), 199. Powell's official report from which this publication was abridged is found in two government document versions, *Exploration of the Colorado River of the West and Its Tributaries, Explored in 1869, 1870, 1871, and 1872, under the Direction of the Secretary of the Smithsonian Institution* (Washington, D.C.: U.S. Government Printing Office, 1875); and U.S. Congress, House, *Exploration of the Colorado River of the West,* H. Misc. Doc. 300, series 1622, 43rd Cong., 1st sess., 1873–1874.

28. The party's itinerary and route are verified by the newspaper accounts of Moran's traveling companion, J. E. Colburn. See, especially, "The Land of Mormon," *New York Times,* August 7, 1873, p. 2, col. 3, reprinted in Anderson, ed., *Thomas Moran,* p. 363. Interestingly, the caption associated with Hiller's photograph at the United States Geological Survey is entitled *Cathedral Butte, Blue Cliffs.* A Jackson photograph entitled *Gunnison's Butte* (USGS no. jwh01265) is actually a scene from the Green River, Wyoming, area and looks nothing like Moran's engraved views of Gunnison's Butte. For more on Powell sharing Hiller's photographs with Moran, see Kinsey, *Thomas Moran,* pp. 117–132.

29. These works are easily confused since the Green River is a tributary of the Colorado River and Moran's Green River pictures are sometimes titled with variations on *Cliffs of the Upper Colorado.* Indeed, in November 1874, Moran wrote to Prang about the portfolio series: "I have the designs ready to work on of *Donner Lake. Twin Lake. Pikes Peak. Summit of the Sierras. Great Salt Lake & Azure Cliffs of* [*Green River* struck out] *Colorado.*" But the later Prang chromo, *Cliffs of the Upper Colorado,* was 11½ × 6½ inches, and the unpublished *Gunnison's Butte,* like the rest of the watercolors in the portfolio series, was 9½ × 14 inches. Moran noted in his ledger book that he was paid $500 in December 1879 for the later work. Moran ledger, GIL 4026.4054, p. 27.

30. Powell, "The Cañons of the Colorado," p. 310; "Glories of Southern Utah," *Aldine* 8 (January 1876): 34. Moran's wood engravings for Powell's *Scribner's Monthly* articles also appeared later in many of Powell's publications. For more on Powell's acquisition of them from the magazine, see Kinsey, *Thomas Moran,* pp. 125–126. Moran's ledger entry of January 15, 1875, noted receipt of $60 from *The Aldine* for a *"Gunnison's Butte,"* which is no doubt the same image (GIL 3626.145, p. 26).

31. "Glories of Southern Utah," p. 35. Gunnison's history is from Goetzmann, *Army Exploration in the American West,* pp. 221–223.

32. Goetzmann, *Army Exploration in the American West,* p. 285.

33. *Prang Auction Catalogue, 1892,* p. 130.

34. I was unable to obtain a reproduction of this painting, *South of Green River, Wyoming,* ca. 1880, but it may be viewed in Harvey, *Thomas Moran and the Spirit of Place,* p. 13.

35. Moran ledger, GIL 4026.4048, p. 54.

36. Wilkins, *Thomas Moran,* p. 121.

37. Moran ledger, GIL 3626.145, pp. 26, 31.

38. See also the Moran wood engraving, *The Narrows (Mu-Koon-Tu-Weap Cañon)*, a title that conjoins both terms "Narrows" and "Cañon," in Powell, "An Overland Trip to the Grand Cañon," p. 662.

39. Lindstrom, *Thomas Moran in Utah*, 18n8.

40. J. E. Colburn, *New York Times*, September 4, 1873. Quoted in Anderson, ed., *Thomas Moran*, p. 364.

41. Powell, "An Overland Trip to the Grand Cañon," p. 663.

42. "Thomas Moran on Utah Scenery," unidentified Utah newspaper, June 9, 1900, AAA, NTM 4, frame 604.

43. Powell, "An Overland Trip to the Grand Cañon," p. 662. The watercolor is entitled *In the Narrows, Zion Valley, The Gate Keeper*, GIL 0236.878. Both of these views compare closely to Hiller's photograph, NA, Still Picture Division, no. 57-PS–553.

44. Powell, "An Overland Trip to the Grand Cañon," pp. 662–663.

45. Langford, "The Wonders of the Yellowstone" (June 1871): 113–128. Moore's original drawing is today owned by Yellowstone National Park, and the original sketches Moran made from them for *Scribner's* are now in the Gilcrease Collection. For more, see *The Art of Yellowstone, 1870–1872* (Tulsa, Okla.: Thomas Gilcrease Museum Association, 1983), 8–9.

46. William Henry Jackson also made photographs of Upper Falls that Moran may have used. For two of these, see NA, Still Picture Division, 57-HS–84 and 57-HS–1205.

47. Cited in Clark, *Thomas Moran, Watercolors*, p. 132n61.

48. Moran ledger, GIL 3626.145, p. 11.

49. Langford, "The Wonders of the Yellowstone" (May 1871).

50. Albert Peale diary, quoted in Merrill, ed., *Yellowstone and the Great West*, p. 136; Langford, "The Wonders of the Yellowstone" (May 1871): 11.

51. Hayden, "Wonders of the West," p. 393. Hayden contradicted himself in the Prang publication, saying in the text accompanying *Tower Falls and Sulphur Mountain* that the Devil's Den is a canyon formed by Tower Creek. Hayden, *The Yellowstone National Park*, p. 27.

52. Hayden, "Wonders of the West," p. 393.

53. For more on this issue, see Kinsey, *Thomas Moran*, pp. 82–83.

54. Moran ledger, GIL 3626.145, p. 32.

55. Grand Teton National Park was established in 1929 but included only the Teton Range and the six glacial lakes at the base of the mountains. Jackson Hole National Monument, decreed by presidential proclamation in 1943, combined Teton National Forest and other federal properties, including Jackson Lake, with 35,000 acres owned by John D. Rockefeller, Jr. The two areas were joined in 1950, forming the present boundaries of today's Grand Teton National Park (http://www.nps.gov/grte/cult/parkhis2.htm).

56. "Mr. Jackson, our persevering photographic artist, took a great number of views of the scenery in this vicinity — including many of the cascades in the Cañon, and the Tetons from all points of the compass." Nathaniel P. Langford, "The Ascent of Mount Hayden," *Scribner's Monthly* 6 (June 1873): 140. The *Scribner's Monthly* wood engraving, *Mount Hayden and Mount Moran from the West*, in the Langford article seems to have been drawn from Jackson's view of the Tetons, a copy of which is now in NA, Still Picture Division, 57-HS–162.

57. The idea of naming one of the Tetons Mount Moran was suggested to Ferdinand Hayden by Moran's friend and *Scribner's Monthly* editor Richard Watson Gilder. Gilder to Hayden, May 23, 1872, NA, roll 2, frame 573. The campfire meeting at which this was decided is recounted in Langford, "The Ascent of Mount Hayden," pp. 152–153.

58. Moran to Hayden, April 4, 1873, NA, roll 3, frame 263.

59. Hayden to Moran, August 25, 1872, AAA, NTM 1, frames 599–600.

60. Moran to Hayden, April 4, 1873, NA, roll 3, frame 263.

61. Langford, "The Ascent of Mount Hayden," p. 143. The composition is also quite similar to a later watercolor entitled *The Tetons*, now in the collection of the Cooper-Hewitt Museum in New York. See Morand, *Thomas Moran: The Field Sketches*, no. 422.

62. This trip is chronicled in Fryxell, "Thomas Moran's Journey to the Tetons in 1879." The Gilcrease also has a single-sheet wood engraving, *The Teton Range* (GIL 1526.347), but where it was originally published remains uncertain.

63. Quoted in ibid., p. 39.

64. Powell, "The Cañons of the Colorado."

65. Powell, U.S. Congress, House, *Exploration of the Colorado River of the West*.

66. Hayden, *The Yellowstone National Park*, p. 43.

67. "Art," *Atlantic Monthly* 34 (September 1874): 374–377. In my book, *Thomas Moran*, I identified the author of this passage as Clarence Cook. Although others have credited him with this as well, I have not been able to verify that Cook wrote for the *Atlantic Monthly* in addition to the *New York Daily Tribune*.

68. "Culture and Progress: 'The Chasm of the Colorado,'" *Scribner's Monthly* 8 (July 1874): 373.

CHAPTER 5. FERDINAND HAYDEN AND THE PRODUCTION AND MARKETING OF *THE YELLOWSTONE NATIONAL PARK*

1. Sanford Gifford to Hayden, July 14, 1871, NA, roll 1, frames 137–139. Gifford had other plans for the summer, but, as he wrote, they were not working out to his satisfaction. It was too late to accompany Hayden, but he wrote, "Could I have foreseen how the summer is likely to shape itself, how gladly would I have been your companion on the Yellowstone."

2. A. B. Nettleton to Hayden, June 7, 1871, NA, roll 2, frames 120–122.

3. For a detailed discussion of these activities, see Kinsey, *Thomas Moran*, pp. 59–62, 81–92.

4. Hayden, *The Yellowstone National Park*, p. iii.

5. Koehler would go on to become a significant figure in the art world, helping found the *American Art Review* and serving as a curator at the Boston Museum of Fine Arts. He also later wrote about the Morans, including an article on Mary Nimmo Moran. Sylvester R. Koehler, "The Work of the American Etchers: Mrs. M. Nimmo Moran," *American Art Review* 20 (1881): 31. For more on Koehler, see Clifford S. Ackley, "Sylvester Rosa Koehler and the American Etching Revival," in *Art and Commerce: American Prints of the Nineteenth Century* (Proceedings of Conference at the Museum of Fine Arts Boston, May 8–10, 1975, Charlottesville: University Press of Virginia, 1978), 143–150.

6. Louis Prang to Hayden, December 16, 1874, June 21, 1875, NA, roll 9.

7. Ibid., September 24, 1875.

8. Some of the original watercolors Moran made for Prang (such as *Tower Falls and Suphur*

Mountain, Yellowstone National Park, at the Westmoreland Museum of American Art in Greensburg, Pennsylvania) have the artist's descriptions of the subjects on the verso. This may have been to provide the publisher with information to be used in the text that would accompany the chromolithographs. The information, however, is limited to the basic location of each site and some descriptive details and does not mention the circumstances of Moran's encounters with them.

9. For information on Hayden's activities throughout this period, see Mike Foster, *Strange Genius: The Life of Ferdinand Vandiveer Hayden* (Niwot, Colo.: Roberts Rinehart Publishers, 1994).

10. L. Prang & Co. to Hayden, October 18, 1875, NA, roll 9.

11. Ibid., January 31, 1876.

12. Ibid., March 9, 1876.

13. Ibid., April 28, 1876.

14. Ibid., June 26, 1876.

15. John Sartain to Moran, March 6, 1876, and Sartain to Louis Prang, January 15, 1876, Harriet Sartain collection, AAA, cited from Ethan Robey, "John Sartain and the Context of Taste at the Centennial," in Martinez and Talbott, eds., *Philadelphia's Cultural Landscape,* pp. 94–95.

16. A photograph of Moran's *Mountain of the Holy Cross* in Memorial Hall may be seen in Kinsey, *Thomas Moran,* p. 142.

17. *Frank Leslie's Historical Register of the United States Centennial Exposition, 1876* (New York: Frank Leslie's Publishing House, 1877); facsimile ed. with a new introduction by Richard Kenin (New York: Paddington Press, Two Continents Publishing Group, 1974), 184.

18. A detailed discussion of the reaction to the Battle of the Little Bighorn is discussed in Richard Slotkin, *The Fatal Environment: The Myth of the Frontier in the Age of Industrialization* (Middletown, Conn.: Wesleyan Press, 1985), 435–476.

19. L. Prang & Co. to Hayden, July 11, 1876, NA, roll 9. The emphasis is Prang's.

20. Ibid., July, 22, 1876.

21. Ibid.

22. Ibid., May 19, 1876.

23. Ibid., May 25, 1876. The emphasis is Prang's.

24. Ibid., July 8, 1876.

25. Ibid., January 31, 1876.

26. Ibid., March 9, 1876.

27. Ibid., June 21, 1876.

28. Ibid., August 2, 1876.

29. The actual amount in 2004 would be $426,480.62, based on the Consumer Price Index calculator at http://www.eh.net/hmit/compare/.

30. L. Prang & Co. to Hayden, January 2, 1877, NA, roll 9.

31. Ibid., January 12, 1877.

32. Ibid., January 27, 1877.

33. "New Publications," *New York Daily Tribune,* February 5, 1877, p. 6, col. 1.

34. L. Prang & Co. to Hayden, February 5, 1877, NA, roll 9.

35. "Fine Arts," *Nation* (February 15, 1877): 107.

36. L. Prang & Co. to Hayden, February 7, 1877, NA, roll 9.

37. Ibid., February 1, 1877.

38. L. Prang & Co. wrote Hayden on February 19, 1877: "*Prof. Dana.* We addressed an earnest appeal to him some time ago, asking him to give us the support of his name by writing a letter, but he does not even reply." On February 24, the editors reported: "From Prof. Dana we have finally heard, but he declines to write a letter. He promises, however, to write a notice soon in the 'Journal.'" Ibid.

39. *American Journal of Science and Arts* 13 (March 1877): 229–230.

40. L. Prang & Co. to Hayden, March 6, 1877, NA, roll 9.

41. *Newark Daily Advertiser,* March 9, 1877.

42. "Two Books," *Harper's Weekly* (April 21, 1877): 303. By the 1870s, Curtis had already had a long literary career and significant experience with art reviews. For more, see Dearinger, ed., *Rave Reviews,* pp. 72–74.

43. "A National Park," *Times* (London), November 23, 1877, p. 3, col. F. This review was reprinted in the *Printing Times and Lithographer* (London, January 15, 1878), 13.

44. L. Prang & Co. to Hayden, February 8, 1877, NA, roll 9.

45. Blackmore was also an amateur ethnographer and would later become a principal financier for the Denver and Rio Grande Railway through Colorado. For more, see Kinsey, *Thomas Moran,* pp. 154–155, 158.

46. L. Prang & Co. to Hayden, December 17, December 18, 1877, NA, roll 9.

47. "The Yellowstone National Park," *Scotsman* (Edinburgh), January 9, 1877, p. 2; reprinted as "The Yellowstone National Park," *A Journal of Outdoor Life, Travel, Nature, Study, Shooting, Fishing, Yachting* (February, 15, 1877): 25. Prang's staff noted that it also appeared in the *Denver News.* For Prang's and Hayden's correspondence about this, see the letters of January 27 and February 17, 1877, NA, roll 9.

48. L. Prang & Co. to Hayden, January 23, 1877, NA, roll 9. Although Prang's letters refer to Archer as "Prof.," he was actually a surgeon, writer on botany, and director of the Edinburgh Museum of Science and Art from 1860 to 1885. I greatly appreciate the assistance of Dr. Graeme D. Eddie at Edinburgh University in Edinburgh, Scotland, with this information and for locating the *Scotsman* article for me.

49. "The Yellowstone National Park," *Scotsman.*

50. L. Prang to Hayden, November 6, 1875, NA, roll 9. The request was made in slightly different form on September 24, 1875.

51. Ibid., August 2, 1876.

52. Ibid., January 2, 1877.

53. Ibid., December 9, 1876.

54. Ibid., January 2, 1877, and December 9, 1876.

55. Ibid., January 19, 1877.

56. Ibid., January 12, 1877.

57. These names are scattered throughout the correspondence from L. Prang & Co. to Hayden in the spring of 1877. Ibid.

58. Ibid., March 14, 1877.

59. Ibid., February 8, 1877.

60. L. Prang & Co. did issue a preliminary circular for the portfolio for the Centennial showing, which the editors mentioned in their letters to Hayden on July 1 and 11, 1876, NA, roll 9. The circular being discussed here, however, in February 1877 was the more elaborate version for which they sought the testimonials. The company's letter of March 19, 1877, described the final product: "Printed in red and black with a red line around it on heavy paper." Unfortunately, I have not located either of the circulars.

61. "Our English agent reports that the 'School of Mines' refuses to take a copy of your book, alleging that it is *'too artistic'* for them!" L. Prang & Co. to Hayden, March 19, 1877, NA, roll 9.

62. Ibid., February 19, 1877. Although it is unclear precisely which geographical society is

being discussed, the journal of the American Geographical Society noted the gift in 1877. The National Geographic Society was not founded until 1888.

63. Ibid., March 6, 1876.

64. Ibid., March 21, 1877.

65. Ibid., April 6 and 8, 1877.

66. Ibid., March 9, 1877.

67. Ibid., December 28, 1876. L. Prang & Co. acknowledged Hayden's achievements as the principal sales agent in a letter of April 24, 1877.

68. Ibid., December 22 and 17, 1877.

69. Ibid. L. Prang & Co. wrote to Hayden on September 29, 1877: "Your favor of yesterday received. Many thanks for your kind expressions of sympathy. We are pretty badly scorched, but nevertheless kept our colors flying. . . . We can not yet tell how many copies of 'Yellowstone' will be available, but certainly have a few of them left." On May 11, 1878, the company wrote: "As you are aware the fire in our establishment last September destroyed the greater part of the edition of the Yellowstone National Park, and we now have but about 50 copies of the work left, which are in perfect condition. Can you not assist us in disposing of these?" The correspondence offers little other indication of the reactions to the portfolio's loss by those who had worked so hard on it.

70. "Fires: Partial Destruction of Prang's Chromo Factory at the Highlands," *Boston Post*, September 28, 1877, p. 3. I am extremely grateful to Jane Winton at the Boston Public Library for locating this article for me. The $50,000 figure was cited, it should be noted, only one day after the fire, and subsequent assessments seem to have doubled the cost of the damage. Sittig reports, for example, that the losses amounted to over $100,000. "Our Portrait Gallery — Louis Prang, Boston, Mass., U.S.A.," *British Lithographer* (August/September 1892); cited in Sittig, "L. Prang & Company," p. 50.

71. Prang was insured for $114,251 in general insurance, $30,000 for the building, and $7,310 for the oil paintings. "Fires: Partial Destruction," *Boston Post*.

72. On March 9, 1878, L. Prang & Co. sardonically commented to Hayden about the twenty-five sets of *The Yellowstone National Park* that remained: "It almost appears to us they ought to command a premium." NA, roll 9.

73. Ibid., January 19, 1877.

74. Ibid., May 4, 1877.

75. Prang's office provided these to Hayden on consignment, paying him $2 for the sale of a $4 print and wrote, "The damaged copies we will furnish to you henceforth at $1.25 per copy mounted if intended to be sold." Ibid., May 16, 1878.

76. *Illustrated Catalogue of Fine Art Studies, Water Color Studies, Pictures, Etc., Published by L. Prang & Co.* (Boston: L. Prang & Co., 1890). This catalog contains thumbnail wood engravings of each of the Moran chromos from the 1876 series, as well as of the two smaller later chromos the company produced from his work.

77. "Old Book of Lists," Moran papers, GIL 4026.4048. Anderson, ed., *Thomas Moran*, reprints several notices of this purchase, p. 235.

78. Marzio, *The Democratic Art*, p. 105.

79. John Ruskin to Moran, AAA, NTM 1, frames 652–653.

80. Probably referring to Moran's more recent painting style, which had loosened considerably from his more linear work of the early 1870s, Ruskin also took pains to offer stylistic advice to his American friend. He had already written, "I do wish with my whole heart you would give up for a while all that flaring and glaring and splashing and roaring business — and *paint*, not etch — some quiet things like that little true landscape absolutely from nature." And in the letter concerning the Prang chromos, he revisited the subject: "And please, in some degree attend to what I wrote of the necessity of giving up flare and splash. Force yourself to show leaves and stones — such as God meant us all to be shaded by, and to walk on — and be buried under — till you see the daily beauty of these and make others see it." Ruskin to Moran, ibid., pp. 659–651, 652–653.

81. The lecture was Ruskin's fourth rather than his first of the season, delivered on May 26, 1883. It is reprinted in John Ruskin, *The Works of John Ruskin*, ed. E. T. Cook and Alexander Wedderburn (London and New York: George Allen, 1908), 14:327.

82. The quote is from Marzio, *The Democratic Art*, p. 105. Ruskin believed that "Art is only in her right place and office when she is subordinate to use; that her duty is always to teach." But he also said, "It is to be further observed that although the skill now directed to the art of chromo-lithotint has achieved wonders in that mechanism, the perfection of illustrated work must always be in woodcut or engraving coloured by hand." The first comment was in Ruskin's *The Laws of Fesole: A Familiar Treatise on the Elementary Principles and Practice of Drawing and Painting*, p. 94, and the second was in "The Black Arts," *Magazine of Art* 6 (January 1888): 73–77. Reprinted in Ruskin, *The Works of John Ruskin*, 14:363.

83. Louis Prang to Hayden, November 20, 1878, NA, roll 9.

84. Prang autobiography, reproduced in Sittig, "L. Prang & Company," p. 155.

85. McClinton, "Thomas Moran's Watercolours," pp. 40–41. The sale was cataloged; see *Prang Auction Catalogue, 1892*. The Moran watercolors are numbers 344–359.

CHAPTER 6. THE END OF AN ERA

1. *Illustrated Catalogue of Fine Arts Studies, Water Color Studies, Pictures, Etc., Published by L. Prang & Company*, 20.

2. Although Carol Clark's catalogue raisonné, *Thomas Moran: Watercolors*, lists *Cliffs of the Upper Colorado* (her no. 104) as a watercolor, it was recently included in an exhibition at the Dallas Museum of Art and is clearly an oil painting. It is reproduced in Harvey, *Thomas Moran and the Spirit of Place*, p. 12.

3. As early as 1865, Prang issued a "Christmas stocking library — six different stories, put up in a nice ornamented paper box." *Scientific American* 13 (December 16, 1865): 387. The sales of Christmas cards is reported in McClinton, *The Chromolithographs of Louis Prang*, p. 81. See also Peck and Irish, *Candace Wheeler*, p. 164.

4. Prang's Christmas cards are discussed in several sources. See especially McClinton, *The Chromolithographs of Louis Prang*, pp. 73–90.

5. A typical Prang Christmas card advertisement may be found in *Scribner's Magazine* 4 (December 1888): 34.

6. Hollingsworth, "How Christmas Cards Are Made," p. 60.

7. Peck and Irish, *Candace Wheeler*, p. 165.

8. Ibid.

9. This ingenious strategy for eliciting public interest is described in "The Prang Competition," *New York Times*, October 9, 1881, p. 10. See also "Christmas Card Designs: The Messrs. Prang & Co.'s Third Competition," *New York Times*, November 3, 1881, p. 16. The third competition had 575 entries.

10. Wilkins, *Thomas Moran*, p. 241.

11. Peck and Irish, *Candace Wheeler*, p. 169.

12. A copy of this card is owned by HCC, Prang B2.6:7.

13. *Boston Daily Evening Transcript,* December 12, 1884. A week earlier the same paper had noted the exhibition of the cards: "There is now on public exhibition in New York a collection of designs for Christmas cards, entered in a limited competition established by Prang & Co. They were all ordered and paid for by the firm, and in addition compete for prizes of $1000, $500, $300 and $200. These prizes were awarded by the votes of about a hundred of the dealers of such cards. The first prize fell to Charles D. Weldon, the second to William H. Low, the third to Thomas Moran and the fourth to Frederick Dielman. There are twenty-three designs in all by twenty-two well-known painters. . . . Mr. Moran['s] is an angel trumpeting through a town at sunrise." *Boston Daily Evening Transcript,* December 4, 1884.

14. Wilkins, *Thomas Moran,* p. 241, based on an unidentified clipping in EHL.

15. BPL and HCC have copies of this card. On the verso is a poem by Celia Thaxter. In a circular vignette in the lower right are the words, "Prang's Third Prize Card by Thomas Moran."

16. BPL has a copy of this card in an 1883–1884 Prang album, p. 47, no. 1353.

17. I discuss this work in my book, *Thomas Moran,* p. 171, and in my article that reproduces the original watercolor, "Sacred and Profane," 17.

18. See Barry Shank, *A Token of My Affection: Greeting Cards and American Business Culture* (New York: Columbia University Press, 2004).

19. William S. Ayres, "Pictures in the American Home, 1880–1930," in *The Arts in the American Home, 1890–1930,* eds. Jessica H. Foy and Karal Ann Marling (Knoxville: University of Tennessee Press, 1994), 149–164.

20. Kirsten Swinth, *Painting Professionals: Women Artists and the Development of Modern Art, 1870–1930* (Chapel Hill: University of North Carolina Press, 2001).

21. This chromolithograph is reproduced as plate 7 in Kinsey, *Thomas Moran.* The original oil is *Grand Canon of the Colorado* (1892–1908, Philadelphia Museum of Art).

22. Moran ledger, GIL 4026.4049, no. 67; Wilkins, *Thomas Moran,* p. 273.

23. Wilkins, *Thomas Moran,* p. 264.

24. Gustave Buek, "Thomas Moran, N.A., The Grand Old Man of American Art," *Mentor* 12 (August 1924): 29.

25. This is discussed in a number of sources. See, for example, Keith Bryant, "The Atchison, Topeka, and Santa Fe Railway and the Development of the Taos and Santa Fe Art Colonies," *Western Historical Quarterly* 9 (October 1978): 437–454; Sandra D'Emilio and Suzan Campbell, *Visions and Visionaries: The Art and Artists of the Santa Fe Railway* (Salt Lake City: Peregrine Books, 1991); Charles C. Eldredge, Julie Schimmel, and William Truettner, *Art in New Mexico, 1900–1945: Paths to Taos and Santa Fe* (New York: Abbeville Press for the National Museum of American Art, 1986); and Joni L. Kinsey, *The Majesty of the Grand Canyon: 150 Years in Art* (Cobb, Calif.: First Glance Books, 1998).

26. General Advertising Agent [William Simpson] to J. M. Connell, January 22, 1915, SFRR.

27. This excursion included a stop in Chicago and dinner with the dealer Rob Roy Ricketts, and it is interesting to speculate if the assembled group may have conceived the unique relationship that resulted in the 1912 *Grand Canyon from Hermit Rim Road.*

28. Kinsey, *Thomas Moran,* p. 134.

29. Zaplin-Lampert Gallery advertisement, *American Art Review* (August 1996).

30. Wilkins, *Thomas Moran,* p. 265.

31. Photolithography began as early as 1858, but the halftone method would not be perfected for some time. In 1877, photomechanical processes began to be more widely available, when the Heliotype Printing Company, the Chemical Engraving Company, and the Forbes company (which specialized in the Alberttype, or collotype) began advertising their services in Boston, all signaling a major change in reproductive technology, replacing the manual methods that had characterized Prang's achievements. Pierce and Slautterback, *Boston Lithography,* p. 12.

32. Some of the publishers listed on such prints of Moran's work include (besides those discussed in the text) Brown and Bigelow, St. Paul, Minnesota (for the Northern Pacific Railroad); Chicago Colortype Co.; the Knapp Co., New York; Charles Tabor & Co., New York; and the Frederickson Co., Chicago.

33. Moran began listing his paintings with information about their copyright sales in his ledger, GIL 4016.4019. Some entries are listed twice in two different ledgers or pages and sometimes contain conflicting information.

34. Ruth Moran to Osborne & Company, Allwood, N.J., AAA, frame 207.

35. "Comment on New Books," *Atlantic Monthly* 69 (May 1892): 712.

36. From an unidentified advertisement, "Art Instruction in Public Schools," in BPL.

37. "Memoranda," *Scribner's Monthly* 13 (March 1877): 733.

38. Freeman, *Louis Prang,* p. 137.

39. McClinton, *The Chromolithographs of Louis Prang,* p.159; Tyler, *Prints of the West,* pp. 146–147; Marzio, *The Democratic Art,* p. 110.

Selected Bibliography

BOOKS, ARTICLES, DISSERTATIONS, AND NEWSPAPERS

Ackley, Clifford S. "Sylvester Rosa Koehler and the American Etching Revival." *Art and Commerce: American Prints of the Nineteenth Century.* Proceedings of Conference at the Museum of Fine Arts, Boston, May 8–10, 1975 (Charlottesville: University Press of Virginia, 1978): 143–150.

Adamson, Jeremy Elwell. *Niagara: Two Centuries of Changing Attitudes.* Washington, D.C.: Corcoran Gallery of Art, 1985.

The Aldine Art Union Prospectus — 1874–75 (November 1874).

Alexander, Thomas G. "Red Rock and Gray Stone: Senator Reed Smoot, the Establishment of Zion and Bryce Canyon National Parks, and the Rebuilding of Downtown Washington, D.C." *Pacific Historical Review* 72 (February 2003): 1–38.

American Journal of Science and Arts 13 (March 1877): 229–230.

Anderson, Nancy, ed., with contributions by Thomas P. Bruhn, Joni L. Kinsey, and Anne Morand. *Thomas Moran.* Washington, D.C., and New Haven, Conn.: National Gallery of Art and Yale University Press, 1997.

Anderson, Nancy K., and Linda S. Ferber. *Albert Bierstadt: Art and Enterprise.* Brooklyn, N.Y.: Brooklyn Museum in association with Hudson Hills Press, 1990.

Antreasian, Garo Z. "Some Thoughts about Printmaking and Print Collaborations." *Art Journal* 39 (Spring 1980): 180–188.

"Art." *Atlantic Monthly* 34 (September 1874): 374–377.

Art and Commerce: American Prints of the Nineteenth-Century. Boston and Charlottesville: Museum of Fine Arts, distributed by the University Press of Virginia, 1978.

The Art of Yellowstone, 1870–1872. Tulsa, Okla.: Thomas Gilcrease Museum Association, 1983.

"An Art Workshop." *Aldine: A Typographic Art Journal* 2 (July 1869): 2.

"Autotypes and Oleographs." *Nation* 11 (November 10, 1870): 317–318.

Ayres, William S. "Pictures in the American Home, 1880–1930." In *The Arts in the American Home, 1890–1930,* edited by Jessica H. Foy and Karal Ann Marling. Knoxville: University of Tennessee Press, 1944.

Barnhill, Georgia B., Diana Korzenik, and Caroline F. Sloat, eds. *The Cultivation of Artists in Nineteenth-Century America.* Worcester, Mass.: American Antiquarian Society, 1997.

Bartlett, Richard. *Great Surveys of the American West.* Norman: University of Oklahoma Press, 1962.

Bassford, Amy O., and Fritiof M. Fryxell, eds. *Home-Thoughts, from Afar: Letters of Thomas Moran to Mary Nimmo Moran.* East Hampton, N.Y.: East Hampton Free Library, 1967.

Bayard Curley, Jane. "The Advent of the American Christmas Card: Prang's Christmas Card Competitions and the Rise of Women Artists." *Nineteenth Century* 22 (Fall 2002): 2–8.

Beecher, Catherine E., and Harriet Beecher Stowe. *The American Woman's Home: Or, Principles of Domestic Science, Being a Guide to the Formation and Maintenance of Economic, Healthful, Beautiful, and Christian Homes.* New York: J. B. Ford, 1869, and Boston: H. A. Brown, 1869.

Benjamin, S. G. W. "A Pioneer of the Palette: Thomas Moran." *Magazine of Art* 5 (February 1882): 89–93.

Benjamin, Walter. "The Work of Art in the Age of Mechanical Reproduction." 1936. Reprinted in *Illuminations,* edited by Hannah Arendt. New York: Schocken Books, 1978.

Boag, Peter C. "Overlanders and the Snake River Region: A Case Study of Popular Landscape Perception in the Early West." *Pacific Northwest Quarterly* (October 1993): 122–129.

———. "Thomas Moran and Western Landscapes: An Inquiry into an Artist's Environmental Values." *Pacific Historical Review* 67 (February 1998): 40–66.

Bogart, Michele H. "Artistic Ideals and Commercial Practices: The Problem of Status for American Illustrators." *Prospects* 15 (1990): 225–281.

———. *Artists, Advertising, and the Borders of Art.* Chicago: University of Chicago Press, 1995.

Boime, Albert. *The Magisterial Gaze: Manifest Destiny and American Landscape Painting, ca. 1830–1865.* Washington, D.C.: Smithsonian Institution Press, 1991.

Boston Daily Evening Transcript, November 25, 1870; April 9, 1875; December 1, 1875; December 6, 1876; December 4, 1884; December 12, 1884.

Bruhn, Thomas. "Thomas Moran's Painter-Lithographs." *Imprint* 15 (Spring 1990): 2–19.

Bryant, Keith. "The Atchison, Topeka, and Santa Fe Railway and the Development of the Taos and Santa Fe Art Colonies." *Western Historical Quarterly* 9 (October 1978): 437–454.

Bryant, William Cullen, ed. *Picturesque America; or The Land We Live In.* 2 vols. New York: D. Appleton and Co., 1872–1874.

Buek, Gustave. "Thomas Moran, N.A., the Grand Old Man of American Art." *Mentor* 12 (August 1924): 29–37.

Cadbury, Warder. *Arthur Fitzwilliam Tait: Artist in the Adirondacks.* Cranbury, N.J.: Associated University Presses, 1986.

Carbonell, Bettina Messias. *Museum Studies: An Anthology of Contexts.* Malden, Mass.: Blackwell Publishing, 2004.

Carr, Gerald. *Frederic Edwin Church: The Icebergs.* Dallas, Tex.: Dallas Museum of Art, 1980.

Catalogue of Louis Prang's Collection, Sold by Private Auction. Boston: Copley Hall, 1899.

Catalogue of Publications Issued by L. Prang and Co., Fine Art Publishers. Boston: Alfred Mudge and Son, 1872.

"Christmas Card Designs: The Messrs. Prang & Co.'s Third Competition." *New York Times,* November 3, 1881, p. 16.

"Chromo-Civilization." *Nation* (September 24, 1874): 201–202.

"Chromo-Lithographs, American, English, and French." *Nation* (October 31, 1867): 359.

"Chromo-Lithography." *New York Times,* October 31, 1874, p. 13.

"Chromo-Lithography." *Putnam's Monthly Magazine of American Literature, Science, and Art* 12 (October 1868): 507–508; (December 1868): 763–764.

"Chromos in Perfection." *Boston Daily Evening Transcript,* November 25, 1870, p. 1, cols. 3–4.

Clapper, Michael. "Art, Industry, and Education in Prang's Chromolithographic Company." *Proceedings of the American Antiquarian Society* 105, no. 1 (1995): 145–161.

———. "'I Was Once a Barefoot Boy!': Cultural Tensions in a Popular Chromo." *American Art* 16 (Summer 2002): 17–39.

———. "Popularizing Art in Boston, 1865–1910: L. Prang & Co. and the Museum of

Fine Arts." Ph.D. diss., Northwestern University, 1997.

Clark, Carol. *Thomas Moran: Watercolors of the American West.* Austin: University of Texas Press for the Amon Carter Museum, 1980.

———. "Thomas Moran's Watercolors of the American West." Ph.D. diss., Case Western Reserve University, 1981.

Codman, John. "The Shoshone Falls." *Century Magazine* 39 (April 1890): 924–927.

Coffin, Charles Carleton. "Labor and the Natural Forces." *Atlantic Monthly* 43 (May 1879): 553–566.

Coffin, William. "American Illustration of Today." *Scribner's Magazine* 11 (January 1892): 106–117.

"Color Printing from Wood and from Stone." *Nation* (January 10, 1867): 36–37.

Cook, Clarence. *Art and Artists of Our Time.* New York: Selar Hess, 1888.

———. *The House Beautiful: Essays on Beds and Tables, Stools and Candlesticks.* New York: Scribner, Armstrong & Co., 1878.

———. *What Shall We Do with Our Walls?* New York: Warren and Fuller, 1881.

Cosmopolitan Art Journal 1 (January 1857): 3.

"Culture and Progress: 'The Chasm of the Colorado.'" *Scribner's Monthly* 8 (July 1874): 373.

Dearinger, David B., ed. *Rave Reviews: American Art and Its Critics, 1826–1925.* New York: National Academy of Design, 2000.

D'Emilio, Sandra, and Suzan Campbell. *Visions and Visionaries: The Art and Artists of the Santa Fe Railway.* Salt Lake City: Peregrine Books, 1991.

"Desultory Thoughts on Wood Engraving and Wood-Cut Printing." *Knickerbocker* 41 (January 1853): 52.

DeVinne, Theodore. "The Growth of Wood-Cut Printing." *Scribner's Monthly* 20 (May 1880): 35.

DiMaggio, Paul. "Cultural Entrepreneurship in 19th-Century Boston." *Media, Culture, and Society* 4 (1982): 33–50, 330–322.

DuBois, Gussie Packard. "Thomas Moran Knows Nature and Paints It." *Pasadena Star-News*, March 11, 1916, p. 6, col. 3.

"The Editor's Easy Chair." *Harper's Monthly* 36 (February 1868): 398.

"The Editor's Easy Chair." *Harper's Monthly* 52 (April 1876): 772–773.

"Editors' Table." *New England Magazine* 16 (May 1894): 391–392.

Eldredge, Charles C., Julie Schimmel, and William Truettner. *Art in New Mexico, 1900–1945: Paths to Taos and Santa Fe.* New York: Abbeville Press for the National Museum of American Art, 1986.

"Fine Arts." *Nation* (February 15, 1877): 107.

"Fine Arts." *New York Daily Tribune*, November 20, 1866, p. 6, col. 1.

"Fine Arts." *Philadelphia Daily Evening Bulletin*, October 25, 1856, p. 2, col. 2.

"Fine Arts: Multiplied Art." *Nation* 1 (July 20, 1865): 90–92; (July 27, 1865): 123–125.

"Fine Arts Items." *New York Daily Tribune*, April 27, 1866, p. 7, cols. 1–2.

"Fires: Partial Destruction of Prang's Chromo Factory at the Highlands." *Boston Post*, September 28, 1877, p. 3.

First Century of National Existence; The United States as They Were and Are. Hartford, Conn.: L. Stebbins, 1875.

Foster, Mike. *Strange Genius: The Life of Ferdinand Vandiveer Hayden.* Niwot, Colo.: Roberts Rinehart Publishers, 1994.

Frank Leslie's Illustrated Historical Register of the United States Centennial Exposition, 1876 (New York: Frank Leslie's Publishing House, 1877). Facsimile ed. with a new introduction by Richard Kenin. New York: Paddington Press, Two Continents Publishing Group, 1974.

Freeman, Larry. *Louis Prang: Color Lithographer, Giant of a Man.* Watkins Glen, N.Y.: Century House, 1971.

Fryxell, Fritiof. "Thomas Moran's Journey to the Tetons in 1879." *Augustana Historical Society Publications* 2 (1932): 36–46.

"Glories of Southern Utah." *Aldine: A Typographic Art Journal* 8 (January 1876): 34–35.

[Godkin, E. L.] "Chromo-Civilization." *Nation* (September 24, 1874): 201–202.

Goetzmann, William H. *Army Exploration in the American West, 1803–1863.* New Haven, Conn.: Yale University Press, 1959.

Griffits, Thomas Edgar. *The Technique of Colour Printing by Lithography, A Concise Manual of Drawn Lithography.* London: Faber and Faber, 1940.

Haines, Aubrey. *The Yellowstone Story: A History of Our First National Park.* 2 vols. Yellowstone National Park, Wyo.: Yellowstone Library and Museum Association, 1977.

Hamerton, Philip Gilbert. *The Graphic Arts.* London: Seeley, Jackson, and Halliday, 1882.

Harris, Neil. *Cultural Excursions: Marketing Appetites and Cultural Tastes in Modern America.* Chicago: University of Chicago Press, 1990.

Harvey, Eleanor Jones. *Thomas Moran and the Spirit of Place.* Dallas, Tex.: Dallas Museum of Art, 2001.

Hayden, F. V. *Annual Report of the United States Geological and Geographical Survey of the Territories, Embracing Colorado and Parts of Adjacent Territories, Being a Report of Progress of the Exploration for the Year 1874.* Washington, D.C.: U.S. Government Printing Office, 1876.

———. *Twelfth Annual Report of the United States Geological and Geographical Survey of the Territories: A Report of the Progress of the Exploration in Wyoming and Idaho for the Year 1878, by F.-V. Hayden, U.S. Geologist. Conducted under the Authority of the Secretary of the Interior.* Washington, D.C.: U.S. Government Printing Office, 1883.

———. "Wonders of the West II: More about the Yellowstone." *Scribner's Monthly* 3 (February 1872): 388–396.

Hollingsworth, M. E. "How Christmas Cards Are Made." *Wide Awake* 20 (December 1884): 59–65.

Horgan, Mary B. "Our Leading Illustrators." *Independent* 59 (December 1905): 1408.

Howells, William Dean. "A Counterfeit Presentiment." *Atlantic Monthly* 40 (October 1877): 448–461.

Hults, Linda. "Thomas Moran's *Shoshone Falls:* A Western Niagara." *Smithsonian Studies in American Art* 3 (Winter 1989): 89–102.

"Idaho Scenery." *Aldine: A Typographic Art Journal* 8 (June 1876): 195.

Illustrated Catalogue of Fine Art Studies, Water Color Studies, Pictures, Etc., Published by L. Prang & Co. Boston: L. Prang & Co., 1890.

"Illustrated Presentation and Gift Books." *American Literary Gazette and Publisher's Circular*, December 1, 1869, p. 489.

"Illustrated Works." *Cosmopolitan Art Journal* 1 (June 1857): 111.

Increased Attractions." *Aldine Press* 2 (May 1869): 34.

Ingersoll, Ernest. *Crest of the Continent: A Record of a Summer's Ramble in the Rocky Mountains and Beyond.* Chicago: R. R. Donnelley and Sons, 1885.

Jackson, Clarence S. *Picture Maker of the Old*

West: William Henry Jackson. New York and London: Charles Scribner's Sons, 1947.
Jacobowitz, Arlene. *James Hamilton, 1819–1878: American Marine Painter.* Brooklyn, N.Y.: Brooklyn Museum of Art, 1966.
James, Henry. "The Bostonians." *Century Magazine* 30, new ser. 8 (May–October 1885): 861–882.
Jarves, James Jackson. *The Art Idea.* 1864. Reprint ed., edited by Benjamin Rowland, Jr., Cambridge, Mass.: Belknap Press of Harvard University Press, 1960.
———. *Art Thoughts.* New York: Hurd and Houghton, 1871.
Jefferson, Joseph. "The Autobiography of Joseph Jefferson." *Century Magazine* 40 (August 1890): 538–556.
Jussim, Estelle. *Visual Communication and the Graphic Arts: Photographic Technologies in the Nineteenth Century.* New York: R. R. Bowker, 1983.
Kainen, Jacob. "Why Bewick Succeeded: A Note in the History of Wood-Engraving." *Contributions from the Museum of History and Technology,* Bulletin 218 (Washington, D.C.: Smithsonian Institution, 1959): 186–201.
King, Clarence. "The Falls of the Shoshone." *Overland Monthly* 5 (October 1870): 379–385.
———. *Mountaineering in the Sierra Nevada.* Boston, 1872. Reprint ed., Lincoln: University of Nebraska Press, 1970.
Kinsey, Joni L. *The Majesty of the Grand Canyon: 150 Years in Art.* Cobb, Calif.: First Glance Books, 1998.
———. "Sacred and Profane: Thomas Moran's *Mountain of the Holy Cross.*" *Gateway Heritage* 11 (Summer 1990): 4–23.
———. *Thomas Moran and the Surveying of the American West.* Washington, D.C.: Smithsonian Institution Press, 1992.
Koehler, Sylvester R. "The Work of the American Etchers: Mrs. M. Nimmo Moran." *American Art Review* 20 (1881): 31.
Langford, Nathaniel P. "The Ascent of Mount Hayden." *Scribner's Monthly* 6 (June 1873): 129–157.
Last, Jay T. *The Color Explosion: Nineteenth-Century American Lithography.* Santa Ana, CA: Hillcrest Press, 2006
———. "The Wonders of the Yellowstone." *Scribner's Monthly* 2 (May 1871): 1–17; (June 1871): 113–128.
Levin, Jo Ann Early. "The Golden Age of Illustration: Popular Art in American Magazines, 1850–1925." Ph.D. diss., University of Pennsylvania, 1980.
Levine, Laurence W. *Highbrow/Lowbrow: The Emergence of Cultural Hierarchy in America.* Cambridge, Mass.: Harvard University Press, 1988.
Lindstrom, Gaell. *Thomas Moran in Utah (68th Faculty Honor Lecture).* Logan: Utah State University, 1983.
"Linton's Hints on Wood-Engraving." *Scribner's Monthly* 19 (April 1880): 793.
Literary World 3 (December 1872): 104.
L. Prang & Co. Illustrated Catalogue of Art Publications for Fall 1876. Boston: L. Prang & Co. Art and Educational Publishers, 1876.
Lyles, Anne, and Diane Perkins. *Colour into Line: Turner and the Art of Engraving.* London: Tate Gallery, 1989.
Lynes, Russell. *The Tastemakers: The Shaping of American Popular Taste.* 1949. Reprint, New York: Dover Publications, 1980.
Mancini, J. M. *Pre-Modernism: Art-World Change and American Culture from the Civil War to the Armory Show.* Princeton, N.J.: Princeton University Press, 2005
Martinez, Katharine. "John Sartain (1808–1897): His Contribution to American Publishing." *Imprint: Journal of the American Historical Print Collectors Society* 8 (Spring 1983): 1–12.
Martinez, Katharine, and Page Talbott, eds. *Philadelphia's Cultural Landscape: The Sartain Family Legacy.* Philadelphia: Temple University Press, 2000.
Marzio, Peter C. *The Democratic Art: Chromolithography, 1840–1900, Pictures for a Nineteenth-Century America.* Boston: David R. Godine in association with the Amon Carter Museum, 1979.
McCarthy, Kathleen D. *Women's Culture: American Philanthropy and Art, 1830–1930.* Chicago: University of Chicago Press, 1991.
McClinton, Katharine Morrison. *The Chromolithographs of Louis Prang.* New York: Clarkson N. Potter, 1973.
———. "L. Prang and Company Chromos." *Connoisseur* 191 (February 1976): 97–105.
———. "Thomas Moran's Yellowstone Watercolours." *Apollo* 124 (July 1986): 38–43.
McKinsey, Elizabeth. *Niagara Falls: Icon of the American Sublime.* Cambridge: Cambridge University Press, 1985.
"Memoranda." *Scribner's Monthly* 13 (March 1877): 733.
Merrill, Marlene Deahl, ed. *Yellowstone and the Great West: Journals, Letters, and Images from the 1871 Hayden Expedition.* Lincoln: University of Nebraska Press, 1999.
Meyers, Amy R. W., ed. *Art and Science in America: Issues of Representation.* San Marino, Calif.: Huntington Library, 1998.
Morand, Anne. "The Camera and the Artist's Eye." *Gilcrease Journal* 10 (Summer 2002): 4–31.
———. *Thomas Moran: The Field Sketches, 1856–1923.* Norman: University of Oklahoma Press for the Thomas Gilcrease Institute of American History and Art, 1996.
Morand, Anne, and Nancy Friese. *The Prints of Thomas Moran in the Thomas Gilcrease Institute of American History and Art, Tulsa, Oklahoma.* Tulsa, Okla.: Thomas Gilcrease Museum Association, 1986.
Morand, Anne R., Joni L. Kinsey, and Mary Panzer. *Splendors of the American West: Thomas Moran's Art of the Grand Canyon and Yellowstone.* Birmingham, Ala.: Birmingham Museum of Art in association with University of Washington Press, 1990.
Morrill, Edward. "Louis Prang — Lithographer." *Hobbies — The Magazine for Collectors* (August 1940): 30–33.
Mott, Frank Luther. *A History of American Magazines.* 5 vols. Cambridge, Mass.: Harvard University Press, 1930–1968.
"Mr. Prang's Defense." *New York Daily Tribune,* December 7, 1866, p. 5, col. 1.
"A National Park." *Printing Times and Lithographer* (London), January 15, 1878, p. 13.
"A National Park." *Times* (London), November 23, 1877, p. 3. col. F.
Neely, Mary E. "Popular Art." *The Ladies Repository: A Monthly Periodical Devoted to Literature, Arts, and Religion* 4 (December 1876): 549–552.
Newark Daily Advertiser, March 9, 1877.
New York Evening Mail, December 3, 1873.
Novak, Barbara. *Nature and Culture: American Landscape and Painting, 1825–1875.* New York: Oxford University Press, 1980.
Orvell, Miles. *The Real Thing: Imitation and Authenticity in American Culture, 1880–1940.* Chapel Hill: University of North Carolina Press, 1989.
Parton, James. "Popularizing Art." *Atlantic Monthly* 23 (March 1869): 348–357.

Peck, Amelia, and Carol Irish. *Candace Wheeler: The Art and Enterprise of American Design, 1875–1900*. New York and New Haven, Conn.: Metropolitan Museum of Art in association with Yale University Press, 2001.

"Photography and Chromo-Lithography: Their Influence on Art and Art Culture." *Philadelphia Photographer* (1868): 114–115.

"The Picture of Commerce." *Harper's Weekly* 33 (May 18, 1889): 403.

"A Piece of History Worth Writing." *Century Magazine* 26, new ser. 4 (May–October 1883): 477.

Pierce, Sally, and Catharina Slautterback. *Boston Lithography, 1825–1880: The Boston Athenaeum Collection*. Boston: Boston Athenaeum, 1991.

Platzker, David, and Elizabeth Wyckoff. *Hard Pressed: 600 Years of Prints and Processes*. New York: Hudson Hills Press, 2003.

Powell, John Wesley. "The Cañons of the Colorado." *Scribner's Monthly* 9 (January 1875): 293–310; (February 1875): 394–409; (March 1875): 523–537.

———. *Canyons of the Colorado*. Meadville, Pa.: Floyd & Vincent, 1895. Reprinted as *The Exploration of the Colorado River and Its Canyons*. New York: Dover Publications, 1961.

———. "An Overland Trip to the Grand Cañon." *Scribner's Monthly* 10 (October 1875): 659–678.

———. U.S. Congress, House. *Exploration of the Colorado River of the West*. H. Misc. Doc. 300, series 1622, 43rd Cong., 1st sess., 1873–1874. Also published as *Exploration of the Colorado River of the West and Its Tributaries: Explored in 1869, 1870, 1871, and 1872, under the Direction of the Secretary of the Smithsonian Institution*. Washington. D.C.: U.S. Government Printing Office, 1875.

Prang, Louis. "Chromo-Lithography, the Handmaiden of Painting." *New York Daily Tribune*, December 1, 1866, p. 6.

———. "On Theories of Chromo-Lithography." *Nation* (November 28, 1867): 437–438.

Prang Auction Catalogue, 16–18 February, 1892. New York: American Art Galleries, 1892.

"The Prang Competition." *New York Times*, October 9, 1881, p. 10.

Prang's Chromo: A Journal of Popular Art. Boston: L. Prang & Co., 1867–1871.

"Publishers' Department." *Bay State Monthly* 2 (December 1884): 175.

Rainey, Sue. *Creating Picturesque America: Monument to the Natural and Cultural Landscape*. Nashville, Tenn.: Vanderbilt University Press, 1994.

Reed, Christopher, ed. *Not at Home: The Suppression of Domesticity in Modern Art and Architecture*. London: Thames and Hudson, 1996.

Rhymes of the Rockies; or What the Poets Have Found to Say of the Beautiful Scenery on the Denver and Rio Grande Railroad, the Scenic Line of the World. 3rd ed. Chicago: Poole Bros., 1887.

Rushford, Edward A. "Lewis [*sic*] Prang: Engraver on Wood." *Antiques* 37 (April 1940): 187–189.

Ruskin, John. *The Works of John Ruskin*. Edited by E. T. Cook and Alexander Wedderburn. London and New York: George Allen, 1908.

Ruud, Brandon, ed. *Karl Bodmer's North American Prints*. Omaha, Nebr.: Joslyn Art Museum, in association with the University of Nebraska Press, 2004.

Sandweiss, Martha A. *Print the Legend: Photography and the American West*. New Haven, Conn.: Yale University Press, 2002.

"The Scenery of Southern Utah." *Aldine: A Typographic Art Journal* 7 (March 1875): frontispiece and pp. 306–307.

Schmidt, Mary Morris. *Index to Nineteenth-Century American Art Periodicals*. 2 vols. Madison, Conn.: Sound View Press, 1999.

Shank, Barry. *A Token of My Affection: Greeting Cards and American Business Culture*. New York: Columbia University Press, 2004.

Sittig, Mary Margaret. "L. Prang & Company, Fine Art Publishers." Master's thesis, George Washington University, 1970.

Slotkin, Richard. *The Fatal Environment: The Myth of the Frontier in the Age of Industrialization*. Middleton, Conn.: Wesleyan Press, 1985.

Stanwood, Edward. *Boston Illustrated*. Boston: James R. Osgood, 1872.

Stephens, Hal G., and Eugene M. Shoemaker. *In the Footsteps of John Wesley Powell: An Album of Comparative Photographs of the Green and Colorado Rivers, 1871–72 and 1968*. Boulder and Denver, Colo.: Johnson Books and the Powell Society, 1987.

Stockton, Frank R. "The Reversible Landscape." *Century Magazine* 28, new ser. 6 (May–October 1884): 434–439.

Stowe, Harriett Beecher. *House and Home Papers*. Boston: Ticknor and Fields, 1865.

———. "What Pictures Shall I Hang on My Walls?" *Atlantic Almanac* (1869): 41–44.

"Street Lithography." *Art Age* (December 1884): 57.

Sweeney, J. Gray. *Artists of Michigan from the Nineteenth Century*. Muskegon, Mich.: Muskegon Museum of Art, 1987.

———. Great Lakes Marine Painting of the Nineteenth Century. Muskegon, Mich.: Muskegon Museum of Art, 1983.

Swinth, Kirsten. *Painting Professionals: Women Artists and the Development of Modern American Art, 1870–1930*. Chapel Hill: University of North Carolina Press, 2001.

"Thomas Moran's Water-Colors." *Scribner's Monthly* 5 (January 1873): 394.

"To the Public: Wood Cuts." *Sartain's Union Magazine* 5 (September 1849): 12.

Townley, D. O. C. "Living American Artists." *Scribner's Monthly* 3 (March 1872): 599–609.

Truettner, William, ed. *The West as America: Reinterpreting Images of the Frontier*. Washington, D.C.: Smithsonian Institution Press, 1991.

Twain, Mark. "A Connecticut Yankee in King Arthur's Court." *Century Magazine* 39 (November 1889): 74–83.

"Two Books." *Harper's Weekly* (April 21, 1877): 303.

Tyler, Ron. *Prints of the West*. Golden, Colo.: Fulcrum Publishing, 1994.

Tyler, Ron, et al. *American Frontier Life: Early Western Painting and Prints*. New York: Abbeville Press, 1987.

"Utah Scenery." *Aldine: A Typographic Art Journal* 7 (January 1874): 14–15.

Valleys of the Great Salt Lake, Describing the Garden of Utah and the Two Great Cities of Salt Lake and Ogden. Chicago: R. R. Donnelley & Sons, 1890.

Wagner, Ann Prentice. "The Graver, the Brush, and the Ruling Machine: The Training of Late Nineteenth-Century Wood Engravers." *Proceedings of the American Antiquarian Society* 105, no. 1 (1995): 167–191.

Waldstein, Charles. "The Lesson of Greek Art." *Century Magazine* 31, new ser. 9 (November 1885–April 1886): 259–271.

Ward, Gerald W. R. *The American Illustrated Book in the Nineteenth Century*. Winterthur, Del.: Winterthur Museum, 1987.

Warner, Charles Dudley. "The Novel and the

Common School." *Atlantic Monthly* 65 (June 1890): 721–731.

Wilkins, Thurman. *Thomas Moran: Artist of the Mountains.* Norman: University of Oklahoma Press, 1966; revised ed., 1997.

Wilson, Edward L. "Chromo-Lithography." *Philadelphia Photographer* 13 (August 1866): 233–234.

Wilson, James B. "The Significance of Thomas Moran as an American Landscape Painter." Ph.D. diss., Ohio State University, 1955.

"With Wheeler in the Sierras." *Appleton's Journal: A Monthly Miscellany of Popular Literature* 3 (October 1877): 289–297.

Wittholf, Brucia. "The History of James Smillie's Engraving after Albert Bierstadt's 'The Rocky Mountains.'" *American Art Journal* 19 (1987): 40–51.

"The Yellowstone National Park." *Journal of Outdoor Life, Travel, Nature, Study, Shooting, Fishing, Yachting* (February 15, 1877): 25.

"The Yellowstone National Park." *Scotsman* (Edinburgh), January 9, 1877, p. 2.

"The Yellowstone Region." *Aldine: A Typographic Art Journal* 6 (March 1873): 74.

Zalesch, Saul E. "What the Four Million Bought: Cheap Oil Paintings of the 1880s." *American Quarterly* 48 (March 1996): 77–109.

WEB SITES (ALL ACCESSED JULY 2004)

http://www.bozemanonline.com/history.php

http://www.colomar.com/ColoradoPlaces/mosquito_pass.html

http://eh.net/hmit/compare

http://gallery.unl.edu/

http://www.gardenofgods.com/history.htm

http://www.geyserstudy.org/midway.htm#excelsior

http://gorp.away.com/gorp/activity/byway/mt_beart.htm

http://libraryphoto.er.usgs.gov/

http://www.nps.gov/grte/cult/parkhis2.htm

http://photoswest.org

http://1traildamage.com.glowball.com/trails/index.php?id=41

http://www.nps.gov/yell/tours/oldfaithful/castleg.htm

http://www.nps.gov/zion/ParkProfile.htm

Index